Personality Psychology

Second Edition

To Rory Ann

SAGE was founded in 1965 by Sara Miller McCune to support the dissemination of usable knowledge by publishing innovative and high-quality research and teaching content. Today, we publish over 900 journals, including those of more than 400 learned societies, more than 800 new books per year, and a growing range of library products including archives, data, case studies, reports, and video. SAGE remains majority-owned by our founder, and after Sara's lifetime will become owned by a charitable trust that secures our continued independence.

Los Angeles | London | New Delhi | Singapore | Washington DC | Melbourne

Personality Psychology

A Student-Centered Approach

Second Edition

Jim McMartin

California State University, Northridge

Los Angeles | London | New Delhi
Singapore | Washington DC | Melbourne

FOR INFORMATION:

SAGE Publications, Inc.
2455 Teller Road
Thousand Oaks, California 91320
E-mail: order@sagepub.com

SAGE Publications Ltd.
1 Oliver's Yard
55 City Road
London, EC1Y 1SP
United Kingdom

SAGE Publications India Pvt. Ltd.
B 1/I 1 Mohan Cooperative Industrial Area
Mathura Road, New Delhi 110 044
India

SAGE Publications Asia-Pacific Pte. Ltd.
3 Church Street
#10–04 Samsung Hub
Singapore 049483

Acquisitions Editor: Reid Hester
Editorial Assistant: Morgan McCardell
Production Editor: Bennie Clark Allen
Copy Editor: Lana Todorovic-Arndt
Typesetter: Hurix Systems Pvt. Ltd.
Proofreader: Rae-Ann Goodwin
Indexer: Wendy Allex
Cover Designer: Michael Dubowe
Marketing Manager: Shari Countryman

Printed in the United States of America

Library of Congress Cataloging-in-Publication Data

Names: McMartin, Jim.

Title: Personality psychology: a student-centered approach / Jim McMartin.

Description: Second Edition. | Thousand Oaks: SAGE Publications, Inc., 2016. | Revised edition of the author's Personality psychology, 1995. | Includes bibliographical references and index.

Identifiers: LCCN 2015039526 | ISBN 9781483385259 (pbk.: alk. paper)

Subjects: LCSH: Personality. | Personality development.

Classification: LCC BF698. M349 2016 | DDC 155.2–dc23 LC record available at http://lccn.loc.gov/2015039526

This book is printed on acid-free paper.

16 17 18 19 20 10 9 8 7 6 5 4 3 2 1

Brief Contents

Detailed Contents

Preface to the Second Edition

Life can only be understood backwards, but it must be lived forwards.

—Soren Kierkegaard (1813–1855)

This textbook is intended to complement (or replace) those traditional theorist-centered texts that examine personality through a successive presentation of theorists, theories, and research. The underlying general question running throughout this concise text is, How do personality theories (and data) help me understand my own personality? Theories and research are presented as answers to the sorts of questions students typically bring to a course on personality psychology. A distinctive feature of this book is that it is student centered rather than theorist centered.

Another distinctive feature of this text is that I divide the reader's life course into his or her past, present, and future selves. I ask basic questions about personality that are relevant to those time frames. Plausible answers to the questions are given through research observations that may be interpreted within one or more of five theoretical orientations: psychodynamic, trait theory, cognitive/social learning, humanistic/existential/narrative, and evolutionary psychology. While acknowledging students from diverse backgrounds and ages, I assume the typical reader to be a 20-ish-year-old college student who has taken at least one prior course in psychology. Research that deal with topics of particular interest to individuals in this age range have been given preferential treatment. Investigations relevant to the concerns of young adults help readers appreciate the practical value of personality theories.

This text amplifies standard personality textbooks in which the foreground is theory and the background is the potential application to interesting questions about personality. By considering what is currently known about each of the questions raised and how these data are interpreted, I encourage readers to evaluate each theory's usefulness for understanding their own personalities and thereby come to a deeper understanding of the personality theories covered here.

Part I. Basic Issues in Personality Psychology

Part I of the text consists of three chapters. The brief introductory chapter defines personality, compares *personality* to *self*, introduces the personality x situation debate, and examines David Funder's comprehensive treatment of the psychological meaning of situations. The chapter concludes with an overview of the five theoretical orientations to familiarize readers with their distinctive terms and key concepts.

Chapter 1 introduces students to the meaning of *theory* as used by scientists in all fields. To help students appreciate the usefulness of any scientific theory, I compare a theory to a map: Both help us get from where we are now to where we want to go. The second half of this chapter continues the Introduction by presenting, in greater detail, the distinctive features of the five orientations that will be referred to throughout the rest of the text.

Chapter 2 covers both the methods used in personality research as well as the purposes and principles of personality assessment. The goal of this chapter is to reinforce the view of Charles Darwin that research observations are valuable only to the extent that they either clearly support or contradict "some view." My aim is to encourage students to adopt the habit of evaluating research outcomes by how well they confirmed or refuted a hypothesis derived from a theory.

Part II. My Past Self

Part II consists of two chapters. Chapter 3 ("Genetic and Temperamental Influences") opens with the question "Did my personality begin in the womb?" The affirmative answer to this question is based on findings from behavioral genetics, personality differences among nonhuman animals, considerations of gene x environment interactions, and differences among infant temperaments. The chapter concludes with a discussion of gender differences in temperament.

While Chapter 3 presents a detailed look at the nature side of the perennial nature–nurture issue, Chapter 4 ("Cultivating Personality") examines the role of early environments as they influence personality development. Three key environmental variables—parenting style, attachment quality, and identification with a caregiver—are evaluated through the results of current theory-driven research. The final section of this chapter discusses the development of gender identity.

Part III. My Present Self

Part III opens with identity and self-esteem (Chapter 5), where Erik Erikson's theory of psychosocial development takes center stage. Additionally, the contributions of Carl Rogers, Dan McAdams, E. Tory Higgins, William Swann, Mark Leary, and Albert Bandura are evaluated via current research findings.

Chapter 6 ("Needs, Motives, and Goals") discusses our present self in terms of our current motives. Human motivation may be understood from many viewpoints. My goal in this chapter is to give students an appreciation for the dazzling diversity of valid answers to the apparently simple question, "What makes us tick?" To this end, I present the views of (a) Alfred Adler; (b) humanistic accounts of self-actualization and self-determination; (c) evolutionary psychology (the need to belong to a group, striving for status, and the mating motive); (d) basic personality dispositions (the need for achievement, the Dark Triad, and sensation seeking); and (e) cognitive approaches (our possible selves, our personal strivings, and our personal projects).

Useful ways of understanding and coping with stress are covered in Chapter 7. Stress may be profitably understood from four points of view: psychodynamic (e.g., Freud, Horney); trait theory (e.g., dispositional optimism); cognitive/social learning theory (e.g., Lazarus, Beck); and humanistic psychology (e.g., Rogers). The chapter concludes with practical information about coping with stress provided by recent developments in positive psychology.

Disorders of personality (Chapter 8) is a relatively recent addition to core textbooks of personality. I compare two distinct ways of understanding these disorders: (1) by counting how many symptoms the individual manifests (the traditional clinical approach) and (2) by observing his or her pattern of extreme scores on two or more personality traits (the newer dimensional approach). The chapter concludes by evaluating the strengths and weaknesses of these two methods for conceptualizing personality disorders.

Part IV. My Future Self

The final two chapters of the book are premised on the understanding that our future selves are determined by the choices we make in the present. Chapter 9 ("Expectations, Plans, and Self-Regulation") covers (a) George Kelly's Psychology of Personal Constructs; (b) how our internal working models guide the quality of our interactions with other people; and (c) four common threats to self-regulation (acting impulsively, hurt feelings, fatigue, and procrastination). Understanding these threats points to practical ways for improving self-regulation skills. Chapter 10 concludes the text by examining personality continuity and change over the life course.

Acknowledgments

I thank the numerous people who helped me at various stages in writing this revised and expanded edition. I thank Annie Hill Rhodes, therapist and dear friend, for joyously sharing her expertise about personality disorders. I also want to thank my colleagues for their thoughtful and generous suggestions (alphabetized names of 16 reviewers) for their valuable and insightful comments on prior drafts of this manuscript.

Thanks also to the people at SAGE Publications for their professionalism and dedication to this project. My talented editor, Reid Hester, identified a group of high-quality reviewers whose informed comments were creative, supportive, and influential. My thanks to you, Reid, and to your editorial staff members, Lucy Berbeo and Morgan McCardell, for your enthusiastic support for this project.

Most of all, I am deeply thankful to Rory Ann McMartin, my wife and best friend, for her invaluable assistance with all aspects of this project, especially for her cartoons that grace these pages. To her I gratefully dedicate this book.

SAGE Publications gratefully acknowledges the following reviewers:

Daniel Bentley, University of Ottawa

Michele Breault, Truman State University

Jennifer Casani, Barry University

Donald W. Daughtry, Texas A&M University-Kingsville

Alisha Janowsky, University of Central Florida

Daniel N. Jones, University of Texas at El Paso

Diane Martichuski, University of Colorado Boulder

Nicole C. Polen-Petit, National University

Daren S. Protolipac, St. Cloud State University

Sean C. Rife, Murray State University

Tara M. Stoppa, Eastern University

Éva Szeli, Arizona State University

Heather Terrell, University of North Dakota

Carrie L. West, Schreiner University

Grace White, The University of Central Florida

Heike A. Winterheld, Washington University in St. Louis

About the Author

Jim McMartin is Emeritus Professor of psychology, California State University, Northridge. He began his career as a Research Associate at the Institute for Developmental Studies in New York City. He helped to collect and analyze seminal data showing the academic benefits of pre-school experiences. The data from this well-controlled field experiment, as well as replicated findings from similar research programs across the United States, led to federal funding for the Head Start Program. He earned degrees in psychology from Fordham University (BS), Brooklyn College (MA), and the University of Minnesota (PhD). He has published in such journals as the *Journal of Personality and Social Psychology*, *Human Relations*, and *Sociometry*, among others, as well as invited articles for the *International Encyclopedia of Psychiatry, Psychology, Psychoanalysis, and Neurology*. He lives in Camarillo, California, with his wife, Rory Ann, who created the illustrations throughout this book, as faithful servants to our fine feline, Samantha, a.k.a. She-Who-Must-Be-Obeyed.

Part I

Basic Issues in Personality Psychology

Introduction

❖*What is personality?*

Definition of Personality

Personality Versus Self

Two Central Issues
   1. The Person x Situation Debate
   2. Five Theoretical Approaches to Personality

*P*ersonality is a term commonly used in everyday life. We hear statements such as "Jill has a *great* personality" or "Jack has *no* personality." These evaluative judgments imply that Jill is outgoing and lively, fun to be around, and consistently distinctive from other people in socially pleasing ways. Jack, on the other hand, rarely expresses himself, is withdrawn and shy, and is consistently distinctive from other people in socially unpleasing ways.

Personality psychologists would agree with one implication of these descriptions of Jack and Jill: Personality refers to the *distinctive* characteristics of the person—characteristics that *consistently* manifest themselves in different situations. Wherever you meet Jill—at school, at the mall, in her home, or in the homes of others—you expect her to be lively and outgoing. Similarly, Jack—almost always quiet and withdrawn—prefers to hang out at the fringes of his social circle. If Jill were not consistent—if she were fun to be around on some occasions, but moody and angry at other times—her personality would probably be described as erratic or volatile.

Not only are Jill and Jack consistent in manifesting their personalities, the fact that Jill is seen to have a great personality but poor Jack has no personality means that both are seen as distinctively different from other people in their dominant traits. Although other people are also fun to be around, Jill stands out in this dimension; similarly, other people may be quiet and reserved, but Jack is so withdrawn that others think he lacks a personality. The point is that if *everyone* in the group were just as outgoing as Jill, or just as quiet as Jack, there would be no basis for their distinctiveness and their personalities would be described in different ways.

"We all thought he had no personality
and now look at him!"

Definition of Personality

Personality is the developing system of those distinctive motivational, emotional, cognitive, and spiritual attributes that manifest themselves in the individual's unique adaptations to his or her environment at any point in the life course.

This definition, derived from common usage of the term, highlights the idea that "personality" refers to consistent and distinctive differences among individuals. It also implies that personality can change within a person over the life course. The key terms in this definition are as follows:

- *Developing*: Personality is a living process. It is not fixed or static. Developing implies that your future personality, your future self, may be organized differently from your present self.
- *System*: Personality is organized. Its various components are integrated. Personality is not an isolated collection of traits, thoughts, and emotions that have nothing to do with each other. We have a past that influenced who we are today, we have present dispositions that influence how we react to our environment, and we have hopes, goals, and expectations for the future that guide our present thoughts, feelings, and actions.
- *Distinctive*: Each individual has a unique way of expressing his or her attributes. Personality refers to both who we *are* and how we *represent* who we are.
- *Motivational*: Our needs, wants, and desires comprise a major part of our personality. Our motives may be conscious (we are aware of what we want) or unconscious (our actual motives are out-of-awareness).

- *Emotional*: Our feelings and moods, consciously experienced or not.
- *Cognitive*: Our thoughts, ideas, and beliefs, including our self-concept, consciously articulated or not.
- *Spiritual*: The meaning we give to our life and the world in which we live, whether the meaning is consciously acknowledged or not.
- *Unique*: We react to the demands of our environment in ways that are similar, but are not identical, to how other individuals react to their environments.
- *Adaptations*: How we respond to the stresses and strains of daily life and how we choose to reach our goals.
- *Any point in the life course*: Your personality manifests itself differently at different stages of your life due to innate developmental factors (e.g., learning to talk) and environmental demands (e.g., social norms within specific environments, such as a library). Personality change over the life course may reflect significant changes in our fundamental motivation, emotional reactivity, self-concept, and/or the meaning we give to our lives.

Personality Versus Self

The organization of this book into past, present, and future selves requires comment. A currently unresolved issue in the field of personality psychology concerns the proper usage of the term *self*. The problem is that some confuse *self* with *self-concept* by using these terms synonymously. Moreover, the term self has been used interchangeably at times with terms such as *ego, self-schema,* and *self-representation.* I agree with Drew Westen (1991) that self refers to *all* of you—your conscious and unconscious aspects. Personality and self are synonymous.

Self-concept, ego, self-schema, and self-representations are narrower terms. Your self-concept is your awareness of who you are, including how you feel about yourself (your self-esteem). Ego refers to your ability to make conscious decisions and be aware of yourself and your environment. Self-schema and self-representation, like self-concept, refer to your conscious picture of yourself. To the extent that you are currently unaware of important aspects of your personality (your self), a discrepancy exists between who you *are* (your personality or your self) and your *idea of who you are* (your self-concept, self-schema, or self-representation). Personality psychologists such as Carl Jung and Victor Frankl hold that the growth of our personality over the life span involves becoming more and more aware of who we truly are. We continue to achieve our personality over our lifespan.

Two Central Issues

1. The Person x Situation Debate

The year 1968 is a pivotal year in the history of personality psychology. This is the fateful year when Walter Mischel published his book *Personality and Assessment,* a book that, for many years, turned the field of personality psychology topsy-turvy.

Mischel found that numerous studies of personality traits revealed again and again that most of us are not consistent in our behavior from one situation to another. Our behavior changes according to the characteristics of our immediate situation. Our personalities are thus irrelevant for understanding why we behave the way we do. Our present physical and social environments sufficiently explain our actions.

Many personality psychologists understood Mischel to mean that *personality* is an illusion. This illusion is caused by repeatedly seeing other people in the same situation (e.g., at work, at school, at home, at the bowling alley), but not in other situations. We observe they behave consistently (conscientiously, goofing-off, talkative), and we naturally attribute these consistencies to their personalities because we are unaware of how much their (and our) behavior is under situational control. Come to think of it, who hasn't been surprised to see a boisterous, somewhat out-of-control pal act politely and with restraint when he is in the presence of his parents? It's like he suddenly morphed into a completely different person, right? Even more dramatically, on TV news, we sometimes see neighbors stunned to learn that the "nice guy next door" is a serial killer.

So is Mischel correct? Is personality just an illusion? Personality psychologists did not, as you might expect, take kindly to this attack on the reality of their field. They were not pleased to think they had spent their professional lives studying something that does not really exist. Their reply to Mischel took three forms:

1. If the immediate situation is important for understanding why we act as we do, what are the relevant *dimensions* or *types* of situations that cause our behavior? Those who argued that personality is an illusion have failed to show which aspects of situations are most relevant for understanding our behavior. Merely noting that personality traits appear to contribute little to understanding why we act the way we do does *not* automatically mean that situational variables account for all the rest. There could be other, unmeasured, personality traits that would explain our behavior had they been measured.

2. Kenneth Bowers (1973) used the term *situationism* to refer to the point of view that our immediate environment is the key determinant of how we act, *not* our personalities. Bowers found 11 investigations that varied both person variables and situation variables. He observed that, across these 11 studies, personality differences accounted for, on average, only 13% of the total variability. But situational differences accounted for even less variability, 10%. The Person x Situation *interaction*, on the other hand, accounted for 21% of the total variability. Both traits and situations, considered alone, seem to be equally poor at accounting for variability. The interaction of the two seems to be more promising.

3. There is a crucial distinction between *states* of personality and *traits* of personality. A state is a temporary condition—like how you feel while you are in the dentist's chair. Do you feel anxious? Of course you do. Everyone feels at least some degree of anxiety while someone is poking around the inside of his or her mouth with sharp instruments and whirring drill bits. Okay, but do you feel just as anxious when enjoying a documentary on early American quilt making? Probably not. Our anxiety in the dental chair is state dependent. It is not necessarily an enduring personality trait.

While states are temporary conditions, traits are more stable aspects of our personalities. A personality trait is an aspect of our personality that we are likely to express consistently across a variety of different situations. Even so, we do not express our traits in the same way across all situations: We typically vary our behavior according to its appropriateness. A life-of-the-party extravert is unlikely to express herself in the same way during her oral exam in molecular entomology.

William Fleeson describes two kinds of personality differences. One kind, the kind people usually talk about, refers to *between-person* differences: Some people are more outgoing than others, some are more adventurous than others, and so on. Another kind of personality difference is *within-person* variability: We vary when, where, and by how much we reveal our personalities. No one acts exactly the same in all conditions— no one, that is, except infants and those who are mentally ill. Even 1-year-old babies usually act differently when Mom is around versus when she is not. People modify their behavior according to where they are as well as how they are feeling—serious pain can put a serious damper on the behavior of the world's happiest extravert.

Fleeson (2001) found that when our traits are measured in multiple ways, consistent differences in personality traits are stable and predictable across situations. Talkative individuals tend to be more talkative, most of the time, than their more reserved peers. However, when we want to understand how a particular person will act in a specific situation, we need to know the details of that situation. Talkative individuals are, as a rule, less talkative when they are sleeping.

Twenty years after its publication, Mischel's (1968) critique of traits has been evaluated as having salutary effects on the study of personality (Kenrick & Funder, 1988). For one thing, trait theorists learned that multiple measures of a trait, aggregated behaviors, show far greater consistency over situations than do single observations. Trait theorists, as a result of this controversy, better understand how to construct more valid personality tests.

Another benefit accruing from this controversy is that trait theorists are reminded that behavior does not occur in a vacuum. An individual's behavior may reflect not her personality by itself, nor the situation by itself, but the *interaction* of the person with her situation.

Arnold Buss (1979) notes that there are three kinds of person x situation interactions:

1. *The effect of one variable depends on the presence of another variable.* In a study of almost 2,000 young adults, risky sexual behavior was influenced by the person x situation interaction across a number of personality variables and types of situations. For example, highly impulsive individuals (compared to less impulsive ones) were less likely to use a condom *only* when they were having casual sex. The personality variable of impulsivity *did not* explain condom use when these individuals were either engaged or married to their sexual partner. In other words, condom use was affected by the interaction of a personality trait, impulsivity, and a situational variable, one's relationship (casual, engaged, or married) with a partner (Cooper, 2010).

2. A second meaning of person x situation interaction is that *people usually select their situations.* Athletes like to be with other jocks on the athletic field or hang out with other gym rats. Studious individuals are often found in the library. Online gamers choose to spend much of their free time gaming.

3. A third meaning of a person x situation interaction is that *personality can change situations*. A dull gathering can turn into an enjoyable experience by the arrival of a "life-of-the-party" individual who is a natural "icebreaker." Conversely, a convivial social evening can turn sour with the arrival of a dominating and aggressive person whose idea of fun is insulting people.

Where do we stand now? Two recent developments are noteworthy:

(A) The important dimensions of situations may have been identified. David Funder and his colleagues have proposed the "Situational Eight DIAMONDS" as a comprehensive taxonomy for clearly identifying which aspects of situations will influence our behavior (Funder, Furr, & Colvin, 2000; Rauthmann et al., 2014). These are the Eight DIAMONDS:

1. *D*uty: The situation calls for a job or a project to be completed.

2. *I*ntellect: The situation affords an opportunity to show intellectual ability.

3. *A*dversity: The situation involves being criticized or threatened in some way.

4. *M*ating: The situation involves members of the opposite sex or romantic partners.

5. p*O*sitivity: The situation is enjoyable, humorous, or playful.

6. *N*egativity: The situation is anxiety arousing, stressful, or frustrating.

7. *D*eception: The situation involves the possibility of being deceived or betrayed.

8. *S*ociality: The situation involves social interaction or being with close friends.

The DIAMONDS taxonomy helps resolve a problem that has long bedeviled situation researchers: How do we specify when one situation shifts into a different situation? For example, a dedicated work group (Duty) may shift into an enjoyable social event (pOsitivity + Sociality) as soon as their work task is completed, thus allowing aspects of personality (e.g., playfulness, humor) to emerge, traits that were inhibited as long as the task remained unfinished. Other advantages of this approach include the possibility of providing standardized situation characteristics as well as a uniform way of classifying situations, thereby allowing researchers to determine how similar or dissimilar they are to each other (Rauthmann et al., 2014).

(B) A second development shows that personality variables by themselves can transcend specific situations and thus play a vital role for various life outcomes. Consider the following general conclusions based on numerous investigations:

– The trait of *extraversion* is linked to happiness, subjective well-being, health, longevity, and resilience. It is also associated with satisfaction in romantic relationships and community involvement.

– The trait of *agreeableness* is linked to spirituality, religious values, and behavior. It is also associated with health, longevity, and a decreased chance of heart disease. Agreeable people have satisfying peer and family relationships and are satisfied with their occupations.

– The trait of *conscientiousness* is also linked to spirituality, religious values, and behavior. Conscientious people are less likely to engage in risky behaviors, abuse substances, or engage in antisocial or criminal activity.

– The trait of *neuroticism* (emotional instability) is linked to unhappiness and an absence of subjective well-being. It is also associated with dissatisfaction, conflicts, and abuse in romantic relationships.

– The trait of *openness to experience* is linked to spirituality, virtues, and forgiveness. It is also associated with artistic interests and a politically liberal attitude (Ozer & Benet-Martinez, 2006).

So is personality real or is it an illusion? Personality is real as long as we remember that situations are equally real. If we "know" someone who we see only in the same type of situation, the consistency we see in his behavior may reflect his personality or it may only reflect how he behaves in that type of situation. We need to keep an open mind.

2. Five Theoretical Approaches to Personality

Throughout this book, I present five theoretical orientations to understanding personality. These theories shed light on basic questions about differences between individuals at similar points over the life span and personality changes within the same person over the life course.

These five theoretical approaches—psychodynamic, trait theory, cognitive/social learning, humanistic/existential/narrative, and evolutionary psychology—contribute uniquely meaningful ideas and hypotheses for understanding personality differences. The complexity of personality is matched by the complexity of those theories designed to explain it. There is no grand unifying theory of personality that encompasses all five approaches. Yet.

These five approaches are covered in greater detail in Chapter 1. Here we take a brief look at the unique purpose of each approach to help us focus on their similarities and differences.

Psychodynamic

The psychodynamic approach to personality arises from the clinical practices of Sigmund Freud and others. It is chiefly, but not exclusively, concerned with our *emotional responses* and *emotional conflicts* aroused by the events of everyday life, especially those that cause dysfunctional overreactions to unpleasant events (e.g., by becoming excessively anxious, depressed, or angry to the point of being unable to cope effectively with the annoying event). Chronic emotional overreactions to the changes of everyday life might indicate the presence of unconscious conflicts. Deep-seated conflicts usually require psychotherapy to bring them to the surface where they may be successfully resolved. Liliane Frey-Rohn (1974) views Freud's emphasis on emotions and feelings in treating neuroses to be his essential contribution. Other theorists who adopt the psychodynamic point of view, such as Carl Jung, point to the lack of meaning in the adult's life as a contributing cause of his or her emotional difficulties. The distinguishing feature of all psychodynamic theorists is the importance they place on the unconscious (out-of-awareness) part of our personalities.

Trait Theory

These theorists consider personality traits to be the *structure* of personality. They hope to discover the fundamental building blocks of personality and how these traits (blocks) fit together. Beginning with Gordon Allport (1937) and continuing today with the extensive research program of Robert McCrae and Paul Costa (2008) and others, many trait psychologists believe that five basic traits—extraversion, neuroticism (emotional instability), conscientiousness, agreeableness, and openness to experience—adequately capture the major ways our personalities are similar and different. While trait theorists disagree about the exact number of traits, all do agree that fundamental personality traits are found in all cultures around the world. Two traits that are virtually always found in cross-cultural research are introversion/extraversion and emotional stability/instability. In contrast to the psychodynamic approach, trait theorists deal with the conscious part of personality that can be accessed through self-reports on personality tests.

Cognitive/Social Learning

The cognitive/social learning approach to personality stresses the importance of cognitions or thoughts as central to our personality. Walter Mischel's (1973, 1990) approach to personality focuses on social-cognitive units of study such as competencies, constructs, expectancies, goals, and self-regulatory systems. Personality theorists who favor this approach underscore the role of thinking, planning, and problem solving as key variables for understanding individual differences.

Humanistic/Existential/Narrative

The humanistic/existential/narrative approach stresses the significance of personal meaning in one's life—the spiritual dimension of personality. Ideas such as self-actualization (Abraham Maslow, Carl Rogers); the search for meaning (Victor Frankl); life narratives (Dan McAdams); and personal constructs (George Kelly) all deal with the central role of meaning for understanding personality.

Evolutionary Psychology

Evolutionary psychology is unique among these five theoretical views because it explains personality by examining the evolutionary origins of the human species rather than by looking at the origin of your individual personality. The central premise of evolutionary psychology is that the human mind is equipped, as in hard-wired equipped at birth, with a set of *evolved psychological mechanisms*. These mechanisms exist because they solved specific problems of survival or reproduction over our long evolutionary history. Moreover, these evolved mechanisms are designed by natural and sexual selection to respond to a relatively small set of stimuli, just as our eyes respond to light waves but not to sound waves and vice-versa for our ears. Identifying these evolved psychological mechanisms is one of the ways evolutionary psychology explains how your personality is both similar to all other people as well as how you are unique (Buss, 2008).

QUESTIONS TO PONDER

1. How can we *measure* someone's personality? Why would we do so? Are any ethical issues involved?

2. Does your everyday behavior largely reflect your *personality,* or is it primarily influenced by the various *social situations* you find yourself in? How about your *friends*? Is their behavior more a reflection of their personalities or of the situations they encounter?

3. Have you ever wished you had a different personality? If so, what stops you from having one?

SUGGESTIONS FOR FURTHER READING

Gladwell, M. (2005). *Blink: The power of thinking without thinking.* New York, NY: Back Bay Books.

Haidt, J. (2012). *The righteous mind: Why good people are divided by politics and religion.* New York, NY: Vintage Books.

Kurzban, R. (2010). *Why everyone (else) is a hypocrite: Evolution and the modular mind.* Princeton, NJ: Princeton University Press.

Nettle, D. (2007). *Personality: What makes you the way you are.* New York, NY: Oxford University Press.

Using Theory and Research to Understand Personality

❖What are theories of personality, and why are they important?

A theory is like a map. Theories are devices to help us get from *here* (our present knowledge) to *there* (a better understanding of nature). Thus, the primary question one asks about any map or any theory is, *Is it useful?* Does it represent reality accurately enough so we can make sense of where we are now? Does it help us get to where we want to go?

Why is it important to know theory? The simplest and most direct answer is that every person is a complex system of feelings, thoughts, goals, plans, and so on. Every person has a unique history, functions (more or less) in the present moment, and has (or despairs of having) meaningful hopes for the future. If we want to understand how *any* complex system works, we need a good theory, just as we need a good map to help us find our way around a complex city. We need good theories of personality to help us answer interesting and important questions about ourselves and other people.

We use personality theory throughout the book to help answer questions concerning our similarities and differences. To appreciate how a theory helps answer questions, we first need a basic understanding of the nature of scientific theories. In the first part of this chapter, we outline what a theory is, what functions it serves, and how to tell a good one from a bad one. All theories, like all maps, are not created equal.

Basic Questions About Theories

What Is a Theory?

A *theory is a conceptual scheme that attempts to organize and explain the facts of nature in terms of general principles or laws.* The facts of nature that the theorist wants to organize and explain fall within the domain or content area of the theory.

Freud's theory of personality, for example, assumes adults' present emotional disturbances originate from their unresolved psychological conflicts that occurred during early childhood. One fact Freud could not explain was why some of his adult women patients showed evidence of impaired neurological functioning (for instance, paralysis of an arm) even though a thorough physical examination found no neurological basis for the impairment. At that time, such cases baffled neurologists (which Freud was at the beginning of his career). If there is no *physical basis* for the impairment, Freud reasoned, there must be a *psychological* reason for it. But what could that be? Why in the world would anyone use her own mind to disable herself? Freud realized that a new theory of neurological functioning was needed.

To say that a theory is a *conceptual scheme* means that it is created in the mind of the theorist. The theory-builder selects what he or she thinks are the most important variables or features of the events to be explained and hypothesizes how these variables relate to each other. As a conceptual scheme, a theory provides an abstract picture of how nature operates, just as a map shows an abstract picture of how the streets and highways of a city intersect. All new theories are new conceptual schemes.

What Are the Functions of a Theory?

A good theory serves three functions:

1. It organizes many different observations with as few variables as possible. This is the *synthesizing function* of a theory. Good theories should organize and integrate known facts from within a single domain (e.g., human behavior) and within a single, over-riding, logically consistent framework (e.g., the specific theory). Freud, for example, attempted to synthesize all of his patients' diverse symptoms (e.g., nightmares, anxiety, associations to dream images, slips of the tongue, etc.) into a coherent story relating all these symptoms to his patients' unresolved childhood conflicts.

2. Moreover, theories may suggest new hypotheses (specific predictions) to be tested against observations not yet made. This is called the theory's *heuristic function*. Hypotheses that are supported by observations increase the scope of the theories from which they were drawn, thereby making the theories even more useful.

   Hypotheses, then, are educated guesses to what should be observed under particular conditions. After reading a map of an unfamiliar city, for example, we predict (hypothesize) the most efficient route from Point A to Point B. We need to drive the hypothesized route to discover if our hypothesis is correct (our map may be out-of-date). Direct observation, after all, is the essence of the empirical method. We can test many more hypotheses with a highly detailed map than we can with a crudely drawn map.

3. A theory should direct our attention to the most important variables of interest. But it should also prevent us from becoming bewildered or distracted by the complexity of the events we want to understand. Hall and Lindzey (1978) refer to this as the theory's *blinder function.* By focusing only on some discrete set of key variables, the theory says, in effect, we can safely ignore all other variables that are part of the complex phenomenon we want to understand. In reading a map of a city, for example, you need to know how the streets inter-connect with one another. Maps do not tell you how these streets were originally constructed or the names of everyone who built them. Such information would just make the map more complicated and would not help you get around any easier. Similarly, all theories reduce the complexity of the events they want to explain by focusing on relatively few variables.

How Can I Tell a Good Theory From a Poor Theory?

For starters, good theories adequately fulfill the preceding three functions. Poor theories fail to integrate all the known facts of a domain, fail to generate interest in testing additional hypotheses, or fail to eliminate unnecessary variables.

In addition, theories differ in the *scope* of what they are designed to explain. The greater the scope, the more events or facts the theory encompasses. Einstein's Theory of Relativity and Darwin's Theory of Evolution are called "grand" theories because of their enormous scopes. The greater a theory's scope, the greater is its potential usefulness. A highly detailed atlas is potentially more useful than a map of a small town.

Within the domain of personality theories, the approaches of Sigmund Freud and Erik Erikson have a wide scope, relatively speaking, because both attempt to explain personality processes that take place over the life span. Other theories of personality have more modest scopes that focus on more circumscribed aspects of the person. At the present time, *no* grand theory of the person integrates, or even tries to integrate, all of our identifiable "parts"—mental, emotional, spiritual—that constitute what it means to be a well-functioning individual. Might you be the person psychology needs to meet this daunting challenge?

Theories also differ in their simplicity, or *parsimony*. The more events a theory can adequately explain *with the fewest possible theoretical constructs*, the more parsimonious it is. At the top of the class of scientific theories meeting this criterion is undoubtedly Albert Einstein's formula connecting the two major variables of our physical world, energy and matter: $E = mc^2$ (c is the speed of light). Parsimony becomes an important criterion when comparing *theories that are otherwise identical* in doing their major job, that of being useful maps. Personality psychology has not yet reached the stage where we can select a good theory *based only* on its parsimony because we still disagree about the relative scientific usefulness of our available theories.

Finally, theories differ in their scientific status on the interrelated criteria of the *testability* of the hypotheses derived from them and the *refutability* or *falsification* of their major claims about the nature of human nature. A testable hypothesis is one in which the observed outcomes will lead us to accept or reject it. An untestable hypothesis is one that will survive any observation.

An example of an untestable hypothesis is a teacher's claim that any student who failed his or her test did so because he or she didn't study "hard enough." Any student who replies, "But I studied very hard" is countered with, "No, you didn't. The proof is that you failed the test. If you had studied hard enough, you would have passed it." Such an explanation for students' failures is irrefutable because the teacher has *no independent measure* of "studying hard." She only observes her students' test scores. She assumes that *all* failing performances are caused by lack of adequate study. But what if some of her students have serious learning disabilities that prevent them from assimilating what they study, no matter how hard or how long they work at it? Her staunch commitment to her untestable hypothesis prevents her from discovering any reasonable alternative interpretation of what she observed.

So it is with scientific theories. Refutable hypotheses allow researchers to collect information and see for themselves which hypotheses should be retained, which should be modified, and which should be discarded. Testing plausible alternative interpretations of existing data permits rapid scientific progress by quickly excluding those interpretations that lead to dead-ends (a sure sign of a bad map!). John Platt (1964) has called this aspect of hypothesis testing "strong inference." But those so-called theories that are based on untestable hypotheses (e.g., "Intelligent Design") are only speculations about human nature. These speculations may be provocative and interesting to some people, but they are *not scientific theories* because they cannot be disproved (Popper, 1959). Nonrefutable hypotheses only provide us with out-of-date, useless maps that lead us around in circles, getting nowhere.[1]

The role of research, then, is to help us evaluate the validity of hypotheses derived from theories. The role of *research design* is to provide useful guidelines for collecting evidence or data that—as unambiguously and clearly as possible—shed light on the truth or falsity of the hypothesis under investigation. A hypothesis, like any declarative sentence about the nature of the world, is either true or false (under the particular conditions of testing). The failure to support a hypothesis derived from a theory in any particular instance does not necessarily mean that the hypothesis is false; nor does it mean the theory is useless. Other interpretations for the failure to support a hypothesis must be examined. For example, the failure might be due to a flawed procedure (e.g., an unreliable personality test) used by the investigator. Useful theories generate novel hypotheses and are supported by the research evidence just as a valuable map allows us to test and evaluate different hypotheses about the most efficient ways to get around town.

As you read this text, consider how the five major theoretical approaches compare on the preceding criteria for evaluating scientific theories. More importantly, consider how these theories relate to your own life. To what extent do they help you create a better understanding of your own personality?

Now that we have a basic background in the nature of scientific theories, we present an overview of five theoretical approaches to personality. The purpose of the overview is to give you an idea of which personality variables the theory considers to be especially important. Each theory will also be covered in greater detail in later chapters.

Five Personality Theories

The Psychodynamic Orientation

Principal Theorists: Sigmund Freud
Alfred Adler
Carl Jung
Karen Horney
Erik Erikson
John Bowlby

The psychodynamic orientation to personality stresses the importance of unconscious components in the human psyche or mind and the relationship of the unconscious to the conscious or aware part of the mind. *Psychodynamic* is an umbrella term that connotes any theory that values the role of the unconscious in determining human personality. Sigmund Freud began this approach at the end of the 19th century. Subsequently, many individual theorists, only a few of whom can be given space in this book, created their own unique versions, each with a new name to distinguish their theories from Freud's psychoanalysis. Thus Freud is our first guide in our journey to the mysterious inner recesses of the mind.

Sigmund Freud

The "father" of modern personality theory, Sigmund Freud (1856–1939), first used the term *psychoanalysis* in 1895 in his *Studies on Hysteria,* coauthored with Josef Breuer (Clark, 1980).

Psychoanalysis today has three distinct meanings. It may refer to a *process of psychotherapy,* a *general theory of personality,* and a *research method* for investigating unconscious processes. Freud assumed that unconscious processes brought into awareness by psychoanalysis are basic to all humans and apply to healthy individuals as well as to those who are emotionally disturbed.

In Freud's monumental *The Interpretation of Dreams* (1900/1965), he proposes that our dreams reveal our unconscious wishes and fears, frequently in disguised form. One of the psychoanalyst's tasks, Freud suggested, is to help his patient decode the *manifest dream symbols* into their *true* or *latent meanings* to bring dark, unconscious wishes into the light of awareness.

Freud's encounters with his adult patients pointed him in the direction of early childhood sexual experiences and fantasies for understanding personality development.[2] Freud first proposed that all neuroses were caused by early sexual abuse of the child by an adult in the child's life (the sexual seduction theory or the trauma theory of neuroses). He later changed his mind and concluded that as small children, his patients unconsciously *wished* to sexually possess their opposite-sex parent (the Oedipus complex). Their inability to renounce this wish, Freud thought, caused emotional problems in adulthood. But some question whether Freud too quickly abandoned his original sexual trauma theory (Esterson, 1993; Masson, 1992).

In any event, Freud generalized his therapeutic conclusions into universal statements about human nature based on a small number of case histories. These Freudian universals include (1) the Oedipus complex, (2) invariant (unchanging) psychosexual stages of development, and (3) his structural model of the personality as composed of the id, ego, and superego.

Freudian Universal #1: *The Oedipus Complex:* The Oedipus complex refers to a deep-seated, unconscious wish for a pleasurable and exclusive relationship with one's opposite-sex parent and the permanent elimination of one's rival, the parent of the same sex. The little boy wants his mommy's exclusive attention and love, and the little girl wants the same from her daddy. This complex appears during the phallic stage of development when young children discover the pleasure of masturbation, during which, Freud presumed, they unconsciously fantasize about possessing the parent of the opposite sex.

Freud thought that the Oedipus complex was eventually resolved by different processes in boys and girls. Little boys are induced to give up masturbating (and fantasizing about possessing mommy) under the threat (real or imagined) of the *castration complex*, especially if they happen to see that girls lack a penis ("Look what happened to them!"). Little girls, however, already know they lack a penis: "From the very first she envies boys its possession; her whole development may be said to take place under the colours of envy for the penis" (Freud, 1940/1989b, p. 76).[3] A little girl, then, often fails to get much pleasure from masturbation (clitoral stimulation being more difficult to achieve regularly than is stimulation of the penis) and soon gives it up "since she has no wish to be reminded of the superiority of her brother or playmate" (p. 76). So the castration complex in girls ("Someone must have cut off my penis!") *precedes* her Oedipus complex, whereas in boys the castration complex follows it. As we will see, this difference led Freud to assume sex differences in how the Oedipus complex gets resolved, resulting in his peculiar view of women's moral sensibilities.

Freud's views about the Oedipus complex were extremely controversial in his lifetime and remain controversial today. On the one hand, Freudians admit that most of Freud's hypotheses are too difficult to test in the laboratory (Westen, 1998, p. 355) and that compelling scientific evidence for the Oedipus complex is still lacking (Luborsky & Barrett, 2006). On the other hand, those with a Freudian orientation report strikingly impressive anecdotes that seem to verify the reality of the Oedipus complex: A father reported that his 4-year-old son said, "Mommy, daddy has to leave. I don't like him anymore." When the boy's mother asked her son why, he replied, "He has a bigger penis than I do" (Westen, 1998, p. 355).

Freudian Universal #2: *The Psychosexual Stages of Development:* The invariant psychosexual stages of development are called the oral, anal, phallic, latency, and genital stages. The Oedipus complex, Freud believed, occurs at about the age of 4 or 5 when children pass through the *phallic stage* of development and first learn of the pleasures associated with self-stimulation of their genitals. Prior to this stage, children's psychic energy or *libido* (which is essentially sexual in nature, according to Freud) expresses itself in pleasurable activities associated with the mouth (*oral stage:* birth to 1 or 2) and anal cavity (*anal stage:* ages 3 to 4).

Freud believed three significant events take place during the phallic stage:

1. The Oedipus complex will be successfully resolved only if the little boy *identifies* with his father and forgoes the wish for the exclusive love and attention of his mother. Fear of castration helps him resolve his Oedipus complex. This fear comes from either direct, external threats from his father ("Stop playing with yourself or I'll cut it off!") or from the unconscious hostility he projects toward his father ("Daddy will cut it off because he's angry at me"). Boys who identify with their fathers are no longer jealous of mommy's attention to daddy. The effect of identification with daddy is to feel, unconsciously, that mommy's attention to daddy is, in a way, attention to him also. Fear of being castrated and the resolution of the Oedipus complex leads the little boy directly into the nonsexual latency stage.

For girls, it is quite a different matter. Freud (1933/1989a) distinguishes two stages in girls' development—pre-Oedipus and post-Oedipus. Pre-Oedipally, the little girl has affectionate feelings for her mother. These feelings are the basis for the daughter's identification with her mother. Post-Oedipally, the girl sees her mother as a rival for her father's attention and love. At this stage, the little girl wants to get rid of her mother so she can take her place with her father. Freud was unable to figure out how a little girl ever successfully resolves her Oedipus complex.[4] In fact, Freud finally concluded that girls *never* adequately deal with their Oedipus complex.[5]

2. Failure to resolve the Oedipus complex during the phallic stage results in a chronic emotional disturbance or *neurosis*, which may last a lifetime unless treated by psychoanalysis. An unresolved Oedipus complex in a neurotic adult frequently manifests itself as chronic unwillingness to take personal responsibility for the consequences of one's actions or inactions (e.g., always blaming someone else when things go wrong). Freud believed that *all neuroses* were due to unsuccessful resolutions of the Oedipus complex (a sweeping but untestable hypothesis).

3. The failure to identify with the parent of the same sex during the phallic stage may result in *confusion of gender identity* and/or homosexuality. Boys who cannot identify with their fathers may identify with their mothers; girls who cannot identify with their mothers may

identify with their fathers. As a consequence, the person may develop a lifelong attraction to members of the same sex as compensation for the missing parental identification.

The *latency stage* (sexually quiet) and *genital stage* (attachment of the sexual drive to an appropriate person of the opposite gender) characterize post-Oedipus development. Freud thought that the three earliest stages (oral, anal, and phallic) represent potential psychic landmines that could result in (a) arrested development (*fixation*), (b) adults returning to a prior stage when under stress (*regression*), or (c) fixed personality characterizations throughout adult life (for example, the "passive oral character" who chronically depends on other people).

Freudian Universal #3: *The Structural Model of the Mind:* Freud's universal structural model proposes that the human mind (psyche) can be divided (analyzed) into three parts—the id, ego, and superego. Thus Freud called his system "psycho-analysis."

The *id*—the unconscious, biological, instinctual part of our personalities—functions according to the *pleasure principle:* It seeks sources of gratification and avoids sources of pain. Infants are pure ids.

The *ego*—the conscious (most of the time), executive part of the personality— operates via the *reality principle*, whereby we are able to postpone gratification of our innate drives until they can be appropriately satisfied. The ego is the part of the personality that tolerates the tensions built up by the id and *decides* when it is appropriate to satisfy them. For example, it is not socially correct in mainstream North American society to slurp your soup during a funeral service, no matter how hungry you might be. Tolerating our hunger pangs until the service is over requires an ego strong enough to inhibit us from shouting out, "Hurry up! I'm starving!"

It is important to distinguish the conscious ego from the *ego complex*, which exists at both the *preconscious* level (Freud's term for the subconscious, which is the "level" of the mind that is relatively accessible to conscious awareness) and the *unconscious* level (the deeper regions of the mind whose contents are not as easily brought into awareness).

The ego complex manifests itself in various ways:

(a) we feel hurt, disappointed, and/or angry whenever we don't get what we want (e.g., it rains on the day of our picnic);

(b) we feel hurt and/or angry when other people fail to give us the special treatment we feel we are entitled to;

(c) we feel hurt and/or angry when someone holds a different opinion than ours; or

(d) we automatically hijack conversations to talk about ourselves rather than continue the topic brought up by someone else. Have you noticed how many people would rather talk about themselves than empathize with the speaker?

The ego complex, then, refers to the many ways we unconsciously see ourselves as the center of the universe. A person in the grip of his or her ego complex tends to be annoyed by the manifestations of someone else's ego complex ("He's so arrogant! He thinks *he's* the center of the universe!"). The challenge for adults is to retain their ego strengths while minimizing the automatic and out-of-awareness influence of their

ego-complex. The intense unconscious grip of the ego complex may be weakened by being willing to become conscious of its scope and presence in our life, whenever it pops up. Consciousness ("There I go again!") gradually dissolves the strength of our unconscious complexes.

The *superego* is the component of the psyche that has incorporated the moral rules, regulations, and values of the child's social group, as first taught by the parents. The superego contains both the ideals we strive to meet (resulting in feelings of pride) as well as the punishments we experience (via guilt feelings) when we know we have violated our moral principles. The superego contains both consciously held ethical principles ("I will treat other people as I would like to be treated by them") as well as unconscious, primitive, unrealistic, and rigid rules ("If I think a bad thought, I must be a bad person"). One of the goals of psychoanalytic therapy is to help the patient distinguish the mature moral code he or she consciously chooses to live by from the inflexible, black-and-white judgments of the immature child. Data obtained from well-controlled randomized trials show that psychodynamic therapies can be effective for treating a variety of psychological disorders such as depression, panic disorder, and substance abuse (Gibbons, Crits-Christoph, & Hearon, 2008).

Freud viewed sex and aggression as innate biological drives that all humans have to control if stable human communities are to survive. This control requires the young child to internalize his or her parents' views about the proper time and place to express these instincts. Freud thought that normal human existence consists of chronic *conflict* between our innate physiological drives and our learned values from society. Our biological and social natures, Freud believed, constantly battle one another:

1. Our instinctual id presses for *immediate satisfaction* ("I want it now!") only to be

2. *turned away* either by a harsh superego ("Thou shalt *not* ...") or frustrated by the unavailability of resources in our immediate environment (e.g., we are hungry but there is no food), or the conflict is

3. *successfully alleviated* by our ego ("I'm very hungry now, but I will nevertheless keep working on this task because I know I can eat in one hour").

Freud believed psychoanalysis effectively helps patients strengthen the executive part of their personality, the conscious ego, so they can successfully (i.e., in a *relatively* stress-free manner) resolve the perpetual demands among the warring components of the id and superego and cope with the demands of external reality. Given the insistent nature of our biological drives, the ego may win the battle of the hour, but the incessant war between our instinctual and social natures continues until we die.

Psychoanalysis does not provide us with a joyous philosophy of life, as illustrated by Freud's belief that its ultimate purpose is to free patients from neurotic suffering so we can experience the normal miseries of everyday life. Those familiar with the basic tenets of Buddhism know that it teaches precisely the opposite: Our egos are the *cause* of our suffering, not the solution to it! Carl Jung, in a way, "split the difference" between these contradictory views. Jung thought that developing an adequate ego is the main task for the first half of life (around age 30–35), while the second half requires relinquishing its grip over the mind: we need to retain our ego strengths but not let our egos rule us. Caring for other people is one way to "get outside of ourselves" and weaken the ego complex.[6]

Conflicts that are not successfully resolved by conscious ego decisions may be temporarily resolved by various defense mechanisms. *Defense mechanisms* are unconscious techniques of the ego designed to lessen or eliminate anxiety by distorting some aspect of reality. The threat to the ego that triggers a defense mechanism may reside in either the external world (e.g., the threat of infection by the HIV virus) or the inner world (e.g., feelings of hatred that threaten one's self-concept of being a "nice" person).

Defense mechanisms are useful in the short run. They prevent us from being overwhelmed. They give us breathing space, time to adapt to the threat. Defense mechanisms become problematic when they prevent us from taking appropriate and realistic actions to deal with the true source of our anxiety. In the long run, however, the continual use of automatic, unconscious defense mechanisms leads us into inevitable difficulties with other people. Why? Because all defense mechanisms distort reality to one degree or another. As a patient of psychoanalyst Karen Horney complained at the beginning of treatment, "If it were not for reality, I would be perfectly all right!" (Horney, 1950, p. 37).

A personal example of how defense mechanisms operate may be helpful. When I first heard that President John Kennedy had been shot, I *immediately* thought, "No, it's a terrible mistake. It's not really the president who was shot. Someone who *looks* like President Kennedy has been shot."

Freud would have interpreted my reaction as manifesting the defense mechanism of *denial.* My immediate and automatic denial of the event served the short-run function of giving me time to adapt to the shocking news. After turning on the television and watching the news coverage, I soon gave up my denial and began to cope consciously with the tragedy. Denial is a commonly used first line of defense against accepting and dealing with especially painful parts of external reality, such as the loss of a loved one or the news that one has a terminal illness (Kübler-Ross, 1969).

Freud attracted a group of followers in the early part of the 20th century, some of whom eventually broke away to form their own versions of psychoanalysis because they disagreed with Freud's insistence that all mental energy or libido was sexual in nature. Influential personality theorists such as Alfred Adler, Carl Jung, and Karen Horney, to name a few, denied the validity of Freud's *pansexualism*, his belief that conscious and unconscious sexual drives are the root cause of all manifestations of mental life (Gay, 1988). We return to Freud in Chapter 4 when we examine how he thinks our early childhood experiences affect our adult personalities.

Alfred Adler

Alfred Adler's (1870–1937) *individual psychology* focuses on the importance of early childhood experiences and on our orientation to the future. Adler maintains that although our past experiences affect the way we view or interpret our current experiences, the goals we strive toward can alone explain our behavior. These goals are motivated by the individual's attempt to overcome *feelings of inferiority* that originated in early childhood. Adler's idea of *fictional finalism* reflects his belief that "the final goal alone can explain man's behavior" (1930, p. 400). This final goal (e.g., peace on earth, equality of all humans, or universal justice) may be impossible to realize, and thus a fiction, but it nevertheless motivates a great deal of our present behavior. Adler's ideas about the relevance of birth order are presented in Chapter 4, and his views about the significance of goals are covered in Chapter 6.

Carl Jung

Carl Jung's (1875–1961) *analytical psychology* differs from Freudian psychoanalysis in its unique premise that the human mind contains *two layers* of unconscious material. Some of the key terms in Jung's theory of personality are personal unconscious, collective unconscious, archetypes, complexes, and individuation.

Along with the *personal unconscious* that Freud analyzed in therapy—that level of the unconscious that is unique to every person—Jung (1965) postulated the existence of a *collective* or *universal unconscious.* Jung believed the personal unconscious is primarily composed of complexes while the collective unconscious—common to all humans—acts as a "storehouse" of great bundles of energy called archetypes.

Archetypes are psychic traces of the human race's earliest and most universal experiences, such as being reared by a parent, living in some sort of shelter, and being attracted to people of the opposite sex. Jung believed archetypes are shared by all humans. Archetypes predispose us to relate to conscious experiences in specific ways, similar to how instincts function in animals (the question about the functions of "archetypes" will reappear as a question about the functions of "modules" when we cover evolutionary psychology).

A *complex* acts like an invisible, emotionally tinged, mental magnet that unconsciously pulls the person's conscious feelings and attention to itself. Complexes disrupt the "flow" of consciousness. The individual is usually unaware of this abrupt change when it happens. To the individual under the influence of an unconscious complex, his sudden shift in conversation topics seems both normal and interesting. The stronger the complex, the more easily it will be triggered by an innocuous remark. "The straw that broke the camel's back" might be a complex: Innocent words can provoke violent reactions. Complexes, like other manifestations of unconscious influence, are more easily observed in others than in oneself.

To illustrate a complex in operation, consider the following true incident. Bob and Jan, a married couple, were seated around a dining room table along with six other adults. While we pleasantly conversed, Jan looked into her purse, intently searching for something that apparently was supposed to be there. After many minutes, Bob asked, "Jan, what's missing?" Jan immediately glared at him and said, loudly, "Shut up, Bob! It's not my fault!" Jan's complex instantly took control of her consciousness as she immediately interpreted her husband's neutral query as one of blame ("It's MY fault something is missing"), and she responded angrily and inappropriately to him. This incident suggests that Jan, like many people, carries a *guilt complex* that can easily "pop out" at the slightest provocation.

Other common unconscious complexes include the *inferiority complex* (feeling ashamed about our real or imagined incompetence), the *ego complex* (seeing oneself as the center of one's social universe, around which other people, like planets around the Sun, must always revolve), the *power complex* (always needing to be in control and in charge), the *sex complex* (shown by an immediate sexual association to any nonsexual stimulus, such as a fresh cantaloupe or banana), and the *money complex* (the only unforgiveable sin in some households is buying retail).

While Freud saw the dream as the "royal road" to the unconscious, Jung identified the complex as serving this function (Jung, 1934/1969a). Complexes manifest themselves in chronic negative emotional reactions—such as anger, hurt feelings, anxiety, shame—to the ordinary events of everyday life (as exemplified by Jan's anger), as well as in the patterns found in our dreams.

Complexes are also revealed by unusual and idiosyncratic associations. A man who instantly makes a sexual comment after seeing a picture of the face of a 75-year-old woman is controlled by his sex complex. Another heterosexual man whose immediate response to a fold-out image of an underdressed, beautiful female model is "I wonder how much money she's paid?" seems to be controlled by his money complex. Note that a sexual response to a stimulus designed to provoke a sexual response provides no information about the presence of a complex. It is only odd or strange reactions that are suggestive of an unconscious complex.

Jung notes that we don't have complexes; complexes have us. Complexes grab our conscious attention at the slightest provocation. Striking shifts in conversation topics may be symptoms of a complex, especially if the same person shifts to the same topic on multiple occasions. Complexes are caused either by (a) unresolved conflicts or (b) by expending a great deal of conscious energy and attention on a single topic over a long period of time or (c) both. Conversations among retired couples tend to center around prior work experiences (retired men) or food (wives of retired men) or health (both) or grandchildren (both).

Individuation refers to Jung's view of the development of personality: "Individuation is a natural process. It is what makes a tree turn into a tree. . . .

Consciousness can . . . block individuation by not allowing what is in the unconscious to develop" (Jung, in McGuire & Hull, 1977, p. 210). Individuation differs from Maslow's self-actualization in the importance Jung places on deliberately allowing our unconscious to play an active role in our life. The opposite of individuation is the one-sided and incomplete development found in those who suppress and deny all unconscious aspects of themselves. Jung (1931/1969b) held that the true goal of personality development is *wholeness*—each individual needs to become the unique whole or complete person he or she was meant to become.

Jung's view of personality is that we all approach life with either an extraverted or introverted attitude. Most people, Jung realized, can adopt either attitude depending on the immediate situation and so are referred to as "ambiverts." It is only those individuals who are at the extremes who always adopt the same attitude—introverted or extraverted—no matter what situation they are in, who are properly labeled as introverts or extraverts.

This attitude, in combination with one of the four distinct ways of dealing with the events of everyday life, results in eight distinct "types" (he meant "traits") of personalities.

The ways we deal with reality, the four functions, are sensation, thinking, feeling, and intuition. These functions exist in a particular relationship to each other with sensation and intuition being opposites as are thinking and feeling. Psychic energy used by one function takes away psychic energy from its opposite. Thinking clearly is virtually impossible whenever we are intensely emotional. Similarly, individuals whose thinking function is dominant often have a difficult time knowing exactly what they are feeling.

Sensation is the function that tells us *something is,* thinking tells us *what it is,* feeling tells us whether *we like it or not,* and intuition tells *us where it came from and what will happen next.* Individuals differ in which one of these four functions we use first, automatically, and most easily in coping with reality. Jung calls this our "superior function." This preference for a particular function (along with a strong aversion to employing its opposite) results in distinct personality types (Jung, 1921/1971).

Are you a fan of *Star Trek?* The original characters in the television production clearly illustrated these Jungian "types." Mr. Spock, brainy and cold, obviously represents the thinking type. Spock would calmly inform everyone, without any emotion, that the crew has exactly 17.43 seconds to live unless the proper buttons on the Gizmo Machine are pushed in the correct sequence. Doctor McCoy represents Spock's opposite. McCoy is pure feelings ("Dammit, man, I'm a doctor, not a Servo-Mechanism device!"), feelings often expressed as anger directed at Spock, precisely because Spock has no feelings. "Feeling" and "thinking" types often have a difficult time living together, as not a few married couples have discovered.

Scotty, the ship's engineer, represents the sensation type. Scotty has to be aware of the engines' conditions at all times lest they suddenly explode when he's not looking. He often warns the captain that the ship's engines are about to "blow" because of Kirk's rash decision to jump start them on cold mornings. Scotty's conflicts with the captain are inevitable because Captain Kirk embodies the intuitive function, sensation's opposite. Kirk comes up with out-of-the-blue solutions to life-threatening problems that no one else, not even the brainy Spock, thought of, intuitive leaps that get them out of jams in the nick of time! Whew, that was close! The interaction and conflicts among these crew members are personifications of what goes on inside each of us as we use, ignore, or suppress any of these four functions. Jung would have loved the show.

Each of us has the capacity to engage in all four functions. But whether through nature or nurture, or a combination of both, all of us settle on one of the four functions as *the* way we prefer to deal with reality. Jung calls this, as mentioned above, our superior function. He hypothesizes that the opposite of our superior function is our inferior function, the one we least like to use, the one we use reluctantly, often with anxiety, and almost always *crudely*. The more we like to engage reality by *thinking* about it, the less likely we are to be aware of our *feelings*. To a "thinking type," his feelings are likely to be experienced only as "good" or "bad," whereas someone's whose feelings are her superior function experiences them as highly nuanced and differentiated. A "feeling type," in the same way, is likely to feel uncomfortable when required to exercise her thinking function. Making fine intellectual distinctions is as difficult for her as nuanced feelings are for the thinking type.

Likewise, highly intuitive individuals resist getting "bogged down" in the boring sensory details of daily living as they long to be free from the chains of sensation. And individuals who live for fresh sensory input, whether it be from traveling to new lands, eating new foods, wandering around flea markets, or whatever, often fail to appreciate the larger picture. Their present sensations are what they value most. Jung held that individuation includes our efforts to come to terms with our inferior function over the life course to become whole persons. We return to Jung's concept of individuation in Chapter 10.

Karen Horney

Karen Horney (1885–1952) was certain Freud did not understand women. Horney clearly saw that Freud's biologically oriented explanations of women's psychology (for instance, his view that women are more insecure than men because they lack penises) completely ignored the restrictive social forces at work in Europe in the 20th century.

Horney was personally familiar with prejudice toward women. As a high school student, she was prohibited from taking an anatomy course because young women of her time were not allowed to view naked corpses. Horney saw that many women of her day lacked self-confidence only because social conditions, not innate biological factors, favored men over women. Horney concluded that if women are affected by "penis envy," then men must be equally influenced by "womb envy." Freud did not like her attitude (Horney, 1967; Quinn, 1987).

Horney's central concept is *basic anxiety*. Basic anxiety arises from early childhood experiences of insecurity. Basic anxiety is the child's "feeling of being isolated and helpless in a world conceived as potentially hostile" (Horney, 1950, p. 18). Many events can produce insecure feelings in a child: being dominated by a parent, unpredictable behavior by parents, being chronically overprotected or ignored, or being required to take sides in chronic parental arguments (Horney, 1945).

All neurotic behavior is a variation on the theme of seeking security by reducing or eliminating basic anxiety (Horney, 1950). She classifies different neurotic "solutions" into the three general procedures of *moving toward others* (being dependent on other people's love, attention, and/or approval to feel secure), *moving against others* (asserting oneself or dominating others to feel secure), and *moving away from others* (withdrawing from others, isolating oneself to feel secure).

It is important to understand that moving toward, against, and away from other people are not, in themselves, neurotic behaviors. Horney points out that in different life circumstances, any one of the three "moves" may be quite appropriate. Indeed, for a person to function normally, all of them are needed, depending on the situation. A person who is not dominated by the need to feel safe can use any appropriate action to reach his or her goals: Sometimes we need to assert ourselves, sometimes we need to rely on others, sometimes we need to be alone. Different problems call for different solutions.

Someone suffering from a neurosis, however, feels anxious at the *mere thought* of behaving in a way that contradicts his false self-image. He attempts to solve all of his problems by using just *one* of these moves (the one that makes him feel safe) in *every* situation. What makes the particular move a neurotic solution is that it is used indiscriminately, based only on what makes the person feel safe, rather than its appropriateness in the situation. It is like trying to fix broken wooden furniture by using only one tool. While a hammer is an excellent tool for putting nails through wood, it is not helpful for sanding purposes.

"Moving toward" others is a psychologically healthy thing to do when we are physically or emotionally ill. Seeking help in that condition is a normal manifestation of our evolved attachment-exploration system. But it is inappropriate whenever we need to stand up for ourselves. A woman whose false self-image requires her to always be nice to others (no matter how they treat her) favors the "moving toward" solution. She feels anxious at the mere thought of standing up to other people. She has great difficulty asserting herself. She confuses acting (properly) assertively with acting (improperly) aggressively. She may feel anxious at the thought of taking time for herself, withdrawing temporarily from social life to collect herself, because others might see her as "selfish." And it is almost impossible for her to deny doing favors for other people no matter how much she may be inconvenienced. The idealized and compulsive self-image is a harsh taskmaster.

Similarly, a man whose false self-image requires him to assert himself in all situations favors the "moving against" solution. He feels at ease as long as he is "top dog" but is visibly anxious when he feels "less than" others in his immediate social environment. He tends to dominate conversations in social gatherings. He psychologically equates asking for help with "being weak." So he often fails to get the help he needs because his false self-image cannot admit to any weakness, such as the "weakness" shown by asking a stranger for directions.

In Horney's view, we achieve emotional freedom only when we recognize and accept our true selves. This entails discarding that false self-image associated with adopting one "solution" to fit all of life's challenges. Only by accepting who we really are can we realistically cope with varying life problems by changing our responses to fit the situation. One size does not fit all. The essence of all "neurotic solutions" is the futile attempt to replace who we really are with who we wish to be (our idealized self). Horney compares the neurotic solution to the canine world: It is as if a cocker spaniel said, "I'm really a Great Dane!" and then acted as if this delusion were true, trying to maintain it in spite of numerous contradictions from everyday reality, and feeling angry and hurt whenever his friends treat him as he really is, a cocker spaniel, rather than who he pretends to be.

Individuals who adopt a neurotic solution have interpersonal difficulties whenever they unconsciously demand that other people treat them as they want to be seen, to support their idealized self-image, rather than respond to them as they really are. A man who compulsively presents himself to others as a loving, exceptionally wise person is terribly offended when he learns people see that his "love" is contingent on being constantly reaffirmed as a "guru." Since he is not ready to acknowledge his neurotic solution, his reaction to this news is to no longer associate with anyone who fails to support his self-flattering self-image. Replacement friends are found. His neurotic solution remains intact. Horney's views are developed in more detail in Chapter 7, "Stress and Coping."

"Pardon me, do I detect a whiff of smug indifference
hiding behind the facade of a wallflower?"

Erik Erikson

Erik Erikson (1902–1994) trained as a child psychoanalyst with Sigmund Freud's daughter, Anna, and was elected to the Vienna Psycho-Analytic Society in 1933. He began his professional career committed to Freud's view of human nature. But Erikson's cross-cultural observations of the Native American Sioux and Yurok peoples eventually led him to reject Freud's notion of unresolved childhood conflicts as the sole explanation of their unusual ritualistic behavior. Instead, Erikson saw that the Yurok and Sioux were undergoing a *series of developmental crises* highly similar to the personal crises experienced by many people in Europe and the United States. In Erikson's theory, the successful resolution of these crises serves to strengthen the individual and ultimately promotes psychological health.

Erikson's distinctive contributions to personality theory lie in his views that

1. ego development takes place over the entire life span,

2. a series of universal stages or crises characterize individual development, and

3. each individual must adapt to specific demands of his or her culture.

Thus Erikson created a *psychosocial approach* for understanding personality. Personality develops, or fails to develop, as we engage, or fail to engage, with each task society sets before us. At the heart of our life-long development is our *identity*, a concept Erikson (1968) introduced in his hugely influential book, *Identity: Youth and Crisis*. While Erikson's life-span view of personality development is presented throughout the rest of this book, Chapter 5 ("Identity and Self-Esteem") focuses on his major contributions to this central concept of personality.

John Bowlby

John Bowlby (1907–1990) studied children's attachments to their caregivers. Bowlby held that from these attachment relationships children develop conscious and unconscious mental images of themselves and others. He called these mental images *internal working models*. Internal working models, Bowlby hypothesized, help us perceive events, forecast possible futures, and construct our plans. Internal working models, formed early in childhood, can influence our choices throughout our lives (Ainsworth & Bowlby, 1991; Bowlby, 1973). Although Bowlby began his professional career as a Freudian psychoanalyst, his unique approach to personality draws from the diverse fields of ethology, cognitive control theory, and psychoanalytic principles of defense and conflict resolution. Bowlby's concept of internal working models applies both to our formative years (Chapter 4) as well as to how we plan to reach our objectives (Chapter 9).

Trait Theory

Principal Theorists: Gordon Allport
Raymond Cattell
Hans Eysenck
Paul Costa and Robert McCrae

Personality traits are organized *dispositions* within the individual. These dispositions are revealed in a person's consistent and distinctive behavior across a variety of different situations. Traits dispose us to behave in similar ways throughout our lives. When we perceive differences in the personalities of our friends and acquaintances,

© Bettmann/CORBIS

Photo 1.1 Gordon Allport (1897–1967)

Allport, a vigorous proponent of personality traits, proposed the distinction between nomothetic and idiographic approaches. Allport is the single most important person in the history of the scientific study of personality.

Key publications:

Personality: A Psychological Interpretation (1937)
The Nature of Prejudice (1954)
Pattern and Growth in Personality (1961)

we are seeing differences in their traits: Jack is friendlier than Tom, but Tom is more conscientious than Jack. Do you want to have a good time? Call Jack. Do you want to get your work done on time? Call Tom.

Traits are sometimes confused with types. In everyday language, we might hear someone say, "He's the type of person who . . ." Strictly speaking, a type refers to a *distinctive category* so that a person either fits into that category or does not. For example, some people have Type A blood, while others have Type B, AB, or Type O. These are discrete, qualitatively different, types of blood. There is no middle ground and there is no range within types. One person with Type A blood does not have more or less Type A blood than others. Adding more Type A blood will not produce Type B blood.

A trait, however, unlike a yes-or-no type, refers to a *range* of possible dispositions. The trait of agreeableness, for example, ranges from extremely agreeable to extremely disagreeable. Everyone's personality will fall somewhere in this range. Most people's personality test scores are near the middle of the range on most traits. When personality psychologists designate a trait by a single term—extraversion, agreeableness, honesty—the designation refers to one pole of the trait, while its opposite pole is implied. All personality traits are bipolar—they range from one extreme to the other.

The Lexical Hypothesis

How can we identify which personality traits are important? One simple way would be to examine the words we use to describe people. If the ways we differ from each other are important and noticeable enough to assign them verbal labels, then examining natural language should tell us a great deal about which personality traits are significant in everyday life. This is the basis of the *lexical hypothesis:*

> *Those individual differences that are most salient and socially relevant in people's lives will eventually become encoded into their language; the more important such a difference, the more likely it is to become expressed as a single word.* (John, Angleitner, & Ostendorf, 1988, p. 174)

Sir Francis Galton (1822–1911) first proposed the lexical hypothesis in 1884. His effort resulted in a list of about 1,000 words. Since then numerous investigators have made a more systematic effort to capture all of the words in a language that describe personality traits. John et al. (1988) provide a comprehensive history of the lexical approach up to the late 1980s.

The prize for the most ambitious attempt to understand personality traits by examining language goes to Gordon Allport and Henry Odbert. They consulted *Webster's New International Dictionary* (1925), which contained about 550,000 words, searching for all words that "distinguish the behavior of one human being from that of another" (Allport & Odbert,1936, p. 24). They found almost *18,000 words* that referred to some aspect of personality.

After removing synonyms and including only those terms that uniquely describe stable personality traits, Allport and Odbert were able to reduce the number of words to 3,000. Raymond Cattell (1905–1998) then used Allport and Odbert's list as a starting point to find common personality "factors" that could account for most of these terms. Cattell later summarized his work with, "the trouble with measuring traits is that there are too many of them!" (1965, p. 55).

Cattell's early work was limited by the unavailability of modern computers and software that can reduce a large set of correlations among many personality variables to a few common factors. (This valuable procedure, *factor analysis*, is described in Chapter 2.) Because of this, and other procedural details, the personality factors that Cattell identified have not been replicated by other investigations (John et al., 1988).

Modern Trait Theory

So how many traits are there? Five. No, six. Wait, maybe there is only one. Or two. Or three! A thorough review of trait theory presents evidence in support of each of these positions (Saucier & Srivastava, 2015). The numerical disagreement is due, in part, to how general or broad one considers a personality trait to be. Welcome to trait theory.

1. There is only one trait: *good versus bad.* This largest global evaluation trait was first identified in 1957 by Charles Osgood and his colleagues as the largest single factor among words in a language. They found, across many different languages, that people use the evaluative dimension of good versus bad as their first and primary dividing principle for categorizing people, things, and events (Osgood, Suci, & Tannenbaum, 1957).

Among studies of the structure of personality traits, the one trait solution has been reported by Saucier (2003) and others (see Saucier & Srivastava, 2015).

2. There are two traits: *individual initiative* (high versus low) and *community solidarity* (high versus low). These two basic personality dimensions, as found by Goldberg and Somer (2000) and others, had been previously described in terms of *agency* versus *communion* (Bakan, 1966) or *getting ahead* versus *getting along* (Hogan, 1983). One dimension applies to characteristics of the individual in the pursuit of his or her goals, while the other dimension describes the individual's connections, positive or negative, to other people.

3. There are three traits: *individual initiative* (high versus low), *honesty and agreeableness* (high versus low) and *conscientiousness and impulse control* (high versus low) (De Raad et al., 2010). The three trait solution splits community solidarity into two smaller traits: one concerned with cooperation with others, the other with self-discipline (Saucier & Srivastava, 2015).

Long before this recent lexical discovery of three traits, Hans Eysenck had proposed three major traits of personality: extraversion, neuroticism, and psychoticism. The trait of *psychoticism* refers to undersocialized individuals who are likely to be involved in criminal activities. Eysenck's psychoticism dimension is most closely allied with the De Raad et al. (2010) conscientiousness and impulse control dimension (Eysenck, 1947; Eysenck & Eysenck, 1976).

4. There are five traits: The "Big Five" (John, Naumann, & Soto, 2008) and the Five-Factor Model (McCrae & Costa, 2003) have, as of this writing, more empirical support than any other trait theory. These five traits have been identified across numerous independent investigations: *neuroticism* (anxious, vulnerable versus easy going, unruffled), *extraversion* (versus introversion), *openness to experience* (imaginative, curious versus uninterested in trying new activities or exploring new ideas), *agreeable* (versus disagreeable), and *conscientious* (versus irresponsible, careless).

The Big Five solution has been replicated across numerous languages. Lexical studies in German, Dutch, Czech, Croatian, Polish, Turkish, and English have found these five traits are sufficient for describing personality differences (Saucier & Srivastava, 2015). The one trait that sometimes fails to replicate is openness to experience. This failure most often occurs when the research is conducted within pre-industrial, rural societies. Perhaps individual differences on the trait of openness are difficult to perceive when daily life revolves around repetitive patterns and innovation is rare or nonexistent (Piedmont, Bain, McCrae, & Costa, 2002).

5. There are six traits: *honesty-humility* has been identified as a sixth personality dimension in addition to the Big Five, yielding a model called HEXACO: honesty-humility, emotionality, extraversion, agreeableness, conscientiousness, and openness (Ashton & Lee, 2001; Ashton, Lee, & deVries, 2014). While the Big Six was originally detected in Korean and French samples, it has been replicated in other languages. The six trait solution may be less tied to the Germanic and Slavic language groups than the Big Five (Saucier & Srivastava, 2015). Future research, we can hope, will settle the question of the independent existence of the honesty-humility trait. Is it truly a separate personality dimension, or is it better understood as a combination of conscientiousness and agreeableness?

Cognitive/Social Learning Theory

Principal Theorists: Walter Mischel
                     Albert Bandura
                     Charles Carver and Michael Scheier

Cognitive/social learning personality theorists recognize the central importance of the thoughts and perceptions we have of ourselves and others. This orientation primarily differs from the humanistic/existential/narrative orientation in its stress on the cognitive component of personality. Personality variables such as *expectancies, personal constructs, self-efficacy, plans, anticipated outcomes,* and *schemas* are some of the concepts encountered within the cognitive/social learning approach.

Walter Mischel

Mischel (1973) proposes five kinds of variables that are relevant to understanding another person. The five variables that comprise the Cognitive-Affective Processing System (CAPS) are influenced by unique events over our life course. Not only do we differ in our characteristic traits or dispositions (which is one aspect of this approach), but we differ in how we *process* the events and experiences of our lives (Mischel & Shoda, 2008). Your personality consists of two fundamental aspects: a static aspect (your personality traits) and a processing aspect (CAPS): How you *process* the objective events in your life creates your unique *experience* of these events.

These five CAPS variables—encodings, expectancies and beliefs, affects, goals and values, self-regulatory competencies and plans—must be taken into account to understand an individual's behavior in any given situation: Our behavior is the result of how we interpret and feel about our experiences. Mischel's five variables comprehensively cover the cognitive/social learning orientation and thus serve well as an overview to this approach.

1. *Encodings:* We all interpret (or *encode*) information from the world to form our unique set of personal ideas about ourselves and others. If you've ever discovered that you and a close friend hold very different interpretations of the "same" event (the behavior of a mutual friend, how enjoyable a movie is, etc.), then you've experienced the reality of personal constructs. It can be quite a shock to find that the *meaning* or *attribution* you give to someone's actions is not shared by a close friend. The same behavior you interpret as "pushy," "aggressive," or "controlling" might be viewed by someone else as "assertive" or "showing leadership."

2. *Expectancies and Beliefs:* An example of expectancies is Albert Bandura's (1977, 1986) concept of self-efficacy. *Self-efficacy* refers to your expectation that you can execute the behavior needed to get what you want. You might understand that to obtain something you want (to go on a date), you need to take certain actions (ask her out). However, you may nevertheless have low self-efficacy regarding your likelihood of actually carrying out the required behavior (you are too shy to ask). Bandura's research demonstrates effective ways of raising people's self-efficacy in particular situations. Expectancies, whether conceptualized as Bandura's self-efficacy or Bowlby's internal working models, are critically important person variables for understanding personality over the life course.

3. *Affects:* Everyone has feelings or emotions (affects) associated with significant events in their lives. These feelings are also aroused whenever we recall these past events. Memory researchers tell us that whenever an experience generates strong emotion, adrenalin and other hormones are released, and the release of these hormones guarantees we will remember this experience for a long time, perhaps forever (McIntire, McGaugh, & Williams, 2012). Thus, if the original event caused us to experience a strong unpleasant emotion (or combinations of emotions) such as embarrassment, shame, guilt, resentment, anger, or sadness, whenever we recall that event in the future, those same feelings will be aroused.

   The concept of affects includes our physiological responses to events. Not only do we differ from each other in how we construe or interpret events in our lives, we also differ in how we feel about those events given a similar interpretation. Loud, boisterous boys at a picnic might annoy some nearby adults, while others shrug their antics off with a "boys-will-be-boys" attitude.

4. *Goals and Values:* What actions we take depend not only on how we perceive the situation and our expectancies, but also on what we want. Our values, purposes, and preferences are among the most stable aspects of our personalities (Mischel, 1984).

5. *Self-Regulatory Competencies and Plans:* In order to achieve your major life goals, you need to (1) know what they are, (2) know you are capable of executing the necessary actions, and (3) develop *plans* to attain them. Self-regulation refers to Mischel's idea that we are capable of directing and controlling our own present behavior toward the goals we hope to realize in the future. When external *feedback* (like grades) is absent or minimal, persistence in the behavior to reach our goals requires internal self-regulation, as Carver and Scheier (1981) have emphasized. For example, to continue to study diligently throughout a course with only one or two exams requires a stronger self-regulatory system than to do so in a course with weekly quizzes. When our "payoffs" (our major goals) exist in the distant future, we need an internal guidance system that regulates and orients our present behavior toward our goals. Self-regulatory systems include our goals and the self-imposed rules that direct our behavior toward them.

Humanistic/Existential/Narrative Theory

Principal Theorists: Abraham Maslow
Carl Rogers
George Kelly
Victor Frankl
Dan McAdams

The humanistic/existential/narrative approach to personality pays far less attention to unconscious motivation and unconscious conflict than does the psychodynamic approach (although it does not ignore it). Rather than view the person as buffeted about by his or her complexes and unresolved conflicts, the humanistic/existential/narrative approach stresses that each individual actively constructs his or her own personality and needs to take responsibility for so doing if maturity is to be reached. Of the five orientations considered in this book, the humanistic/existential/narrative approach is the one most concerned with the spiritual dimension of personality as manifested in a person's search for the meaning of his or her life.

Abraham Maslow

Abraham Maslow (1908–1970) distinguished between deficiency needs and growth needs. Sometimes our perceptions of another person are motivated by *deficiency needs:* We want something from her, something we don't have, but we think we need. Consequently, we see her as either providing or withholding, generous or stingy, useful or useless. Under these conditions, we do not see her as she really is. Our perception of her is sharply limited by our own *frame of reference.* When we operate from deficiency, we see other people *as if* they are objects, either objects blocking our way or objects we hope to manipulate to our satisfaction.

In contrast, the special way we perceive the world during *peak experiences* (wonder-filled events of awe and ecstasy) is *Being-cognition:* the other person or object "tends to be seen as a whole, as a complete unit, detached from relations, from possible usefulness, from expediency, and from purpose" (Maslow, 1968, p. 74).

Maslow's concept of Being-cognition shares much in common with philosopher Martin Buber's (1970) concept of the *I-Thou* relationship (in which we see others as they are in themselves). Similarly, Maslow's notion of deficiency motivation is similar to Buber's *I-it* relationship, which occurs whenever we see other people as objects or "its" in our world. Buber proposes, interestingly, that whenever we see another person as an "it," we become an "it" as well! Buber and Maslow agree that how we see other people deeply reflects our own personality.

Maslow's approach to personality, then, sharply distinguishes deficiency motivation from growth motivation. Growth motivation is reflected in a person's concept of self-actualization, the tendency to reach one's highest potential. The self-actualized person agrees with Shakespeare's advice (in *Hamlet*), "to thine own self be true."

Carl Rogers

Carl Rogers (1902–1987) maintained that each person exists in the center of a *phenomenal field,* the totality of his or her past and present experiences. To understand other people requires that we let them reveal their own phenomenal field as they understand it, from their own internal frame of reference. Rogers (1951) developed *client-centered* or *nondirective therapy* as a means for letting the client (no longer referred to as a patient) be in charge of the therapeutic process. This includes encouraging the client to take responsibility for his or her own growth toward healthy functioning. Roger's view of the *fully functioning person* has much in common with Maslow's self-actualizing person. Rogers's views are examined in more detail in Chapter 5, "Identity and Self-Esteem."

George Kelly

George Kelly (1905–1967) placed great emphasis on the way we perceive or *construe* our world. Kelly's (1955) theory, called the *psychology of personal constructs*, holds that we attempt to make sense of our world by developing constructs, or personal lenses, through which we perceive "objective" reality. These constructs are like flawed glass: They do *not* allow our perceptions to reflect reality with perfect accuracy. There are always new and improved ways of matching our constructs to reality, which Kelly calls *constructive alternativism.* Throughout the life course, we modify, change, and revise our constructs so they might better reflect our actual experiences.

Kelly's basic premise is that everyone is keenly interested in anticipating future events. Knowing how and what a person predicts will happen in the future is crucial for understanding that person's present behavior. Kelly's *fundamental postulate* is, *A person's processes are psychologically channelized by the ways in which he anticipates events.*

Our anticipation of future events sets in motion psychological processes to deal with them. A clear example of this is the *self-fulfilling prophecy:* If I (mistakenly) anticipate that tomorrow you will be angry with me, I may consequently feel angry and unfriendly toward you even before our meeting. When we do meet tomorrow, I might act in a cold or harsh way toward you. As you experience my unfriendly attitude, your attitude toward me becomes unfriendly. At that point I think to myself, "I knew this would happen" and feel justified for my initial unfriendly behavior. Unfortunately, I do not see that it was precisely my own faulty anticipation of your angry feelings (and my subsequent behavior toward you) that influenced your reaction. Kelly's view is that daily life consists of a series of anticipations and the psychological processes they generate. Kelly's theory is covered in greater detail in Chapter 9.

Victor Frankl

Victor Frankl (1905–1997) initially wrote of his experiences as a holocaust survivor shortly after his release from a Nazi concentration camp in 1945. Out of these horrific experiences, Frankl constructed his own style of psychotherapy, which he calls a *therapy of meaning* or *logotherapy.* Frankl (1984) holds that not only is each person solely responsible for the meaning he or she finds in living, but each person must answer to life by *"answering for* his own life; to life he can only respond by being responsible. Thus logotherapy sees in responsibleness the very essence of human existence" (pp. 113–114, italics in original). Logotherapy is discussed further in Chapter 10.

Dan McAdams

Dan McAdams proposes that individuals give their lives purpose and unity by creating *narratives* or stories about themselves. A person's identity is found within the *life story* he or she creates. In McAdams's approach, the life story is one of three levels of personality.

One level consists of our basic *dispositions or traits* such as agreeableness or conscientiousness. Another level consists of our *characteristic adaptations* to our environment such as our goals and coping strategies. The third level is how *we integrate all aspects of ourselves* into our life story. McAdams's view of personality is useful for understanding how we form, maintain, and perhaps alter our sense of who we are, our identity, over the course of our lives. The theme of *redemption* is central to many life stories (McAdams, 2006).

Evolutionary Personality Theory

Principal Contributors: Richard Alexander
                                        William Hamilton
                                        David Buss
                                        Steven Pinker
                                        Leda Cosmides
                                        John Tooby

The time is ripe for the field of personality psychology to mature into an explanatory science.

—David Buss and Lars Penke (2015, p. 5)

Evolutionary psychology applies to personality in two ways. First, it attempts to explain those aspects of human behavior that are universal. As expressed by evolutionary psychologists John Tooby and Leda Cosmides: "The long-term scientific goal toward which evolutionary psychologists are working is the mapping of our universal human nature" (2005, p. 5).

How did the human mind evolve? One possibility is that competition and conflict with other human tribes caused our brains to evolve the way they did. (Alexander, 1989; Flinn, Geary, & Ward, 2005; Irons, 2005). A hominid tribe that could out-think its enemies, even slightly, possessed a vital advantage. The ability of your tribe to imagine and predict where and when a hostile enemy tribe might strike, and plan accordingly, gives your tribe a significant military advantage. The human mind became a weapon in the struggle for survival, a weapon far more decisive than any before it. And this mental advantage was applied, over and over, within each succeeding generation. The tribe that could out-think its opponents was more likely to succeed in battle and would then pass on the genes responsible for this mental advantage to its offspring. You and I are the descendants of the winners.

Over our long 5- to 6-million-year history as a separate species, the ability to out-think our opponents eventually resulted in the formation of the prefrontal cortex, whose functions include *imagining future scenarios* (mental time travel), *planning,* and *decision making* (Fuster, 2008). We carry within our genes the same adaptive mechanisms that enabled our ancestors to be successful. Evolutionary psychology (EP) seeks to identify and provide ultimate explanations for such universal human adaptations as fear of the dark, care for our young, and ethnocentrism (Brown, 1991).

EP gives us a blueprint to identify situations that really matter—situations that involve *adaptive problems.* Universal human adaptive problems include finding and attracting a mate, detecting and punishing cheaters within an ongoing social group, discriminating friends from foes, negotiating status hierarchies, avoiding being ostracized by the group, and so on. EP affords a systematic way of selecting meaningful situations to investigate because they involve known problems of adaptation (Buss & Penke, 2015; Pinker, 1997).

The second way evolutionary psychology applies to personality is by explaining the ubiquitous presence of personality differences. There are two opposing views within EP about the meaning of personality differences:

1. Some evolutionary psychologists argue that variability in human personality traits means that these traits are *not important* from an evolutionary point of view: Trait variability is only *random noise* since neither extremity of the trait has been naturally selected for either survival or reproduction purposes. This point of view notes that the end result of natural selection is *uniformity* of a characteristic across individuals within a species, not variability. Millions of years ago natural selection determined that humans need exactly two ears, two eyes, and one nose to survive. Thus all healthy human babies are born with precisely those numbers of facial features. We do not observe variability in these facial features from one person to the next (Tooby & Cosmides, 1990).

2. Other evolutionary psychologists disagree. The presence of a species-wide evolved adaptation is compatible with individual differences in how that adaptation is expressed. Each of us have a number of adaptations that help us get along in groups, but we vary on such personality dimensions as agreeableness, extraversion, and conscientious, traits that influence how we function and adapt within these groups: Some people are more cooperative than others, some easily adopt leadership roles, some people are more dependable. There are numerous ways we can adapt to and fit into the social groups that are important to us. Lars Penke states the case directly: "There is absolutely no reason to assume a one-to-one match between adaptations and dimensions of individual differences" (2011, p. 245). The challenge of evolutionary psychology is to explain both what we have in common and how and why we differ.

Two general approaches are used in EP to explain personality differences:

Life history theory focuses on individual differences in inclusive fitness (Kaplan & Gangestad, 2005). *Inclusive fitness theory* was first proposed in 1964 by William Hamilton (1936–2000) to extend Darwin's original idea of fitness (those genes which you pass to your children) to the care you provide to your own children (if any) *plus* the care you provide to your brothers' and sisters' children *plus* any care you give to any offspring related to you. By your altruistic actions, you help to spread a portion of your genes to the next generation. Since you share, on average, 50% of your genes with your siblings, any children of your siblings, your nieces and nephews, will carry, on average, 25% of your genes. Hamilton's brilliant idea was to see that Darwinian fitness (parent-to-child) was too narrow. Your inclusive fitness refers to the *total reproductive success of your entire family,* immediate and extended (Buss, 2012). So it is not a surprise, then, to find that some human groups *prescribe* altruism to one's kin, no matter how distantly related, genetically speaking, they may be (Burnstein, 2005).

The importance of personality within inclusive fitness theory has been demonstrated in a study of nearly 11,000 individuals. Those persons who scored higher on extraversion, lower in conscientiousness, and lower in openness to experience were associated with having more children and more grandchildren. Higher agreeableness was associated with having more grandchildren. Personality traits were thus shown to be related to reproductive success over three generations (Berg et al., 2014).

The second way that evolutionary psychology understands individual differences in personality is by the idea of *conditional adaptations.* Adaptations are conditional when the same genetic structure (genotype) results in a different appearance (phenotype) due to environmental conditions. A compelling example of this is *first language acquisition.* Although we all are born with the same hard-wired propensity to learn language, a propensity Steven Pinker (1994) calls the *language instinct,* the actual languages we first learn to speak reveal a remarkably diverse set of distinct vocal sounds. We easily learn to speak the first languages we hear. But learning a new language later in life is far from easy for most people.

Other examples of conditional adaptations that explain individual differences in personality include differences in the quality of children's attachment to caregivers (e.g., secure versus insecure), enduring situational differences (e.g., raised by a single parent versus two parents), and selecting particular positions or niches within one's larger environment to spend one's energy (Bronfenbrenner, 1979). Exposure to different niches may encourage the expression of different aspects of one's personality (e.g., extraverted salesman versus conscientious bookkeeper versus aggressive athlete versus curious researcher). Variability in personality traits can lead to an understanding of how personality interacts with situations (Buss & Greiling, 1999).

Evolutionary psychology is covered in more detail later in this book. Chapter 3 presents an evolutionary understanding of the traits of the five-factor model. Chapter 6 shows EP's contribution to understanding such universal human motives as the need to belong to a social group, striving for social status, and mate selection.

Table 1.1 summarizes the five approaches to personality including the key contributors and concepts associated with each.

❖ **Table 1.1**   Summary of the Five Theoretical Approaches to Personality

Approach	Major Contributors	Key Terms
Psychodynamic	Freud, Adler, Jung, Horney, Erikson, & Bowlby	Unconscious conflicts, inferiority feelings, defense mechanisms, complexes, psychosocial crises, internal working models
Trait Theory	Allport, Cattell, Eysenck, Costa, & McCrae	Types vs. traits, trait domains vs. facets, manifest vs. latent traits, factor analysis
Cognitive/Social Learning	Mischel, Bandura, Carver, & Scheier	Plans, self-efficacy, self-regulation
Humanistic/Existential/ Narrative	Maslow, Rogers, Kelly, Frankl, & McAdams	Self-actualization, personal constructs, meaning of life, life story
Evolutionary Psychology	Alexander, Hamilton, Pinker, Buss, Cosmides, & Tooby	Adaptations, inclusive fitness, life history theory, differential reproduction, modularity of mind

❖

QUESTIONS TO PONDER

1. Of the five orientations to personality covered in this chapter, which one do you find most appealing? Which one is least appealing? Might your initial reactions be related to your personality?

2. How would you describe the psychological differences between your ego and your ego-complex? Are there certain situations when your ego complex is likely to be activated? How do you feel at those times? Would you like your ego complex to be activated more often than it is now?

3. Over the past 5 years, has your personality changed at all? In what ways? How much do you expect it to change over the next 5 years?

4. From the standpoint of evolutionary psychology, in what ways will human personalities be different 1,000 years from now? What assumptions must be true for these changes to occur?

❖

NOTES

1. An engaging report of Intelligent Design's spectacular failure as a science may be found in Lauri Lebo's *The Devil in Dover: An Insider's Story of Dogma v. Darwin in Small-Town America* (2008, The New Press).

2. The orthodox view is that Freud observed sexual conflicts in his patients and then developed his theory from these observations. But revisionist views of the beginnings of psychoanalysis suggest that Freud began his treatment by *assuming* sexual conflicts lay at the heart of their emotional disturbances and then attempted to *convince his patients* that sexual conflicts were at the root of their troubles. For detailed information on this point see *The Memory Wars: Freud's Legacy in Dispute* by Frederick Crews (and 18 others) published in 1995 by *The New York Review of Books.* Also check Frank Sulloway's (1992) intellectual biography of Freud: "Freud's initial fascination with establishing sexuality's omnipresent part in the neuroses was inspired by his highly ambitious vision in the 1890s [of transforming psychology into biology or physiology]" (p. 90). It would seem that 100 years after the origin of psychoanalysis, we continue to debate what Freud actually observed in his patients versus what he hoped to observe.

3. References to publications (e.g., Freud [1940/1989b]) that give both the date of initial publication and the date of the currently available translated version indicate when these seminal ideas were first made public.

4. Sometimes the Oedipus complex in girls is referred to as the Electra complex. But the term may have first been used by Carl Jung, not Freud. In fact Freud argued against using different terms for boys and girls. See Freud (1940/1989b, p. 77, footnote 6).

5. Because Freud couldn't figure out within the structure of his biologically based drive theory of personality how girls successfully resolve their Oedipus complex, it is not surprising that he also held many unfavorable views about women. He believed, among

other things, that women have "little sense of justice," are "weaker in their social interests," and have "less capacity for sublimating their instincts than men" (1933/1989a, p. 166). Freud was blind as a bat when it came to seeing the powerful effects of cultural forces and social situations in shaping personality and behavior. He was remarkably unaware that the women of his era, the Victorian age, were placed under a severe set of restraints, both physically (corsets, etc.) and socially (norms and expectations). See Quinn (1987) for more information on this point.

6. An informative illustration of the difference between the *ego* and *ego-complex* occurred many years ago on an episode of the TV series, *The Wonder Years*. The older sister of the show's main character said to her brother that she wanted to tell him something about himself, but she didn't want this knowledge to go to his head. Her brother agreed. She then informed him that girls thought he was good-looking. In one sentence, we can see the difference between the ego (self-knowledge) and the ego-complex (allowing that knowledge to "go to your head."). An enlightening way to discover the strength and scope of one's ego complex is to try to go a full day without saying the words *I, me,* or *mine.*

❖

SUGGESTIONS FOR FURTHER READING

Frankl, V. (1959). *Man's search for meaning.* Boston, MA: Beacon Press.
Freud, S. (1933/1965). *New introductory lectures on psycho-analysis.* New York, NY: Norton.
Kroeger, O., & Thuesen, J. M. (1988). *Type talk.* New York, NY: Dell.
McAdams, D. P. (2006). *The redemptive self: Stories Americans live by.* New York, NY: Oxford University Press.
Pinker, S. (1997). *How the mind works.* New York, NY: Norton.

❖

INTERNET RESOURCES

Disclaimer: The below media resources are provided to enhance your interest in the material in the text. Please be aware that Internet tests are often not validated. They are for educational purposes only and certainly not for accurate self-diagnostic measures of your personality. Should you choose to take one or all of them, you should interpret your results as something you might want to think about rather than necessarily indicating anything definitive about your personality. IOW, interpret your results with a large grain of salt and do not hesitate to LOL.

1. For information about the Big Five personality traits, see http://www.outofservice.com/bigfive/.

2. For a tour of the Freud Museum, see http://www.freud.org.uk/.

3. To take the Myers-Briggs test of Jung's four functions, go to http://www.humanmetrics.com/cgi-win/jtypes1.asp.

2

Research Methods and Personality Assessment

How do psychologists learn about personality? Why should I care?

Research Methods
    Experiments
    Correlational Research
    Case Studies

Personality Assessment
    Purposes of Assessment
    Settings for Assessment
    Test Reliability and Validity
    Types of Assessments

Ethical Issues in Research and Assessment

Summing Up: How Should I Interpret My Score on a Personality Test?

Chapter 1 outlined a number of useful ways to think about personality. These ways are called theories: conceptual maps to help us understand the complexities of personality and point us in fruitful directions to learn more. This chapter peeks inside the research psychologist's toolbox to examine the methods and techniques used to discover how we are similar and different from one another.

The major point of this chapter has been succinctly expressed by Charles Darwin:

"How odd it is that anyone should not see that all observation must be for or against some view if it is to be of any service."

Darwin's epigram calls our attention to the point of research. What views (e.g., guesses, hypotheses, theories) do our observations (e.g., measurements) support, fail to support, or contradict? Darwin correctly noted if observations are to be of real value, they need to be closely connected to *some view* in the sense that either our observations confirm what we expect to find or they fail to support, perhaps even contradict, this point of view. Useful scientific observations are like signposts: They point us in one direction or another. We learn from them.

Research Methods

Personality psychologists draw upon a variety of different kinds of observations to help them understand the full extent of individual differences. The particular kind of observations frequently depends on the type of research she is doing: an experiment, correlational work, or a case study. The type of research depends on the specific hypotheses she is investigating.

Experiments

When the goal of the research is to determine if there is a *causal* relationship between two variables, the researcher must conduct an *experiment*. Among all the tools in the researcher's toolbox, only experiments can identify cause-and-effect relationships.

The essence of an experiment is that the researcher assigns participants to two or more groups in such a way (e.g., by simple random assignment) that these groups are probably equivalent to each other on all relevant variables. She then treats these (presumably) equivalent groups differently by assigning them to different levels of her *independent variable* (the variable that might cause differences in behavior). She then observes some aspects of personality (her *dependent variable*—those behaviors that might be influenced by her independent variable) to see if they differ. If her groups, on average, differ significantly (in a *statistical* sense), she then concludes that her independent variable caused those differences she observed in her dependent variable.

A quick example of an experiment: A teacher randomly assigns students to different amounts of time (her independent variable) to finish their exams to see if those who were allowed only 25 minutes will receive, on average, a different grade (her dependent variable) than those who were allowed the full 50 minutes.

Three conditions must be met before we can logically conclude that changes in independent Variable A *cause* changes in dependent Variable B:

1. *Variable A comes before Variable B.* The cause always precedes the effect.

2. *Variable A and Variable B covary.* Changes in the independent variable are reliably associated with changes in the dependent variable.

3. *Other plausible causes are eliminated.* By randomly assigning participants to different *treatment groups* (i.e., *levels* of the independent variable) and controlling for all other relevant variables, the researcher concludes that any differences found on the dependent variable are due only to differences in the ways these groups were treated—and nothing else.

*"Getting the results we wanted was so much easier
before we had to control for experimenter bias!"*

Experiments that involve human participants need to be designed with care because the third criteria, eliminating other plausible causes, is often quite challenging. Can you guess why? The major reason goes right to the heart of our subject matter: the reality of personality differences.

Participants may differ in how they understand the instructions by the experimenter, for example, some hearing that they will be competing, others interpreting what they hear as they will be cooperating. The instructions often have to be pretested to ensure that they are understood in the same way by everyone. Individual differences are typically thought of as *noise* or *uncontrolled error variance* by experimental psychologists. From the experimental point of view, it is a shame we are not clones of each other—there would be no uncontrolled error variance due to personality differences!

A pertinent example of experimental work in personality was reported by William Revelle and his colleagues in their study of how well introverts and extraverts[1] perform on a test of verbal ability (Revelle, Amaral, & Turriff, 1976). Drawing on Hans Eysenck's (1967) theory that introverts and extraverts differ in their normal brain activity, they hypothesized that increased arousal will impair the verbal performance of introverts (too much arousal) but will improve the verbal performance of extraverts (they will not be overly aroused). Participants' personalities were assessed with the Eysenck Personality Inventory (Eysenck & Eysenck, 1964/1975), and their arousal levels were manipulated by randomly assigning them to a placebo (nonarousal) or caffeine (arousal) treatment condition.

These investigators predicted that personality (introvert versus extravert) and level of arousal (placebo versus caffeine) will *interact* to determine an individual's verbal performance. An interaction means that the behavior (verbal performance) of the participants will be affected by *both their personality and their arousal level*: Increased arousal will have a *negative* impact on the verbal performance of introverts, but additional arousal will have a *positive* impact on the verbal performance of extraverts, assuming Eysenck's (1967) theory is correct. This is precisely what they observed, as shown in Figure 2.1.[2]

What would Darwin think about this experiment? I think he would be pleased. As it was designed, the observations, one way or the other, would support or would not support a hypothesis derived from a theory.

What did they find? Exactly what they expected to find: the interaction of personality × arousal on verbal performance. Additional arousal (induced by caffeine consumption) interfered with the verbal performance of introverts, while it facilitated the verbal performance of extraverts, precisely in line with Eysenck's theory. This interaction has been replicated in many laboratory experiments. It is one of the most robust findings in personality research (DeYoung & Gray, 2009; Eysenck, 1990).[3]

It is worth noting that the data showed that introverts and extraverts, on average, scored the same on the test of verbal performance. Neither personality "type"

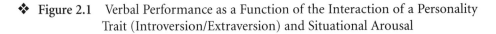

❖ **Figure 2.1**   Verbal Performance as a Function of the Interaction of a Personality Trait (Introversion/Extraversion) and Situational Arousal

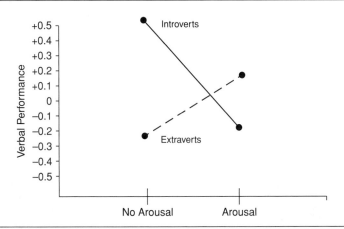

Source: Adapted from William Revelle, Phyllis Amaral, and Susan Turiff (1976). Introversion/Extraversion, Time Stress, and Caffeine: Effect on Verbal Performance. *Science, 192,* 149–150.

was superior to the other on this measure. Within the context of an experiment, this comparison is called a *main effect*. The average score of all individuals in one treatment group (introverts) is compared to the average score of all individuals in the other treatment group (extraverts) across all levels of the other variable (arousal in this case). In this study, there was no main effect of personality "type."

Neither was there a main effect of the other independent variable, arousal level: Both aroused and nonaroused participants performed, on average, the same on the test of verbal performance. Only the *personality x arousal interaction* was statistically significant. What does this mean?

Whenever two or more variables interact in determining behavior, we need to specify the levels of each variable. In this example we need to know *both* personality and arousal conditions to understand what was found: Introverts score higher than extraverts under low arousal, while extraverts score higher than introverts under high arousal. Mentioning either personality or arousal by itself fails to capture what was observed.

Types of Independent Variables

There are two kinds of independent variables. Each kind is illustrated in the Revelle et al. (1976) study.

(a) An experimentally *manipulated* independent variable is one that the experimenter applies to all the participants in her research. She randomly assigns each participant to one of the levels of her independent variable (IV). She is in control of which participant experiences which level (2) or levels (3 or more) of all IVs. In the Revelle et al. (1976) study, arousal (caffeine) versus nonarousal is the IV under experimenter control.

(b) What about the other independent variable, introverts versus extroverts? This is called a *subject variable*. Participants brought their personalities, along with all their other personal characteristics, to the experiment. While our personal characteristics (e.g., age, ethnicity, gender, etc.) cannot be experimentally manipulated, they can be measured and compared.

Participants in the Revelle et al. (1976) study first took a psychological test, the Eysenck Personality Inventory, to measure how introverted or extraverted they are (most people score near the middle). The researchers then compared those individuals who scored at the extreme ends of the scale. Their test scores indicated they were probably either highly introverted or highly extraverted.

Virtually all experiments in personality psychology involve both experimentally manipulated independent variables and subject variables. The point of experimental research in personality is to see if some aspect of behavior will be affected by the *situational variable x personality variable* interaction. The random assignment of participants to situations allows us to conclude, when the observations warrant it, that these situations *cause* individuals to behave as they do. And the point of including subject variables is to discover if these manipulated situations affect some personality "types" more than others. The experiment, to repeat the point because it is important, is the *only* tool in the personality psychologist's toolbox to allow a *causal* interpretation of the data.

As important as experiments in personality research can be, the experimental method is, however, the *least* used tool in the personality psychologist's toolbox (Robins, Tracy, & Sherman, 2007). We now turn to the most frequently used tool, our new best friend, the correlation coefficient.

Correlational Research

A correlation is an association between two variables. Consider the variables of height and weight. Not only do humans differ on how tall we are and how much we weigh, there is an association or correlation between these subject variables: Taller adults, on average, weigh more than shorter ones. There is a *positive correlation* between these variables: As one variable increases in value so does, usually, the other.

There can also be a *negative correlation* between two variables. This occurs when larger values of one variable are associated with smaller values of the other. If individuals with high self-esteem complain of fewer psychosomatic ailments than individuals with low self-esteem, this would be evidence of a negative correlation between these variables. *Positive* and *negative* refer only to the *direction* of the association of two variables.

The major statistic in personality psychology research is the *correlation coefficient*. A coefficient is a number. A correlation coefficient, then, is a number, ranging anywhere from −1.0 to +1.0, that expresses the *strength* (if any) and *direction* (positive or negative) of the relationship between two variables. A correlation coefficient of zero means that there is no correlation or association between the two variables.

Figures 2.2 and 2.3 show scatterplots of fictitious data from 10 participants. The X and Y variables in Figure 2.2 positively correlate, $r = +.861$. The X and Y variables in Figure 2.3 negatively correlate, $r = −.767$.

The correlation coefficient was co-developed by Sir Francis Galton (a cousin of Charles Darwin). It is one of Galton's many seminal contributions to psychology. Galton selected the symbol r to represent the correlation coefficient.[4] Galton's seminal

❖ **Figure 2.2**   Scatterplot Showing Positive Correlation Between Two Variables

❖ **Figure 2.3**   Scatterplot Showing Negative Correlation Between Two Variables

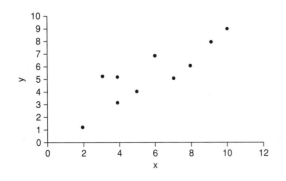

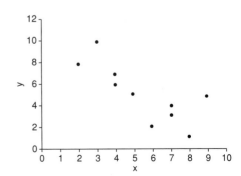

Photo 2.1   Sir Francis Galton (1822–1911)

Galton is the father of the study of individual differences and psychometrics. He introduced the terms nature versus nurture, co-developed the correlation coefficient, and was the first proponent of the lexical hypothesis of personality.

Key publications:

Hereditary Genius (1869)
Inquiries into Human Faculty and Its Development (1883)

idea that the words we use to talk about personality reflect the importance of personality traits continues to spark lexical research (e.g., Wood, 2015).

The highly useful correlation coefficient allows us to answer such questions as the following:

Which personality variables are associated with which other personality variables?

How strong are these associations?

What is the direction of their association, positive or negative?

When researchers find consistent answers to these questions from different investigations (i.e., the results are *replicated*), they can then address more important questions:

Why do these personality variables correlate with each other?

Which theory of personality best accounts for the relationships among these variables?

While some aspect of our behavior is the dependent variable in experiments, scores on personality tests typically provide the data in correlational research. Why do investigators administer and correlate results of personality tests?

Your score on a personality test is assumed to be an indicator or a sample of one of your personality *traits*. Is this assumption valid? Stay tuned. For now, let's begin at the beginning by noting that a researcher wants to know if two or more traits are systematically related to one another.

Types of Personality Variables

The traits that are measured are called *manifest variables*. The score you obtain on the test is assumed to be a manifestation of your position (high, middle, low) on that trait. Should we find that this trait correlates with other manifest traits, this is evidence they have something in common, called a *latent variable*. A latent variable is a broad personality variable that lies below the surface that manifests itself in different specific ways.

For example, suppose we want to know if there's a correlation between the traits of extraversion and *sensation-seeking*, a personality trait proposed by Marvin Zuckerman. Sensation-seeking refers to the desire to experience frequently a variety of new sensations such as those produced by

1. engaging in dangerous outdoor activities (e.g., downhill skiing, mountain climbing), and/or

2. adopting an unusual, nonconforming lifestyle, and/or

3. seeking excitement by going to parties, drinking, using drugs, and engaging in sexual activities, and/or

4. avoiding as much as possible all routine activities because unchanging environments or interacting with unexciting, predictable people quickly leads to feeling bored and restless. (Zuckerman, 1979, 2005)

In the prior section on experimental research, we saw that extraverts' verbal performances improved under arousal. Those high in sensation-seeking regularly choose activities that are psychologically and physiologically arousing. If extraverts and high sensation-seekers prefer external stimulation, then these traits should correlate positively: Those who are above average on one should be above average on the other. Please note that it is not necessary that this correlation be a perfect $r = +1.0$ to reveal an association between the two. Sometimes even small observed values of correlation coefficients can further our understanding of personality.[5]

An investigation into a possible extraversion–sensation-seeking correlation meets Darwin's standard for empirical observations: The observation of a positive correlation suggests that the need for arousal underlies both traits. The absence of a positive correlation indicates that these traits have little or nothing in common. Either way, we learn something about personality. The observation will be a signpost. The research question is, Do extraverts engage in more sensation seeking activities than introverts?

We need ways to measure both extraversion and sensation-seeking. When we refer to a trait by only one of its end points, it is understood that this is just a shorthand way of referring to the trait's full range, introversion–extraversion or low-to-high sensation-seeking.

With regard to extraversion we have any number of tests available to us. An early conception of extraversion was developed by Hans Eysenck (1916–1997) in 1947. The Eysenck Personality Questionnaire (EPQ; Eysenck & Eysenck, 1964/1975) measures Extraversion as well as two other major traits, Neuroticism (or emotional instability) and Psychoticism (undersocialized individuals who are often convicted of criminal offenses). The EPQ has been found to be a reliable and valid measure of extraversion. To measure how important sensation-seeking is to a person, we could ask him or her to fill out the Sensation Seeking Scale (Zuckerman, 1971).

Having decided on our measurement instruments, the next step is to obtain a sample of individuals who are willing to fill out both scales. In personality psychology, it is not unusual for a researcher to obtain data from hundreds of participants. This is because individuals are often tested in group settings that allow the researcher to collect large amounts of relevant data within a relatively short time span (a class meeting, for example).

The time-saving feature of the correlational method stands in sharp contrast to the experimental method, which can be quite time-consuming (needing a full hour to test one participant, for example). Once we have completed the data-collection phase, we are ready to compute the correlation coefficient.

This was the general procedure used by Eysenck and Zuckerman (1978) to find out if these two variables, extraversion and sensation-seeking, are positively correlated, as expected by arousal theory. Testing approximately 350 men and 750 women from both the United States and England, they found a positive correlation between extraversion and sensation-seeking for both American men ($r = +0.25$) and English men ($r = +0.32$) as well as for American women ($r = +0.44$) and English women ($r = +0.23$). All of these correlation coefficients differed from zero, statistically speaking. Thus, these positive correlations are a signpost that physiological arousal might underlie both extraversion and sensation-seeking.

Do these positive correlations *prove* that physiological arousal induces both extraverted behaviors and sensation-seeking? No, unfortunately it is not that simple. Whenever we observe what we expected to observe, we know we are going in the right direction but it is far from conclusive. Confirmatory observations like these are *necessary* but not *sufficient* conditions for the unqualified acceptance of a theory. These observations need to be replicated with other samples to see if there is a general pattern. Moreover, correlation does not by itself necessarily imply causality. A third variable, such as arousal in this example, could be the hidden cause of both of them.

On the one hand, such observations are necessary because if they do not occur when the theory expects them to (not just once but repeatedly), we rightly suspect there is something wrong or missing from the theory. Those signposts would tell us we are not moving in the right direction. However, even when the signpost tells us we are moving in the right direction, it does not rule out the possibility we are on a common path with two or more different theories. We require additional signposts, and perhaps other methods of research, to tell us which competing theory better accounts for all the data.

But for now, we are happy to observe what is expected by arousal theory. Since arousal theory does not specify the magnitude of the correlation between extraversion and sensation-seeking, any observed sample value that significantly departs from zero in the positive direction is consistent with the theory.

Do researchers always test their observed correlation coefficient against the hypothesis of zero relationship? No. Suppose brain arousal theory predicted (it doesn't) that the correlation between extraversion and sensation-seeking is higher in women than in men. If that were true, an individual's biological sex would be a moderator variable. A *moderator variable* is one that gives the answer of "it depends" to scientific questions:

Question: "How strongly do extraversion and sensation-seeking correlate?"

Answer: "It depends on the sex (gender) of the individual."

If that were true (again, it isn't), then a person's gender would be called a moderator variable for understanding the correlation of extraversion with sensation-seeking (Chaplin, 2007). In the Eysenck and Zuckerman (1978) study, the data reveal that those traits do correlate more highly for American women than for American men. However, these traits correlate less highly for English women than English men. The signpost gives a mixed message. Bad signpost.

Since an individual's biological sex is not really a moderator variable of the extraversion–sensation-seeking relationship, but we pretended it was for teaching purposes, we do not need to concern ourselves with trying to figure out why nationality seemed to make a difference. But that *would* be the next step if sex were a moderator variable.[6] "It depends" is often the correct answer to questions about the nature and extent of individual differences. The precise specification of "it depends" is the moderator variable. A moderator variable could be any variable on which individuals differ: gender, age, nationality, religious affiliation, prior bowling experience, and so forth.

Factor Analysis: Congregation of Correlation Coefficients

Eysenck and Zuckerman (1978) found that extraversion and sensation-seeking are positively correlated, albeit modestly. This outcome has been replicated many times over the ensuing years. When research psychologists want to understand *why* two personality variables correlate, they may utilize an important research procedure called *factor analysis*.

We know that correlation does not necessarily imply causality. From the observation that extraversion and sensation-seeking are positively correlated, we cannot conclude that differences in extraversion cause differences in sensation-seeking nor can we conclude that differences in sensation-seeking cause differences in extraversion.[7]

What we can do is administer tests of other personality variables that might be related to both extraversion and sensation-seeking. Drawing on Eysenck's theory that physiological arousal underlies both of these traits, we could select tests that relate to different manifestations or forms of arousal. Administering a battery of tests to the same participants can yield interesting results about the structure of personality traits. Below is an *intuitive introduction* to factor analysis. A more detailed overview of factor analysis is provided by Goldberg and Velicer (2006) and by Lee and Ashton (2007).

Let's imagine we select six paper-and-pencil tests, labeled A through F, of different personality variables. Choosing *which variables to measure* is the most important decision in factor analytic work. The variables selected should be guided by theory or prior research results. Okay, so each participant takes all six tests.[8] We then compute the correlation coefficient of the scores of each participant on each test with his or her scores on every other test. We enter each correlation coefficient into the appropriate place in a 6 × 6 matrix, yielding 21 individual correlation coefficients. The fictitious data might look this:

❖ **Table 2.1** Hypothetical Correlation Matrix for Six Variables (A–F)

	A	B	C	D	E	F
A	+.86	_+.80_	_+.83_	+.15	+.21	+.15
B		+.81	_+.87_	+.14	+.17	+.18
C			+.80	+.10	+.21	+.22
D				+.82	_+.85_	_+.84_
E					+.80	_+.88_
F						+.84

The correlation coefficients below the diagonal are not entered to avoid unnecessary clutter. The correlation of test A with test B is the same as the correlation of test B with test A. Should an investigator suspect that a moderator variable (sex of participants, for example) is important, she would report the results for one gender above the diagonal and the results for the other below the diagonal. This allows readers to see at a glance if the gender of the participants influences how strongly these six personality traits intercorrelate. In this example, there is no moderator variable and thus no need to repeat the same numbers above and below the diagonal.

The six numbers in bold represent typical correlations of each test with itself (A with A, B with B, etc.). These numbers tell us how *reliable* these tests are based on prior test-retest results. One hopes that the reliability coefficient of each test is at least .80 (Anastasi, 1988), as they are in this made-up example. Out of the 21 correlations in the matrix, six of them are reliability coefficients. This leaves us with 15 correlations of each test with every other test.

It is the numbers that are underlined that are important for our purpose. Take a moment to look at the six underlined correlation coefficients. Does it look like one big jumble of numbers to you or can you detect a pattern?

I do hope you see a pattern: Tests A, B, and C intercorrelate highly with each other. Scores on tests A, B, or C do not, however, correlate highly with scores on tests D, E, and F. These latter values are slightly above zero, which indicates that these personality variables might be, at best, only weakly related to each other. Also note that while scores on tests D, E, and F intercorrelate highly with each other, they only weakly correlate with scores on tests A, B, and C.

This pattern of correlations indicates that there are two underlying factors connecting extraversion with sensation-seeking. One factor seems to be related to scores on tests A, B, and C (but has little to do with the other three tests), while a second factor is related to scores on tests D, E, and F (but has little to do with the scores on tests A, B, and C).

Two factors are easier to understand than 15 separate coefficients. In an actual investigation with these six personality tests, the 15 individual correlation coefficients would be entered into a computer program that is designed to detect and measure the strength of any factors present in the data set. For our purposes, we just need to get a general idea of what factor analysis is and why it is useful in personality research.

After the factors have been identified, the next task is to decide what to name them. The investigator reviews the individual tests and test items and looks for what tests A, B, and C have in common with each other (but not with D, E, and F). He also seeks to find what tests D, E, and F have in common (but not with A, B, or C).

Suppose tests A, B, and C ask respondents to rate themselves on such items as "I like to leap before I look," "I usually do the first thing that comes to mind," and "It annoys me if I have to think about a problem too much." If the other items on these three tests are similar to those, it seems reasonable to characterize individuals who agree with such items as "impulsive."

Suppose further that tests D, E, and F ask respondents to rate themselves on items such as "I very much enjoy hanging out with my friends," "When it comes to throwing a party, my motto is 'The more the merrier,'" and "My favorite memories are of the good times I had with my family and friends." Individuals who agree with these and other similar items could be fairly characterized as "sociable."

So factor analysis allows us to reduce the 15 individual correlations among these six personality tests to two factors: *impulsivity* and *sociability*. The relatively small correlations among these two factors suggests that these personality factors are not totally independent of each other but are weakly related. This is exactly what has been found. Scores on sociability and impulsivity factors correlate +0.25 (Sipps and DiCaudio, 1988).

The next step in a factor analytic study of personality traits, after the factors have been identified, is to statistically determine how strongly or weakly each test correlates with each identified factor. These values are called *factor loadings*. Continuing with our intuitive approach, the factor loadings for the six tests might look something like this:

❖ Table 2.2   Hypothetical Factor Loadings for Six Variables (A–F) on Two Factors

Test	Factor 1 (*Impulsivity*)	Factor 2 (*Sociability*)
A	**.65**	.15
B	**.71**	.20
C	**.68**	.17
D	.11	**.72**
E	.18	**.69**
F	.22	**.65**

The pattern of these loadings is consistent with what we found earlier. Tests A, B, and C correlate (load) more highly on Factor 1 than on Factor 2. Tests D, E, and F load considerably higher on Factor 2 than they do on Factor 1. Thus, it would seem clear from these observations that impulsivity and extraversion, while weakly correlated, nevertheless are two distinct ways that individuals seek external stimulation: by acting impulsively and/or by seeking social connections.

Factor analysis has been a major tool in personality research for many years. With the use of statistical factor analytic programs, researchers have been able to develop tests of personality by discovering which potential items highly correlate with other items. High inter-item correlations suggest that these manifest items are measuring or tapping into the same underlying latent personality trait.

The items that comprise a personality test might initially come from almost anywhere. A researcher, you, for example, might make up your own items that seem to "tap into" the construct you want to measure. You might ask friends, family, and strangers on the street to contribute their ideas and/or you might "borrow" items from existing personality scales. You then ask individuals (college students are often handy) to take your test. You then enter all their scores into a factor analysis computer program and discover which items correlate highly enough to suggest they share a common factor. Most of the items on this initial test might be eliminated because they do not correlate with any other items.

A statistical program will tell you how many factors (if any) are in your data set as well as the factor loadings of each individual item with those factors. You will then be able to whittle down your initially large set of items until your test contains only those items that have significant factor loadings. At this point you administer these retained items to a new sample of participants to see if the same factors and factor loadings occur again. This last step is a necessary research process generally called *cross-validation* or, more specifically in this case, *confirmatory factor analysis.*

Factor analysis has been used to identify the fundamental traits that form the structure of personality. Different research programs have arrived at different answers. Raymond Cattell discovered 16 fundamental traits (Cattell, 1957). Hans Eysenck (1976) discovered three. Currently there is widespread agreement that five major traits—extraversion, neuroticism, openness to experience, conscientiousness, and agreeableness (the "Big Five")—are sufficient to cover the major ways our personalities differ (John, Naumann, & Soto, 2008; McCrae & Costa, 1987).

Widespread agreement about the validity of Big Five does not, however, mean that the issue of the number of fundamental personality traits has reached universal agreement (Block, 1995). A factor analytic study aimed at identifying personality attributes not assessed by these five traits—such as sense of humor, frugality, and cunning—found 10 additional factors (Paunonen & Jackson, 2000). Other researchers conclude that the Big Five ignores the important trait of honesty-humility, leading them to favor a model they call HEXACO, which adds Honesty-Humility (H) to the existing Big Five traits (Ashton & Lee, 2005).

What in the world is going on? How can such a sophisticated tool as factor analysis give such divergent results across different investigations? The answers to these questions help us understand the limits of this procedure.

First, different investigators may select slightly different personality variables or they may differ in terms of the number of items tapping the same construct. Lewis Goldberg and Wayne Velicer (2006, p. 212) flatly state that selection of variables is the single most important consideration by investigators using factor analysis.

Second, investigations differ in how they select participants. Did the investigator attempt to obtain a representative sample of individuals living in, say, the United States or, as is far more likely, were the data obtained from a sample of convenience (e.g., college students)? Moreover, some investigators may target a relatively homogeneous population such as a clinical sample. Even though studies have found no systematic differences in factor structure between samples of clinical and normal individuals (O'Connor, 2002; Widiger & Costa, 2013b), nevertheless a particular clinical sample could be overrepresented by, say, depressed patients, which could influence the outcome of the factor analysis.

Third, the way personality traits are measured varies across different investigations. Some ask the participants to rate aspects of their personalities on a 5-point or 7-point rating scale. Other investigators may choose a "yes-no" (i.e., dichotomous) format such as *true versus false* or *agree versus disagree*. Or participants are given a list of adjectives and asked to check all those that apply to themselves. While this latter way of assessing personality is easiest for the participants, it also is the most prone to careless responding. Participants who want to finish as quickly as possible may inadvertently (or not) skip over whole chunks of adjectives. This is a likely explanation for the typical finding of huge differences in the total number of adjectives checked by participants (Goldberg & Velicer, 2006).

These three differences in procedural details, then, may account for the variability in the number of fundamental traits identified by various investigators. Until there is agreement among researchers about how to standardize selection of tests to be analyzed, selection of participants to take the tests, and the measurement units employed by the tests, we may expect investigators to continue to disagree about the number of fundamental traits characterizing human personality.

Factor analysis, it should be noted, is prone to other potential problems. What to call or label a factor is a highly subjective enterprise. Factor analysis can tell us that one or more factors exist and it can reveal each item's factor loadings. Fine. But the investigator needs to decide what these factor loadings mean and give the factor an appropriately descriptive label. What shall I call the factor? For example, labels such as "ego-strength,' "conscientiousness," and "dependability" seem to be synonymous, yet there are still meaningful connotative differences among them that imply they are referring to different personality constructs. There is no Factor Analysis Clearing House standard for naming factors.

A final limitation is that an obtained factor might make no sense. The items that load on a factor seem to have nothing in common. It can include odd combinations of different traits that are difficult to pin down under one descriptive label (Block, 1995).

In summary, then, factor analysis can be a very valuable tool to identify the relatively few *latent* variables that underlie the many apparently different *manifest* variables seen in personality tests. These latent variables, when replicated by factor analyses by other investigators, tell us something important about the structure of personality traits. Although there is disagreement about the precise number of latent variables, all agree that *introversion–extraversion* and *emotional stability–instability* are two of them.

The two methods covered so far, experiments and correlations, both look at one or only a few aspects of a person. Neither method looks at how a person's behavior or traits connect to other aspects of his personality such as his aspirations for the future, how his personality was affected by early childhood experiences, or the content of his nightly dreams. These drawbacks are corrected by the final method in the personality psychologist's toolbox, the case study.

Case Studies

The most important distinction in personality psychology is between nomothetic and idiographic research (Allport, 1937). The *nomothetic* approach seeks to discover *general laws and principles* about personality, laws that are true for all people in all cultures. The research questions we have looked at so far in this chapter, questions answered by either experimental or correlational methods, are examples of the nomothetic approach.

The association between brain arousal and extraversion, for example, is assumed to be true for all humans. An essential aspect of the nomothetic approach is searching for the *conditions under which* such associations hold true. Is it really a cross-cultural universal? Perhaps there exists a group of people living in some remote part of the earth for whom the arousal–extraversion relationship is not true. Discovering this fact would not disprove the arousal–extraversion relationship. It would qualify it. Additional research would be required to discover why the arousal–extraversion association does not hold for this group of humans.

In contrast to the nomothetic search for general laws is the desire to understand the *whole person* in all of his or her distinctiveness. What makes this person unique? The *idiographic* approach to personality is characterized by the *case study* of a single individual. After reading an extensive case history of a particular individual, we would feel that we know this person far better than before. "A psychology of individuality would be essentially idiographic" (Allport, 1937, p. 22).

While a psychology of the individual would be idiographic, would it be scientific? What is the role of the case history within a scientific framework? Doesn't the case study method contradict science's goal of finding *general* laws and principles? In a word, no.

An important distinction within the scientific enterprise is the context of discovery versus the context of justification. The *context of discovery* refers to the initial stages whereby the investigator sees reality in a new way, imagines how this new way might explain existing data more usefully, and thinks of new potential observations that are consistent with this new way of interpreting reality. In brief, the context of discovery gets the scientific ball rolling.

In contrast, the *context of justification* involves a systematic testing of these new ideas to see if they are really useful (Reichenbach, 1938). Darwin's epigram at the beginning of this chapter directly applies to the context of justification: The most useful observations are those that help us decide which interpretation of existing data is more likely to be correct. The context of justification helps us know, one way or the other, if the ideas generated in the context of discovery are valid, need to be modified, or wrong.

Case studies are valuable as sources of hypotheses to explain human behavior. The life of a single person, examined in detail, can provoke many ideas about how a particular person developed his or her personality. This point is illustrated with great clarity in Robert White's (1952) classic in-depth study of the "natural growth of personality" as exemplified in the lives of three individuals. More recently, Rae Carlson proposed the formation of an "invisible collaboration" between excellent biographical studies, that provide the raw data of a person's life, and personality psychologists who then make sense of these data by applying an appropriate theory of personality. Carlson illustrates this by applying Silvan Tomkins's *script theory* to illuminate aspects of the personalities of Nathaniel Hawthorn and Eleanor Marx (Carlson, 1988, p. 105; Tomkins, 1979).

Case histories are usually more interesting to read than dry statistics because they discuss the whole person rather than test scores. Any meaningful discussion of a person's life requires that the reader understand the various environmental situations the person had to deal with in his life. Biographies and psycho-biographies situate the person in a particular time and place. In sharp contrast, the correlation of test scores is context-free. The data are presented, as it were, in a vacuum.

The history of psychology is replete with single case studies (Dukes, 1965). Freud, after all, built his theory and methods of psychoanalysis around the lives of some of his patients. The difficulty, it must be noted, is that Freud presented these case histories as both *inspiration for* and as *proof of* his theory of psychoanalysis. Freud conflated the context of discovery with the context of justification. Is it plausible, given the multitude of ways we differ from each other, that what is true about my personality is *necessarily* true for yours? No. The single case study does not permit us to generalize what we observe to be true for one person to be true for all people. Thus, case histories are valuable within the context of discovery but have no value within the context of justification.[9]

Within personality psychology, the case study is the method of choice by those interested in the related approaches of *psychobiography* (e.g., Elms, 1994, 2007; Erikson, 1958, 1969; Runyon, 1982, 1997) and the *narrative study of lives* (e.g., McAdams, 1985, 1993, 2013).

Psychobiography is a form of biography that examines and interprets key events in a person's life by the application of psychological theory. Psychobiography is one aspect of psychohistory. Rather than focus on historical events, psychobiography emphasizes the lives and the psychology of historically important individuals.

The first psychobiography was Sigmund Freud's psychoanalysis of Leonardo da Vinci (Freud, 1910/1964). While a well-written psychobiography is interesting to read, nevertheless there lurks the sneaking suspicion that the author's own psychological issues may have unwittingly informed his psychobiological analysis of his subject. In other words, there is a strong personal element inherent in all psychobiography that readers should keep in mind (Song & Simonton, 2007).

As we saw in Chapter 1, the personal narrative approach to personality seeks to understand your personality through the life story you have created. The most important component of your life story is your *narrative identity* or your "internalized, evolving, and integrated story" of yourself, of who you are (McAdams, 2007, p. 242). While the study of personal narratives and narrative identities is clearly idiographic, McAdams points out that the methodology employed in this area typically involves quantitative measures to test hypotheses. Idiographic work in personality need not, in other words, rely exclusively on qualitative analysis (McAdams, 2007). One quantitative measure useful for idiographic research is the experience sampling method.

Experience sampling methods (ESMs) are procedures that permit participants to reveal their thoughts, emotions, and behavior in real time across a variety of situations. Three qualities characterize an ESM: The experience occurs in a *natural setting*, the experience is recorded in *real time* (or as close as possible to it), and experiences are *recorded repeatedly* over time (Connor et al., 2007).

McAdams and Constantian (1983) used the experience sampling method to find out if participants' results on a projective test (the Thematic Apperception Test [TAT], covered below) was consistent with their real-world thoughts and feelings. They paged 50 college students seven times a day for one week. These participants were asked to answer a brief set of questions as soon as possible (when it was safe to do so) after they received the page. They were asked to reveal what they were thinking about, how they were feeling, and what they were doing when they were paged.

The results of this real-time, real-world investigation showed that those participants who were strong in intimacy and affiliation motivation, as measured by their TAT responses, were more likely to be engaged in conversations and letter writing than those who were low in these motives. Their results showed that human motivation, as revealed on personality tests, correspond to real-world behaviors. So while the ESM may be used to investigate a single personality ideographically, tentative nomothetic conclusions may be drawn when numerous individuals participate in the research (McAdams & Constantian, 1983). These tentative conclusions require sufficient replications, of course, before they can be considered to be factual.

Were he alive today, Gordon Allport would certainly be pleased by such research. Allport thought that the nomothetic versus idiographic dichotomy is "too sharp: it requires a psychology divided against itself" (Allport, 1937, p. 22). Allport's unifying view is that it is better to regard the two approaches as complementary—they contribute to each other. The idiographic approach can suggest interesting hypotheses to test on a general cross-section of people to seek nomothetic confirmation. Nomothetically discovered relationships may be applied to the lives of specific individuals to learn how plausibly these relationships may be generalized across individuals who differ in age, sex, race, ethnicity, or nationality. Both nomothetic and idiographic research help us understand a person. It is not either/or. It is both.

We have now completed our look at the three distinct ways personality psychologists can gather observations: by conducting experiments, doing correlational studies, and/or examining a single life in depth via the case history. Next on the agenda is how personality may be measured and how psychologists demonstrate that these measures are accurate.

Personality Assessment

Purposes of Assessment

Assessment refers to the systematic measurement of any aspect of personality that is of interest. Possible aspects include (a) our wants and goals, such as our need for love, achievement, and care for others; (b) problematic aspects of our personality, such as excessive anxiety or depression; (c) personality traits, such as extraversion or impulsiveness; and (d) styles of development and self-regulation, such as attachment styles and how we cope with daily stress. The purpose of assessing any of these aspects of personality varies with the setting and the circumstances of measurement.

Settings for Assessment

My first encounter with a personality test occurred in my freshman year of college. My major field, physics, was not working for me, and I needed to find a new major. I went to the Counseling Center and took a test called the Strong Vocational Interest Blank (SVIB). After the test was scored, I learned that I had interests similar to those of psychologists. The vocational counselor suggested I pick up any intro psych book, see if the topics are interesting, and if so, take a course in it. This reasonable advice led me to discover that I had a long-standing interest in trying to understand other people's behavior as well as my own. So I switched my major to psychology and have been grateful to the SVIB ever since.

Vocational personality tests are routinely employed in high school, college, and guidance centers. The purpose of testing in these settings is to help individuals discover which professions and occupations are suitable for someone with their particular set of interests, their likes and dislikes. Two tests that are available for this purpose are the Jackson Vocational Interest Survey and the Strong Interest Inventory (an updated version of the SVIB).

Other settings where personality tests are routinely given are clinical or counseling offices, mental health centers, or hospitals. The primary purpose of tests such as the Minnesota Multiphasic Personality Inventory (MMPI-2-RF) is to help the clinician diagnose and treat those suffering from emotional, behavioral, and/or chronic interpersonal difficulties.

Legal settings often employ personality tests to help determine if the defendant is legally responsible for his actions (i.e., is sane) or is not (i.e., is insane). The judgment of sanity or insanity is based on more information than just test results, of course. Personality tests may be usefully employed in legal settings to help detect those defendants who want to "fake bad." Some test items have been found to reliably discriminate between those who really are insane versus those who are trying to fake insanity to avoid hard jail time. Since the test taker has no way of knowing the "right" answer to these items, a profile demonstrating faking bad, along with other evidence, can persuade authorities that the defendant is indeed sane.

Personality tests are a staple in many business settings to determine the best fit between the applicant and the positions available. Personnel departments may also employ tests to help with promotion and relocation decisions.

Finally, personality tests may be given in any setting where the purpose is to do basic research. This is most apt to occur on college campuses and in psychology courses. Paper-and-pencil tests are easy to administer and allow for the efficient collection of a large amount of data in a short period of time.

Test Reliability and Validity

Test reliability refers to consistency. A test is considered to be reliable if it meets two criteria: (1) Are all the items of this test measuring the same trait? This question is directed at the *internal consistency* of the test items. To answer it, the researcher finds the correlation of the answers to each item with answers to every other item. A test's *alpha coefficient* or *Cronbach's alpha*, tells us how internally consistent are its items (Cronbach, 1951). A personality test is considered to be internally consistent when its alpha coefficient equals or exceeds 0.80 (Anastasi, 1988). We are confident that all the test items are measuring the same personality construct (e.g., extraversion, agreeableness, etc.).

(2) A second criterion for test reliability is consistency over time: Do the respondents achieve the same, or nearly the same, score when they take the test again at a later time? This question is answered by demonstrating that the test–retest correlation of scores is reasonably high. Again, a reliability coefficient of at least 0.80 is desirable to show that individuals' relative ranking on the trait is consistent over time when the two tests are given in close temporal proximity. As a general rule, as the time interval between test and retest increases, the lower is the test's reliability coefficient (Anastasi, 1988).

Test validity refers to the extent to which a test measures the construct it is designed to measure. If you take a personality test to measure how introverted or extraverted you are, the score you receive on the test should reflect your actual position on this trait. It is the responsibility of the test constructor to show that her personality test really measures what she says the test is suppose to measure. How can she do this?

The validity of a test can be demonstrated in a variety of ways. Using extraversion as an example, the first criterion concerns the appearance of the test items: Do the items on her test *look like* they are measuring extraversion? If so, the test passes the *face validity* criterion.

Second, do the items on the test seem to tap the *entire range of the meaning* of the construct? Individuals who are extraverted may express this trait in a variety of ways: They are friendly and like to be with other people, they can be assertive, they prefer to be active, and they usually display positive emotions. A test that contains items measuring all these aspects is one that has *content validity* for extraversion.

Third, do the scores on her test correlate highly with scores on established tests of extraversion? *Criterion validity* refers to this aspect of the validation process. For example, one potential criterion is how often a person prefers to work as part of a team versus working alone. Other things being equal, we expect that more extraverts than introverts prefer working as part of a team.[10]

Criterion validity can take the form of a more or less simultaneous measurement of both the test and the criterion (*concurrent validity*) or the test may be given some days, weeks, or months before the criterion is assessed (*predictive validity*). In either case, the correlation between test score and criterion is the test's *validity coefficient*.

Construct validity, the grandaddy of all validity measures, may be demonstrated in a variety of ways. The essential idea is that: (1) we start with a construct to be measured by defining it as carefully and as comprehensively as we can (e.g., extraversion); (2) we develop test items to measure this construct; and (3) we compare test scores with as many other criteria (that reflect the construct) as is feasible. Our test will demonstrate its construct validity by the following outcomes:

(a) groups that are expected to differ in the average value of this construct (e.g., salesmen versus librarians) are indeed found to differ in the expected direction;

(b) test scores correlate highly with other (valid) measures of this construct;

(c) the test's alpha coefficient is impressively high, demonstrating the test measures a single construct;

(d) experimental conditions designed to change average levels of this construct produce these predicted changes (e.g., pretend you are an extreme introvert [or extravert] while taking this test).

Should all or most of these efforts produce the expected data, we are confident that the test measures what it is intended to measure, that is, it has sufficient construct validity (Cronbach & Meehl, 1955; Hogan & Nicholson, 1988).

Finally, another way to demonstrate a test's construct validity is to show that a new test designed to measure a construct possesses both *convergent* and *discriminant validity*. Suppose you create a new measure of extraversion (because, perhaps, you'd like a shorter test with fewer items). You can establish your test's convergent and discriminant validity by administering your new test along with different tests (to the same participants) that measure extraversion along with other personality constructs, such as perfectionism and anxiety, traits which are not related to extraversion. Your new test demonstrates its convergent validity by correlating highly with the existing (valid) tests of extraversion. It establishes its discriminant validity by *not* correlating highly with tests designed to measure perfectionism or anxiety. Should your test achieve both of these outcomes, we have confidence that your new test really does measure what you wanted it to measure (Campbell & Fiske, 1959).

Types of Assessments

Self-Report Tests

You've probably taken a self-report test at some point in your life. These tests are answered either true-false, agree-undecided-disagree, or you might be asked to rate an aspect of your personality on a scale of *1 to 5* or *1 to 7* or *1 to whatever*. In this type of assessment, you are asked to report on some aspect of yourself, hence the clever title of *self-report*.

Self-report tests are also referred to as *objective* tests because they are scored the same way by all examiners—by counting which items you endorsed or did not endorse as indicative of your personality. Objectively scored personality tests stand in contrast to *projective tests*, for example, whose scoring and interpretation may vary from one examiner to the next.

There are three types of self-reports (Paulhus & Vazire, 2007):

First, there is the *direct self-report* whereby respondents are asked direct questions about themselves, as in true or false: "My favorite food is broccoli." Second, there are *indirect self-reports* that typically obscure the personality dimension being measured. For example, one measure of narcissism asks respondents about their leadership skills, their physical attractiveness, and their ability to tell an engaging story (Narcissistic Personality Inventory, Raskin & Hall, 1981). The rationale behind such indirect questions is that since narcissists are self-deluded, asking a direct question (Are you narcissistic?) would be a waste of time. Finally, there are self-reports that are *open-ended*. This kind of self-report imposes no questions at all but simply asks a general question such as "Please describe your personality." The major difficulty with open-ended self-reports is how to code and compare the wide diversity of responses. Perhaps for this reason, the open-ended self-report is the least used of these three types of self-reports. Researchers almost always have a set of target behaviors or attitudes they want to measure.

There are many advantages of direct and indirect self-report tests: They are easy to administer, they can ask about multiple aspects of personality, the respondents are typically motivated to fill them out (people usually like to talk about themselves), many respondents may be tested at the same time (as in a college classroom).

Finally, if the results can be taken at face value, they will be easy to interpret. For example, if you ask respondents if they are "dog people" or "cat people" or "both" or "neither," the percentages of respondents in each of the four categories probably corresponds to reality, assuming that the respondents can read English.

The primary disadvantage of self-reports concerns the accuracy of what is reported. When the test items delve into more personal issues—drug use, sexual activity, financial matters—the responses may reflect other motives than the one to report accurately. Motives such as *self-presentation* ("I want the test giver to think well of me"), *self-enhancement* ("I want to think well of myself"), and *consistency* ("I don't want this answer to contradict how I answered a similar previous item") may arise during the testing session. Finally, the accuracy of responses to self-report items may be compromised by various *response biases*, such as social desirability and the acquiescent response set.

Responding to items in a *socially desirable* way means that the test-taker answers in terms of what is socially acceptable or desirable rather than truthfully. Responding to items in this way challenges the validity of the test. If asked, for example, "How often do you lie?" the respondent may give the socially acceptable answer of "never or rarely" instead of the truthful answer. How do test constructors deal with this problem? One way is to match items on social desirability and ask respondents to choose which item more accurately describes them. If the items are equally socially desirable or equally socially undesirable, the answer will reflect something other than the tendency to answer in socially desirable ways.

Another potential problem with self-report tests is the *acquiescent response set*. This is the tendency to agree with an item irrespective of its content. This type of response bias can be eliminated in advance by writing test items in such a way that the presence of the personality trait is signified by responding "agree" to half of the items and "disagree" to the other half.

Response biases are potential flaws that personality test constructors take very seriously (e.g., McGrath et al., 2010). Fortunately, response bias indicators can be built into these tests to detect it (Rohling et al., 2011). The presence of an acquiescent response set, for example, is indicated by consistently agreeing with highly improbable events ("I like everyone I've ever met," or "I have never been sick.").

Three Self-Report Tests

Three examples of self-report tests that have been and are widely used are the Minnesota Multiphasic Personality Inventory (MMPI; Hathaway & McKinley, 1943a), the California Personality Inventory (CPI; Gough, 1957), and one test of the five-factor model of personality, Neuroticism, Extraversion, Openness—Personality Inventory—Revised (NEO-PI-R; Costa & McCrae, 1992a).

The MMPI was designed to diagnose individuals who present a variety of psychological problems. Respondents answer true or false to a large number of items that have been found to be associated with one or more psychiatric problems such as depression or paranoia. The test also contains items designed to ferret out those individuals who are defensive (those who "fake good") and those who try to appear more troubled than they really are by "faking bad" (malingerers).

Over the ensuing years the MMPI has gone through multiple editions as items are deleted and new scales added. The MMPI-2-RF, for example, contains scales designed to measure such aspects of personality as anxiety, cynicism, and substance abuse, among others. It also features nine validity scales that help to interpret a person's personality profile. Someone who scores highly on one or more of these scales has given unreliable answers throughout the test. His or her overall results are untrustworthy (Ben-Porath, 2012).

The California Personality Inventory contains 20 scales to measure such personality traits as dominance, sociability, self-control, and psychological-mindedness. Like the MMPI, the CPI is a true-false test that has been administered to thousands of normal individuals. Individual scales have shown high reliability and validity (Gough, 1987).

The Five-Factor Model (FFM) of personality, described in Chapter 1, proposes that most of the ways that individuals differ in their personalities are adequately described in terms of five major traits: neuroticism, extraversion, openness to experience, agreeableness, and conscientiousness. Since the FFM approach to understanding personality traits is covered throughout this book (Chapters 1, 3, and 8), it is appropriate here to evaluate the reliability and validity of one of the instruments used to measure these basic traits, the NEO-PI-R (Costa and McCrae, 1992a).

The test-retest reliability of the NEO-PI-R has been found to be high over a span of 3 to 6 years. The test-retest correlation coefficients of the five major factors ranged from .83 (neuroticism and openness), .82 (extraversion), .79 (conscientiousness) to .63 (agreeableness) (McCrae & Costa, 1990, p. 88). These data indicate both that the test is reliable and that these personality traits are stable over the time span between the two testings.

Numerous investigations have shown that the NEO-PI-R is a valid measure of these personality traits. One report, based on varying sample sizes of hundreds of adults, found that the correlations of trait scores across *different raters* (self, friend 1, friend 2, spouse), ranged from a low of .26 (a friend and spouse ratings on extraversion) to a high of .63 (self and a friend ratings on openness). All correlations are statistically significant (McCrae & Costa, 1990, p. 38). These data indicate the test's validity in that different raters show statistically significant agreement when rating the same traits of the same person. Taken together with these and numerous other investigations of the properties of the NEO-PI-R, we can be confident that it is a reliable and cross-culturally valid self-report measure of personality.[11]

In summary, then, self-report personality tests are valid in research settings where the respondents, answering anonymously, do not have a personal stake in the outcome. Self-report tests are of more doubtful value, however, in those settings where the respondent knows that his or her responses may seriously impact the future, as in employment interviews, clinical settings, or as part of the judicial process. In those situations, results of self-report tests should be checked against results obtained by other methods, such as a personal interview and reports from prior employers (Paulhus & Vazire, 2007).

Projective Tests

The idea behind projective tests is that when a scene we are viewing is ambiguous, we automatically and nonconsciously resolve the ambiguity by "projecting" our unconscious associations, motives, and feelings into it. If an individual were given a series of 20 different photographs, one at a time, each depicting a different scene—a man by himself, a woman and a child, a man and a woman, etc.—and asked to write or tell a short story about each scene, we could read through these 20 productions to see if there is a common theme that runs through them. The presence of one or more themes suggests that these are issues that are presently at or below the conscious surface of the person's mind. Unlike a self-report test, a projective test is designed to ferret out those motives and feelings that lie below the level of conscious awareness.

The above description is taken from the procedure involved in the Thematic Perception Test developed by Henry Murray and his colleagues (Morgan & Murray, 1935), probably the second most widely used projective test behind the Rorschach Inkblot Test.

Murray (1943) provided some guidelines for interpreting the stories created in response to the pictures. Particular interest should be paid, Murray suggested, to the needs expressed in the story. Is the protagonist concerned about keeping or losing friends (the affiliation motive)? Is he or she expressing a desire to achieve something—to complete an important project, obtain a college degree, or excel at a difficult task (the achievement motive)? Murray was clear to stress that the interpretations by the examiner of the meaning of these imaginative productions should be thought of as hypotheses. These hypotheses should be evaluated by alternative methods, not assumed to be the absolute truth.

The Thematic Apperception Test (TAT) has been successfully adopted to study personality in experimental situations. David McClelland and his colleagues initially aroused a motive (e.g., hunger) in the participants and then observed how their responses to the TAT cards were affected. By carefully examining how the participants' responded to the cards when a specific motive was activated, they were able to devise scoring schemes for that motive (McClelland, Atkinson, Clark, & Lowell, 1953). This use of the TAT has resulted in our increased understanding of the achievement motive (e.g., McClelland, 1961), intimacy and affiliation motives (e.g., McAdams & Constantian, 1983), and the power motive (e.g., Winter, 1973). Current research on these human motives includes the creative attempt to build them into computational models of motivation (e.g., Merrick & Shafi, 2011).

Are you old enough to remember the TV show *Password*? A team consists of a "sender" and a "receiver." The sender's task is to prompt his or her partner to say the hidden word (hidden from the receiver) as quickly as possible with the first word that comes to mind. The sender does this by saying a stimulus word, a clue, one at a time that will allow the receiver to find the hidden word by association (e.g., father-mother). The team that successfully "passes" the hidden word in the shorter time period (needing fewer clues) is the winner.

"Password" (it is available as a board game) is based on one of the earliest projective tests, developed in 1879 by Sir Francis Galton, the Word Association Test. Carl Jung (1906) used word association with his patients to unearth areas of chronic emotional disturbances, called *complexes*.

Jung observed that a complex may be inferred from the responses to stimulus words by any or all of the following: (a) the person takes a long time to respond, (b) the person makes no response, (c) the stimulus word is repeated, (d) the response is strange—an idiosyncratic association to the stimulus word, (e) responses referring to the same theme (e.g., sex, guilt, inferiority) are provoked by different stimulus words, and (f) the person shows nonverbal indications of being uncomfortable.

Jung's extensive work with the word association test led him to view complexes as relatively autonomous unconscious forces that are independent of the conscious ego and thus are liable to override the ego's intentions. In social situations, this can result in funny and/or embarrassing experiences when the "wrong word" is uttered, and we glimpse how someone really feels. When we hear a tired hostess say to her last remaining guests, "Can't you go? Must you stay?" we understand her feelings while knowing that she revealed them unintentionally.

Probably the most well-known projective test is the one developed by Hermann Rorschach in 1921. The Rorschach Inkblot Test consists of 10 cards, each card displaying a blot of ink. These blots are random shapes that allow someone looking at them to "see" something in them: a face, a butterfly, whatever. Rorschach designed the test to assess three dimensions of personality: conscious intellectual activity, externalized emotions, and private wishes. An evaluation of the Rorschach Inkblot Test concludes that it is valid for diagnosing distorted thinking, intelligence, therapy prognosis, and dependency (McGrath & Carroll, 2012).

Nevertheless, projective tests remain controversial. On the one hand, many clinical psychologists maintain that an understanding of personality is woefully incomplete without them. Research psychologists, on the other hand, are dismayed by their lack of demonstrated reliability and validity.

This is not a new issue. Over 60 years ago, the complaint was raised that a comprehensive handbook of projective techniques (Bell, 1948) presented scant evidence of the reliability and validity of these tests (Macfarlane & Tuddenham, 1951). Clinicians counter these concerns by pointing out that, unlike personality traits, unconscious issues are subject to change when they are brought to the surface as part of the therapeutic process. Post-therapy retest results for any projective technique, then, *should* differ from the pretest if psychotherapy is effective. The standard ways of evaluating the reliability and validity of self-report tests do not apply to projective tests. Can these conflicting viewpoints be reconciled?

Perhaps. Research on the "cognitive unconscious" (Kihlstrom, 2008) conducted over the past 30 years (e.g., Bargh, 1982) has shown that much of our conscious processing of social information is both automatic and unconscious. And the characters that are "seen" in various projective tests are likely to be drawn from this level of the unconscious (Westen, Gabbard, & Ortigo, 2008). The implication is that the personality data gathered from projective tests may show far more validity than was formerly presumed (Westen, Feit, & Zittel, 1999). A marriage of contemporary experimental research into automatic nonconscious processes with insightful clinical interpretations might eventually result in strong offspring capable of demonstrating healthy psychometric properties of projective tests. We can hope.

Behavioral Measures

Here we make an inference about a person's personality by observing what he or she does. Since psychology is concerned with understanding human behavior, one might assume that behavioral measures dominate research in personality psychology. Alas, they do not. Why not?

Earlier we saw how easy it is to administer self-report personality tests. Data can often be collected *efficiently*: quickly and inexpensively. Behavioral measures of personality, however, fall at the other extreme of the efficiency dimension. Behavioral measures typically require a serious time commitment for both data collection and analysis. Data analysis may be dauntingly time consuming because of the difficulties in developing reliable coding standards that permit independent observers to agree on which aspects of personality have been revealed.

All nonverbal behavior is inherently ambiguous. Suppose you observe a person at a social gathering who is off by himself in a corner, his nose buried in a book. Can you safely draw any inferences about his personality? He could be seriously socially avoidant. Maybe he is just introverted. Or maybe he is looking up something for his hostess. He might be reviewing the procedures for the ice-breaking game he's about to initiate. We need more information before safely drawing any credible conclusions about his personality.

The direct observation of behavior is not the easiest way to study personality. But if the field of personality psychology is to continue to make progress, new ways to observe how personality manifests itself in the real world are needed. Multiple ways of observing personality that lead to the same conclusions give us confidence that our understanding applies to the real personalities in the real world and not just to how persons respond on self-report, paper-and-pencil tests (Furr & Funder, 2007).

Physiological Measures

My first hands-on experience with psychological research occurred when I volunteered during my sophomore year. The research was concerned with the personality correlates of anxiety reduction.

After completing a true-false personality test (the MMPI), I was asked to look at a screen that flashed either a red or green card, one at a time. While a device measuring my galvanic skin response (GSR) was attached to my left palm, with my right hand I was instructed to press the appropriate colored button, red or green, as soon as the card flashed on the screen. Flash, press, flash, press, flash, press, and so forth. Boring.

After doing this for about 20 minutes, a loud piercing noise suddenly blasted my eardrums, scaring the wits out of me! It took me quite a while to calm down from being so startled. That was the only time, fortunately, that the highly aversive noise occurred during the remaining 30 minutes of button-pushing. I was unhooked from the GSR device, thanked, and ushered out. I never found out the results of this research.[12]

A *galvanometer* is a device for measuring a person's galvanic skin response (GSR). It measures how much moisture is on the skin (i.e., sweat), which is presumed to be caused by fear or anxiety. A galvanometer is often used as one of the physiological measures when conducting a lie detection procedure, as part of a *polygraph* (poly = many, graph = measure).

If it were true that everyone's sweat glands (or any other physiological measure) automatically responded whenever they lied, then polygraph results might be admissible evidence in a court of law. But that is not true. Some individuals show no changes in how much they sweat when they lie, while other individuals sweat copiously even when telling the truth because they imagine the other person *thinks* they are lying.

The purpose of measuring a person's physiological reactions is to obtain additional sources of data beyond self-report, ratings by observers, and so on. Our full understanding of anxiety, for example, requires multiple sources of information: what a person says about himself, what others observe about him, the conditions that cause him to feel anxious, and the bodily changes that occur during anxiety.

Other physiological measures include the following:

The EEG: The electroencephalograph measures the electrical activity of the brain in terms of different "waves" that occur throughout the day and night. The EEG allowed researchers to discover that we all go through predictable degrees of sleep during the night and that one of our brain waves is associated with REM (rapid eye movements), a sure sign of dreaming.

Differences in EEG patterns have been observed in individuals suffering from borderline personality disorder (BPD) compared to individuals diagnosed with major depressive disorder (MDD). These two disorders share a number of symptoms: irritability, risk of suicide, and heightened sensitivity to real or imagined interpersonal rejection. They differ in the typical reaction to perceived rejection. While MDD individuals are likely to withdraw from contact and isolate themselves, those with BPD respond with increased approach (e.g., stalking) and overt hostility ("I will *not* be ignored"). Differences at the physiological level substantiate a differential diagnosis of MDD versus BPD (Beeney et al., 2014).

The EKG: The electrocardiogram measures changes in the electrical activity of the heart. Heart rate changes are associated with states of psychological and physiological arousal. Some personality traits have been found to be risk factors for stroke and coronary heart disease. On the basis of longitudinal data covering over 24,000 individuals over a time period of 3 to 15 years, extraversion was found to be associated with a higher risk of stroke but not coronary heart disease (CHD). Neuroticism, on the other hand showed the opposite pattern: greater mortality from CHD than stroke. Highly conscientious individuals were found to have *lower* mortality from both CHD and stroke (Jokela et al., 2014).

Finally, the field of *physiological measures of personality* refers to all of the specific measurement tools found within the growing field of psychobiology of personality (Zuckerman, 2005). These include examining the role of various neurotransmitters, hormones, and genes on personality development and traits. Gordon Allport pointed out in 1937 that "personality is neither exclusively mental nor exclusively neural.

The organization entails the operation of both body and mind, inextricably fused into a personal unity" (p. 48). Psychobiology promises to help us more clearly understand how this fusion of mind and body into a personal unity takes place.

In summary, physiological measures allow personality psychologists to look closely at the biological basis of our attitudes, traits, and temperaments. Understanding the ways we differ physically allows us to appreciate more fully the reasons we differ psychologically.

Ethical Issues in Research and Personality Assessment

Ethical issues in personality arise whenever a test taker's identity is known to the test giver. For virtually all of the research reported in this text, this ethical issue does not arise because the participants' personality scores are anonymous: Personality researchers do not usually ask their participants to identify themselves by name. No one but the test taker knows how he or she responded to each item.

When an individual test taker's identity is known, potential ethical issues arise out of the concerns for privacy, concerns for the validity of the test, and concerns for fairness.

Privacy: The test giver is ethically obligated to obtain your informed consent before administering the test. This means you should be told the purpose of the test and who will have access to your results. You have the right to ask, "If someone else besides those you already named wants to see my test results, will I be notified in advance so I can grant or refuse this person's access to my answers?"

Finally, you have the right to know for how long your test results will be on file. If, for example, you take a personality test as part of seeing a counselor in your freshman year in college, how long will the school keep your results? The ethically correct answer is that the college should destroy your records when you are no longer a student there. Legal issues, however, may require the school to hold onto your records for a fixed number of years after you leave. It does no harm for you to ask and learn your school's policy on this issue.

Validity: When personality tests are used as part of the hiring process, employers have the obligation to show that the test results are a reasonably valid indicator of job performance. In the United States, this legal requirement of test validity traces back to the Equal Employment Opportunity Act of 1972. Without this requirement, an employer could administer a bogus test to an applicant and use the bogus results as the bogus reason for not hiring him or her, an obviously unfair practice.

Fairness: Employers are also mandated, by the same 1972 law, to ensure that the test does not unfairly discriminate against any particular ethnic, racial, or sexual group. For example, an applicant from another culture may obtain a low score on a test not because she is unqualified, but only because she is unfamiliar with some of information on the test due to cultural differences. From this point of view, the ethical concern for fairness falls under the ethical concern for test validity: The employment screening test should be valid for all those who apply for the position.

Summing Up: How Should I Interpret My Score on a Personality Test?

Your score on any personality test is like a snapshot. A snapshot of your face reveals, *maybe*, how your face looked at the moment the shot was snapped. All sorts of photographic technical details, however, are involved in that snapshot, details that could distort your image. Lighting conditions and the quality of the camera are just two of the variables involved in rendering a true photographic image. If this were not true, we'd have to conclude that all grandparents had red eyes.

Similarly, your score on a test reflects how you responded on the day and time you were tested. This score *may* tell you something about your personality. If your score tells you something you already knew about yourself, then no further discussion is necessary: The snapshot seems to be accurate. But if your score tells you something new about yourself, then you would be wise to find out if this new information is accurate, especially if it is important.

Learning, for example, that your vocational interest test result indicates you would enjoy being a dentist has life-altering implications should you act on it. What you want to know is, Is *my* test result valid for *me*? Actions to help you answer that question are well worth your time and effort. You could, for example, ask to retake the test to see if you obtain similar results. Personality test results can lead to meaningful life changes when the possibility they are valid is carefully tested by the thoughtful test taker.

❖

QUESTIONS TO PONDER

1. Most personality psychologists today favor the five-factor solution (The Big Five; The Five-Factor Model) to the problem of the number of fundamental traits needed to describe individual differences in personality. Some favor a six-factor solution, as in the HEXACO model (where H = honesty-humility). How can this discrepancy be resolved?

2. Want to develop your own personality test? This is the best way to learn how tests are constructed and validated. You could start by going online and checking out the huge selection of public-domain personality test items available at http://ipip.ori.org. The Oregon Research Institute hosts a large selection of over 2,000 items for any researcher to use freely to construct his or her own personality test. These items, called the *International Personality Item Pool (IPIP)*, have been used by multiple researchers around the world (Goldberg et al., 2006).

3. An easy way to collect data is through the Internet. After you select those items from IPIP that seem to measure the personality trait you are interested in, you could begin to collect data by publishing your test on the Internet. Chris Fraley (2007) tells you how to do so along with guidelines about how such data should be interpreted. Samuel Gosling and Winter Mason (2015) offer suggestions for using the Internet in novel ways to study traditional topics. Finally, Facebook can be an important research tool for personality research as well as for social science research in general (Kosinski et al., 2015).

NOTES

1. *Extravert* is the preferred spelling by the American Psychological Association. The word may also be spelled with an *o* instead of an *a*.

2. The conditions of the experiment by Revelle et al. (1976) are more complicated than I presented them. My simplification of their experimental design (for clarity purposes) does not, however, change the shape of the interaction the authors hypothesized and observed.

3. While the *finding* of the Extraversion x Arousal interaction is robust, research has yet to isolate the specific brain systems activated by different kinds of external stimulation (DeYoung & Gray, 2009).

4. Galton selected *r* to represent the correlation coefficient because of correlation's connection to the statistical concept of *regression*. Virtually all introductory statistics textbooks explain the association between correlation and regression.

5. The extreme values of the correlation coefficient, +1 and −1, are never found in actual practice. Personality researchers use statistical tests of significance to determine if the magnitude of the observed correlation coefficient is likely to have occurred by chance. When the sample size is large, in the 100s, even small values of r can indicate there is *some* (non-zero) relationship between the variables. *Statistical significance* does not mean by itself that the finding is particularly meaningful or important. The value of the correlation coefficient, *r,* can be interpreted as the *magnitude* or the *effect size* of the association between the two variables. Some researchers, however, prefer r^2 for this purpose. Daniel Ozer (2007) discusses the meaning of effect size as it applies to correlation coefficients.

6. Researchers in personality psychology, as well as in all other fields of science, often have to act like detectives to figure out "Who done it?" As Sherlock Holmes (Arthur Conan Doyle) famously said, "When you have eliminated the impossible, whatever remains, however improbable, must be the truth." In the case of the data reported by Eysenck and Zuckerman (1978), there is a confound between nationality of the participants and the method of testing: The data of the American sample were collected at the same time in a classroom, but in the English sample, the EPQ data were collected from 1 to 3 years before the sensation-seeking scale was filled out. Thus we do not know if the different results from the two samples are due to national differences, procedural differences, or both.

7. Please note that the correlation between two variables does not rule out the possibility that one *might* cause the other. The well-replicated finding of a positive correlation between cigarette smoking and lung cancer was eventually understood (on the basis of additional data as well as the correlation) to mean that cigarette smoking is indeed one of the *causes* of cancer. The mental leap from correlation to causality is never justifiable, though, without corroborating data from relevant experiments. It is useful to remind ourselves that the frequent erroneous mental leap from correlation to causality is one of the most common cognitive biases of the evolved human mind.

8. If there is reason to believe that the *order* in which these six tests are taken is important (will people who take test A or test B first give different responses on test C?), then the order in which participants take these tests should be systematically counter-balanced. After all the data are collected, order effects can be determined and, if they are present, the data need to be analyzed separately. If there is no evidence that order made a difference, the data are pooled.

9. There is one exception to this rule. When the hypothesis asserts that a relationship *always* exists between two variables, we need only *one* disconfirming observation to disprove it. While such disconfirmations have been observed in other areas of psychology (e.g., perception, language development), personality psychology is not one of them (Dukes, 1965).

10. In the real world, "other things" are never equal. The choice of working conditions (team versus alone) is affected by other personality variables (e.g., conscientiousness, need for affiliation) in addition to extraversion—as well as by the requirements of the task. So it is not realistic to expect to find a strong correlation of extraversion with work choice in all work settings. But we do expect the correlation to be usually greater than zero (more extraverts than introverts prefer to work in a team).

11. The reliability and validity of the NEO-PI-R is examined in some detail only because it is the most widely used measure of the Big 5. Many studies of the Big 5 have been and are conducted using other self-report measures. Their reliabilities and validities are demonstrated in the same way as explained in the text for the NEO-PI-R. The result is that most personality researchers presently believe that these major traits—neuroticism, extraversion, openness, agreeableness, and conscientiousness—account for most of the individual differences observed at the level of traits or dispositions. Please note that the *order* in which these traits are presented vary across different researchers. Oliver John and his colleagues, for example, prefer to order them: extraversion, agreeableness, conscientiousness, neuroticism, and openness (John, Naumann, & Soto, 2008).

12. Ethical standards today require that academic researchers first clear their procedure with, and get approval from, their university's Institutional Review Board before any data may be collected. Moreover, after the research is complete, participants should be debriefed and told the purpose of the research along with a summary of the results (which could be posted on an accessible bulletin board).

❖

SUGGESTIONS FOR FURTHER READING

Gosling, S. D., & Mason, W. (2015). Internet research in psychology. *Annual Review of Psychology, 66,* 877–902.

Kosinski, M., Matz, S. C., Gosling, S. D., Popov, V., & Stillwell, D. (2015). Facebook as a research tool for the social sciences: Opportunites, challenges, ethical considerations, and practical guidelines. *American Psychologist, 70,* 543–556.

Platt, J. R. (1964). Strong inference. *Science, 146,* 347–353.

Robins, R. W., Fraley, R. C., & Krueger, R. F. (Eds.). (2007). *Handbook of research methods in personality psychology.* New York, NY: Guilford.

Runyon, W. M. (1982). *Life histories and psychobiography.* New York, NY: Oxford University Press.

❖

INTERNET RESOURCES

1. For a list of current psychological projects, see
   http://www.psych.hanover.edu/research/exponnet.html.

2. To participate in psychological research online, see
   http://www.onlinepsych.co.uk.

3. To assess your "Big Five" personality traits, see
   http://www.youjustgetme.com.

Part II

My Past Self

3

Genetic and Temperamental Influences

❖Did my personality begin in the womb?

In what ways are you more like your mother than your father? This question occurred to me as a teenager when I noticed that my sister and father shared certain personality traits, whereas my mother and I were similar in other ways. For example, my sister and father were usually easygoing and relatively unflappable when challenged by life's frustrations and disappointments. Their favorite phrase at such times was "This, too, shall pass." In contrast, my mother and I tended to overreact to these same challenges as if they were impending catastrophes.

These clear differences in emotional responsiveness to changing events sparked my curiosity about their causes. Were they due to genetic similarities between me and my mother versus my sister and father? Or did the fact that I was the first-born child in our family have anything to do with it? Or did a combination of hereditary influence and unique early experiences cause my sister and me to have such different personalities?

In Part II, we view our past self by examining genetic and temperamental factors (this chapter) and early environmental influences (Chapter 4). The basic question we want to answer in Part II is to what extent can we attribute differences in our personalities to our genetic makeup, our early family experiences, or the interaction of genes and early environment? We begin our quest with a look at what the field of behavioral genetics says about personality differences.

Behavioral Genetics: The Seeds of Personality

For countless years before Gregor Mendel (1822–1884) discovered the laws of genetic inheritance, farmers around the world practiced "selective breeding" to help ensure that the new generation would have the traits they wanted for that species. For example, they would breed their best milk-producing cows with those males whose past female offspring were good producers of milk.

Since virtually no one knew the basic laws of genetics until the 20th century,[1] farmers and other selective breeders were puzzled whenever the new generation did not "breed true"—the desirable characteristic seen in the parents does not appear in the offspring. Where did it go?

A common human example of not "breeding true" is eye color. Two brown-eyed parents occasionally have a blue-eyed baby. How and why this happened was a mystery before Mendel, based on his extensive research with variations of peas, discovered that genes come in pairs (alleles) and offspring inherit one allele from each parent. Moreover, these genes (which Mendel called "heredity units" or "factors") are either "dominant" or "recessive" (Mendel's terms).

In the case of eye color, the two relevant alleles may be coded for either brown or blue, with the allele for brown eyes being dominant. But not all brown eyes are genetically identical. Some people with brown eyes inherited both dominant alleles from each parent (they have homozygous brown eyes). Other brown-eyed people inherited the dominant brown allele from one parent and the recessive blue allele from the other (they have heterozygous brown eyes). Their eye color, the phenotype (the observed trait), is brown, while their genotype (their unseen inherited genetic structure) contains alleles for both brown and blue eyes. Two partners, each with heterozygous brown eyes, will have, on average, children with blue eyes in 25% of their conceptions.

This example of a failure to "breed true" does not work in the other direction. All children of two blue-eyed parents will have blue eyes since both parents lack the dominant allele for brown eyes. So the genetic principle is that visible phenotypes may not "breed true" whenever the invisible genotypes of both parents consists of heterozygous alleles for that trait.

The laws of genetic inheritance were unknown to Charles Darwin (1809–1882). One of Darwin's hobbies was to attend shows by "pigeon-fanciers," people who raised and bred pigeons as a hobby. Darwin was delighted to learn about the slight anatomical variations between different breeds as well as the slight differences among birds of the same breed.

Pigeon-fanciers would hold contests to see who could breed the best example of some new predetermined feature. They might breed for a potential trait of upright feathers on the top of the pigeon's head, instead of the feathers laying smooth, making it look like the pigeon is wearing a feathered hat. By cross-breeding those pigeons whose head feathers look a tad unruly, within a few generations, pigeon-fanciers hoped to be able to breed a new variety of hat-wearing pigeons.

While Darwin did not breed pigeons for these contests himself, he was quite interested in the new varieties that appeared. He thought of the whole process as *artificial selection*—artificial because the new traits that appear after selective breeding are selected by humans, not by the birds themselves. The essence of Darwin's theory of evolution by *natural selection*, in contrast, depends on animals being "selected" (in a sense) by nature if they have the necessary physical characteristics that allow them to survive and reproduce, favorable characteristics they then pass on to their offspring. Darwin realized that very slight differences among animals of the same species can result, over thousands of generations, in dramatic anatomical changes, changes so dramatic as to result in a new species.

Darwin introduced the phrase *natural selection*[2] in 1859 with the publication of *On the Origin of Species by Means of Natural Selection* (Browne, 1995). Today, the combination of Darwin's theory of evolution via natural selection, combined with our knowledge of the laws of genetics, is called the Modern Evolutionary Synthesis or simply the Modern Synthesis (Gould, 2002).

Animal Personalities

We know animals within the same species differ on any number of physical characteristics. Do they also differ in their personalities? Are personality differences, which are so obvious at the human level, also found in animals?

Ivan Pavlov (1849–1936) knew about personality differences in animals (Pavlov, 1906). He observed that some of the dogs in his classical conditioning experiments easily learned to connect the unconditioned stimulus (meat powder) with the conditioned stimulus (sound of a bell), while others failed to do so. Pavlov adopted Galen's temperament typology to classify the dogs' personalities. Galen's seminal ideas about temperament are covered later in this chapter. As important as Pavlov's observations of the personality differences among dogs are, the number of systematic investigations of animal personality since then have been few and far between.

One reason for the reluctance by personality psychologists to study animal personality has been the fear that their conclusions will be dismissed as nothing but *anthropomorphism*—ascribing human traits to animal behavior. Since animals lack the ability to use words, observations of their behavior may reflect only the personality biases of the observer and not the animal. Systematic research, however, has shown that the ratings of personality traits of animals by independent observers are as valid as their ratings of the personality traits of humans (Gosling, Kwan, & John, 2003). By taking ordinary methodological precautions in investigations of animal personality, the specter of anthropomorphism may be laid to rest.

The first major review of research of animal personality was published in 2001 by Samuel Gosling. By dint of enviable persistence, Gosling (2001) identified 187 useful studies of animal personality in 64 different species among research papers published across an extraordinarily wide variety of professional journals, from agriculture to zoology.[3] Gosling's impressive review can leave no doubt in the mind of even the most skeptical critic of animal research that animals have personalities and that these personalities can be reliably and validly assessed.

Okay, but why study animal personality? What can be gained that we cannot learn from investigating personality differences among humans? There are a number of advantages to researching animal personality:

First, animals can be studied in more detail and over a greater length of time than is possible for humans because there is greater control of their environments.

Second, because many animal species have shorter life spans than humans, complete longitudinal studies over an animal's entire life are possible.

Third, studies of animal personality permit ethical physiological interventions to measure such internal processes as neurotransmitters, enzymes, and hormones (Vazire et al., 2007).

Fourth, for many species one can obtain detailed quantitative and molecular genetic information. A thorough review of how the trait of curiosity and exploratory behavior manifests itself across different species revealed an association between specific gene alleles and exploratory behavior (Pisula, Turlejski, & Charles, 2013).

Fifth, animal research can shed light on the evolutionary processes that influenced both personality structure and encouraged personality differences (Weinstein, Capitanio, & Gosling, 2008). For example, friendship among chimpanzees has been found to be related to their similarity in the traits of sociability and boldness (Massen & Koski, 2014). Given that the single most well-documented finding in social psychology is the similarity–attraction relationship—we are most attracted to those individuals who are most similar to us (Byrne, 1971)—this observation in a sample of chimpanzees suggests the relationship might have an evolutionary basis. Indeed, investigations of friendships within many animal species—horses, elephants, hyenas, dolphins, monkeys, as well as chimpanzees—reveal that friendships are adaptive. Having friends helps males compete successfully and produce more offspring; having friends helps females experience less stress and live longer, as well as have more infants who survive (Seyfarth & Cheney, 2012).

"He was raised by a guy named Darwin. Now all he does is spy on us!"

Finally, research based on animal models can shed light on a number of issues in personality psychology that cannot, for one reason or another, be conducted with humans. A few examples will illustrate this point:

1. Research with monkeys demonstrated the crucial significance of early attachment to the mother for their development into fully mature, healthy animals (Harlow & Harlow, 1962). Manipulating the early postnatal environment to study the lifelong effects of early social experiences can, of course, only be done ethically with animals.

2. What experiences of the mother shortly before birth might affect the personality of her offspring? Pregnant rhesus monkeys experienced three unpredictable loud noises lasting for 1 second each time (over a 10-minute interval). They experienced this 5 days a week for a few weeks before they gave birth. The effects of this stressful experience on their newborns include (compared to the offspring of nonstressed mothers) impaired coordination, attention deficits, less exploratory behavior, and excessive clinging behavior when exposed to stress (Schneider, 1992a, 1992b).

3. The molecular basis underlying gene x environment interactions can be investigated more easily. Rhesus monkeys were at greater risk for poor visual tracking and poor attention spans when they inherited a short allele of a particular gene *and* they were raised in a nursery, not by their natural mothers. Both conditions had to be present for these developmental deficits to occur (Champoux et al., 2002).

4. Finally, health-related outcomes can be identified with the use of animal models. The personality trait of sociability has been found to protect the animal's health by producing antibodies in response to SIV (simian immunodeficiency virus). Animals rated as

low in the trait of sociability produced fewer antibodies to combat the virus (Capitanio, Mendoza, & Baroncelli, 1999).

Might the Five-Factor Model (FFM) of personality apply to animal personalities as well as humans? Yes, it does. In a study of hundreds of chimpanzees and orangutans, researchers observed that the traits of extraversion and neuroticism could be reliably measured and that both traits declined with increasing age (as is commonly found with humans). Agreeableness increased in older chimpanzees (also true for humans) but declined in orangutans. The researchers interpreted these data as support for the genetic/evolutionary basis of the FFM (Weiss & King, 2015).

Moreover, in a review of 19 studies of personality across 12 nonhuman species, there was clear evidence for four of the five major traits. Extraversion, neuroticism, agreeableness, and openness to experience were found in most species (Gosling & John, 1999).

Conscientiousness, the fifth dimension of the FFM, was observed only in chimpanzees. A chimpanzee who displayed lack of attention and goal directedness, as well as erratic and disorganized behavior, was rated at the low end of conscientiousness. Since planning, thinking before acting, following rules, and controlling impulses require the brain capacity to do so, these traits should be most easily observed in animals with a sizable frontal cortex—humans and our genetically closest relatives, chimpanzees (Gosling & John, 1999).

A compelling explanation for the difficulty of controlling impulses to act while we are in the grips of intense emotional arousal is that there are many *more neural connections* in our brain that run *from* our emotional center, the amygdala, *to* our prefrontal cortex than run from our cortex to the amygdala. This means that the battle between our thoughts and feelings is an unfair fight: It is much easier for our emotions and feelings to influence our thoughts than it is for our thoughts to influence our feelings (LeDoux, 1996).

Brain anatomy supports the wisdom of slowly counting to 10 before we act whenever we feel angry (or are under the spell of any powerful emotion). By deliberately recruiting our prefrontal cortex, we give ourselves time to think about the consequences of any rash actions we might later regret (because we did not first consider their consequences). Thinking allows us to plan an effective response rather than thoughtlessly reacting to the provocation. Self-control and self-regulation are important components of the trait of conscientiousness—probably the most recent personality characteristic to appear on the scene because it is the trait most dependent on cortical control. Information about the ability to self-regulate is given in Chapter 9.

Our brief look at studies of animal personality shows that: (1) they have personalities and (2) the traits that have been identified are similar to the personality traits we see among humans. Does this mean that human personality traits have an evolutionary basis? Let's take a closer look at the units of evolutionary and hereditary transmission, the genes.

What Are Genes?

At the moment of our conception, we inherited 50% of our genes from our father and 50% from our mother. Genes are found in varying numbers on 23 pairs of chromosomes in the nucleus of virtually every cell. Genes are strands of DNA (deoxyribonucleic acid) that form a double helix, a spiraling ladder whose sides are connected by rungs of chemicals called nucleotides. It is the particular arrangement or order of these nucleotides that determines such physical characteristics as a person's gender, skin color, height, and predisposition to genetically determined diseases like sickle-cell anemia, hemophilia, and Huntington's chorea.

Such is the standard or traditional view of the structure of the DNA molecule. Recent work in microbiology, however, suggests that this standard view is oversimplified. It appears that the DNA molecule is not in actuality the fixed entity implied by the traditional view, but acts more like a metabolic molecule that biochemically responds to its environment. This new way of thinking about the basic unit of hereditary transmission, the DNA molecule, strongly suggests that the conceptual differences between "nature" and "nurture" are far less distinct than generally recognized (Rennie, 1993).

Whatever the actual structure and properties of the DNA molecule turn out to be, it is important to note that at the instant of conception, the zygote (the initial union of sperm and ovum, or fertilized egg) begins to develop in the environment provided by the mother's womb. Understanding the principles of behavioral genetics means understanding that all genetically determined development always takes place under particular environmental conditions. Changes in early environment can affect later gene operation as seen in those sad cases of deformed babies who resulted from the mother ingesting alcohol or other drugs during pregnancy. Whatever the prospective mother takes into her body *at any stage of pregnancy* automatically becomes part of her fetus's initial environment.

To determine the relative influence of heredity and environment, behavioral geneticists take advantage of what might be called "Nature's experiment" by comparing the resemblances of two kinds of twins, identical and fraternal. The co-twin method is a powerful procedure for sorting out the respective roles of heredity and environment in accounting for differences among our personalities.

Twin Studies

All identical twins share 100% of their genetic inheritance. Identical twins are referred to as monozygotic or MZ twins because they come from the same fertilized egg or zygote. Fraternal twins, more accurately referred to as dizygotic or DZ twins, begin life as two different fertilized eggs growing together in their mother's womb. Dizygotic is a more accurate term than "fraternal," because a brother–sister pair can be dizygotic twins as readily as two brothers or two sisters. Dizygotic twins are genetically related to the same degree as ordinary brothers and sisters, sharing 50% of their genes (on average). This method of studying twins is called *co-twin* because it involves comparing two sets of twins, MZ versus DZ pairs.

Nature, then, provides us an opportunity to compare the personality resemblances of MZ twins, who are 100% genetically identical, with DZ twins, who are, on average, 50% genetically similar. The logic behind the co-twin method is quite direct: If genes affect personality, then MZ twins should be more similar to each other than DZ twins are to each other, everything else being equal. Similarity of trait scores is measured by our friend from the prior chapter, the correlation coefficient. All personality psychologists agree with the logic of the co-twin method.

Controversy, however, stirs about the plausibility of the assumption that the environments of MZ twins are as equally similar as the environments of DZ twins. Many believe that MZ twins tend to be treated more similarly than are DZ twins (e.g., MZ twins are more likely to be dressed identically in early childhood). If they are treated more similarly than DZ twins, then MZ twins are more similar to each other on both genetic and environmental dimensions, compared to DZ twins. The point here is simply that if the "equal environments" assumption proves not to be true, the validity of the co-twin method would be challenged.[4]

Heritability

Heritability is the key concept in behavioral genetics. *Heritability* refers to the extent to which observed variability in a trait is attributable to variability in genetic background. Heritability can theoretically vary between 0% and 100%. Zero percent heritability means that none of the observed differences in personality relate to genetic differences. One hundred percent heritability means that all observed variability is due to genetic differences. Heritability can also be expressed in decimal form (ranging from .00 to 1.0).

We can define heritability another way through the biological concepts of phenotype and genotype, terms introduced earlier in this chapter. A phenotype, you recall, is the observed characteristic, trait, or behavior (e.g., brown or blue eyes). A phenotype is the result of the underlying genetic structure (the genotype) and the sequences of environments we have experienced throughout life. For example, although we all inherited genes that strongly determine how tall we will grow to be, the environmental factor of our dietary habits certainly affects our actual final adult (phenotypic) height. A genotype is the original genetic structure we inherited from our parents. Heritability, then, can be defined as that proportion of the variability of a trait's phenotype that is explained by variability in the underlying genotype.

Exercise 3.1 Computing Heritability

You can compute any trait's heritability (h^2) estimate for yourself if you know the magnitude of the correlation of this trait for identical twins (r_{MZ}) and its correlation for fraternal twins (r_{DZ}).

Suppose on the trait of extraversion, the correlation from a sample of identical twins is r_{MZ} = .50, while the correlation of scores from a sample of dizygotic twins is r_{DZ} = .30. How large or small is the heritability of extraversion according to these samples?

The formula for heritability is

$$h^2 = 2 \times (r_{MZ} - r_{DZ})$$

So if identical twins' scores correlate r = .50 while fraternal twins' scores on the same trait correlate r = .30, the heritability estimate for this trait would be

$$2 \times (.50 - .30) = 2 \times .20 = .40 = 40\% = h^2$$

Thus, 40% of the variability of extraversion scores can be attributed to genetic differences.

Photo 3.1 Carl Jung (1875–1961)

Jung used the Word Association test in 1904 to detect unconscious complexes. He was the first to introduce, in 1915, the terms *introversion* and *extraversion*. Jung viewed the complete development of personality as an achievement that takes a lifetime.

Key publications:

Psychological Types (1921/1971)
Two Essays on Analytical Psychology (1953)
Memories, Dreams, and Reflections (1965)

Investigators using the co-twin method typically find a heritability component of about 40% to 50% for many personality traits. But with the two dominant personality traits of extraversion-introversion (outgoing versus quiet and reserved) and emotional instability-stability (also called neuroticism), heritability estimates exceeding 50% or more have sometimes been obtained.

Most of the research concerning the heritability of personality traits has involved at least one of the five traits of the FFM (McCrae & Costa, 2008). Each trait is identified by only one of its two extremes or poles. Thus, Trait I in the FFM is neuroticism (N) or emotional instability. Individuals who score high on this trait are thin-skinned, anxious, and irritable. Low scorers are described as calm, relaxed, and comfortable with themselves. Most of us are somewhere between these extremes. Trait II is extraversion (E) rather than extraversion-introversion; Trait III is openness to experience (O) rather than open-closed; Trait IV is agreeableness (A) rather than agreeableness-disagreeableness; and Trait V is conscientiousness (C) rather than conscientious-irresponsible. While McCrae and Costa (2008) present these traits in the order of N, E, O, A, C, it may help to remember them by noting that these letters form the anagram OCEAN.

The main point is that each trait refers to a particular dimension of personality in which some people are high, some are low, and most are in the middle. Table 3.1 displays the five traits of the FFM, the six facets within each trait, and their average heritabilities across different investigations.

The heritability estimates of the five traits of the FFM, shown in the last column of Table 3.1, range from a low of 40% for the trait of agreeableness to a high of 55% for the trait of openness to experience. Table 3.1 gives you an idea of the strength of the heritabilities of five major personality traits, as estimated by the co-twin method.

❖ Table 3.1 Average Heritabilities of the 5 Traits and 30 Facets of the Five-Factor Model

Trait/Facet	High Scorers	Low Scorers	Heritability
Neuroticism			**.47**
Anxiety	nervous, worried, tense	calm, relaxed	.43
Angry Hostility	angry, frustrated, bitter	easy-going	.53
Depression	sad, lonely, hopeless	not easily discouraged	.46
Self-consciousness	easily embarrassed	not shy or socially anxious	.45
Impulsiveness	cannot control cravings	high tolerance for frustration	.29
Vulnerability	feel unable to cope	feel capable to cope	.53
Extraversion			**.53**
Warmth	affectionate, friendly	reserved, distant	.53
Gregariousness	enjoy being with others	loners, socially avoidant	.53
Assertiveness	dominant, forceful, talkative	keep to the background	.51
Activity	energetic, busy	leisurely, relaxed	.38
Excitement Seeking	seek sensations, thrills	low need for thrills	.62
Positive emotions	happy, laugh easily, cheerful	not exuberant	.42
Openness to Experience			**.55**
Fantasy	vivid imagination, daydream often	practical minded	.43
Aesthetics	appreciate art, music, beauty	uninterested in art	.66
Feelings	discriminates different emotions	feelings are unimportant	.45
Actions	try new foods, activities	find change difficult	.55
Ideas	intellectually curious	little or no interest in new ideas	.66
Values	examine existing social values	conservative, dogmatic	.48
Agreeableness			**.40**
Trust	assume other people are honest	skeptical of others	.34
Straightforwardness	sincere, disingenuous	manipulative	.40
Altruism	generous, willing to assist	unwilling to help others	.30
Compliance	mild, forgive and forget	competitive, uses anger	.48
Modesty	humble, self-effacing	arrogant, conceited	.30
Tender-mindedness	sympathetic, empathetic	tough-minded	.37
Conscientiousness			**.47**
Competence	feel capable and effective	feel unprepared and inept	.36
Order	neat, well-organized	not methodical, careless	.39
Dutifulness	ethical, scrupulous	undependable, unreliable	.37
Achievement Striving	set high goals	lack ambition, lackadaisical	.41
Self-discipline	complete tasks	procrastinate, quit easily	.40
Deliberateness	think before acting	hasty, speak before thinking	.30

Sources: Traits: Average heritabilities of five co-twin studies reviewed by Bouchard and Loehlin (2001). Facets: Average heritabilities of three co-twin studies reported in Jang et al. (1996, 2002). The descriptions of the two poles of each facet are taken from Widiger and Costa (2013, pp. 445–448).

The consensus at this time is that the heritability of these traits ranges between 40% and 50% (South et al., 2015).

Different co-twin investigations can yield different heritability estimates. Why? Each estimate depends on such variables as the sample size, the variability of the scores within the sample, and the specific personality test employed. Note that the individual heritabilities of the *six facets* of each trait (shown in Table 3.1) may be smaller than the overall, domain-level trait. This is particularly true for the trait of conscientiousness, which shows an average heritability of 47% even though none of the facets of this trait reveal an average heritability over 41%. This difference can be explained by the measurement principle covered earlier: Aggregate measures of traits are more reliable than single measures. When the correlations for the facets are corrected for reliability of the measurements, heritability estimates are equivalent to those of the traits, about 50% (Turkheimer, Pettersson, & Horn, 2014).

Researchers using the co-twin method have found that various attitudes have their roots in differential heritability (Feather, 1975). For example, the attitude toward capital punishment has a higher heritability component than the attitude toward co-ed education. Highly heritable attitudes have been found to be "stronger" than less heritable ones. Highly heritable attitudes, for instance, are less easily modified by external persuasion (Tesser, 1993).

Political attitudes have a genetic basis. MZ twins' attitudes toward social inequality and the need for changes in the economic system are more similar than the attitudes of DZ twins on these issues (Kandler, Bleidorn, & Riemann, 2012; Tuschman, 2013).

Traits that are related to temperament have substantial heritabilities. Individual differences in activity, emotional reactivity, endurance, and sensitivity to changes in the environment were found to be strongly related to differences in genetic background with heritabilities ranging from 62% to 83% (Kandler, Riemann, & Angleitner, 2013).

Moving from traits to behavior, a review of studies of adolescent sexual behavior found that heritabilities for *age at first intercourse* ranged between 0 and 72%, with an average heritability of 40% (Harden, 2014). Another study of adolescent twins found that *affiliating with delinquent peers* has a genetic component with heritabilities of 26% for males and 32% for females (Button et al., 2007). Finally, a study of adolescent girls found that *substance use* (alcohol, tobacco, marijuana) had a genetic basis with heritabilities of 44% and 49% at ages 14 and 18, respectively (Bornovalova et al., 2013).

Other Research Methods

Identical Twins Reared Apart: The most convincing evidence of the importance of genetics for understanding personality differences comes from studies of identical twins reared apart. Much of these data come from the Minnesota Study of Twins Reared Apart, which began in 1979 and has tested over 100 pairs of identical twins (MZ) who were reared apart (Bouchard et al., 1990). The well-replicated finding is that, for major personality traits, the degree of similarity of MZ twins is the same whether they were raised together or apart.

For example, for the trait of *constraint,* on which high scorers describe themselves as cautious, avoidant of dangerous activities, and conventional, the scores of MZ twins

❖ **Table 3.2** Correlation Coefficients for Identical Twins Raised Together Versus the Correlation Coefficients for Identical Twins Reared Apart on Seven Personality Traits

Trait	Identical Twins Raised Together	Identical Twins Raised Apart
Constraint	.58	.57
Negative emotionality	.54	.61
Distress	.52	.30
Fear	.49	.37
Anger	.37	.33
Activity level	.38	.27
Sociability	.35	.20

Sources: Tellegen et al. (1988) and Plomin et al. (1988).

reared together correlated .58, while the scores of MZ twins reared apart correlated .57. Table 3.2 shows the magnitudes of the correlation coefficients for constraint and six other personality traits for MZ twins reared together versus MZ twins reared apart.

The correlation coefficients for the seven personality traits in Table 3.2 do not statistically differ between the MZ together twins versus the MZ apart twins, suggesting that their similarity is primarily due to their similarity in genetics (each MZ twin pair shares the same genome). Indeed, a comprehensive report of 31 personality traits revealed that the similarity of personality scores of MZ twins was the same whether they were raised together, average $r = .50$, or apart, average $r = .49$ (Bouchard et al., 1990).

In summary, then, whether the observations are based on comparing identical twins to fraternal twins or they are based on comparing the personality similarity of identical twins who were reared apart to that of identical twins reared together, the conclusion is the same: Differences in genetic background accounts for about 40%–50% of observed personality differences.

Adoption Research: The logic of adoption research is straightforward: If genes are important determinants of personality traits, then biologically related siblings (who share, on average, 50% of their genes) should resemble each other to a greater extent than genetically unrelated siblings who were adopted in infancy into the same families. As with the co-twin method, personality resemblance is measured by the correlations of the siblings' scores on various personality tests.

Unlike the typical heritability of about 40%–50% estimated by the co-twin method, adoption studies usually yield smaller personality heritability estimates (Loehlin, Willerman, & Horn, 1988; Vukasovic & Bratko, 2015). One widely accepted explanation for this difference in heritabilities is that genetic influences may be *nonadditive*—they are a result of either dominant genes or interactions among specific genes. Nonadditive effects means that the correlations for MZ twin pairs would be larger than twice the correlations for DZ twin pairs. Research using extended family designs (e.g., twin pairs, twins versus siblings, biological versus adopted siblings) may clarify the exact magnitude of the heritability of personality traits (South et al., 2015). Interestingly, some behavior geneticists believe that the precise strength of trait heritability is not particularly important to know, as long we know the heritability is greater than zero and less than one (Turkheimer et al., 2014).

Molecular Studies

The issue of *how much* genes affect personality (heritability) is different from the issue of *which* individual genes affect personality. The study of the molecular genetics of personality began in 1996 with reports of associations between specific genes and personality traits. A link between a dopamine receptor gene and extraversion was found as was an association between a serotonin transporter gene and neuroticism. Additional research found that while discovering the precise genetic links to extraversion has proven to be elusive, the finding of an association of serotonin and neuroticism has been replicated: There is a small but meaningful role of the 5-HTT serotonin gene for the personality trait of neuroticism (Canli, 2008).

To date, molecular studies have been able to account for only a small percentage of the variability of a trait, personality or otherwise. For example, while it is known that 90% of the variability of height can be accounted for by genetics, only 10% of that variability is known to be associated with identifiable genes (180 alleles). The huge gap between the heritability identified by behavioral genetics (40%–50% for personality traits) and by studies at the molecular level (1%–2% for personality traits) is known as the *missing heritability problem* (Maher, 2008). As Robert Plomin noted, "Gene hunters are still recovering from the shock of finding that the largest associations account for so little variance in the population." (Plomin, 2013, p. 109).

What's going on? The missing heritability may be due to a number of factors. In the first place, the genetic basis of a given personality trait may be the result of thousands of separate genes, each with a small effect size, acting in concert. Because there are so many genes making up the genetic influence, isolating them individually is obviously a daunting task. Second, some heritable variation could be due to rare allele variants that exert large effect sizes but are difficult to detect by typical DNA sequencing protocols. Third, unknown gene–gene interactions might contribute to the similarity of personalities in identical twins. Finally, the possibility of a *gene x environment interaction* means that the gene might express itself more easily in some environments than in others, causing greater variability in its phenotype than in its molecular structure (Manuck & McCaffrey, 2014). What do gene x environment interactions mean in this context?

Gene x Environment Interactions

Students are often surprised to learn (I was!) that the field of behavior genetics is as important for understanding environmental influences as it is for understanding genetic ones. If genetic (**G**) differences account for 50% of the variability of personality traits, the other 50% must come from variability across environments (**E**). Importantly, there are two kinds of environments for twins: environments they *share in common* and environments that are *unique* to each twin. The general formula that guides genetic behavioral research is:

Trait variability = **G** variability + **Shared E** variability + **Unique E** variability,

where shared environment refers to growing up in the same family, going to the same school, and so forth. Unique environmental differences refer to experiences of the individual that are not shared by one's twin or siblings (e.g., having different hobbies, different friends).

The surprising finding in personality behavior genetics is that shared family experiences account for only a tiny part of the total variability, a part so tiny that it is more convenient to conclude that shared environment accounts for *none* of the variability of personality traits (Turkheimer et al., 2014). Accounting for the highly replicated observation that shared environments have no effect on personality differences has led behavior geneticists to rethink the concept of "environment" and wonder if gene x environment interactions might be involved.

There are a number of ways that our genetic endowment might interact with our various environments to produce our unique personalities. John Loehlin has comprehensively outlined the 18 different ways behavior geneticists are concerned with the environment (Loehlin, 2010). I present a few of these ways to illustrate the complexity of the gene x environment issue.

First off, there are *three gene–environment correlations:* active, passive, and reactive (Scarr & McCartney, 1983).

Consider the idea of "Experience-Producing Drives" (Bouchard, 1997): individuals who, for example, inherited the genetic configuration that underlays the need for excitement and sensation-seeking are more likely to engage in such pursuits than those low in this need. These experiences, in turn, help shape their personalities: The correlation of genes with environmental experiences has a *potentiating effect* on personality above and beyond the genetic influence by itself and thus falls in the category of *active gene–environment correlation.*

The *passive gene–environment correlation* refers to those situations where parents pass on their genes to their children *and provide an environment* that supports the expression of those genes. Parents who are musically inclined are likely to pass on genes relevant to music appreciation and performance as well as providing their growing children with a rich musical environment in the form of the availability of musical instruments, music heard in the home, and/or music lessons. Similarly, athletic parents could both pass on their athletic genes and provide an environment that supports athletic activities.[5] Loehlin (2010) points out that adoption studies are one way to disentangle the confound between genes and environments that correlate passively: Adoptive parents are less likely to provide the same degree of gene-supporting environment as natural parents.

The *reactive gene–environment correlation* refers to the reactions of other people to genetically based traits. The behavior of parents is often a reaction to the genetically driven characteristics of their child. Infants who are easy to soothe, for example, are more likely to evoke positive, loving responses from their parents compared to those who are difficult to soothe (Avinum & Knafo, 2014; Bell, 1968; Lewis & Rosenblum, 1974).

Other examples of the reactive gene–environment correlation include the following: (1) A field experiment found that when waitresses wore blond wigs they received larger tips from their male customers (Gueguen, 2012); (2) in general, physically attractive people are treated better than those who are less attractive (Langlois et al., 2000). Such continually favorable attention, beginning in early childhood, might result in a physically attractive person developing a sense of "deserving" special privileges, or acting, as we say, "stuck up." Narcissism could be one outcome of the reactive gene–environment correlation; (3) preschool children who are temperamentally outgoing evoke more prosocial and friendly responses from an unfamiliar peer (DiLalla, Bersted, & John, 2015).

Next, there are the environmental influences that are shared by family members, two prenatal and four postnatal:

Prenatal

Shared uterus: DZ twins share the same uterus. Ordinary siblings do not. Loehlin (2010) points out that the hypothesis that left-handedness is caused by prenatal crowding has not been supported since DZ twins are not more likely to be left-handed than siblings who are not twins.

Shared chorion: The chorion is the outermost layer of the membranes that protect the developing embryo. Some MZ twins share the same chorion; others do not. Does this type of shared environment really make a difference for personality? Results are mixed. Sokol et al. (1995) found that MZ twins who shared a chorion were slightly more similar to each other than those MZ twins who did not. But another investigation into these types of shared environments found that both types of MZ twins were equally similar (Riese, 1999).

Postnatal

Sharing environments outside the family (e.g., same friends): Judith Rich Harris (1995, 1998) proposes that a child's peer group has a greater effect on his or her personality than the child's parents. Modest support for this hypothesis was obtained in a comparison of 500 MZ twin pairs (Loehlin, 1997). Further, Harris (2006) hypothesizes that the peer group is the major reason that MZ twins usually develop different personalities: Needing something to tell the twins apart, their friends seize on any difference between them (You're the one who likes ravioli?) and reinforces it. This reinforcement of personality differences is accepted by the twins because every child wants to be accepted for his or her unique self.

Environments that differ by age: Twins experience their environments at the same age, but siblings experience them at different ages. A study of American and Australian twins versus siblings, however, found no evidence that the environments shared by twins were more similar than environments experienced by siblings (Keller et al., 2005).

Environments that differ by sex: On a measure of neuroticism, adopted siblings of the same sex showed a correlation of .31 compared to a correlation of .14 for adopted siblings of the opposite sex. This modest difference in the size of the correlations (.31 versus .14) implies that sex-related environmental differences are worthy of further study (Loehlin, Willerman, & Horn, 1987).

Siblings as each other's environment: The above-mentioned study by Keller et al. (2005) did not find that sibling environment made any difference for the personality traits that were measured.

Finally, the complexity of personality is due in part to the reality that *humans evolved in one environment,* the *environment of evolutionary adaptedness* (Tooby and Cosmides, 2005), *but live today in another.* This crucial difference is easily illustrated via observations of toddlers who immediately recoil in fear at the sight of a crawling snake but happily play with a revolver, which may or may not be loaded (Ohman & Mineka, 2001, 2003). The investigations of animal personality covered earlier in this chapter suggest that at least some components of human personality might have deep evolutionary roots.

In summary, Loehlin's detailed examination of the numerous ways we can speak of "the environment" (only some of which are given here) shows how complex this seemingly simple concept is. So the next time someone tells you how important "the environment" is for understanding personality, you may politely inquire, "Of which environments do you speak?"

Conclusions

We can draw three conclusions from the body of research into the genetic basis of personality:

1. There is a significant genetic component to many personality traits.

2. This component accounts for at least 40% of the variability observed among individuals' personalities.

3. Our personalities begin in the womb.

Before we leave the topic of personality's heritability, it is not a bad idea to check our understanding of the meaning of a heritability component of 40%. Please decide if each of the following three statements is true or false:

1. At least 40% of my personality is due to traits I inherited from my biological parents.

2. At least some portion of human behavior is known to be inherited.

3. Genetic influence is at a maximum at birth and declines in importance as we age.

These are three common misconceptions regarding genetic influence. The correct answer to each statement is false!

1. Heritability is a population concept, not an individual one. For example, the average height in a population of people may be 66 inches, but some individuals in that population will be much shorter and others will be much taller than average. In a different population, the average height may be quite different, and again different individuals in that population would be expected to deviate from that average.

In the same way, heritability estimates are expected to vary across different populations of people. Heritability estimates are related to such variables as the size of the sample and the variability of the trait within the sample.[6] Your own unique personality may be under much more or much less genetic influence. Behavioral geneticists cannot pinpoint exactly to what extent *your* specific personality traits are related to genetic influence from your parents. This difference between what we know at the *group level* (average heritabilities for different aptitudes and personality traits) versus what can be said with confidence about how *any particular individual* is affected reflects a basic tension throughout all research in personality psychology. The two statistical ways to describe any data set, its *average* and its *standard deviation* (the size of the variability around that average), are equally important.

2. We do not inherit behavior or personality traits. The genes we inherit from our parents are codes to create sequences of amino acids. From conception onward, these genetic actions take place within sequences of particular environments. The observed expressions of genetic influence in our behavior or personality traits depend on both the underlying genetic structures and the sequences of environments we have encountered, starting with our mother's womb. Our personalities depend on both nature and nurture.

3. Many people believe the influence of genes on behavior is at a maximum at birth and declines over the life course. Evidence does not support this belief. In the first few months of life, the infant's behavior is quite variable. It is difficult to observe any meaningful genetic influence. But by 6 months of age, genetic influences are seen in the broad personality traits of activity, sociability, and emotionality, and by 9 months of age, a number of temperamental traits such as activity and regularity show genetic influence (Riese, 1990). Investigations of older adults show strong genetic influence for such life experiences as serious conflicts with one's children, divorce, and improvements in married life (McGue & Lykken, 1992).

The data on this issue are mixed. A longitudinal analysis of twins in adulthood concludes that personality stability is strongly associated with genetic factors, whereas personality change largely reflects environmental influences. This analysis is consistent with longitudinal observations of adopted children (McGue, Bacon, & Lykken, 1993). However, a large-scale investigation of more than 15,000 twins, who ranged from 18 to 59 years in age, revealed significant *decreases* in the heritability of the extraversion and neuroticism traits as they grew older. Even so, there was significant genetic influence at all age levels (Viken et al., 1994). Thus, whether genetic influences on personality increase, decrease, or remain the same over the life span has yet to be well established.

The genetic "seeds" of personality, then, are not limited to the period of early childhood, but persist throughout the life course. Those personality traits that do appear very early in life are commonly thought to reflect those biological components of personality we call temperament, the next topic of this chapter.

Temperament

Are you temperamental? What does it mean to be temperamental? In everyday English usage, we think of a temperamental person as someone who is high-strung, easily excitable, prone to quick changes in mood, and/or fickle. A diva, perhaps?

The concept of *temperament* has a long history. It was the first dimension of personality to be identified by the early Greeks and Romans. While the physician Galen (2nd century CE) is often given credit for the four types of *humors* (presented below), these ideas were already floating around during his lifetime. The full fourfold typology was not seen until later (Diamond, 1974). Remarkably, three aspects of this earliest approach to individual differences are still current today:

1. Biological factors influence the personality differences we see among people.

2. Emotions are the essence and defining feature of temperament.

3. The four temperament humors merge well into the four quadrants formed by crossing the two super-traits of neuroticism and extraversion (Clark & Watson, 2008). Figure 3.1 shows the relationship between the Greek humors and the two super-traits.

The upper left-hand quadrant of Figure 3.1 displays how the Greek humor of *melancholia* fits in with modern trait theory: These sad individuals would score high

❖ **Figure 3.1** How the Four Humors Relate to the Traits of Emotional Stability (Neuroticism) and Extraversion

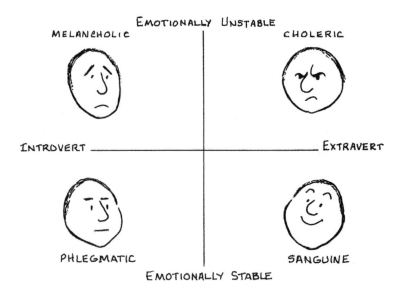

on neuroticism (emotionally unstable) and low on extraversion (i.e., they are highly introverted). The upper-right hand quadrant displays the *choleric* temperament: Emotionally unstable extraverts who are often angry. The lower right-hand quadrant shows where a *sanguine* person connects to the two traits: She is extraverted and emotionally stable (low neuroticism). Finally, the lower left-hand quadrant shows the *phlegmatic* temperament: An emotionally stable and introverted personality. The Greek idea, it should be noted, is that a balanced or healthy person is a *blend* or *mixture* of the four humors. The English word *temperament* is derived from the Latin word *temperamentum*, a mixture (Rothbart, 2011). Only when one of these four humors is found in excess do we see the emergence of one of the above four types.

Child and personality psychologists approach the study of temperament from different perspectives: Child psychologists are primarily interested in those individual differences, such as reactivity and self-regulation, that appear early in life. They reserve the term temperament to these early-appearing, genetically caused differences among infants and babies. Personality *traits* refer to stable individual differences that appear later in childhood and are under the influence of environmental experiences as well as genetics (Rothbart & Bates, 2006). Personality psychologists, in contrast, are interested in individual differences in temperament that predict, or show continuity with, personality traits in later childhood, adolescence, and adulthood. Since not all temperamental traits are stable in early life (Rothbart, 2011), personality psychologists prefer to focus on those that are (Shiner, 2015).

Infancy and Early Childhood

The first systematic study of infants' temperament was conducted by physicians Alexander Thomas and Stella Chess. They initiated the New York Longitudinal Study in 1956 (Thomas, Chess, & Birch, 1968). Although this early work has been called bold and influential (Kagan & Fox, 2006), it was ultimately determined to be flawed because it relied solely on parents' ratings of their infants' temperaments. Later work discovered that such ratings partly reflect *the temperament of the parents* (Matheny, Wilson, & Thoben, 1987).

If parental ratings are flawed measures of their child's temperament, how else can temperament be assessed? Jerome Kagan believes a psychology laboratory is the best place to observe how toddlers react to a new situation.

Whenever you meet a new person, or you are in an unfamiliar situation, how do you typically behave? Do you hold back until you can assess what's going on? Or do you act pretty much the same way in both familiar and unfamiliar surroundings? According to Kagan, your typical response to unfamiliar people and events reveals a key element of your temperament.

Kagan and his colleagues have demonstrated that in the unfamiliar situation of a psychology laboratory, some 20- to 30-month-old children consistently become quiet, timid, and reserved as they scope out their new environment. Other children boldly and fearlessly immediately begin to explore their novel surroundings. These two behavioral tendencies, inhibited and uninhibited, are obvious to parents: The tendency to approach or to avoid unfamiliar people and places is one of the most striking differences among several thousand 4- to 8-month-old infants (Sanson et al., 1987).

Longitudinal research shows that the majority of inhibited children (about 10% of those studied) and uninhibited children (about 25%) maintain these behavioral styles from ages 2 though 7. About 75% of the inhibited children at age 7 have one or more unusual fears (e.g., attending summer camp, going alone into their bedroom at night), compared to only 25% of the uninhibited children. Among children observed from birth through age 25, inhibited behavioral qualities remain the most stable of all identified traits (Kagan, 1989).

Kagan's research program continues to document behavioral differences in infants and young children that are due to differences in temperament. To account for the full range of behavioral diversity seen in his laboratory, Kagan expects as many as 23 temperament dimensions will eventually be found. These temperamental differences are due to differences in brain activity (Kagan, 2010).

Finally, an ongoing major research program to identify temperaments in infants and young children has been conducted by Mary Rothbart and her colleagues (e.g., Derryberry & Rothbart, 1988; Rothbart, 2011; Rothbart & Bates, 2006). Data collected from the Children's Behavior Questionnaire for 3- to 7-year-olds showed *three broad temperament factors* encompassing a number of specific traits:

Factor 1. Surgency. Includes the traits of *activity* (running rather than walking); *positive excitement* (positive anticipation for expected pleasurable events); *high-intensity pleasure* (enjoys highly stimulating activities); *impulsivity* (rushes into new situations); and *smiling and laughter* (responds with positive affect in response to situational changes).

Factor 2. Negative Affectivity. Includes the traits of *anger/frustration* (in reaction to interruption of activities); *discomfort* (negative affect brought about by being overstimulated); *not easily soothed* (takes longer to recover from distress or arousal); *fear* (negative reaction to potentially negative events), and *sadness* (negative affect in response to disappointment or object loss).

Factor 3. Effortful Control. Includes the traits of *focused attention* (can concentrate without being distracted); *inhibitory control* (can plan an activity yet also shift behavior when needed); *low-intensity pleasure* (enjoys nonstimulating situations such as sitting on parent's lap); and *perceptual sensitivity* (aware of slight changes in the external environment). (Rothbart, 2011)

Earlier investigations of personality in childhood also uncovered a three-factor solution. Jack Block (1971) identified three personality types: *Resilient* (self-confident, able to concentrate, adaptable), *overcontrolled* (shy, introverted, inhibited), and *undercontrolled* (impulsive, disagreeable). David Watson and Lee Anna Clark (1993) identified a similar model of temperament. They labeled their three dimensions *negative temperament, positive temperament,* and *disinhibition.* A number of independent investigations using different methodologies within different populations also found these same three dimensions (e.g., Caspi, 1998; Vroman, Lo, & Durbin, 2014).

So do these three temperamental dimensions found in very young children equally apply to adults? No. The five major traits (e.g., OCEAN) offer a better fit to the data (Caspi & Shiner, 2006). This brings us to the study of temperament from the perspective of personality psychologists.

Older Children, Adolescents, and Adults

In one study of the development of the three temperament traits seen in young children, six personality factors were identified in the older children. Five factors were similar to those of the five-factor model, while a sixth factor was similar to the high-intensity pleasure of Rothbart's Surgency factor (De Pauw, Mervielde, & Van Leeuwen, 2009). Moreover, another investigation concluded that the three temperamental traits found in young children expanded into five traits in adulthood (the five traits of the five-factor model). The *Effortful Control* temperamental dimension developed into a complex combination of conscientiousness and agreeableness. The trait of openness to experience appeared later than the others. Differences in curiosity, for example, are first seen among older children (Clark & Watson, 2008; Markon, Krueger, & Watson, 2005).

Stability and Change

The main finding from behavior genetic research is that genetic influences account for the largest percentage of the stability of temperament traits over time. Changes in childhood temperament traits are mainly accounted for by both genetic factors and nonshared environmental influences that are unique to the individual child (Shiner, 2015).

For example, changes in infants' positive emotionality are related to the quality of the marital relationship of their parents. Infants whose parents had healthier marital relationships showed increases in positive emotionality (Belsky, Fish, & Isabella, 1991). In other studies, children's negative emotionality decreased when their caregivers related to them with sensitivity (Bates, Schermerhorn, & Petersen, 2012), but their negative emotionality was made worse by noisy and chaotic home environments (Matheny & Phillips, 2001), or when parents punished then for expressing their negative feelings (Eisenberg et al., 1999).

Gender Differences

A meta-analysis of 189 investigations of children's temperaments (3 months of age to 13 years old), found that girls were rated higher in *Effortful Control* than boys. Girls were better able to regulate their *attention* and to *ignore/inhibit impulses* to wander away. Given that these abilities are important developmental tasks, these data suggest that boys undergo a maturational lag in self-regulation that lasts through middle childhood.

In the same investigation, boys were rated higher than girls on the temperament dimension of *Surgency* and its sub-traits of *activity* and *high-intensity pleasure.* School yard observations of the different kinds of play of boys and girls support this conclusion: rough-and-tumble play is more characteristic of boys than it is of girls. Rothbart's temperament factor of *Negative Affectivity* showed a small difference in *fear,* with girls rated as slightly more fearful than boys (Else-Quest et al., 2006).

Another meta-analysis of sex differences in emotional expressions found that girls and women were more likely to express feelings of *guilt* and *shame,* particularly about their bodies, sexual activities, and food or eating, than were boys or men (Else-Quest et al., 2012). Research has shown that young girls' dissatisfactions with their bodies begins between 6 and 8 years old (Ruble, Martin, & Berenbaum, 2006).

Conclusions from this large data set are consistent with another meta-analysis of emotional expressions in children that found small but significant differences between the sexes: Girls are more likely than boys to show both *positive emotions* as well as *sadness, anxiety,* and *sympathy*. Young boys were more likely to show *anger,* but this sex difference reversed in adolescence when adolescent girls displayed more anger than boys (Chaplin & Aldao, 2013).

The results of three large cross-cultural studies of sex differences in personality traits in adulthood are consistent with what has been observed in young children. Women reported more frequent and more intense feelings of *affection* and *sadness* than did men. This was true, on average, for a sample of over 2,000 participants from Australia and over 6,800 participants internationally (Brebner, 2003). Similarly, a large-scale study of sex differences across 55 cultures found that women scored noticeably higher than men on the traits of *neuroticism* and slightly higher on the traits of *extraversion, agreeableness,* and *conscientiousness* (Schmitt et al., 2008). Finally, a third cross-cultural study of gender differences in emotional expressions found that women, in general, reported more *sadness, fear, shame,* and *guilt,* while men reported more *anger* (Fischer et al., 2004). Such data suggest that these gender differences are universal (Ruble et al., 2006).

In conclusion, if we compare personality development to the growth of a plant, the genes that influenced how characteristically active, happy, or anxious we are can be considered to be the seeds of our personality. But for personality to blossom, these seeds must take firm root in the soil provided by our early environment—a fact acknowledged by all behavioral geneticists and temperament theorists. Your past self was affected by both seeds and soil. The next chapter covers three key ingredients found in the soil of your early childhood: the style of parenting you experienced, the quality of your attachments to your caregivers, and the processes that led to your identification (or not) with these caregivers.

❖

QUESTIONS TO PONDER

1. Many people do not accept the premise that researchers are ethically permitted to treat animals in ways that would be unethical if applied to humans. What is your view on this issue? What ethical guidelines are followed by those departments that house animals at your school? A fresh approach for appreciating the role that animals play in human life is provided by Catherine Amiot and Brock Bastian in their 2015 paper, "Toward a psychology of human-animal relations" (*Psychological Bulletin, 141,* pp. 6–47).

2. In what ways are you more similar to one of your parents than to the other? Do you think this is due to your genetic inheritance or to the way you were raised? If you know your grandparents, how similar is your mother to her parents and your father to his? Are you more similar in some ways to one of your grandparents? What accounts for this similarity?

3. If you have brothers or sisters, how similar are you to them? Have you ever thought that either you or they must have been adopted because you are so different? Have you observed striking differences in personality among siblings in other families? How can such large differences in personality between siblings raised in the same family be explained?

4. Suppose in the near future genetic engineering reaches the point where prospective parents will be able to decide whether to have a boy or a girl, how smart he or she will be, and which major personality traits he or she will have. Would you take advantage of this technology for your own children-to-be? Why or why not? If most parents did this, what might be the long-term consequences for society as a whole?

5. Suppose within the next 10 years a pill is developed that allows you to permanently modify any aspect of your personality. The pill will make you more extraverted, for example, or whatever trait is most important to you. Would you take such a pill? What trait would you like to change?

❖

NOTES

1. Although Mendel published his two-factor theory in 1866, no one seems to have commented about the significance of his paper until 1900.

2. Right from the start Darwin regretted his choice of language. Many thought *natural selection* signified that the Creator selected which animals would survive. Darwin meant, of course, that those animals who happened to be advantaged by nature with "favorable heredity" was a matter of chance, the roll of the genetic dice. After the publication in 1859 of *On the Origin of Species by Means of Natural Selection* and the ensuing (and continuing) confusion and attacks on the book, Darwin wondered if the phase *Natural Preservation* might have been less anthropomorphic. He scribbled a note about this to his close friend Charles Lyell, who misread Darwin's atrocious handwriting as *Natural Persecution*. Given how personally Darwin took these attacks, Lyell's misreading gave him a good laugh (Desmond & Moore, 1991, p. 492).

3. I advise all new researchers to read Gosling's (2001) paper to (1) see how a thorough literature review is conducted and (2) appreciate the numerous decisions researchers sometimes have to make (which prior research to include, which to omit) before beginning their own investigations.

4. The assumption that identical twins who were raised apart experienced different environments (so that any similarity in their personalities must be due to genetics) needs to be carefully evaluated. Being "raised apart" does not necessarily mean being raised differently. Some twins "raised apart" were adopted by close relatives who lived next door. These twins grew up knowing each other, spent time together, went to the same school, and had the same friends. Without an independent quantitative measure of environmental differences, it is difficult to attribute personality similarity to genetics alone.

5. The (unconfirmed) story goes that former NFL football coach Don Shula, before asking his wife, Dorothy, to marry him, asked her to *run backward as fast as she could!* Don, a former defensive back, hoped they would have an athletic son skilled enough to play

the same position in the National Football League. Dorothy passed Don's running backward speed test. One of their sons, Dave, played for one season in the NFL.

6. Heritability can be a tricky concept because it always refers to *how much variability* in an observed trait can be explained by variability in genetic structure, the genome. If there is little or no variability in a trait, then its heritability must be small even if we know the characteristic is under genetic control. Consider, for example, this question: What is the heritability of the *number of ears* people have? If heritability is a new concept to you, your immediate answer will probably be 100% because it is obvious that how many ears humans have is determined by heredity. But because everyone, or nearly everyone, inherits exactly two ears, there is essentially *zero variability* in this physical characteristic, and thus its heritability is zero. (This is a different question than how well we use our ears to hear what other people are really saying, a personality characteristic whose heritability may well be above zero.)

SUGGESTIONS FOR FURTHER READING

Harris, J. R. (2006). *No two alike: Human nature and human individuality.* New York, NY: Norton.

Kagan, J. (2010). *The temperamental thread: How genes, culture, time, and luck make us who we are.* New York, NY: Dana Press

Rothbart, M. K. (2011). *Becoming who we are: Temperament and personality in development.* New York, NY: Guilford.

Tuschman, A. (2013). *Our political nature: The evolutionary origins of what divides us.* Amherst, NY: Prometheus Books,

Zuckerman, M. (2005). *Psychobiology of personality* (2nd edition revised and updated). New York, NY: Cambridge University Press.

INTERNET RESOURCES

1. For information on evolutionary psychology, see http://www.psych.ucsb.edu/research/cep/index.html.

2. For information about the Minnesota study of twins, see http://www.psych.umn.edu/psylabs/mtfs/.

3. For information on birth order, see http://www.pbskids.org/itsmylife/family/birthorder/.

4

Cultivating Personality

What kinds of early childhood experiences affected my personality?

Ingredient #1: Parenting Styles
   Nurturance and Control
   Importance of the Family
   Psychosocial Stages of Development

Ingredient #2: Attachment
   Evolution of Attachment
   Types of Attachment
   Internal Working Models

Ingredient #3: Identification
   Freudian Theory
   Bandura's View of Imitation
   Development of Gender Identity

Our early childhood environment provides three critical ingredients for the soil in which our personalities grow and blossom: parenting styles, attachment, and identification.

Ingredient #1: Parenting Styles

Nurturance and Control

How would you describe your parents' typical behaviors and attitudes in raising you? Were they basically warm and accepting? Or were they usually cold and rejecting? What about the issue of control? Did they generally insist you meet their standards, or did they let you do whatever you wanted? Research indicates that the parenting dimensions of *nurturance* (warm versus cold) and *control* (setting firm limits versus not setting limits) influence personality development (Baumrind, 1972; Maccoby & Martin, 1983). The first part of this chapter describes research on parenting styles and relates these findings to the theories of Alfred Adler and Erik Erikson.

Some parents can be described as **authoritarian:** They demand to be obeyed. Authoritarian parents want to control their child. Although parents who adopt this parenting style frequently *tell* (or order) their child, "Act your age," the child *hears* their admonition as, "Stop being a child," or even worse, "Stop being yourself!" These parents rarely explain the reasons for their decisions; they are not particularly communicative or nurturant. The authoritarian parenting style is high in control and low in warmth.

There are two forms of control. **Psychological control** consists of inducing guilt in the child, withdrawal of love, and parental intrusiveness. Parents who adopt this control style are authoritarian, manipulative, and insensitive to their child's emotional needs. Research has found that some of the effects of psychological control on children include low self-esteem, anxiety, and depression (Barber, 2002).

Behavioral control consists of monitoring the child's activities, setting nonarbitrary, reasonable rules for their child to follow, and enforcing these rules fairly. Parents who adopt this control style are warm and sensitive to their child's needs. Behavioral control is associated with *fewer* behavioral problems in children: There are fewer incidences of drug abuse, truancy, and antisocial behaviors (Barber, 2002; Crouter & Head, 2002). Parents who adopt behavioral control programs lead Diana Baumrind to classify them as **authoritative** (see below).

Permissive parents do not make many demands on their child. They nurture the child but remain passive in setting and communicating standards for their child to achieve. Their implicit message is, "Do what you want." The permissive parenting style is low in control and high in warmth.

Uninvolved parents are uninterested in their child's development. They set few standards for their child's behavior and provide minimal nurturance and support. The uninvolved parenting style is low in both control and warmth.

Authoritative parents raise their children within a context of high nurturance and realistic maturity demands. These parents prefer to use rewards rather than punishments. They communicate their expectations clearly and frequently provide explanations for their decisions. The authoritative parenting style is high both in control and in warmth. And, as mentioned above, the type of control exerted by authoritative parents is described as behavioral in that it consists of observable actions that the child is expected to comply with (e.g., set the table before dinner).

Research shows that different parenting styles affect children's personalities. For example, the authoritative parenting style is consistently associated with children who demonstrate autonomy, high self-esteem, and superior academic performance. Children reared in authoritative homes tend to be friendly and popular with their peers, cooperative with adults, independent, and achievement oriented. They also display a high degree of self-control (Crockenberg & Litman, 1990; Dekovic & Janssens, 1992).

Baumrind (1973) refers to this cluster of personality characteristics as *instrumental competence*. A vast literature shows that adolescents from authoritative homes tend to be more self-assured, more creative, more responsible, more adaptable, more curious, more socially skilled, and more successful in school. All in all, the evidence linking authoritative parenting practices and raising positive, healthy adolescent children is exceptionally strong and has been replicated across a wide variety of ethnic groups, family structures, and countries around the world (Collins & Steinberg, 2006).

"I bet kids who are raised by wolves don't have to eat their spinach!"

In contrast, the other three parenting styles have been found to detrimentally affect children in various ways. For instance, preschool children of authoritarian parents have been observed to be withdrawn, unhappy, anxious, and insecure when interacting with peers. These children are likely to act aggressively when frustrated. Teenagers from authoritarian families, especially boys, obtain poorer grades in high school than teenagers from authoritative families (Parke & Buriel, 2006; Putallaz, 1987). Moreover, adolescents reared by authoritarian parents tend to be more passive, less self-assured, more dependent, less curious, and less socially skilled (Collins & Steinberg, 2006).

Children from permissive families were observed to be more immature than others and had difficulty controlling their impulses (Baumrind, 1971). They also have been characterized as more irresponsible, more conforming to peer pressure, and less likely to become leaders.

The most consistently negative outcomes have been associated with the uninvolved parenting style. Consistently uninvolved parents are guilty of the form of child maltreatment called *neglect*. Uninvolved parenting is associated with such child personality characteristics as low self-esteem, increased aggression, reduced control over impulses, and insecure attachment (Collins & Steinberg, 2006).

Parental depression is a frequent cause of uninvolved parenting. A depressed parent may feel overwhelmed by his or her problems and may not make any deep emotional connection to the child. Intergenerational research finds that parental depression has long-term effects: the children, as adults, are likely to be depressed and/or inadequate parents themselves. Never having been emotionally connected to their own parents, the grown children of depressed and uninvolved parents oftentimes cannot emotionally bond with their own offspring (Whitbeck et al., 1992).

The scriptural warning about the "sins of the father" being passed on to his children is supported by evidence of the intergenerational transmission of parenting style (Sroufe, Egeland, Carlson, & Collins, 2005; Whitbeck et al., 1992). Children who eventually become parents tend to raise their children the same way they were raised. Their parents taught them how to parent. What else would you expect? Which parenting style do you now use, or think you will some day use, with your children?

Two quotes from The Minnesota Study of Risk and Adaptation vividly illustrate this point. The two parents who are quoted first took part in this impressive longitudinal investigation when they themselves were very young children:

> Serena, age 2, works hard on the lever problem, following her mother's leads until, finally, she gets the candy out of the box by weighting down the board. Her mother Jessica smiles and says in an animated voice: "There, now you've got the candy out! You got it!" Two decades later, Serena watches Dustin, her own 2-year-old, as he works hard to solve the same problem. At last he solves the problem and smiles brightly. "There you go. Good job!" she says, and smiles warmly at him.
>
> When Ellis seeks help from his mother as he struggles with the problem, she rolls her eyes at the ceiling and laughs. When he finally does manage to solve the problem, his mother says, "Now see how stubborn you were." Two decades later, as Ellis watches his son Carl struggle with the same problem, he leans away from the child, laughing and shaking his head. Later, he taunts the child by pretending to raise the candy out of the box, then dropping it as the child rushes to try to get it. In the end, he has to solve the problem for Carl and says, "You didn't do that. I did. You're not as smart as me." (Sroufe et al., 2005, p. 287)

Mary Main (1999) explains this intergenerational link in terms of a parent's state of mind that is stabilized by giving *minimal attention to attachment cues* from her or his child. The insecure adult's primary goal is to continue holding a *false* sense of security. The parent does this by ignoring and/or rejecting a distressed infant's signals for physical contact. And so it goes.

The kind of soil provided by the quality of parenting experienced in early childhood clearly affects the development of personality. How do theories of personality explain these findings? The views of Alfred Adler and Erik Erikson are especially relevant.

Importance of the Family

Alfred Adler believed that early childhood experiences are critically important in the development of the individual's *style of life* (Adler, 1929). By style of life Adler meant the unique way each of us pursues our individual goals. Adler held that people form their style of life very early in childhood, by the age of 4 or 5. Adler stressed the role of the parents and the child's birth-order position in the family constellation as important influences for shaping adult personality.

Role of the Parents

Adler identified two errors by parents that can cause a child to develop a faulty or neurotic style of life: pampering the child and neglecting the child. The pampered child is the result of a permissive parenting style, and the neglected child is the result of an uninvolved parenting style. Research clearly supports Adler's views regarding the detrimental effects of these two styles. Adler did not distinguish between the authoritarian and authoritative parenting styles.

Adler felt that because the basic problems of life revolve around developing accurate ideas about work, friendship, and love, it is the parents' role to enable their child to do so successfully (Ansbacher & Ansbacher, 1956). The person who develops a healthy lifestyle, Adler believed, is one whose parents treated him or her with consideration and respect. A healthy life style involves choosing personal goals that are consistent with social interest.

Social interest refers to our built-in need to adjust to the conditions of our social environment. Adler's (1939) basic assumption is that it is human nature to cooperate and be interested in the welfare of others. "Mirror neurons" in the human brain seem to bear Adler out. *Mirror neurons* are triggered both when a person performs an action and when merely observing another individual performing the same behavior. Seeing another person pick up something with his hand and/or bring food to his mouth activates the same neurons in the brain that become active when the person does these actions himself. Mirror neurons are thought by some psychologists to be the biological basis of human imitation and empathy (Kilner et al., 2009; Rizzolatti & Craighero, 2005; Siegel, 2012). Other psychologists, however, believe that mirror neurons arise from associative learning processes in early development and do not necessarily have a specific evolutionary purpose (Cook et al., 2014). Clearly, more research is needed to settle this important question about the functions of mirror neurons.

Although Adler thought social interest is innate, he realized it does not emerge automatically. It needs to be cultivated in the soil of early family environment. Both pampering and neglect distort or thwart the child's social feelings. Pampering makes it difficult for the child to develop social feelings and appreciate that other people have their own needs. Neglected children, on the other hand, feel unwanted and rejected, causing them psychologically to withdraw from the responsibilities of social life. In support of Adler's hypothesis is the observation that neglected 3- to 6-year-old children socially withdraw and emit fewer prosocial behaviors than nonneglected children (Hoffman-Plotkin & Twentyman, 1984).

Birth Order

Unfortunately for Adler's theory, the data do *not* unequivocally support his other major contention that the child's position or birth order in the family constellation is a key determinant of his or her adult personality.

Only-born children, according to Adler, should be more self-centered than those who have brothers and sisters because they never have to share their parents' attention. Do you believe that only-born children are spoiled? If so, you are not alone. The idea that only-born children are more spoiled or pampered than other children is widely accepted throughout the general population, even though careful research consistently *fails* to support it! For example, one study observed exactly the opposite of what one might expect to find: Only-born children were *more cooperative* compared to either firstborns with younger siblings or last-born children. Moreover, an analysis of 115 studies of only-born children revealed that they were *higher* on measures of character and were just as sociable and well-adjusted as other children (Falbo & Polit, 1986).

Research is mixed regarding Adler's ideas about other aspects of the family constellation. Empirical research does support his contention that firstborn children tend to be concerned with power and authority; one way they can attain these goals is through outstanding achievement in some field of endeavor (Ansbacher & Ansbacher, 1956).

Firstborns tend to be overrepresented both in lists of eminent people as well as among those who achieved educational and occupational success in a variety of fields. For example, firstborns are overrepresented among U.S. presidents and among women who hold doctorate degrees (Mellilo, 1983; Wagner & Schubert, 1977). Consistent with Adler's view, firstborns score higher on the need for achievement and hold greater educational aspirations. Across 41 countries, firstborns had better knowledge of science than later-borns (Chiu, 2007; Glass, Neulinger, & Brim, 1974).

Although Adler did not address birth-order differences in emotional arousal, Stanley Schachter found that firstborn women reported greater fear and anxiety when anticipating receiving electric shocks (which were never actually delivered) than did later-born women. Firstborn women also had a higher need to affiliate with other women who were in the same situation (Schachter, 1959). Schachter explained this observation by assuming children learn when to be emotionally aroused from their parents: New parents are likely to express anxiety whenever their first child shows any sign of a health risk, no matter how slight ("She burped! Call 9-1-1!"), whereas by the time a third or fourth child arrives, experienced parents' attitudes are more casual: "Don't bleed on the new carpet!"

Frank Sulloway invokes an evolutionary psychological explanation for birth-order differences. Just as Darwin saw that all biological species exploit specific ecological niches, Sulloway views each birth-order position as its own niche within the family, and he assumes that firstborns tend to identify strongly with their parents' values. Research backs this up: Firstborn adolescents report they feel a stronger obligation to their families than do later-born adolescents (Juang & Cookston, 2009). The primary message of firstborns to their younger siblings is, "This is how we do things around here!"

Consequently, second-born children need to find their own unique niche within the family. They do this, according to Sulloway, by becoming more rebellious and more open to new ideas. In support of this hypothesis, Sulloway found that, historically, adults who are second-born in their family tend to be strong advocates of new scientific ideas and are in the forefront of scientific revolutions (e.g., Copernicus, Darwin), whereas firstborns strongly resist these changes to scientific thinking. Sulloway also notes that Adler, himself a second-born, rebelled against Freud's (a firstborn of his mother) parent-child theory (the Oedipus complex) by developing his own theory centered around sibling rivalry and the feelings of inferiority frequently experienced by those who are second-born (Sulloway, 1996).

Adler's views about the personality characteristics of last-born children have received mixed empirical support. Adler felt that a typical last-born, being the baby of the family, is most likely to be pampered (Ansbacher & Ansbacher, 1956). As a consequence, last-born children are most likely to depend excessively on others and seek quick and easy solutions to their problems. In support of this idea, last-borns have been found to be overrepresented among populations of alcoholics (Barry & Blane, 1977). Contrary to Adler's notions, however, is the finding that last-born children are *more* popular than first- or second-borns, a result we would not expect if last-borns are as "babied" as Adler speculated (Miller & Maruyama, 1976).[1]

In any event, the bottom line is that birth-order differences, when they are observed, tend to be very small. For example, in a large-scale investigation of over 377,000 high school students, the average correlation of personality traits with birth order was found to be a miniscule *.02*. This means that only 2% of the total variability in a personality trait can be attributed to birth order position in the family. Based on this and related findings, the authors conclude "the attention given to the role of birth order on personality is, at best, disproportionate to its importance to the development of personality" (Damian & Roberts, 2015, p. 104).

Even so, Adler's stress on the critical significance of our early childhood experiences with our parents is well placed. Erik Erikson's theory also connects what happened to us in infancy and childhood to invariant (unchanging) stages of development. To Erikson, both *what* we experience and *when* we experience it affect our future personality.

Psychosocial Stages of Development

Like Adler's theory, Erikson's theory applies to numerous points across the life course. Adler and Erikson agree that we all make active contributions to growing our personalities by understanding who we are and who we want to become.

Unlike Adler, though, Erikson holds that the effects of our early social experiences depend on when they occur. Also unlike Adler, Erikson (1963) sees personality growth as following the epigenetic principle: Development is genetically determined and operates in stages that unfold in an invariant or unchanging sequence for all individuals. Epigenesis determines "the proper rate and sequence" of development (Erikson, 1968, p. 93). **Epigenesis**[2] is an extremely important idea. It means that what comes later in development totally depends on all that preceded it. Our first social encounters lay the groundwork for everything that follows.

Finally, Erikson, unlike Adler, points to the specific maturity demands made by our cultural and social groups at each stage of life, demands that provoke us to respond in some way, adaptively or maladaptively. Because each society has its own view of the ideal characteristics of the mature individual, all of society's socializing agents, particularly the parents, promote these valued personal characteristics. Personality development is the ongoing product of the interaction of our individual needs with societal expectations.

Erikson's theory involves a total of eight stages, with each stage centering on a particular crisis of development. Erikson uses the term *crisis* to denote a developmental turning point, a decisive period during which the individual either acquires new capacities for vitality or fails to grow and thrive. A positive resolution of each crisis strengthens the growing ego; a negative resolution weakens it. Moreover, a positive resolution of a crisis at one stage increases the chances of positive resolutions of crises at later stages.

A positive resolution, to Erikson (1968), means that, on balance, the *ratio* of positive to negative experience is favorable. But a positive resolution does not necessarily mean the crisis is settled forevermore. New conflicts may resurrect old crises.

Consider the identity crisis that typically occurs in adolescence. During adolescence, the growing person prepares to leave the soil of his or her family and live independently. To do so, the young man or woman needs to determine who he or she is and what he or she deeply values. The crisis is resolved positively to the extent that these issues can be decided. Positive resolutions result in new ego strengths; failures to resolve crises result in core pathologies. Failure to resolve the identity crisis, for example, will result in the continuing negative experience of identity confusion and repudiation of values that are needed for a firm sense of identity.

This chapter on the cultivation of personality considers Erikson's views on the first four psychosocial stages of personality. Table 4.1 summarizes the key elements of Erikson's theory.

Trust versus mistrust: Who do you trust? Everyone? No one? It depends on the person? Erikson (1968) sees the attitude of basic trust toward oneself and toward the world as the most important prerequisite of mental vitality.

The infant who achieves basic trust shows this in easy feeding and deep sleeping. The attitude of basic trust is learned primarily from the infant's mother by her sensitive care and sense of personal trustworthiness. By experiencing the mother's trust in herself and in her world the infant learns to trust his mother, his world, and himself. The parenting style most consistent with Erikson's prescriptions for establishing basic trust is clearly the authoritative one. The personality outcome that develops from basic trust is the adaptive ego strength of **hope**.

❖ **Table 4.1** Summary of Erikson's Eight Stages of Development

Life Stage	Psychosocial Crisis	Adaptive Ego Quality	Ego Core Pathology
Infancy (0–2 years)	Trust vs. Mistrust	Hope	Withdrawal
Toddler (2–3 years)	Autonomy vs. Shame and Doubt	Will	Compulsion
Early School Age (4–5 years)	Initiative vs. Guilt	Purpose	Inhibition
Middle School Age (6–12 years)	Industry vs. Inferiority	Competence	Inertia
Adolescence	Identity vs. Identity Confusion	Fidelity	Repudiation
Young Adulthood	Intimacy vs. Isolation	Love	Exclusivity
Adulthood	Generativity vs. Stagnation	Care	Rejectivity
Old Age	Integrity vs. Despair	Wisdom	Disdain

Source: Erikson (1963, 1978, 1982). Reprinted from *The Life Cycle Completed* by Erik H. Erikson, with the permission of W. W. Norton & Company Inc. Copyright © 1982 by Rikan Enterprises, Ltd.

On the other hand, mothers (or primary caregivers) who act in unreliable, arbitrary, and rejecting ways create a sense of basic mistrust. People manifest mistrust in symptoms of depression, grief, rage, excessive demands for attention, and withdrawal from social exchanges (Erikson, 1963, 1968). These same sorts of behaviors have been found to be associated with the nonoptimal authoritarian, permissive, or uninvolved parenting styles that we saw in the beginning of this chapter. Erikson's speculations about the first psychosocial stage are consistent with empirical studies of the effects of parenting styles on the developing personality.

Successful resolution of this first psychosocial crisis enables the infant to hold an attitude of basic trust and be capable of mistrust when the other person and/or the situation warrants it. An indiscriminately trusting child is one who is gullible, easily taken advantage of by others, and potentially at risk. As Erikson (1968) puts it, "A person devoid of the capacity to mistrust would be as unable to live as one without trust" (p. 325).

Research shows that an attitude of distrust can *reduce* automatic stereotyping of a newly met person. Distrust may elicit a sense of dissimilarity from the person one mistrusts, a sense which then carries over to perceiving other people as potentially dissimilar, unique individuals rather than automatically stereotyping them as identical group members. Distrust may require greater cognitive effort, the sort of effort needed to overcome automatic (i.e., unthinking) stereotypic responses (Posten & Mussweiler, 2013).

Autonomy versus shame and doubt: In the crisis of toddlerhood (ages 2 to 3), the growing child begins to assert her new capacities by attempting to do things on her own. "I can do it myself" is the recurring refrain that follows the initial sign of this stage, the ubiquitous "No!" A growing autonomy presupposes a well-developed sense of basic trust. The child must be sure that her faith in the world will not be undermined by her wish to have her way. As the wishes get translated into new activities (e.g., running), and the new activities are successfully completed, the child feels a growing sense of autonomy and pride.

The ego strength that follows from successful accomplishments is **will**, the desire to exercise free choice and self-restraint (Erikson, 1964). This is likely to occur if the parents are able to guide their child's behavior appropriately and firmly, neither rushing the child to master tasks beyond his abilities nor neglecting to set standards at all. The authoritative parenting style describes Erikson's views on what is needed for the successful resolution of this crisis. A child's sense of autonomy is essential for the development of a healthy conscience and self-directed behavioral standards (Grusec, 2011; Maccoby, 2007).

Parents who are too harsh or too permissive are likely to generate feelings of doubt and shame in the child. Authoritarian parents usually set unrealistic, unreachable standards that cause chronic feelings of failure in the child. Permissive or uninvolved parents fail to guide the child into those new activities and challenges appropriate for her age level, thereby inviting feelings of shame and doubt when failure occurs repeatedly (as when a toddler repeatedly attempts unsuccessfully to imitate the behavior of an older sibling).

Unsuccessful resolution of this crisis means that failure experiences outweigh successful ones, thereby leaving the child with a lasting propensity for self-doubt and shame. Such doubts frequently manifest themselves in *obsessions* (chronic, unwanted thoughts and ruminations) and *compulsions* (repeating the same behaviors over and over, such as handwashing) in vain attempts to master the environment in all its minute detail. Compulsion is the specific core pathology Erikson (1968) associates with failure to achieve a sense of autonomy.

Initiative versus guilt: The third psychosocial crisis (ages 4 to 5) concerns the child's increasing abilities to move about more freely, ask questions incessantly, and fantasize about being an adult. If caregivers support the child's new range of activity, she will emerge at about the beginning of the fourth year with a sense of initiative as a basis for realistic ambitions and goals. Erikson sees **purpose** as the ego strength achieved at this stage of development.

Parents who severely punish their children are likely to make them feel guilty for expressing their newfound enthusiasms. If authoritarian parents force their children to suppress most of these expansive initiatory impulses, the children might feel anger and rage toward their parents, feelings they are likely to repress. The unconscious anger and rage may then turn into guilt for having such "bad" feelings. Guilt can also be induced by uninvolved or depressed parents who withdraw their love when the child misbehaves (Zahn-Waxler et al., 1990).

Adults, then, whose early social environments did not support the successful resolution of this crisis, may manifest their conflicts over initiative in various ways: *self-restriction,* which prevents the adult from living up to his or her potential; *severe anxiety* about ambitious strivings; *overcompensatory showing off* by a tireless initiative that results in numerous bodily stresses and strains (e.g., ulcers, headaches, high blood pressure); and *inhibitions* that foreclose initiating new activities (Erikson, 1963, 1968).

Industry versus inferiority: Children who have successfully negotiated the first three crises and thus possess the ego strengths of hope, will, and purpose are now ready to deal with the challenge of school. The fourth psychosocial crisis (ages 6 to 12) involves adjusting to the external demands of teachers, parents, and peers for learning new and necessary skills for survival in one's culture. The ego strength to be acquired by successful resolution of this stage is a sense of **competence**.[3] The strength of a child's motivation to be successful in life is well-established at the conclusion of this stage (Atkinson & Birch, 1978).

The danger here is developing a sense of inferiority, a concept promoted earlier by Adler (1927/1957). The cultivation of personality through the school years is heavily influenced by the prior (and current) parenting style experienced at home. Erikson (1968) neatly illustrates the epigenetic model of personality development with his view that the child's sense of inferiority may be caused by inadequate resolutions of the three prior crises:

> *The child may want his mommy more than knowledge; he may still prefer to be the baby at home rather than the big child in school; he still compares himself with his father, and the comparison arouses a sense of guilt as well as a sense of inferiority. (p. 124)*

In addition to the child's "readiness" to feel inferior by her less than optimal prior experiences with her parents, the school experience itself may contribute to lifelong feelings of inadequacy:

1. Children discover they cannot easily master every skill valued by their culture. They find that, compared to some of their schoolmates, they do not get grades as high, play sports as well, or learn a musical instrument as easily. Feelings of inferiority generated by such unfavorable comparisons generalize to new situations. Children may refuse even to try a new activity, fearing they will not do as well as their peers. Regrettably, by failing to try, children prevent themselves from discovering new talents and skills that could help alleviate budding feelings of inferiority (Crooks, 1988).

2. The social environment generates feelings of inferiority by its negative and punitive evaluations for any kind of failure. The long-term effects of failure in school importantly depend on the explanations for it provided by the child's social group (teachers, peers, parents). A child who believes she failed only because she did not exert enough effort is likely to try harder next time. But a child who is told she is stupid or unmusical or uncoordinated may stop trying altogether out of feelings of shame. Chronic and negative ability attributions for failure may result in a generalized sense of learned helplessness that precludes future learning about one's actual competencies throughout life (Abramson, Seligman, & Teasdale, 1978; Lewis, 1992; Weiner, 1985).

3. School-age children's feelings of self-worth strongly relate to their self-perceived physical attractiveness and popularity. Attractive and popular children exhibit higher degrees of self-worth than less attractive and/or less popular children. Interestingly, a positive relationship exists between physical attractiveness and self-esteem, not just among children, but among adults across the life span (Harter, 1990a).

It has been proposed that a key reason, perhaps *the* reason, students achieve or fail to achieve academic success in school is to protect their sense of worth, especially in competitive situations. Martin Covington's (1989) self-worth theory proposes that "academic achievement is best understood in terms of students attempting to maintain a positive self-image of their own ability, especially when risking failure" (p. 88). Supporting Covington's theory of children's sensitivity to ability evaluations is the finding that even a few remarks about lack of ability can cause children to take a pessimistic view of their future success (Holloway, 1988).

Thus failure in school plays a significant role in forming a negative self-image, especially when the child's self-concept is negative to begin with, a finding totally consistent with Erikson's epigenetic theory of personality development. Further support for Erikson's theory comes from a 34-year longitudinal study where the results are consistent with his views of the long-term effects of the trust, autonomy, and initiative stages of growth (Whitbourne, Sneed, & Sayer, 2009).

In conclusion, Baumrind's (1973) idea of authoritative parenting "has been notably successful in distinguishing effective from ineffective parenting" (Maccoby, 1992, p. 1012). Moreover, the research evidence on the long-term effects of parenting style on personality development is consistent with the theoretical views of Adler and Erikson. Parenting style is one of the key ingredients in the soil of personality development.

Ingredient #2: Attachment

Attachment refers to an enduring emotional tie between a baby and its caregiver. The infant's first manifestation of attachment to the caregiver occurs somewhere between 4 and 12 months of age. The infant demonstrates attachment by becoming distressed when the caregiver leaves him alone and by showing delight upon his or her return (Bowlby, 1969/1982).

John Bowlby distinguishes attachment from attachment behavior, as ends are distinguished from the means to those ends. A child (or anyone) who is attached wants to be in close proximity to or have physical contact with the attachment figure. Attachment is likely to be activated when the child (or anyone) is frightened, sick, or fatigued. *Attachment* refers to an internal state of the person. The purpose of all attachment behaviors is to secure protection from danger. Once this secure base is attained and the danger has passed, the child is free to leave her attachment figure to explore her surroundings. Bowlby (1969/1982) conceptualizes this as an *attachment/exploratory system*.

Attachment behavior refers to any actions a person uses to attain a desired proximity to another. Common attachment behaviors by infants (e.g., crying, howling, cooing, and smiling) usually differ from common attachment behaviors by adults (giving gifts, calling on the telephone, getting a hug, and saying, "I love you"). Although the forms of attachment behaviors may vary, the underlying desire for attachment is the same in the infant and the adult (Ainsworth, 1989; Bowlby, 1988).

Evolution of Attachment

John Bowlby began his understanding of infant attachment from an evolutionary perspective. When newborns of a species are unable to care for themselves, their survival depends on being cared for and protected by a caregiver. The attachment system evolved to help infants survive. Bowlby noted that across human cultures and in many primate species young and vulnerable infants display a *specific and universal series of reactions* to separation from their caregiver:

(a) *Protest:* Immediately following separation, most infants vehemently protest by crying, screaming, and/or throwing temper tantrums. This strategy evolved to draw the caregiver's attention to the infant and to re-establish contact. Infants who protested were thereby more likely to stay in close proximity to their caregiver, survive to maturity, and pass on those genes responsible for the protest to their own offspring.

(b) *Despair:* When protests fail to bring the caregiver back into contact, infants enter a second phase during which they fall silent and their activities cease. Bowlby speculates that this strategy helps the unattended infant to remain unnoticed by predators.

(c) *Detachment:* Bowlby noted that after a period of despair infants who are still not connected to their caregivers enter a third phase in which they resume normal activities. In this phase they learn to be independent and self-reliant. Emotional detachment from their original caregivers allows them, in theory, to form emotional bonds with potential future caregivers. (Bowlby 1969/1982, 1973, 1980)

Physiological measures of infants and their mothers support the view that the human attachment system evolved. Specific areas of the brains of both mothers and their infants—the orbitofrontal cortex (OFC)—"light up" when they see each other. The OFC is associated with both rewarding activities and rewarding thoughts. It has been observed to function in similar ways in primates. The OFC has been called "The Social Brain Network" (Adolphs, 2003; Elliott et al., 2003; Grossmann, 2015).

When infants are 6 months old, their brains show positive reactions to their mother's face, but not the face of a stranger. Moreover, the *same brain regions* within the OFC of both the infants (at 1 year) and their mothers become particularly active when they see each other's faces (de Haan & Nelson, 1999; Minagawa-Kawai et al., 2009). This similarity of localization within the OFC strongly suggests that the attachment system co-evolved in mothers and their infants to release positive and rewarding feelings for each other as part of the bonding process. These rewarding feelings help ensure the mother's continued care over the long period of her child's dependency.

Modern evolutionary thinking includes life history theory. *Life history theory* is the study of how members of a species allocate their resources to enhance their *inclusive fitness*. Life history strategies are examples of gene x environment interactions since specific reproductive efforts within a species change when their environment changes (Kaplan & Gangestad, 2005). A dramatic example of a life history strategy within the animal kingdom is the reef-living cleaner fish. These fish have permanent territories ruled by a dominant male who controls a harem of females. When the dominant male dies, the female who is most dominant (within the female hierarchy) takes over the territory and quickly (within an hour) begins acting as a male toward the other females. About two weeks later this once-female male begins producing sperm and fathers new offspring. Similarly, in another species of fish living in the Red Sea, females are sensitive to the proportion of males in the group. When this proportion reaches dangerously low levels, some females become males. These remarkable transformations help ensure the survival of their species (Belsky, 1999; Charnov, 1982, 1993). What would human life be like if spontaneous biological sex changes like these regularly occurred in our species?

Attachment theory combined with life history theory explains why some women, beginning at an early age, have many children, while other women, starting later, have fewer children. The central assumption is that the child-rearing behavior of the parent conveys some information to the infant/child about the environment he or she is entering. On the one hand, parents who are rejecting, insensitive, and inconsistent communicate that their environment is harsh and unpredictable. Unpredictable environments lead individuals to feel they have little or no control over their immediate environments (Mittal & Griskevicius, 2014). These kinds of early unpredictable experiences, whether in their homes or neighborhoods (Copping & Campbell, 2015) lead children, when they mature, to adopt a "fast" reproductive strategy: Begin early and have as many children as possible. This is the quantity over quality solution.

On the other hand, parents who raise children with sensitive and responsive care communicate that the environment is benign and predictable. This kind of early experience leads their children at maturity to prefer a "slow" reproductive strategy: Develop your own skills first and only then have few well-cared for children. This is the quality over quantity solution. Data show that, as predicted, authoritative parenting styles are positively correlated with a slow life history strategy (Belsky, Steinberg, & Draper, 1991; Dunkel et al., 2015).

Research stimulated by life history theory has identified a cluster of traits that vary along the "fast-slow" life history strategies, traits found in both human and non-human animals. These data demonstrate the powerful role that life history strategies play in the organization of behavior. Individuals who favor a *fast* life history strategy tend to have sex at earlier ages, be more sexually active, have more sexual partners, be less cooperative with peers, be more materialistic, be more aggressive, be less altruistic, take more risks, value present benefits over future rewards, prefer to "hook up" rather than become romantically attached to a partner, and not value parenting as highly (del Giudice & Belsky, 2011).

The application of evolutionary psychology to the understanding of attachment includes ambitious attempts to appreciate how the various *kinds* of attachment came to be naturally selected (Belsky, 1999; del Giudice, 2009). Research programs to test these promising ideas are in their infancy. The essential distinction is between secure and anxious types of attachment.

Types of Attachment

Secure Versus Anxious Attachment

Bowlby (1973) observed that not all children are attached to their caregivers in the same way. Some children are more easily comforted and settled by the return of their caregivers than others. After being frightened by mommy's absence, these children's tears quickly dry when she holds, rocks, and soothes them on her return. They then quickly return to play and explore their environment. Other children, however, are not settled so readily. They cling excessively to their caregiver and do not resume playing with their toys. They seem afraid that she might suddenly abandon them again. These two types of attachment are called secure and anxious (Ainsworth & Bowlby, 1991).

The Strange Situation is a procedure devised by Mary Ainsworth (1913–1999) to measure the quality of an infant's attachment to his or her mother. In this procedure, the mother and her 12-month-old infant are brought to a playroom, which the child is free to explore. In a standardized series of steps, the child is first exposed to a strange adult in the presence of mother and then in her absence, is left alone briefly, and then is reunited with mother. How the infant behaves in the Strange Situation reveals the quality of attachment to mother (Ainsworth, Blehar, Waters, & Wall, 1978).

Securely attached infants separate easily from mother to explore the playroom. As they discover the exciting toys and treasures strewn about the floor, they look at their mothers and smile to share their delight. When the stranger enters the room, they are not overly wary and may even seek to engage this new adult in interaction. Those who are upset when mother leaves the room seek mother at reunion, are soothed readily, and return to exploring the playroom. Securely attached infants consistently show positive emotional responses to their mothers throughout the procedure.

Anxiously attached infants, in contrast, show in various ways that they are unable to use their mothers as a secure base for exploration of the playroom. Anxious attachment disrupts the attachment/exploration system.

Three Types of Anxious Attachment

1. *Anxious/avoidant* infants differ noticeably from securely attached children in their behavior at reunion with mother. Even though they were upset by her absence, they avoid and ignore mother when she reenters the playroom, as if they are angry at her. Unlike the secure group, anxious/avoidant infants remain distressed following mother's return, as shown by their accelerated heart rates (Sroufe & Waters, 1977).

2. *Anxious/resistant* infants, unwilling to explore their new surroundings, get quite upset by mother's absence, yet are not easily comforted by her upon return. These infants reveal strong ambivalence toward mother by their alternating bids to be picked up and comforted followed immediately by squirming and pushing her away. This type of pattern is also called *anxious/ambivalent* attachment.

3. *Disorganized/disoriented* infants appear depressed, dazed, or disoriented. Contradictory behaviors toward mother (e.g., approach followed by an abrupt, about-face withdrawal), freezing behaviors in midplay, and confusing sequences of rapid emotional changes in the first seconds of reunion are some of the characteristics of this pattern. These infants appear to be severely conflicted. They simultaneously display activation of incompatible approach and avoidance behavioral tendencies (Main & Hesse, 1990; Main & Solomon, 1990).

Parental Sensitivity and Quality of Attachment

A child's attachment quality is related to the parent's behavior toward their infant. Caregivers who are consistently sensitive and responsive to their infants' needs are likely to raise children who are securely attached to them (e.g., Rosen & Rothbaum, 1993). While the majority of studies have examined the effects of maternal sensitivity on her child's attachment security, a sufficiently large number of investigations have concluded that paternal sensitivity is also reliably associated, albeit more weakly, with raising a securely attached child (Brown, Mangelsdorf, & Neff, 2012; Lucassen et al., 2011; Thompson, 2006). The association between parental sensitivity and children's attachment security is one of the most highly replicated findings in the field of child psychology (e.g., De Wolff & van IJzendoorn, 1997; Rosen & Rothbaum, 1993; Sroufe et al., 2005; Thompson, 2006; Weinfield et al., 2008).

It is easy to relate those parental qualities associated with secure attachment to Baumrind's (1973) authoritative parenting style. For example, securely attached children are more likely to respond to parental directives and to comply with boundaries set by their parents. These findings, in concert with those discussed below, suggest parental control needs to be exercised within a context of warm, sensitive, and responsive care, qualities that are lacking in the authoritarian style (Londerville & Main, 1981; Sroufe, 1988).

Caregivers who are not sensitive and responsive are likely to raise a child who is described by one of the three patterns of anxious attachment. Although parents of securely attached babies are likely to be emotionally expressive by touching them, smiling, and using their voices, parents of anxious/avoidant children are often inaccessible and unresponsive to their babies' behavioral cues (Egeland & Farber, 1984). These parents report they dislike physical contact with their children. Their children may have learned to expect a rebuff from their caregiver in times of stress. Consequently, to avoid rejection, they may turn away from the caregiver who has been unresponsive to them in the past. The pattern of anxious/avoidant attachment appears to be common among children whose mothers suffer from depression (Field, 1989; Main & Weston, 1982).

In terms of the previously discussed parenting styles, anxious/avoidant infants are likely to have been reared by parents who are uninvolved or neglectful. School children who had been classified in infancy as avoidantly attached tend to be aggressive with their peers. They are more likely to engage in antisocial behavior and exhibit conduct problems. Even though they may be distinctively forward in new social situations, they rarely form close friendships as school children (Aguilar et al., 2000; Keller, Spieker, Gilchrist, 2005; McElwain et al., 2003; Sroufe et al., 2005).

The pattern of anxious/resistant attachment is associated with inconsistent caregiving (Ainsworth et al., 1978; Sroufe, 1988). Children with this attachment style are generally more fearful and anxious than children raised under the other attachment patterns. Moreover, the observation that they are more likely to be diagnosed with an anxiety disorder has been well replicated (Kochanska, 1998; Warren et al., 1997). "Resistant attachment in infancy was uniquely and specifically associated with anxiety disorders at age 17 ½" (Sroufe et al., 2005, p. 246).

It seems these children's anxiety is related to how their mothers react to the sound of a crying baby—with anxiety. While mothers whose children were avoidantly attached reacted with anger to the sound of a crying baby, the mothers of resistantly attached children were more likely to become anxious (Leerkes, Parade, & Gudmundson, 2011). In a 32-year longitudinal study, 32-year-old adults who had been classified as anxious/resistant as infants were more likely to report the kinds of nonspecific physical symptoms associated with chronic anxiety (e.g., upset stomach, headaches, muscle tension) than adults who had, as infants, experienced other attachment patterns (Puig et al., 2013).

Moreover, insecurely attached (childless) women show heightened activation in the amygdala part of the brain to the sounds of a crying infant (compared to women who are securely attached). Excessive activity in the amygdala indicates that these insecure women experience infant crying as highly aversive. This suggests, in turn, that excessive amygdala excitability causes insecure parents to respond inconsistently and ineffectively to their infants' signs of distress; they themselves become overly distressed, which interferes with thinking clearly about how to alleviate their child's discomfort (Reim et al., 2012).

Finally, maltreated children have been found to manifest the disorganized/disoriented pattern of attachment (Carlson et al., 1989; Crittenden & Ainsworth, 1989). This classification is associated with mothers who have experienced the loss of a family member prior to completing high school and have failed to resolve this loss. It is not loss, per se, that is associated with this attachment pattern, but *unmourned* loss. Main and Hesse (1990) speculate that a parent still suffering from unresolved mourning may remain frightened by that loss. Consequently, the parent may experience random episodes of anxiety, episodes that frighten her child because of their unpredictability and complete unrelatedness to the external environment.

This line of thinking implies that the disorganized/disoriented pattern of attachment is due to being raised by a ***scaregiver***. Speiker and Booth (1988) found these mothers were less socially competent, both in adult–adult interactions and in interactions with their children. Specifically, such mothers are more likely to disrupt an interaction with their infant by, for example, laughing when the infant is crying or distressed, handling her infant like an inanimate object, arbitrarily removing a toy the infant was playing with, and/or using a loud or angry voice (Madigan et al., 2006).

Dissociation is a psychological symptom in adolescence and adulthood that is reliably related to disorganized attachment. Infants who are both attached to and afraid of the same caregiver are in an impossible bind. Their only recourse is to mentally leave the situation. Dissociation is a defensive, protective function that helps the infant detach from the conflicting approach-avoidance desires in precisely the same way that dissociation protects children who are physically abused (Carlson, 1998; Liotti, 2004; Sroufe et al., 2005; Zelikovsky & Lynn, 1994).

Although numerous studies have demonstrated a *correlation* between parental sensitivity and the child's quality of attachment, these results do not necessarily mean that parental treatment *causes* children to be either securely or anxiously attached. It may be, for example, that some children are more temperamentally difficult than others (see Chapter 3), and that the child's attachment quality relates both to characteristics of the child and to how the child is treated by the parents (Vaughn et al., 1992). However, newer research that explicitly considers both temperament and attachment variables tends to show that attachment quality moderates the effect of temperament rather than temperament influencing the effects of attachment (Vaughn, Bost, & IJzendoorn, 2008). In other words, attachment quality seems to be more important for positive personal and social outcomes than the infant's inborn temperamental characteristics. Attachment, like parenting style, is a key ingredient in the soil of personality.

"What makes you think I have attachment issues?"

Correlates of Attachment Patterns

What are the long-term effects of your earliest attachment to your caregiver? Let's see what research has found so far.

1. *Parent–child relationship*: Securely attached infants showed, as 2-year-olds, greater enthusiasm, cooperation, and positive affect during shared tasks with their mothers (Thompson, 2006).

2. *Childhood friendships*: Securely attached children at 1 year of age are more likely (than anxiously attached children) to be in positive friendship relationships at age 5. Moreover, securely attached children get along better with their peers, are more popular, and have

more friends than anxiously attached children (Berlin, Cassidy, & Appleyard, 2008; Booth-LaForce & Kerns, 2009; McElwain, Booth-LaForce, & Wu, 2011).

3. *Self-esteem:* The cumulative evidence consistently shows that securely attached children have more positive self-esteem than anxiously attached ones (Cassidy et al., 2003; Collins & Steinberg, 2006). Four- and five-year-old children, for example, have been found to be more *ego resilient*—that is, more confident and flexible in managing impulses—than anxiously attached children. Moreover, the self-knowledge of securely attached 3-year-olds is more complex and cognitively advanced than that of anxiously attached children (Arend, Gove, & Sroufe, 1979; Pipp, Easterbrooks, & Harmon, 1992).

4. *Empathy:* Securely attached children are more empathetic with other children. Greater prosocial behavior has been observed in those 6- to 11-year-old children whose parents are more sensitive to their signals. Empathetic parents raise empathetic children (Dekovic & Janssens, 1992; Sroufe, 1990). Empathy requires the reasonably accurate perception of other people's feelings. Securely attached children can identify emotions in other children more accurately than insecurely attached children. Securely attached 12-month-old infants could more accurately recognize facial expressions of emotion when they were 6 and 11 years old (Raikes & Thompson, 2006; Steele, Steele, & Croft, 2008; Thompson, 2008). Any limitation in children's ability to feel empathy reduces the probability they will feel guilt or remorse when they harm others (Fonagy et al., 1997).

5. *Emotional regulation:* Children who are securely attached regulate their emotional experiences more capably than those who are insecurely attached. In a longitudinal study over the first 3 years of life, insecurely attached children showed progressively greater fear and anger than securely attached ones (Kochanska, 2001). In another investigation, boys who were securely attached at age 1 ½ used more constructive anger management strategies at age 3 ½ (Gilliom et al., 2002). Moreover, 5- to 6-year-old children, who had been classified as securely attached three years earlier, were rated by their kindergarten teachers as higher in impulse control as well as other measures demonstrating successful cortical control of behavior (Bernier et al., 2015). Finally, fifth-grade children, who were securely attached as infants, were rated by their fifth-grade teachers as better able to (1) control their tempers, (2) compromise in conflict situations, (3) receive criticism well, and (4) cooperate with peers, compared to those children who were insecurely attached in infancy (Drake, Belsky, & Pasco Fearon, 2014).

In addition, *retrospective accounts* of childhood attachment patterns have been observed by a number of investigators to be related to the quality of *adult* marital and work relationships. These data clearly suggest the possibility that the type of early attachment pattern in childhood has deep-seated effects throughout the life course (Collins & Read, 1990; Simpson, 1990).

How can we account for the pervasive influence of these childhood attachment patterns? There are at least four plausible explanations (Weinfield et al., 2008):

1. Early attachment experiences could affect the developing brain.

    (a) The entire brain may be thought of as a neural attachment system because so many different neural structures (e.g., sensory systems, memory systems, regulatory systems, the neocortex) are directly involved in attachment behavior (Coan, 2008);

(b) The growth of the right hemisphere is affected by the child's attachment experiences (Minagawa-Kawai et al., 2009; Schore, 2002).

(c) Excessive childhood stress—as a result of insecure attachment—could cause the death of those neurons connecting the neocortex to the limbic system. Such a neural disconnection would cause lifelong difficulties with emotional regulation (Schore, 1997, 2009; Siegel, 2012).

2. Attachment relationships may serve as the basis for self-regulation.

Securely attached infants may learn a variety of ways to deal with distress by experiencing their mothers' acceptance as they express a range of different emotions. Avoidantly attached infants learn to minimize emotional expressions of distress and thus never learn how to properly regulate them. Resistantly attached infants learn that only maximum distress signals will be attended to and thus find emotional modulation and regulation to be difficult (Grusec, 2011). And infants whose attachment is categorized as disorganized are the least capable at managing their emotions (Berlin & Cassidy, 2003; DeOliveira et al., 2004; Diener et al., 2002).

3. An infant learns what behaviors are involved in the give-and-take of a relationship.

Sensitive parenting teaches the infant that communication depends on sending clear signals to the other in a synchronized, predictable pattern. Insecurely attached infants experience communication as an uncoordinated interaction that may or may not be responsive to the infant's needs. The interactional skills that are learned within a secure attachment relationship may be applied to new relationships with peers, and so on.

4. Attachment affects the child's internal working models.

Internal working models of self and other may be unconsciously applied to new attachment relationships in adulthood. The continuity of our *internal working models* from infancy to adulthood, then, is the fourth explanation for the continuity of our personality throughout the life course.

Internal Working Models

Bowlby believed that each of us, in the course of our initial interactions with our caregivers, constructs our internal working model of important aspects of our world. Our internal working models have three functions: They help us (a) to perceive and interpret our experiences, (b) to forecast the future, and (c) to construct plans. The more accurately your internal working models map your world, the more realistic are your ensuing forecasts and plans.

Bowlby (1973) proposed that working models of ourselves and our attachment figures are especially important throughout our lives. He hypothesized that they emerge from actual patterns of child-caregiver interactions sometime around the end of the first year of life. If your caregivers were emotionally available and supportive, you were likely, as an infant, to develop an internal working model of yourself as lovable and competent. If, however, your caretakers frequently rejected your efforts to be comforted, you were likely to develop an internal working model of yourself as unworthy and incompetent.

Fortunately, early inadequate parenting can be corrected by later positive inter-personal experiences. Internal working models, although formed early in life, are modifiable later in life. Positive social experiences outside the family can cause ini-tially faulty working models to be replaced by more accurate mental representations of yourself and other people. Being involved in a caring relationship seems to be the critical variable in instances in which an early dysfunctional internal working model is replaced with more accurate and positive images of self and others. This positive relationship may be with a spouse, the spouse's parents, or a therapist (Bowlby, 1988; Bretherton, 1992; Rutter & Quinton, 1984).

Because children use their internal working models to predict their attachment figures' behavior, their models of themselves and others have significant conse-quences over the life course. Bowlby (1973) views internal working models as central to the intergenerational transmission of attachment patterns. Supportive parents who encourage their children to be independent are likely to raise children who grow to be emotionally stable and self-reliant adults. And when these children grow to adult-hood and become parents, they will probably treat their own children as they have been treated because (1) their internal working models of themselves are that they are competent and (2) their internal working models of children are that children need a secure base to explore their environment.

Children rejected by their parents are likely to become rejecting parents them-selves if subsequent positive social experiences do not correct their dysfunctional models. Bowlby (1973) thought that the "inheritance of mental health and of mental ill health through the medium of family microculture is certainly no less important, and may well be far more important, than is their inheritance through the medium of genes" (p. 323).

Internal working models, then, can be thought of as "*mental genes*" acquired after birth that affect the personalities of future generations through familial influence, unless they are modified before the onset of parenthood. The quality of the child's attachment determines her internal working model of herself and her attachment figures. These mental genes, in turn, affect how she is likely to raise her own children.

How can we know which "mental genes" influence how a person chooses to parent his or her child? The most direct way is to ask them which one of the following three types of relationships best describes how they feel:

1. "I am somewhat uncomfortable being close to others. I find it difficult to trust them completely, difficult to allow myself to depend on them. I am nervous when anyone gets too close, and often, love partners want me to be more intimate than I feel comfortable being."

2. "I find that others are reluctant to get as close as I would like. I often worry that my partner doesn't really love me or won't want to stay with me. I want to get very close to my partner, and this sometimes scares people away."

3. "I find it relatively easy to get close to others and am comfortable depending on them. I don't worry about being abandoned or about someone getting too close to me." (Brennan, Clark, & Shaver, 1998; Hazan & Shaver, 1987)

This straight-forward procedure has been used to identify a parent's style of child-rearing. Adults who select the first alternative reveal an avoidant attachment style; those who select the second alternative show an anxious/ambivalent attachment style; and those who choose the third alternative display a secure attachment style. A review of numerous investigations of parents' *self-reported attachment styles* found that reported security of attachment was consistently related to positive parenting outcomes, while reported insecurity was related to more unfavorable outcomes. A parent's "mental genes" are not difficult to identify (Jones, Cassidy, & Shaver, 2015).

Even if adults' own childhood care was less than optimal, Bowlby (1988) suggests that a coherent, easily accessible account of attachment-related information (i.e., their internal working model) signifies they have come to terms with their upbringing and have "earned" a secure status for themselves. When parents are asked to describe how they were raised, the coherence and organization of their accounts of their own childhood is the best predictor of their infant's attachment security. Coherence means that their account makes sense, all of the parts fit together, and there are no obvious missing gaps.

So can insecure working models of attachment, models initially formed in early childhood, be modified by later positive social experiences? Can children who were inconsistently raised by their caregivers change their "mental genes" if they experience a loving, supportive, reliable romantic partner in adulthood? Yes. The quality of later close relationships—with teachers, friends, and romantic partners, for example—may shift an insecure internal working model of oneself to a secure one. However, the precise psychological pathways for such positive developmental changes are not yet well understood (Bretherton & Munholland, 2008).

Ingredient #3: Identification

Identification by the child with his or her parents is the third ingredient in the soil of personality. Psychoanalytic and cognitive-social learning theories offer alternative explanations for the processes children use to identify with their parents. We present the influential views of Sigmund Freud and Albert Bandura to account for the significance of identification for personality development.

Freudian Theory

Sigmund Freud based his theory of infancy on unfortunate analogies with the psychotic states of schizophrenia and mania as well as the biological conceptions of development from German idealist philosophy (Sulloway, 1992; Westen, 1990). Freud held that

> infants are oblivious to their social surroundings, hallucinate experiences of gratification, believe that they are omnipotent and omniscient, confuse self and other ... and only begin to engage with the social world because wish-fulfillment is not successful and drive gratification is not available in any other way. (Westen, 1990, p. 48)

Photo 4.1 **Sigmund Freud** (1856–1939)

Freud's theory divides the human mind into three parts: *id* (instinctive, childish), *ego* (rational decision making), and *superego* (conscience). Psychoanalytic therapy aims to strengthen the ego's ability to handle internal conflicts as well as deal effectively with external reality.

Key publications:

The Interpretation of Dreams (1900)
The Psychopathology of Everyday Life (1901)
New Introductory Lectures on Psycho-Analysis (1933)

With such an odd view of normal human infancy, it is no wonder Freud saw adult psychological life as a perpetual battle to remain sane by avoiding regression to the "psychotic-like state" of our beginning months of life.

Several psychoanalysts have challenged the validity of such sweeping generalizations (e.g., Horner, 1985; Lichtenberg, 1981). Daniel Stern (1985), in a major effort to integrate psychoanalytic theory with methodologically sound findings from infancy research, concludes that normal infants *do not* confuse themselves with other people or show other symptoms of psychosis. Freud's view of infancy is wrong. Nevertheless, is there any evidence to support his assumption of the five stages of human development?

Freud's Psychosexual Stages of Development

As noted in Chapter 1, Freud thought personality develops across five invariant psychosexual stages. He called these the oral, anal, phallic, latency, and genital stages of development. At each stage (except the latency stage), the child associates pleasurable sensations with particular parts of the body. Normal development in the genital stage results in an adult who achieves sexual pleasure by engaging in intercourse with a person of the opposite sex. Any other form of sexual activity, Freud believed, reflects a *fixation* (or blockage) of psychic energy or libido at an earlier stage of development. Under conditions of stress, an apparently normal adult might undergo *regression* to an earlier stage by manifesting infantile behavior (e.g., thumbsucking, babytalk), overeating, or overdrinking.

Freud held that the child identifies with his or her parents during the *phallic stage*, at about 4 to 5 years of age. Before examining Freud's thoughts on identification, we should first examine the significance he attaches to the two stages that precede it.

Oral stage: The infant's primary focus of pleasurable sensations is the mouth. Freud thought that parents—the primary sources of gratification for the infant—who overindulge or abruptly stop weaning could cause libido to fixate at the oral stage. How parents deal with their infant's needs determines whether the infant will experience personality difficulties related to the oral stage later in life. The phrase *oral character types* refers to people whose sources of pleasure remain focused on or around their mouths (e.g., smoking, chewing gum, thumbsucking).

There are two versions of the oral character—the oral receptive and the oral aggressive person. The *oral receptive character* fixated at the earliest stage of infancy. In theory, such a person was overindulged in infancy and depends excessively on others as adults (Blum, 1953). Oral receptive characters tend to be naive, overly trusting, and gullible—in other words, they will "swallow anything." The *oral aggressive character* refers to anyone who fixated at the biting stage of infancy and tends to have sadistic, exploitative, and verbally manipulative attitudes toward others. Verbally, such people frequently use biting sarcasm to verbally attack others, especially those they envy and want to dominate.

Anal stage: At about the ages of 2 or 3, the young child's pleasurable sensations shift from the mouth to the other end of the tube, the anal cavity. Freud speculated that children at this stage derive their chief pleasures by retaining or expelling feces. The primary source of conflict involves issues surrounding toilet training.

Fixations at this stage result in adult personality constellations of either the anal retentive character or the anal expulsive character. The *anal retentive character* reveals three dominant personality traits: He or she is stingy, obstinate, and excessively neat or orderly (Blum, 1953). These traits are thought to derive from overly strict toilet training sessions in which the young child learned to hold back his feces as if they were prized possessions, not to be given away lightly. Overly strict toilet training may also have the opposite effect: The child may learn to express anger and rage by expelling his feces at the most inappropriate times and places. An adult manifests the traits of the *anal expulsive character* by being chronically messy and readily throwing temper tantrums to get his way.

Phallic stage: During ages 4 to 5, the child, whose sexual pleasures shift to the genital area, discovers the pleasures of self-stimulation. The character traits associated with fixation at the phallic stage differ between boys and girls because sex-role behavior begins to be learned at this age. The *phallic character type*, in adult males, is revealed through traits such as narcissism (extreme self-involvement and rapid shifting between high and low self-esteem), exhibitionism, competitiveness, an insatiable interest in "conquering" as many women as possible (Don Juanism), and a desire to prove he is a "real man." Women fixated at this stage are also exhibitionistic, but they manifest their adult personalities by being flirtatious and seductive. At the same time, they most likely deny they send out sexual signals and may appear to be rather naive. Both adult men and women of the phallic character type, whether married or single, share an abiding interest in continually attracting the attention of members of the opposite sex.

As you read these descriptions, did anyone you know leap to mind? When that happens we feel almost compelled to think, "Yes, it's really true! So-and-so is just like that!" Unfortunately, such subjective reactions, as strong as they might be, do not prove Freud was right. Is there any objective evidence to support the existence of these character types?

In his review of the literature on the empirical status of Freud's character types, Malcolm Macmillan (1997) concludes that in spite of a great deal of energy expended to find personality traits clustering in the ways Freud proposed, little or no empirical support has been found for his proposals. The evidence, such as it is, is limited to anecdotal case histories rather than systematic research that controls for extraneous or confounding variables. Many have concluded there is no persuasive evidence for Freudian concepts or for the effectiveness of psychoanalysis as a therapeutic procedure (e.g., Crews, 1995; Esterson, 1993; Webster, 1995).

Identification, which occurs during the phallic stage, is Freud's mechanism to explain the young child's internalization of parental values. Identification is a key ingredient of the soil of personality because without it, the child is morally disconnected from the norms and values of his or her social group. If identification fails to occur, the child's ideas of right and wrong conduct will be defective. The child's superego or conscience will lack the necessary "internal guidance system" for regulating conduct. A person who failed to identify with his parents may well base his adult decisions of whether to violate society's laws solely on evaluations of the likelihood of being caught, not on the harm he inflicts on others. Identification is a key ingredient for developing our emotional connection to other people.

Freud used the term *identification* in various ways. With regard to describing the child–parent relationship, it can refer to *similarity in behaviors* between the child and parents, the *process* that brings about that similarity, or the *motive* to imitate and identify with an important person in the child's life. Here we focus on the two motives Freud proposed as the basis of the child's identification with his or her parents—anaclitic identification and defensive identification.

Anaclitic identification is based on the child's dependence on his or her caregivers. The child identifies with the parents to be able to reproduce, in fantasy and behavior, the mother's and father's words and actions. Anaclitic identification allows the child to maintain, in fantasy, a continual positive relationship with the parents and therefore protects the child against the fear of losing the mother or father's love.

Defensive identification is caused by fear of one's parents. Children imitate their parents, Freud held, to protect themselves from harm inflicted by these powerful giants. Defensive identification gives the small child a "magical" feeling of power and control over a situation in which she is, in reality, powerless.

Anna Freud (1936), Sigmund's daughter, proposed **identification with the aggressor** as a defense mechanism to ward off intolerable anxiety against threat of harm. A contemporary example of this is the *Stockholm syndrome*—the positive feelings some victims of kidnapping develop toward their captors. Such positive feelings emanate from unconscious defensive identification with the aggressors ("They won't hurt me because I'm just like them."). This is a good example of the short-run survival value of defense mechanisms.

Sigmund Freud believed identification to be a pivotal event in the development of personality. Identification with a parent allows the child to resolve successfully the

Oedipus conflict, adopt a gender identity consistent with his or her biological sex, and internalize the values of society, as transmitted by the parents.

"The way I see it--If nature is right, I can blame my genes.
If nurture is right, I can blame my parents. Either way, I'm golden!"

Failure to identify with a parent, accordingly, will cause the person to experience one or more of the following difficulties:

1. The child is unable to psychologically separate or detach from the same-sex parent. The person will experience lifelong difficulties in regulating his emotional states—in short, he will become neurotic. Freud believed that unsuccessful resolution of the Oedipus conflict lies at the heart of *all* neuroses: "In neurotics . . . this detachment from the parents is not accomplished at all. . . . In this sense the Oedipal complex is justifiably regarded as the kernel of the neuroses" (1924/1952, p. 346). In other words, the adult neurotic unconsciously clings to childish wishes to be protected by his parents and is unwilling to take personal responsibility for his or her own life.

2. The person may develop gender confusion and/or become homosexual (Freud, 1924/1952). Boys who do not identify with their fathers may identify with their mothers; girls who do not identify with their mothers may identify with their fathers. Such children will be sexually attracted to people of the same sex to replace the parent with whom they could not identify. Such is the Freudian view. We'll present other views of the development of gender identity a bit later in this chapter.

3. A child who is unable to identify with his or her parents will develop a defective superego or conscience. Disturbances in superego formation are manifested by either narcissism or failure to internalize the values of society (Freud, 1914/1959b). In psychoanalytic thinking, the child's idealization of the parents includes idealizing the parents' code of conduct. She constructs her own internal sense of morality by identifying with idealized parental standards. Without such an identification process, the child will not begin to internalize the values and norms of her society (Hartmann, Kris, & Lowenstein, 1946).

Freud saw identification as a critical determinant of adult personality. What led him to believe that identification is so important? Primarily, Freud hypothesized that identification is how a child resolves the Oedipus conflict (1923/1959c). As mentioned in Chapter 1, the Oedipus conflict refers to the child's wishes and fantasies for the exclusive love and attention of the opposite-sexed parent and the elimination of his or her chief rival, the parent of the same sex. By identifying with his father, the little boy preserves his father's love (anaclitic identification), prevents his father from retaliating against the boy's anger (defensive identification), and no longer feels jealous when Mommy shows she loves Daddy because, through identification, Mommy's love of Daddy is also, in a way, love toward him as well. Through identification, children begin to form a stable sense of their own masculinity or femininity and internalize their parents' ideals and values.

Contradicting Freud's views on identification, however, research shows that boys develop a stronger identification with their fathers and a firmer sense of masculinity when their fathers are nurturant and warm rather than punitive or threatening (Hetherington & Frankie, 1967). A systematic review of Freudian hypotheses concludes that there is no compelling evidence for the Oedipus complex (Luborsky & Barrett, 2006). Moreover, there is no research justification for the view that boys are motivated by Oedipal fears. Finally, research shows that girls and women have at least as strong a superego (conscience), if not stronger, than boys and men (Fisher & Greenberg, 1996).[4]

Several psychoanalytic observers have also commented on the importance of the mother's role in gender identification. Excessive gratification, inconsistent mothering, or failure to set limits may be detrimental to superego development and, by implication, to successful identification. Excessive mothering and an absent father have been psychoanalytically implicated as one of the key causes of gender confusion in boys, whereas excessive fathering and an absent mother play the same role in developing gender confusion in girls (Stoller, 1985; Tyson & Tyson, 1990).

While Freud and other psychoanalysts explain identification by focusing on factors internal to the child, Albert Bandura and the social learning theorists examine the developmental significance of the child imitating role models in his or her external environment.

Bandura's View of Imitation

In his observations of young children, Bandura noted that they were likely to imitate a model under a wide variety of conditions after simply observing what the model did (due to mirror neurons?). Bandura held observational learning and imitation to be centrally important in the acquisition of new behaviors (Bandura & Walters, 1963). Acquiring a new behavior means learning how to execute it. Bandura (1971) identified four processes required for imitation: We need to pay attention, we need to retain what we attended to, we need the necessary motor skills, and we need motivation to perform what we saw.

In his research program, Bandura was interested in determining the conditions that lead to imitation. Given that children have a wide variety of potential models to imitate—at home, on TV, in the playground—what determines who they will imitate? Experimental evidence shows that children will probably imitate models who are rewarding, affectionate, and nurturing (Bandura & Huston, 1961); are perceived to be powerful in controlling resources (Bandura, Ross, & Ross, 1963); and are similar to the child, especially with regard to sex (Bandura, Ross, & Ross, 1961). For Bandura, then, the child's identification with his or her parents comes naturally from the child's tendency to imitate rewarding, powerful, and similar persons—the parents.

Development of Gender Identity

One of the most important events of your past self was identifying yourself as a boy or a girl, that is, your gender identity. Research shows that most children can correctly discriminate pictures of boys and girls by age 2½ or 3, about the same age they begin to hold sex-role stereotypes. Sex-role stereotypes are beliefs that define particular tasks, behaviors, or traits as either feminine or masculine. The most clearly stereotypic traits for women are weakness, gentleness, and soft-heartedness; the most clearly stereotypic traits for men are aggressiveness, strength, and cruelty. These particular traits have been found to be sex-stereotyped across many cultures (Williams & Best, 1990).

How do children learn to apply the label "boy" or "girl" to themselves? The Freudian theory of identification, as we have seen, stresses the importance of resolving the Oedipus conflict at around the age of 4 or 5. But empirical studies of young children's sex-role behaviors have not supported the Freudian view: "Pre-Oedipal" children as young as 2½ or 3 prefer to play with same-sex playmates (LaFreniere, Strayer, & Gauthier, 1984).

More strikingly, age 2½ seems to be a sensitive period for developing gender identity, as seen from studies of children whose genitals were ambiguously formed at birth. Unfortunately, these children are sometimes assigned to the wrong gender (i.e., infant boys are mistakenly thought to be girls; infant girls are erroneously thought to be boys). Investigations of the long-term effects on boys who were raised as girls because of their misfortunate anatomical beginnings reveal mixed results. Some boys who were raised as girls thought of themselves as boys (Reiner & Gearhart, 2004), while other boys self-identified as girls (Meyer-Bahlburg, 2005), even though sometimes their interests were more masculine than feminine (Bradley et al., 1998). Thus the precise conditions under which gender reassignment will be successful are unknown as of this writing.

The biological basis of gender identification is supported by the results of a study of 314 twins. In a small percentage of those twins, 2.3%, there was evidence of gender identity disorder (GID). *Gender identity disorder* is diagnosed when an individual persistently identifies with the opposite biological sex and experiences chronic discomfort with one's own biological sex (Docter, 1988). The strong genetic basis for this disorder is shown by the finding that 62% of the variability was due to heredity, leading the researchers to conclude "gender identity may be much less a matter of choice and much more a matter of biology" (Coolidge, Thede, & Young, 2002, p. 251).

The social learning view of Bandura (1986) and Walter Mischel (1966, 1970) is that children learn their sex roles by being reinforced directly to engage in appropriate sex-role behavior and imitate same-sex models. There is support for this view. Parents do encourage their young children to engage in sex-typed activities. Moreover, toddlers whose parents more consistently reward sex-typed play learn accurate gender labels earlier than toddlers of inconsistent patterns (Lytton & Romney, 1991).

Several studies show that children are more likely to imitate same-sex than opposite-sex models (Bussey & Bandura, 1984; Bussey & Perry, 1982). Observing and imitating same-sex parents, peers, and media characters promotes gender identification. Moreover, cognitive processes play a central role in gender development that go beyond simple imitation. Children also learn abstract rules that govern appropriate gender behavior, and when these rules are internalized, the children administer self-praise for correct gender conduct (Bussey & Bandura, 1999).

Gender-schema theory (Bem, 1981) is a cognitive approach that explains how children learn sex-role behaviors. Gender-schema theory proposes that as children develop, they form an idea or schema about masculine and feminine sex roles. By observing Mommy and Daddy do different things and act in slightly different ways, young children begin to form initial impressions or ideas of what it means to be a man or a woman. By the age of 18 months, children categorize people, objects, and activities by gender. Children also differ in how fully developed and accessible their gender schemas are and how readily these schemas influence their behavior (Egan & Perry, 2001; Lieben & Bigler, 2002; Ruble, Martin, & Berenbaum, 2006). Perhaps children do not learn sex roles by imitating their same-sex parents as much as they are sensitive to reinforcements for sex-appropriate actions from same-sex adults and children. Gender identification seems to be best explained from a cognitive-social learning viewpoint (Serbin & Sprafkin, 1986).

However it is learned, gender identification remains a vital component of our self-concept. Idiosyncratic features of our primary role models and peer groups of childhood shaped our individual connotations of what it means to be a man or a woman. It is clear that cognitive-social learning theory does a better job accounting for what is known about the acquisition of sex roles than does psychoanalysis.[5]

The two fundamental questions posed in Part II, "Did my personality begin in the womb?" and "What kinds of early environmental experiences affected my personality?" have now been answered. Research on the genetic basis of personality, covered in Chapter 3, shows that individual differences in personality have a biological basis. Our genetic inheritance can be thought of as the "seeds" of our personality. Temperament refers to those personality traits—such as emotionality, activity, and sociability—that have an especially strong biological basis. Temperamental differences appear early in life and persist throughout the life span.

At the same time, our early environment is equally important. As we found in this chapter, parenting styles, attachment, and identification are three basic ingredients of the "soil" of personality. These ingredients contribute to the cultivation of adult personality.

But humans are not plants. Unlike plants, the young child becomes increasingly mobile, demanding, and creative in asserting his or her wants and needs. Raising children who will develop into self-sufficient and caring adults is an obviously greater challenge than growing healthy plants. After all, when plants are neglected, they quietly wilt; when babies are uncared for, they scream. A screaming infant is so unpleasant to hear that parents will usually expend almost any effort to get their child to stop.[6]

Yet there is more. We are not passive pawns watching helplessly as heredity and environment shape us willy-nilly. We have a choice, a say, in the kind of self we are creating. Our future is open and will reflect the choices we make today. As Marc Bornstein (2014) notes, "Individuals contribute to their own development, and we are increasingly aware that people are agents in their own lives" (p. 144).

❖

QUESTIONS TO PONDER

1. Which of the four parenting styles apply to how your mother and father were raised by your grandparents? Did those styles influence how they raised you? Do you think how you were raised will affect how you will raise your own children?

2. How might the different attachment styles of childhood manifest themselves in adulthood? How could an adult who recognizes that she was insecurely attached as a young child change her internal working models of herself and others?

3. In 2014, a professional athlete was arrested on charges of child abuse and child endangerment because he frequently used a belt or a "switch" to severely beat his 4-year-old son for misbehavior. The athlete pleaded guilty to a lesser charge to avoid jail. In his initial statements to the press, however, the athlete defended his actions on the grounds that he did to his son only what his father had done to him. He expressed no remorse over his behavior—either before or after sentencing. What would it take for this person (or anyone whose early personal mistreatment pathologically warped their view of proper child-rearing) to stop denying that they themselves are victims of child abuse?

❖

NOTES

1. If last-born children are as spoiled and self-centered as Adler thought they are, they could not adjust easily to the give-and-take of childhood play. Thus they would not be as popular as empirical research indicates.

2. Please note that the term *epigenetics* (or *epigenesis*) has additional meanings than Erikson's. In the field of genetics, epigenesis can refer to (1) the idea that an observable phenotype can be the result of the *interaction* of a gene x environment (rather than either genes or environment alone) or (2) the occurrence of a heritable change in gene function not attributable to the organism's DNA. A monthly, peer-reviewed journal, *Epigenetics*, began publication in 2006 to report current research on this important topic.

3. A self-report measure of industry among children 8- to 13-years-old has been developed by Kowaz and Marcia (1991).

4. As noted in Chapter 1, Freud's theory does not apply to understanding how little girls come to identify with their mothers. Because Freud believed *his* theory was correct, this difficulty led him to erroneously conclude that something must be wrong with women!

5. Other views of the development of gender identification go beyond the scope of this text. For additional information see Bem (1985), Docter (1988), and Ruble, Martin, and Berenbaum (2006).

6. The noxious sounds of the upset human infant are undoubtedly of great evolutionary significance. If *homo sapiens* had evolved a variety of human infants who made pleasant cooing noises when they were uncared for or were in danger, this variety would have quickly become extinct. Parents would have slept soundly through their infant's discomfort and thus been unable to protect their child from predators or other dangers.

SUGGESTIONS FOR FURTHER READING

Bowlby, J. (1988). *A secure base: Parent–child attachment and healthy human development.* New York, NY: Basic Books.
Grossmann, K. E., Grossmann, K., & Waters, E. (Eds.) (2005). *Attachment from infancy to adulthood: The major longitudinal studies.* New York, NY: Guilford.
Hrdy, S. B. (2009). *Mothers and others: The evolutionary origins of mutual understanding.* Cambridge, MA: The Belknap Press of Harvard University Press.
Siegel, D. J. (2012). *The developing mind: How relationships and the brain interact to shape who we are.* New York, NY: Guilford.
Sroufe, L. A., Egeland, B., Carlson, E. A., & Collins, W. A. (2005). *The development of the person: The Minnesota Study of risk and adaptation from birth to adulthood.* New York, NY: Guilford.

INTERNET RESOURCES

1. To take a survey that measures your attachment style, go to http://www.web-based-design.net/cgi-bin/crq/crq.pl.

2. For a slide presentation of the basics of Bowlby's views on attachment, see http://www.slideshare.net/preethibalan9/bowlbys-theory-of-attachment.

3. To take a test of your gender identity, go to http://www.hemingways.org/GIDinfo/sage/.

Part III

My Present Self

❖

5

Identity and Self-Esteem

❖Who am I? Why is it important for me to like myself?

Introduction
  What Is Self-Esteem?
  How Is Self-Esteem Measured?

Psychosocial Theory of Identity
  Adolescence: Identity Versus Identity Confusion
  Early Adulthood: Intimacy Versus Isolation
  Adulthood: Generativity Versus Stagnation

Humanistic/Narrative Approaches to Identity and Self-Esteem
  The Person-Centered Approach of Carl Rogers
  The Narrative Approach of Dan McAdams

Single-Variable Research Programs
  Self-Discrepancy Theory
  Self-Verification Theory
  Identity Fusion Theory
  Sociometer Theory
  Self-Efficacy Theory

Can you recall when you first became aware of your self, that is, when you became self-conscious? My earliest memory is being in a scary situation when I was 4 years old (separation anxiety). At that point, I was already self-conscious, as are all children. But I do not remember precisely when I initially became self-aware. Whenever it first originated, our sense of identity and feelings about our self-worth are essential parts of our present selves.

Introduction

What Is Self-Esteem?

Self-esteem, our evaluation of ourselves, can range between feeling that we are worthy and valuable members of society to feeling we are worthless and valueless. William James (1890) offered a simple yet profound definition:

$$\text{Self-esteem} = \text{Successes/Pretensions}$$

This formula says we can raise our self-esteem in two ways: by accumulating successes and by reducing our pretensions. Reducing our pretensions means accepting ourselves for who we are without holding unrealistic expectations. When our pretensions chronically exceed our actual successes, we feel dissatisfied with ourselves and experience low self-esteem. Note that this sort of low self-esteem is completely self-induced by our own pretensions. But when our successes exceed our pretensions, we feel good about ourselves and experience high self-esteem. Thus, James's formula could be restated:

$$\text{Self-esteem} = \text{Successes achieved/Successes expected}$$

To understand this formula imagine how you would react after getting a grade of "B" on an exam or term paper. James's formula tells us that your reaction depends completely on your prior expectations: If you expected to receive an "A," you will be disappointed by the "B" and will experience (momentary) lowered self-esteem. But if you expected a grade of "C," you will feel good and experience higher self-esteem. James's simple formula raises the meaningful question of how often the ultimate cause of our own happiness or sadness lies within our own expectations for ourselves.

James (1890) further hypothesized that "staking our salvation" on those particular aspects of our identity contributes the most to our overall level of self-esteem. For example, the student who hoped to receive an "A" may have staked her salvation on her identity as an excellent student. Receiving a grade of "B" would be a bigger blow to her self-esteem than to another student whose salvation lies in off campus pursuits.

Is James's hypothesis correct? Yes, research findings support it. Consistent with James's hypothesis, Rosenberg (1965) showed that adolescents who hold negative self-concepts are likely to have overall low self-esteem only when they feel their flaws are personally important. To see yourself as a poor athlete, for instance, does not lower your self-esteem if you don't particularly value athleticism. Similarly, Pelham and

Swann (1989) found a strong relationship between identity and self-esteem: The more people value those skills they excel at, the higher is their overall self-esteem.

How Is Self-Esteem Measured?

Psychologists and nonpsychologists alike place a special significance on self-esteem because it is, they believe, an important determinant of our behavior. Children who become pregnant, drop out of school, or use drugs are believed to do so, at least in large part, because they have low self-esteem. The same belief applies to adults who maltreat their children, commit crimes, are chronically unemployed and dependent on welfare, or are addicted to alcohol and/or other drugs. Individuals with high self-esteem are unlikely, it is assumed, to engage in such self-defeating or deviant behavior. Therefore, it is reasoned, those who commit such deviant acts must have not felt good about themselves beforehand.

Numerous investigators have tested the hypothesis that low self-esteem is one of the reasons behind so many social problems. If this hypothesis were to be supported by observations in the real world, preventive social measures protecting (and even elevating) at-risk children's self-esteem could be enacted to prevent problematic behaviors down the time track. Obviously, this is a far from trivial issue. What have the investigators found?

The typical outcome has been disheartening. Most research on this issue has *failed* to find evidence in support of the hypothesis that self-esteem is systematically related to problematic behavior (Mecca, Smelser, & Vasconcellos, 1989). How can this be? Are our beliefs about the importance of self-esteem wrong? Or is it something else?

One plausible explanation for research failures to demonstrate the social importance of self-esteem lies in the inadequate measurement tools used by most investigators. There are three problems with most research efforts:

First, simple self-report measures of self-concept and global self-esteem (overall, all-inclusive self-esteem) are at best imprecise measurement devices (see Wylie, 1974, 1979 for a full discussion of this point).

Second, self-concept scales usually consist of standard questions that all participants answer. A person's self-esteem score is mechanically determined by computing the total favorable self-ratings minus the total unfavorable self-ratings. Because all items are scored the same way for everyone, they are not usually weighted to represent their relative importance to each individual. The typical self-esteem scale does not identify those specific aspects of the self-concept that the person values most highly.

Third, the absence of a universal, standardized definition of self-esteem has resulted in self-esteem scales multiplying like rabbits. More than 200 self-esteem scales are available. Most of them are not comparable to one another! It is no wonder that such little progress has been made in demonstrating the relationship of self-esteem to real-world behaviors (Scheff, Retzinger, & Ryan, 1989).

A major issue concerning how we should study personality, as mentioned in Chapter 1, is known as the nomothetic versus idiographic debate. The term nomothetic comes from the Greek *nomothetikos*: the giving or enacting of laws; idiographic derives from the Greek *idios*: one's own, as in idiosyncratic (Allport, 1937).

Nomothetic research involves testing large numbers of participants and averaging their scores on the variable or variables of interest. The goal of nomothetic research is to discover general laws that apply to everyone. Idiosyncratic responses (sometimes called "outliers") are either considered part of error variance, ignored, or dropped from the data set.

Idiographic research efforts are designed to discover the unique pattern of traits and motives that exist within an individual person. The goal of idiographic research is to understand in depth a particular individual in all his or her uniqueness.

Most research efforts that have failed to show the relationship of self-esteem to behavior have been nomothetic. High self-esteem individuals are identified as those who score above the average of all participants tested on that occasion. Low self-esteem individuals are those whose total score is below the group average. The group average on these tests tends to be very high because most normal individuals hold overly positive self-evaluations to begin with (Taylor & Brown, 1988). Being below average, then, doesn't necessarily mean one suffers from low self-esteem—in all likelihood, most of these research participants suffer from low self-esteem only in the minds of nomothetically minded researchers.

Idiographic research that takes the time to study each individual's unique self-concept and determine his or her own level of self-esteem apart from comparison to any group is far more likely to successfully demonstrate the importance of self-esteem Regrettably, such careful, time-consuming investigations are few and far between (Asendorpf, 2015; Pelham, 1993; Pelham & Swann, 1989).

Methodological issues aside, there is another possibility for the failure of self-esteem research to show that any single social problem has its roots in individuals' low self-esteem. Perhaps those teenagers who abuse drugs, drop out of school, become pregnant, and so on, have not yet formed a satisfying personal identity. If a person is not sure who he or she is, temptations to avoid immediate responsibilities by getting high, and so forth, are not countered by opposing personal values that serve to inhibit such behavior. Your identity, after all, resides at the core of who you think you are. What do we know about identity?

The Psychosocial Theory of Identity

The sense of ego identity is the accrued confidence that one's ability to maintain inner sameness and continuity ... is matched by the sameness and continuity of one's meaning for others.

—Erik Erikson (1959, p. 89)

Erik Erikson is the major theorist from the psychodynamic tradition who stresses the vital importance of identity. For deeply personal reasons, Erik Erikson (1902–1994) needed to develop a coherent understanding of psychosocial identity to solve his own severe identity crisis. Erikson was born out of wedlock to his Jewish–Danish mother in 1902. His mother never told him who his father was, an issue which haunted Erikson throughout adolescence and well into adulthood. Boundary issues fascinated Erikson because they permeated his life: Was he German, like his stepfather (Theodore

Homburger), Danish (like his mother), or American (his adopted home)? Asked whether he was Protestant or Jew, his answer was, "Why both of course!" (Friedman, 1999, p. 345).

Erikson's lifelong preoccupation with personal and social boundaries led him to one of his most important ideas, ***pseudospeciation***: ethnocentrism makes every tribe, clan, or nation feel it is the *center* of the universe and *superior* to all other tribes, clans, or nations (e.g., "*American Exceptionalism*"). Consequently, members of every tribe, consciously or unconsciously, may view members of other tribes *as if* they belong to a different, inferior species than their own (Erikson, 1970, p. 431).

In coming to America in 1938, Erikson changed his name to Erik H. Erikson. He later explained, "I made myself into Erik's son. It is better to be your own originator." At age 73 Erikson revealed, "Without a deep identity conflict I would not have done the work I did" (Friedman, 1999, pp. 147, 433). Erikson originally trained as a Freudian analyst before developing his own theory of personality, which accepts the major premises of traditional psychoanalysis. Erikson built on such Freudian ideas as unconscious conflict and psychosexual stages of development by situating the developing person within a social context. Thus his approach is called ***psychosocial*** because it emphasizes both psychological variables within the developing person as well as those external social pressures to which individuals must adapt over the life span.

We presented Erikson's first four stages of development in Chapter 4. Table 5.1 summarizes the important elements from Erikson's next three stages.

In this chapter, we present Erikson's theory regarding the stages of adolescence, early adulthood, and adulthood. Erikson's last stage, Old Age, is covered in Chapter 10.

❖ **Table 5.1**   Summary of Erikson's Stages of Development

Life Stage	Psychosocial Crisis	Adaptive Ego Quality	Ego Core Pathology
1. Infancy (0–2 years)	Trust vs. Mistrust	Hope	Withdrawal
2. Toddler (2–3) years	Autonomy vs. Shame and Doubt	Will	Compulsion
3. Early School Age (4–5 years)	Initiative vs. Guilt	Purpose	Inhibition
4. Middle School Age (6–12 years)	Industry vs. Inferiority	Competence	Inertia
5. Adolescence	Identity vs. Identity Confusion	Fidelity	Repudiation
6. Young Adulthood	Intimacy vs. Isolation	Love	Exclusivity
7. Adulthood	Generativity vs. Stagnation	Care	Rejectivity
8. Old Age	Integrity vs. Despair	Wisdom	Disdain

Source: Erikson (1963, 1978, 1982). Reprinted from *The Life Cycle Completed* by Erik H. Erikson, with the permission of W. W. Norton & Company Inc. Copyright 1982 by Rikan Enterprises, Ltd.

Adolescence: Identity Versus Identity Confusion

Erikson's fifth stage of development occurs during adolescence. The *identity versus identity confusion* crisis begins to be resolved at this time. Establishing an identity, in Erikson's view, requires both an *intrapersonal process* (within ourselves) and an *interpersonal process* (relating to other people). The intrapersonal process of identity formation involves experiencing internal continuity of one's self over time as well as mentally integrating those new social roles—occupational, sexual, ideological—one is beginning to play. The interpersonal process involves finding our individual niche among the opportunities offered by society and being rewarded by society for doing so. The paycheck we receive for working symbolizes the worth society places on the value of our contribution. The individual needs to find his or her place in society and the society must provide opportunities to do so. Anyone who achieves a stable sense of identity experiences "a feeling of being at home in one's body, a sense of 'knowing where one is going,' and an inner assuredness of anticipated recognition from those who count" (Erikson, 1968, p. 165).

The key to understanding Erikson's view of the identity crisis is to recall that he proposes an epigenetic theory. This means, in this context, that how the adolescent handles the issue of who he or she is depends importantly on the resolution of the four prior life stage crises. In the ideal case, the four prior stages will result in the four ego strengths of hope, will, purpose, and sense of competence. Because each step is grounded in all of the prior steps, a person's identity intimately relates to these first four adaptive qualities. When the identity crisis makes its first conscious appearance, the adolescent who has already accrued these four primary ego strengths can resolve the identity crisis more easily and more favorably than someone who has not.

Erikson's theory is clear enough. Is there any evidence to support it? Yes. However, due to the inherent difficulty of testing his ideas, the methodologies employed are less than ideal. A convincing test of Erikson's idea would involve administering valid measures of the resolution of each crisis at the time it occurred and then observing how well or poorly each person resolved his or her identity crisis 15- to 20-years later. Such an ideally ambitious longitudinal investigation has yet to be reported.

The good news is that research results do support the reasonableness of Erikson's claims. College students who were ready to decide on their career paths demonstrated both more successful identity resolutions as well as successful resolutions of the prior four stages (Cohen, Chartrand, & Jowdy, 1995). These results were consistent with the observation that those college students who were more successful in resolving earlier psychosocial crises developed more mature career attitudes than those who did not (Munley, 1975).

An earlier cross-sectional study of college students found significant differences between seniors and freshmen on scales measuring industry, inferiority, and identity (Constantinople, 1969). A cross-cultural study using a self-report questionnaire to measure the personality components identified by Erikson found, as expected, these components to be strongly interrelated (Ochse & Plug, 1986). Also consistent with Erikson's ideas is research showing that college students' identity formations are related to their present feelings of competence, trust, and autonomy (Damon,

1983; Harter, 1990b). While each of the above studies are imperfect investigations of Erikson's main epigenetic hypothesis, all of their outcomes are at least consistent with his psychosocial theory of development.

Erikson holds that *fidelity* is the specific ego strength that emerges as the adolescent begins to resolve the crisis of identity versus identity confusion. The infant's adaptive quality of trust foreshadows the adaptive quality of fidelity. Fidelity refers to the adolescent's commitment to trust those role models one identifies with, the ideologies or social causes one finds worthy, and oneself as a competent, purposeful, intentional (willful), and hopeful person. Erikson (1982) notes that "hope connotes the most basic quality of 'I'-ness, without which life could not begin or meaningfully end" (p. 62). Erikson's epigenetic theory predicts that the ego strength of fidelity is more likely to be attained in those whose first crisis resulted in acquiring the ability to hope. The central significance of hope has been demonstrated by the extensive research program of Charles "Rick" Snyder (1944–2006) who summarized his key findings in *The Psychology of Hope* (2003).

Additional research supports Erikson's central premise that identity, or a well-defined self-concept, is important for a well-functioning personality. A 34-year-longitudinal study found that favorable identity solutions at age 20 correlated with favorable intimacy measures at ages 21, 34, 42, and 54, as well as overall satisfaction with one's own life at age 54 (Sneed et al., 2012). Moreover, individuals with a strong sense of identity, compared to those with tentative identities, are better able to regulate and control their own feelings and actions, set and successfully achieve their goals, have higher self-esteem, and project a consistent and socially desirable self-image to other people (Sedikides, 1993). Identity is unquestionably a key dimension of personality.

That Erikson holds our past to be an important determinant of our present functioning is, of course, quite in keeping with his psychoanalytic orientation. But the principle of epigenesis also looks to the future. Although the crisis of identity comes to the forefront during adolescence, its ultimate solution extends well into adulthood: "Epigenetically speaking, of course, nobody can quite 'know' who he or she 'is' until promising partners in work and love have been identified" (Erikson, 1982, p. 72). The adolescent's initial effort to find his or her place in the world represents a starting point toward resolving the identity crisis. Experience in the world is indispensable before we can discover who and what we love, the skills we possess, the kinds of work we enjoy, and our allegiance to particular ideologies—religious, political, intellectual, whatever. By successfully resolving the identity versus identity confusion crisis, we gain the ego strength of fidelity that gives us another strength to deal with ensuing psychosocial crises.

Erikson views identity development as a process over time. It may be a bumpy process for those adolescents who are unable or unwilling to commit themselves to a particular set of self-images. The core pathology associated with role confusion is *role repudiation,* an unwillingness to identify with any of the potential roles offered by one's society. Role repudiation may appear as diffidence which reflects a slowness in settling on any particular set of identity images. More seriously, role repudiation might result in a systematic defiance or marked preference for a *negative identity* (socially

unacceptable yet stubbornly held self-images). A juvenile delinquent, for example, might take pride in being a social "outcast" (Erikson, 1982) rather than being characterized as having low self-esteem.

A variation of negative identity is **toxic social identity**. A person displays a toxic social identity when his or her personality is centered around hating and dehumanizing one or more different social groups. The purpose of dehumanizing other groups is to allow the person to think of and treat them as if they are a different, lower species than human, thereby manifesting Erikson's previously mentioned concept of pseudospeciation. The motive (conscious or unconscious) supporting a toxic social identity is the building up and maintenance of one's self-esteem by derogating others (Fein & Spencer, 2000).

The tendency to dehumanize other social groups is associated with the following:

- Disagreeable personality characteristics such as psychopathy, narcissism, ultra-nationalism, and hostile attitudes
- An automatic emotional aversion to unfamiliar persons
- Hierarchical ideological positions, a social dominance orientation, and a strong belief in human dominion over animals. A social dominance orientation is a general attitude supporting the domination of particular groups over other groups, no matter how the domination originated (Sidanius & Pratto, 1999)
- Social disconnection from other people (Haslam, 2015; Haslam & Loughnan, 2014)

Erikson (1968) views adolescence as a period of **psychosocial moratorium** allowing the young person to experiment with different social roles before finding his or her niche in society. As a psychoanalyst, Erikson does not assume that we consciously experience moratorium as such. Only in retrospect do we realize that what we took so seriously as adolescents was in fact a needed experimentation with a particular identity image. The moratorium fails only if the young person remains chronically unwilling to select and affirm particular social roles (identity confusion) or prematurely settles on an identity before taking the time to explore different social roles. Some adults put social pressure on teenagers by asking, "What do you want to be when you grow up?" This pressure pushes some teenagers to foreclose their identity crises prematurely by overidentifying with all parental values and wishes instead of taking time to discover what is right for one's authentic self.

Empirical studies of Erikson's theory of adolescent identity have been heavily influenced by James Marcia's related proposal of four identity status positions. In drawing on Erikson's theory, Marcia (1980) hypothesized that there are two essential components to adolescent identity formation: (1) a *crisis* during which old values and old choices are reexamined, and (2) a *commitment* to a particular social or occupational role and ideology. By combining these two components, four possible outcomes are generated:

1. *High crisis, high commitment*: Following a crisis of identity, the person firmly commits to a particular occupation and ideology. This positive outcome is called *identity achievement*.

2. *High crisis, no commitment*: The identity crisis remains in progress. This outcome is called *moratorium*.

3. *No crisis, high commitment*: The person precludes the experience of an identity crisis by prematurely committing to an occupation and ideology. Past decisions are not reevaluated. This outcome is called *foreclosure*.

4. *No crisis, no commitment*: The person is not presently experiencing an identity crisis (although an unresolved one may have been experienced in the past) and has not made an occupational and ideological commitment. This outcome, usually found very early in the process, is called *identity diffusion*.

Investigations of Marcia's classification scheme have found that the highest levels of self-esteem are often (but not universally) found among identity achievers, followed by the moratorium group, then foreclosure, and last by those in the identity diffusion group (Damon, 1983). Successful identity achievers also have been found to be less self-preoccupied with how others evaluate them and more self-assured than other adolescents (Adams, Abraham, & Markstrom, 1987).

College students with diffuse identity styles are likely to employ procrastination (see Chapter 9), wishful thinking, and tension reduction strategies when faced with stressful situations. They prefer to cope with their own anxious feelings rather than directly attack the problem causing their stress. In contrast, students whose identity styles are consistent with Marcia's identity achieved status are more likely to use direct, problem-focused attempts to solve their personal problems (Berzonsky, 1992).

College years are, to some extent, a continuation of psychosocial moratorium. So it is not surprising that high school graduates, who work full-time and do not go to college, report higher levels of identity achievement in establishing stable religious and political identities than do college students (Munro & Adams, 1977). Moreover, it is not unusual for college students to regress from identity achievement to moratorium at some point during their academic careers. Many students switch their majors at least once (Adams & Fitch, 1982). For most students, the moratorium period does not last forever. Most college graduates emerge from the Ivory Tower with a college degree in hand and a firmer identity in mind than they had as entering freshmen (Waterman, 1982, 1985). Having faith in themselves and their ideals, they are now ready to enter the adult world of love and work.

General support was found for Waterman's (1999) proposition that more young adults are likely to change their identity status *from* foreclosure or diffusion *to* identity achievement status than changing in the opposite direction (Kroger, Martinussen, & Marcia, 2010). These data are consistent with Erikson's premise that identity achievement is a central life task for the individual no matter how long he or she takes to achieve it.

Moreover, identity achievement may be but one of the steps for continued *identity development* over the life span. Identity development means that as we gain new experiences throughout life, we discover new aspects about ourselves that change our sense of who we are. An individual may discover relatively late in life, for example, that she loves to paint, thereby opening up new aspects of her self-concept. Continual identity development is needed for our sense of identity to remain flexible and adaptive to our changing experiences (Carlsson, Wangqvist, & Frisen, 2015). The idea of continual identity development over the life course is totally consistent with Erikson's (1982) psychosocial view of the complete life cycle. Identity achievement does not mean our identities are set in stone.

Early Adulthood: Intimacy Versus Isolation

Young adults who successfully emerge from adolescence with stable identities "can be eager and willing to fuse identities in mutual intimacy" (Erikson, 1982, p. 70). The psychosocial crisis of young adulthood is the crisis of *intimacy versus isolation.*

Following, as it does, the establishment of a personal identity and stable self-esteem, intimacy depends on young adults' perceptions of themselves as competent and valuable individuals (epigenesis, again). Intimacy is a fundamental sharing of our innermost being with another person (McAdams, 1989). An intimate relationship between two adults requires both of them to be willing and able to recognize and empathize with each other's needs.

Gender differences in intimacy during adolescence are easily observed. Girls' friendships are characterized by greater knowledge of each other and greater sensitivity to each others' feelings. Girls engage in more talking, sharing, and giving than boys. Boys more often engage in mutual intimacy in the context of shared activities and sports. Intimacy within opposite-sex friendships emerges relatively late in adolescence (Collins & Steinberg, 2006).

Barriers to intimacy include all the ego core pathologies that have resulted from the unsuccessful resolutions of the earlier crises: chronic mistrust of others, a tendency to withdraw when stressed, feelings of shame, guilt, and/or inferiority, as well as identity confusion.

Isolation means remaining separated and unrecognized. The greatest psychological danger associated with chronic isolation is a continual reliving of one's identity conflict and the potential return to identity confusion. Erikson, as shown in Table 5.1, identifies *exclusivity* as the extreme core pathology associated with isolation. Exclusivity refers to an elitist attitude the individual uses to shut out others not worthy of his or her attention and involvement in a relationship. As with the other Eriksonian stages, the presence of a core pathology disturbs further psychosocial growth.

Loneliness is a common symptom of isolation. Surveys indicate that as many as 25% of adults feel very lonely during any given 30-day period (Weiss, 1974). Loneliness may be short-lived or chronic. Either way, loneliness causes numerous specific effects in the brains of both humans and animals (Cacioppo, Capitanio, & Cacioppo, 2014). Chronic loneliness is a well-established risk factor for the onset of depression (Aanes, Mittlemark, & Hetland, 2010; Cacioppo, Hawkley, & Thisted, 2010).

People who are lonely are often socially anxious and often select social strategies that make intimacy difficult. For example, they are likely to verbally put themselves down and be passive in social interactions. They let others establish the direction and purpose of their joint activities (Langston & Cantor, 1989). The tendency to be self-deprecating is a sign of low self-esteem and chronic negative affect.

Chronically self-deprecating individuals make it difficult for others to enjoy their company. The gloom of negative affect makes it difficult to have a good time. Moreover, other people usually do not provide direct feedback regarding their negative reactions to hearing someone verbally berate himself. Since we're often unsure what will "set off" a person, it is safer to say nothing than provide potentially helpful feedback. Consequently, self-deprecators "turn off" other people, yet they do not know it, and thus they deprive themselves of information that would allow them to improve their social skills (Swann, Stein-Seroussi, & McNulty, 1992). This phenomenon is a special case of the more general one of individuals who are so unaware of their inadequacies that they see no need for improvement—an ironic case of being too ignorant to realize one is ignorant (Kruger & Dunning, 1999). Those who reveal their low self-esteem to others implicitly demonstrate that they cannot accept themselves—they have an identity problem.

These findings indirectly support Erikson's assumption that identity resolution relates to our ability to resolve the intimacy-isolation conflict. More direct tests of Erikson's claim, although few in number, also tend to be supportive. Orlofsky, Marcia, and Lesser (1973), for example, found that the more mature their male participants scored on a test of their identity status, the more mature they scored on a measure of intimacy. A similar positive correlation between identity and intimacy was found for women (and replicated for men) (Tesch & Whitbourne, 1982). Moreover, adolescents who were advanced on Marcia's (1980) classification system were also more likely to have formed intimate relationships (Dyk & Adams, 1990; Fitch & Adams, 1983).

Not everyone agrees with Erikson's hypothesis that intimacy follows identity. Some female psychologists view this sequence as male-centered. Carol Gilligan (1982), for example, argues that for women, "identity is defined in a context of relationship and is judged by a standard of responsibility and care" (p. 160). A woman, in other words, is more apt to define herself by her intimate relationship with a partner. Supporting Gilligan's analysis is the observations that men's self-esteem is associated with success in personal achievements whereas women's self-esteem depends to a greater extent on her connections and attachments to other people (Josephs, Markus, & Tafarodi, 1992). Thus identity and intimacy may not be as sequential for women as they are for men.

Consistent with Gilligan's views, romantically involved college women feel little conflict over intimacy and seem to have few, if any, problems balancing their identity-pursuits with their intimacy needs (Cantor, Acker, & Cook-Flanagan, 1992). Do these results also apply to men? Unfortunately we do not know because men were not included in this study. Obviously, additional research is needed.

Erikson postulates *love* as the ego strength that develops from a successful resolution of the intimacy versus isolation conflict. He defines love as the capacity for mutuality that transcends childhood dependency. *Mutuality*, his key term, refers to a voluntary interdependence of the lives of two individuals. Various meanings of love have attracted the attention of serious thinkers for thousands of years.

What Is Love?

The question of whether love is some single, unified process or is composed of distinctly different elements has been investigated by numerous researchers since the early 1970s (e.g., Berscheid & Hatfield, 1974; Hatfield, 1988; Hendrick & Hendrick, 1992; Rubin, 1970; Sternberg, 1986). Their research has focused on three basic questions: Are there different kinds of love? If so, what are they? How are they related?

I present two answers to these questions for your consideration. First, we look at the work of John Alan Lee. Lee (1973) describes, on the basis of extensive interviews of more than 4,000 adults, various "colors" of love that reflect different meanings and connotations to different people. Lee begins by identifying three "primary colors" of love:

Eros stresses the supreme importance of love in a person's life. Eros is based strongly on the physical attractiveness of one's partner and seeks early sexual relations with that partner.

Ludus (pronounced loo-dus) is the playful aspect of love. Ludic love is love practiced as a game or pastime. Ludic lovers may have more than one partner at any point in time and do not make deep emotional commitments to any of them. All ludic lovers, boys as well as girls, just want to have fun.

Storge (pronounced store-gay) is based on the love that grows out of friendship. Storgic lovers enjoy each other's company and share many interests and activities. The passionate element of love so crucial to erotic and ludic lovers is not that important to storgic lovers.

From these three "primary colors" of love, Lee identifies three "secondary colors" that represent combinations of two primary ones: *mania* is composed of eros and ludus, *pragma* combines ludus and storge, and *agape* is composed of eros and storge. Lee's major point is that creating a mutually fulfilling love relationship is "not a question of *how much* love the partner returns, but *which kind*" (1988, p. 53, italics in original).

Another answer to questions about the nature of love has been provided by Ellen Berscheid (2010). Based on her analysis of numerous empirical investigations of love and intimate relationships, Berscheid posits there are four basic kinds of love:

Romantic-passionate love is activated by desirable qualities (e.g., physical attraction, sense of humor, etc.) in the other person, sexual desire, and the belief that one is liked by the other. Romantic-passionate love is Lee's *eros*. Behaviors associated with this form of love include those that encourage the other to initiate sexual relations.

Companionate love is friendship love, strong liking, and Lee's *storge*. It arises from proximity, familiarity, and similarity—variables that facilitate friendship formation. The actions that are associated with companionate love include spending time together, engaging in activities involving similar interests, and expressing liking to each other.

Compassionate love includes altruistic love, Lee's *agape*, and community involvement. Behaviors found in this type of love vary depending on the nature of the needs of the other.

Attachment love is a strong affectionate bond with an attachment figure. Behaviors connected with attachment love are those that promote proximity, as Bowlby (1969/1982) initially noted.

Research on Lee's and Bersheid's prototype models of love has been hampered by the lack of precise measuring instruments that clearly discriminates one type of love from another. This area clearly needs precise and validated measures of love to provide the empirical basis for these interesting proposals about love's nature (Campbell & Fiske, 1959; Fehr, 2015).

"It was love at first Tweet!"

Childhood Correlates of Intimacy and Love

Erikson's theory of the psychosocial stages of development implies that the different types of adult love are related to different types of childhood attachment patterns. If we assume that securely attached children are likely to resolve favorably Erikson's first psychosocial crisis—basic trust versus basic mistrust—then data that show the expected connection between (1) quality of early attachment to parents and (2) quality of love in adulthood can be taken as support for Erikson's epigenetic approach.

For example, how would you describe your single most important love experience? From their responses to a newspaper "love quiz," adults were classified into one of three attachment styles: 56% of the respondents indicated it was relatively easy for them to get close to others, and they did not especially worry about being abandoned. They were classified as "secure." 25% indicated they felt uncomfortable getting close to others and found it difficult to trust them completely. They were classified as "avoidant." 19% perceived that other people are reluctant to get as emotionally close to them as they would like, and they worried that their partners did not really love them. They were classified as ambivalent (Hazan & Shaver, 1987).

In comparing these three groups on their answers to questions about their single most important love experience, these investigators found distinct differences: Secure lovers described their experience as happy, friendly, and trusting. They accepted their partner in spite of his or her faults. Avoidant lovers experienced a fear of intimacy, emotional ups-and-downs, and jealousy. Ambivalent lovers revealed that their relationship involved obsession, desire for reciprocity, and extreme sexual attraction and jealousy.

Moreover, the three love style groups were observed to differ in their self-reported attachment history in childhood: Secure lovers perceived their parents to have been caring and affectionate; they saw their mothers as respectful, confident, and accepting; and they remembered their fathers as having been loving and humorous. Avoidant lovers described their mothers as cold and rejecting; ambivalent lovers were especially likely to remember their fathers as being unfair.

This observation of a connection between attachment history and quality of present romantic relationships has been replicated by other investigators (Collins & Read, 1990; Simpson, 1990). Other well-replicated findings include (a) avoidantly attached adults tend not to believe in romantic love; and (b) ambivalently attached adults are not confident they can establish a successful romantic relationship, and they fear their behavior could be destructive (Mikulincer & Shaver, 2007).

Research has also found an association between attachment styles and Lee's six styles of love. Securely attached adults favored the *eros* and *agape* love styles—the styles that encourage lasting romantic bonds. Avoidantly attached adults preferred lower *eros* and higher *ludus* (game-playing) styles. Ambivalently attached adults were more likely to favor *mania* as their preferred style of love (Mikulincer & Shaver, 2007). Consistent with both Bowlby's attachment theory and Erikson's psychosocial theory, people who report a secure attachment history tend to show greater trust and commitment in their present romantic relationships than those whose attachment histories are insecure.

"They say free-range husbands are healthier but they tend to wander off!"

All of the above data are consistent with the views of both Bowlby and Erikson. But we need to note that these data do not constitute definitive proof for either theoretical position, because of their methodological limitations: The observations depend on the adult participant's *memory* of his or her childhood relationship with the parents. Retrospective studies such as these can yield observations that are at best consistent with theoretical expectations, but the observations do not conclusively prove the theory's usefulness. The general principle is straightforward: In retrospective studies, selective memory and other variables—unmeasured and uncontrolled—might account for the observed correlations. Consequently, we cannot assume such observations are compelling evidence in support of any particular hypothesis. But at the very least these data are in line with theoretical expectations.

Out of their love for each other, then, young adult partners typically produce one or more children. This directly leads to Erikson's seventh psychosocial stage of development, adulthood.

Adulthood: Generativity Versus Stagnation

Adulthood, according to Erikson (1982), is the time when the crisis of *generativity versus self-absorption and stagnation* makes its appearance in our lives. "Generativity . . . encompasses *procreativity, productivity,* and *creativity,* and thus the generation of new beings as well as of new products and new ideas, including a kind of self-generation concerned with further identity development" (Erikson, 1982, p. 67, italics in original).

We find new dimensions to our personalities by caring for others, whether we narrowly define others as members of our immediate family or broadly embrace the family of mankind, including the earth with its flora and fauna, its mountains, oceans, and deserts. Failure to care about the next generation leads to increasing stagnation and self-involvement that can result in the ego core pathology of ***rejectivity:*** a chronic unwillingness to include other people in one's generative concerns. This pathology may be shown by being compulsively self-preoccupied within one's narrow world of work and hobbies and/or obsessively concerned with one's public image. Feeling they had not been cared for in childhood by the key adults in their lives, these individuals are unwilling as adults to bestow care on others.

Adulthood, Erikson points out, is the time of life linking the present to the future generation. The new ego strength arising from the generative versus stagnation crisis is *care*—a widening commitment to help and sustain those persons, products, and ideas that are important to us. Erikson (1982) notes that all the ego strengths from earlier crises are needed for the intergenerational task of cultivating strength in the next generation of young people by teaching, guiding, and nurturing them. Active generative concerns often first surface when young adults begin raising their own children (Peterson & Stewart, 1993).

Abundant research supports Erikson's views on the significance of this stage. Parents who score high on generativity favor an authoritative, child-centered parenting style (Peterson, Smirles, & Wentworth, 1997). Generative adults are more politically involved and actively work for social change (Cole & Stewart, 1996). Generativity is consistently associated with various measures of mental health: Generative adults are more likely to show high levels of life satisfaction, happiness, and self-esteem (McAdams, Hart, & Maruna, 1998).

A major reason for the welcome emergence of research on generativity over the past 25 years is the availability of the Loyola Generativity Scale (LGS) to measure it (McAdams & de St. Aubin, 1992). The LGS consists of 20 statements that respondents evaluate on a 4-point scale, from 0 (the statement never applies to you) to 3 (the statement applies to you very often).

Scores on the LGS range between 0 and 60. Three representative items of the LGS are

1. *I try to pass along the knowledge I have gained through my experience.*

2. *If I were unable to have children, I would like to adopt children.*

3. *I feel as though my contributions will exist after I die.*

One longitudinal investigation of midlife generativity in women showed that a generative concern at age 43 was associated with greater investment and concern for intergenerational roles (daughter and mother) 10 years later (Peterson, 2002). Another found that generativity scores of women at age 52 correlated positively with three of the "Big Five" personality traits 10 years later: higher scores on extraversion, agreeableness, and openness to experience were related to higher scores on generativity. Higher scores on generativity are also associated with lower scores on neuroticism. Moreover, the higher the scores on generativity, the greater is one's satisfaction with life 10 years later (Peterson & Duncan, 2007).

As Erikson predicted, young men's generative concern significantly increased over the decade from their mid-20s to their mid-30s. Corresponding scores of women did not change, however, since women showed as much generative concern in their mid-20s as did men in their mid-30s (Einolf, 2014).

Finally, the results of three more investigations support Erikson's epigenetic approach:

- A 22-year sequential study tested individuals ranging in age from 20 to 42 years. As subjects aged, there was increased resolution for the first seven psychosocial crises (Whitbourne et al., 1992).
- Young adults who are more skilled at self-regulation scored higher on generativity concerns; higher generativity concerns, in turn, were associated with increased sense of the purpose of life (Busch & Hofer, 2012).
- The positive association between generativity and experiencing a meaningful life was replicated in a study of elderly adults across four cultures (Hofer et al., 2014).

Numerous positive associations between generativity and social responsibility, active involvement with civic, political, and/or religious groups, and breadth of friendship connections have been found (McAdams, 2006). Generativity is a crucial stage in the development of personality.

Humanistic/Narrative Approaches to Identity and Self Esteem

The Person-Centered Approach of Carl Rogers

The goal the individual most wishes to achieve, the end which he knowingly and unknowingly pursues, is to become himself.

—Carl Rogers (1961, p. 108)

Have you ever said to someone, or even thought to yourself, "I'm not myself today"? We seem to understand intuitively what phrases such as "wanting to become myself," "trying to find myself," or "I'm not myself" mean. Still, don't you find something odd about these common expressions? When I say, "I'm not myself," am I really saying that an aspect of myself that "I" don't want to identify as "me" has made an unwanted appearance? Such curious phrases raise the question of how "I" and "me" got to be such strangers in the first place.

Self-Alienation

There are two general answers to how self-alienation develops:

1. From a historical perspective, the "self" seems to have first become a social problem in the early days of the 20th century. Only within the past 100 years or so has there been widespread cultural understanding that the "self" is an elusive, hidden, inner quality that is not identical to one's public actions (Baumeister, 1987).

2. From the psychological perspective, Carl Rogers (1951, 1961) traces the development of individual self-alienation to the conditions of early childhood socialization. Our

self-concept develops from initial interactions with significant people in our lives. When our parents praised us for being "good" and blamed us when we were "bad," we internalized these experiences into our earliest sense of ourselves. Furthermore, pleasing powerful caretakers takes clear precedence over expressing our authentic but contrary feelings and perceptions that might anger them. As a consequence, Rogers notes, infants easily learn to exclude all threatening self-perceptions. These are threats caused by discrepancies between what they really feel (such as anger) and what their parents want them to feel (happily compliant).

Is self-alienation inevitable? No. Rogers (1951) believes parents who (a) accept their child's wants and feelings can (b) accept their own feelings about the child's undesirable behaviors and they can communicate to the child their *acceptance of him or her as a person* (as distinguished from their repudiation of his or her unacceptable behaviors). This vital distinction enables their child to develop healthy self-esteem as an integral part of his or her undivided self-concept.

The acceptance of a person irrespective of how he or she behaves is called **unconditional positive regard**. Accepting a *person* need not imply a blanket approval of that person's *actions*. A father can tell his child, "I love you but what you did is wrong," and still provide unconditional positive regard. From repeated experiences of receiving unconditional positive regard from his or her parents, a child learns to feel the same way toward himself or herself, which Rogers calls **positive self-regard**. Positive self-regard is Rogers's term for positive self-esteem.

In sharp contrast, when a child's self-concept and self-esteem depend almost entirely on always acting the right way, the child learns to seek approval from adults for "being good" and avoid disapproval by not "being bad." When this occurs, the child has internalized **conditions of worth:** the value that other people (and ultimately the child) place on specific actions. Conditions of worth develop as children feel they have value in the eyes of significant adults *only* if they behave the way adults want them to. In other words, conditions of worth develop out of children's experiences of **conditional positive regard** (Rogers, 1959).

© Corbis

Photo 5.1   Carl Rogers (1902–1987)

Carl Rogers initiated a sea change in thinking about personality. He showed that we are not passive victims of either our biological urges or our prior reinforcement history. Rather, we are active agents seeking to enhance our lives by means of self-actualization.

Key publications:

Client-Centered Therapy (1951)
On Becoming a Person (1961)

So what's the problem? Aren't most children raised this way? Yes, answers Rogers, and that's precisely why self-alienation is so widespread. Rogers holds that conditions of worth and conditional positive regard split a person between her true self and the mask she wears to get the approval of others

To Rogers (1959), there is one fundamental human motive—the ***actualizing tendency***—which is "the inherent tendency of the organism to develop all its capacities in ways which serve to maintain or enhance the organism" (p. 196). As a result of this actualizing tendency, infants engage in the ***organismic valuing process***. This is their use of the actualizing tendency to decide how to evaluate each experience: Is it good or bad?

Rogers maintains that whatever the infant perceives is the infant's reality. By trusting our own experiences, Rogers believes that we would naturally do what's right for our own growth. Typically, however, parents impose their values on the child, restricting him or her from those actualizing experiences they judge to be unsafe, socially unacceptable, unprofitable, or morally wrong. If parents communicate they will not love the child if he or she persists in these unacceptable behaviors, the child faces a conflict between two powerful realities: the internal actualizing tendency and external conditions of worth. Because all children have a strong need for ***positive regard*** (that is, to be loved), they solve the conflict by accepting the conditions of worth and denying their organismic valuing tendency. The child, at some level of awareness, learns: "Other people know better than I do what's good for me." The seeds of self-alienation are planted early and deep.

Self-Concept and Self-Esteem

Rogers uses the terms ***self*** and ***self-concept*** synonymously.[1] He distinguishes how we actually see ourselves (actual self-concept) from how we would like to see ourselves (ideal self-concept). Rogers notes that if our actual self-concept matches or is congruent with our ideal self-concept, then we are likely to have a healthy level of self-esteem and be on the path of self-actualization. But if our actual self-concept is incongruent with our ideal self-concept, then we are likely to feel anxious, experience low self-esteem, and/or feel self-alienated. Rogers (1954) reported that in one case, a particular client's self-ratings of her actual and ideal self correlated more highly after a year of therapy than at the beginning of therapy. This indicates that her perceived self matches more with her ideal self, and she is less self-alienated. Her ideal self-concept became more realistic. Similar increased agreements between the actual self and the ideal self from pre- to post-therapy were found within a group of 25 clients (Butler & Haigh, 1954). Rogers interprets these data as indications of positive mental health.[2]

Self-concept and self-esteem are related. People who are certain of their positive self-attributes, attributes they deem important, have higher self-esteem than those who are uncertain of their own attributes (Pelham & Swann, 1989). Okay, but what is the real value of having high self-esteem? Studies show that high self-esteem helps us to persist after an initial failure. Self-esteem seems to act as a buffer against premature discouragement. Like *The Little Engine That Could*, we keep trying (Baumeister et al., 2003).

A strong sense of identity encourages a person to feel in control of his or her future outcomes ("I know what I want and I know I have the skills to get it"). Thus identity promotes feeling self-confident and good about oneself. Conversely, people with low self-esteem tend to hold less clearly defined self-concepts (and are less certain about their own attributes) than people with high self-esteem. Those who do not like themselves very much apparently prefer to live with a certain degree of mental fuzziness about who they are and they thereby remain uncertain about their feared personal inadequacies (Baumgardner, 1990; Campbell, 1990).

The Narrative Approach of Dan McAdams

Narrative identity is the internalized and changing story of your life that you begin to work on in the emerging adult years.

—Dan McAdams (2006, pp. 83–84)

Dan McAdams (1993) proposes a theory of personal identity that centers on the proposition that each individual "comes to know who he or she is by creating a heroic story of the self" (p. 11). In other words, you create your own identity by constructing a story, a narrative, that integrates your past experiences, your present situation, and your hopes and plans for the future into a coherent, meaningful whole (McAdams, 2006).

We begin to fashion the material for our personal narrative identity from our earliest childhood experiences. McAdams agrees with Erikson that infants develop unconscious attitudes of hope or despair out of their earliest experiences of love and trust with their caregivers. In McAdams's theory, our earliest attachment relationships affect our *narrative tone*. On the one hand, securely attached children are more likely to create narrative identities that are essentially optimistic and hopeful about the future; insecurely attached children, on the other hand, are more likely to adopt identities that are pessimistic and doubtful about the future (McAdams, 1993).

McAdams hypothesizes that those unconscious *images* that pervade an adult's identity are based on preschool experiences. These images are a synthesis of our early experiences within the family, with our childhood friends and relatives, and from exposure to portrayals in movies, television, the Internet, and other media. In his view, narrative tone and imagery are the essential contributions of early childhood to adult identity.

Narrative identity is the key concept in the narrative study of lives. Narrative identity is the individual's "internalized, evolving, and integrative story of the self" (McAdams, 2008, p. 242). The stories we create reflect our attempt to weave a coherent account of who we once were, who we are now, and who we could become within our relationships to our family, friends, and the wider community. In accord with Erikson's psychosocial approach to personality development, McAdams maintains "the self comes to terms with society through narrative identity" (McAdams, 2008, p. 243).

Our life-story themes are related to our personality dispositions. Individuals who score high on the trait of neuroticism tend to tell stories with more negative emotion, less positive emotion, and less growth. People who score high on openness to experience tend to tell stories that are highly coherent (McAdams & Manczac, 2015). Studying personality via the life narrative approach may be organized around six common principles (McAdams, 2008):

1. *The Self Is Storied*: Human beings are natural story tellers. When we talk about our lives to others, we do so via stories. ("Guess who I met today!")

2. *Stories Integrate Lives*: Stories connect disparate elements of our lives into satisfying integrated and coherent narratives.

3. *Stories Are Told in Social Relationships*: We narrate the events in our lives differently to different audiences. We take account of characteristics of our audience and tailor our stories accordingly (e.g., telling the same event to a child versus an adult).

4. *Stories Change Over Time*: Since our lives are not stagnant, neither are our narrative identities. Personality development, new experiences, and unavoidable lapses in memory all contribute to changes to our narrative identities.

5. *Stories Are Cultural Texts*: Stories reflect the culture in which we developed. For example, memories of North Americans are usually more self-focused than memories of people from East Asia, which center around social interactions (Wang, 2001; Wang & Conway, 2004).

6. *Some Stories Are Better Than Others*: Narrative psychologists investigate the characteristics that create a good life story and how these features are associated with maturity and psychological health (e.g., Bauer, McAdams, & Sakaeda, 2005; King, 2001). Moreover, some psychotherapists see the therapeutic process as one of life story revision and repair. Narrative therapists help individuals transform their damaged and disorganized life stories into new ones that promote coherence, growth, and health (Angus & McLoud, 2004; Singer, 2005).

The research program of McAdams and his colleagues focuses on Erikson's seventh stage of development, generativity versus stagnation. Generativity in adulthood is often found in those adults whose life narratives are characterized by *redemption*. These adults, in one way or another, work to promote the welfare of future generations. The discovery that generative adults share similar narrative identities was made within one of the few research programs that combine idiographic and nomothetic approaches to investigations of personality (McAdams, 2006).

Single-Variable Research Programs

This final section of the chapter presents five research programs that emphasize single important aspects of identity and self-esteem. These variables are self-discrepancy, self-verification, identity fusion, the sociometer, and self-efficacy. These research programs are notable because they make major contributions to our understanding of identity and self-esteem. We begin with the research program of E. Tory Higgins and *self-discrepancy*.

Self-Discrepancy Theory

E. Tory Higgins (1987) wants to understand the psychological significance of discrepancies between various aspects of our mental self-representations. The essence of his *self-discrepancy theory* is that in addition to your *actual* self-concept and your *ideal* self-concept, you also possess an *ought* self-concept: Your beliefs about your present duties, responsibilities, and obligations.

Self-discrepancy theory predicts and finds that different sorts of discrepancies are associated with different emotional states:

1. The discrepancy between how we perceive our *actual* self versus our *ideal* self (we are not the person we would *like* to be) causes us to feel one or more of the *dejection-related* emotions: We feel disappointed, ashamed, or sad. If we fail to make the honor roll, cheerleading squad, or chess team, when the hopes and dreams of our ideal self are tied to such outcomes, we will probably feel depressed.

2. Any discrepancy between perceptions our *actual* self versus our *ought* self (i.e., we are not the person we think we *should* be) will cause us to feel anxious, guilty, or fearful of receiving punishment. If we don't attend class, don't do our assignments, and don't study, we might feel anxious about such dire outcomes as failing the course, flunking out of school, and needing to choose another career.

Self-discrepancy theory also includes your *can* self, which refers to beliefs about your potential, and your *future* self, which refers to beliefs about the type of person you are likely to become. Participants' actual, ideal, ought, can, and future selves are measured, and discrepancies, if any, are noted. Research finds that the most depressed and dejected people are those whose can or future self is the same as their ideal self, *but* their actual self chronically falls short of their ideal. In other words, when we are not the person we would like to be, yet we still feel we could be that sort of person, we feel especially sad (Higgins, Tykocinski, & Vookles, 1990).

Self-discrepancy theory has been successfully applied to increase our understanding of eating disorders such as *bulimia* (binge-and-purge eating) and *anorexia nervosa* (compulsive, unhealthy dieting). Because people suffering from bulimia have been found to be chronically depressed (e.g., Lee, Rush, & Mitchell, 1985), self-discrepancy theory predicts that these individuals will show a discrepancy between their *actual* and *ideal* self-concepts. Moreover, because people suffering from anorexia have been observed to be anxious, prone to feeling guilty, and conscientious in meeting the demands of others (e.g., Bruch, 1973), self-discrepancy theory predicts that these people will reveal a discrepancy between their *actual* and *ought* self-concepts. Support has been found for both hypotheses. People suffering from bulimia are likely to feel depressed that they are not who they would like to be, whereas those suffering from anorexia are likely to feel anxious that they are not the person they think they ought to be (Strauman et al., 1991).

Since anxiety and depression usually correlate with each other (*comorbidity*), it is challenging to hypothesize differential results due to the specific type of self-discrepancy. The comorbidity of anxiety and depression might explain the inconsistent support that self-discrepancy theory has received across eight separate investigations (Watson, Bryan, & Thrash, 2014).

Although the relative magnitudes of the two self-discrepancies are stable over a 3-year period (Strauman, 1996), it is frequently found that *both* kinds of self-discrepancies are associated with *both* anxiety and depression. Larger self-discrepancies are associated with greater social anxiety, greater negative affect (e.g., irritability and fearfulness), and decreased positive affect, such as pride and interest (Hardin et al., 2007; Watson, Bryan, & Thrash, 2014).

The above findings are consistent with the view of Carl Rogers (1959) that positive therapeutic changes in self-esteem are due to a reduction of the client's discrepancy between the real self and the ideal self. The more specific hypotheses of self-discrepancy theory offer a promising approach to understanding the conditions under which particular sorts of discrepancies within the self result in predictable sorts of emotional experiences (anxiety or depression). Persuasive support for self-discrepancy theory awaits improved measures of ideal, ought, and actual selves as well as new measures of anxiety and depression characterized by greater discriminatory precision (Campbell & Fiske, 1959).

Self-Verification Theory

William Swann's (1987) *self-verification theory* assumes we all prefer to receive feedback from others that confirms or verifies our view of ourselves. Feedback from you that supports my self-concept allows me to predict the course of future social interactions with you and others. If I think of myself as socially adept and charming, I hope you'll agree with my self-assessment. But if I learn that you really think I am an insensitive oaf, I am likely to have two reactions: My feelings will be hurt and I will become uncertain about this aspect of my self-concept.

Whenever we receive social disconfirmation about a *positive* (and valued) self-attribute, these two reactions are likely. But how would you react if you received disconfirmation concerning a *negative* self-attribute? Suppose you think of yourself as a poor dancer. Then, after dancing with a new partner, you are told you are a *marvelous* dancer. What would you think? Will you instantly revise your self-concept and adopt the nickname "Twinkletoes"? Or might you wonder if your dance partner had too much to drink and so there is no need to modify your unflattering (but accurate) choreographic self-concept?

Self-verification theory assumes, as did Prescott Lecky's (1945) self-consistency theory, that our need for information verifying or supporting the correctness of our self-concepts can sometimes override *self-enhancement*, our wish to obtain favorable information about ourselves from others. Yes, we feel good when others compliment us. But do we feel good when we doubt the compliment is true? No, of course not.

Self-verification theory predicts that when our self-concept is unambiguously negative about a certain attribute, we prefer that other people confirm this view rather than flatter (and confuse) us with false information. Much research supports this hypothesis. Married people with negative self-concepts are more committed to those spouses who think *poorly* of them than to spouses who disconfirm their negative self-concepts by thinking highly of them (Swann, De La Ronde, & Hixon, 1994; Swann, Hixon, & De La Ronde, 1992).

Self-verification theory has been successfully applied to social identity. Your social identity consists of those aspects of yourself that connect you to a social group, such as your ethnic group, religion, political ideology, sports team, and so on. Your social identity is as real and important as other aspects of your identity (Turner & Onorato, 1999). Will your desire for self-verification appear when your social identity is made salient?

Studies of gender identity reveal that participants prefer to interact with someone who verifies a negative aspect of group identity (e.g., women can be melodramatic) to someone who does not (Chen, Chen, & Shaw, 2004). Similarly, group members who verify one another's self-views create greater group cohesion than when members fail to verify one another's self-concepts (Swann, Milton, & Polzer, 2000). Moreover, people prefer to interact with those who verify their ingroup identities more than with those who flatter them (Gomez et al., 2009).

Some people identify so strongly with their collective identity that it becomes equivalent to their personal identity. Insulting their social group is as painful for such individuals as insulting them personally. These individuals are considered to be in a state of **identity fusion**. Individuals who express a willingness to sacrifice their own lives for the sake of their group have fused their collective identity with their personal identity. Their strong emotional attachment to their social group overrides their instinct for self-preservation. How do individuals who exhibit identity fusion differ from those who do not?

Identity Fusion Theory

Identity fusion theory is an extension of self-discrepancy theory. William Swann and his colleagues hypothesize that when an individual has fused the personal and social identities, these identities become functionally equivalent. This means that a challenge to either personal or social identity will motivate increased willingness to engage in extreme behavior (e.g., fighting and dying) for his group. Such extreme behavior will not be found among those individuals who do not show identity fusion. Not only did the results of three experiments strongly support this hypothesis (Swann et al., 2009), it has been replicated 13 times across three ensuing investigations (Swann et al., 2014; Swann, Gomez, Dovidio, et al., 2010; Swann, Gomez, Huici, et al., 2010).

Identity fusion theory is based on four principles (Swann & Buhrmester, 2015):

1. *The Self as Agent Principle.* We experience ourselves as *agents* whenever we feel we are in control of our actions and, by our actions, we control events in the world (Haggard & Tsakiris, 2009). Wanting to buy something and then purchasing that item is an everyday example of acting as an agent. Identity fusion theory predicts and finds that increases in a highly fused person's sense of agency (engaging in physical activity, for example) intensifies pro-group behavior (Swann, Gomez, Huici, et al., 2010).

2. *The Identity Synergy Principle.* A challenge (e.g., disrespect, insult) to a highly fused individual's personal or social identity will result in increased pro-group behavior. Data supporting this principle has been reported by Swann et al. (2009) and has been replicated at least 13 times, as mentioned above.

3. *The Relational Ties Principle.* Highly fused individuals will be more inclined to sacrifice their lives for fellow group members than will less-fused individuals. Research supporting this principle has been cited above. Moreover, even if they are ostracized from their group, highly fused individuals nevertheless showed increased endorsement of extreme behavior in support of that group, which was not true for those whose identities were not fused (Gomez et al., 2011).

4. *Irrevocability Principle.* Once a person has fused his personal identity with his social identity, he or she will always have a fused identity with that social group. Research into the stability of identities over periods of 1 to 18 months found that the test-retest correlation for highly fused individuals was significantly higher (r = .60) than the test-retest correlation (r = .28) for those whose identities are not fused (Swann, Jetten, et al., 2012).

Of these four principles, the weakest empirical support to date is for the Irrevocability Principle. A test-retest correlation of .60 indicates that the identities of a substantial number of individuals did *not* remain fused to their social group.

Identity fusion can result in good or bad social outcomes. Being the target of an identity-fused suicide bomber is obviously a terrible outcome for his victims and their families. Positive benefits of identity fusion can be seen in such pro-social actions as risking one's life to save others during a disaster or caring enough about one's community to volunteer time and money for its welfare. For example, those Americans who were strongly fused with their country were especially likely to provide support to the victims of the bombing attack at the Boston Marathon on April 15, 2013 (Buhrmester et al., 2015). Identity fusion can also be beneficial to an individual in that a strong bond with a social group can fulfill belongingness needs and help to provide a meaningful, satisfying life (Jetten, Haslam, & Haslam, 2011).

Our motives for self-esteem and self-enhancement may be satisfied by identity fusion. But, self-enhancement, please note, can be a two-edged sword: On the one hand, it can be beneficial to remind ourselves of our strengths whenever our self-esteem has taken a temporary "hit." On the other hand, self-enhancement can also artificially enlarge an already inflated ego to the point where anyone who does not enthusiastically confirm such egotistical delusions risks a hostile, even violent reaction (Baumeister, Smart, & Boden, 1996). This ambivalent connection between self-enhancement and self-esteem is explained by *sociometer theory* proposed by Mark Leary and his colleagues (Leary & Baumeister, 2000; MacDonald & Leary, 2012).

Sociometer Theory

Sociometer theory accepts one of evolutionary psychology's key assumptions: The human mind consists of distinct, dedicated brain circuits, called *modules*, which were naturally selected because they aided human survival and/or reproduction. These modules are hard-wired at birth. Each module is dedicated to one specific domain relevant to survival and/or reproduction (Kurzban, 2010; Tooby & Cosmides, 2005).

Consider the facial recognition module. Almost all humans have the ability to know instantly if a person they see is familiar or unfamiliar. We do not need to take Face Recognition 101 to develop this skill. Nor do we need to exert conscious energy to use it. As soon as we see a human face, we automatically and instantly classify it into one of two categories: familiar or unfamiliar. That is how all modules function—they work automatically and without conscious effort.

Even so, the facial recognition module is not 100% accurate. We may be fooled by a stranger who looks like someone we know or we may be unable to recognize a familiar face, even our own. This is a medical condition called *prosopagnosia*, described vividly by Oliver Sacks in *The Man Who Mistook His Wife for a Hat*. Nevertheless, like other biological systems, the facial recognition module works reasonably well most of the time. Accumulated evidence from many disciplines (e.g., psychology, neuroscience, genetics, primatology) strongly suggests that face recognition is an adaptation (Ploeger & van der Hoort, 2015). Our survival might depend on our ability to distinguish quickly between a familiar friend and a dangerous stranger.

At the neurological level, there are a number of different methods used to detect modules in brain networks (Sporns & Betzel, 2016). The ongoing research challenge is to connect these neurological modules with those postulated by evolutionary psychologists, such as modules for (a) detecting cheaters, (b) identifying potential mates, (c) detecting threats to mate-poaching, and (d) ostracizing those group members who might be carrying a contagious disease (Buss & Penke, 2015). Sociometry theory assumes that (1) human social life is essential for survival, (2) all individuals need at least minimal acceptance by other people, and (3) humans possess a hard-wired brain circuit—*the sociometer*—that screens and monitors our social environment for cues relevant to our *relational value* in the eyes of people who matter to us. *Social acceptance* and *social rejection* are the end points on a scale of relational value (Leary & Guadagno, 2011).

Sociometer theory further assumes that whenever we detect and experience social acceptance and social rejection, we feel good or bad about ourselves. These self-relevant feelings—our self-esteem—are an important part of this modular system. All modular systems are activated only by those specific stimuli that are relevant to that module. The modular system of vision, for example, is activated by light waves but not by odors (Fodor, 1983; Pinker, 1997). Since we evolved to function within a social group, a modular sociometer expects individuals to be sensitive to subtle cues to changes in their social value.

Data supporting the sociometer hypothesis were obtained in a study of overweight women. The experimenter, a woman of normal weight, wore either (a) a t-shirt that depicted relatively heavy women holding hands with the statement "everyBODY is beautiful" or (b) a plain white t-shirt. One week later, the women who saw the "everyBODY is beautiful" t-shirt had significantly higher self-esteem than the women who saw the plain white t-shirt, but *only* when the second testing was done by the *same* experimenter (who wore a plain t-shirt on second testing). As expected by sociometer theory, self-esteem is sensitive to signals of being valued by others and is relationship specific. Women who were exposed to the "everyBODY" t-shirt on week one but were tested by a different experimenter on week two did not show an increase in self-esteem (Weisbuch et al., 2009).

Do you think your self-esteem would change if you spent a year in a foreign country? Changes in the self-esteem of over 800 German high school students who participated in a year-long international exchange program were related to the students' feelings of social inclusion by the host country. As predicted by sociometer theory, there was a significant positive increase in a student's self-esteem when he or she felt socially included by the host country. These positive changes in self-esteem were especially pronounced among those students whose intial self-esteem was low (Hutteman et al., 2015).

Finally, sociometer theory directly applies to those situations where a person, based perhaps on inadequate parenting in childhood, sets his or her sociometer too low. A "too-low" setting means that the individual detects less social support and approval than what is true in reality and consequently experiences low self-esteem. A person whose self-esteem is chronically low (i.e., low trait self-esteem) is likely to react to ambiguous evaluations as if they were negative (Koch, 2002). This is doubly unfortunate because individuals who feel they have less value to others may act on this erroneous assumption by withdrawing from the relationship or by becoming angry. In either case, the other person may want to end the relationship. Moreover, those individuals who suppress expressing their emotional reactions in social situations are viewed by others as socially avoidant. Consequently, other people do not want to affiliate with them. A "too low" sociometer setting can result in an unintentional self-fulfilling prophecy (DeHart, Pelham, & Murray, 2004; Leary & Toner, 2015; Tackman & Srivastava, 2015).

At the other extreme, an individual may set his sociometer too high. While the illusion that he is more popular, better liked, held in higher esteem than is factually true contributes to his feeling good about himself in the short run (Taylor & Brown, 1988), the long-run consequences can be disastrous. Individuals who act conceited, snobbish, or "stuck up" are disliked or may be socially rejected. They may react aggressively when confronted with the feedback that they are not as superior and talented as they think they are (Baumeister, Smart, & Boden, 1996). When high self-esteem reaches narcissistic levels, there is the potential for violence should the feedback be interpreted as an "insult" (Bushman & Baumeister, 1998). Moreover, when a person's narcissism becomes seriously problematic for *other* individuals in that person's life, there are grounds for a diagnosis of Narcissistic Personality Disorder (see Chapter 8). There *is* such a thing as *too much* self-esteem.

Self-Efficacy Theory

> There is a growing body of evidence that human attainments and positive well-being require an optimistic sense of personal efficacy.
>
> —Albert Bandura (1989, p. 1176)

Bandura's concept of self-efficacy refers to our expectation that we have the capability to enact the behaviors needed to reach our goals. Self-efficacy is our *belief* that we have the behavioral skills needed for success in a particular situation. Simply *possessing the skill* to give an entertaining public speech is not sufficient to do so. We need to *believe* we have the skill. Our efficacy beliefs vary for different tasks. High self-efficacy refers to my strong belief that I can execute a particular behavior (e.g., write and send an email); low self-efficacy refers to my belief that I cannot perform the behavior (e.g., remove a virus from my computer).

Bandura (1989, 1997) focuses his attention on the individual as a causal *agent* in bringing about (or failing to bring about) desired outcomes. As we saw in Chapter 1, Bandura draws an important distinction between *efficacy* expectations and *outcome* expectations. Let's say Jack wants to go on a date with Jill. Jack's *positive outcome expectation* is his knowledge that a specific action (asking her out) might bring about the outcome he desires (she might say "Yes"). But, alas, Jack is too shy and cannot bring himself to perform the required behavior. His efficacy expectation is too low for him to ask Jill. As a consequence, they never date. Efficacy and outcome expectations are not the same.

These two types of expectations might differ in the other direction as well. I could hold a *negative outcome expectancy* (the behavior will *not* produce the desired result) and at the same time have high self-efficacy (I know I can execute the behavior). For example, I know I can explain the many fascinating strategies of baseball to my wife, but my outcome expectation (based on past experience) is that she will continue to politely try to suppress her yawning reflex. Again, efficacy and outcome expectations are not the same.

Where does self-efficacy come from? Bandura (1986) identifies four sources of our expectations in our behavioral competence:

- *Successes and failures associated with our own past performance:* Prior successes lead to self-efficacy; past failures lead to the absence of self-efficacy in similar situations. *Mastery experiences*, in which we try and succeed at accomplishing our goals, are usually the most important factors in determining self-efficacy.
- *Inferences based on observing the effects of others' actions:* Observing others learn to succeed by executing the necessary behavior can lead us to believe that we also can learn to do these behaviors.
- *Encouragement and persuasive efforts by others:* Exhortations such as "You can do it!" most effectively change another person's self-efficacy when they are combined with precise information about *how to execute* the behavior. Persuasion by itself is usually ineffective (and often annoying).
- *Reinterpreting the meaning of physiological arousal:* We may interpret feeling anxious while doing a new behavior as a signal that we are not very good at this task, which can decrease self-efficacy; task failure therefore becomes more likely. But if we reinterpret the symptoms of anxiety as excitement, or we learn that "everyone in this situation feels butterflies," the experience of physiological arousal is less likely to instigate those intrusive negative thoughts (e.g., "I'm just no good at doing this.") that interfere with the behavior's execution.

Consider this example of practical research generated by Bandura's self-efficacy theory: The goal of this study was to increase women's empowerment over the threat of physical violence (Ozer & Bandura, 1990). Forty-three women, ranging in age from 18 to 55 years (average = 34), enrolled in a self-defense program. These women received training in a mastery model program from a female instructor who taught them how to ward off attacks by men. Detailed instructions and practice with simulated attacks were provided in 5 weekly sessions, for a total time of about 23 hours. Six months after the training sessions ended, 35 women completed various measures of self-efficacy.

The researchers found that the mastery modeling program enhanced numerous dimensions of self-efficacy relevant to self-defense. The women perceived they could cope better with an attack. They were better able to control intrusive negative thoughts of failure. They also felt less vulnerable to physical assault and engaged in more public activities that they previously avoided out of fear of attack. The authors conclude, "The results of this study indicate that empowering people with the means to exercise control over social threats to their personal safety serves both to protect and liberate them" (Ozer & Bandura, 1990, p. 485). These positive results were replicated in another self-defense program: Many women felt more confident when in potentially dangerous situations, they were more comfortable when interacting with strangers, and experienced more positive feelings about their bodies (Hollander, 2004).

Bandura (1989, 1997) summarizes much of the growing literature on the relationship of self-efficacy to other personality variables. For example, people with high self-efficacy *persist longer* at a task in the face of obstacles, are more inclined to *anticipate successful future outcomes*, are better able to *"turn off" negative thoughts* associated with potential failure, and are more likely to *enter risky situations* in which they might fail even though they feel just as anxious as their low self-efficacy counterparts. These characteristics are also associated with high self-esteem.

With regard to beginning and continuing with a physical exercise program, self-efficacy "has represented the strongest, most consistent psychological correlate of physical activity behavior" (Higgins et al., 2014, p. 891). Self-efficacy predicts adherence by coronary heart patients to an exercise program (D'Angelo et al., 2014) as well as sobriety for (former) substance abusers (Kelly & Greene, 2014).

It is clear that self-efficacy is an important way to conceptualize identity and self-esteem. Indeed, self-efficacy seems to bridge these two concepts. By conceiving ourselves as self-efficacious in those areas of life that we value, we thereby feel in control of our fate, at least to some extent. We thereby identify ourselves as competent. This makes us feel good about ourselves. Increasing our self-efficacy changes both our identity and our self-esteem.

❖

QUESTIONS TO PONDER

1. Have you ever been asked, verbally or in writing, to answer the question, "Who are you?" Do you like or dislike to answer this question? Why? Have you ever thought of answering "Who wants to know?"

2. If William James is correct that your self-esteem is a ratio of your actual successes to your "pretensions" about yourself, what are the two ways you can increase your

self-esteem? Is it easier to increase the numerator or to decrease the denominator? Is it possible to identify your pretensions *before* they adversely affect your self-esteem? Where did your pretensions come from?

3. In the Declaration of Independence of the United States of America, all individuals are presumed to have the inalienable right to life, liberty, and the pursuit of happiness. Is the pursuit of happiness the same as the pursuit of self-esteem? If not, how do they differ? Would U.S. history be any different if Thomas Jefferson had written that all people have the inalienable right to high self-esteem?

NOTES

1. As mentioned in Chapter 1, Rogers is by no means the only personality theorist to obfuscate the issue by writing as if who we *are* (our self) is identical to our *concept* of who we are. See Westen (1991) on the need to distinguish clearly between the concept of "self" and the "self-concept."

2. It is important to note that the "self-ideal discrepancy" measure used by Rogers and his colleagues is now known to be seriously flawed and is no longer used by sophisticated investigators. A discussion of these flaws takes us beyond the scope of this text. The interested reader is referred to Cronbach and Furby (1970) and Wylie (1974, 1979).

SUGGESTIONS FOR FURTHER READING

Erikson, E. (1968). *Identity: Youth and crisis.* New York, NY: Norton.
Hoover, K. (1996). *The power of identity.* Chatham, NJ: Chatham House.
Maalouf, A. (1996). *In the name of identity: Violence and the need to belong.* New York, NY: Arcade Publishing.
Sen, A. (2006). *Identity and violence: The illusion of destiny.* New York, NY: Norton.

INTERNET RESOURCES

1. For information about confidence and well-being, see http://www.centreforconfidence.co.uk/.

2. To take the Rosenberg Self-Esteem scale, go to http://personality-testing.info/tests/RSE.php.

3. To take a brief test of identity and the identity crisis, go to https://www.psychologytoday.com/blog/fulfillment-any-age/201203/are-you-having-identity-crisis.

Needs, Motives, and Goals

❖ *What do I want? Why does it matter?*

Do you ever eat when you're not hungry? Have you shopped for things you don't need (or even want)? Ever wasted time watching a brain-numbing TV show? If you answered yes to any of those questions, why did you do those things?

The question of *why* we want what we want is a question of motivation. Our motives have been called the "springs of action"—they move us to get something or avoid something. Human motivation is a complex subject. Not only do we have many different motives—biological, social, uniquely personal—that change over the life course, our motives also differ in their accessibility to awareness. Sometimes we know clearly what we want and why we want it. At other times, the actual motives for our behavior are hazy, indistinct, or simply unknown.

Unconscious motivation underlying a particular action may be inferred whenever an individual *sincerely* responds "I don't know" when asked *why* he or she engaged in that behavior.[1] Unconscious motivation, as noted in Chapter 1, is a key distinguishing feature of the psychodynamic orientation, represented in this chapter by the views of Alfred Adler.[2] The path to full awareness of the motives behind our actions begins by realizing that we are not always as aware of them as we could be.

Alfred Adler's Fundamental Human Motive

> *The psychic life of man is determined by his goal.*
>
> —Alfred Adler (1927/1957, p. 29)

Adler's changing views of *the basic* human motive that moves all of us to action were heavily influenced by his own dramatic childhood experiences. The death of his younger brother in the next bed when Adler was only 3, multiple serious childhood accidents, nearly dying of pneumonia when he was 5, and growing up as a weak and sickly child—all of these led to his early decision to become a physician. This future goal, Adler later recounted, meant that "I had set a goal from which I could expect an end to my childhood distress, my fear of death" (Ansbacher & Ansbacher, 1956, p. 199). To Adler, then, goals are therapeutic because "by means of this concrete aim or goal, the individual can think and feel himself superior to the difficulties of the present because he has in mind his success of the future" (1929, p. 2).

During childhood, Adler was painfully aware of his feelings of inferiority in comparison with his athletic older brother. From this distressing personal experience, Adler formulated a general law of development: All children, healthy or not, feel inferior in comparison with their bigger and more powerful parents. The painful feeling of inferiority (the inferiority complex) is compensated for by the child, whose desire for recognition and superiority "determines the goal of an individual's existence" (1927/1957, p. 67). Thus Adler holds that the motive to be superior to others is simply a way of dealing with the more basic and more threatening inferiority complex.

"Striving for superiority" is Adler's expression for what Abraham Maslow later called "self-actualization." In a healthy person, striving for superiority means the individual is motivated by the goals of self-realization and self-perfection. But for anyone in the grip of a neurosis, striving for superiority is distorted into a drive to be superior to other people and have power over them. Adler coined the term *masculine protest* to describe the power-oriented behaviors by men and women in reaction to their feelings of inferiority.

In sum, Adler (1929) strongly emphasized the significance of the goal-directed aspect of our personalities, which he referred to as "the mysterious creative power of life … that power which expresses itself in the desire to develop, to strive, and to achieve" (p. 2). His emphasis on the importance of the motive to create ourselves has also been stressed by theorists from the humanistic/existential/narrative orientation, such as Abraham Maslow and Carl Rogers.

Three Humanistic Approaches to Motivation

Abraham Maslow's Hierarchy of Needs

In the ideal instance, inner requiredness coincides with external requiredness, "I want to" with "I must."

—Abraham Maslow (1971, p. 302)

Abraham Maslow, as we saw in Chapter 1, distinguishes between *deficiency motivation* and *growth motivation* (Maslow, 1968). In general, deficiency motivation refers to those basic human needs whose chronic nonfulfillment lead to illness. Maslow's (1970) deficiency needs are

- *Physiological needs* (food, water, oxygen)
- *Safety* (shelter, security, protection, freedom from fear)
- *Belongingness and love* (companionship, affiliation, intimacy)
- *Self-esteem* and *esteem from others* (recognition, appreciation, status)

Needs that are continually unfulfilled can lead to various illnesses and difficulties. Continued lack of food or water can result in death. Continual threats to safety can

Photo 6.1   Abraham Maslow (1908–1970).

One of the founding fathers of Humanistic Psychology, Maslow distinguished growth needs from deficiency needs. He presented the image of needs arranged in a pyramid, with our physiological needs at its base and self-actualization at the pinnacle.

Key publications:

Motivation and Personality (1954)
Toward a Psychology of Being (1968)
The Farther Reaches of Human Nature (1971)

result in generalized anxiety and neurosis. The thwarting of the needs for love and belongingness is commonly found at the core of severe pathology (Maslow, 1970). And the absence of esteem may result in deep-seated feelings of inferiority. For these reasons, Maslow considers basic needs to be motivated primarily by their absence or deficiency.

Growth motivation, also called the *need for self-actualization,* refers to a person's desire to do those activities that he or she is individually fitted for: "What a man can be, he *must* be. He must be true to his own nature" (Maslow, 1970, p. 46, italics in original). Self-actualization means that the individual desires self-fulfillment in ways that are unique to him or her. For one person, self-actualization may take the form of being the best father he can be to his children; to another person, self-actualization means providing the best possible service to those who are sick; to a third person it means creating the best product she can, whether it is in art, architecture, or animation. Maslow (1970) notes that individual differences are at their maximum when it comes to the specific ways we express our need for self-actualization.

Behaviors Leading to Self-Actualization

There are some commonalities across the idiosyncratic expressions of self-actualization. Maslow (1971) lists eight characteristics:

1. Doing the chosen task with total absorption and full concentration. This complete attention to the task at hand blocks out all self-conscious thoughts.

2. Choosing to grow, daily, rather than playing it safe. "*Self-actualization is an on-going process*" (p. 45, italics in original).

3. Paying respectful attention to our inner selves to determine whether or not we really like something rather than responding automatically in terms of how we think we should respond.

4. Being honest rather than not.

5. If the previous four steps are taken on a daily basis, the individual will come to know what his or her mission in life is.

6. "Self-actualization means working to do well the thing one wants to do" (p. 48).

7. Recognizing peak experiences—transient moments of ecstasy that accompany activities performed under growth motivation.

8. Being willing to become aware of one's characteristic defense mechanisms and having the courage to give them up.

Personality Characteristics of Self-Actualizing People

Maslow (1970), on the basis of sampling his personal friends and acquaintances, his biographical knowledge of historical figures, and sampling the healthiest 1% of college students, determined the 15 major personality characteristics of self-actualizing people. These are the following:

1. More efficient perception of reality: They are better able to spot phonies and judge people correctly.

2. Acceptance of self, others, and nature: Because they see reality for what it is rather than wishing it were different, they possess a deep-seated acceptance of who they (and others) are. They are not free of feelings of guilt and anxiety, but these feelings are confined to their *improvable* shortcomings.

3. Spontaneity, simplicity, naturalness: They are free to adopt or to ignore the social conventions of everyday living when they express themselves.

4. Problem centered: They have a mission in life, devoting themselves to an important human problem outside of narrow self-interest.

5. Need for privacy: They like privacy and solitude to a greater extent than most people.

6. Self-sufficiency and autonomy: They are not dependent on other people or their culture for their main sources of satisfaction in life.

7. Continued freshness of appreciation: They have the capacity to reexperience as new and beautiful what to others are just the ordinary events of everyday life (a sunset, a human baby, music).

8. Capacity for peak experiences: Some self-actualizers commonly experience those feelings of wonder, awe, and ecstasy that have been called *mystical experiences* by William James (1961). Other self-actualizers rarely or never have such experiences.

9. Deep feeling of identification for mankind: They exhibit what Adler (1939) called "social interest," a genuine desire to help other people.

10. Interpersonal relations: They tend to have deep relationships with a small number of close friends, who are likely to be self-actualizers themselves.

11. Democratic character structure: They are friendly with people from all walks of life and backgrounds.

12. Transforming means into ends: They have the capacity to distinguish the end or aim of some activity from the means to that end, yet they often treat the means as if it were an end in itself. They enjoy the journey on the way to their destination.

13. Philosophical, nonhostile sense of humor: They do not enjoy jokes made at the expense of others. Their sense of humor is responsive to "the human condition" that applies to all of us: They prefer to *laugh with*, not *laugh at*.

14. Creativeness: They all demonstrate an originality akin to that seen in healthy children.

15. Resistance to enculturation: They maintain a certain detachment from the norms and mores of their culture. They are "ruled by the laws of their own character rather than by the rules of society" (Maslow, 1970, p. 174).

Measures of Self-Actualization

These 15 characteristics reported by Maslow make it seem desirable to be a self-actualizer. It is pleasing to believe Maslow has correctly unearthed the distinguishing characteristics of the most evolved members of our species. Yet his own methodology prevents other investigators from independently confirming or disconfirming his findings. For example, we cannot be sure how Maslow decided some historical figures were self-actualized and others were not; we wonder at the inclusion of some of his historical personages as self-actualizers who are known to have suffered from mental depression or other psychological disorders (e.g., Abraham Lincoln, Ludwig van Beethoven); we don't know how various personality tests of his college students were scored to determine which students were self-actualized; and, finally, we don't know to what extent Maslow simply and unconsciously selected people he admired—people who reflected his own value system—and labeled them "self-actualizers."

To surmount these difficulties, two measures of self-actualization have been developed. The first is called the Personal Orientation Inventory or POI (Shostrom, 1963). The POI is a self-report test consisting of 150 pairs of forced-choice items. The person taking the POI is asked to select the one item in each of the pairs that best reflects himself or herself.

The POI provides scores on two major scales—time competence and inner direction (autonomy)—and ten subscales. High self-actualizers are time-competent people who live fully in the present. They meaningfully relate their past and expected future to their current lives. They do not dwell on what happened to them in the past nor do they avoid the present by fantasizing what joys or difficulties will befall them in the future. They use their past experiences to help them make effective choices in the present. Time incompetence, in sharp contrast, characterizes those who are not self-actualized. It is manifested by living "primarily in the past, with guilts, regrets, and resentments, and/or in the future, with idealized goals, plans, expectations, predictions, and fears" (Shostrom, 1974, p. 4). Time-incompetent people tend to split their past and possible futures from their present. They find it difficult to integrate their past, present, and future selves into a coherent whole.

On the inner-directed dimension, high self-actualizers demonstrate autonomy in their decisions. At the same time, they are not insensitive or unaware of the social demands associated with living as part of a group. Yet, on balance, high self-actualizers tend to be more self-directed than other-directed.

Research indicates the POI has reasonable reliability and validity. Individuals who are high self-actualizers tend to score low on measures of neuroticism or emotional instability. High self-actualizers also tend to be highly creative (Damm, 1969; Knapp, 1965).

As an alternative to the 150-item POI scale, Jones and Crandall (1986) developed a brief measure of self-actualization. Respondents are asked to rate each of 15 statements on a 4-point scale, where 4 = *agree*, 3 = *somewhat agree*, 2 = *somewhat disagree*, and 1 = *disagree* (except for those items that are reverse-keyed in which 1 = *agree*, etc.). Jones and Crandall administered both their 15-item scale and the POI to over 500 college students. They found that the overall self-actualization scores on both tests correlated positively. Moreover, scores on their short scale were found to correlate positively with self-esteem and negatively with neuroticism. Table 6.1 presents the 15 items of this measure of self-actualization. Items followed by (R) have been reverse-keyed: disagreement indicates greater self-actualization.

Self-actualization correlates positively with the importance of self-acceptance and negatively with the importance of financial success. The greater the importance of self-acceptance, affiliation with others, and community feeling (making the world a better

❖ **Table 6.1**   A Brief Measure of Self-Actualization

1. I do not feel ashamed of any of my emotions.
2. I feel I must do what others expect of me. (R)
3. I believe that people are essentially good and can be trusted.
4. I feel free to be angry to those I love.
5. It is always necessary that others approve of what I do. (R)
6. I don't accept my own weaknesses. (R)
7. I can like people without having to approve of them.
8. I fear failure. (R)
9. I avoid attempts to analyze and simplify complex domains. (R)
10. It is better to be yourself than to be popular.
11. I have no mission in life to which I feel especially dedicated. (R)
12. I can express my feelings even when they result in undesirable consequences.
13. I do not feel responsibility to help anybody. (R)
14. I am bothered by fears of being inadequate. (R)
15. I am loved because I give love.

Source: Adapted from Jones and Crandall (1986, p. 67). Reprinted with permission.

place to live), the greater is a person's psychological well-being and self-actualization (Kasser & Ryan, 1993).

The greater the importance college students attached to financial success as their main goal in life, the less self-actualized they were. Subjects motivated primarily by financial success were found to be less self-actualized, showed less vitality in living, were more depressed, and experienced greater anxiety. Additionally, individuals who placed a high priority on materialistic values incurred more debt, had lower-quality interpersonal relationships, and reported decreased personal and physical well-being. Finally, people valuing financial goals over other goals were affected more by extrinsic rewards in the situation than by intrinsic ones within themselves. Thus it appears that the greater the motive for financial success (over all other possible motives), the less the person may be described as *fully functioning*, the term used by Carl Rogers to indicate self-actualizing individuals (Kasser, 2016; Kasser & Ryan, 1993).

Carl Rogers' Actualizing Tendency

The person who is psychologically free moves in the direction of becoming a more fully functioning person.

—Carl Rogers (1961, p. 191)

Carl Rogers (1961) thought of self-actualization as the "mainspring of life" (p. 35). He believed that there is only one basic human motive, a motive he called "the actualizing tendency." Rogers defines the self-actualization motive as "the urge ... to expand, extend, become autonomous, develop, mature—the tendency to express and activate all the capacities of the organism" (1961, p. 35). A person in the *process* of self-actualizing himself or herself is a person who is fully functioning. Rogers (1961) describes the personality characteristics of the fully functioning person as follows:

1. *An increasing openness to experience.* This is the *opposite* of defensiveness. As we saw in the last chapter, in Rogers' view, defensiveness is the person's response to threatening experiences. Fully functioning people are willing and able to experience all of themselves, nondefensively. They are open to *all* of their feelings, their fears and pain as well as their courage and tenderness.

2. *An increasing tendency to live fully in each moment.* Fully functioning people are responsive and adaptable to the changes occurring in themselves and in other people. By living fully in the present, fully functioning persons do not attempt to rigidly impose their preexisting views of what should be on their own experience. Rather, they allow their experiences to be whatever they are.

3. *An increasing trust in oneself.* Instead of relying on fixed rules and past decisions, fully functioning individuals learn to trust what feels right to them in every situation. Because a fully functioning person is open to experience, any error of judgment can be quickly corrected.

The effect of becoming a fully functioning person is to live an enriched life filled with meaning, challenge, and excitement. It involves stretching and growing one's potentialities. Fully functioning individuals are not primarily motivated by such external inducements as money, fame, or the approval of others. Fully functioning people are primarily motivated by their intrinsic interest in their chosen activities and by the challenge of successfully accomplishing their chosen tasks. The actions of fully functioning people, then, are more likely to be intrinsically motivated rather than extrinsically motivated. The distinction between these two sources of motivation lies at the heart of self-determination theory.

Edward Deci and Robert Ryan's Self-Determination Theory

The Self-Determination Theory (SDT) of Edward Deci and Richard Ryan assumes that all humans possess the inner resources for the growth and self-regulation of their personalities. SDT identifies three needs that promote the development and integration of personality: *competence* (I am capable), *relatedness* (I am connected to other people), and *autonomy* (I choose my own goals). These needs are innate, essential, and universal (Ryan & Deci, 2000, 2008).

Can you see how SDT connects to Erikson's ideas? *Will* is the strength attained by the successful resolution of the *autonomy versus shame and doubt* crisis in toddlers; *Competence* is the adaptive ego quality that develops from the successful resolution of the *industry versus inferiority* crisis during the middle school years; and *Love* is the ego strength that accrues from successful resolution of the *intimacy versus isolation* crisis of young adulthood.

SDT's research program began by investigating two different kinds of motivation, intrinsic versus extrinsic. *Intrinsic motivation* is conceptualized in terms of the person's needs for competence and self-determination. Although White (1959) made the need for competence the essence of intrinsic motivation, Deci and Ryan believe that it is not only competence but also self-determined competence that forms the basis of intrinsic motivation. They are focusing on the difference between learning to play the piano only because your parents want you to versus learning to play the piano because you love the sound of beautiful melodies (Deci & Ryan, 1985, 1991; Ryan, 1993).

Self-determination, like the concept of self-actualization favored by Maslow and Rogers, stresses the importance of *choice* as a determinant of our actions. Observations consistent with Deci and Ryan's (1985) formulation reveal that intrinsically motivated college students are persistent: They are more likely to complete their courses of study than students who are not intrinsically motivated (Vallerand & Bissonnette, 1992).

Intrinsic motivation, then, refers to doing some activity simply because one wants to do it and chooses to do it. Extrinsic motivation refers to engaging in the same activity for an external reward (e.g., money; praise or avoiding blame from others; meeting a deadline). Both forms of motivation may be involved simultaneously: A person may work hard at a task both because she extrinsically hopes to reap a financial windfall *and* because she intrinsically finds the task to be challenging.

These two forms of motivation, considered singly, have quite different psychological effects on the individual. Intrinsically motivated individuals experience greater self-confidence, interest, and excitement while doing the chosen task, which typically results in superior performance, persistence, creativity, vitality, self-esteem, and general well-being. Extrinsic motivation, since it refers to doing an activity for the rewards (separate from the activity itself), can be associated with feeling alienated and inauthentic (Ryan & Deci, 2000). Our sense of well-being is enhanced when intrinsic, but not extrinsic, goals are reached (Sheldon & Kasser, 1998).

Can intrinsic and extrinsic sources of motivation affect each other? Yes. Suppose you like to solve anagram puzzles (ranamag zelzups) because you enjoy the challenge. Suppose further that a research psychologist offers you a monetary reward for each correct solution. After the money was paid and you could return to solving them just for fun, would you do so? Research indicates you might not. The *overjustification effect* refers to situations that inadvertently turn play into work by controlling intrinsically motivated behavior via external rewards. The highly replicated effect of extrinsic rewards under these conditions is to *decrease* intrinsic interest in the activity (Deci, Koestner, & Ryan, 1999). Moreover, people are likely to produce *less creative* work (Amabile, Hennessey, & Grossman, 1986; Deci & Ryan, 1985). Moreover, threats, deadlines, and imposed goals can diminish intrinsic motivation. Like external rewards, they serve to focus the person's attention on the consequences of the behavior rather than experiencing the satisfaction of self-directed autonomy.

Can extrinsic rewards increase intrinsic motivation? Surprisingly, yes. The critical variable is how the reward is interpreted. If the person sees the reward as an attempt to *control* his behavior, intrinsic motivation decreases. If, however, the reward is seen not as control but as *positive feedback* about one's competence, intrinsic motivation increases (Ryan, Mims, & Koestner, 1983). Similarly, what began as an external regulation can become internalized if its rationale is understood, other individuals accept it as reasonable, and the person feels a degree of choice about compliance (Kuhl & Fuhrmann, 1998).

Thus situational influences (e.g., external rewards) can affect future intrinsic motivation for that task. A college student, for example, might initially be motivated solely by the extrinsic reward (incentive) of attaining a college degree. Her academic experiences, however, might be so interesting that she begins reading the optional assignments to satisfy her curiosity. At that point, her motivation to remain in college would be for both internal and external reasons.

The research stimulated by Self-Determination Theory has contributed important insights into the complex relationships between intrinsic and extrinsic motivation. Moreover, the accumulated data support the basic assumption of SDT: Intrinsic motivation is likely to be present when the person chooses his or her activities (autonomy), feels capable of carrying them out (competence), and these activities occur within a context of security and connection to other people (relatedness). Those who have authority over other people (e.g., supervisors, educators, etc.) are more likely to promote positive outcomes by attending to the basic psychological needs of those they supervise. Such desirable outcomes may be achieved by allowing them as much autonomy as possible, fostering competence, and treating them with respect (Ryan & Deci, 2000).

In general, research has shown that the *quality* of our performance is more likely to be affected by our intrinsic motivation, while the *quantity* of our work output is more predictable by our extrinsic motivation (Cerasoli, Nicklin, & Ford, 2014).

Evolutionary Psychology's View of Motivation

A basic assumption of evolutionary psychology is that over our 5- to 6-million-year journey as a separate species, we gradually acquired many hard-wired cognitive units that aided our survival and reproduction. One example is our ability to recognize faces (as mentioned in Chapter 5). These units, called *modules*, evolved to (a) react to a specific stimulus (seeing a human face) and (b) effortlessly produce an immediate specific response (we instantly classify the image as familiar or unfamiliar). Modularity is a property of all living organisms at every level of organization and may well be indispensible for understanding the human mind (Barrett & Kurzban, 2006).

Evolutionary psychology (EP) assumes that each human motive evolved to deal with a specific need. Human motivation from the EP point of view wants to identify (a) the specific stimuli behind each motive that cause us to "spring into action" and (b) the conditions that satisfy that motive (Kurzban & Aktipis, 2006). The modular point of view denies that the human brain is a "general problem solving device." Why? Because in nature there is no such thing as a "general" problem. Each and every problem is specific and requires its own unique solution (Cosmides & Tooby, 2013; Tooby & Cosmides, 1992). Thus feeling hungry motivates us to find something to eat (rather than hide); feeling frightened motivates us to freeze, flee, or fight (rather than mate); feeling tired motivates us to rest (rather than explore). A thorough understanding of any particular motive, then, requires that we understand

1. Its functional significance: How does this motive help us survive or reproduce?

2. Its developmental course: How and when does this motive become active?

3. Its triggers: What determines which motives become active at any specific point in time? (Kenrick et al., 2010)

While evolutionary psychology can help us understand numerous human motives (Neel et al., 2015), in this section we examine how it applies to three fundamental social motives: the need to belong to a group, the need for social status, and the need to select a mate.

The Need to Belong

The desire for interpersonal attachment may well be one of the most far-reaching and integrative constructs currently available to understand human nature.

—Roy Baumeister and Mark Leary (1995)

The view that humans need to belong to a social group is incontrovertible. In Chapter 3, we saw the adaptive value of friends within many animal species. In Chapter 4, we saw how essential is an infant's attachment to a caregiver for its survival and growth. In Chapter 5, we saw how much self-esteem is affected by friendship and social acceptance.

The evolutionary story of the human species involves the coevolution of genes, social structure, and culture. All human beings are born into an existing social group and grow up as members of that group. We are unable to survive and reproduce outside of the active support by a social group (Brewer & Caporael, 2006). Moreover, caring and close relationships are necessary for us to thrive and develop to our full potential (Feeney & Collins, 2015; Greenaway et al., 2015).

How do we know this? One intriguing piece of evidence shows a strong relationship, over the long evolutionary history of our species, between changes in the size of our ancestors' neocortex and the size of the groups they lived in. As neocortex size increased, so did the number of individuals in the group. This relationship is one of *coevolution*: both variables changed at the same time (without implying that either variable caused the other to change). Robin Dunbar estimates that we evolved a neocortex large enough to handle living in a group of about 150 people (Dunbar, 1993, 1998, 2010).

We evolved to be aware of both *who* is in our social circle as well as the *relationships* among these people. You don't want to invite mortal enemies to your party. We usually can keep track of the friends and enemies of our friends. However, as group size increases, the number of possible relationships between any two people grows even faster. If you invite 20 people to your party, there are 190 possible conversations (relationships) between any two guests.[3] Humans need a brain big enough to keep track of all that potential social information.

Other evidence of our need to belong includes

- How readily we form into *cohesive groups* with strangers

- How effortlessly we categorize our social world into *us versus them*

- How quickly we *detect cheating* within the group

- How much it *hurts to be excluded* from our group

  ○ The impressive research program of Henri Tajfel and his colleagues has demonstrated repeatedly that individuals assigned to a social group by the most trivial of reasons (e.g., a coin flip) will immediately show favoritism to that group. When asked to divide resources between two groups, individuals consistently show favoritism to their arbitrarily assigned group (Tajfel, 1970; Tajfel & Billig, 1974). These data show that the human mind is well prepared for living in groups.

  ○ Along with ingroup favoritism there is often, but not always, prejudice and discrimination against outgroups. Throughout our evolutionary history, members of unfamiliar tribes might have posed real threats to health by carrying diseases against which the invaded group had no natural immunity (Makhanova, Miller, & Maner, 2015). Intergroup anxiety is correlated with avoidance of outgroup members (Stephan, 2014). And the less we know about the "others," the easier it is to stereotype them. In fact, we humans negatively stereotype outgroup members so easily that it seems we evolved a "tribal mind" (Berreby, 2005) with its own dedicated tribalism circuit in the brain.

This possibility is supported by the observation that the ability to stereotype is located in the brain's orbitofrontal cortex. We know this because damage to this area prevents individuals from stereotyping (Milne & Graffman, 2001). Erikson, as we have seen, proposed the concept of *pseudospeciation* to describe the common but erroneous assumption that some social groups are so different from us, are so *other*, that we react to them as if they are a lower and inferior species. *Dehumanization* is a frequent reaction to individuals from other racial and ethnic groups (Haslam, 2015). Blatant dehumanization is likely to occur after incidents of intergroup violence (Kteily et al., 2015). Moreover, there is the possibility that the human brain evolved to react to different ethnic groups as if they really are different biological "species" (Gil-White, 2001).

We remember information about ingroup members differently than outgroup members. Outgroup members are categorized in memory according to their attributes (traits, duties), while ingroup members are remembered as distinct persons (Ostrom et al., 1993). Moreover, we experience divergent emotional and hormonal reactions to outgroups depending on the kind of threat they pose. Outgroups seen as threats to safety evoke fear, while outgroups seen as obstacles evoke anger (Cottrell & Neuberg, 2005; van der Schalk et al., 2011). Hormonal reactions to outgroups also differ. Testosterone levels of men playing violent video games significantly increased only when they were competing against outgroup members (Oxford, Ponzi, & Geary, 2010).

Finally, we tend to attribute fewer emotions to outgroups in the same way that we assume animals have fewer emotions than we do, a process called *infrahumanization*—we think that outgroup members are less human than we are (Haslam & Loughnan, 2014; Leyens et al., 2007). Susan Fiske's neurological research program shows that dehumanizing is most likely to occur when we both dislike and disrespect an outgroup—such as homeless people and drug addicts—whose images, she finds, evoke the same brain activity in the amygdala as when we feel disgust (Harris & Fiske, 2006).

The ease with which we categorize individuals into ingroups or outgroups leads some evolutionary psychologists to assume the existence of "in-group" and "out-group" modules as innate structures of the mind (Geary & Huffman, 2002; Neuberg & Cottrell, 2006). In support of this possibility is the observation that when a person is reminded that he belongs to a distinct social group, he is more willing to express his prejudicial attitudes toward outgroups (Effron & Knowles, 2015). Our need to belong to a group is so important that we readily classify outgroups, even with minimal knowledge, as threats to our existence (Neuberg & Cottrell, 2006). Regrettably, it appears that pseudospeciation continues to influence how we feel, think, and react to individuals of different racial and ethnic backgrounds than our own. What will it take for us to transcend our tribal mind?

> ○ Group living requires that individuals trust one another. But philosophers like Nicolo Machiavelli (1469–1527) and Thomas Hobbes (1588–1679) advise us not to trust strangers we may never meet again (Hobbes, 1997; Machiavelli, 2003). Many modern economists agree with this way of thinking. Trusting people we do not know and may never see again only puts us at risk of being exploited by these strangers because it is in the stranger's self-interest (under this one-shot meeting scenario) to take from us more than he or she will return (Berg, Dickhaut, & McCabe, 1995; Bolle, 1998).

In spite of this rational analysis that directs us not to trust people we meet for the first time, studies show that most individuals do trust strangers at their first meeting. Are we so dense that we don't realize we can be exploited? Or is something else going on? David Dunning and his colleagues believe something else is going on—the presence of a social norm mandating that we begin social encounters assuming the other person will act with good will. Over a series of six investigations, they found that even when participants rated the stranger (based on a photo) as *less* trustworthy, they still extended initial trust. Why? Consistent with an evolutionary view of our need to belong, the authors conclude that "trusting others is what people think they should do" (Dunning et al., 2014, p. 122).

Belonging to a group means that sometimes individuals have to help the group and forego, at least temporarily, their own preferences for how to spend their time and energy. Selfish and clever individuals, however, realize it is to their advantage if they can manage to avoid the personal costs (e.g., time, effort, risks) of aiding the group yet somehow still enjoy the benefits produced by others. Such a person is a *cheater*—an individual who fails to reciprocate within the group. He or she accepts the benefits (e.g., food) of the implied social contract but fails to deliver (e.g., ducks out of the hunting party) the requirement that the benefit was based on—everyone contributes to the effort (Cosmides & Tooby, 2005). But if everyone in the group were to cheat, the group's survival would be in peril.

How often do you hear someone say, "That's not fair"? The research results of Leda Cosmides and her colleagues suggest that we are equipped with a *cheater-detection module* that is triggered whenever we suspect someone is trying to get away with something—trying to gain a personal benefit at the expense of the work of other people (Cosmides, 1989; Cummins, 1999). These individuals are also known as *free riders*—they ride along without paying their fair share.[4] Abundant research shows that when free-riders are detected, they are punished by their group, although physically attractive free-riders may be punished less severely than unattractive ones (Putz et al., 2016). In any event, the sheer frequency of the words, "That's not fair!" suggests that there is a lot of cheating, as well as cheating detection, in everyday life.

In addition to detecting cheaters, research suggests that natural selection may have made it easier to identify potential physical threats from facial cues alone. Brief glimpses of photographs—observed for only 2 seconds each—were sufficient for participants to distinguish violent from nonviolent sex offenders. Features indicating high masculinity were associated with participants' accurate judgments (Stillman, Maner, & Baumeister, 2009).

Other data suggest we use facial cues to identify individuals who are trustworthy. Decisions that a stranger is trustworthy are made quickly and effortlessly. For example, we are more likely to trust a smiling stranger when we judge that his smile is sincere. An authentic smile seems to be an honest (valid) signal that one can be trusted (Centorrino et al., 2015). Other research finds that the human face gives reliable clues about a stranger's trustworthiness when we can observe the person's face at the moment the stranger decides to cheat or not. The effortlessness with which trustworthiness is judged suggests that trustworthiness detection is a modular process (Bonnefon, Hopfenzitz, & De Neys, 2013). Future research, one hopes, will pinpoint the facial cues we use to decide effortlessly if someone is trustworthy or a cheater.[5]

"Your brain's face recognition and cheater detection modules have merged and that's why everyone you see looks like a cheetah!"

○ Finally, if group participation is essential to human growth, one would expect individuals to be vigilant to signs of being excluded from the group and to feel hurt when they are ostracized. This is exactly what happens.

Babies, as we know from the work of John Bowlby, Mary Ainsworth, and others, protest at signs of abandonment by crying loudly and persistently. Children, teenagers, and adults feel hurt when they are excluded from the groups that are important to them. These painful feelings are adaptive for survival in that they motivate us to try to be reinstated into the group. Other reactions to exclusion include anger, aggression, sadness, a decrease in self-esteem, increased physiological stress, and, if the exclusion is chronic, depression and helplessness. The particular attempts used by ostracized individuals to be readmitted are influenced by cultural norms (Uskul & Over, 2014; Williams, 2007).

The particular emotions that are generated by exclusion from the group depend on the reasons for being ostracized. Individuals excluded because they were free riders tend to feel guilty, ashamed, and sorry for their actions, while those who were excluded because they might carry a contagious disease tend to feel anger, disgust, and betrayal by the group. The strategies they employ to be readmitted also vary with the cause of exclusion. Free riders promise to be a "team player" and "work twice as hard," while those with a pathogen infection remind the group of their prior positive contributions and try to make the group feel guilty for excluding them (Robertson et al., 2014). In addition, the pain of social exclusion motivates ostracized individuals to pay close attention to the unique characteristics of those who can help them be readmitted and, consequently, stereotype them less, compared to individuals who were not excluded (Claypool & Bernstein, 2014).

The pain caused by social exclusion follows the same neural pathways as pain caused by physical injury. How do we know this? While participants were undergoing fMRI scans, they played a game of "Cyberball" on a computer monitor in front of them. At first they watched two other participants (in reality a prearranged software program) "toss" a ball back and forth on the computer monitor, while their own monitor was being hooked up (this delay was a ruse to obtain their pretest fMRI). After the participant was connected to the computer, the other two simulated participants "threw" the Cyberball to him a total of seven times, followed by excluding him from the game for the remainder of the scan (about 45 throws to each other). Participants reported feeling ignored and excluded during this period. Most importantly, their fMRI scans showed the same pattern of brain activation that is seen in patients undergoing physical pain (Eisenberger, 2015; Eisenberger, Lieberman, & Williams, 2003; MacDonald & Leary, 2005). It appears we evolved an ostracism detection system (Spoor & Williams, 2006) that causes us to feel pain whenever we are socially rejected in order to (1) focus our attention on our rejection and (2) motivate us to end our pain by trying to get readmitted to the group (Williams, 2007).

Participants who suspect they might soon be socially excluded pay special and prolonged attention to smiling faces as signals they are liked and thus will not be excluded (DeWall, Maner, & Rouby, 2009). Ostracized individuals with low self-esteem blamed themselves and showed they felt stressed by their increased cortisol reactivity (Ford & Collins, 2010). Individuals who are anxiously attached showed greater sensitivity to physical pain when they were excluded from a group, but not when they were included, indicating that the ostracism hyperactivated their attachment system and thereby increased their pain of exclusion (Frias & Shaver, 2014).

In other experimental circumstances, socially excluded individuals reacted with anger and acted aggressively only toward those who had excluded them, not to bystanders

(DeWall et al., 2009; Twenge et al., 2001). Detrimental psychological effects of being ostracized in a Cyberball game lasted for at least 55 minutes after the game was over (Buelow et al., 2015). However, a 10-minute online conversation with a person of the opposite sex was sufficient to replenish the battered self-esteem of those who had been excluded. New and positive social contact was sufficient in this study to restore the hurt feelings caused by the earlier exclusion (Gross, 2009).

Not putting all our eggs into the same social basket might be an effective way of coping with ostracism. Natural selection, it seems, solved some the problems associated with living in groups—dealing with free riders and avoiding contact with those who might carry communicable diseases—by banishing them from the group[6] (Kurzban & Leary, 2001). Unlike our tribal ancestors, however, today we are likely to be connected to two or more social groups (e.g., immediate family, work, neighborhood, church groups, friends from childhood, etc.), providing us with social alternatives and thereby softening the blow of being ostracized from any single one of them.

The explosive growth of online social media might be due, in part, to the power of being "friended" by as many people as possible.[7] Facebook usage, however, can come with psychic costs: The longer individuals are active on Facebook, the more depressed they feel afterward (even though they opened Facebook to feel better). Nevertheless, they continued to use Facebook (Blease, 2015; Sagioglou & Greitemeyer, 2014). Further research identified envy (e.g., "It is so frustrating to see some people always having a good time") as the likely culprit for their depressed mood. When envy was controlled for, Facebook usage resulted in less depression (Tandoc, Ferrucci, & Duffy, 2015). Facebook, it is worth noting, has become a valuable research tool for psychology and the social sciences in general (Kosinski et al., 2015).

In summary, the evolutionary approach to understanding the strength of our need to be connected to a group is strongly supported by observing (1) how we easily identify with a group, (2) how readily we see our social world in terms of "us" versus "them," (3) how quickly we detect untrustworthy ingroup members, and (4) how much it hurts to be socially excluded. As the epigram that began this section noted, the need to belong to a group is one of the most far-reaching and important constructs to help us understand human nature (Baumeister & Leary, 1995).

Striving for Status

Another motive that may be understood from an evolutionary point of view is that of seeking social status (via popularity, prestige, leadership, and/or dominance). Who doesn't want to be popular? It feels good to know that other people like us and want to hang out and be friends with us. We might not have ever asked ourselves why being popular feels good. Wanting to be popular seems self-evident—what's to understand?

Evolutionary psychology seeks *ultimate explanations* for any given behavior—its survival and/or reproductive value. These ultimate explanations are sufficient to explain what functions the behavior serves. Whether or not we are conscious of these functions is not important as far as EP is concerned. It doesn't matter that we do not wonder why we like to be popular. It only matters that being popular or influential in our social circle matters to us. The loss of popularity, like the feeling of being excluded, is also painful because our social status is directly tied to our success at *inclusive fitness*, our ability to survive, reproduce, and take care of ourselves, our offspring, and our relatives. Higher status individuals, in most species, including ours, are less likely to die of starvation and more likely to leave living offspring (Cummins, 2005; Marmot, 2004). The desire for status is indeed a fundamental human motive (Anderson, Hildreth, & Howland, 2015).

Evolutionary psychology also wants to understand the *proximal causes* of behavior. What environmental changes cause us to be concerned with our popularity and status?

Since status is connected to ultimate fitness, natural selection has provided us with alarm bells that automatically go off whenever we perceive a loss of popularity or decreased social influence: We feel *stressed*. Our bodies react to this loss as if it were a matter of life-or-death. Perception of decreased status causes the brain to activate the autonomic nervous system, which causes the release of two hormones, adrenalin and cortisol. Adrenalin is a fast-acting hormone valuable for fight-or-flight reactions: our heart rate and blood pressure rises, and we are physiologically prepared for immediate action. Cortisol acts more slowly. It increases blood sugar and fat storage. Circulating cortisol is often used as a measure of stress (Sapolsky, 2004).

Animal research identifies additional hormones that are related to social status. Status correlates positively with androgen and serotonin levels: higher status individuals show higher levels of both hormones. Changes in social rank are reflected in changes in these hormone levels. While defeated males show a sharp decrease in androgen levels, androgen levels increase in the winners. Subordinate rats who were at the receiving end of frequent beatings from those at the top of the dominance hierarchy showed persistently elevated cortisol levels (Blanchard et al., 1993). Serotonin levels increase in those subordinates who rise in social status (Sapolsky, 1990).

Similar changes are found in humans. Male winners of athletic contests, both the athletes themselves as well as fans of the winning team, show increased levels of testosterone, while female winners show lower levels of cortisol (Cummins, 2005). High status male executives reveal *both* high levels of testosterone *and* low levels of cortisol (Sherman et al., 2015). Moreover, the relationship between changes in social status and hormone levels works in both directions. College students who were administered a Prozac-like drug, citalopram, were rated by their roommates as less submissive and more cooperative. They also spontaneously adopted a dominant pattern of direct eye contact when talking to strangers. Serotonin clearly influences social behavior (Tse & Bond, 2002).

What these studies add up to is that neuroendocrine changes reflect a signaling system that informs us about changes in our social status. How we feel communicates where we are in the pecking order and how we respond to social challenges communicates our self-perception to others (Cummins, 2005). What's so important about social hierarchies that any change in our social standing produces these automatic hormonal reactions?

Sex is what's so important. High status men gain greater access to women through two roads. Women prefer high-status men because these men offer women greater protection and ample resources for them and their children (Hill & Hurtado, 1996). A second road to sexual access is through intrasexual domination. High status men might take the wives or mates of low-status men for themselves without fear of retaliation (Buss, 2012). History is replete with examples of kings, emperors, and other high-status males who amassed large harems of women simply because they could. The earliest known civilizations, as identified by Laura Betzig (1993), beginning in 4,000 BCE and lasting about 4,000 years, showed a consistent pattern of women-gathering by the rulers, ranging from the 332 women in the harem of the Maharaja of Patiala to over 10,000 women of the Chinese emperor Fei-ti (overcompensate much?).

What about today? Surely things have changed, right? Not really. Socially dominant men have more affairs than less dominant men, and high status men are preferred as partners in extramarital affairs (Baker & Bellis, 1995; Egan & Agnus, 2004; Perusse, 1993). But social dominance, and the status associated with "manhood" itself, are not forever fixed. They require effort to achieve and maintain. Men at the top are challenged by younger men below them in the hierarchy. "Precarious manhood" refers to the ease with which a man's status in his social hierarchy may be threatened and the steps he takes to reestablish it—steps which make him appear more "manly." Men whose "manhood" is threatened tend to become more aggressive, have low tolerance for the alternative lifestyles of others, and show increased support for warfare to solve international problems (Winegard, Winegard, & Geary, 2014).

It's not surprising that many young men compete with each other to jockey for social dominance. They want to get the attention and interest of women. These displays apparently pay off. Dominant behavior in young men increases female sexual attraction even though the women may not like these men very much (Sadalla, Kenrick, & Vershure, 1987). Sex is but one of the perks associated with being at or near the top of the social hierarchy. Higher status group members exert more influence within the group, have better access to scarce resources, obtain more social support, enjoy better health, live longer, and have better reproductive success (Ellis, 1994). All that sounds great. So how can a person get closer to the top?

One way to move up a rung or two of the social ladder is to become more valuable to your group. Two characteristics associated with increased social status are *competence* and *acting generously* toward others in the group. Those who take the initiative and self-confidently offer solutions to their group are seen as more competent than others (even though on objective measures they are average). Visibility within the group is a necessary condition for a change in status (Anderson & Kilduff, 2009).

In groups that are impressed by signs of wealth, conspicuously wearing luxury brands can help improve one's social standing. Evolutionary psychology's *costly signaling theory* (Miller, 2009; Saad, 2007) or *handicapping principle* (Zahavi & Zahavi, 1997) predicts that *conspicuous consumption* (Veblen, 1899/1994) signals to others that one has "money to burn." Individuals who wore luxury clothes were consistently treated better and raised more money for charity than those wearing ordinary, nonluxury clothes (Nelissen & Meijers, 2010). Acting as if one already has high status may be one way to be treated like someone who actually has high status.

Some personality characteristics are associated with high social status. In groups where the status hierarchy is based on prestige rather than dominance, individuals who display the traits of self-esteem, agreeableness, conscientiousness, and helpfulness to others tend to have higher social status. A *prestige hierarchy* is based on freely given deference to those who merit it by their achievements, talents, or excellence in some valued sphere of social life. In contrast, a *dominance hierarchy* is based on force or the threat of force (Henrich & Gil-White, 2001). In dominance hierarchies, the traits associated with high status individuals are narcissism, aggression, and disagreeableness (Cheng, Tracy, & Henrich, 2010). Since these are the same traits that make people unpopular, it seems that dominant leaders prefer to be feared rather than liked (which was Machiavelli's advice in *The Prince*).

Individuals who use abstract (as opposed to concrete) language are seen as more powerful and having higher status. Those who use abstract language are also perceived as more distant and judgmental. These are traits associated with being more socially powerful (Wakslak, Smith, & Han, 2014). Other language features that signal higher status are speaking in a lower pitched voice (Carney, Hall, & Smith LeBeau, 2005) and speaking rapidly (Miller et al., 1976). Speaking abstractly, rapidly, and with a low-pitched voice probably leads to perceiving the speaker as possessing high status more easily in some environments than others (e.g., a college classroom versus a playground).

Sex: The Mating Motive

When Charles Darwin published *On the Origin of Species* in 1859, he believed he had solved "the mystery of mysteries," how one species evolves into another. His answer: by natural selection. Individual animals who are equipped at birth—by nature—with the "right stuff," have a better chance of surviving and passing on their genes to their off-spring than do individuals who lack these qualities. As long as the selection pressure to survive always acts in the same direction (e.g., a major shift in climate causes a once fer-tile area to receive very little annual rainfall), then even slight variations in the heritable qualities that aid survival in this new environment could, over many generations, result in a new species that is *well adapted to that environment* (e.g., lizards are well adapted for living in deserts). Nature is the independent variable (so to speak), species change over time is the dependent variable.

But if natural selection solves the problem of how evolution occurs, why did Darwin write in 1860 that "the sight of a feather in a peacock's tail, whenever I gaze at it, makes me sick!"(Coyne, 2009, p. 145)? Darwin was not made sick by the beauty of the peacock's tail when it is fully opened and shimmering while he struts in front of admiring peahens (the peacock, not Darwin). No, Darwin was mightily annoyed because he did not understand how this large cumbersome apparatus the peacock drags around behind him could possibly help him survive. It's more the opposite—his huge tail is a clear impediment to walking without effort let alone trying to get airborne to escape a predator. Yes, the feathers are beautiful, and the peahens really like them, but the peacock's feathers also attract predators. The existence of peacocks mocked Darwin's solution of "survival of the fittest."[8]

The peacock did help Darwin eventually realize that natural selection is only one part of evolution. Darwin's 1871 publication, two books in one, *The Descent of Man, and Selection in Relation to Sex*, completed the picture. Evolutionary change requires both *natural selection* and *sexual selection*.

Sexual selection takes two forms. In *intrasexual selection*, members of the same sex compete with each other to gain access to mates. In almost all species, males do the competing, while females cheerlead on the sidelines and mate with the winners. Why is that?

Parental investment theory is the answer. The sex that invests more time and energy raising the young chooses who to mate with. The sex that invests less time and less energy competes. Across all species, it is almost always the female that invests more time and energy rearing her offspring. Relative parental investment and sexual selection are the root causes of sex differences (Bjorklund & Kipp, 1996; Buss, 1995).

In humans, we see sex differences in risky behaviors that can be explained by intrasexual competition: Young men want to impress young women by displaying their bravery, dominance, skill, and self-confidence—attributes that women find attractive in men. Men take more risks than women. Risk-taking by adolescent males to impress adolescent females is so prevalent that it has been labeled "The young male syndrome" (Wilson & Daly, 1985). If he is successful in attracting a female, the result is that the physical and mental qualities that contributed to winning—strength, coordination, cunning—will be inherited by his offspring. And *differential reproduction* is at the heart of evolutionary theory—the heritable traits associated with successful reproduction are passed on to the next generation, while the heritable traits of the losers are not.

Young men take risks even when women are not present. In those cases intrasexual competitions serve to establish dominance hierarchies (Who is the biggest chicken? Who is the best athlete?) and reveals skills valued for future leadership roles, team participation, and coalition formation (Byrnes, Miller, & Schafer, 1999). Adolescents of both genders take more risks in the presence of peers, compared to when they are alone, and when such decisions have an emotional component (Figner et al., 2009; Smith, Chein, & Steinberg, 2014).

Intersexual selection is the second way sexual selection operates. If there is consensus among the members of one sex about what are the desirable characteristics of the other, then individuals of the opposite sex who possess those qualities will tend to be chosen as mates. Those who do not show the desired traits will not be chosen. Assuming that the consensus of valuable qualities remains stable over time, then evolutionary change will occur as the desired qualities become more frequent in the population and the undesired traits will be seen less and less often until they vanish altogether.

Because the females of many species are choosy about their sexual partner, Darwin used the term *female choice* to refer to intersexual selection. Since peahens prefer to mate with peacocks with large, brilliant, shimmering tail feathers, those peacocks with the largest and most visually striking tail feathers are selected, and they, in turn, will produce sons whose tail feathers will be attractive to peahens when they became sexually mature. A comprehensive investigation of sexual selection across 186 species reveals that many different male characteristics are correlated with mating success, and they almost always involve female choice (Anderson, 1994).

Women's Mate Preferences

Given the enormous difference in time and energy that men and women make in bringing a child into the world, evolutionary psychology expects women, more than men, to be more concerned with her potential mate's *economic resources.* This sex difference was found without exception

(a) in 37 cultures around the world, sampling over 10,000 individuals (Buss et al., 1990),

(b) among participants in speed dating (Asendorpf, Penke, & Back, 2011),

(c) in studies of personal ads (Gustavsson & Johnsson, 2008), and

(d) in studies of computer dating services (Bokek-Cohen, Peres, & Kanazawa, 2007).

> Different samples, different methods, different countries, same result: Women have evolved a strong preference for those long-term mates who can show they have the ability to support them. Modern women are the descendants of generations of women who had this mate preference, a preference that contributes to their own and to their children's survival.

Women also prefer men with high social status, who are slightly older than themselves, who are ambitious and dependable, who are taller than they are, who are in good health, who love and are committed to them and their children, and who are kind, have a sense of humor, and are generous (Buss, 2012).

Men's Mate Preferences

Physical attractiveness is more important to men than it is to women (Li et al., 2013). There is an important exception to this well-replicated finding, however. When it comes to *short-term relationships*, women rate the importance of physical attractiveness of their partner almost as highly as men do (Buss & Schmitt, 1993; Gueguen & Lamy, 2012; Hald & Hogh-Oleson, 2010).

Physically attractive women are preferred by men worldwide and this has been true for as long as these preferences have been measured (Buss et al., 2001). Why? Evolutionary psychologists assume that a woman's physical attractiveness has been naturally selected as a cue or marker to indicate she enjoys good health. Of course that may or may not be true in any individual case. Aren't there billions of healthy women around the world who may or may not be especially physically attractive? Yes, but evolutionary processes work on what is true on average for that species, not on what is true for each member of the species.

If physical beauty has been selected because it signals good health, we would expect this trait to be relatively more important to men in those areas around the world where pathogens are highly prevalent but relatively less important in geographical areas where pathogens are rare. This is precisely what has been observed (Gangstad & Buss, 1993).

In addition to physical attractiveness, men prefer women who are younger than they are and who are preferably at the beginning of their reproductive years (historically about 22 years long). Mating with a woman at the beginning of these years allows more time to sire many offspring. Men prefer women who are shorter than they are, who have long hair, clear skin, who walk slowly and fluidly, and whose faces and bodies are symmetrical (Buss, 2012).

A woman's weight is more important in some cultures than others. In societies that experience frequent food shortages, women with more body fat are preferred. Plumper women are also preferred in non-Western societies with subsistence-based economic systems. Men from various countries around the world report the ideal woman's waist-to-hip ratio is about 0.7 (e.g., 18 inch waist/26 inch hips; 25 inch waist/36 inch hips; 30 inch waist/43 inch hips; etc.). Finally, human breasts are large relative to those in closely related species and for that reason are assumed to be the result of sexual selection. Men do prefer women with larger breasts, but only if they are symmetrical. Larger breasts tend to be asymmetrical and are associated with reduced fitness (fewer offspring). Asymmetrical breasts are not preferred by men. Large and symmetrical breasts are markers of successful fitness and are preferred by men (Sugiyama, 2005).

Self-Actualization

Now that we have looked at how evolutionary psychology understands the importance of the need to belong to a group, the need for social status, and the need to mate, how does EP understand self-actualization? Is the need for self-actualization the same sort of need as the need for food or shelter? How does self-actualization contribute to reproductive fitness? Are men and women attracted to each other because they are self-actualized? Or is their attraction based on the same activities and products generated by motives for status and mate selection?

Creative displays by humans are attractive to the opposite sex just as the peacock's tail is attractive to peahens. Male artists are more likely to draw attention to their creative output than are female artists. When mating motives are salient, males are more likely to display their creative outputs (Griskevicius, Cialdini, & Kenrick, 2006). Women are likely to choose creative men as mates (Miller, 2000). Okay, but what does the motivation behind the creative output have to do with it? Whether these creative outputs were motivated by the desire to be a multi-millionaire or by the desire to express one's deepest feelings, their sexual selection value lies in *what* was produced rather than *why* it was produced.

It is still fine to speak about our desire to self-actualize or to admire others for their personal growth in becoming more self-actualized individuals. EP does not change that. But EP does help us realize that the functional value of any motive ultimately lies in its contribution to survival and reproductive fitness. From this point of view, the self-actualization motive does not deserve a privileged place at the top of Maslow's pyramid (Kenrick et al., 2010).

Error Management Theory

Our final topic under evolutionary psychology's approach to motivation is error management theory (Haselton & Nettle, 2006; Haselton, Nettle, & Andrews, 2005).

This theory is an outgrowth of what is known about parental investment, sexual selection, and the psychological differences they create between men and women (e.g., the above section on gender differences in mating motivation). Error management theory predicts that these sex differences lead men and women to make different kinds of mistakes in thinking or cognition. The error each gender is likely to make follows from differences in reproductive fitness.

A man's contribution to reproduction may be exceedingly minimal in time, effort, and the use of personal resources (a wee bit of sperm). A woman's contribution to reproduction is always the opposite: It is time consuming (9 months), quite effortful, and increasingly depletes her resources. This biological difference, from an evolutionary point of view, leads to two quite different reproductive strategies: A human male's reproductive fitness is maximized by fathering as many different children with as many different women as possible. A woman's reproductive fitness, however, is maximized by raising fewer, healthy children who will eventually become parents. Quantity versus quality.

From this point of view, men should be ready to mate with as many women as often as possible. This tendency, error management theory says, leads men to misperceive women's platonically friendly behavior as a sign of sexual attraction. Men's minds are biased in the direction of minimizing the cost of missed sexual opportunities. It is better for him to *overestimate* her actual interest, and get shot down, than to not act on a true sexual signal and miss an opportunity to mate.

Women, however, are more concerned with the potential outcome of their sexual relations than are men. As we have seen above, women value men who have the resources to care for them and their children. But these resources are useless to her if the man doesn't stay around after she becomes pregnant. Error management theory predicts women are unwilling to have sex with a man she suspects is not committed to her. This is true to such an extent that she is likely to *underestimate* a man's true intentions to stay. Women's minds are biased in the direction of requiring solid evidence that her partner will be faithful so she will avoid the far more costly error of having to raise her child by herself. It is better for her to be really sure about him than to be sorry. Thus women are more likely to make the error of rejecting men who in fact would be faithful.

To test these hypotheses, written dating scenarios were given to men and women undergraduates. These students were asked how they would respond to various possibilities regarding sexual signals and commitment to the relationship (e.g., "If a woman touches a man's arm on a date, how likely is it that she is interested in having sex with him?"; "How much do you agree or disagree that a typical woman needs to know that a man loves her before she is willing to have sex with him?"). The researchers anticipated that men and women's ratings would differ as expected by error management theory. And they did. Men rated various behaviors by women as signaling greater sexual intent than women did; women underestimated a prospective mate's commitment more than men (Haselton & Buss, 2000).

Error management theory has been successfully applied to the study of mate poaching. Since men's resources are greatly valued by women, the threat of a mate being successfully poached by another woman is highly threatening. Thus, women should be more sensitive than men to cues that other women are poaching as well as more sensitive to all cues of infidelity. This is what was found in a series of four studies of mate poaching. Women were quicker and more accurate in detecting poaching and cues of infidelity. Women focused more attention on what other women are doing (and less attention on how their mate was responding to them), while men focused their attention on their partner and who she might be interested in (rather than on what male poachers are doing). Consistent with error management theory, these results suggest men and women have developed different ways of dealing with the threat of mate poaching to achieve the same result—mate retention (Ein-Dor et al., 2015).

Dispositional Approaches to Motivation

In this section, we'll see that the dispositional approach looks at motivation as an enduring part of our personality. A dispositional motive is like a trait with an action component. It influences us to interpret events and to respond in consistent ways. I've selected three to look at in some detail: the need for achievement, the Dark Triad, and sensation seeking.

Need for Achievement

*The primary goal of the achievement motive is **efficiency**.*

—David McClelland and Carol Franz (1992, p. 680, emphasis in original)

Henry Murray published *Explorations in Personality* in 1938 and dedicated it to Sigmund Freud and Carl Jung (among others). Having been analysed by Jung, Murray was impressed with the reality of unconscious motivation, motives that can influence us without our conscious awareness. He wanted to study those wants and needs that lie outside (below?) full awareness and to do so in a systematic, scientific way. Working with Christiana Morgan, Murray developed the Thematic Apperception Test (TAT) as a means to accomplish this. The TAT consists of 20 ambiguous pictures, 19 of which depict one or more people. Participants are asked to make up a story concerning each picture, a story that answers questions such as "What led to this situation?" "What is happening now?" "What will happen in the future?" The TAT is a *projective test* in that it assumes the story reflects our current *covert* needs, wishes, and conflicts (Morgan & Murray, 1935).

Murray (1938) listed a number of psychological needs that we all have. These needs vary in strength between people and they also vary in strength within the same person at different times. Three of these needs have been well researched: the need for achievement, the need for affiliation, and the need for power. In the prior section we touched upon the need for affiliation (the need for belongingness) and, slightly, the need for power (striving for status). Here we cover the need for achievement.

David McClelland and his associates defined the achievement motive through observations of their research participants. College men who had a strong motive to achieve showed "a concern with doing things better, with surpassing standards of excellence" (McClelland, Atkinson, Clark, & Lowell, 1953, p. 228). McClelland (1985) later revealed that he wished he had called it the "efficiency motive" instead of the achievement motive because efficiency more accurately describes the distinctive feature of this motive, that of wanting to "do things better."

Achievement as an Intrinsic Form of Competence Motivation

Koestner and McClelland (1990) point out that three major characteristics of intrinsic motivation are usually present in individuals who have a strong motive to achieve. Individuals high in the achievement motive have been found to prefer to

1. *Engage in Moderately Difficult Challenges.* Easy tasks do not provide the incentives to feel gratified by their successful completion (virtually everyone can do them) and very difficult tasks involve a low probability of success (virtually no one can do them). Individuals characterized by a high achievement motive, like those who are intrinsically motivated, prefer to engage in moderately difficult challenges.

2. *Act in a Self-Determined Manner.* In the absence of external constraints, individuals strongly motivated to be successful typically outperform those with a low achievement motive. But when external controls are present, individuals high in achievement motivation do not outperform those who are low. The externally controlling variables that undermine the effects of achievement motivation also undermine intrinsic motivation. Pressures to hurriedly complete the task, the presence of external rewards such as money, and competition with others have all been shown to reduce intrinsic motivation and eliminate the performance advantages otherwise shown by individuals high in achievement motivation. McClelland (1985) concludes that only a highly motivated person who feels personally responsible for her successful outcomes will experience satisfaction from doing something more efficiently.

3. *Receive Feedback About Their Performance.* Individuals strongly motivated to achieve success, like those who are intrinsically motivated, desire and profit from learning how effective their behavior is for reaching their goals.

A final similarity between the motive to achieve and intrinsic motivation concerns the type of parenting behaviors that seem to lead to each. Parents who emphasize independence training of their children, especially in decision making, and who set challenging standards for their children to reach, are likely to foster both the motive to achieve and intrinsic motivation (Koestner & McClelland, 1990).

McClelland's research into the achievement motive has been extremely wide-ranging. From the study of college students' achievement fantasies in the laboratory to the prediction of the economic growth of 23 countries over 21 years (McClelland, 1961), the need for achievement has been shown to affect the lives of individuals as well as entire nations.

The Dark Triad

Delroy Paulhus and Kevin Williams (2002) identified a personality cluster of three traits they called the *Dark Triad.* The three personality traits that make up the Dark Triad are psychopathy, narcissism, and Machiavellianism (at the subclinical level). Paulhus and Williams referred to this cluster as "dark" because each of the three traits can show up in nasty or unpleasant behaviors. They are considered to be *subclinical* because none of these traits dominate a person's personality in an extreme way. Extremity of traits, as we will see in Chapter 8, can be a diagnostic symptom of a personality disorder. Nonextreme versions, however, are traits we may encounter in everyday life such as when we meet individuals who constantly brag, are emotionally cold, verbally aggressive, and insincere.

Psychopathy at the subclinical level is characterized by low empathy, impulsivity and thrill-seeking, and low levels of anxiety. Subclinical narcissism is described by such traits as vanity, grandiosity, entitlement, dominance, and feeling superior to others. Machiavellianism, first described in the psychological literature by Richard Christie and Florence Geis in 1970, is the trait of being manipulative, exploiting others, and doing whatever it takes to get what you want.

Paulhus and Williams (2002) found that while these three traits positively inter-correlate, they do not correlate so strongly that we should think of them as synonyms for each other. Their initial results led them to conclude (a) there is a common core among these three traits and (b) each trait contributes unique elements. An individual characterized by the Dark Triad is someone who scores above average on the three traits of psychopathy, narcissism, and Machiavellianism. As of 2014, there were over 700 publications dealing with some aspect of the Dark Triad (Paulhus, 2014).

How Does the Dark Triad Relate to HEXACO?

As covered in prior chapters, HEXACO is a conception of personality traits that adds the sixth trait of "Honesty-Humility" to the five "super-traits" of the Five-Factor Model. Research shows this sixth trait is related to the Dark Triad. The more highly individuals score on measures of the Dark Triad, the less honest and humble they are. The core of the Dark Triad is the opposite of Honesty-Humility (Lee & Ashton, 2005). This core is called *callousness;* it describes someone who is *callous-manipulative* as well as someone who is disagreeable and dishonest (Furnham, Richards, & Paulhus, 2013). Across a series of six experiments, individuals who scored low on Honesty-Humility were found to cheat more often than those who scored high on this trait. Low scores on Honesty-Humility were the only personality scores on any trait that consistently predicted cheating (Hilbig & Zettler, 2015). These results are consistent, of course, with the view that the core of the Dark Triad is callousness and dishonesty. How else does the Dark Triad show up in everyday life?

Behavioral Correlates of the Dark Triad

Workplace behavior: Counterproductive work behaviors (CWB) such as abusive supervision, making fun of a coworker, and excessive office politicking create aversive workplace environments and result in losses of billions of dollars per year (Bennett & Robinson, 2000). How is the Dark Triad implicated in CWBs? A meta-analysis found that two traits of the Dark Triad are associated with CWBs: narcissism and Machiavellianism. Individual workers who score highly on these traits are more likely to be involved with CWBs and thereby contribute to an aversive work environment (O'Boyle et al., 2012).

Cheating, lying, and mate poaching: In a study of the Dark Triad and self-reported cheating by college students, all three Dark Triad traits correlated positively and significantly with cheating, especially psychopathy. A second investigation found that the three traits significantly correlated with plagiarism with psychopathy again showing the strongest relationship (Williams, Nathanson, & Paulhus, 2010). Another study found a small but statistically significant positive association between frequency of lying and the traits of psychopathy and Machiavellianism (Baughman et al., 2014).

Mate poaching, as we saw above, is the attempt to form a romantic relationship with a person who already is in a romantic relationship with someone else. Studies have found that about 50% of men and women admit to trying to mate poach at some point in their lives and the overwhelming majority of adults (85%) report that someone has tried to poach them away from their current relationship (Schmitt & Buss, 2001).

The Dark Triad is implicated in mate poaching. In an online survey, individuals who scored highly on the Dark Triad made more poaching attempts than those lower on the scale. They also were more likely to have their own mate poached away from them. This latter finding may be due to the costs of mate poaching: One cannot pay as much attention and "guard" one's own mate if one is on a quest to poach the mates of others (Jonason, Li, & Buss, 2010; Kardum et al., 2015). Each of the traits of the Dark Triad positively correlated, for both men and women, with poaching attempts and with being the victim of poaching by someone else.

More generally, when it comes to long-term mating, individuals, both men and women, prefer romantic partners who are low in the traits of the Dark Triad. But for one-night stands, individuals who are high in those traits are preferred. An exception to these preferences was found for those, both men and women, who score high on psychopathy: These individuals rated partners who were high on the traits of the Dark Triad as more attractive for both one-night stands and long-term relationships (Jonason, Lyons, & Blanchard, 2015).

"So he's a narcissistic Machiavellian psychopath. What's not to like?"

Cyber-aggression and violence: Cyber-aggression consists of such acts as sending insulting comments to someone, spreading rumors online to damage a person's reputation, posting embarrassing photographs of someone (like a former girl friend) and other anti-social acts. An online survey of adolescents found that 36% admitted to one or more acts of cyber-aggression over the past three months. Each of the three traits of the Dark Triad correlated positively with cyber-aggression with psychopathy revealing the strongest relationship (Pabian, De Backer, & Vandebosch, 2015).

Other investigations concur. In one of them, the strongest predictor of cyber violence was scoring low on the trait of Agreeableness—violent actions are more likely to be perpetrated by those who who are disagreeable. The next strongest predictors of violence were psychopathy, Machiavellianism, impulsivity, and narcissism (Pailing, Boon, & Egan, 2014).

The correlations of the Dark Triad with aversive behaviors in the workplace, with cheating, lying, and mate poaching, and with acts of cyber-aggression and violence demonstrate its wide range of influence. While the Dark Triad traits help individuals be reproductively successful (Mealy, 1995; Schmitt & Buss, 2001; Wilson, Near, & Miller, 1996), they come with a price tag. Two studies reveal the Dark Triad's darker side:

1. Using functional magnetic resonance imaging (fMRI), one investigation found that photographs of people who had two of the personality characteristics of the Dark Triad—psychopathy and Machiavellianism—activated the amygdala, the brain structure that reacts to fearful or threatening stimuli in the environment. Perhaps natural selection has provided us with a facial cue warning us to be careful when interacting with those whose Dark Triad is pronounced (Gordon & Platek, 2009).

2. Have you ever been cheated, taken advantage of, or had your trust betrayed? I have. What happens next? After we become aware we were cheated, our cheater-detection module activates the amygdala, adrenalin is released, and the adrenalin causes our memory of being cheated to last a lifetime. Once a person has been identified as a cheater, the ensuing distrust is difficult to change even if we later learn that our identification was a mistake. Once a person is branded as a cheater, distrust lingers. We do not forget who cheated us. This memory, painful though it may be, helps us avoid being exploited again by this person in the future (Mealy, Daood, & Krage, 1996; Suzuki, Homma, & Suga, 2013).

Sensation Seeking

Sensation seeking is the personality trait that reflects how strongly or how weakly we want to experience a variety of novel and intense sensations. Sensation seeking is negatively correlated with the trait of conscientiousness of the Five-Factor Model (Zuckerman, 2009).

The Sensation Seeking Scale (SSS; Zuckerman, 1971) consists of four subscales:

1. *Thrill and Adventure Seeking*: engaging in extreme sports and taking risks. Items indicate a person's *intentions* rather than what he or she has actually done (e.g., "I would like to go skydiving someday").

2. *Experience Seeking*: wanting new experiences through the mind and the senses, travel, music, etc. Individuals who score high on this subscale are drawn to social nonconformity. They prefer to associate with unconventional people.

3. *Disinhibition*: seeking intense experiences in parties, social drinking, and sex.

4. *Boredom Susceptibility*: an intolerance for repetitive experiences and boring people. Those who are high in sensation seeking quickly feel restless and antsy when they are in such situations (Zuckerman, 2009).

A number of different kinds of risky behaviors are associated with sensation seeking. Soldiers who volunteer for combat duty are higher in sensation seeking than other soldiers (Hobfoll, Rom, & Segal, 1989). Individuals who engage in unprotected sex are higher in sensation seeking than those who do not (Hoyle, Fejfar, & Miller, 2000). People who like to drive fast and furiously by speeding, tail-gating, and/or driving while intoxicated tend to be high sensation seekers (Jonah, 1997). Those who enjoy high-risk sports such as mountain climbing and downhill skiing typically score high on the SSS (Goma-i-Freixanet, 2004). Finally, individuals who are drawn to occupations that involve physical risk—paratroopers, airline pilots, firefighters, and so on— are above average sensation seekers (Zuckerman, 2007).

Many studies have shown that individuals who report frequent marijuana use, smoking cigarettes, and/or bouts of heavy drinking tend to score high on sensation seeking. A comparison of personality tests found that the SSS was the best predictor of the use of most kinds of drugs (Jaffe & Archer, 1987). This test also predicted treatment failures for individuals addicted to cocaine: the higher an individual's SSS score, the lower the prognosis for successful recovery (Ball, 1995).

Violent criminals score higher on the SSS than those who engage in risky sports (Goma-i-Freixanet, 1995). The Disinhibition subscale scores of early adolescents predicted delinquent behavior when they became older (Horvath & Zuckerman, 1993; Newcomb & McGee, 1991).

Why is this? Zuckerman (2005) prefers a psychobiological explanation to account for these relationships. Behavior genetics research shows that sensation seeking is highly heritable and that a specific gene for the dopamine receptor (DRD4) is associated with novelty seeking. Forms (alleles) of this gene are also associated with strength of response to novel stimuli, heroin use, alcohol abuse, and compulsive gambling. Zuckerman's psychobiological model of sensation seeking assumes there is a genetic predisposition toward acting impulsively as well as a relatively weak arousal system to risk and dangerous situations. Indeed, individuals who are low in sensation seeking are more easily aroused and upset by aversive stimuli (e.g., unpredictable loud noises) than those who are not (Lissek et al., 2005). Many individuals are biologically predisposed to seek novelty and excitement without being inhibited by fears of injury or other potentially negative consequences. For them, mountain climbing is more about the thrill of victory than the agony of the feet.

Cognitive Approaches to Motivation

We conclude the chapter with three cognitive treatments of the significance of motives and goals for understanding personality. As mentioned in Chapter 1, goals are one of the five classes of personality variables proposed by Walter Mischel (1973). A *goal* is a present mental image, associated with positive or negative feelings, directing your actions to bring about a desired outcome in the future (Pervin, 1989). Your present goals are self-constructed highways to your future self.

The following three treatments of goals are cognitive because they are organized around your *major beliefs* about your present self (and current situation) as well as your potential future self (and a different situation). To hold and pursue realistic goals means you have faith in your abilities and efforts as well as hope for the future. To have no goals worth pursuing is to live in despair. It is your "possible selves" (Hazel Markus), your "personal strivings" (Robert Emmons), and your "personal projects" (Brian Little) that give meaning to the present events of your life.

Our Possible Selves

Hazel Markus and her colleagues refer to *possible selves* as our cognitive representations of our hopes, fears, and goals. Possible selves are our imagined ideas of what we hope to become and what we fear we might become. Possible selves are incentives that guide present behavior (Markus & Nurius, 1986; Markus & Wurf, 1987).

The most important element of any goal is its *concrete meaning* for the person. A goal will influence a person's behavior to the extent that she can make it personal by building a bridge of self-representations that span her current state and her desired future state (Markus & Ruvulo, 1989). Thus a close and inherent connection exists between a person's goals and his or her present self-concept. An essential part of how I see myself today includes who I hope to become tomorrow.

The theory of possible selves has been successfully applied to understanding some aspects of juvenile delinquency. Researchers suggest that a desirable expected self ("I will be able to get a good job") has maximum motivational significance when it is *balanced* by a feared possible self in the same domain ("I will be unemployed"). Youths, ages 13–16, were asked to describe their possible selves. Nondeliquent youths showed the expected balance between their hoped-for self and their feared-self. Delinquent youths, however, did not. These youths lacked images of positive expected selves that could serve as incentives for avoiding criminal activity in the future (Oyserman & Markus, 1990; Oyserman & Saltz, 1993).

These results suggest that the theory of possible selves might usefully be applied to other problematic domains of adolescent life (e.g., dropping out of school, using drugs, becoming pregnant unintentionally). The theory of possible selves explains how the mental image of a hoped-for future self can function as an incentive that guides present behavior. Prospective first-time fathers, whose possible future selves included being actively involved in child care were indeed more active after the birth of their children. A possible self of competence in a particular domain can serve as a buffer against feedback that one has failed on a task-relevant domain. The feedback apparently does not cause one to get discouraged by the failure compared to someone else whose possible self does not include competence in that domain (Strauss & Goldberg, 1999).

Our Personal Strivings

Robert Emmons (1989) defines a *personal striving* as an idiographically coherent pattern of goals that represent what a person is trying to accomplish. The term *idiographically* is an important qualifier of this approach to goals because Emmons is interested in focusing on how each individual's distinctive goals make sense (are coherent) within the overall life course of that person. The concept of personal strivings is a unifying construct that organizes different single goals around a common theme. For example, an individual who personally strives to "make a good impression" might have specific goals such as to "get good grades," "be a cool dresser," and "show the boss I can handle more responsibility." Other examples of personal strivings include "get to know new people" and "avoid arguments when possible" (Emmons, 1989).

Personal strivings relate to a person's physical and psychological well-being. People who rate themselves as happiest are those who, in general, successfully attain their personal strivings (Emmons, 1986). This is especially true when a person's strivings do not conflict with each other. When one personal striving ("to appear more intelligent than I am") conflicts with another personal striving ("to always present myself in an honest light"), individuals are likely to feel distressed and report more physical illness and visits to the doctor (Emmons & King, 1988). As Erikson would expect, the well-being of older people has been found to be positively related to their personal strivings for generativity and ego integrity (Sheldon & Kasser, 2001). When individuals select goals for which they have the necessary resources, subjective well being increases. The greater the congruence between your goals and the resources available to you (such as family support, close friends, or social skills), the higher your subjective well being is likely to be (Diener & Fujita, 1995).

Moreover, the *degree of generality* of our personal strivings appears to be an important determinant of our happiness or distress. *High-level strivers* are individuals who describe their goals in abstract and expansive ways ("become the best manager in the company") whereas *low-level strivers* tend to frame their goals in concrete terms ("meet next week's sales quota"). Emmons (1992) found that high-level strivers experience more psychological distress but less physical illness whereas low-level strivers show the opposite pattern (less distress, greater risk of illness). High-level strivers are better able to deal with their conflicts in the long run (although they experience more distress while doing so). Low-level strivers, on the other hand, do not feel distress—because they repress conflicts among their personal strivings—but at the long-term cost of an increased risk of physical illness (Emmons, 1992).

Our Personal Projects

Brian Little defines *personal projects* as extended sets of actions designed to reach some goal. These projects may vary along several dimensions. For example, they may be relatively important or unimportant to us, chosen by us or assigned by someone else, solitary concerns or ones shared with others, and highly specific or most general. Like the prior approach, Little (1989) stresses the idiographic nature of an individual's *personal* projects: They have meaning and significance to the person.

Little's research program begins by asking college students to list the projects they are currently working on. Examples of such projects include "finish my psychology essay," "make new friends," and "lose 10 pounds." They then rate each project along a series of dimensions.

Little (1989) finds that the three dimensions that reveal the strongest correlations with overall present life satisfaction are stress, outcome, and control. Those who rate their projects as highly stressful show *less* overall life satisfaction, whereas those who rate themselves as being in control of and making progress toward a desired outcome tend to be more satisfied with their present lives. Little's findings support Bandura's concept of *self-efficacy* as mediating between our personal projects and our sense of competency and well-being. Not only is personal project efficacy associated with happiness, but also the meaningfulness of the project is strongly related to how well it allowed the students to "be themselves." Individuals whose personal projects are consistent with core aspects of their identity report higher levels of meaning than those whose projects are less related to their identity (McGregor & Little, 1998).

Moreover, Palys and Little (1983) found that the time dimension of personal projects relate to one's present subjective well-being. Projects extending very far ahead in time (a college student who wants to become head of a major corporation) are less likely to be related to present life satisfaction and well-being than projects that can be realized sooner. It is important for our present well-being that our personal projects strike the right balance between being personally meaningful as well as manageable in the here-and-now to provide us with the satisfaction of seeing them successfully realized.

QUESTIONS TO PONDER

1. Is it possible to live a full life without goals? Can a person realistically have the goal of "having no goals"? What would be the psychological consequences?

2. How do people decide which particular goals to pursue? How are goals related to a person's needs and motives?

3. What are the differences between a "want" and a "need"? List five things you want and five things you need. Which list is more essential to achieve your present goals?

4. From the standpoint of evolutionary psychology, do humans really have a *need* for self-actualization? Why or why not?

5. Carl Jung postulated that *archetypes* are unconscious bundles of energy found in all humans that help us deal with reality. Is archetype a synonym for what evolutionary psychologists call *modules*? If not, how do these concepts differ?

NOTES

1. Responding "I don't know" does not imply the presence of unconscious motivation if the question concerns *how* one performed a certain behavior. If you are asked to explain how you tie your shoelaces, for example, you may be hard-pressed to articulate consciously the precise sequence of your actions. All well-rehearsed, overlearned, habitual

behaviors may be performed more or less automatically with minimal awareness. But the question of unconscious motivation is relevant should a person *honestly* answer, "I don't know" to the query, "*Why* did you tie your shoelaces?" Of course, "I don't know" may simply be short-hand for "It's none of your business."

2. Adler is sometimes mistakenly identified as a "Neo-Freudian." This error probably traces back to Hall and Lindzey's (1957) first edition of their hugely influential *Theories of Personality* that lumped Adler, Horney, Fromm, and Sullivan together in a chapter labeled "Neo-Freudians" because that's how each *began* their careers, as followers of Freud. But an examination of their mature theories shows they have little in common with the basic drive-reduction premises of psychoanalysis. Hall and Lindzey's third edition (1978) now classifies these theorists as "Social Psychological," a more accurate depiction because their theories replaced Freud's biological reductionism with our social environment as a more important influence on our personality development.

3. The formula that connects the number of people in a group (N) to the number of possible two-person relationships (R) is $R = N(N-1)/2$. So for the 20 lucky people at your party, there are $20 \times 19/2 = 10 \times 19 = 190$ possible 2-person conversations.

4. Will the cheater-detection module eventually eliminate cheating? No. Natural selection tells us that the really good cheaters will go undetected and pass along their clever cheating genes to their offspring. But so will those who are skillful cheater detectors. As some get better at detection, some cheaters get better at avoiding detection. And so forth and so on. This is an example of an evolutionary arms race (Pinker, 1997).

5. Bonnefon et al. (2013) report that while trustworthiness detection is a reliable skill, it is easily overridden by distractions from irrelevant variables such as clothing and facial hair. If these findings are replicated, the implication is that we need to learn to trust our intuitive (i.e., modular) judgment because any conscious analysis only makes it worse. All modular processes are impenetrable or opaque to conscious analysis. We can experience this fact for ourselves by trying to consciously articulate all of the processes that allow us to see. Vision is modular.

6. Informal evidence of how highly we value being part of group appears in the strong ratings in numerous countries around the world of the long-running TV show (it began airing in Europe in the late 1990s; the United States in 2000) depicting strangers who form into tribes and vote each other off islands.

7. Dave Eggers dystopian novel, *The Circle*, takes obsession with social media to its logical and creepy conclusion.

8. "Survival of the fittest" was first introduced by British philosopher Herbert Spencer in 1864. He used it to replace Darwin's term, "natural selection." Darwin accepted this phrase in 1868 to mean "better designed for an immediate, local environment." Regrettably, Spencer's phrase was inappropriately extended to refer to British society as a whole. "Survival of the fittest" became a convenient rationalization by those born at the top of the social class system to justify their superior standing ("We're simply more fit, don't you know!"). "Social Darwinism" has interfered with some people's understanding of Darwin's exclusively *biological* meaning of "survival of the fittest." Any examination of Darwin's life clearly shows he certainly was *not* a "Social Darwinist."

SUGGESTIONS FOR FURTHER READING

Deci, E. L., & Ryan, R. M. (1985). *Intrinsic motivation and self-determination in human behavior*. New York, NY: Plenum.

Ellenberger, H. F. (1970). *The discovery of the unconscious: The history and evolution of dynamic psychiatry*. New York, NY: Basic Books.

Lieberman, M. D. (2013). *Social: Why our brains are wired to connect*. New York, NY: Crown.

Miller, G. (2000). *The mating mind: How sexual choice shaped the evolution of human nature*. New York, NY: Anchor Books.

Wright, R. (1994). *The moral animal: Evolutionary psychology and everyday life*. New York, NY: Pantheon.

INTERNET RESOURCES

1. For information about the relationship between rejection and self-esteem, see http://www.psychologytoday.com.articles/200707/dumped-not-down.

2. Mark Leary has provided a number of personality scales to measure such characteristics as our need to belong, our fear of being negatively evaluated, and so on, go to http://people.duke.edu/~leary/scales.html.

3. To take a personality test that measures the three components of the Dark Triad, go to http://personality-testing.info/tests/SD3.php.

7

Stress and Coping ❖

❖What is stress? How can I cope with it?

Interpretational Approaches

    The Person-Centered Approach

    The Cognitive Approach

    The Depressive Self-Schema Approach

Dispositional Approaches

    The Five-Factor Model (FFM)

    Optimism

    Ego Control and Resiliency

    Hardiness

Psychodynamic Approaches

    Anxiety and the Mechanisms of Defense

    Three Neurotic Solutions to Anxiety

Positive Psychology and Coping

L ife is stressful. So might the first universal truth of Buddhism be applied to contemporary life.[1] Stress is as much a part of living as breathing. Chronic stress, however, can contribute to numerous life-threatening illnesses such as ulcers and heart disease, particularly those diseases that are associated with inflammation. Stressful childhoods are associated with increased levels of inflammation and increased susceptibility to chronic diseases in adulthood. In turn, inflammation is associated with a variety of illnesses such as cardiovascular disease (CVD), Type 2 diabetes, and Alzheimer's disease (Fagundes & Way, 2014; Miller, Chen, & Parker, 2011). Moreover, individuals with CVD have been shown to be at increased risk for dementia if their typical response to stressful situations takes the form of the Type A behavior pattern characterized by anger (Bokenberger et al., 2014).

In addition to these documented physical effects of prolonged stress, our emotional reactions may include excessive anger, anxiety, and/or depression, among others. One of the most well-documented effects in research on depression is the relationship between stress and depression: Stressful life events markedly increase an individual's risk for Major Depression Disorder (MDD). In fact, major life events are the single most important risk factor for MDD (Kendler, Gardner, & Prescott, 2002).

George Slavich and Michael Irwin (2014) have proposed a stress-related theory of the causes of MDD, the *social signal transduction theory of depression*. They hypothesize that experiences of social rejection and adversity activate those components of the immune system that are involved in inflammation. Specific, identifiable forms of inflammatory activity, in turn, elicit depression, fatigue, and other reactions. The causal chain they propose is the following: social rejection → stress → inflammation → depression.

If their theory is right, does this mean that anti-inflammatory drugs might alleviate both inflammation and depression? Yes. Preliminary work indicates that aspirin and other anti-inflammatory drugs can be both psychologically and physically beneficial. Slavich and Irwin are properly cautious in their recommendations: ". . . although targeting inflammation to alleviate depression sounds intuitively promising, additional research is needed to understand when exactly these pharmacologic interventions are beneficial" (2014, p. 799).

When did health professionals first realize that stress is a major factor in disease? The father of stress research, Hans Selye (1907–1982), published his first book for the general public, *The Stress of Life*, in 1956. His work focused on the *physiological* effects of stressors. A *stressor* is any factor that results in stress—rushing to meet a deadline, preparing for a job interview, or experiencing simultaneous demands from coworkers, family, and friends. Selye (1973) conceptualized stress as responses of our bodies to demands made upon it. Selye's pioneering research demonstrated the existence of the biological stress syndrome (also known as the general adaptation syndrome) that is our body's evolved response to all stressors.

This chapter is concerned with the *psychological* aspects of stress and their relation to personality and coping. We'll look at three distinct ways of conceptualizing psychological stress and their suggestions for coping effectively with it. Stress is multidimensional and may be profitably understood from more than one perspective.

The *interpretational approach* focuses on how we portray or explain to ourselves those external events that precede stress. Within this approach, we find *phenomenological* (e.g., Carl Rogers) and *cognitive* (e.g., Richard Lazarus and Susan Folkman; Aaron Beck) theorists who agree that it is how we interpret important changes in our lives that most influences how stressful we experience those changes to be.

Dispositional theorists (e.g., Paul Costa and Robert McCrae) want to identify those broad-based personality traits or dispositions that leave some of us more vulnerable to stress than others. We also cover three single-trait approaches to stress and coping: optimism, ego resiliency, and hardiness.

Psychodynamic theorists (e.g., Sigmund Freud, Karen Horney) assume that stress signals the presence of one or more unconscious conflicts. For us to make sense of this signal, we first must become aware of it. However, one of the most defensive ways many individuals deal with their chronic stress is to simply deny that it exists (Breznitz, 1983). Psychodynamic theorists want to help individuals recognize how stressed they really feel and then work with them to identify and become aware of those parts of their minds that are at war with each other. Such awareness can help them resolve their internal conflicts and thereby directly reduce their self-induced stress. The unmistakable sign that an important internal conflict has been successfully resolved is dramatically increased vitality (Blanck & Blanck, 1974; Hartmann, 1958; Peterson & Seligman, 2004).

We conclude the chapter by looking at how recent developments in *positive psychology* can help us cope with stress.

Interpretational Approaches

The Person-Centered Approach

Curiously enough a positive evaluation is as threatening in the long run as a negative one, since to inform someone he is good implies that you also have the right to tell him he is bad.

—Carl Rogers (1961, p. 55)

To tell someone she is good implies you can withdraw the praise should she fail to live up to your expectations. When praise is conditional for certain behaviors, we experience conditions of worth. As we saw in Chapter 5, Carl Rogers believes conditions of worth and the actualizing tendency place humans in a state of self-conflict: To secure the love of others, we often deny our inborn impulse to develop all of our capacities and talents. Consequently, we desire experiences that bring us positive regard from others rather than experiences that will actualize our full potential. For example, because developing a new skill or talent may result in failure and criticism from others ("You're wasting your time!"), we may choose to forego such experiences in spite of their ultimate value for our own self-actualization (e.g., what we learn about ourselves in the process). One of the saddest examples of this kind of denial is when a person chooses to live out his or her parents' wishes for them instead of following his or her own true interests.

Furthermore, experiences that are *incongruent* with, or threaten, our self-concept can result in anxiety. Rogers defines threat as a perception of an incongruity between an experience and the self-concept. A person whose self-concept is centrally organized around being a good student, for example, would be threatened by failing an important examination. Whether the person in that situation would experience anxiety depends on how the threat is handled. When anxiety becomes excessive, the individual may require help from others to alleviate it.

Rogers (1959) holds that we engage in defensive processes to maintain consistency between our self-concept and our experiences. There are two basic types of defensive processes. First, we can *perceptually distort* the experience to make it more compatible with our self-concept. The student in the earlier example could decide that the examination was unfair and not a true measure of what he or she actually knows. On the other hand, we can *deny* that the experience took place at all. This is very difficult when other people know we took the exam (and we know they know). But we humans are so sly, we can begin the denial process even *before* the exam or any other potentially threatening event occurs, as shown by research on the defensive process of self-handicapping.

Self-Handicapping

The stress associated with maintaining a particular self-image is well-illustrated by *self-handicapping*. Self-handicapping is the term given to those extreme defensive maneuvers to protect one's self-concept and self-esteem, manuevers used at the likely risk of self-induced failure to reach a desired goal. Denial is illustrated by choosing to self-handicap in the first place (Higgins, Snyder, & Berglas, 1990; Schwinger et al., 2014).

Self-handicappers behave in such a way that if they fail to get what they want, they can easily attribute the failure to the handicap rather than to a more central aspect of their self-concept. Many behaviors have a self-handicapping function. Drug or alcohol use, lack of practice, test anxiety, listening to distracting music, and lack of effort can all be used as excuses to explain poor performance and protect self-esteem. For example, a self-handicapping ploy of some job applicants is to not dress appropriately for the job interview. If they are not offered the position, they can attribute their failure to the fact that they didn't have time to dress properly rather than to the more ego-threatening attribution that they are not as qualified as they think they are. Self-handicapping permits individuals to shift their attributions for a poor performance from their abilities to their handicaps and thus protect their self-esteem from taking a hit (McCrae & Hirt, 2001).

Research has shown that people who self-handicap have higher self-esteem after learning they failed than those who did not self-handicap beforehand (Rhodewalt et al., 1991). Moreover, if self-handicappers should somehow succeed, in spite of not putting forth their best effort, it can only mean they are exceptionally talented! Thus self-handicapping can be motivated by self-enhancement as well as self-protective concerns. Men are more likely to self-handicap via reduced effort than women, probably because women place more value on giving their best effort than men (McCrae, Hirt, & Milner, 2008).

Both defensive and enhancement motives are involved in self-handicapping behavior, depending on the person's initial level of self-esteem. When a task, such as a new test of intelligence, was identified as important and either success or failure (but not both) was experimentally manipulated to be the only meaningful test result, self-handicapping varied with the initial level of self-esteem.

High self-esteem people were likely to self-handicap (by not practicing very long) only when they could *enhance their self-image* by succeeding on the task (when they were told beforehand that the test was only a valid measure of very high IQ, but was not valid for measuring low IQ). But if the only possible meaningful outcome was to show they *were not* very intelligent (they were told beforehand that the test was a valid

SELF-HANDICAPPERS GOLF ASSN.

TODAY'S OPTIONS (CHOOSE ONE)

1. Use the monkey caddy.
2. Replace driver with hockey stick.
3. Replace putter with pool cue.
4. Wear ferret on head.
5. Wear mice under golf cap.

measure of below average IQ but was not valid for measuring high IQ), high self-esteem participants *did not* self-handicap. They apparently had enough self-confidence in their own intellectual abilities to not be threatened by possible negative test results.

Low self-esteem people in the same situation, however, showed the opposite tendency. They were likely to self-handicap when the only meaningful result was to fail the test and thereby demonstrate low intelligence. The self-handicapping behavior of low self-esteem individuals indicates they were motivated to *protect themselves* against the loss of self-esteem caused by failure (Tice, 1991).

It seems that high self-esteem people feel good enough about themselves to believe they can deal effectively with any future failure; thus, they do not self-handicap simply to protect their self-image. High self-esteem people are more likely to self-handicap when success will result in enhanced self-esteem as when a bright student doesn't study for a test and still hopes to succeed despite his lack of effort. High self-esteem self-handicappers are more likely to make increased ability attributions after a success than low self-esteem self-handicappers (Rhodewalt et al., 1991). Low self-esteem people, in contrast, appear not to have sufficient self-confidence to believe they can handle failure very effectively. Primarily motivated by self-protection, they are more likely to self-handicap to provide themselves with less threatening attributions for failure.

A great deal of failure in school is related to students needing to protect their self-worth, even at the expense of dropping out (Covington, 1989). Self-handicapping is especially likely among those students who view intelligence as some "fixed quantity" rather than an ability that can grow with practice (Dweck, 1999; Rickert, Meras, & Witkow, 2014). Students who hold such an "entity" theory of intelligence tend to get lower grades, just as those who chronically self-handicap do (Blackwell, Trzesniewski, & Dweck, 2007; Urdan, 2004; Zuckerman, Kieffer, & Knee, 1998).

Chronic denial, whether through self-handicapping or any other defensive maneuver, can have severe consequences for the life path.

Although phenomenologists like Carl Rogers focus on our immediate *perception of events* as important determinants of stress, the cognitive approach deals more explicitly with our mental configurations of those perceptions. *How we think about what we perceive* is how cognitive theorists understand stress.

The Cognitive Approach

Because psychological stress defines an unfavorable person-environment relationship, its essence is process and change rather than structure or stasis.

—Richard Lazarus (1993, p. 8)

All stressful events involve change. How much stress we feel depends on (a) the environmental change itself and (b) our expectations for coping successfully with that change. Richard Lazarus and Susan Folkman (1984) define stress as a relationship between a person and his or her environment: "Psychological stress is a particular relationship between the person and the environment that is appraised by the person as taxing or exceeding his or her resources and endangering his or her well-being" (p. 19).

Lazarus and Folkman's approach identifies our *appraisal* of some changing event as the key determinant of our stress response. As seen in their definition, the two variables that affect stress involve our appraisal that the event (a) taxes our personal resources to deal with it and (b) endangers our well-being.

Lazarus and Folkman distinguish two kinds of appraisal processes:

Primary appraisal classifies the environmental event as either *irrelevant* to our well-being, *positive*, or *stressful*. Stress appraisals are further divided among those that have already caused some *harm or loss*, might cause loss in the future (*threats*), or could result in some positive gains (*challenge*).

Secondary appraisal refers to our evaluation of what *we might do to manage* the stressful event. Whereas primary appraisal asks, "How bad is it?" secondary appraisal asks, "What can I do about it?" Secondary appraisal has much in common with Bandura's concept of self-efficacy expectations covered in Chapter 5.

Lazarus and Folkman (1984) make the point that our primary appraisals of the stressful event's meaning and our secondary appraisals of our coping options *interact* with one another in determining our degree of stress and the strength of our emotional response to the event. If the event is life-threatening, we may become emotionally aroused even if we know we have the skills to cope with it (e.g., a professional driver during a high speed skid). On the other hand, even a mildly threatening event can be highly stressful if we feel we are helpless to cope with it (e.g., being surrounded in a crowded bus or subway by sneezing, coughing people).

How do you typically cope with stressful situations? Do you usually try to tackle the problem directly, or do you first deal with your emotional reactions? Or does your coping style depend on the situation?

Consider the stress caused by noisy neighbors. You could cope with this annoyance by appraising the situation as one that requires action. You could inform your neighbors about how much noise they're making and ask them to dial it down. This action may be sufficient to change their behavior, thus eliminating that source of stress. Lazarus and Folkman (1984) call this ***problem-focused coping***: We make a direct effort to change or modify stressful aspects of our external environment. If our first coping effort does not have the effect we desire (i.e., our neighbors continue their noisy ways), we would then need to try other problem-focused coping responses.

Or you might adopt a different way to cope with the noise. You could interpret it as due to the lively exuberance of youth and realize the noise is only temporary. In this case you've changed your appraisal of the situation, and by so doing, you've removed the need to take action. This is ***emotion-focused coping***: We change our interpretation of the external event. Emotion-focused coping refers to the many ways we can choose to deal with our subjective reactions to the event, rather than the event itself. Emotion-focused coping, like the defense mechanisms covered below, may be useful in the short run by allowing us breathing space to adjust to the stressful event. But if the party next door is still going full blast at 2 a.m., you might change your interpretation of the event and switch to a problem-focused approach.

How we cope with stress in our lives has been investigated through The Ways of Coping Questionnaire (Folkman & Lazarus, 1985). This 68-item instrument consists of eight scales to measure our tendencies to use eight strategies for coping with stressful events.

Scale 1 is the only scale that assesses our tendency to use a problem-solving coping strategy:

1. *The problem-focused coping* scale contains 11 items. ("I'm making a plan of action and following it.")

   Scales 2 through 7 assess different *emotion-focused coping* strategies:

2. *Wishful thinking* ("I wish that the situation would go away or somehow be over with.")

3. *Distancing* ("I try to forget the whole thing.")

4. *Emphasizing the positive* ("I try to look on the bright side of things.")

5. *Self-blame* ("I realize I brought the problem on myself.")

6. *Tension reduction* ("I try to make myself feel better by eating, drinking, smoking, or using drugs or medications.")

7. *Self-isolation* ("I keep others from knowing how bad things are.")

   Scale 8 measures our tendency to use a combined problem- and emotion-focused strategy:

8. *Seeking social support* ("I talk to someone to find out more about the situation.")

Lazarus (1993) summarizes the major findings about coping as revealed by The Ways of Coping Questionnaire:

- *Coping is complex.* People tend to use most of the eight coping strategies during every stressful event.
- *Coping strategies depend on the appraisal* of whether any actions will effectively change the situation. Problem-focused coping is more likely when appraisal indicates something can be done; emotion-focused coping is more likely when appraisal indicates nothing can be done to reduce the source of stress.[2]

We use some coping strategies more consistently than others. The strategy of thinking positively, for example, is relatively stable across a variety of different kinds of stressful events. Those who think positively in one stressful situation are likely to think positively in another (the personality trait of optimism will be covered later). Men and women adopt similar coping patterns when researchers control for the type of stressful encounter (e.g., work- or family-related stress). The strategy of seeking social support is not particularly stable. A person who seeks social support for help with one kind of stressful event may not seek social support to deal with another kind of stress (Lazarus, 1993). Which kinds of stressful events, if any, lead you to seek advice and/or consolation from your family, friends, and/or professional counselors?

"I knew you'd understand!"

Our coping strategies mediate our emotional responses to stressful events, sometimes in complex ways. For example, in testing the hypothesis that "coping is personality in action under stress" the coping efforts of premed students before and after a highly stressful medical school entrance exam were surveyed. Results showed that students who used wishful thinking and self-blame became increasingly anxious before and after the test. In contrast, students who distanced themselves from the outcome reported decreased anxiety after they took the test (Bolger, 1990, p. 525). The effects of talking to others appear to depend on *when* we report how we feel. Anxiety increased immediately after talking to others but was reduced 2 days later, compared to no-talk controls. The positive benefits of coping take time (Mendolia & Kleck, 1993).

The usefulness of any one coping strategy depends on (1) the type of stressful event, (2) the personality of the person who is stressed, and (3) which possible outcome is studied (e.g., health, subjective well-being, or social functioning). "What works in one context may be counterproductive in another" (Lazarus, 1993, p. 9).

The Depressive Self-Schema Approach

The negative appraisals of the depressed are global, pervasive, and exclusive. Depressives ... expect failure to continue well into the future.

—David Clark and Aaron Beck (1989, p. 393)

Aaron Beck proposes that depression and other emotional difficulties associated with stress are largely produced by cognitive distortions in the *cognitive triad* of how people think about themselves, their world, and their future. In his observations of depressed patients' thoughts, Beck (1984) notes three common themes: *self-dislike* ("If something bad happens, it must be my fault because I'm just no good."); *negative interpretations of external events* ("If something bad happens, it's a catastrophe."); and *pessimistic views of the future* ("It will never get better.").

According to Beck's analysis, these *cognitive distortions* are due to a common group of logical errors. These errors include (a) *personalizing*, or interpreting negative events as always due to oneself; (b) *catastrophizing*, the error of overstating the negative consequences of disappointing events; and (c) *hopelessness*, the error of assuming that improvement is impossible.

Beck (1976) observes that depressive self-schemas form a vicious downward spiral: Negative interpretations of oneself result in lowered self-esteem, which increases the likelihood of negatively interpreting other events, which further lowers self-esteem. Do you know anyone who exhibits this vicious cycle? How can it be broken?

Beck (1983) proposes there are two subtypes of depression. *Sociotropic* depressives depend excessively on others and are preoccupied with thoughts about social deprivation and loss. Their self-esteem is highly sensitive to even minor forms of social rejection. For example, adolescents who sought and found social support on Facebook reported they felt less depressed, while adolescents who failed to find social support on Facebook reported they felt even more depressed (Frison & Eggermont, 2015).

Autonomous depressives are primarily concerned with achieving their goals. They value personal autonomy and control and are described as perfectionistic, goal-oriented, and authoritarian. They tend to avoid interpersonal entanglements because these may interfere with their autonomy and pursuit of their individual goals.

Beck's distinction between sociotropic and autonomous depressives suggests that stress itself can be conceptualized as a personality trait. Are certain clusters of personality traits associated with experiencing greater stress than other trait clusters? Yes.

Dispositional Approaches

It has never been the goal of Robert McCrae and Paul Costa to study stress per se. Their Five-Factor Model of personality, as we have seen, is concerned with describing the *structure* of personality. Nevertheless, their Five-Factor Model contributes to our understanding of stress and coping.

The Five-Factor Model (FFM)

Each of the five traits of the FFM is related to stress and coping. Let's start with extraversion-introversion. Extraverts typically report they feel good about themselves and life in general to a greater extent than do introverts. Positive affect is the emotional core of extraversion (Watson & Clark, 1997). Their positive affect may act as a "buffer trait" against the stresses and strains of everyday living. This is shown by responses from a large sample of adults who reported a recent stressful event in their lives (such as the loss of a loved one, illness in the family, or the challenge of marriage). Extraverts were more likely to deal with the stress by engaging in positive thinking, taking rational actions, and finding satisfaction in other areas of their lives (Connor-Smith & Flachsbart, 2007; McCrae & Costa, 1986). Extraverts are more likely to engage in problem-focused coping with stress and to cognitively reframe the stressful event so as to give it a more positive "spin" (Smith, Williams, & Segerstrom, 2015).

The second trait of the FFM that relates to stress and coping is neuroticism (or emotional instability). People who report they frequently feel fearful, sad, angry, worried, or guilty score high on measures of negative affect. Such individuals exhibit the low emotional stability associated with the trait of neuroticism (Larsen & Ketelar, 1991; Watson & Clark, 1992). The trait of neuroticism seems to accentuate stress and inhibits effectively coping with it (Carver & Connor-Smith, 2010). Individuals who score high on the neuroticism scale are likely to use emotion-focused solutions rather than dealing directly with the problem. Adults who score highly on this trait cope with stress by withdrawing into escapist fantasies, procrastinate in making decisions, abuse alcohol and/or drugs, or eat to excess (Connor-Smith & Flachsbart, 2007; McCrae & Costa, 1986).

Neuroticism or emotional instability is a general trait that is composed, as we saw earlier, of six facets: anxiety, hostility, depression, self-consciousness, impulsiveness, and vulnerability. This last facet is especially relevant to stress and coping because vulnerability "designates an inability to deal adequately with stress" (McCrae & Costa, 1990, p. 43). Moreover, high scores on neuroticism are associated with slower cardiovascular recovery in responses to stressors used in controlled laboratory studies (Chida & Hamer, 2008). People high in neuroticism experience more intense and more longer lasting stress than those who are not as emotional unstable.

Naturalistic observations of people in everyday life support the idea that emotionally unstable people are more vulnerable to stress (Bolger & Schilling, 1991). Over a period of 6 weeks, married people provided daily reports about the occurrence of, and their reactions to, various stressful events. It was found that those who were above average in neuroticism (more emotionally unstable) experienced greater distress in response to the hassles of everyday life than those who were below the group average. Moreover, the most distressing type of daily hassles for emotionally unstable people was interpersonal conflict. Interpersonal conflict is the most commonly reported source of stress (Bolger et al., 1989; Smith et al., 2015). As we have seen, individuals who score high on tests of neuroticism tend to adopt emotion-focused strategies in dealing with their stress. Perhaps they feel unable to take direct, problem-focused actions to deal with the stressful situations in their daily lives (Suls & Martin, 2005).

The *Type D* personality disposition consists of selected facets of extraversion and neuroticism. Specifically, this disposition is found in individuals who chronically experience negative affectivity in terms of any or all of five facets of neuroticism (anxiety, angry hostility, depression, self-consciousness, vulnerability) and two facets of extraversion (low warmth, low gregariousness). "Socially inhibited worrier" is an apt characterization of this disposition (Denollet, 2005; Horwood, Anglim, & Tooley, 2015). Employees with this personality disposition experience greater emotional exhaustion as well as being less engaged with their work. Perhaps such individuals chronically experience many negative emotions but rarely express them out of fear of social disapproval or rejection. Their continuous effort to inhibit these feelings and put on a "happy face" is a compelling explanation for their emotional exhaustion (Cheung & Miu-Chi Lin, 2015; van den Tooren & Rutte, 2015).

The third trait related to stress and coping is openness to experience. Individuals scoring high on this trait are creative, imaginative, curious, and have broad interests. Low scorers are described as down to earth, conforming, traditional, and have relatively few interests. McCrae and Costa (1986) found that adults who scored high on this trait handled the stress in their lives by trying to find humor in the situation while low scorers coped by putting their faith in God or other people. Individuals high in openness tend to choose problem-focused strategies to handle stress (Carver & Connor-Smith, 2010), and they have fewer negative social interactions than people who are less open (Smith et al., 2015).

Agreeableness is the fourth trait of the FFM. It is also associated with low interpersonal conflict as well as an increased use of social support when stress occurs. Individuals high in agreeableness report greater subjective well-being and enjoy better health outcomes than those low on this trait (Carver & Connor-Smith, 2010).

Conscientiousness, the fifth trait of the FFM, is associated with lower stress exposure, problem-focused coping, lower rates of divorce, decreased risk for illnesses such as diabetes and tuberculosis, and increased longevity (Goodwin & Friedman, 2006; Kern & Friedman, 2008; Roberts & Bogg, 2004). Conscientious individuals are more likely to use problem-solving coping methods. They also try to look at the problem's bright side (Connor-Smith & Flaschsbart, 2007).

While it is convenient for authors of personality textbooks to pigeonhole theories into this approach or that approach, life outside of textbooks is a bit more complex, as you may have noticed. I mention this truism as a way of introducing research that showed changes in personality traits depended on how the events were interpreted. In other words, both interpretational and dispositional viewpoints are needed to understand what was found in this longitudinal investigation (Sutin et al., 2010).

Middle-aged adults were asked to describe the most stressful event in their lives within the past 10 years. They were also asked to evaluate this event in terms of whether it was a learning lesson, a turning point in their lives, or both. (These participants had already completed a measure of the FFM traits both before and after the stressful event.) Thinking about the event afterward, those who saw the event as a negative turning point in their lives showed an increase in neuroticism. Those who saw the event as a lesson learned increased in extraversion and conscientiousness. The authors conclude that changes in personality traits are more strongly related to how individuals interpret stressful events rather than their simple occurrence (Sutin et al., 2010). Shakespeare would agree: "There is nothing good or bad but thinking makes it so."

Optimism

Do you generally expect good things will happen in your life? If so, you are characterized by the trait of *optimism*, described by Charles Carver and Michael Scheier as a stable, generalized disposition to anticipate positive outcomes across all areas of life. An optimistic personality disposition enables us to better cope with adverse events. Optimists are more likely to cope actively by selecting a problem-focused approach. Pessimists either choose an emotion-focused approach or they avoid thinking about the stressful situation. Optimists tend to *reframe* the stressful situation more positively ("If life hands you a lemon, make lemonade."). Optimists tend to accept the situation as it is, use less denial, defuse the stress with humor. Optimists carry a sense of hope that their efforts to deal with the problem will pay off (Carver & Scheier, 2009; Solberg Nes & Segerstrom, 2006).

However, the unconditional belief that an optimistic attitude will always improve performance may lead to disappointment. Reality always puts limits on what is actually possible in any given situation, no matter how optimistic we may be (Tenney, Logg, & Moore, 2015). That essential qualifier aside, though, the real-world benefits of having an optimistic attitude for coping with stress are well replicated. A small sample:

- An optimistic personality disposition helps women cope with the stress of discovering they have breast cancer (Carver et al., 1993). Women who were optimistic before they received the diagnosis of cancer showed a better quality of life at the 1-year follow up (Schou, Ekeberg, & Ruland, 2005).
- Students who are more optimistic of attaining the grade they want were less threatened before and after an important examination than less optimistic students (Carver & Scheier, 1994).
- Optimistic, soon-to-be lawyers felt less stress during the tense 4-month waiting period between taking the California bar exam and learning if they passed (Sweeny & Andrews, 2014).
- Optimistic individuals who were falsely told their stress levels were higher than normal secreted less cortisol than those who were not optimistic. Optimism served to buffer the physiological stress response to the stressful news (Jobin, Wrosch, & Scheier, 2014).
- Dispositional optimism is a valuable personal resource for mothers facing economic adversity. Optimistic mothers in those circumstances provided more nurturance, were more involved with parenting, and demonstrated higher levels of effective child rearing.

These results were replicated in both African-American and Mexican-American households (Taylor et al., 2010; Taylor et al., 2012).

The real-world benefits of optimism are great news for optimists and their merry friends. But what about those of us whose natural disposition is not bright and sunny? Are we doomed to perpetually anticipate soggy picnics? Maybe not. The last section of this chapter, positive psychology, offers a variety of personality strengths that are valuable coping strategies for everyone.

Ego Control and Resiliency

Unexpected changes in the environment can lead us to feel stressed and frustrated. The ability to tolerate frustrating events first appears when we're about 2 years old and improves over the years. *Ego control* refers to the extent to which people inhibit, modify, or express their impulses and desires. Some people cannot delay gratification. They express their wants and desires immediately, without any concern for its appropriateness in their current situation. These people are called *undercontrolled* (Block and Block, 1980). Undercontrolled is a synonym for impulsive. At the other extreme are individuals who are *overcontrolled*. They are rigid, inhibited, and nonspontaneous. Neither extreme is particularly helpful for dealing with stress. Ego undercontrol shows relative consistency in both sexes over the time span of 3 to 23 years of age (Block, 1993). Children who are relatively impulsive (compared to their peers) are likely to be impulsive adults.

Block and Block's (1980) construct of *ego resiliency* refers to the flexibility of ego controls. Highly flexible people can vary their degree of control depending on the situation. People who lack ego resiliency have a more difficult time coping with stressful events. They tend to act either rigidly or impulsively, even if their chosen course of action is not effective. Jane Loevinger's (1976) concept of ego development (i.e., becoming increasingly able to resist impulses and exert self-control) has been found to be associated with increased levels of ego resiliency (Westenberg & Block, 1993).

Ego resiliency (ER) is fairly stable throughout childhood. Eighteen-month-old children's level of ego resiliency correlated with their ER ratings when they were 42 to 84 months old. Additionally, ER ratings at 18 months were related to social competence at 84 months of age (Taylor et al., 2014). ER is also related to attachment quality. Five-year-olds rated as highly resilient by their teachers had earlier been classified as securely attached (Arend, Gove, & Sroufe, 1979). Similarly, maternal warmth in economically challenged families promotes children's resilience and positive adjustment (Kim-Cohen et al., 2004).

Additional support for the view that attachment quality contributes to ego resilience includes (a) resilient college students were less anxiously attached compared to those rated not as resilient (Galatzer-Levy & Bonanno, 2013) and (b) fathers who are avoidantly attached are less ego resilient in dealing with the stresses of caring for their newborn children than fathers who are not avoidantly attached (Fillo et al., 2015).

The pattern of drug use among 18-year-olds appears to be related to ego resiliency: Those who occasionally experimented with drugs were more likely to be rated by other people as ego resilient. In contrast, frequent drug users were seen as undercontrolled, and total abstainers were rated as overcontrolled (Shedler & Block, 1990). And among adult women, ER predicted their overall well-being, satisfaction with their romantic relationship, engagement with work, and the state of their physical health 9 years later (Klohnen, Vandewater, & Young, 1996). Finally, ego resiliency correlates with each trait of the five-factor model, especially conscientiousness. Ego resilient individuals combine the traits of high conscientiousness with low neuroticism (Huey & Weisz, 1997).

The data are clear: Ego resilience is a protective factor against stress. What is far from clear is explaining its origins. How can those who lack it get it? Multiple theorists agree that dispositional, relational, and situational variables are necessary ingredients in the development of ego resilience, but its final recipe has yet to be written. David Fletcher and Mustafa Sarkar (2013) review the promising contenders for the winning *pièce-de-résilience*.

Hardiness

The trait of hardiness consists of three interrelated tendencies of control, challenge, and commitment that can help us cope with stressful events (Kobasa, 1979). *Control* is our general expectation that our outcomes are predictable and controllable by our own efforts. *Challenge* is the belief that changes are a normal part of living and they thus challenge us to employ our abilities effectively. *Commitment* is the belief that our activities are meaningful and important rather than meaningless and trivial. In theory, the greater our sense of control, challenge, and commitment, the greater we exhibit the trait of hardiness in meeting life's changes, which are then experienced as less stressful.

Executives of a large company who were high in hardiness were observed to have fewer serious illnesses than those who were low in hardiness (Kobasa, Maddi, & Kahn, 1982). This finding was replicated among service members of the Norwegian Armed Forces. Hardiness predicted the likelihood of absences due to illness as well as the number of times an individual missed work (Hystad, Eid, & Brevik, 2011). Hardiness is also positively associated with being engaged with work assignments and negatively associated with cynicism and job burnout. Dispositional hardiness appears to be a health buffer against stressful events (Bue et al., 2013).

Which personality traits are associated with hardiness? A meta-analysis found that hardiness typically correlated positively with extraversion and openness to experience but negatively with neuroticism. Emotionally unstable individuals are less hardy than those who are emotionally stable. Other personality correlates of hardiness include optimism, extraversion, high self-esteem, and positive social relationships (Eschleman, Bowling, & Alarcon, 2010).

As a tool for understanding stress, Sigmund Freud and Karen Horney agree that analysis is indispensable—the psychoanalysis of emotional distress caused by unconscious conflicts. The purpose of analysis is to bring these conflicts into awareness so they may be resolved once and for all.

Psychodynamic Approaches

Anxiety and the Mechanisms of Defense

The problem of anxiety is a nodal point, linking up all kinds of most important questions.

—Sigmund Freud (1924/1952, p. 401)

Freud's word for stress is anxiety. Anxiety serves as a danger signal to the ego. Freud (1926/1959a) believed that the ego can experience anxiety from three sources: the external world, the id, and the superego. We cope with these painful feelings of anxiety by unconsciously adopting various mechanisms of defense, some of which are more adaptive than others.

Anxiety

Objective anxiety (or reality anxiety) is what Freud meant by *fear*, the fear of real dangers in the external world. Should you spot a speeding truck heading right at you, your fear will help you to move quickly out of the way. Once the external danger has passed, your fear will subside. Fear is the basic type of anxiety from which the other two forms are derived.

It's important to note, though, that fear and anxiety are not identical emotional experiences. *Fear* refers to emotional arousal that is automatically elicited by an external stimulus (Öhman & Mineka, 2001). *Anxiety* applies to either emotional arousal that is not caused by some external event or to cases when our arousal far exceeds that which is warranted by objective reality (i.e., we emotionally overreact to a trivial event).

Freud distinguishes two forms of anxiety:

Neurotic anxiety is the fear that our instinctual impulses and desires will overwhelm our ego's ability to control them and we will do something we will be punished for later. Because we were punished for trying to gratify ourselves when we were small children (reaching for yummy cookies before dinner), we unconsciously associate anxiety with both the punishment we received and the temptation to engage in similar behaviors. Even though we have forgotten those particular early childhood experiences, the anxiety we feel in the present is related to the earlier dangers we experienced in our past.

Moral anxiety is the superego's warning to the ego that some thought or behavior is unacceptable. Moral anxiety is the early warning signal that, if not heeded by the ego, will result in feelings of guilt and self-blame. Sometimes it does not take much to set off these alarm bells and we feel anxious even though we have absolutely no intention to act on a passing thought (e.g., taking revenge after being insulted). Why is that?

Randolph Nesse uses the analogy of a smoke detector to explain how anxiety and our defense mechanisms might have evolved: Smoke detectors are set to go off at the slightest indication of smoke (causing many false alarms) to prevent the possibility of a failure to detect a disastrous life-threatening fire (a false negative). In the same way, anxiety is often a false alarm in that we are not in any real danger but this annoyance (the cost of a sensitive warning system) is offset by the advantage that the anxiety prepares us for action (or nonaction) when the appropriate behavior is actually needed (Nesse, 2005).

People with inappropriately strong superegos feel guilty at the mere thought of violating some well-internalized moral precept or failing to live up to their ego ideal. Like neurotic anxiety, moral anxiety originates from childhood experiences when we were punished for our transgressions. A conscience-stricken person is someone who chronically feels guilty over minor transgressions or failures to be perfect.

Individuals who strongly identify with their ideal images of themselves (i.e., who they think they should be) are at risk for becoming perfectionists. Perfectionists are likely to endorse such irrational beliefs as "There is one perfect solution to every problem and it is essential that I find it" and "I must be competent in all possible respects if I am to consider myself worthwhile" (Ellis, 1962). Gordon Flett and Paul Hewitt discuss the types of perfectionism and treatments available to individuals who struggle with this type of neurosis. Some perfectionists are at risk for becoming incapacitated by depression (Flett & Hewitt, 2013).

"Therapy's working. I used to get angry and upset.
Now I just get angry!"

Neurotic anxiety and moral anxiety are sometimes referred to as *free-floating anxiety* because they are not as directly tied to present external stimuli as objective anxiety (= fear). Neurotic and moral anxiety are associated with past, forgotten traumatic events. These types of anxiety do not go away simply because the external danger has passed. They have an internal base of operations that can dominate consciousness whenever the present situation triggers a memory of prior traumatic events.

The good news is that our chronic emotional overreactions can be a key to awareness if we recognize that we are overreacting. Once I became aware that I was making an emotional big deal out of an ordinary classroom event, I was able, by letting my mind wander in association to this classroom trigger, to recall vividly my childhood trauma that was the root cause of my excessive emotional reactions. Identifying the source of these inappropriate overreactions enabled me to be free of them forever.[3] Once we clearly know the original source of our emotional molehills, we can stop making mountains out of them because we will see they are only molehills.

Defense Mechanisms

Strong anxiety threatens the ego's primary function as the personality's executor. In such instances the ego will *unconsciously* protect itself by adopting one or more defense mechanisms to cope with the threat. These defense mechanisms *distort reality* to make it more acceptable to the ego. Defense mechanisms are examples of Lazarus and Folkman's emotion-focused coping strategies (changing our interpretation of the external event) except that they occur unconsciously and automatically. Defense mechanisms give us time to adjust to the stressful event and think of possible problem-focused solutions. Defense mechanisms become problematic when they become our consistent reactions to all stressful events.

Following Anna Freud's (1936) concept of hierarchical levels of defenses, George Vaillant (1977, 1993) classifies defense mechanisms into four levels, depending on their degree of maturity (I = least mature, IV = most mature). See Table 7.1.

Under Level IV, Vaillant (2000) identifies five "high adaptive level" defenses. *Sublimation,* as described above, is one of them. The others include *suppression,* the ability to postpone gratification ("I'll put these thoughts aside for now and think about them later"), and *anticipation,* the ability to expect future emotional reactions ("I'll probably feel nervous during the interview"). In addition, *altruism* is a mature defense because it can dramatically reduce anxiety caused by past traumatic events as

❖ **Table 7.1**   Representative Defense Mechanisms at Each of Vaillant's Four Levels

Mechanism	Definition	Example
Denial (I)	The external danger is not consciously perceived or acknowledged.	An alcoholic denies that alcohol causes many problems in his life.
Projection (II)	Seeing one's own unacceptable feelings, attitudes, or behaviors in other people but not in oneself.	A worker, unaware of her own angry feelings toward her boss, perceives her boss to be angry with her.
Reaction Formation (III)	Overemphasizing the opposite trait of one's true but unacceptable feelings.	A mother resents having to care for her child and "smothers it" with love.
Sublimation (IV)	Redirecting unacceptable thoughts and impulses into socially acceptable and useful behavior.	A egotistical man becomes a college professor who is the center of attention whenever he lectures.

Source: Adapted from Vaillant (1993).

well as transform the lives of both the giver and receiver. For example, a victim of past abuse who altruistically volunteers to help similar victims thereby empowers all concerned to face life's challenges with more strength and wisdom than before the abuse occurred. Finally, Vaillant agrees with Freud (1905/1960) that *humor* is the highest of these adaptive defensive processes. Mature humor (i.e., self-deprecating, not hostile) allows the person to look squarely at what is painful but without additional discomfort or putting others in an uncomfortable position (Vaillant, 2000). A longitudinal investigation of defense mechanisms found that adults generally moved in the direction of more adaptive coping from adolescence to early old age (Diehl et al., 2014).

Phebe Cramer distinguishes coping mechanisms from defense mechanisms. While both coping and defense mechanisms are evoked by substantive changes in one's world, coping efforts are explicitly directed at solving the problem that caused the disequilibrium. Coping efforts are problem focused. In contrast, defense mechanisms, operating automatically and without conscious participation, prevent the ego from being overwhelmed by anxiety, and thus are always concerned with the individual's emotions rather than the external problem that provoked excessive anxiety (Cramer, 1998, 2006). Anxiety, and how we handle it, lies at the heart of Karen Horney's understanding of stress.

Three Neurotic Solutions to Anxiety

Every neurotic is driven to maintain the status quo.

—Karen Horney (1945, p. 234)

Because the process of living involves change, and change can be stressful, anyone suffering from a neurosis is especially prone to feeling stressed out. Horney views neurosis as the ongoing process of trying to replace one's actual self with an unrealistic *idealized self-image.* The neurotic person is deeply motivated to protect this false image

© Bettmann/CORBIS

Photo 7.1 Karen Horney (1885–1952)

Although originally trained as a Freudian, Horney replaced Freud's drive reduction approach to motivation with three ways we can reduce anxiety: by moving against other people, by moving away from other people, or by moving toward other people.

Key publications:

The Neurotic Personality of Our Time (1937)
Self-Analysis (1942)
Neurosis and Human Growth (1950)

against any change in spite of the stresses and strains entailed by constantly needing to prop up a delusional self-image. Why would anyone do this to himself?

As mentioned in Chapter 1, Karen Horney's (1950) central idea is basic anxiety: "[The] feeling of being isolated and helpless in a world conceived as potentially hostile" (p. 18). Basic anxiety leads the child to cope with the powerful adults in her life by hiding her true feelings (feelings that are or could be unacceptable to adults) and coping with these adults in any way that does not arouse anxiety. Both temperamental and environmental factors determine her specific coping attempts. Horney classifies these coping solutions as either *moving toward, moving away from*, or *moving against* other people.

Each solution works in that it can reduce basic anxiety. But the person who gains a certain modicum of security in this way pays the terrible price of self-alienation: The idealized, false self-image compulsively determines what is desired for the continual construction of this psychic idol rather than the individual's real needs: *"The energies driving toward self-realization are shifted to the aim of actualizing the idealized self"* (Horney, 1950, p. 24, italics in original). Moreover, the idealized self competes with the actual self for the individual's feeling of identity, creating great uncertainty about who one really is. *Self-alienation* is the nuclear problem in all cases of neurosis (pp. 187–188).

In each of the three neurotic solutions, one of the dimensions involved in basic anxiety is overemphasized (Horney, 1945). Those who "move toward others" overemphasize their childlike *helplessness*. People who need people are not the "luckiest people in the world," but are the most dependent. People who "move away from others" overemphasize *isolation* ("I am a rock. I am an island."). They fear entanglement and restriction of their imagined freedoms. People who "move against others" overemphasize the *hostility* they see pervading the world ("Do unto others before they do unto you."). Their idealized self-image calls for them to compulsively prove they are superior to other people. They frequently steer ordinary conversations into verbal competitions from which they, in their own minds, emerge victorious.

Horney observes that people suffering from a neurosis back up their idealized self-images with a number of unconscious "neurotic claims." A *neurotic claim* is a *wish* whose nonfulfillment "is felt as an unfair frustration, an offense about which we have a right to feel indignant" (Horney, 1950, p. 42). Those whose solution to anxiety is to move toward others claim that friends and/or family members should always be available to them whenever they are needed. Otherwise, these so-called friends are being "selfish." Those whose solution is to move away claim they should be free from being inconvenienced by others, even including the inconvenience of needing to say no to requests. Since they themselves do not "bother" anyone, no one should bother them. Those who move against others often feel annoyed if they have to wait in line just like everyone else when it should be obvious to everyone that they have important work to do. They deserve and thus should receive preferential treatment. Not receiving it violates their neurotic claim, leading them to feel anxiety and, perhaps, anger.

The difference between a neurotic claim and a nonneurotic preference is seen in our reactions to its nonfulfillment. How do you typically react when you *don't* get what you want? When a nonneurotic preference fails to be realized, we accept reality and make alternative plans without feeling that some grave injustice has been perpetrated. Even though we might feel disappointed, we can still learn from the experience to increase our chances for success the next time (e.g., call ahead to make sure the store is open). We can easily let go of any negative emotional reaction to the nonfulfillment.

Reactions to the nonfulfillment of neurotic claims, however, are another story. These claims are often revealed by the word *should*. A neurotic person feels deeply that other people *should* do this or that and is offended when they don't. The unconscious power of neurosis is graphically illustrated by the neurotic sufferer who utterly fails to see the direct cause-and-effect connection between his unrealistic neurotic claim of what other people *should* do and his feelings of hurt, disappointment, anger, or anxiety when they fail to behave in those ways. Whenever we emotionally overreact to the ordinary frustrations of life, we have a chance to discover something important about ourselves. Making unreasonable demands on others or holding unrealistic expectations does not change reality—these demands only create additional stress in our lives.

For example, consider a mother who demands that her grown children should continue to cater to her whims and wishes, even if these interfere with her children's own plans and activities. Whenever her children fail to heed her beck and call, this woman feels her children don't love her and are ungrateful for all she has done for them. She will likely feel hurt, angry, anxious, or depressed. She's unable to see that these negative emotions arise from her own unrealistic neurotic demand that she should be the center of other people's lives.

The chronic stress experienced by people suffering from a neurosis is, to a great extent, self-induced. The accurate perception of cause-and-effect relationships in one's emotional life, on the other hand, eliminates self-induced stress. Table 7.2 presents the idealized images and typical unconscious neurotic claims of Karen Horney's three neurotic solutions.

These are neurotic solutions because they unconsciously serve to perpetuate the status quo of the idealized self-image at the expense of living a full, creative, love-filled life. The neurotic person attempts to solve all the diverse problems of living by adopting the identical neurotic solution. When, as is bound to happen, the solution fails to work, additional stress is experienced. To the neurotic person, the neurotic solution is his *only* solution: He feels a sense of panic if he has to behave otherwise.

In contrast, a healthy person feels free to use any of the three solutions as situations change and call for different solutions. Horney tells us that, as different circumstances arise, we should be capable of cooperating with others, of asserting ourselves by standing up to others, and of keeping to ourselves when we need peace and quiet. These three possible actions complement each other and allow us to be whole or complete (Horney, 1945).

Although Horney's ideas are interesting and provocative, they share the same problem endemic to all psychodynamic perspectives: They are difficult to test empirically. Consequently, Horney's distinctive hypothesis that there are exactly three neurotic solutions has yet to be supported by research observations.

❖ **Table 7.2** Idealized Self-Images and Typical Neurotic Claims of Karen Horney's Neurotic Solutions to Anxiety

Solution	Ideal Self-Image	Typical Neurotic Claims
Moving Against	I am master of my fate. I can solve any problem.	Because I am superior, I am entitled to have my neurotic needs respected by you and to disregard your rights. You should admire, respect, and obey me.
Moving Toward	I am unselfish, good, modest, generous, noble, saintly, helpless, and a martyr.	Because I have suffered so much for you, I am entitled to special treatment from you. You should take care of me.
Moving Away	I am self-sufficient, independent, free of desire, stoic, and fair.	Because I want nothing from you, I am entitled not to be bothered by your expectations and requests. You should leave me alone.

Source: Adapted from Horney (1950). In her last work, Horney identifies the major appeal of the moving against solution as the appeal of mastery, of the moving toward solution as the appeal of love, and the moving away solution as the appeal of freedom.

Empirical research does support Horney's general idea that "moving toward" others is a problematical way of going through life. Vicky Helgeson and her colleagues, for example, have developed an "Unmitigated Communion" scale to identify those whose focus on other people is clearly unhealthy. Such individuals are likely to endorse such items as "I always place the needs of others above my own" and "I can't say no whenever anyone asks me for help" (Helgeson, 2015, p. 526). While the concept of "unmitigated communion" is not identical to "moving toward others," the two constructs seem to have much in common, including identifying those who are low in self-esteem (Helgeson & Fritz, 1998).

Longitudinal Research

Other findings are also compatible with Horney's hypothesis. Longitudinal research suggests that some children who are aggressive, shy, or dependent show continuities across the life course that are consistent with their initial personality trait. For example, 8- to 10-year-old boys who frequently threw severe temper tantrums (a manifestation of Horney's "moving against") were rated 20 years later as significantly more irritable than other 28- to 30-year-old adults. Girls who threw severe temper tantrums were rated as ill-tempered parents 20 years later. Moreover, ill-tempered children of both sexes were more likely to divorce or experience a great deal of conflict in their marriages (Caspi, Elder, & Bem, 1987).

Does this continuity of a certain personality style *prove* that Horney's concept of "moving against" is valid? Not at all. There are numerous plausible explanations for such consistency over time, explanations that do not assume these children tried to reduce their basic anxiety. For example, the continuity of maladaptive behavior can plausibly be explained by the fact that ill-tempered behavior will likely evoke corresponding negative behavior in other people, thus creating a pattern of negative reciprocal social interaction. In spite of viable alternative interpretations, these longitudinal research observations are at least consistent with Horney's theory.

Similarly, shy boys (an example of Horney's "moving away") were found to delay entering marriage, becoming fathers, and establishing stable occupational careers. Shy girls over the same 30-year time period, however, were *not* found to delay marriage compared to nonshy girls. In fact, shy women were more likely to marry men who had high occupational status at the age of 40 than were nonshy women. Whether this is due to highly ambitious men preferring to marry shy women, or whether shy women may have aided their husband's careers by staying at home and fulfilling the traditional homemaker role, is not clear from these data (Caspi, Elder, & Bem, 1988).

This difference in adult outcome between shy boys and girls may be related to differential sex-role norms regarding the social appropriateness of chronic nonassertive behavior. Shy men may be seen as wimps; shy women may be seen as pleasant and agreeable. Personality does not reveal itself in a social vacuum. The long-term effects of any personality style always depend on the values and norms of the social setting in which the personality is manifested.

What about Horney's concept of "moving toward"? Here the longitudinal data are less clear. Boys rated as "dependent" were more likely as adults to have an intact first marriage. Their wives expressed more satisfaction with their marriages than did other wives. "These men seemed to have transformed their childhood dependency into a mature, nurturant style in adulthood that serves them particularly well in the intimate interpersonal world of home and family" (Caspi, Bem, & Elder, 1989, p. 397).

Dependent girls, however, were not so fortunate as adults. At age 30, these women were seen as having a low level of personal aspiration for the future. Moreover, they lacked personal meaning in their lives, had narrow interests, and were rated as moody, unassertive, and self-pitying. The social context once again may be important for understanding these gender differences. These girls may have been *oversocialized* into the female role of dependency. As adults, they ended up leading constricted and cramped lives (Caspi et al., 1989). For females, then, the data are more consistent with Horney's view of "moving toward."

Each view of stress suggests its own optimal coping strategy. From various interpretational perspectives, we cope best with stress by becoming aware of and modifying any unrealistic perceptions and cognitive appraisals. From the dispositional perspective, we know that some people are more likely to experience stress than others: Neuroticism and negative affectivity predispose us to experience stress; optimism, hardiness, and ego resiliency buffer us against stress. Knowing our own dispositions can be useful in helping us to avoid stressful situations. Finally, from the psychodynamic point of view, stress is caused by internal, unconscious conflicts. The anxiety that is symptomatic of unconscious conflict can be alleviated by any process, such as psychotherapy, that brings the conflict to such crystal clear awareness that its solution is obvious.

A person plagued by a chronic internal conflict is like someone trying to drive a beat-up car with one foot pressing the gas pedal firmly to the floor while his other foot presses equally firmly on the brake pedal. What happens? The engine turns over rapidly, the car shakes violently, expending enormous energy, but the car goes nowhere. Much energy is exhausted, but the car doesn't move. A person consumed by a major conflict feels exhausted without knowing why.

But when the conflict is fully resolved, all the psychic energy, both conscious and unconscious, that had gone into its maintenance is now released and is consciously available. The conflict-free person experiences an unexpected and vigorous uprush of vitality. His clunker has turned into a sports car. Zooooooooom!

The advent of positive psychology in 2000 (e.g., Seligman & Csikszentmihalyi, 2000) ushered in a new stage in psychology's evolution. Positive psychology focuses on those positive features of human nature that make life worth living: hope, creativity, courage, wisdom, spirituality (to name but a few). A person whose life is grounded on any psychological *strength* (the meaning of *virtue*) can cope with the stresses and strains of daily living from a different vantage point than those we've considered so far. We end this chapter by looking at some of the ways positive psychology helps us cope with stress.

Positive Psychology and Coping

As we have seen, Erik Erikson's psychosocial theory holds that personality development is a life-long process. It consists of eight stages or crises. As previously mentioned, Erikson felt that the growth of personality is epigenetic: How we handle our present crisis depends in part on how well or poorly we handled our prior ones. Erikson (1959) thought that each crisis will result in either a new personality strength (virtue) or a personality defect, depending on whether the resolution was favorable or unfavorable to future growth. Fifty years later, many personality psychologists have come to agree with Erikson that understanding an individual's strengths and virtues is essential for knowing who the person is and how she uses these strengths to cope with life's challenges. Positive psychology has arrived (Seligman & Csikszentmihalyi, 2000).

In the remaining pages of this chapter, we'll look at the eight strengths (virtues) that Erikson proposes accrue from successfully negotiating each crisis. How do these eight strengths help us cope with stress? Research psychologists in this new field of positive psychology (e.g., Peterson & Seligman, 2004) hope to understand how the entire range of personal strengths and virtues, not only Erikson's eight, help us navigate around the stresses and strains of daily living.

Hope is the virtue we gain from successfully resolving our first crisis of *trust versus mistrust*. How hope helps us cope with stress was covered in the preceding section on optimism. Like research on optimism, research on hope finds that individuals who express more hope show greater academic and athletic accomplishments, better physical and psychological health, and superior interpersonal relationships (Rand & Cheavens, 2009). Since hope is a *forward-minded attitude*, it is not surprising that individuals who adopt a distant-future perspective experience less distress than those who do not. Their stress is reduced because a distant-future perspective reminds them of the impermanence of the present stress-inducing negative event. In other words, the attitude "this too shall pass" can be an effective way of coping with stress (Bruehlman-Senecal & Ayduk, 2015).

Will is the strength we obtain from resolving Erikson's second psychosocial crisis of *autonomy versus shame and doubt.* Will enables us to exercise free choice (autonomy) and allows us to engage in self-restraint and self-control. *Self-regulation,* the modern term for self-control, is such an essential part of personality development that I've devoted a big chunk of Chapter 9 to it. For now, though, I'll note that one way self-regulation enables us to cope more effectively is by being able to reinterpret or reappraise a stressful situation from *threatening* (and highly stressful) to *challenging* (not quite as stressful). These reappraisals, along with reducing stress, also result in more positive emotional reactions, fewer negative emotional reactions, greater task persistence, and more focused thinking (Tomaka et al., 1997).

Purpose, the ego-strength that accrues from successful resolution of Erikson's *initiative versus guilt* crisis, permits the child to venture into the new, the unknown, by engaging her curiosity (Erikson, 1959). Having achieved a sense of autonomy at the prior stage of development, the child discovers she can use her will to explore her environment and follow with purpose wherever her curiosity leads—into new experiences and new knowledge. Exploring new events encourages learning new things and developing new skills. Curiosity is intrinsic motivation in its purest form. We know that a sense of well-being usually accompanies actions that are intrinsically motivated (Ryan & Deci, 2000). Curiosity is associated with greater learning and performance in both academic (Harackiewicz et al., 2002) and work settings (Reio & Wiswell, 2000).

How does curiosity relate to stress and coping? Curiosity has been found to increase tolerance for otherwise distressing experiences resulting from behaving outside one's usual comfort zone (Kashdan, 2007). Curiosity is one of the facets of openness to experience. Individuals who are high in openness, when trying to resolve marital difficulties, tend to adopt a problem-solving approach, while those who are low in openness to experience employ either distancing strategies or ignore the problem (McCrae & Sutin, 2009). Curiosity has also been found to correlate with greater psychological well-being, increased intelligence, and longevity (Kashdan & Silvia, 2009), suggesting that curiosity, by increasing one's sense of well-being and active engagement with life, functions as a general buffer against the stresses of everyday life.[4]

Competence, the virtue Erikson hypothesizes comes out of the successful resolution of the *industry versus inferiority* crisis, is another term for *self-efficacy* (discussed in Chapter 5). Numerous studies have shown that the generalized sense of self-efficacy either helps buffer the effects of stress or it directly enables the individual to effectively cope with the stressors in his or her life. For example, post-deployment self-efficacy was found to be inversely related to how much distress combat veterans experienced (Smith, Benight, & Cieslak, 2013). Among adults 65 to 75 years of age, those who scored higher in self-efficacy showed fewer symptoms of maladjustment in reaction to the stress caused by daily hassles (Holahan, Holahan, & Belk, 1984). Competence is an invaluable strength for coping with stress.

Fidelity, the virtue Erikson identifies as the result of the successful resolution of the *identity versus identity diffusion* crisis, is the strength of being true to oneself. An individual who is true to herself is a person who has *integrity*. Being true to herself also means that she is *autonomous*—she chooses her actions rather than acting just because someone else tells her to. Self-determination theory maintains that *autonomy* is a universal human need.

How does integrity or autonomy help us cope with stress? Autonomous individuals devote their attention to the task at hand because they chose to do it. They are intrinsically motivated to accomplish what they set out to do. Should their workload be suddenly and unexpectedly increased (a stressful event), they continue to focus their attention on their task. They cope with the new demand by creating more efficient procedures to get the additional work accomplished. In contrast, individuals doing the same work, but not autonomously, experience the changed workload as highly stressful and adopted emotion-focused strategies to deal with their anxiety (Parker, Jimmieson, & Amiot, 2013). When we act with integrity we have more psychological energy available to us. None of our energy is drained away in maintaining a "front" we think we need for self-protection, self-enhancement, or as resistance to doing things we don't want to do. We don't feel emotionally exhausted (van den Tooren & Rutte, 2015).

Love, the virtue accruing from the successful resolution of Erikson's sixth crisis, *intimacy versus isolation*, is a multi-faceted diamond. *Attachment* is the facet that provides a consistent protective benefit against stress. Securely attached individuals have a greater sense of self-efficacy, are more ego-resilient, perceive themselves to be able to cope effectively, expect they can control their negative moods, are confident they can solve life's problems, are more optimistic and hopeful, and have hardier, more stress-resistant attitudes (Mikulincer & Shaver, 2007). Another facet, *romantic love*, appears to buffer against physiological stress reactions and helps regulate our emotions. Individuals who had recently fallen in love showed reduced autonomic reactions to stressful films compared to those who were single (Schneiderman et al., 2011). Whether this stress-buffering effect persists after the initial rosy bloom of falling in love fades away is an important question for future research.

The ability to *care* is the strength that emerges from the adult crisis Erikson calls *generativity versus stagnation*. Synonyms for this ego-strength are kindness, altruism, compassion, empathy, and nurturance. Empathy, feeling what another person feels, is an ego-stregth that is most likely to be activated when we understand why the *situation* caused the other person to feel the way he or she does. Being able to appraise someone else's situation (as one that typically causes anyone to feel a particular emotion, such as anxiety, sadness, joy, etc.) allows us to feel what they feel (Wondra & Ellsworth, 2015).

The research program of Dan McAdams has documented the numerous positive characteristics associated with a generative and caring life style. Highly generative adults, for example, reveal higher levels of life satisfaction and lower levels of anxiety and depression, compared to less generative adults. Thus, giving what we can to those who need our help seems to be naturally self-rewarding (McAdams, 2006), a finding consistent with the view that humans evolved to be in close connection with each other (Lieberman, 2013).

Wisdom is the virtue that accompanies our last developmental crisis, *integrity versus despair.* Erikson notes that as we approach the end of our lives, we cannot help looking back to see what we have accomplished or have failed to accomplish. During this last stage, the life cycle weaves back on itself and integrates maturing forms of hope, will, purpose, competence, fidelity, love, and care into an integrated sense of wisdom (Erikson, Erikson, & Kivnick, 1986).

What is wisdom? Many ideas have been offered. Erikson proposes that wisdom "is detached concern with life itself, in the face of death itself" (1964, p. 133). He means that wise elderly individuals are those who remain personally involved with human problems in spite of any bodily decline. They do not succumb to the anxiety and despair of impending death. Successful resolution of this final crisis entails accepting without regret our life decisions or uselessly ruminating on "what if" we had chosen different paths.

A number of theorists distinguish two forms of wisdom, personal and general. Personal wisdom refers to the understanding and insights about life that come from your personal experiences (subjectively). General wisdom concerns understanding life from an observer's point of view (objectively). One approach to general wisdom describes five criteria for its attainment:

(1) Have rich factual knowledge about human nature, lifespan development, interpersonal relations, and social norms.

(2) Possess rich procedural knowledge about how to conduct oneself, how to give advice, how to resolve interpersonal problems.

(3) Understand the context of problems (e.g., school, work, family, etc.) and put these problems into a lifetime perspective of past, present, and future.

(4) Accept individual differences in value systems, while being ready to help everyone reach their potential.

(5) Recognize and manage uncertainty without undue stress (Baltes & Staudinger, 2000; Staudinger & Gluck, 2011).

How many of these five criteria have you achieved? I'm making some progress on the first one. I wonder if these are ideals rather than realistic criteria that can be actually met by any single human person over one lifetime. What do you think?

Finally, Peterson and Seligman (2004) consider the strength of wisdom to consist of five components: creativity, curiosity, open-mindedness, love of learning, and perspective. By perspective they mean the ability to see and make sense of the overall picture and to use this ability to improve the well-being of oneself and others.

Are these components of wisdom related to stress? Yes, mostly. In a study of working adults, the more strongly these components characterized a person's personality, the lower was his or her stress. This was particularly true for the component of curiosity (which, as we saw earlier in the chapter, can serve as a buffer against stress). The only component in this study that was unrelated to stress was creativity (Avey et al., 2012).

All-in-all, individuals who have achieved the strength of wisdom experience less stress than those who are not as wise (yet).

While the experience of stress is a universal experience, we cope with it with varying degrees of effectiveness. When a major life change causes us to feel stressed, some of us adopt a problem-focused approach to deal with it. Others, however, feel so overwhelmed that they can only deal (at first anyway) with the emotions incited by the change—anxiety, sadness, anger, and so forth. In the next chapter we look at personality differences from the standpoint of those whose ability to cope with stress has been compromised. The personalities of these individuals are described as disordered because they cannot effectively deal with the stresses of daily living. Their attempts to do so result in either increased stress for themselves, increased stressed for the people in their lives, or both. Disorders of personality is the subject of Chapter 8.

❖

QUESTIONS TO PONDER

1. What purposes does stress serve? Would your life be better or worse if you never experienced stress?

2. How would you define stress? Does knowing and understanding the meanings of stress help you to deal with it?

3. Can a person be chronically stressed and not know it? Does anyone you know appear more stressed than he thinks he is? Do your friends think of you as more or less stressed than you think you are?

4. What was the most stressful event you've experienced over the past year? How did you cope with it? Are you any wiser for having had this experience?

5. Is there any downside to wisdom? Can wisdom be lost after it is attained?

❖

NOTES

1. The four universal truths of Buddhism are usually described as suffering, the cause of suffering, the end of suffering, and the path that leads to the end of suffering (*The Dhammapada*, 1973).

2. The research of Lazarus and his colleagues supports the psychological value of the Serenity Prayer: "Lord, grant me the serenity to accept the things I cannot change, the courage to change the things I can, and the wisdom to know the difference."

3. Early in my teaching career while giving a lecture, I felt furious (which I never expressed) whenever a student failed to understand me. After this inappropriate reaction happened a few times, I recalled (in the quiet of my home) those incidents that ignited this weird anger. I realized that I was reacting to being misunderstood as if it were a matter of life and death ... *life and death* ... those words reverberated around in

my head until they brought back memories of being trapped in a burning house when I was 6 years old.

The smoke filling up my bedroom led me to put on a realistic-looking toy rubber gas mask (to help me breathe, I childishly thought). After the fireman carried me next door, he asked if there was anyone else in the flaming building. I shouted, "MY BABY SISTER IS IN THE HOUSE!" but the stupid rubber mask prevented him from understanding me. The woman holding me in her lap, thinking I needed the mask to breathe, prevented me from taking it off. The fireman left the room. I was crying, frightened, and angry … in great emotional turmoil. But the fireman had read my body language. A few minutes later he brought my sleeping two-year-old sister safely into the house. She slept through the whole incident with no health consequences.

My memory of this traumatic event lingered below awareness until it was released 20+ years later with the help of my students. After I remembered this incident, student failures to understand my lectures no longer provoked my fury. I knew I was not wearing a gas mask.

4. Curiosity has a curious history. There was a time in Western history when curiosity was viewed extremely negatively. Curiosity was the vice of ocular lust! If you are curious about curiosity's redemption, see Barbara Benedict's *Curiosity: A Cultural History of Early Modern Inquiry* (2001), Hans Blumenberg's *The Legitimacy of the Modern Age* (1983), and/or Roger Shattuck's *Forbidden Knowledge* (1996).

SUGGESTIONS FOR FURTHER READING

Fredrickson, B. L. (2009). *Positivity.* New York, NY: Three Rivers Press.
Lazarus, R. S. (1999). *Stress and emotion.* New York, NY: Springer.
Sapolsky, R. M. (2004). *Why zebras don't get ulcers* (3rd ed.). New York, NY: St. Martin's Griffin.
Seligman, M. E. P. (2006). *Learned optimism: How to change your mind and your life.* New York, NY: Vintage Books.

INTERNET RESOURCES

1. For information about positive psychology, see http://www.positivepsychology.org/.

2. To see how vulnerable you are to stress, go to http://www.stress.org.uk/stresstest.aspx.

3. To see how resilient you are, go to http://resiliencyquiz.com/index.shtml.

Disorders of Personality

What are the signs that my usual ways of coping with stress are maladaptive?

What Is a Personality Disorder?

Thinking About Personality Disorders: Syndromes or Dimensions?

Ten Personality Disorders
   Cluster A: Paranoid, Schizoid, and Schizotypal Disorders
   Cluster B: Antisocial, Borderline, Histrionic, and Narcissistic Disorders
   Cluster C: Avoidant, Dependent, and Obsessive-Compulsive Disorders

Syndromes Versus Dimensions: Strengths and Weaknesses
   Syndromal Approach of the DSM-5
   Dimensional Approach of the Five-Factor Model

Sources for Diagnosis

Personality Disorders Over the Life Span

As noted in the previous chapter, life is stressful and we cope with stress in a variety of ways. Some people develop a coping style that (1) consistently reflects their entire personality and (2) creates pervasive ongoing difficulties for themselves, other people in their lives, or both. When these two conditions are met, we may speak of someone who displays or has a disordered personality.

The exact ways that someone with a personality *disorder* differs from someone with a unique personality *style* are difficult to pinpoint. The differences between style and disorder are most likely to appear when we are under stress. Those whose personalities are styles cope with stress in a variety of ways depending on the demands of their situation. If our stress is caused by being disrespected in the workplace, we could cope with it by clearly and assertively expressing our discomfort and talking it over with the source of the disrespect. Should our stress be caused by taking on too many tasks at the same time, we could make a conscious choice to eliminate one (or more) of these tasks even if our decision might disappoint someone.

Individuals whose personalities are more disordered than stylistic are stressed more easily than others, and they have fewer ways to cope effectively. A salesman who chronically reacts with vindictive anger to any frustration—including the frustration of needing to cut back on making new sales until manufacturing can fill his back orders—angrily insults the company's owner to such an extent that it gets him fired.

Suppose this happened to you. What would you do next? If your personality style borders on the inappropriately aggressive side of assertiveness, you could learn how to manage your anger. Courses in anger management skills are readily available. You could learn how to act assertively without acting aggressively.

In the case of this salesman, however, his extreme intolerance of frustration led him to repeat this pattern (frustration → anger → verbal aggression) with other employers. He was fired so often that he could no longer find employment in sales (Just imagine what his letters of recommendation from former employers looked like!). When an individual's personality style leads to repeated acts of self-destruction, it's easy to conclude that his personality is disordered. The unique symptoms and personality traits associated with 10 disorders of personality are the subject of this chapter.

What Is a Personality Disorder?

A precise definition of a personality disorder is not clear-cut. Why? Some personality disorders are not experienced as problems by the person herself. She experiences herself as doing just fine, thank you. It is always the *other* people in her life who are the source of her problems. As noted earlier, a woman patient of Karen Horney complained, "If it were not for reality, I would be perfectly all right!" (Horney, 1950, p. 37). Since her daily, ongoing experience of herself is pain free (i.e., she is not plagued by guilt feelings, does not feel especially anxious, is not depressed, etc.), she has no reason to see a therapist. She does not feel she needs anyone's help. Her symptoms are *ego-syntonic*: all of her thoughts, feelings, and behavior are totally compatible with her self-concept. She is comfortable with herself (American Psychological Association, 2007).

An irate salesman sees a world filled with incompetents who deserve to be the target of his scorn. If they were competent, he'd have no reason to be angry with them. Individuals diagnosed with antisocial personality disorder often feel comfortable with themselves. As they see it, their justifiable anger is just part of who they are, dynamic go-getters. It is not their fault that so many people are ineffectual. Their symptoms are also ego-syntonic.

"Could you please lower your voice. I can still hear you!"

A person diagnosed with obsessive-compulsive personality disorder, on the other hand, experiences many difficulties on a daily basis. She does not like having to engage in ritualistic acts every day, acts such as making sure, over and over again, that her doors and windows are locked. In more severe cases, simply the huge chunk of time the person needs just to go through her compulsive rituals (e.g., cleaning the house over and over) makes accomplishing ordinary daily tasks extremely difficult. Such symptoms are experienced as totally unwanted by the suffering individual. She does not want to clean over and over. But she must.

Unwanted symptoms are *ego-dystonic.* Fans of the long-running and re-running television show, *Monk,* may be amused, as I was, by many of Monk's relatively harmless compulsive rituals. But my amusement came to an abrupt halt when I viewed the episode where Monk endures the pain of excruciating thirst even though ample bottled water is at his fingertips. He could not drink it because the water was a different brand than the only one he is compelled to drink. This episode dramatically portrayed compulsions for what they can be: potentially life-threating.

Who is more likely to reach out for help, someone with ego-syntonic or ego-dystonic symptoms? Individuals with ego-dystonic symptoms are far more likely to seek professional help because their symptoms are problematic for themselves. On a daily basis they experience the pain of excessive anxiety, depression, and so forth. They know they are not functioning well.

Ego-syntonic symptoms, as mentioned above, are those that are compatible with a person's self-image. But other individuals suffer from them. Surveyed participants reported that antagonistic people are most bothersome when they try to engage with others. People want to avoid them. More generally, we don't like to be close to anyone who irritates us, regardless of the specific form of the irritation. Having to deal with people who are *compulsively* domineering, needy, or attention-seeking is extremely tiresome. Individuals with ego-syntonic symptoms may feel good about themselves, but they typically lack insight into how much they irritate other people (Williams et al., 2014).

A perfectionistic executive, for example, may be virtually impossible to please. He cannot distinguish between trivial and serious mistakes. He demands that every flaw be fixed immediately, no matter the cost to morale or to the larger goals of the project. His perfectionism makes work unbearable. He may eventually be asked by his supervisor to visit the Human Resource department because of repeated interpersonal difficulties.

This executive, however, fails to understand why he needs help. His perfectionism is such a central part of his personality that it feels normal to him. From his point of view, if his employees were as conscientious as he is, there would no problems. He is unaware that he is the source of office tension because his perfectionism stems from an ego-syntonic personality trait: He likes seeing himself as conscientious and responsible. It is who he is.

Physical analogues of ego-syntonic psychological traits are those symptoms of illnesses known as "silent killers." An individual may have dangerously high blood pressure, for example, and yet be completely unaware of it. His wake-up call to this threat to his health may arrive in the form of a heart attack. This analogy breaks down, however, when we consider its effect on other people. His high blood pressure, per se, does not impact those around him since neither he nor they know about it. But all personality disorders, including those with ego-syntonic symptoms, always negatively affect other individuals in the person's life.

A general personality disorder, then, is defined as

> an enduring pattern of inner experience and behavior that deviates markedly from the expectations of the individual's culture, is pervasive and inflexible, has an onset in adolescence or early adulthood, is stable over time, and leads to distress and impairment.

This definition comes from the most recent edition of the *Diagnostic and Statistical Manual of Mental Disorders*, 5th ed., conveniently referred to as DSM-5 (American Psychiatric Association, 2013, p. 645). Please note that this definition explicitly acknowledges personality disorders are manifested within the individual's culture and its norms. An individual who might be perceived as socially avoidant in a culture that features social events on a daily basis would be understood as normal in a different culture that values privacy.

The DSM-5's criteria for a diagnosis of a *general personality disorder* include the following six provisions:

A. The person shows an enduring pattern of behavior and inner experience that deviates noticeably from the individual's culture in two or more of the following ways:

1. His or her *thinking processes* markedly deviate from what is considered normal.

2. The range, intensity, and appropriateness of his or her *emotional expressions* are outside the cultural norms. In addition, the *lability* (the ease of changing from one emotion to another) of emotional expression is unusual, either because the person

never changes his emotional state (e.g., *The Hulk* is always angry) or because these emotional changes are so abrupt (e.g., crying-laughing-crying) that it is impossible for others to know what the person is really feeling.

3. *Interpersonal functioning* is problematic. The person frequently (almost always) has serious conflicts with one or more persons in his or her life.

4. *Impulse control* is lacking. The individual consistently engages in one or more impulsive behaviors (e.g., drinking, drug use, sex, gambling, shopping, etc.) without considering either the immediate or long-term consequences of these actions.

B. This enduring pattern of behavior and/or experience occurs independently of the particular social situations the person finds himself in. In other words, the pattern is inflexible across situations. It is not confined to any one particular environment, such as being at work, preparing taxes, or visiting one's in-laws.

C. This pattern leads to distress (ego-dystonic symptoms) or impairment in functioning in some area or areas of the person's daily routine (e.g., home, work, social life). Note that "impairment in functioning" covers those cases where individuals whose ego-syntonic symptoms make life difficult for others around them (Stone, 2013).

D. The behavior and/or experience pattern is stable and has been a part of the person's personality for years. Moreover, its onset can be traced at least back to adolescence or early adulthood.

E. This pattern cannot be plausibly explained as a consequence of some other disorder.

F. This pattern is not due to the effects of either a substance (e.g., drugs, medication, alcohol) or some other medical event (e.g., head trauma).

Thinking About Personality Disorders: Syndromes or Dimensions?

What does it mean when we say a person "has" a disordered personality? Does it mean that the person is *qualitatively* different from normal people in the same way that a person diagnosed with, say, tuberculosis, is qualitatively different from those of us fortunate enough not to have tuberculosis? When we think in terms of qualities (or attributes), a person either *has* or *does not have* tuberculosis—it is not a matter of having a little, some, or a lot of tuberculosis.

Or does "disordered personality" refer to the set of personality differences between those who are "disordered" and those who are not, differences that are better understood as differences in *degree* rather differences in *kind*? Under this conception, someone with a disordered personality has the same personality traits that everyone else has—he just has some of them to an extreme degree. These two alternate ways to think about personality disorders are called the *syndromal* and the *dimensional* approaches.

If we adopt the *syndromal approach,* we would consult the DSM-5 (American Psychiatric Association, 2013). In addition to defining a general personality disorder, as in the six criteria covered above, 10 personality disorders are identified. A person is classified as manifesting one (or more) of these disorders if he or she displays some of its presenting symptoms. The exact number (three, four, five, or more) of symptoms needed for a diagnosis depends on the specific disorder. The syndromal model is the counting symptoms method for understanding personality disorders (Zapolski, Guller, & Smith, 2013). The applications of the syndromal model to each of these 10 disorders are given in Table 8.1 through Table 8.10.

Conceptualizing a personality disorder (PD) as a cluster of syndromes is consistent with the medical model that diagnoses any illness, physical or mental, by (1) noting its specific presenting symptoms, (2) selecting those illnesses or diseases that could cause this pattern of symptoms, and by means of a *differential diagnosis*, (3) determining which specific illness or disease best accounts for all (or most) of the patient's presenting symptoms. If the individual manifests symptoms of two or more disorders, these disorders are called *comorbid*. The assumption of this way of thinking about PDs is that psychological problems may be usefully diagnosed in the same way that doctors diagnose threats to our physical health. Whether or not the medical (syndromal) model is the most fruitful way to understand PDs is the major question of this chapter.

Conceptualizing PDs as continuous *dimensions* (traits) of personality is a newer way to think about them (Widiger & Trull, 2007). The dimensional approach assumes that personality traits are the building blocks of everyone's personality. The conception of traits as fundamental to individual differences traces back to the beginning of the modern psychological understanding of personality (Allport, 1937; Stagner, 1937).

From the dimensional or trait point of view, an individual with a disordered personality is *not* qualitatively different from normal. He or she is displaying an extreme position on one or more personality traits at the time of testing. These traits are not only extreme. They constitute core difficulties for the person and/or other individuals in that person's life.

Consider, for example, the trait of neatness or orderliness. Neatness is one of the six facets of the broader trait of Conscientiousness in the Five-Factor Model of personality (Widiger & Costa, 2013b). This facet reflects individual differences in organization or orderliness. It is one thing to be neat and organized but quite another to obsess so constantly about it that there is little time for anything else. An individual who is *compulsively* neat and well-organized, who scores high on most or all of the other facets of Conscientiousness, would be a strong candidate for a diagnosis of obsessive-compulsive personality disorder (OCPD). A normal or non-disordered personality would fall somewhere between super neat-freak Felix Unger and carefree total slob Oscar Madison, the oddest of fictional couples as depicted by playwright Neil Simon in *The Odd Couple*. Extreme scores on any of the (manifest) facets of any of the traits of the Five-Factor Model suggest the possibility of an underlying (latent) personality disorder.

Therapists and researchers who favor the dimensional approach to understanding personality disorders may choose between at least three self-report personality tests: The Five-Factor Model or FFM (e.g., Presnall, 2013), the Temperament and Character Inventory (Cloninger, 2006), and the Shedler-Westen Procedure-200 (Shedler & Westen, 2004).

In a comprehensive review of available dimensional procedures for classifying and assessing PDs, the Five-Factor Model was considered to have the strongest overall support (Clark, 2007). Consequently, the FFM will serve as our representative of the dimensional approach to personality disorders throughout the rest of this chapter. As we saw in Chapters 1 and 3, the five basic domains of the Five-Factor Model are Neuroticism (**N**), Extraversion (**E**), Openness to Experience (**O**), Agreeableness (**A**), and Conscientiousness (**C**). Each of these five broad domains consists of six facets (more specific traits). These facets are defined in Chapters 1 and 3 (see Table 3.1).

A consensus of experts (numbering between 25 and 30 for most personality disorders) agree that the below FFM trait descriptions for the 10 personality disorders are accurate (Lynman & Widiger, 2001). The facets of the FFM that are associated with each personality disorder are provided by Widiger, Costa, Gore, and Crego (2013, Table 6.1, p. 79). For the sake of clarity, I capitalize these traits only when referring to their understanding within the FFM; an uncapitalized trait refers to its more general or everyday usage.

Tables 8.1 through 8.10 consist of a side-by-side comparison of how these conceptualizations understand the 10 personality disorders identified in DSM-5. The strengths and weaknesses of the syndromal versus dimensional approaches are compared at the end of the section.

Ten Personality Disorders (PDs)

DSM-5 organizes the 10 disorders of personality into three groups or clusters:

Cluster A: paranoid, schizoid, and schizotypal PDs. Individuals in Group A appear peculiar, eccentric, or strange.

Cluster B: antisocial, borderline, histrionic, and narcissistic PDs. Individuals in Group B appear emotional, dramatic, or unpredictable.

Cluster C: avoidant, dependent, and obsessive-compulsive PDs. Individuals in Group C appear anxious or fearful.

Note that the DSM-5 admits the A, B, and C clustering system "has serious limitations and has not been consistently validated" (DSM-5, p. 646; American Psychiatric Association, 2013). Nevertheless, this clustering system allows us to present these PDs in bite-sized portions rather than gulping them down in one sitting.[1]

Cluster A: Paranoid, Schizoid, and Schizotypal Personality Disorders

(Individuals who appear peculiar, eccentric, or strange)

Paranoid Personality Disorder (PPD)

A person suffering from paranoid personality disorder (PPD) lives a lonely life. He trusts no one. He is wary of other people's motives. He suspects that some hidden agenda lurks behind commonplace statements. In the most serious cases, the individual suffering from PPD totally closes himself off to considering any new evidence, no matter how compelling it appears to other people, evidence that would disprove his fears and suspicions. The term *para noia* means "against knowledge" (Shapiro, 1965).

Table 8.1 shows the seven DSM-5 symptoms of PPD in the left-hand column. The right-hand column displays the *facets* on each **FFM domain** that are thought to be typical of an individual diagnosed with paranoid personality disorder.

The paranoid personality disorder appears most often on the Agreeableness (A) domain (four facets) with low scores indicating the individual is suspicious, aggressive, deceptive, and tough-minded. PPD is the least studied and understood personality disorder perhaps because paranoid individuals are least likely to volunteer to allow a stranger to "study" them.[2] Thus there is relatively little evidence in the research literature for the reliability and/or validity of the PPD diagnosis (Triebwasser et al., 2012).

All of us have been prepared by natural selection to be vulnerable to PPD. It's conceivable that our distant ancestors found that fearing harmless people is less costly in the long run than failing to avoid truly dangerous individuals. After all, it takes only one mistake of trusting someone we shouldn't to suffer serious consequences (Ellett & Wildsschut, 2014). From the standpoint of evolutionary psychology, then, perhaps we should be surprised that the prevalence of PPD in the general population has been estimated to be only between 2.3 and 4.4% (DSM-5; American Psychiatric Association, p. 651).

Even if PPD is a relatively unlikely occurrence, a single severely disturbed PPD individual can inflict great harm. A careful reading of the diaries and other written materials by four mass shooters lead investigators to conclude that the shooters suffered from paranoid personality disorder.

❖ **Table 8.1**   Paranoid Personality Disorder (PPD)

DSM-5: Four or More of the Following Symptoms	FFM Domains: *Significant Facets*
1. Suspects others are deceptive	N: *Angry*
2. Wonders if he or she can trust friends and other people	E: *Cold, unfriendly, negative attitude*
3. Reluctant to confide in friends for fear of betrayal	O: *Inflexible behavior and values*
4. Interprets benign remarks as personally threatening when other people do not see them as threats	A: *Suspicious, aggressive, deceptive, tough-minded*
5. Holds grudges over past slights	
6. Perceives attacks on his or her character and reputation which other people do not	
7. Suspects, without evidence, his or her sexual partner has been or is unfaithful	

Photo 8.1 Theodore Millon (1928–2014)

A founding figure in the study of personality disorders, Millon developed a number of objective personality inventories that bear his name such as the Millon Clinical Multiaxial Inventory (MCMI) and the Millon Adolescent Personality Inventory (MAPI).

Key publications:

Modern Psychopathology (1969)
Disorders of Personality (1981)
Masters of the Mind (2004)

The writings of the following mass shooters consistently reveal an obsession with being rejected by "elites" who unfairly achieved their high status. The shooters convinced themselves (via their closed paranoid thinking) that these elites fully deserve the vengeance to be inflicted upon them (Dutton, White, & Fogarty, 2013).

- Eric Harris: shot 27 people, killing 13 at Columbine High in 1999

- Seung-Hui Cho: shot and killed 32 people at Virginia Tech in 2007

- Kimveer Gill: shot 20 people, killing one, at Dawson College, Montreal, in 2006

- Anders Breivik: killed 89 people by a bomb and by shooting in Norway in 2011

Are we sure that those four disturbed shooters suffer from paranoid personality disorder? Some have suggested that they are psychopaths (e.g., Cullen, 2009). Such diagnostic disagreements are not unusual. A constant refrain throughout all informed discussions of PDs is the difficulty of arriving at a correct *differential diagnosis.* How can we know which is the correct diagnosis?

Dutton, White, and Fogarty (2013) note that the writings of these shooters reveal features not associated with psychopathy: The killers displayed intense emotions over their perceived "rejection" by others, revealing a deep unfulfilled wish that they should have been a highly esteemed member of the group. Psychopaths do not form emotional bonds and rarely obsess about being rejected by others. Psychopaths dismiss other people as not worthy of their time or energy. Moreover, the diaries of those shooters reveal their intense anxiety over social rejection. Psychopaths, however, are characterized by low, not high, states of negative emotional arousal (Patrick, 2007). Thus, the available evidence suggests these four killers suffered from paranoid personality disorder.

A correct differential diagnosis is important because of its implications for selecting the most beneficial course of therapeutic treatment and/or management of a personality disorder. According to Theodore Millon (1996), the prospects for successful treatment for individuals suffering from PPD are "not promising," but "it is possible to put them on a road to recovery, providing them with a glimpse of a positive, healthy way of relating" (pp. 722, 727).

Schizoid Personality Disorder (SZPD)

If someone really has "no personality," the ideal candidate for this derogatory epithet would be a person suffering from SZPD. They shun close relationships. When they must interact with someone, they are cold and withdrawn. These individuals seem to wish they were socially invisible. The left-hand column of Table 8.2 shows the seven DSM-5 symptoms associated with this disorder. The right-hand column presents the only two domains of the FFM, Extraversion (E) and Openness (O), that characterize this disorder. A person characterized by SZPD is expected to score heavily in the introverted direction (i.e., show low scores) on the Extraversion domain. Someone who is that extremely introverted might be considered to be problematically *detached* from all social connections (Crego et al., 2015).

A person diagnosed with SZPD fails to exhibit *positive emotions*, the central defining facet of extraversion (Watson & Clark, 1997). Moreover, individuals diagnosed with SZPD are expected to score on the low end of four other facets of extraversion: They are cold, withdrawn, passive, and indifferent to seeking out exciting activities.

The personality profile of SZPD reveals individuals who are at best indifferent to the company of other people—they can take it or leave it—and at worst might combine with other personality disorders to constitute a genuine threat to people. While the majority of those diagnosed as SZPD do not pose a threat, when this disorder is

❖ **Table 8.2** Schizoid Personality Disorder (SZPD)

DSM-5: Four or More of the Following Symptoms	FFM Domains: *Significant Facets*
1. Neither wants or likes close relationships	E: *Cold, withdrawn, passive, does not seek excitement, does not show positive emotions*
2. Usually chooses solitary activities	O: *Closed to feelings, does not initiate new behaviors*
3. Not interested in sexual experiences with others	
4. Few, if any, activities are pleasurable	
5. Lacks close friends except for first-degree relatives	
6. Indifferent to the praise or criticism of others	
7. Shows emotional coldness or indifference	

comorbid with other disorders, the combination can be lethal. Michael Stone (2013), in his studies of serial killers, reports that 40% were diagnosed as SZPD comorbid with another disorder. Stone (1998) singles out Jeffrey Dahmer as an American serial killer whose diagnosis was schizoid PD comorbid with sadism[3] (Schwartz, 1992). The prevalence rate of SZPD ranges between 3.1 and 4.9% with males slightly more at risk than females (DSM-5, p. 654). The prognosis for this disorder is not promising since these individuals present a profound form of "passive resistance" to change. But if their deficits are mild and their life circumstances are favorable, they do stand a reasonable chance of maintaining adequate social relationships (Millon, 1996).

Schizotypal Personality Disorder (STPD)

This personality disorder is characterized by a certain oddness of behavior and speech. A person diagnosed with STPD might reveal *ideas of reference*, the belief that other people are sending him secret messages. While everyone else thinks they are listening to the weather report, he is convinced that the weather person is actually sending him a coded message that only he can decipher.[4] The first listed symptom in Table 8.3 under the DSM-5, "Thinks the actions of others refer particularly to him," describes the symptom of ideas of reference.

The domains of Extraversion (E) and Openness (O) dominate the FFM profile of this disorder. The afflicted person appears cold and distant, has an active fantasy life, and is highly curious. In addition, the facets of high anxiety and high self-consciousness indicate the domain of Neuroticism (N) is represented here as well.

Of the 10 personality disorders in DSM-5, schizotypal personality disorder is the most controversial. The controversy centers on this question: Is it a *qualitatively* distinct condition, one that is discontinuous from normal personality, or does it consist

❖ **Table 8.3** Schizotypal Personality Disorder (STPD)

DSM-5: Five or More of the Following Symptoms	FFM Domains: *Significant Facets*
1. Thinks actions of others refer particularly to him or her	**N**: *Anxious, self-conscious*
2. Engages in magical thinking beyond the cultural norm	**E**: *Cold, withdrawn, does not show positive emotions*
3. Has unusual perceptual experiences	**O**: *Active fantasy life, engages in new activities and ideas, highly curious*
4. Displays odd thinking and speech patterns	**A**: *Mistrusts other people*
5. Highly suspicious of others	
6. Inappropriate or constrained emotional expressions	
7. Behavior or appearance that is peculiar or odd	
8. Lacks close friends other than first-degree relatives	
9. Extreme social anxiety centered on paranoid fears	

of a set of continuous (dimensional) personality traits whereby the individual reveals extreme attitudes and behaviors on an identifiable set of them?

The syndromal or *taxon* approach to STPD has been vigorously promoted by Paul Meehl. *Taxa* (plural of taxon) are the different discrete categories within any system of taxonomy (Meehl, 1992). The most widely known, ground-breaking taxon system was developed by Carl Linnaeus (1707–1778), the father of modern taxonomy, to categorize all forms of life on earth in terms of their genus and species (e.g., *homo sapiens*).[5]

In Meehl's view (1962, 1990), STPD is a discrete disorder of personality that affects about 10% of the general population. (This estimate is considerably higher than the prevalence rate of 3.9% in DSM-5.) Moreover, Meehl expects that about 10% of these individuals will eventually decompensate into the major mental illness of schizophrenia, thereby accounting for the approximate 1% prevalence rate of this poorly understood brain disease. Meehl hypothesizes that STPD is caused by a single dominant "schizogene" that disrupts normal development. It is the presence of this gene, were it found, that would justify viewing this disorder as a discrete category or taxon. A thorough discussion of the relationship of STPD to schizophrenia has been provided by Eran Chemerinski and colleagues (2013).

The categorical understanding of STPD is supported by the observation that of 13 investigations of STPD, the majority have backed the taxonomic model. However, more recent research shows that when the items on the openness domain are reworded to reflect its maladaptive variants (e.g., "morbid curiosity" replaces "curiosity"), the expected correspondence between openness and STPD is obtained.

It seems fair to conclude that STPD may be fruitfully conceptualized as a set of traits consisting of high neuroticism (anxiety and self-consciousness), low extraversion (cold, withdrawn, not exhibiting positive emotions) and high openness when the openness facets are clearly identified as maladaptive (Edmundson & Kwapil, 2013; Saulsman & Page, 2004). Keeping an open mind about a contentious issue is usually a good idea and is a sign of a healthy personality. But when our minds are so open that we lose our ability to distinguish reality from nonsense (e.g., "Everything is true!"), the maladaptive aspect of this trait reveals itself. Unless the individual suffers from only the mildest form of this disorder, the overall prognosis for STPD is poor (Millon, 1996).

Cluster B: Antisocial, Borderline, Histrionic, and Narcissistic Personality Disorders

(Individuals who appear emotional, dramatic, or erratic)

Antisocial Personality Disorder (ASPD)

The list of symptoms given by DSM-5 for a diagnosis of antisocial personality disorder is unique among these 10 disorders: Six of the seven symptoms shown in the left-hand column of Table 8.4 are observable behaviors. Engaging in criminal acts that could lead to being arrested (e.g., petty theft), chronically lying, acting impulsively,

❖ **Table 8.4** Antisocial Personality Disorder (ASPD)

DSM-5: Three or More of the Following Symptoms	FFM Domains: *Significant Facets*
1. Repeatedly acting in ways that are grounds for arrest	**N:** *Angry, impulsive, not anxious, not self-conscious, not vulnerable*
2. Patterns of deceitfulness: lying, conning others	**E:** *Assertive, active, seeks excitement*
3. Chronic impulsivity and failure to plan ahead	**O:** *Engages in new activities*
4. Aggression and irritability as shown in repeated assaults	**A:** *Mistrusts others, deceptive, exploits others, aggressive, arrogant, tough-minded*
5. Recklessly ignoring safety issues (e.g., drives recklessly)	**C:** *Irresponsible, lacks self-discipline, acts rashly rather than deliberately*
6. Chronically acting irresponsibly as in failing to honor debts	
7. Lack of remorse over hurting or stealing from another	

assaulting people, acting irresponsibly, and acting recklessly are all behavioral symptoms of this disorder.

The only symptom that is not observable is the lack of remorse for wrongdoing. While we can observe someone who *says* he's sorry, it's hard to know how sincere that apology really is. The seventh DSM-5 symptom refers to how an individual *feels* about hurting someone. An individual suffering from ASPD is not likely to feel true remorse. Individuals who are truly sorry for their wrongdoings do not repeat them.

The FFM personality traits associated with ASPD are shown in the right-hand column of Table 8.4. The domains of Neuroticism (N) and Agreeableness (A) are represented by such facets as anger, impulsiveness, mistrust, frequently using or exploiting other people, arrogance, and tough-mindedness.

DSM-5 points out that the antisocial personality disorder is also called *psychopathy, sociopathy,* or *dysocial personality disorder* (DSM-5, p. 659; American Psychiatric Association, 2013). However, a number of research psychologists strongly disagree: Antisocial personality disorder is not synonymous with psychopathy. While it is true that both disorders share the symptoms of exploiting others and acting impulsively, nevertheless there are additional personality characteristics of the psychopath—superficial charm, callousness, and a complete lack of empathy—which are not found in those with ASPD. While all psychopaths would also be diagnosed with ASPD (comorbidity), not all ASPD individuals are psychopaths.

The results of four investigations support the premise that ASPD and psychopathy are not identical. Two studies examined the relationship between these disorders and criminal behavior. Rider and Kosson (2013) found that those individuals whose symptoms qualified them to be diagnosed as ASPD with comorbid psychopathy engaged in more violent criminal activity than those individuals who were diagnosed with ASPD alone. With regard to nonviolent crimes, ASPD individuals with comorbid psychopathy were charged more often than those ASPD individuals without psychopathy. These results replicated the pattern observed by Kosson et al. (2006) that individuals presenting symptoms of both ASPD and psychopathy commit more crimes than those with ASPD alone.

Moreover, research comparing brain activity of those diagnosed with ASPD versus those diagnosed with psychopathy supports the view that these are different disorders.

Participants were asked to view photographs of angry or fearful faces while undergoing a *functional magnetic resonance imaging* (fMRI) procedure. This procedure measures brain activity by detecting changes in blood flow to all areas of the brain that are active. The logic behind these investigations is straightforward: On the one hand, if the *same* area of the brain shows increased blood flow for both those with ASPD and those diagnosed with psychopathy, the identical underlying disorder appears to have two different names. On the other hand, if *different* areas of the brain become active under the same environmental conditions (i.e., looking at faces), then ASPD and psychopathy would appear to be different disorders. The presence or absence of an emotional reaction was determined by activity in the *amygdala*, the structure in our brains responsible for processing our emotional reactions (LeDoux, 1996).

Two investigations found that those participants with ASPD responded with a heightened emotional reaction to the faces displaying emotions while those diagnosed with psychopathy responded less emotionally. The *more* symptoms of ASPD that an individual presented, the *more* his amygdala reacted. The reaction of those with ASPD to angry faces is consistent with the observation that individuals who have been socially excluded from their groups are likely to react aggressively and are more likely to place aggressive interpretations on ambiguous words (DeWall et al., 2009; Twenge et al., 2001). Future research into the origins of ASPD might show a consistent pattern of rejection by his or her family.[6]

The opposite was found for those diagnosed with psychopathy: the *more* symptoms they presented, the *less* active was their amygdala when they looked at photographs of angry or fearful faces (Hicks & Patrick, 2006; Hyde et al., 2014). These results suggest that the presence of psychopathy suppresses the reactivity of the amygdala to those stimuli that non-psychopaths find emotionally engaging. It is also possible that individuals whose amygdala is non-reactive to normal emotional stimuli are more likely to be diagnosed as psychopaths. Or, conceivably, some presently unknown third factor might account for the presence of both psychopathy and amygdala nonresponsiveness to emotional events. In any event, these data clearly support the view that ASPD and psychopathy are different personality disorders.

The prevalence rates of ASPD in the general population range between 0.2% and 3.3%. It is diagnosed more often in males than females. As individuals grow older, some of their more abusive and impulsive symptoms may undergo remission (DSM-5, pp. 661–662; Millon, 1996).

Borderline Personality Disorder (BPD)

A person diagnosed with borderline personality disorder is primarily characterized as *unstable*: There is a marked lack of continuity in his interpersonal relationships, his self-image, his emotional states, and behavior (highly impulsive). Table 8.5 presents the nine DSM-5 symptoms in the left-hand column.

In terms of personality domains, individuals diagnosed with BPD present high levels of Neuroticism (N) as well as low levels of Conscientiousness (C) and Agreeableness (A) (Stepp, Whalen, & Smith, 2013).

Research indicates that how individuals deal with embarrassing, humiliating, or shaming events in their lives plays a major role in the development of this disorder. Specifically, individuals who spend much time ruminating over a shaming event are more likely to show symptoms of BPD when their rumination takes the form of angry thoughts directed at the person or persons who shamed them. While anger rumination may provide short-term relief from the pain of shame, its continued use exacerbates such BPD symptoms as increased emotional instability, identity confusion, and negative relationships with others (Peters et al., 2014). Additionally, women who manifest multiple symptoms of BPD are likely to consume more food to ameliorate their negative moods and are thus at risk for developing problems with binge eating (Ambwani & Morey, 2015).

The good news is that shame prone individuals who are candidates for the development of BPD can avail themselves of useful therapeutic processes. Marsha M.

❖ **Table 8.5** Borderline Personality Disorder (BPD)

DSM-5: Five or More of the Following Symptoms	FFM Domains: *Significant Facets*
1. Frantically avoids real or imagined abandonment	**N**: *Anxious, angry hostility, depressed, self-conscious, impulsive, vulnerable*
2. A pattern of unstable relationships alternating between extremes of idealization and derogation	**O**: *Active fantasy life*
3. Identity confusion: extremely unstable self-image	**A**: *Mistrustful, deceptive, aggressive*
4. Engages in two or more potentially self-damaging actions such as reckless driving, substance abuse, binge eating	**C**: *Acts rashly*
5. Threats of suicide, self-mutilation (e.g., self-cutting)	
6. Emotional instability	
7. Chronically feeling empty	
8. Inappropriate intense anger, frequent displays of temper, recurrent physical confrontations (fighting)	
9. Temporary paranoid thinking due to stress or signs of a split personality (dissociation)	

Linehan's (1993) Dialectical Behavior Therapy teaches individuals to process their emotions in various constructive ways that reduce the time they spend ruminating over past perceived injuries. By using a combination of individual therapy sessions, practicing social skills in groups, learning how to tolerate distress, coaching over the telephone, and consultations with a team of therapists, BPD patients are better able to emotionally self-regulate. Also, individuals enrolled in a Dialectical Behavior Therapy–based skills group were observed to be less depressed than those in a comparable control group (Feldman et al., 2009). Prevalence rates of BPD in the general population range between 1.6% and 5.9%. Seventy-five percent of those diagnosed as BPD are females (DSM-5, pp. 665–666).

Histrionic Personality Disorder (HPD)

"Drama Queen" or "Drama King" characterizes someone diagnosed with HPD. Needing always to be the center of attention, she or he typically overreacts emotionally to events that most of us brush off as "one of those things." Small changes in daily life can result in more drama, time, and energy than those changes require. The DSM-5 symptoms of HPD are presented in the left-hand column of Table 8.6.

She or he displays at least one facet on each of the five domains of the FFM. Extraversion (E)—warm, gregarious, excitement seeking—and Agreeableness (A)—trusting, deceptive, arrogant—are her or his strong suits. But underneath these mostly positive traits lurks a vulnerable person whose fragile self-esteem can be shaken easily.

What makes the histrionic personality disorder unique among the 10 PDs is that it is not immediately clear why this is a "disorder." Empirical investigations of the symptoms of HPD find that these characteristics do not consistently hang together as they

❖ **Table 8.6** Histrionic Personality Disorder (HPD)

DSM-5: Five or More of the Following Symptoms	FFM Domains: *Significant Facets*
1. Feels ill at ease in social situations unless he or she is the center of attention	N: *Vulnerable*
2. Inappropriate seductive or provocative actions	E: *Warm, gregarious, seeks excitement*
3. Shows rapidly alternating and shallow feelings	O: *Active fantasy life, open to his or her feelings*
4. Uses physical appearance to draw attention to self	A: *Trusting, deceptive, arrogant*
5. Speech is characterized by general impressions, lacking specific details	C: *Disorderly, acts rashly*
6. Drama Queen/King: Exaggerates emotional experiences for dramatic effect	
7. Easily influenced by other people	
8. Believes his or her relationships are more intimate and deeper than they really are	

would if this were a naturally occurring personality disorder (Clark, 1990; Livesley, Jackson, & Schroeder, 1989). For example, some individuals diagnosed with HPD are characterized much the same way that you would describe an extravert—someone who enjoys social interaction and seeks excitement.

If it is not obvious that HPD is a "real" disorder, then what's it doing in the DSM-5? The answer is that histrionic personality disorder had previously been called *hysterical personality*, a syndrome that traces back to the 1895 publication by Breuer and Freud (McCrae, 2006). So why is it not called "hysterical personality disorder"? According to some psychoanalytically oriented theorists, the decision to omit hysterical personality disorder arises from a combination of a lack of solid empirical data and unspecified "political factors" (Kernberg & Caligor, 2005, p. 119). The direct answer to why this disorder changed names is that *hysteria* is derived from the Greek term for *uterus:* This disorder was initially assumed to be found only in women. In reality, of course, men are also subject to HPD. The label of hysteria is inaccurate and needed to be replaced.

The disordered aspect of HPD behaviors shows up in their *inflexibility* and *persistence*. HPD is characterized by an insatiable striving for attention and approval. When these needs are not met, the individual feels devoid of an inner self as he lacks a core identity apart from other people. He requires constant admiration and approval. He is not self-sufficient. He is unable to bolster his rickety sense of identity by himself. He requires *indiscriminant* social approval irrespective of its appropriateness in the situation (e.g., telling a joke during a funeral service) or from the person (e.g., a total stranger) whose attention he needs. Anyone's attention will do whenever he feels empty (Millon, 1996). The prevalence rate of HPD in the general population is estimated to be 1.8% with females receiving this diagnosis more often than males (DSM-5, p. 668). Millon (1996) notes that individuals with HPD rarely seek therapy.

Narcissistic Personality Disorder (NPD)

Narcissism and *narcissistic* are such commonplace words for modern Americans that rarely does a day go by without encountering these terms in one form (e.g., professional literature) or another (e.g., popular media) or another (e.g., best-selling book) or another (e.g., gossip). I seem to be surrounded by narcissists wherever I go (except when I gaze in the mirror, of course).

Our cultural fascination with narcissism began with social critic Christopher Lasch's best selling *The Culture of Narcissism* in 1979. This was quickly followed by Alice Miller's succinct treatment in her 1981 book, *The Drama of the Gifted Child*, a book eagerly consumed by gifted children of all ages. The commercial success of these well-written works opened the floodgates for a tsunami of books on narcissism, some written by highly trained professionals (e.g., Masterson, 1988; Morrison, 1986), others by amateurs whose coworkers were difficult narcissists.[7] A highly popular television sit-com in Great Britain and the United States, *The Office*, centered around the chronic difficulties working for someone displaying symptoms of NPD.

What about today? Is the present generation more narcissistic than previous ones? Jean Twenge thinks so. In her book, *Generation Me* (2006), she presents data indicating that today's teenagers and young adults feel more self-important than ever.

For example, in the early 1950s, only 12% of teens (14–16 years old) agreed with the statement "I am an important person." But by the late 1980s, an astonishing 80% of teens agreed.

Consistent with Twenge's premise is the finding that frequent postings on social network sites of "selfies" (self-taken photographs of oneself) correlate with narcissism. The more selfies that were posted, the higher were individual's scores on the Vanity and Superiority aspects of narcissism (Barry et al., 2015). Individuals who score high on narcissism post a higher quantity and more revealing photos of themselves (Bergman et al., 2011; DeWall et al., 2011). Indeed, the frequency of selfie posting by men correlates with all three traits of the Dark Triad covered in Chapter 6: narcissism, Machiavellianism, and psychopathy (Fox & Rooney, 2015). The explosive growth of selfies across the social media landscape certainly looks like a generation in love with itself.

But not everyone agrees with Twenge. Her critics raise two issues: (1) Because her samples were not drawn randomly from the general population, her results could be biased. Consequently, the increased average score she found on the Narcissistic Personality Inventory (NPI; Raskin & Terry, 1988) could reflect a change only among those college students she selected rather than characterizing an entire generation; (2) her measurement instrument, the NPI, contains scales tapping into both positive aspects of narcissism, such as Self-Sufficiency, as well as negative aspects such as Vanity and Superiority. Other survey data (not reported by Twenge) find generational *increases* in Self-Sufficiency as well as slight generational *decreases* in Vanity and Superiority (Trzesniewski, Donnellan, & Robins, 2008). Finally, the correlation of frequency of selfies posting and narcissism is weak ($r < .20$), and in one study, this relationship was observed only for men. Frequency of selfie posting by women was unrelated to their scores on the NPI (Sorokowski et al., 2015).

So are today's young people really more narcissistic than previous generations? No one knows. Maybe if our grandparents had access to today's technology, they'd have posted as many or more selfies as this generation does. But whatever turns out to be the correct answer, it's important to understand that not everyone who is above average on the trait of narcissism would be diagnosed with narcissistic personality disorder. When does the trait of narcissism become a disorder?

In common parlance, a person with NPD is described as "stuck up" by his friends and family. Possessing an outsized ego, the NPD individual frequently displays an attitude of arrogance as he assumes he is entitled to special and favorable treatment.[8] Table 8.7 gives the symptoms of this personality disorder according to DSM-5.

For individuals with NPD, their most dominant domain is Agreeableness (A), where they obtain *low* scores on five facets: They use others to get what they want, they are mistrustful, deceptive, arrogant, and tough-minded.

Research indicates that this disorder consists of two primary factors—*grandiosity* (e.g., bragging, manipulative, egotistical) and *vulnerability* (shy, craving, thin-skinned) (Campbell & Miller, 2013). While a vulnerable narcissist may initially display a grandiose or bombastic facade, even mild criticism can cause it to crumble (Miller & Campbell, 2008).

The FFM can distinguish between these two versions by showing that grandiose narcissists score high on the Extraversion (E) domain and low on Agreeableness (A).

❖ **Table 8.7** Narcissistic Personality Disorder (NPD)

DSM-5: Five or More of the Following Symptoms	FFM Domain: *Significant Facets*
1. Has a grandiose sense of self-importance	N: *Angry, extreme self-consciousness swings, vulnerable*
2. Fantasizes about unlimited power, beauty, success	E: *Gregarious, assertive, seeks excitement*
3. Believes he or she is special	O: *Fantasizes about power, success, being admired, etc.*
4. Needs unlimited admiration	A: *Exploits other people, does not trust easily, deceptive, arrogant, tough-minded*
5. Feels entitled to receiving automatic special treatment	C: *Not orderly, impulsive*
6. Uses others to get his or her way	
7. Lacks the ability to empathize with others	
8. Is frequently envious	
9. Displays arrogant actions or attitudes	

Vulnerable narcissists show a different pattern: They score high on the Neuroticism (N) domain and low on both Extraversion and Agreeableness. They tend to be disagreeable introverts (Miller et al., 2011).

The prevalence rate of NPD in the general population can run as high as 6.2% (DSM-5, p. 671). A meta-analysis of gender differences found that with respect to grandiose narcissism, men tended to be more narcissistic than women, particularly in their tendencies to exploit other people as well as feeling entitled to special treatment. This raises the possibility that more men than women are diagnosed with NPD (the DSM-5 reports that 50%–75% of those diagnosed with NPD are male). Men and women did *not* differ on vulnerable narcissism, which is characterized by low self-esteem in addition to the above mentioned high neuroticism, and introversion (Grijalva et al., 2015). Narcissistic individuals rarely seek professional help since their pride prevents them from admitting that they need anyone else's help. "Most are convinced they can get along quite well on their own" (Millon, 1996, p. 427).

Cluster C: Avoidant, Dependent, and Obsessive-Compulsive Personality Disorders

(Individuals who appear anxious or fearful)

Avoidant Personality Disorder (AVPD)

"Anxious loner" characterizes an individual diagnosed with AVPD. He constantly fears being judged harshly by others. He is inhibited in social situations, fearful that others will laugh at him or will dismiss or derogate his comments. If a social engagement cannot be skipped, he may avoid displaying what he really thinks or feels by hiding behind a mask of expected social conventions. Table 8.8, left hand column, shows the symptoms of this disorder given in the DSM-5.

Individuals diagnosed with AVPD score highly on five facets of Neuroticism (N): they are anxious, depressed, self-conscious, and careful (not impulsive). Moreover, they feel vulnerable much of the time, particularly around others. Other people are avoided to reduce the anxiety and vulnerability they feel about the real (to them) possibility of being rejected. They score quite low on the Extraversion (E) domain since their avoidant style of coping with stress leads them to withdraw from social contact whenever withdrawal is an option.

When escape from others is not possible, individuals suffering from AVPD wish they had Harry Potter's cloak of invisibility: They appear passive, unassertive, and do not seek excitement, particularly if the exciting activity involves actively engaging with other people. Avoidant personality disorder is an extreme reaction to the mere possibility of social rejection. Just the threat of being ignored, snubbed, or socially rejected is sufficient for a person with AVPD to skip a social event. Perhaps such individuals have lower pain thresholds for rejection than most people. They are extremely thin-skinned.

Social exclusion is painful for everyone. This fact is explained by evolutionary psychology: From infancy, all human beings need the support of others for survival. Being an accepted part of a social group is so vital that natural selection has endowed us with a mechanism that is exquisitely sensitive to any sign of social rejection: **pain.** Pain signals that something is wrong. Severe pain motivates us to take care of the problem immediately. Our brains respond to the pain of ostracism in the same way

❖ **Table 8.8** Avoidant Personality Disorder (AVPD)

DSM-5: Four or More of the Following Symptoms	FFM Domains: *Significant Facets*
1. Avoids working in settings involving contact with people due to fear of criticism or rejection	**N:** *Anxious, depressed, self-conscious, not impulsive, vulnerable*
2. Unwilling to meet new people unless certain he or she will be liked	**E:** *Withdrawn, passive, unassertive, does not seek excitement*
3. Holds back in intimate relationships from fear of being shamed, ridiculed, or embarrassed	**O:** *Does not engage in new behaviors*
4. Worries about being criticized or rejected	**A:** *Modest*
5. Inhibited socially by his or her feelings of inadequacy	
6. Self-image characterized by feeling inferior to others, being socially inept	
7. Reluctant to begin new activities out of fear he or she will embarrass himself or herself	

they respond to pains caused by physical injury (MacDonald & Leary, 2005; Williams, 2007). Moreover, as we saw in Chapter 6, laboratory research demonstrates how easy it is to hurt someone's feelings by excluding him from interacting with strangers for only a few minutes (Eisenberger et al., 2013).

Such demonstrations suggest the possibility that those with AVPD have an overly sensitive brain system that makes the smallest sign of social rejection especially painful. The availability of technology such as fMRI allows researchers to search for and eventually discover the extent to which each personality disorder reveals a distinctive biological pattern. The prevalence rate of AVPD in the general population is estimated to be 2.4% for both males and females (DSM-5, p. 674). Theodore Millon (1996) notes that "avoidant personalities are among the most frequent disorders that therapists encounter … [but] … the prognosis for the avoidant personality is often quite poor" (p. 281).

Dependent Personality Disorder (DPD)

"Clingy" describes how individuals suffering from dependent personality disorder appear to their friends and acquaintances. These individuals feel they are inadequate to take care of themselves. They become anxious at the slightest sign of separation. Table 8.9 gives the DSM-5 symptoms of the dependent personality disorder.

The FFM domains of Neuroticism (N) and Agreeableness (A) dominate the personality characteristics of individuals diagnosed with DPD. Such individuals are

❖ **Table 8.9** Dependent Personality Disorder (DPD)

DSM-5: Five or More of the Following Symptoms	FFM Domains: *Significant Facets*
1. Needs excessive reassurance for everyday decisions	**N:** *Anxious, depressed, self-conscious, not impulsive, vulnerable*
2. Needs other people to assume responsibility for most areas of his or her life	**E:** *Warm, unassertive*
3. Hesitates to disagree with others out of fear of losing their support or approval	**A:** *Trusting, altruistic, compliant, modest*
4. Avoids initiating new projects out of lack of confidence in his or her abilities or judgment	**C:** *Does not feel competent, lacks self-discipline*
5. Goes to extreme lengths to be nurtured and supported, even to the point of volunteering for unpleasant activities	
6. Feels anxious when alone out of fear he or she is unable to take care of himself or herself	
7. Urgently begins a new relationship when a close relationship comes to an end	
8. Is preoccupied with fears about being abandoned and left to take care of himself or herself	

anxious to please. They are expected to score highly on most facets of both those domains. Research has found that dependent persons, as expected, are described as highly agreeable (Gore & Pincus, 2013; Mullins-Sweatt & Widiger, 2007).

If dependent people tend to be highly agreeable, then people who are highly agreeable must be overly dependent on others, right? Nope. Four separate meta-analyses of the association of agreeableness to dependency have *failed* to find a consistent relationship between them (Bornstein & Cecero, 2000; Miller & Lynman, 2008; Samuel & Widiger, 2008; Saulsman & Page, 2004). So what's going on?

What's going on is that the personality test most often used to measure the domains and facets of the FFM, the NEO-PI-R (Costa & McCrae, 1992a), was designed to assess variations among the personalities of normal, non-disordered individuals. Consequently, almost all of the items designed to measure high agreeableness are worded to express *adaptive manifestations* of this trait. Not surprisingly, then, individuals who describe themselves as trusting, altruistic, straightforward, compliant, modest, and tender-minded are not necessarily seen by others (or by themselves) as being overly dependent on other people.

What if we write new items to express the *maladaptive aspects* of excessive agreeableness? Instead of asking participants to rate themselves on the item, "I think of myself as a charitable person," the item is rewritten as "I am so charitable that I give more than I can afford." Similarly, the original item, "I believe most people are well-intentioned," is modified to read, "I tend to be gullible regarding the intentions of others." When the maladaptive variants of agreeableness are made explicit by these reworded items, the expected relationship between agreeableness and DPD is found (Lowe, Edmundson, & Widiger, 2009). Theodore Millon (1996, pp. 336–337) coined the term "The Accommodating Dependent" to describe the adult subtype of those DPD individuals who are submissive, extremely agreeable, and lean on other people for affection and security.

We saw in Chapter 6 how much we need to be included within a social group. Strong social bonds are essential for human survival and reproduction (Baumeister and Leary, 1995; Neuberg, Kenrick, & Schaller, 2010). DPD individuals take the importance of social connection to such an extreme that, out of fear of social rejection, they avoid criticizing their family and friends even when criticism is warranted. They seem to think that even their friends and family will "shoot the messenger" who brings bad news. So they avoid being that messenger.

When we are afraid, we seek the company of others. In a series of classic experiments, Stanley Schachter (1959) observed that individuals who feared an impending strong electric shock near-universally desired to be with other people. Individuals with DPD seem to live in a more-or-less constant state of fear of being unable to care for themselves. They need other people—who are seen as stronger, more competent and more capable—to satisfy their needs for safety and security.

DPD is relatively rare in the general population as its prevalence rate is estimated to be less than 1%. Gender differences are unclear: They either do not exist or more women than men receive this diagnosis (DSM-5, p. 677). The therapeutic prognosis for individuals diagnosed as DPD is relatively good (Millon, 1996).

Obsessive-Compulsive Personality Disorder (OCPD)

The need to be perfect, orderly, and in control of his environment describes a person diagnosed with obsessive-compulsive personality disorder. He is seen as a workaholic by his coworkers and as impossible to please by those he supervises. He delegates reluctantly because he fears other people will not do the work to his precise specifications. The left-hand column of Table 8.10 presents the symptoms of the obsessive-compulsive personality as given by DSM-5.

As seen in Table 8.10, the facets of Conscientiousness (C) dominate the traits on the FFM that characterize individuals with OCPD. Individuals with this disorder live with such unrealistically high standards that they work under intense anxiety. Their self-induced tension over their work not being "perfect" easily leads to procrastination and, frequently, a failure to produce anything at all. The latter possibility is unfortunate because these individuals often have much to offer despite their contributions falling short of "perfection."

Do all perfectionists suffer from OCPD? No, perfectionism is just one symptom of it. But perfectionism can be a deeply ingrained personality style that hinders the course of treatment of OCPD. There are a large number of comorbid disorders associated with perfectionism: depression, suicide attempts, social anxiety, eating disorders, various

❖ **Table 8.10**   Obsessive-Compulsive Personality Disorder (OCPD)

DSM-5: Four or More of the Following Symptoms	FFM Domains: *Significant Facets*
1. Gets so preoccupied with rules and details that the essential purpose of the activity is lost	N: *Anxious*
2. Perfectionistic to the point of being unable to complete a project because it fails to meet his or her unrealistic standards	E: *Cold, does not seek excitement*
3. Is a workaholic who has little or no time for leisure or friendships	O: *Does not express feelings, not interested in new activities, dogmatic*
4. Is overconscientious, scrupulous, and/or inflexible	C: *Feels competent, highly orderly, takes responsibilities seriously, sets high standards and works to achieve them, self-disciplined, cautious, and deliberates before acting*
5. Unable to discard worthless objects even when they hold no sentimental value	
6. Cannot or only reluctantly delegates tasks unless subordinates do them exactly as specified	
7. Hoards money as a protection against unseen disasters	
8. Stubborn to the point of rigidity	

somatic disorders, as well as OCPD (Egan, Wade, & Sharfran, 2011).[9] In different people, perfectionism can range between being nonproblematic to being so profoundly central to the personality that it would show up as one of the symptoms of OCPD. The prevalence rate of OCPD is estimated to be between 2.1 and 7.9%. It is diagnosed twice as often in males (DSM-5, p. 681). Successful therapy for those suffering from OCPD can lead to both fewer obsessive behaviors and a greater joy in living (Millon, 1996).

Three varieties of perfectionism that may or may not be problematic have been identified:

1. *Self-oriented perfectionism* is diagnosed when an individual makes demands for perfection in all of his or her work. "If *my* work is not perfect, it's worthless" seems to be the all-or-none thinking error that permeates this sort of perfectionism. The person confuses the wish to excel with the wish to be perfect. Problematic self-oriented perfectionism is a risk factor for other psychological disorders (e.g., depression, eating disorders) rather than a disorder in and of itself (Hewitt & Flett, 2007).

2. *Other-oriented perfectionism* is the tendency to require perfection from family, friends and co-workers. Their motto seems to be "If *your* work is not perfect, it's worthless." This variety of perfectionism is associated with interpersonal difficulties and is damaging for intimate relationships.

3. *Socially prescribed perfectionists* hold the erroneous belief "I *must* be perfect to earn your respect and admiration." This type of perfectionism becomes problematic when individuals consistently try, across *all* situations, to function under this unrealistic burden. They are at risk for depression and suicide. An obsession with perfection can result in a counter-productive loss of efficiency, sleep deprivation, increased use of alcohol and/or drugs, and exhaustion (Ayearst, Flett, & Hewitt, 2012).

Fortunately, perfectionists can help themselves. Clinical psychologists find that even small changes in behavior can reduce perfectionism's vice-like grip over the

"So Doc, what's wrong with me?"

entire personality. These changes include (a) finding sources of satisfaction in simple everyday pleasures (e.g., "Stop and smell the roses."); (b) finding and pursuing enjoyable hobbies; (c) taking care of yourself—a healthy diet, adequate sleep, and so on; (d) focusing on the *process* of goal achievement rather than the imagined outcome of that process; and (e) valuing yourself by making time to be alone and become better acquainted with your real wishes and interests (Doctor, Kahn, & Adamec, 2008).

The preceding 10 disorders of personality have been described in two ways: as syndromes identified by DSM-5 and as dimensional traits assessed by the Five-Factor Model. The next section discusses the strengths and weaknesses of these two approaches to understanding personality disorders.

Syndromes Versus Dimensions: Strengths and Weaknesses

We have seen throughout Tables 8.1 through 8.10 that these personality disorders may be conceptualized in two different ways: the symptom-counting (syndromal) approach of the DSM-5 and the personality trait (dimensional) approach of the FFM. What are the advantages and disadvantages of these two approaches?

Syndromal Approach of the DSM-5

There are two clear advantages of conceptualizing personality disorders as syndromes:

1. Specifying and identifying the unique symptoms of a particular personality disorder provides an *objective depiction* of that psychological problem in the same way that physicians diagnose physical illnesses and diseases—through the set of symptoms the patient displays.

2. Whether it's everyday conversation, writing about personality disorders, or selecting a diagnosis for an insurance company, a *label* is essential for us to understand each other. The 10 disorders of personality of the DSM-5 are needed as names that provide a commonly understood starting point for discussion and research as well as for continuity with prior published works.

Against these advantages, however, there are a number of weaknesses with the DSM-5 way of conceptualizing personality disorders:[10]

1. Both the *reliability* and the *validity* of the DSM categorical approach to personality disorders have been poor (Lawton, Shields, & Oltmanns, 2011; Pull, 2014; Zapolski, Guller, & Smith, 2013). As we saw in Chapter 2 on research methods, both the reliability and validity of any test or classification system is essential for us to be confident that it corresponds to reality.

2. A patient may show characteristics of multiple disorders. Consequently, an accurate differential diagnosis can be daunting. It is not surprising to find that the most frequent diagnosis is "Personality Disorder Not Otherwise Specified" (Verheul & Widiger, 2004). Such a system would be totally unacceptable for the diagnosis of a physical illness (e.g., "Patient is unhealthy—not otherwise specified"). In brief, the *discriminant validity* among the 10 PDs is poor (Zimmerman, Rothschild, & Chelminski, 2005).

3. Two individuals receiving the same diagnosis and sharing the same personality disorder may nevertheless appear to be noticeably different. This is due to the diagnostic requirement that an individual need show, say, only five of nine possible symptoms. Two individuals could share only *one* of the nine symptoms yet receive the same diagnosis. Again, this would be unacceptable for diagnosing physical ailments. Dozens of different conditions and illnesses share "headache" as one of their symptoms. A headache can be a sign of caffeine withdrawal. It is also one of the symptoms of a brain tumor (Griffith, 2012). We do not think of those two conditions as remotely similar even though they share a single symptom. A more refined system for the differential diagnosis of personality disorders is needed before the medical model of symptom counting can be reliably and validly applied to psychological disorders.

4. Experienced clinicians are well aware that there are far more than 10 ways an individual's personality may be disordered. In spite of the almost numberless ways an individual's personality may be implicated in his or her difficulties with himself or herself and others, the treatment provider is required by insurance companies to select which single *one* is most appropriate (Stone, 2013).

5. Personality disorders are among the most stigmatizing illnesses within the DSM-5. Being labeled with a PD implies that a person *is* his or her disorder (Millon, 2011).

Dimensional Approach of the Five-Factor Model

There are seven advantages to conceptualizing disorders of personality on a continuum of traits as identified by the FFM:

1. Abundant research conclusively shows that the FFM accurately and distinctively describes the 10 personality disorders of the DSM-5 (e.g., Samuel & Widiger, 2008; Saulsman & Page, 2004; Widiger & Costa, 2013b). A study of those diagnosed with borderline personality disorder supported the validity of its trait profile (Anderson et al., 2015). Spouse and self-ratings showed excellent agreement when applied to personality disorders described by the trait domains of negative affectivity, detachment, and antagonism (Jopp & South, 2015).

2. The FFM conceptualizes personality traits on a continuum, ranging from normal to disordered, not as something found only in qualitatively different "types" of people. Individuals diagnosed with a PD reveal extreme positions on some personality traits. Thus, our understanding of personality applies to everyone. We do not need a separate set of constructs to understand the personalities of those who are labeled (stigmatized) "disordered." The same basic factors of personality are found in both clinical and nonclinical populations (O'Connor, 2002).

3. The FFM can reveal the ways that individuals who are in the same diagnostic category differ from each other. The pattern of personality traits provides more useful information about each client's personality than is available within a single diagnostic code.

4. The FFM shows the ways that a client's diagnosed personality disorder might overlap with other personality disorders. A therapist could plan her treatment/management program more effectively by knowing which alternate disorders could also be present (the comorbidity problem).

5. By identifying which set of facets or subtraits show extreme positions, personality researchers can begin to understand each PD from the "bottom up" (Lynman, 2013, p. 278). Research will eventually identify which facets are most central to a given PD and which may be safely ignored. We might find that some facets need to be subdivided into even more specific traits to gain a more accurate understanding of a given disorder.

6. The FFM permits the therapist to identify the client's personality strengths as well as those extreme traits that are problematic. These strengths might then be specifically recruited to aid the client's therapeutic progress. For example, a client who displays a strong and healthy curiosity might feel empowered by engaging her curiosity to help her understand those aspects of her personality that seem to be involved in chronic interpersonal difficulties (Widiger & Mullins-Sweatt, 2009).

7. Finally, by conceptualizing PDs as a constellation of specific traits, the FFM implicitly recognizes that individuals are more than his or her PD diagnosis and thus avoids the possible stigmatizing effect associated with the DSM-5 labels.

Against these advantages, the disadvantages of the FFM are the following:

1. It is a personality test that must be given and scored by the therapist. This is a time-consuming process. This issue has been addressed somewhat by the development of a structured interview protocol to assess FFM traits verbally (Trull et al., 1998). Therapists would need at least minimal training before using the FFM for diagnostic purposes.

2. At present, clinicians cannot recognize a personality disorder if they are given only descriptions of a person's traits from the FFM (Rottman et al., 2009). Again, additional training is needed.

3. There are as yet no diagnostic codes associated with the FFM for clinicians to provide to the client's insurance company. The issue of which *labels* should characterize individuals who show maladaptive personality profiles has yet to be finalized.

One proposal suggests that terms describing extreme (problematic) poles of the five domain traits might work. Thus

- *negative affectivity* is the problematic pole of neuroticism (worry, anxiety, anger, etc.);
- *detachment* is the problematic pole of extraversion (so extremely introverted that one has zero emotional connection to other people);
- *antagonism* is the problematic pole of agreeableness (alienating everyone);
- *disinhibition* is the problematic pole of conscientiousness (no concern for meeting obligations, etc.); and
- *psychoticism* is the problematic pole of openness to experience (totally ungrounded).

Evidence supports this proposal for the first four problematic traits, but not for the proposed problematic pole (psychoticism) of openness to experience (Crego et al., 2015).

4. In fact, the domain of openness to experience has been the *least* helpful in identifying personality disorders. Openness is a complex trait. Openness to experience includes *fantasy proneness*, a trait that can lead to the creation of something new and valuable, or it can lead to a retreat from reality, or *both*. Openness to experience characterizes both

genius and madness. And even within personality disorders themselves, high scores on the fantasy facet of openness to experience are symptomatic of both the dissociative tendencies associated with borderline personality disorder as well as the grandiose fantasies associated with narcissistic personality disorder (Widiger, 2015). Thus, the items tapping this dimension need to be rewritten, so we can distinguish those aspects of openness which are adaptive from those which are clearly maladaptive (Chmielewski et al., 2014; DeYoung, Grazioplene, & Peterson, 2012).

5. A diagnosis of personality disorder is necessarily incomplete if it is only based on the individual's traits. How the person *functions* on a day-to-day basis needs to be carefully evaluated as a part of the overall assessment of his personality. Connecting the person's dysfunctional behaviors with independent measures of his personality traits would provide a more complete picture of the nature of his personality disorder (Clark, 2007).

6. Most important of all, the FFM assumes that a person's self-rating of his or her personality traits is accurate. However, individuals diagnosed with antisocial personality disorder are characterized by engaging in a pattern of deceptive acts. As with the other personality disorders, they are likely to hold distorted views of themselves. Should we take their self-descriptions at face value? Clinicians do well to be properly skeptical whenever self-report measures are the only basis for personality assessment (Oltmanns & Carlson, 2013). Research identifying the conditions under which self-reports are valid is needed.

More research is exactly what is proposed in Section III of the DSM-5 (pp. 761–781). Dimensional assessment measures of personality disorders are acknowledged as being "consistent with current diagnostic practice" (DSM-5, p. 733). It is not far-fetched to imagine that the next edition of the DSM will feature a new diagnostic system, one based on *multiple sources* of independent information about an individual's personality. It is to this topic that we now turn.

Sources for Diagnosis

As we saw in Chapter 2, we may be more confident in the accuracy of any judgment of someone's personality if that judgment is based on the integration of multiple and independent sources of information. Any single source of information about a person may be biased, misleading, or wrong. And if two sources of information are not independent of one another, then an erroneous opinion from informant A is not made more accurate by obtaining another opinion from informant B, if B formed his opinion from A's testimony.

There are four sources of information about a person that could lead to a diagnosis of personality disorder:

1. A *semi-structured interview* by a trained professional might reveal information relevant for a diagnosis. A face-to-face interview allows the therapist to learn what the client *says* in response to the interview questions as well as observe any *nonverbal behaviors* that support or contradict the client's verbal report (e.g., strained voice, sweating, avoiding eye contact, etc.). *Semi-structured* means that the interviewer is free to veer away from the standard protocol to explore important disclosures by the client. The problem with

this method is that different interviewers might choose different aspects to explore more fully and thus could end up with markedly different descriptions of the same person.

2. There are many *self-report personality tests* available for diagnostic purposes. The Minnesota Multiphasic Personality Inventory (MMPI), although initially developed in the late 1930s and early 1940s (Hathaway & McKinley, 1943b), still remains the most frequently administered test battery by clinical psychologists (Camera, Nathan & Puente, 2000). MMPI-2-RF was released in 2008 (Tellegen & Ben-Porath, 2008/2013). Two other self-report tests of personality disorder include the Millon Clinical Multiaxial Inventory-II (Millon, 1987) and the Personality Diagnostic Questionnaire-Revised (Hyler & Rieder, 1987). Self-report tests, as noted under the disadvantages of the FFM, assume the person knows himself well enough to answer the questions accurately and is motivated to be truthful.[11]

3. The purpose of a *structured interview* is to increase the objectivity of the information obtained such that two different interviewers will obtain the same (or virtually the same) information. All interviewers are required to ask the same questions in the same way. This requirement should increase the reliability of the procedure. But just as with any self-report procedure, someone who wants to conceal the truth may do so verbally in a structured interview as well as on paper-and-pencil tests.

4. *Informant reports,* such as found in the descriptions of personality traits by family or friends, may be a valuable source of information. Informant reports can usually be obtained efficiently and inexpensively (Vazire, 2006). Informants close to the person being evaluated—romantic partners, friends, parents—can and do report those pathological and problematic personality traits they observe. The accuracy of informant reports depends on how well the informant knows and likes the individual being evaluated (Carlson, Vazire, & Oltmanns, 2011; Leising, Erbs, & Fritz, 2010).

As expected under the general hypothesis that combining independent sources of information leads to more accurate prediction, a major depression event was predicted most accurately when multiple sources of personality assessment were available. Semistructured interviews, self-reports, and informant reports each improved the accuracy of the prediction (Galione & Oltmanns, 2013). On the other hand, when multiple sources of information are available, there is always the possibility that these sources will be discrepant from each other and point in opposite directions regarding the presence of personality dysfunction. Specifying the conditions under which informant reports are most likely to be accurate is an active area of research (Oltmanns & Carlson, 2013; Oltmanns & Turkheimer, 2006).

Personality Disorders Over the Life Span

Research into the developmental course of serious personality disorders implicates adolescence as the period of greatest risk for their onset (Johnson et al., 2000). Longitudinal studies of individuals diagnosed with PDs tend to show an overall amelioration or lessening of symptoms over time (Cooper, Balsis, & Oltmanns, 2014;

Lenzenweger, Johnson, & Willett, 2004; Skodol et al., 2005). A 10-year longitudinal investigation of borderline personality disorder, for example, found that 88% of the patients no longer met the standard for a diagnosis of BPD (Zanarini et al., 2006).

"I wasn't always afraid of heights!"

But just as individual differences among our personalities is a fundamental fact of life, so too is the fact that this overall, *on average*, decrease in the number of symptoms masks different life trajectories for separate segments of this population.

The first investigation to identify qualitatively distinct trajectories of change in personality disorders was reported by Michael Hallquist and Mark Lenzenweger in 2013. Based on multiple sources of data collected from 250 college students over their 4-year college experience, they report three distinct patterns of change of PD symptoms: a rapid decline, a slow decline, or a relative absence of symptoms.

The disorders that were most associated with a rapid decline of symptoms (from freshman to sophomore year) were borderline, histrionic, and obsessive-compulsive PDs. At the same time, across all trajectory patterns, those initially diagnosed with antisocial PD showed a slight but significant *increase* in symptoms over time (Hallquist and Lenzenweger, 2013). These important findings require replication, of course, before we draw any firm conclusions about the course of specific personality disorders.

Personality disorders may be thought of as a failure in self-regulation: The individual has adopted a way of being-in-the-world whereby his or her primary coping mechanism (i.e., the disorder) is so inflexible and rigid as to be chronically problematic for himself or herself and/or others. Those whose personalities are not disordered have a variety of ways of successfully regulating their thoughts, feelings, and actions. Self-regulation is the topic of our next chapter.

QUESTIONS TO PONDER

1. Why is a clear-cut diagnosis of personality disorders so difficult?

2. "The straw that broke the camel's back" is a well-known adage suggesting that insignificant external events may sometimes cause large psychological and/or physical effects. Have you ever been surprised by someone dramatically overreacting to something you said, something you intended as a trivial remark? Why do you think he or she overreacted? Have you ever emotionally overreacted to a comment made by someone else, a comment you later understood was trivial? What did you learn about yourself from that experience?

3. It is a well-known phenomenon that if a stranger begins to tell us, perhaps while we are standing on line at the supermarket or waiting at any other public setting, some upsetting interpersonal difficulties he is having with a person who is not present, we invariably agree (or at least do not directly disagree) with the person who initiated the one-way conversation. Does the information in this chapter shed any light on why we do that? Why would an individual share personal information with a stranger?

4. Can you think of any situations where you might act *as if* you had a disordered personality? Suppose a loved one unexpectedly needed immediate medical attention in a crowded place. Might you act in that situation like someone who has been diagnosed with histrionic personality disorder? Can you imagine other situations that might induce you to display symptoms of the other disorders? What, for example, might induce you to act as if you are socially avoidant? The point of these exercises is to develop empathy for individuals with these disorders by imagining the ways they chronically misperceive themselves and their social world.

NOTES

1. The American Psychiatric Association's system for clustering the 10 personality disorders is not the only way to group them. Theodore Millon (1996) prefers to group the disorders in terms of those that are "pleasure deficient" (schizoid, avoidant); "interpersonally imbalanced" (dependent, histrionic, narcissistic, and antisocial); "structurally-defective" (schizotypal, borderline, paranoid); and "intra-psychically conflicted" (obsessive-compulsive).

2. A publicly announced study of personality would seem to preclude, almost by definition, individuals with PPD from volunteering. Hearing someone say, "Step into my laboratory, I want to examine you," is more likely to drive them in the opposite direction.

3. Stone (2013) mentions sadism as comorbid with the schizoid personality disorder. The DSM-5 does not classify sadism as a personality disorder. It is covered under the *paraphillic disorders*: Obtaining sexual excitement and satisfaction from sources other than sexual intercourse and its usual preliminary behaviors and is labeled "sexual sadism disorder." The rationale for this classification is that some of the paraphillic disorders, like sadism, entail physical harm to other people and can also be classified as criminal offenses.

4. I experienced a person gripped by ideas of reference early in my teaching career. One of my students, a woman in her early 30s, sent a handwritten letter to my home to let me know that she was receiving the secret signals I was sending to her during my lectures. She also wanted me to know that she was attracted to me as strongly as I was to her. She became aware of my feelings for her via my secret signals. After our next class meeting, I met privately with her to let her know that I was not sending any signals to her. She then claimed I was in denial about my love for her. After learning she was in therapy, I strongly advised she inform her therapist about these delusions. She appeared to be suffering from *Clérambault's Syndrome*, a form of erotic paranoia (American Psychological Association, 2007, p. 178).

5. *Homo sapiens* is usually translated as "wise man."

6. The early childhood experiences of the excessively angry salesman described at the beginning of this chapter were characterized by numerous brutal rejections by his mother.

7. Lasch's book was not the first *anyone* wrote about this personality disorder. Pathological narcissism has been on the psychoanalyst's couch for many years. Sigmund Freud (1916), Otto Fenichel (1945), Heinz Kohut (1971), and Otto Kernberg (1975) discussed their insights about this condition before Lasch popularized it in his 1979 book.

8. Many teachers have had the regrettable experience of granting a student an exception to a standard classroom policy (e.g., "The highest grade for any overdue assignment is a B") only to find that, rather than expressing gratitude, the student presumptuously pushes for additional special treatment (e.g., "Can I handwrite my late paper?"). Hearing his professor say, "I'll make this exception just for you," only confirms a narcissist's sense of entitlement.

9. Comorbidity is one of the limitations of the categorical approach, an acknowledged limitation that motivates a search for a viable alternative dimensional approach to disorders of personality (DSM-5, p, 733; American Psychiatric Association, 2013).

10. The weaknesses of DSM-5 listed here are those that specifically apply to the treatment of personality disorders. The DSM-5 has been criticized more generally for pathologizing many normal behaviors (e.g., temper tantrums, "senior moments," and grief, among others). Books by psychiatrists Gary Greenberg (*The Book of Woe*, 2013) and Allen Frances (*Saving Normal*, 2014) give their detailed concerns over the DSM-5's widening definition of "mental illness."

11. The original MMPI included scales designed to detect outright lying, the tendency to fake looking better than you are (defensiveness), and the tendency to fake looking worse than you are (e.g., feigning insanity), as might be the motivation of someone facing serious jail time if convicted of a felony. MMPI-2-RF includes additional scales to detect careless responding and other sorts of errors by respondents. Extreme scores on any or all of these scales challenge the validity of the entire test result.

❖

SUGGESTIONS FOR FURTHER READING

Ellenberger, H. F. (1970). *The discovery of the unconscious: The history and evolution of dynamic psychiatry.* New York, NY: Basic Books

Millon, T., & Davis, R. (2000). *Personality disorders in modern life.* New York, NY: John Wiley.

Oldham, J. M., & Morris, L. B. (1995). *The new personality self-portrait: Why you think, work, love, and act the way you do.* New York, NY: Bantam.

Shapiro, D. (1965). *Neurotic styles.* New York, NY: Basic Books.

Singer, M. (2005). *Character studies: Encounters with the curiously obsessed.* Boston, MA: Houghton Mifflin.

INTERNET RESOURCES

1. To take a test that may indicate the presence of a personality disorder, go to http://www.4degreez.com/misc/personality_disorder_test.mv.

2. To learn about Marsha M. Linehan's background in borderline personality disorder, see http://www.nytimes.com/2011/06/23/health/23lives.html?pagewanted=all&_r=0.

3. To take a test that may indicate the presence of narcissism, go to http://psychcentral.com/quizzes/narcissistic.htm.

Part IV

My Future Self

Expectations, Plans, and Self-Regulation

What determines whether I will persist or give up trying to reach my goals?

During my junior year in college, I faced a difficult decision. I could either keep my current job delivering groceries or teach part-time at a private school. On the one hand, teaching was engaging, satisfying, and part of my career plans. On the other hand, delivering groceries was more financially rewarding. I opted to forego present economic benefits in favor of taking my first steps toward a career. I'm glad I did.

We all face critical decisions at certain points in our lives. The major point of this chapter is that your future self is affected by your present goals and your persistence in attaining them. By your persistence to attain any major goal (e.g., completing your education, successfully balancing a demanding school/work/family schedule, losing weight and keeping it off), you create a future self that will differ from the one that will occur without such goal-directed persistent behavior. Your present choices create your future self.

To reach our major goals in life, it is not enough merely to have them. Something else is needed. Consider the often-made-but-seldom-kept New Year's Resolution. Many people adopt goals or resolutions on December 31, such as losing 25 pounds, getting a better job, or dating more interesting people, only to give up reaching those goals before the end of January. By themselves, goals clearly do not guarantee success. We also need effective *plans* for achieving them.

But even well-thought-out plans are often not enough. Many people, in spite of having realistic action plans, get sidetracked and give up when obstacles arise. Others successfully achieve their goals despite encountering similar difficulties. Why do some people successfully overcome obstacles while others experience defeat? Many personality psychologists think it is our *expectations* about ourselves, other people, and our obstacles that frequently determine the difference between reaching our goals and giving up. Other psychologists focus on specific threats to *self-regulation:* our ability to stay focused and on track in spite of potential distractions.

In this chapter, we explore those cognitive approaches to personality that directly apply to our expectations and self-regulation. I present the useful ideas of George Kelly, John Bowlby, Walter Mischel, Charles Carver and Michael Scheier, Roy Baumeister, and E. Tory Higgins. I hope the information in this chapter will help you persevere when the going gets tough.

The Psychology of Personal Constructs

> *A person's processes are psychologically channelized by the ways in which he anticipates events.*
>
> —George Kelly (1955, p. 46)

Kelly's fundamental postulate, presented above, says that we anticipate future events in order to predict more accurately what will occur next. It is the content of our anticipations that sets our thoughts and feelings going in particular directions. Imagine how different you would feel if you read a letter that (a) invites you to a surprise birthday party for a good friend versus (b) orders you to contact your dean, your supervisor, or the IRS. Anticipating these different kinds of events will set different psychological processes—feelings and thoughts—into motion.

The ability to anticipate events develops during childhood. Five-year-olds are willing to share their toys because they've learned from past experience that toy-sharing will be reciprocated. They can *anticipate* future sharing and their anticipation affects how they perceive the present situation ("I'll share my toys with you now and you'll share your toys with me later."). Three-year-olds in the same situation are unable to anticipate reciprocity and so they are unwilling to share (Sebastian-Enesco & Warneken, 2015).

Kelly wants to understand how different individuals anticipate their possible futures. He views humans as problem-solving scientists, seeking to get what they want by anticipating events and modifying their behavior accordingly. Successful college students anticipate what areas of the assigned readings and lecture notes will most likely be covered on the upcoming quiz. Their anticipations lead them to study those areas more diligently than material deemed less likely to be on the test. Kelly thinks such anticipations go on constantly, in all areas of life, from anticipating whether a person we like will go out on a date with us, a parent will give us permission to borrow the family car, or our child's school is adequate for her needs.

Medical research provides evidence that Kelly's fundamental postulate is even more fundamental than he anticipated. Our expectations alone can have a profound effect on brain activity. Patients with Parkinson's disease showed similar altered brain activity to just the expectation of medication as they did to actual administration of dopamine (Schmidt et al., 2014). While placebo effects have been known for a long time, it is only recently that researchers have attempted to understand (a) how placebos work on the brain and (b) which personality variables are associated with their effectiveness (Lu, 2015).

OK, so how do we form these anticipations? Kelly elaborates his fundamental postulate by presenting a series of corollaries, only some of which are presented here. His *Construction Corollary* (1955) states, "A person anticipates events by construing their replications" (p. 50). *Construing* is Kelly's term for "placing an interpretation." We do this by noticing the *similarities and differences* between related events. To construe a

Photo 9.1   George A. Kelly (1905–1967)

George Kelly's cognitive approach to personality focuses on the importance of thinking. How we interpret the events in our lives influences how we feel about them as well as what actions we could take.

Key publication:

The Psychology of Personal Constructs (1955)

particular college course as "hard" or "easy," for example, requires having prior experience in similar situations and developing applicable constructs, such as the amount and difficulty of the required reading, the number and quality of term projects, interest in the course material, difficulty of the exams, and so forth. Given a background in similar situations, students anticipate early in the semester how easy or difficult the course will be.

Replications refer to recurrent themes in the events of our lives that allow us to predict in a general but useful way some of the key features of tomorrow's events. If the event is attending tomorrow's class, we might anticipate how interesting or boring it will be based on our experiences with the class. Other students in the same class may anticipate how much or how little new information they will learn rather than how interestingly the information is presented. Other students may anticipate meeting the cute person who sits across the aisle.

Differences among different individuals in the same situation lead to Kelly's *Individuality Corollary:* "Persons differ from each other in their construction of events" (1955, p. 55). To one student, the most important construct may be the entertainment skills of the teacher; to another student, the most important construct may be how much work is required to earn a passing grade; to a third student, the most important construct may be whether class attendance is required for a passing grade. If these three students construe the course in *only* their unique ways, they are taking *subjectively different* courses while physically sitting in the same classroom. Individual differences can arise from different backgrounds in culture, language, social class, family norms, and so on. (Stephens, Markus, & Phillips, 2014).

Kelly points out that the individuality corollary does not preclude individuals from sharing experiences if they are willing to accept other people's frames of reference. If you value a course because of how much you are learning, you can still understand that another student is dissatisfied because he is bored by the material. In Kelly's system, people are similar to the extent that their constructs are similar.

To know another person, then, is to know how he or she construes the world. To gain access to his patients' ways of construing their worlds, Kelly developed the **Role Construct Repertory Test** (or Rep Test). This test assumes that the most important constructs we hold concern the important people in our lives. The Role Title List describes 24 different social roles. Examples of these roles are a teacher you liked, your wife (husband), your mother, your father, a girl or boy you didn't like in high school, and the most interesting person you know. The Rep Test taker writes the names of the specific individuals in his or her life who are described by these roles.

After completing the Role Title List, the person is next asked to consider three of these people at one time and indicate in what way two of them are similar and differ from the third. For example, an undergraduate male might be asked to compare his mother, father, and girlfriend. If he responds by saying that two of them are women and one is a man, the examiner will agree that they are alike in that way and will ask again how two are similar yet differ from the third person. The student may then say, "Well, both my girlfriend and father are curious about a wide variety of things, but my mother seems to be interested only in taking care of the house." The way that his girlfriend and father are similar is called the *similarity pole* of the construct (high curiosity) and the way that the mother differs is called the *contrast pole* (low curiosity).

After repeating this procedure with different groups of three people, the person gradually reveals the key people in his or her life. By allowing individuals to describe people in any way they like, the Rep Test can apply to anyone who is able to verbalize how he perceives his significant others. The Rep Test is an *idiographic* approach to personality because the *individual selects* those concepts that are most important rather than being presented with constructs of interest to the researcher (e.g., "Compare three people you know on how inquisitive they are." The trait of curiosity may be unimportant to the person being tested.).

Another triad might be a boss, your best friend, and a favorite teacher. In what way are two of these individuals alike and differ from the third? Examining a person's responses to all triads that are presented reveals how many different constructs that person uses in construing his or her world. A woman who uses many constructs, for example, possesses cognitive complexity and flexibility. She can call upon a greater variety of constructs to understand and anticipate events in her world. Should the Rep Test reveal that a different woman uses the same construct in all comparisons, it indicates that this single construct "seems to carry the burden of her dealings with the people in her interpersonal world" (1955, p. 249). Having a limited number of constructs means that a person construes all events within a tightly restricted frame of reference (e.g., people and events are either good or bad). Such a person could be described as having "tunnel vision."

The Rep Test is useful for assessing which constructs we use to anticipate future interactions and the degree of self-imposed limits through which we see our world. Our persistence in trying to reach our goals is affected by how we construe the difficulties we encounter along the way. If we construe these difficulties in a way that permits us to anticipate that our efforts will be successful, we are more likely to persist than if we construe the difficulties as insurmountable. Similarly, if our frame of reference includes many relevant constructs, it may be easier to persist despite obstacles that occur in a new situation (e.g., a job in a new field) than if our frame of reference is restricted. A wide variety of constructs gives us more mental options. To George Kelly, how we construe ourselves, our goals, and our obstacles are the keys for understanding our persistence in reaching our goals.

Expectancies and Internal Working Models

If an individual is to draw up a plan to achieve a set-goal not only must he have some sort of working model of his environment, he must have also some working knowledge of his own behavioral skills and potentialities.

—John Bowlby (1982, p. 82)

Internal working models help us perceive and interpret our experiences, forecast the future, and construct plans. These models are determined in large part, according to Bowlby, by our early childhood experiences with our attachment figures. Our general expectation that other people will respond to us and our needs is reflected by two key aspects of these internal working models: (1) our self-concept of whether we are the sort of person anyone is likely to respond to in a helpful way, and (2) our concept of other people in general (and our attachment figures in particular) as willing to respond to our requests for support and protection (Bowlby, 1973).

Research indicates that our working models develop from very simple structures during the preschool period into far more complex cognitive structures by adolescence (Bretherton, 1991). Bowlby thought that our internal working models become stable aspects of ourselves that guide our interpretations of social interactions and expectations about ourselves and others. Although they originate in our earliest attachment relationships with our caregivers, these internal models of ourselves and others continue to influence the quality of our relationships throughout adulthood.

How many internal working models do we have? No one knows. Bowlby discusses two general models: one model for ourselves and another for our views of other people. Ainsworth and her colleagues discuss three types of attachment and their (presumably) corresponding internal models.[1]

Abundant research reveals the range and robustness of the concept of internal working models.[2] For example, while children who are brought up in unpredictable, chaotic environments tend to score lower on tests of intelligence and memory (Goodman, Quas, & Ogle, 2010), their internal working models ("expect the unexpected") might enable them to perform more effectively as adults when faced with *situational* variability. Data support this hypothesis: Adults who grew up in harshly unpredictable environments outperformed adults who grew up in stable environments on tasks that required them to mentally shift quickly between various alternatives. Their early childhood experiences apparently prepared them to cope with situational variability in adulthood (Mittal et al., 2015). Thus, in addition to internal working models of self and other, perhaps we also have one or more internal models that are activated by situational characteristics. What other situational features might activate internal working models?

We are likely to reveal our expectations of self and others in many aspects of everyday social life, whether we are interacting with a stranger, a friend, a serious dating partner, or our marriage partner.

Interacting With Strangers

An example of how our internal working models affect how we interact with strangers is provided by Avril Thorne's thought-provoking study of the conversational styles of introverts and extraverts. Thorne (1987) paired 19-year-old women with dispositionally similar or dissimilar strangers of the same age and sex. Three different conversational dyads were formed: An extravert was paired with an extravert, an introvert was paired with an introvert, or an extravert was paired with an introvert.

Introverts, Thorne found, preferred to talk to an extravert rather than a fellow introvert. Extraverts, however, were evenly divided in their preferences for talking with either an extravert or introvert. Conversations between two introverts tended to stay focused on the same topic (e.g., school, living situation), while conversations between two extraverts were more wide-ranging.

By analyzing their 10-minute conversations, Thorne found a tendency for the typical extravert to expect that she and her partner shared much common ground. The main point of the conversation, from the extravert's point of view, was to explore the extent of their similarity and make personal connections. The most unusual reach for similarity came from an extravert who responded, "You have a turtle? A friend of mine has a kitty!" (p. 720). Introverts, however, did not seem to expect their partners to be similar to themselves. When interacting with an extravert, the typical introvert tended to adopt the role of "interviewer." In this role she attempted to elicit, rather than share, the other person's experience. Thorne (1987) notes that the interviewer role adopted by introverts "seems to express an underlying expectation that experience cannot be shared so much as appreciated as different" (p. 725). Introverts and extraverts seem to differ in their internal working models of the social rewards they expect from initial interactions with strangers.

Interacting With Friends

A clear example of how internal working models affect friendship patterns is shown in the highly cited paper of Kim Bartholomew and Leonard Horowitz (1991). They hypothesized that (1) a person's internal model of himself may be essentially positive ("I am worthy of love and support.") or negative ("I am not worthy of love and support."), and (2) his model of other people may also be essentially positive ("Other people are trustworthy and available.") or negative ("Other people are unreliable and rejecting."). Combining these two models yields four friendship attachment patterns: Secure, Preoccupied, Dismissing, and Fearful, as shown in Table 9.1

If you hold a positive view of yourself (i.e., you are worthy of being loved) and other people are usually responsive to you, your internal working mode is called *Secure*.

❖ **Table 9.1**   Model of Adult Attachment

		Model of Self	
		Positive	Negative
Model of Other	Positive	**Secure** *Comfortable with intimacy and autonomy*	**Preoccupied** *Preoccupied with relationships Overly dependent*
	Negative	**Dismissing** *Dismissing of intimacy Denial of attachment*	**Fearful** *Afraid of intimacy Socially avoidant*

Source: Adopted from Bartholomew and Horowitz (1991). Attachment styles among young adults: A test of a four-category model. *Journal of Personality and Social Psychology, 61,* 226–244. Copyright by American Psychological Association.

If your view of yourself is negative (i.e., you are not worthy of being loved), while your view of others is positive, this type of internal working model is called *Preoccupied*: You are overly concerned with being accepted by other people. On the other hand, if you value yourself highly but hold generally negative opinions about the worth of others, you are likely to protect yourself against disappointment by avoiding intimate relationships, an internal working model called *Dismissing*. Finally, if your view of both yourself and others is negative, your internal working model is called *Fearful*, and you probably prefer to avoid social relationships.

Bartholomew and Horowitz (1991) obtained support for the existence of these four types of internal models from a variety of sources: family and peer ratings, interviews of the subjects, written self-reports, and reports from friends. There was agreement between family and peer ratings, and among the data obtained from interviews, self-reports, and friend's reports, that individuals could indeed be described as holding one of these four internal working models of self and others. Both (a) how we think of ourselves and (b) what we expect from others influence how we are perceived by those who know us well.

Bartholomew and Horowitz (1991) also found that these four attachment patterns were associated with different types of interpersonal problems. Those who were classified as Dismissing saw themselves as particularly cold, competitive, and unexpressive (withholding their feelings); those classified as Preoccupied rated themselves as overly expressive of their feelings and autocratic; Fearful participants saw themselves as passive, introverted, and frequently exploited by others. Those classified as Secure did not report any systematic interpersonal difficulties.

Research suggests that those who are Preoccupied with relationships often end up in a self-fulfilling prophecy. They express a heightened need to belong to, and to be accepted by, their peer group. They feel shame when they fail to meet their unrealistic perfectionistic standards. They pretend to be flawless to gain the group's acceptance. Sadly, however, these perfectionistic self-presentations often create the opposite of what they want. Their peers easily detect their false front and are put off by it (Chen, Hewitt, & Flett, 2015; Chen et al., 2012).

The findings of Bartholomew and Horowitz (1991) are also consistent with additional research on the relationship between internal working models and perceived social support. College students who perceived they had numerous sources of social support tended to believe that this was true of the "typical student" as well. Similarly, those who rated themselves as lacking present social support believed that this was also true of the "typical student." Interestingly, those who felt they had ample social support available to them were more accurate in estimating their peers' perceptions of social support than those who perceived low levels of support. Moreover, students who were satisfied with their presently available social support tended to be satisfied with the care and affection provided by their parents, especially their fathers (Sarason et al., 1991).

Moreover, self-perceptions of college-age participants relate more strongly to the depth of their current friendships than with that of either parent (Sarason et al., 1991). This finding supports Bowlby's belief that we can modify internal working models by experiences after childhood. Meaningful and supportive relationships beyond childhood—such as with a close friend or spouse—can positively affect a person's internal model of himself and what he can expect from other people (Bowlby, 1988; Bretherton, 1992; Rutter & Quinton, 1984).

A child's attachment status (secure versus insecure) is related to the quality of his or her peer relationships (satisfactory or unsatisfactory). Securely attached children are more likely to be satisfied with their relationships with their friends (Pallini et al., 2014; Schneider et al., 2001). Securely attached individuals of all ages (children, teens, adults) have friendships characterized by trust, self-disclosure, closeness, and the ability to resolve conflicts in ways that strengthen the relationship. Attachment insecurity, on the other hand, is associated with less satisfying relationships with friends. Those who are avoidantly attached, for example, are less likely to use Facebook than those with other attachment styles (Hart et al., 2015; Mikulincer & Shaver, 2007).

So how are these two variables—attachment security and friendship satisfaction—connected? Nancy McElwain and her colleagues found that those mothers who asked their 2-year-olds about their *thoughts* (e.g., "What do you think this book is going to be about?") were more likely to have securely attached children and these children, in turn, were more likely to have satisfying friendships when they were 4 to 5 years old. Children who begin to understand the minds of their friends and who can verbalize their ideas and thoughts have more harmonious friendships. An important ingredient of maternal sensitivity, then, is the mother's ability and willingness to engage her child with speech that elicits the child's mental activity about thinking (McElwain, Booth-LaForce, & Wu, 2011).

Finally, supporting Bowlby's contention that internal working models of self and significant others complement one another, individuals who hold a positive self-image are confident that others will be responsive to their needs, whereas those who hold a negative image of self are not (Sarason et al., 1991). Do those who reach their goals simply expect that social support will be available, while those who fail to attain their goals lack, or assume they lack, a supportive group they can rely on?

Interacting With Romantic Partners

Kirkpatrick and Davis (1994) asked over 350 couples involved in serious dating relationships to answer some questions about their attachment styles. One purpose of the study was to determine which attachment styles were paired with each other. On the basis of written responses, all subjects were classified into one of three attachment categories: secure, avoidant, and anxious. Individuals with a secure attachment style are comfortable with intimacy, describe their romantic relationship as happy and trusting, and accept their partner despite his or her faults. Avoidantly attached individuals are uncomfortable with intimacy and are less trusting of their partner. Those who are anxiously attached worry about being abandoned and are preoccupied with the relationship (Hazan & Shaver, 1987). The results of a 4-year prospective study indicate that these three attachment styles are highly stable (Kirkpatrick & Hazan, 1994).

Kirkpatrick and Davis (1994) found, as expected, that the most common pair consisted of securely attached dating partners. Of the dating couples in which at least one partner was insecurely attached, Kirkpatrick and Davis's most striking observation was that "there were no avoidant-avoidant or anxious-anxious pairs. Instead, avoidant participants tended to be paired with anxious partners and vice versa" (p. 506).

This observation dramatically supports Bowlby's hypothesis that internal working models of self and others are complementary. Individuals choose partners who match their expectations and complement their own attachment styles. Those with avoidant attachment styles expect their partners to be dependent and clinging (which characterizes the style of the anxiously attached person); those with anxious attachment styles expect their partner to avoid intimacy, be rejecting, and withdraw from them (which characterizes the style of the avoidantly attached person). Individuals who are either avoidantly or anxiously attached are *not* attracted to individuals who are similarly attached because such similarity violates their expectations of how a romantic figure should act.

Moreover, Kirkpatrick and Davis (1994) observed that the highest break-up rates 3 years later occurred among anxiously attached men and avoidantly attached women. Overall, anxious women were less likely to break up than securely attached women. Expectations, determined by our internal working models of self and others, affect what we expect out of a romantic relationship and how persistent we are in attaining it.

The previously mentioned fourfold categorization of attachment developed by Bartholomew and Horowitz (1991) has been adopted for studying how undergraduate women assess the quality of their dating relationships (Carnelley, Pietromonaco, & Jaffe, 1994). Women scoring high on the fearful attachment style reported less satisfaction in their romantic relationships, less support from their partners, and less constructive conflict resolution. Women who scored high on the preoccupation attachment style were also less satisfied with their relationships and had fewer supportive exchanges with their romantic partners.

Insecure individuals interpret ambiguous messages from their partner in ways that threaten the viability of the relationship. They assume the message was negative and nonsupportive. These data show that individuals are predisposed to evaluate support from their partner in ways consistent with their internal working model. Believing they are not worthy of support, insecure individuals fail to perceive the support that is offered. These internal models, then, (1) predispose us to anticipate upcoming events in biased ways and (2) shape how we interpret new information in the present (Collins & Feeney, 2004).

Early in a dating relationship, securely attached people disclosed more about themselves when their partner was also highly disclosing. Moreover, they elicited more self-disclosures than those who were insecurely attached and they expanded upon the information expressed to them in their own replies. So it is not a surprise that numerous studies have found most people are more attracted to secure partners from the very start of their relationship. College students who were preoccupied with attachment issues were less likely to be married 5 years later. While trying to resolve an interpersonal conflict, securely attached individuals display less negative behavior than those who are insecurely attached (Creasy, 2002; Mikulincer & Shaver, 2007;

Tarabulsy et al., 2012), and those who are securely attached are turned off by casual sexual relationships (Jonason, Hatfield, & Boler, 2015).

Finally, internal working models of attachment have been observed to be stable. In a longitudinal study covering the transition period from a dating relationship to marriage, 78% of the participants received the same attachment classification 18 months into their marriage that they had received 3 months before they were married (Crowell, Treboux, & Waters, 2002). In a review of 30 investigations of the stability of attachment styles over varying lengths of time, the average correlation coefficient was +0.56, showing both substantial continuity, while also implying internal working models are subject to change (Mikulincer & Shaver, 2007).

Interacting With Spouses

Internal working models of oneself and others both affect and are affected by marriage. Kobak and Hazan (1991) found that the more husbands and wives agreed about each other's working models of themselves, the better their communication skills in solving mutual problems and the better their marital adjustment. Knowing what they can expect from each other, couples with more accurate pictures of their partner's internal models listen more to each other and arrive at mutually satisfying solutions, compared to those couples who are unable to update or accommodate their images of one another. Open communication between husbands and wives fosters increased accuracy about each other's working models.

Since Kobak and Hazan's (1991) initial report, the link between attachment security and the quality of one's marriage has been replicated numerous times. What variables might account for this connection? Research has identified the following possibilities:

(a) Secure individuals express their emotions more openly; they engage in more self-disclosure. In general, securely attached individuals have better communication skills.

Better communication skills and the willingness to use them promote increased marital satisfaction with one's spouse. Communicating what you are actually feeling eliminates the need for your spouse to guess at what you *might* be feeling and *why* you are feeling it. "Mind reading" is not only a poor substitute for words, but it often adds unnecessary fuel to the conflict and escalates it dramatically (e.g., "*How* in the world could you *possibly* think I'm feeling *that* [subtext: *you moron!*]?" And, voila! A second conflict arises.).

(b) Secure individuals tend to give their spouses the benefit of the doubt in explaining a negative behavior (e.g., "She shouted at me because she's had an exceptionally stressful day") rather than attributing it to a character flaw (e.g., "She shouted at me because she's emotionally unstable"). Benefit-of-the-doubt explanations are called *relationship-maintaining*. Your explanation does not make your spouse feel attacked or misunderstood (Feeney, 2008).

(c) Securely attached individuals are more likely to forgive transgressions by their spouses and less likely to hold grudges. Being able to express fully one's feelings about a present marital difficulty—and to listen to your spouse's feelings—makes it less likely that this difficulty will be brought up in the future if it can be mutually resolved. The inability to forgive makes it difficult to forget (Kachadourian, Fincham, & Davila, 2004).

(d) Securely attached individuals are less likely to feel psychologically distressed. Individuals are more likely to feel satisfied in their marriage when their spouses are not distressed (Meyers & Landsberger, 2002). It is a different picture for insecurely attached spouses. Couples where the wives are anxiously attached and their husbands are avoidantly attached show increased levels of cortisol in anticipation of conflict. Moreover, they reveal distinctive behaviors during their conflict: Anxious wives do not easily recognize their avoidant husbands' distress; avoidant husbands find it difficult to approach their anxious wives for help (Beck et al., 2013).

Fortunately, women who received little social support as children can change their negative internal working model of themselves for the better if they develop a strong relationship with a stable partner (Bretherton, 1990). A woman's current attachment style is a better predictor of the quality of her marital relationship than is her retrospectively reported relationship with her parents (Carnelley et al., 1994). While any given person's internal working model of attachment may last a lifetime, these mental models are not written in stone. A consistently supportive relationship can, over time, erase the cognitive and emotional damage done by early childhood mistreatment (Mikulincer & Shaver, 2007).[3]

Finally, we all know that many marriages end in divorce. Can attachment theory help us understand why couples divorce? Yes. While attachment theory does not explicitly address divorce, it certainly deals with the psychological consequences of *separation* from someone to whom we were once attached (Bowlby, 1973, 1979, 1980). A comprehensive understanding of divorce (and its possible prevention) from an attachment theory perspective has been provided by Brooke Feeney and Joan Monin (2008).

For our healthy growth and functioning, attachment theory assumes that two elements are always required:

1. The *availability of a trustworthy person* who provides both a *safe haven* for when we are ill or otherwise unable to engage in our usual activities as well as a *secure base* from which we can explore the unknown (including our unknown talents);

2. The *capacity to identify a trustworthy attachment figure* with whom we can have a mutually rewarding relationship.

From an attachment theory perspective, the lack of one or both of these elements in either marriage partner is the beginning of a dysfunctional relationship that might end in divorce (Bowlby, 1979). Let's take a closer look at these elements:

1. The chronic unavailability of one's spouse is one of the primary causes of feeling frustrated, angry, and/or anxious. Although his or her unavailability could be the result of a defective internal working model of attachment learned in early childhood (Bowlby, 1979), it nevertheless hurts the partner who needs a safe haven. Unavailability can show up as (a) being chronically unresponsive to signals indicating care is needed, (b) acting in a rejecting and cold manner, (c) threatening to abandon the family as a tactic to get one's way, and/or (d) not being predictably available (as is usually the case when one's partner is dependent on alcohol or other drugs).

   The response by the partner to any of these signs of unavailability include feeling angry or resentful (resentment is a symptom of unexpressed anger), attempting to shame the unresponsive partner (i.e., you hurt me, so I'll hurt you), becoming compulsively self-reliant, coping with stress by overeating, substance abuse, infidelity, or engaging in addictive behaviors (Bowlby, 1979).

2. A marital relationship can develop problems when one spouse fails to recognize signs of an untrustworthy partner. If one cannot consciously recognize symptoms that one's partner is not trustworthy, one cannot take any corrective actions to address the problem. These failures of recognition are due to faulty internal working models learned in childhood and unconsciously applied to the present relationship.

It is a major premise of attachment theory that an internal model can be so deep-rooted that it continues to influence our perceptions, thoughts, and feelings even though it is dysfunctional and out-of-date. Changing (or updating) a person's faulty internal working model is usually slow because the model has seemingly "worked" for the person for so long. Susan Johnson (2008) shows how attachment theory may usefully apply to couple and family therapy systems.

If a couple decides to divorce, how do the individuals cope with this major change in their lives? It depends in part on their attachment history. Secure individuals are likely to cope with this life change by seeking social support through family and friends. Anxiously attached individuals, on the other hand, tend to display dysfunctional coping strategies such as being preoccupied with their former partner, fruitlessly attempting to reunite, becoming angry when these efforts fail, and showing other signs of emotional distress. Finally, avoidant individuals are likely to rely on distancing and self-reliant strategies as in avoiding new romantic possibilities or being unwilling to seek social support (Pietromonaco & Beck, 2015).

In a marital relationship, the key "environmental" variable is one's partner. Planning a successful marriage requires, as Bowlby's quote at the beginning of this section indicates, reasonably accurate knowledge of both your own and your partner's internal working models of attachment. The more accurately we can anticipate how our actions will affect our partner, the more accurate our internal working models are, thereby increasing the likelihood we will achieve the goal of a mutually satisfying marriage.

Our expectations, anticipations, and plans begin our journey toward achieving our goals. Our ability to self-regulate helps us stay on track. But there are many threats to self-regulation. What are they?

Self-Regulation: Threats and Theories

Self-regulation means self-control. How is your self-control? My self-control, while better than it was when I was younger, still has room for improvement, particularly when I still have room for dessert.

Our self-control usually improves from adolescence to adulthood because changes in specific brain circuits (e.g., circuits connecting the prefrontal cortex, amygdala, and the ventral striatum) during adolescence—but not during childhood or adulthood—make self-regulation more challenging. Three changes are particularly noteworthy:

1. For one thing, pleasurable activities are experienced as especially rewarding during adolescence. Heightened brain responses to positive stimuli make it more difficult for adolescents to avoid these rewarding (and perhaps dangerous) activities. Potentially rewarding activities (e.g., "Let's cut class!") are much more tempting during adolescence.

2. The *mere presence* of a peer group member increases risky decision making in adolescence more so than in children or adults.

3. Finally, adolescents have greater difficulty suppressing their attention toward emotional stimuli compared to children or adults. A perceived insult, for example, is more difficult for an adolescent to ignore.

These three brain changes peak at about 15 years of age (Casey, 2015).

Mortality rates among human adolescents show a 200% rise in preventable deaths due to accidents, suicide, and homicide (Paus, Keshaven, & Giedd, 2008). Adolescence is a time when our brain predisposes us to (a) seek novel experiences, experiences we expect to be highly rewarding, (b) spend more time with our peer group, and (c) fight more with our parents. These three behavioral dispositions are typical of both human adolescents as well as adolescents across a wide variety of mammalian species (Spear, 2010).

Self-regulation helps adolescents avoid exciting activities that are potentially dangerous. Self-control is also associated with less everyday stress: Using a daily diary method, adolescents who scored higher on measures of self-control reported less exposure to daily stress over a two-week period. Why? Perhaps greater self-control enables adolescents to proactively avoid events they expect will be stressful (Galla & Wood, 2015).

Self-regulation refers to the internal processes we need to pursue our goals in spite of the variety of threats—personal, interpersonal, and/or environmental—that could disrupt attaining our desired outcome (Hoyle & Gallagher, 2015). The benefits of self-regulation are well-documented. Those with self-control do better in school, earn more money, enjoy better physical health and better social relationships. The relationship between self-control and positive life outcomes seems to be due to the better habits—better sleeping habits, better eating habits, better study habits, etc.—of those with good self-control (Galla & Duckworth, 2015; Wood & Runger, 2016). Moreover, individuals who are high in self-control tend to avoid those situations that are likely to distract them from their goals. By doing so, they do not need to exert willpower to resist a temptation to go off-task since they have already minimized the presence of enticing opportunities (Ent, Baumeister, & Tice, 2015).

Self-regulation is required whenever we want to achieve any long-term goal, whether the goal is to complete our education, lose a significant amount of weight, or raise healthy children. The sheer length of time it takes to complete these ambitious projects virtually ensures we will encounter obstacles and temptations along the way that, should we succumb to them, will sidetrack us for varying lengths of time, eventually leading us to settle for less or to give up. Because understanding what aids and what hinders our efforts to control ourselves has obvious practical importance, I've organized the rest of this chapter around four common threats to self-regulation. Knowing what can cause self-regulation failure is a good first step for dealing with these potential pitfalls.

Acting Impulsively (CAPS Theory)

If acting impulsively is never an issue for you, I'd like to offer my congratulations. It certainly is for many people. Right behind subjective distress, impulsiveness is the second most frequent diagnostic symptom found in the *Diagnostic and Statistical Manual of Mental Disorders* (Whiteside & Lynam, 2001). However, it is not a problem for everyone. Some people rarely act impulsively. The opposite of acting impulsively is to obsessively go over one's thoughts and plans, again and again, before any action is taken (if it ever is). Healthy mental functioning lies between the extremes of thinking obsessively (but not acting) and acting impulsively (but not thinking).

The personality trait of impulsivity is the tendency to act on impulses or urges without, or even despite, consideration of likely negative consequences (DeYoung, 2011). Impulsive actions have three distinctive qualities: They are speedy, abrupt, and unplanned. Speedy means that there is only a brief time interval between the thought and the impulsive action. Abrupt means the impulsive action is different from what we were doing before we acted. And unplanned means that the impulsive action is not something we had intended to do—the idea suddenly springs into our mind and we suddenly spring into action.

Whenever impulsivity is problematical, serious long-term planning is absent. Moreover, an individual whose personality is dominated by impulsivity is impaired in the other thought processes of concentration, reflection, and judgment. Planning, judgment, and self-reflection are abilities found in normal functioning. These qualities prevent erratic and impulsive behavior from controlling our lives (Shapiro, 1965).

Chronically impulsive individuals produce low levels of the neurotransmitter serotonin. Serotonin helps us to restrain our impulses as well as to inhibit them from forming in the first place. Low levels of serotonin are also associated with suicide, depression, anxiety, and alcoholism (Carver, Johnson, & Joorman, 2008; Zuckerman, 2005).

Impulsivity is one of the facets of the Five-Factor Model's trait of Neuroticism. A factor analysis of numerous personality tests, including the FFM, revealed that impulsivity consists of four independent factors[4] (Whiteside et al., 2005):

1. *Urgency* = the Impulsiveness facet of Neuroticism.

2. *(absence of) Premeditation* = the Deliberation facet of Conscientiousness.

3. *(absence of) Perseverance* = the Self-Discipline facet of Conscientiousness.

4. *Sensation Seeking* = the Excitement-Seeking facet of Extraversion.

An impulsive individual who scores highly on all these facets would be someone who lacks the ability to (1) deliberate and (2) exercise self-discipline when an (3) excitement-seeking (4) urge enters consciousness so that he immediately stops acting for his long-term goal and switches to a new behavior that is more momentarily interesting.

How does knowing this aid self-control? Anyone who is aware of acting too impulsively can be equally aware of how to inhibit temptations to act: Those facets of Conscientiousness that are correlated with acting impulsively are specific facets that we can work to change. We can become more *Deliberate* by deciding to use our mental capacities before acting on our next whim, even if we begin by promising ourselves we'll count to 10 (s-l-o-w-l-y) before we act. This self-imposed time-out gives us the chance to decide (i.e., *to think*) if the tempting behavior is really worth the risk. *Self-discipline*, our ability to carry tasks to completion, might improve if we often remind ourselves how important our long-term goals are.[5]

But wait, there's more! There are times when we receive extremely good news that causes us to feel really happy, joyful, and so forth. Intensely positive affect can also interfere with our long-term goals, as when it leads to a prolonged celebration at a most inopportune time (e.g., the night before a final exam). Positive affect can also artificially increase our optimism to the point where we fail to prepare sufficiently for the outcome we hope to achieve (e.g., "I don't need to study, the test won't be that hard."). Finally, positive affect can make us more distractible and lead to poorer decision making (Smith & Guller, 2015). Self-regulation, then, refers to the ability to stay on track despite any distraction, pleasant as well as unpleasant.

The difficulty with long-term goals is that we tend to discount the value of rewards that are very far in the future. Shiny immediate rewards more easily capture our attention than distant ones. This unfair fight between present and future rewards can be equalized by using a few of our present moments to vividly imagine the future we want to create for ourselves. These vivid self-created pictures can override the seductive power of present distractions. In the next chapter, we'll see how Victor Frankl creatively used his powerful imagination to deal effectively with the utterly evil situation that had been imposed upon him.

Understanding impulsivity began with the ground-breaking research of Walter Mischel on *delay of gratification*. In Mischel's initial research into self-regulation, children were asked to choose between getting an immediate, less desirable reward (e.g., a candy bar) or waiting for a better reward (e.g., two candy bars) to come later. Mischel's research program showed that those children who delayed getting immediate gratification did so by distracting themselves.

For instance, Mischel and Ebbesen (1970) gave preschool children the option of immediately receiving their *less* preferred food treat (e.g., pretzels) or waiting alone for an unspecified amount of time for their *more* preferred treat (e.g., cookies). Children were randomly assigned to one of four conditions. Either both food treats were present while the child waited, neither food was present in the room during the waiting period, or just one of the two treats was present. The study found that children in the *neither food present* condition were able, on average, to wait the longest to receive their preferred treat. Children in this condition, more so than in the other conditions, *distracted themselves* by singing to themselves, inventing games, or trying to take a nap. By distracting themselves from the pleasure of immediately eating the treat, these children were able to postpone gratification longer (average waiting time of about 11 minutes) than children in the other three conditions.

Which group do you think was *least able* to postpone gratification? Mischel and Ebbesen (1970) observed that when *both* food treats were present, children were least able to resist waiting very long (average waiting time of less than 2 minutes) and settled for the less preferred treat. When only one food was present, children waited an average of 5–6 minutes.

The data of Mischel and Ebbesen (1970) show that situational factors help children manage their impulses. The proverbial adage, "Out of sight, out of mind," seems to apply here. Putting this adage into practice, some "perishable" faculty members deliberately refuse to own a television set while they strive to publish. Situational control can be a marvelously effective tool to aid self-regulation. Personality characteristics are also important for tolerating the frustration of delayed gratification as shown by the results of two longitudinal investigations.

One longitudinal investigation found that 4-year-old boys who were able to delay gratification were rated at age 11 as more deliberate, attentive, and cooperative. Girls who were able to delay gratification at age 4 were rated at age 11 as more intelligent, resourceful, and competent (Funder, Block, & Block, 1983).

Similarly, Mischel and Peake (1982) observed that delay competency in 4- to 5-year-olds correlated with cognitive and social competence at ages 16–17. Those preschool children who tolerated relatively long delays were better able to concentrate and to plan ahead as adolescents. In general, they were rated highly by their parents as self-confident, resourceful, and trustworthy. Children who had been unable to delay gratification, however, were rated immature, unpredictable, and stress-prone as adolescents. These observations were replicated in another longitudinal study over a similar age range (Mischel, Shoda, & Peake, 1988).

Building upon these research results, Mischel and his colleagues propose a model of self-regulation given the acronym *CAPS*: the **c**ognitive-**a**ffective **p**rocessing model of **s**elf-regulation. This model sees self-regulation (self-control, willpower) as a contest between two systems within our personality, a *cognitive cool* system and an *affective hot* system (Metcalfe & Mischel, 1999). Our cool system consists of the knowledge and information available for use in self-regulation (e.g., the knowledge that one piece of chocolate cake contains 900 calories). Our hot system is a "go" system. It allows us to process events quickly and with feelings (affect). Our hot system instantly anticipates how the cake tastes. Once our hot system is fully activated, it is difficult to recruit our cool system to help us avoid the temptation.

How does CAPS help us self-regulate? Timing is critical. Mentally distracting ourselves before the hot system has a chance to become active is an effective way to avoid temptation. Another technique is to mentally change your image of the temptation to a *picture* of the temptation: It is not a piece of chocolate cake, it is a *photograph* of a piece of chocolate cake. Since we are not tempted, as a rule, to eat photographs, we are more likely to resist this temptation (Mischel & Moore, 1973). It is also helpful to be prepared in advance for the activation of our hot system. *Implementation plans* allow us to (a) know how to avoid temptations and (b) know what to do when they arise (Gollwitzer, 1999, 2014).

Finally, an *attitude of detachment* has been found to be an effective buffer against the stresses associated with hot system activation. An attitude of detachment is the frame of mind that removes our personal involvement from the situation. I've used it successfully to reduce the pain caused by a cortisone injection into my knee by imagining that the needle is not going into *my* knee but into *a* knee. Sounds strange, but it works (Mischel & Ayduk, 2011).

Mischel (1990) thinks that the ability to delay gratification is a basic personality competence that remains reasonably stable throughout life. This conclusion is supported by findings concerning a concept similar to delay of gratification, *consideration of future consequences*. This refers to our tendency to consider potential distant outcomes of our current behaviors as well as our tendency for our current behavior to be influenced by these imagined future outcomes (Strathman et al., 1994).

For an indication of how high or low you are on this trait, decide how characteristic (or uncharacteristic) each of the following three statements is of you:

1. I consider how things might be in the future and I try to influence those things with my day-to-day behavior.

2. I am willing to sacrifice my immediate happiness or well-being in order to achieve future outcomes.

3. I think it is more important to perform a behavior with important distant consequences than a behavior with less important immediate consequences.

If these statements characterize your view of life, you would be described as high in the trait of consideration of future consequences (CFC). If these statements do not characterize you, you would be described as low on this trait. Strathman and his colleagues (1994) report that their 12-item measure of CFC correlates positively with measures of such similar psychological concepts as the tendency to delay gratification and the trait of conscientiousness.

Individuals who consistently anticipate future consequences differ in a number of ways from those who do not: For example, those high on CFC are more willing to commit their time to join a pro-environment rally (Demarque, Apostolidis, & Joule, 2013), show an interest in eating healthier foods (Gick, 2014), and demonstrate greater moral behavior in the workplace (Cohen et al., 2014). Vividly focusing on future goals is a useful technique for neutralizing the threat of acting impulsively.

Hurt Feelings and Bad Moods (Control Theory)

It is far easier to make progress toward a distant goal if we can avoid feeling strong negative affect. *Negative affect* is psychological lingo for (1) unpleasant emotional feelings such as anger, sadness, or hurt and (2) unpleasant emotional moods such as depression, irritability, or grumpiness that can linger for days (moods last longer than feelings). Negative affect, the collective term for these kinds of emotional states, is a well-established threat to self-regulation. First I review research showing that unpleasant feelings and moods can lead to self-regulation failure. Then I present the Control Theory of Charles Carver and Michael Scheier that explains why negative affect (NA) can be an impediment to our goals.

Whether the research occurs inside the research laboratory (where different moods can be induced by listening to different types of music), or outside the laboratory (asking volunteers to report their moods several times over the course of a day, week, or month), NA consistently leads to self-regulation failure. When they are in a bad mood or have hurt feelings, dieters are likely to break their diet and go on eating binges, recovering alcoholics are likely to relapse, drug users are apt to re-use, and compulsive shoppers are likely to use their credit cards (Wagner & Heatherton, 2015). Women who tried to quit smoking were more likely to relapse within their first week of abstinence if their negative, nicotine-deprived mood was especially aversive (Cofta-Woerpal et al., 2011).

Experiences within our social groups can sometimes be painful. Being snubbed or excluded is one of the most painful psychological experiences we can have. Social exclusion can result in immediate feelings of hurt and/or anger, as well as longer lasting moods of depression and irritability. As we saw in Chapter 6, the same neural pathways that are activated whenever we are in physical pain are also involved when we experience the pain of social ostracism. Social rejection can result in a variety of disagreeable effects: increased aggression, decreased cooperation, impaired clarity of thinking, discounting the value of important future rewards, avoiding self-awareness, as well as failing to self-regulate (Baumeister et al., 2005). The hurt feelings brought about by being socially excluded can lead individuals to act in self-destructive ways through a variety of risky and/or self-defeating behaviors (Twenge, Catanese, & Baumeister, 2002).

Why do bad moods and hurt feelings lead to self-regulation failure? There are three possibilities (Wagner & Heatherton, 2015):

1. Negative affect impairs our memory. The function of *working memory* is to store information temporarily while we attend to the verbal and visual features of our recent experiences (Baddeley, 1986). Individuals who experience negative affect show deficits in their working memory of recent events, possibly because the NA interferes with giving our undivided attention to those events (Brose et al., 2012). Perhaps NA interferes with our memory of how to deal effectively with distractions.

2. Negative affect causes us to change our priorities. We pay greater attention to the surface characteristics of our immediate situation thereby making the long-term consequences of our actions seem less important. It is more imperative to remove the negative affect associated with food deprivation, or nicotine or alcohol withdrawal, than to continue to strive for the long-term consequences of weighing less or being free from drugs.

3. Emotional distress can increase the reward value of the substance we are trying to avoid: Food becomes more enticing to the dieter under additional stress, nicotine to the abstaining smoker, alcohol to the drinker wanting to quit (Wagner & Heatherton, 2015).

*"What I'm gonna say might hurt your feelings,
but hey it's for my own good."*

So we know that negative affect can seriously interfere with self-regulation. But since we cannot know when some unpleasant event will crash into our lives, an event to which we might react with anger, sadness, anxiety, or any negative emotion, it makes sense to be prepared for these possibilities by learning how to regulate our feelings. A number of techniques have been found to be of practical help in this matter.

Response modulation techniques are aimed at getting us back to an even keel as soon as possible. Controlled breathing and focusing on our breath help to distract us from the upsetting event by centering our attention on the natural process of breathing (Philippot, Chapelle, & Blairy, 2002). Similarly, the technique of progressive muscle relaxation in which we systematically tense and relax specific muscles has been found to decrease the intensity of negative affect (Pawlow & Jones, 2002). Above and beyond the relief that occurs, these techniques also reduce the amount of time we spend in negative emotional states. This is important because NA states mobilize numerous mental and physical resources, resources we might be able to use more effectively to cope with the actual cause of our NA (Sapolsky, 2007).

Expressive writing is a useful procedure that can be employed after the immediate crisis is no longer a threat (Pennebaker & Chung, 2007). Putting our feelings on paper can turn initially distressing emotional experiences into organized, meaningful stories, relieve emotional suffering, and promote self-insights that can make us feel even stronger than before the upsetting event took place (Klein & Boals, 2001). These feelings do not have to be written to have a positive impact on future emotional self-regulation. Adults who were interviewed about a high and a low point in their lives and were able to make some sense out of these events (giving them meaning) were found to be better at regulating their emotions 2 years later (Cox & McAdams, 2014).

Finally, three other emotion regulation procedures have been found to be effective. A regular physical exercise program can lead to both a reduction in stress and a greater ability to control one's temper (Oaten & Cheng, 2006). *Mindfulness meditation training* encourages people to focus their attention on the present moment while refraining from negatively evaluating their initial difficulties to remain focused. This kind of training can reduce symptoms of stress, depression, and anxiety (Bishop, 2002).

Similarly, the stress that students felt when they anticipated giving a public speech was significantly reduced by anticipating laughing at funny cartoons when the speech was over. If we can imagine doing anything fun and rewarding after our stressful event is finished, we can take the edge off the negative affect associated with the unpleasant task and reduce it to manageable levels. More generally, the negative affect generated by the anxiety of giving a speech may be minimized by finding meaning in the event and/or being able to experience positive emotions (e.g., curiosity, interest) in spite of the stress (Monfort, Stroup, & Waugh, 2015; Tugade & Frederickson, 2004).

Charles Carver and Michael Scheier's *Control Theory of Self-Regulation* has for many years (Carver & Scheier, 1981, 1990b, 1998) helped us understand why negative affect so often interferes with reaching our goals. Their theory zeros in on why NA is a problem.

At the heart of their theory is the idea of *feedback*. Given that a person has a specific goal in mind (e.g., to lose 20 pounds), negative feedback refers to the discrepancy between her present condition (a weight of X pounds) and the condition she intends in the future (X − 20 lbs.). A *negative feedback loop* refers to (1) the comparison of her present state to the desired future state, and (2) any behavioral adjustments needed to reduce the discrepancy between the two. So if you want to lose 20 pounds, but your daily reading of the bathroom scale tells you that you are not losing weight, then you must adjust your behavior (e.g., consume fewer calories, exercise more, or both) to reach your goal. The process of comparing your present state to the future goal state and adjusting your behavior to reduce the discrepancy serve to "control" your behavior.

Actually achieving and maintaining the desired weight loss, however, is much more difficult and complex than the simple idea of a negative feedback loop. Carver and Scheier recognize that people frequently run into obstacles when trying to meet their important goals. What determines whether we continue toward our goals in spite of obstacles?

Consider the following example: Suppose you wish to achieve high grades. You plan to study diligently to do so. But the night before an important exam, close friends from out of town unexpectedly stop by for a visit.

Carver and Scheier (1990a, 1990b) specify the conditions under which self-regulation will or will not be successful when obstacles to your goals arise. If difficulties interrupt your progress, the critical question is whether you believe you can still reach your goal with additional effort. Your continued self-regulation, then, turns on the question of whether you are hopeful or confident that you can still get what you want in spite of the obstacle.

The answer to this question in a particular case importantly depends on the precise nature of the obstacle and your prior experiences dealing with it. If you have a history of successes in such cases, you will probably continue to try to achieve your goal. You could, for example, decide to see your friends in the early part of the evening, and then cram like crazy afterwards.

But if you do not feel confident of reaching your goal when the difficulty arises, Carver and Scheier's model says you stop trying and withdraw either behaviorally (e.g., drop the course) or, if this is not possible, disengage mentally (e.g., decide to accept one poor grade and concentrate on doing well in your other courses). Thus your expectation about your ability to reach your goal despite the presence of obstacles is a critically important determinant of self-regulation. Those who are confident of ultimate success in spite of the temporary setback will persist. Those who doubt they can still succeed are at risk of self-regulation failure. What is needed, in that case, is a realistic assessment, perhaps in consultation with other people, of one's chances for success. Disengagement from an unrealistic pursuit, after all, is healthier than continuing to put time and energy into straining to reach an unattainable goal.

Control Theory also discusses affect, both positive and negative, as by-products of making progress toward our goals. Control Theory assumes that we all have some kind of internal standard against which we judge our *rate of progress*. When there is a positive discrepancy—when we make more progress than we expected to—we have positive feelings and feel confident our goal is within reach. Feeling confident of ultimate success, people sometimes decide they can coast for a while.

But when there is a negative discrepancy—either we are making no progress at all or our rate of progress is slower than we anticipated—then feelings of dejection, disappointment, and other forms of negative affect are inevitable. Carver and Scheier propose that the negative feelings that accompany the perception of slow progress are the most common reason individuals interrupt their goal-seeking behavior. Holding a realistic expectation of how quickly and easily we will reach our goal is essential for avoiding such disappointments.

The solution to the threat of slow progress, then, is to recalibrate all of the relevant variables and come up with a more realistic plan. Personal health and/or family factors might require us to stop pushing ourselves so hard. Also, long-term goals often involve external factors out of our control (e.g., the course won't be offered again for another 2 years), factors that limit our rate of progress. A plan that takes longer to implement but is more realistic at least will eliminate feelings of dejection due to "slow" progress.[6] We need only accept the new rate of progress as one that is the best for us under our circumstances. Slow progress at least avoids the third threat to self-regulation, fatigue or ego depletion, which we cover next.

Fatigue (Resource Depletion Theory)

Let's say you'd like to lose a few pounds. So you plan to skip dessert and modify your general food intake until those pounds come off. After doing this for a while, you notice that skipping dessert is pretty easy some days but way more difficult on others. Sometimes it takes a huge effort to just say no. Why is that? Why isn't it equally easy or equally difficult all the time? Let's see what's been found in some clever psychology experiments.

Imagine you've volunteered to participate in an experiment described as a study of taste perception. As your individual research session is scheduled, the researcher requests that you skip one full meal before you arrive and that you refrain from eating for at least 3 hours before you arrive. You agree.

When you arrive at the laboratory, the first thing you notice is the delicious aroma of freshly baked chocolate cookies. Yum. As you sit down at the table, you notice there are two bowls of food nearly: a batch of chocolate cookies (supplemented with a few chocolate candies) and a bowl of radishes. Before your arrival, you were randomly assigned to one of two conditions: You are asked to taste either a few cookies *or* a few radishes and to refrain from eating the other food. The researcher leaves you alone in the room for 5 minutes and surreptitiously spies on you to make sure you have the willpower not to eat the other food while you taste the assigned food. Just like all the other participants who were assigned to eat radishes, you do not eat the cookies even though you'd really like to.

The researchers assumed that it takes more willpower to refrain from eating chocolate cookies than it does to refrain from eating radishes. If willpower is a limited resource, then, those assigned to eating radishes should show less of it on the following task. At this point the friendly researcher tells you that the taste perception experiment will begin in a few minutes and, while waiting, would like your help on a second, unrelated study comparing the perceptual skills of college students to those of high school students. This test requires you to trace a complicated maze without lifting your pencil off the paper and without retracing any drawn lines. You are told to take as much time as you like and you can use as many sheets of paper as you need. If you want to stop before you solve the puzzle, ringing the provided bell will bring the experimenter into the room and the tracing task will be over.

As you probably guessed, this second "unrelated" task was actually the dependent variable. The researchers predicted that those who ate the radishes used up more willpower than those who ate the chocolate cookies and would quit the tracing puzzle sooner (which was actually impossible to solve).

What did they find? A control group who ate neither food but went directly to the tracing task took 21 minutes, on average, before they gave up. Those lucky participants who ate the chocolate cookies took 19 minutes, on average, before they said "Enough." The radish-eating hungry participants, whose willpower had been depleted by (a) forcing themselves to eat radishes and (b) refraining from eating chocolate chip cookies, gave up after only 8.5 minutes. In the world of psychological research, this is a huge difference from the other two conditions! Willpower looks like it is a limited resource. Fatigue is a threat to its continued use (Baumeister et al., 1998).

In a naturalistic field experiment, the stress of taking academic examinations appears to be an ego-depleting resource. Students taking exams, compared to their own behavior 4 weeks earlier, as well as to a control group of students who were not taking exams, performed more poorly on an experimental task requiring willpower. Moreover, they reported less healthy eating, less control of their emotions, less physical activity, and other self-care maintenance that requires attention and effort. It appears that the stress of taking exams can deplete the resources we need for everyday healthy functioning (Oaten & Cheng, 2005). Mental fatigue by itself impairs our ability to regulate our emotions (Grillon et al., 2015).

Finally (among the hundreds of studies on this topic), the act of making choices appears to deplete willpower. Undergraduate students were asked either (a) to choose between consumer products in various categories or (b) to rate, without choosing, those same products. The researchers expected that the act of choosing between products, over and over, would be more resource depleting than simply rating each product without choosing between them. The undergraduates were then brought to another room where 20 small paper cups, 1 ounce each, were lined up. The cups were filled with an unpleasant tasting liquid mixture of orange drink, water, vinegar, and a small amount of sugar. The participants were told that this was a study of motivation and they would be a given a nickel for each cup they drank. It was made clear that how many cups they drank was up to them.

The researchers found, as expected, that those who made choices between products drank far fewer cups (average of less than 2) than those who did not have to choose (average of almost 7 cups). Decision making seems to decrease motivation to engage in effortful tasks (Vohs et al., 2008).

Sigmund Freud believed that willpower relies on the ego's use of a limited amount of energy (Freud, 1923/1961). It seemed obvious to him that our egos need sufficient energy to manage both the tasks of daily living and to settle the interminable pushes and pulls between our ids ("Gimmie!") and our superegos ("No!"). Freud's view that the mind works by a kind of psychophysical energy traces back to his early 1890s work on hysteria with Josef Breuer (Sulloway, 1992). Freud developed psychoanalysis to help his patients regain the necessary ego strength needed to manage the stresses and strains of ordinary life without getting overwhelmed by them or by their id versus superego conflicts. To Freud, the ego is the executive of our personality (Westen, Gabbard, & Ortigo, 2008).

While Freud is the conceptual originator of willpower as a finite resource,[7] it took a hundred years before this idea was systematically evaluated by quality empirical research. Since the time that resource depletion was initially proposed by Roy Baumeister and his colleagues (e.g., Baumeister & Heatherton, 1996; Baumeister, Heatherton, & Tice, 1994; Muraven, Tice, & Baumeister, 1998), hundreds of studies have consistently supported the resource depletion view of self-regulation.

This research shows that our capacity for self-control can be fatigued in a variety of ways: resisting temptations, suppressing thoughts, inhibiting emotions, resisting group pressure, managing the impression you're trying to make, making decisions, to name a few (Wagner & Heatherton, 2015). Self-control depletion can result in reduced effort, subjective fatigue, perceived difficulty, and lowered blood glucose levels (Hagger et al., 2010). The conclusion? Self-control resembles a muscle (Mischel, 1996; Muraven & Baumeister, 2000).

Ego depletion also leads to an increase in alcohol consumption (Christiansen, Cole, & Field, 2012) and drinking alcohol, whether due to ego depletion or not, is a well-documented threat to self-regulation. Alcohol intoxication is the largest single cause of relapses among those attempting to quit smoking or reduce their food intake. Alcohol consumption is also associated with unrestrained social behaviors such as inappropriate self-disclosure to strangers, engaging in unsafe sexual activity, and acting aggressively to slight provocations (Wagner & Heatherton, 2015). While alcohol may be a "social lubricant," it can also grease the skids under our capacity for self-regulation.

Since muscle (and willpower) overuse predictably leads to muscle (and willpower) failure, is the opposite also true? Can our willpower be strengthened in the same way that muscles are made stronger, by focused training and exercise? Yes!

The positive effects of training on willpower has been shown in a study where participants agreed to practice a specific exercise for 2 weeks. Two willpower training exercises prevented ego depletion. These exercises involved either (1) improving one's posture or (2) keeping a food diary. Those participants who dutifully complied with these self-control exercises showed improved self-regulation. They increased willpower just as we would expect if willpower is similar to a muscle (Muraven, Baumeister, & Tice, 1999).

Other training programs have also resulted in improved self-control. Participants who volunteered for a 2-month physical exercise program were better able to self-regulate on a visual tracking task despite a comedy video playing nearby. Positive side effects of this physical exercise program included reduced cigarette smoking and alcohol use, eating less junk food, and less impulsive spending. In a second study, the training involved a 4-month program on financial planning and awareness. As in the first study, positive side effects on self-regulation included less cigarette, caffeine, and alcohol consumption (Oaten & Cheng, 2004a, 2004b, as cited by Baumeister, Gailliot, DeWall, & Oaten, 2006).

Finally, the muscle simile for willpower is also supported by data showing that exercising self-control in one area in of life improves self-control in different areas. For example, successful dietary self-control can lead to less impulsive decision making. Data across 18 studies implies self-control (willpower) is like a muscle in that strengthening it in one domain has beneficial effects for successful self-control in other domains (Tuk, Zhang, & Sweldens, 2015).

I wonder how far such training programs might take us. Could we develop our self-control to conquer that *King of Threats* to self-regulation, procrastination?

Procrastination (Regulatory Mode Theory)

I can't keep putting this off forever. I might as well get to it just in time to meet my publisher's deadline. I've had plenty of practice. Isn't that what school is for?

Ninety-five percent of us admit we sometimes procrastinate. The remaining 5% are visitors from another planet. Kidding aside, procrastination is a serious problem when it impacts delaying getting the health treatments we need (Bogg & Roberts, 2004), putting off saving for retirement (O'Donoghue & Rabin, 1999), and making costly mistakes because we hastily filed our taxes at the last minute, mistakes that resulted in over $427 million in overpayments in 2002 (Kasper [2004] cited by Steel, 2007). Procrastination is a major form of self-regulation failure.

Procrastination is the deliberate delay of an intended course of action despite knowing that the delay could make the outcome less desirable. College students, for example, who report that they typically procrastinate in starting class projects and studying for exams, achieve, on average, significantly lower grades than those who do not typically procrastinate (Steel, 2007). Moreover, a meta-analysis of over 4,000 participants found positive correlations between procrastination and such maladaptive coping behaviors as denial, substance abuse, and self-blame (Sirois & Kitner, 2015). Learning what causes procrastination is a first step to understanding how to deal with it.

In the opening chapters of this book we talked about how we can understand human behavior by (a) understanding personality differences, (b) understanding how different situations influence what we do, and (c) understanding the interaction of personality x situation (see Figure 2.1 in Chapter 2).

Both personality and situational factors are involved in procrastination: Some people procrastinate almost all the time across all situations, while almost all of us procrastinate some times in some situations. Table 9.2 summarizes the replicated research findings in terms of those situational factors (#1 and #2) and personality variables (#3–#10) that make it more or less likely we will procrastinate.

Looking at the 10 variables in Table 9.2 that affect procrastination, do all of them make sense to you? All of them make sense to me except #4 *Fear of Failure* (Harrington, 2005; Solomon & Rothblum, 1984). If I'm afraid of failing the assignment, why doesn't

❖ **Table 9.2** Situational and Personality Factors Implicated in Procrastination

You Are *Most Likely* to Procrastinate When	You Are *Least Likely* to Procrastinate When
1. Your project is due in 2 months	1. Your project is due in 2 hours
2. Your project is boring or unpleasant	2. Your project is interesting and important
3. You feel acting conscientiously and responsibly is not very important	3. You want to act in a conscientious and responsible way
4. You are afraid of failing or being negatively evaluated	4. You are more motivated by hope for success than by fear of failure
5. You have a history of self-handicapping	5. You rarely, if ever, self-handicap your chances for success
6. You are easily distractible	6. You usually stay focused on the task at hand despite outside distractions
7. You are impulsive	7. You usually control any impulse to move away from the task at hand
8. You get bored easily	8. You rarely feel bored
9. You lack self-efficacy for the task	9. You know you have what it takes to get the task accomplished
10. Your need for achievement on this task is low	10. You want to do as well as possible on this task

Source: Adapted from Steel (2007), pp. 65–94.

that fear motivate me to *stop* procrastinating and start working? A puzzle, yes? Does the fear of failure lead you to procrastinate or to spring into action?

I'm sure fear of failure motivates some people to get to work and thus, for them, it is not a threat to self-regulation. For others, though, procrastination may reduce their anxiety about failure by temporarily forgetting about the assignment for a while and doing something pleasurable. Maybe those enjoyable activities help to refill depleted ego tanks that became exhausted by resisting the assignment. Might there be some benefits to procrastination?

Whenever we avoid real or potentially unpleasant circumstances, we experience a feeling of relief. *Negative reinforcement*[8] refers to the rewarding effect of eliminating, reducing, or avoiding an unpleasant or fearful stimulus. Any action (e.g., telling a lie) that leads to the elimination of a negative stimulus (e.g., you avoid attending a stressful meeting) will be reinforced by the feeling of relief. That same action is likely to recur under similar circumstances in the future precisely because it has been reinforced—it alleviated or avoided pain, anxiety, uncertainty, or any other unpleasant psychological state. It is called *negative* reinforcement because the aversive stimulus is eliminated or reduced. In contrast, a *positive* reinforcement occurs when the rewarding stimulus is given or presented after the behavior occurs (e.g., food, money, a giggle at a joke).

Whenever the behavior *increases* in frequency under similar conditions, that increase might be due to either the presentation of a positive stimulus (positive reinforcement) or to the removal of a negative stimulus (negative reinforcement).

Procrastination provides temporary relief from an aversive (unpleasant) psychological condition. If we loved what we were doing, we would not procrastinate. So when we are faced with any obnoxious task in the future that reactivates our fear of failure, we know that procrastination—filling our minds with anything else—provides temporary relief. And doing something enjoyable for a little while might restore the energy we need to attack the disagreeable task with renewed gusto, energy needed to cope with any additional stress caused by our procrastinating (Tice & Baumeister, 1997). We expect that any activity that puts us into a positive mood will restore our mental energy to deal with the unpleasant task (Egan, Clarkson, & Hirt, 2015). Procrastinators can use their renewed energy to offset the time they lost by avoiding the disagreeable task.

Regulatory Mode Theory explains procrastination by looking at the relative strengths of two possible orientations toward action, *locomotion* and *assessment.* Locomotion emphasizes movement toward a goal (do something), while assessment emphasizes evaluating the effectiveness of possible movements (which one do I do?) to reach the goal. In assessment mode, we generate a large *number* of possible ways to achieve the goal while in locomotion mode we generate these means *quickly.* Research finds that both locomotion and assessment are independently related to procrastination, but in different directions. Those who are high in locomotion orientation tend to procrastinate less, while individuals who are high in assessment orientation tend to procrastinate more often than average (Higgins, Kruglanski, & Pierro, 2003; Pierro et al., 2011).

Moreover, since locomotion is a form of approaching or promoting an action to reach a goal, while assessment is motivation primarily focused on avoiding or preventing errors from being made, procrastination should result in different emotional reactions. In Promotion and Prevention Self-Regulation Theory (Higgins, 1997), when we are motivated to promote or to achieve some objective, procrastination causes a discrepancy between our actual self and our ideal self. This kind of discrepancy results in feeling *dejected* or *depressed.*

But when our primary motivation centers around preventing unpleasant events from occurring, we are operating from our actual self, and our *ought* or *should* self (e.g., "I should have counted the beans more carefully . . ."). The effect of that discrepancy is that we feel *anxious* (Higgins, 2000). Thus, when we procrastinate, the kind of emotion we experience, depressed or anxious, tells us which sort of self-discrepancy (actual versus ideal or actual versus ought) is more important to us. The intensity of either emotion reflects how much we identify with our ideal self or our ought self.

Clearly appreciating the cause-and-effect relationship between procrastination and its ensuing negative affect may result in procrastination becoming less of a problem as we age and acquire wisdom. People procrastinate less as they get older (Steel, 2007). Wisdom, the adaptive ego strength Erikson identifies as accruing from the successful resolution of the eighth crisis, integrity versus despair, is one of the topics of Chapter 10.

QUESTIONS TO PONDER

1. In your experience, what are the key differences between those times when you success-fully reached your goals and those times when you did not? Are these differences related to any of the ideas in this chapter? If not, what is your theory of why you succeeded in reaching your goals sometimes but not always?

2. How can you tell if a person's internal working model corresponds to reality? Isn't thinking about oneself such a private, personal affair that everyone's internal model is necessarily right for them? When is it appropriate to correct someone else's internal working model?

3. How can we identify which aspects of situations are likely to activate someone's internal working model? How might the DIAMONDS taxonomy of situations, covered in the introduction, be used to find this out?

4. Consider one major goal you are currently pursuing. What obstacles do you expect to encounter? What plans, strategies, or self-regulating activities will you employ to deal with these obstacles? What is your back-up plan?

NOTES

1. See Chapter 4 for a review of secure, anxious/avoidant, anxious/resistant, and disorgan-ized/disoriented attachment styles.

2. The concept of *internal working models* has been criticized on the grounds that it is too broad and can be applied post hoc to almost any research outcome (Dykas & Cassidy, 2011; Hinde, 1988; Rutter, 1995). The undeniable usefulness of the construct, however, should lead to its refinement as future research specifies its boundary conditions.

3. The data showing that early insecure attachment styles may be modified by later positive relationship experiences have, regrettably, not been consistent from study to study. While a number of investigations have observed this change, a number of others have not. These inconsistencies obviously require additional research (Mikulincer & Shaver, 2007).

4. Impulsivity remains an incompletely understood trait. How many factors are needed to encompass its domain has yet to be determined (e.g., Sharma et al., 2013; Stahl et al., 2014).

5. I saw an illustration of this near the end of a basketball game. The losing team, with a few minutes to go, called time-out. As the five exhausted, sweating, out-of-breath play-ers trudged to the bench, their coach said to them, individually and collectively, over and over, "How much do you want it?" The "it" meant winning the game. The coach was trying to take their mind off their fatigue and help them mentally focus on their goal.

6. A former student of mine, a thin woman in her early 40s, lost 30 pounds when she was in her 20s, and successfully kept it off. Her plan, which worked to perfection, was to lose one pound per month, 30 pounds in 30 months. Since she did not expect to lose weight rapidly, she eliminated the threat of being disappointed by "slow" progress. Her rate of progress was obviously right for her. It also allowed her body ample time to adjust to the reduced calorie intake.

7. Even if willpower *is* a finite, limited resource, humans may persist longer on challenging tasks if they believe that willpower is not a finite resource (i.e., willpower is not limited). Research by Carol Dweck and her colleagues suggests that those who hold a "nonlimited" view of willpower show better self-control after completing demanding tasks. They found that those who believed willpower is not a limited resource performed more diligently and procrastinated less than those who believed willpower is a finite resource that needs to be conserved (Job et al., 2015).

8. Please do not confuse *negative reinforcement* with *punishment*. These terms refer to different operations and have different effects. The trick is to remember that *reinforcement* usually results in an *increase* in the frequency of the behavior that was reinforced. Reinforcement refers to either giving something good (positive reinforcement) or taking away something bad (negative reinforcement). Many superstitious behaviors are learned because something bad did *not* happen after the behavior occurred. When an expected negative event does not occur, we feel relief. Any behavior that preceded this nonoccurrence is thereby reinforced. Thus the behavior is likely to recur in similar situations in the future.

   One form of punishment is the *application* of any negative stimulus (e.g., being physically hit, yelled at, shamed) for the purpose of *decreasing or eliminating* the offending behavior. Negative reinforcement and punishment are often confused as when someone incorrectly describes a spanking as "The child received negative reinforcement." Wrong, wrong, wrong. The child was *punished*. The other form of punishment is the removal of something desirable (e.g., cell phone, Internet access, dinner) to try to eliminate an inappropriate behavior.

SUGGESTIONS FOR FURTHER READING

Bandura, A. (1997). *Self-efficacy: The exercise of control.* New York, NY: Freeman.
Baumeister, R. F., & Tierney, J. (2011). *Willpower: Rediscovering the greatest human strength.* New York, NY: Penguin Books.
Ellis, K. (1998). *The magic lamp: Goal setting for people who hate setting goals.* New York, NY: Three Rivers Press.
Reivich, K., & Shatte, A. (2002). *The resilience factor.* New York, NY: Three Rivers Press.

INTERNET RESOURCES

1. A battery of questionnaires designed to assess your ability to self-regulate in various domains of your life (e.g., academic, health, etc.) can be found at http://www.selfdeter mintiontheory.org/self-regulation-questionaires/.

2. To take a test of your tendency to procrastinate, go to http://psychologytoday.tests .psychtests.com/take_test.php?idRegTest=1333.

3. To take a test to see how impulsive you are, go to http://www.okcupid.com/tests/ the-impulsivity-test.

10

Continuity and Change Over the Life Course

❖*In what ways can I expect my personality to remain the same or change over the course of my life?*

Personality Stability and Change
> Absolute Stability
> Differential Stability
> Structural Stability
> Ipsative Stability
> Coherence

Levels of Personality
> Habitual Behaviors
> Traits and Dispositions
> Personal Concerns
> Life Narratives and the Making of the Self

Humanistic and Existential Approaches to Continuity and Change
> The Fully Functioning Person
> The Will to Meaning

Psychodynamic Approaches to Continuity and Change
Jung and the Process of Individuation
Individuation and the Stages of Life
Aging and Wisdom

Do you think it's true, "You can't teach an old dog new tricks"? Or do you believe the opposite proverb, "It's never too late to learn"? If, on the one hand, "The leopard cannot change its spots," why, on the other hand, does "Hope spring eternal in the human heart"? The ready availability of contradictory proverbs allows us to select the most convenient one to explain any outcome—*after* the outcome is known. All proverbs fail to specify the conditions under which some event will occur. Researchers hope to discover to what extent, and under what conditions, personality changes in adulthood.

The simplest answer to the question of whether personality changes over the life course is that it depends on what we mean by "personality" and "change." As unsatisfying as this answer is, its elaboration in this chapter serves to clarify the ways that people can and do change over the life course, the levels or aspects of personality that are involved in both continuity and change, and how personality and change are assessed or measured. We will see that a complete answer to the question involves appreciating both the continuity of certain levels of personality from youth to old age and simultaneously recognizing that other aspects of personality can be modified or reorganized. The complexity of the elaborated answer to the question of continuity and change over the life span matches the complexity of the concept of personality itself.

Our personalities consist of our habitual behaviors, our traits or dispositions, our personal concerns, and our life narratives (for an in depth discussion of three of these levels, traits, concerns, and narratives, see McAdams, 1994; McAdams & Olson, 2010). Although these four levels of personality are not independent of one another, they do require different ways of answering the question of continuity and change over the life course.

The first level of personality is the level of our habitual behaviors. Our habitual response patterns are the basic elements of our personalities that form our traits and types. If personality is equivalent to our habitual acts or overt behaviors, then much of personality can and does change over the life course. We can stop engaging in habitual behaviors such as smoking, drug use, or unhealthy eating. We can start to build new healthy habits such as exercise or meditation (Wood & Runger, 2016).

The second level of personality, that of traits or dispositions, is the level at which we discover the consistencies in behavior over time and situations. It is also the level where we manifestly differ from one another. For example, the trait of extraversion-introversion neatly summarizes a major personality difference between individuals. It also characterizes how we expect a person to act in the future. Trait theorists, and those who adopt the behavioral genetics approach, favor this level of personality. Research at the trait level indicates that while there is significant continuity of personality over the life course, personality change is also possible.

The third level of personality is what McAdams and Olson (2010) refer to as the "agent" or "striving" level of personality. What do you want and how do you plan to get it? It is the level of personality specifically addressed by those who favor the cognitive/social learning approach to personality. As your particular goals and strivings change over time and circumstances, new aspects of your personality may develop to meet these new challenges of living.

To adapt successfully to the demands of being a new parent, for example, mothers and fathers need to develop a level of care and concern for the well-being of their newborn baby. In caring for their children, parents may develop aspects of their own personalities that otherwise might not come to fruition.[1] Feldman and Aschenbrenner (1983), for instance, found many first-time fathers were happily surprised to discover their capacity to function effectively as a mother. Those new fathers who are avoidantly attached to their mates need to modify their internal working model of relationships if they wish to fully participate in their child's growth to maturity (Fillo et al., 2015). A new mother writes, "Becoming a mother changed every fiber, every feeling, and every relationship for me. I am constantly in the process of evaluating, recognizing, and repudiating the upheaval of motherhood" (Kort, 1981, p. 127). At this level, then, personality change over the life span is expected to occur due either to the impact of external life events or to internal maturational processes.

The fourth level of personality is the one whereby we give meaning to our lives. This "life narrative" level refers to your own created story of your life, as you currently understand it (McAdams, 2008; McAdams & McLean, 2013). McAdams conceives of adult identity as an evolving story that weaves a reconstructed past, perceived present, and anticipated future into a coherent and vitalizing life story. His research program finds that adults can and do change and reorganize their stories of themselves through their 50s and beyond (McAdams, 1993, 1994). This level of personality is most compatible with both the humanistic/existential and the psychodynamic orientations. Because we have the ability to reconceptualize "who we are and what we are doing here" at any point in time, we have the ability to change our personalities at this level.

Personality Stability and Change

Just as personality can be conceptualized in different ways, so too can the concept of change. As an illustration, take a few moments to consider the questions: In what ways have you changed over the past 3 years and in what ways are you the same?

Your answers to these questions will depend on what you mean by "change" versus "the same." Caspi and Bem (1990) suggest that five different meanings of stability (versus change) can be applied to personality.

Absolute Stability

Only if you can *compare the same behavior* or *personality attribute* over the 3-year interval, can you answer the question of absolute stability one way or the other. You might say, for example, "Yes, I've changed. Three years ago I felt insecure and unsure of myself almost all the time, whereas now I very rarely feel insecure." Or you might say, "No, I haven't changed. I'm just as outgoing and friendly as I was then." Absolute change is what most people have in mind when they think about "change." Absolute stability, then, is constancy in a specific personality attribute over time.

Differential Stability

By comparing yourself to some selected group of individuals, you can decide whether your personality has changed. You might answer the question by saying, "Yes I've changed somewhat. In the past, I always was the most outgoing, extraverted person in my social group, whereas now, two or three other people are usually more outgoing than I am." Note that the absolute level of extraversion may or may not change when one uses one's relative standing in a group as the basis for comparison. Differential stability refers to the retention of a person's *relative placement within the group* on the personality attribute under consideration.

Structural Stability

By comparing the *relative changes of related facets within a trait,* you can decide whether there has been structural change over the 3-year interval. For example, in McCrae and Costa's theory of personality, agreeableness is composed of the following six facets: (1) trusting versus suspicious; (2) socially straightforward versus socially tactical; (3) altruistic versus selfish; (4) compliant versus competitive; (5) modest versus arrogant; (6) tender-minded versus tough-minded (Widiger & Costa, 2013a). You might be just as agreeable as you were 3 years ago in spite of marked changes in the structural stability of this trait. This would occur if you become, say, less trusting of others but more modest than you were 3 years ago. In other words, if you change in the less agreeable direction on one facet as much as you change in the more agreeable direction on another facet, your overall position on the trait of agreeableness would not change. Nevertheless, there would be structural change in this trait's makeup within your personality.

Ipsative Stability

If you presently see yourself as more conscientious and less extraverted than you were 3 years ago, this is evidence of an ipsative change between these traits. What would have changed is the *relative importance* of these different traits within your personality. Any change among the ordering of your most salient personality attributes is a manifestation of ipsative change. Note that ipsative change may occur along with absolute change: Not only is extraversion less important to you, but you could also be absolutely less extraverted than you were in the past (as well as absolutely more conscientious).

Coherence

Gordon Allport thought of coherence as the *unity of personality.* Allport further thought that the most critical problem for the psychology of personality is understanding the *nature of growth.* He proposed there is one law that admitted of no exceptions: "*[e]very personality develops continually from the stage of infancy until death, and throughout this span it persists even though it changes*" (Allport, 1937, p. 102, italics in original).

Coherence of personality may be evident even though someone changes his behavior. A person who no longer drinks to excess but snorts cocaine daily has only switched deck chairs on the *Titanic*. He has not confronted his intrapersonal conflicts, personality dispositions, and/or identity issues that underlie his addictive behaviors.[2]

Heterotypic continuity refers to the connection between different behaviors at different ages. An example of heterotypic continuity that reflects personality coherence is a young child's ability to delay gratification. The capacity to delay gratification has been found to be associated with dealing successfully, years later, with the stresses and frustrations of adolescence. The early-appearing competence to delay gratification is coherently related to handling well the frustrations often experienced during the teenage years (Mischel, 2004).

Unfortunately, such a clear instance of coherence is the exception, not the rule. Other claims of personality coherence typically appeal to intuition as opposed to being rigorously derived from a theory. Moreover, the different theoretical approaches to personality do not agree on a common definition of coherence (Fournier et al., 2015). Sad to say, "the field of personality development remains without a coherent theory of development" (Roberts, Wood, & Caspi, 2008, p. 384).

Let's review. In addition to *five* meanings of personality change that can apply to *four* levels of personality, the question of stability versus change has three further complications. The answer also depends on (1) *who decides* whether change has occurred; (2) *how socially desirable* is this change; and (3) *when* does the change occur.

Self-ratings and observer ratings of change are most likely to differ on those personality traits that are socially desirable. On desirable traits such as conscientiousness and agreeableness, self-ratings and observer ratings show the *least* agreement. While individuals rate themselves as significantly more conscientious and agreeable than they were in the past, observers do not concur: Observers see them as unchanged on these traits. Self-ratings and observer ratings are more likely to agree, however, for more neutral traits such as how talkative or how emotional the person is.

Even over a fairly short interval of 2 years, reported changes in self-rated traits were not supported by spousal ratings of those traits. While individuals saw themselves as *more* conscientious than they were 2 years earlier, their spouses saw them as significantly *less* conscientious. Similarly, middle-aged adults perceived that they had become, over a 25-year span, better adjusted to the demands of living to a far greater extent than did others who had observed them. Personality change seems to depend on who you ask (John & Robins, 1993; Watson & Humrichouse, 2006; Woodruff & Birren, 1972).

Finally, self-perceptions of change are also influenced by *when* this change occurred. Please answer the following two questions about your personality:

1. How much *has* your personality changed in the past 10 years? A lot? A little? No change?

2. How much do you think your personality *will* change over the next 10 years? A lot? A little? No change?

When these two questions were posed online to over 19,000 adults, it was consistently found that while individuals perceived they *had changed* a great deal over the past 10 years, they expected to change very little, if at all, in the future. The study's authors call this the *End of History Illusion*: Individuals readily acknowledge that they have changed in the past but deny they will change in the future (Quoidbach, Gilbert, & Wilson, 2013).

Why acknowledge you have changed but deny you will change? There are two possibilities: First, most of us hold very positive self-concepts. We like to think of ourselves as attractive, friendly, and competent. To imagine that change might take place in the future threatens this rosy self-portrait. Once we imagine that we rest atop the pinnacle of self-perfection, future change can only mean we will slide downhill. So we reject that possibility. The end of history illusion protects our pleasing self-image (Greenwald, 1980; Tavris & Aronson, 2007; Taylor, 1989).

Second, the process of recollecting our past personality and comparing it to our present one is far easier than the process of imagining in what unknown ways we might change in the future. If a psychological process is difficult to carry out, we might conflate its difficulty with the actual unlikelihood of change: We conclude we are unlikely to change in the future (Quoidbach, Gilbert, & Wilson, 2013).

Thus, self-reports of change need not be taken at face value. Do you know anyone who brags they have changed for the better even though their thoughtless and selfish behavior remains unchanged? Most people, I think, are acquainted with at least one dramatically self-delusional person. Self-reports of personality change need to be corroborated by others before assuming the change is real.

Levels of Personality

Habitual Behaviors

Psychologists who adopt the position of *behaviorism* tend to see human behavior as completely modifiable or changeable. To change a person's habitual behaviors, they maintain, all we need do is manipulate the relevant environmental conditions and the desired behavior will change. The oft-repeated quote from behaviorism's founder, John Watson (1924), concisely illustrates this point:

> Give me a dozen healthy infants, well-formed, and my own specified world to bring them up in and I'll guarantee to take any one at random and train him to become any type of specialist I might select—doctor, lawyer, artist, merchant-chief, and yes, even beggarman and thief, regardless of his talents, penchants, tendencies, abilities, vocations, and race of his ancestors. (p. 104)

No knowledgeable psychologist today, behaviorist or not, would agree with Watson's extreme view of the environment's impact. We know now that all environmental effects depend on the innate properties of the individual. No sane behaviorist would try to teach a turtle to fly.

With respect to personality change, therapists who practice behavior modification hold that since maladaptive behaviors initially come into being through *learning*, those behaviors can be modified and replaced by more adaptive responses through *relearning*. The question then becomes this: Which habitual behaviors are relatively easy to modify and which ones are not?

Martin Seligman's (1994) theory of behavior change distinguishes various behavioral problems according to their *depth*. Simply put, deep problems are more difficult to change than superficial ones. Seligman is not a behaviorist. He considers how we *think* about our problems to be a major determinant of how deep the problem is. *What we believe* about a problem affects how easy or difficult it is to change.

Abundant research supports Seligman's view. Teenagers, for example, who believe that personality traits can be modified report less stress, better health, and higher grades in freshman year of high school than those who believe personality traits are fixed or unchangeable. Believing that we are not doomed by some personality trait we dislike in ourselves, but, on the contrary, believing we have the power to modify it, leads to better health outcomes and adjustment to the stresses of high school (Yeager et al., 2014).

Seligman's theory holds that three components characterize deep behavioral problems:

1. They have a *biological* basis and are heritable.

2. It is difficult to get *evidence that will disabuse* the patient that his or her behavior is maladaptive. A woman who suffers from agoraphobia and is afraid to leave the house because she might be attacked can easily obtain evidence supporting her decision to remain at home. By simply turning on TV news, she learns that innocent people can get mugged, raped, or murdered in the street. Moreover, it is impossible to prove to her that she will *never* be injured should she leave the sanctuary of her home. Deep problems are those associated with underlying beliefs that are difficult to disconfirm by evidence.

3. Deep behavioral problems are associated with very general beliefs (e.g., "I am unlovable") that pervade most or all of daily life. More superficial problems are associated with beliefs that are narrower in scope (e.g., "My boss is the only person I don't get along with."). The more general the beliefs underlying a problem, the more difficult the problem is to change. Seligman calls this component *power*. Very powerful beliefs affect almost everything we do; less powerful beliefs are confined to one aspect of living (e.g., work situations only) that do not "spill over" to affect other aspects of our lives.

Seligman evaluates a variety of psychological problems on each of these three components to determine how changeable each behavior is, given proper therapy. Table 10.1 summarizes Seligman's analysis of the degree to which biological, evidentiary, and power components are associated with selected behavioral problems. The right-hand column displays his conclusions about how easily each behavioral problem can be changed (i.e., cured). For example, the first problem listed, Sexual Identity or Transsexualism, refers to individuals who identify with the opposite sex. A transsexual male feels like a woman trapped in a man's body; a transsexual female feels like a man trapped in a woman's body. Seligman's point is that no amount of psychotherapy can effectively change a person's sexual identity. Thus, sexual identity is unchangeable.

❖ **Table 10.1**   Probability of Being Able to Change Various Behavioral Problems

Problem	Biology	Evidence	Power	Change
Sexual identity	Very high	Very high	Very high	Unchangeable
Alcoholism	Moderate	Moderate	High	Change possible but not easy
Anxiety	Moderate	Moderate	Moderate	Change possible but not easy
Depression	Low	Moderate	High	Change possible but not easy
Agoraphobia	Low	High	Low	Change possible but not easy
Specific phobias	Moderate	Moderate	None	Almost curable
Panic attacks	None	Moderate	None	Curable

Source: Adapted from Seligman (1994, pp. 247–252). Reprinted with permission.

Seligman (1994) concludes

> Optimism, the conviction that you can change, is a necessary first step in the process of all change. But unwarranted optimism, the conviction that you can change what in fact you cannot, is a tragic diversion. . . . My purpose is to instill a new, warranted optimism about the parts of your life you can change. (p. 253, emphasis in original)

At the level of habitual behaviors, then, psychologists agree that we can change certain aspects of personality (behaviors), given that (1) we want to change them and (2) we receive the proper therapeutic help. Moreover, successful change at this level of functioning might lead to changes at other levels of personality. When the substance abuser stops using, his brain begins to resume normal functioning. The positive feelings of a body returning to health, along with other major lifestyle changes (e.g., proper diet, sleep, etc.), could well lead to a new life narrative centered around redemption (McAdams, 2006).

Traits and Dispositions

Absolute trait changes have been observed in a number of longitudinal studies. These statistically significant changes in average scores tend to be small, however, rather than dramatic. At the same time, the size of the stability coefficients indicates that differential stability is the order of the day.

These two outcomes are not necessarily contradictory. Imagine five children in the third grade arranged by height (A, B, C, D, E). Four years later, these same five children are again ordered by height. We find that the tallest of the five now in the seventh grade was also the tallest 4 years earlier. Likewise for the other children: They all retain their same relative rank (A, B, C, D, E). Thus the stability coefficient would be a perfect $r = +1.0$. Does this mean that the height of these children is the same as it was 4 years earlier? Of course not. All of the children are taller. Absolute change has occurred. It is their rank order that is unchanged. Jack Block's (1971) *Lives Through Time* gives examples of how both personality consistency and change occur from high school through middle age.

Absolute Change

Longitudinal studies have found absolute change in some personality traits in individuals in different age brackets: adolescence, adulthood, and the elderly. Absolute changes in personality traits can occur at any age.

Change in adolescence: In a longitudinal study of adolescents from 12 to 20 years of age, nonresilient individuals were far more likely to become resilient, compared to the number of resilient children who became less resilient. These newly resilient individuals were more extraverted, more emotionally stable, more conscientious, and more agreeable than they had been. These results characterized 27% of the total sample. The majority (73%) of the sample were assigned to the same personality classification (undercontrolled, overcontrolled, or resilient) at the end of the study that they had at its start. Thus this study found both meaningful absolute changes in a sizable portion of the sample as well as finding that the majority of children did not change (Meeus et al., 2011).

In another longitudinal study of over 500 Italian boys and girls (age range 13 to 21 years), absolute changes in some traits were observed: Children who became more conscientious, agreeable, and open to experience were more likely to describe themselves as helpful and caring (Luengo Kanacri et al., 2014). These two longitudinal studies of personality change during adolescence indicate that trait change, when it occurs, is in the direction of becoming more agreeable, more conscientious, and more resilient.

Change in adulthood: Investigations of trait change in adulthood fall into four categories: (a) normative changes due to the normal aging process, (b) changes connected to specific life experiences, (c) research programs that combine both of the above, and (d) investigations of the effects of deliberate efforts to change our traits.

(a) *Normative trait change*

A meta-analysis of 92 studies found that the longer the time period between two measurements, the larger were the changes in three personality traits: Older adults became more agreeable, more conscientious, and had less social vitality compared to their earlier scores (Roberts, Walton, & Viechtbauer, 2006). These results were partially replicated in a combined longitudinal/cross-sectional investigation of 13,000 Australians aged 15 to 84. Over a 4-year time span, participants became less extraverted, less open to experience, more emotionally stable, and more agreeable (Wortman, Lucas, & Donnellan, 2012).

(b) *Trait change due to life experiences*

(i) A 16-year-study of the relationship between neuroticism (i.e., emotional instability) and life experiences found that those who scored high on neuroticism experienced more negative events and, reciprocally, negative life experiences predicted small increases in neuroticism. Increases in the trait of neuroticism brought about by unfortunate life experiences lasted over a decade (Jeronimus et al., 2014).

"I started out as an extravert. Then I was an introvert.
Now I don't know what-the-heck kind of -vert I am!"

(ii) A 4-year-study of the effects of being unemployed found small absolute changes in three traits. Those who were unemployed over the 4-year interval became less agreeable, less conscientious, and less open to experience, compared to 4 years earlier. These trait changes were relatively small (averaging about 1.5 to 2.0 scale points where the scale ranged from a minimum of 3 to a maximum of 21). For those who eventually did find employment, their trait scores reverted to pre-unemployment levels (Boyce et al., 2015).

(c) *Trait changes due to a combination of normative change and life experiences*

Documenting the reality of personality change as well as trying to understand how personality changes have been the overarching questions guiding Ravenna Helson and her colleagues' comprehensive research program of personality change in adulthood. The bottom line is that (1) personality change in adulthood does occur and (2) the traits of extraversion, neuroticism, and openness to experience usually decline, while the traits of conscientiousness and agreeableness typically increase (Helson, Jones, & Kwan, 2002; Helson, Kwan, John, & Jones, 2002; Mottus, Johnson, & Deary, 2012).

The Social Clock Project

The Helson et al. data reveal consistent personality changes from youth to middle age (Helson & Moane, 1987). In an ongoing longitudinal study of women who were first studied as college seniors (age = 21) in 1958 and 1960, Helson (1993) finds evidence of three kinds of personality change in adulthood:

1. *Normative personality change* indicates that most women change in the same way. For example, from ages 27 to 43, most women in the sample became less dependent on other people for emotional support (Wink & Helson, 1993).

2. A second kind of change is associated with *particular personality types*. Different patterns of personality change between ages 21 and 43 were observed within three subtypes

of highly self-involved women. *Hypersensitive* narcissistic women became more self-centered, pessimistic, and moody; *willful* narcissistic women became more socially poised and confident; and *autonomous* narcissistic women showed increased resourcefulness and creativity (Wink, 1992).

3. A third kind of change is associated with the adoption of *different social roles and obligations* in adulthood. Helson and her colleagues have found personality change to be related to a woman's adherence or nonadherence to what they call the "social clock."

A *social clock project* occurs within a socially prescribed time period for young and middle adulthood women. A social clock project is similar to Erikson's idea of psychosocial demands made on the young adult in all cultures to begin a career and/or family. Helson, Mitchell, and Moane (1984) conducted a follow-up study of 132 women who were between 42 and 45 years old. From their questionnaire responses, these women were classified as having followed one of two social clock projects:

Feminine Social Clock (FSC) adherents were women who had started their families within 6 years after graduating from college. Women who later became mothers were classified as Late Adherents. Women who did not adhere to the FSC project were classified either as on the *Masculine Occupational Clock* (MOC) project or as *Not Undertaking Either Social Clock* (NSC).

MOC adherents were women who by age 28 had chosen a field of work (except for elementary school teacher or clerical worker) and had shown persistence and advancement in their chosen field from ages 28 to 42 or only at age 28. Women who were on neither social clock by age 28 were classified as NSC.

What were the personality traits of college women who adopted one of these social clock projects?

Feminine Social Clock Women

These women, as seniors, had a strong desire to do well, were responsive to what others did and thought, characteristically met the obligations of social life, effectively used their intelligence, felt optimistic and trusting, and were in good physical and psychological health. Women who started their families on time were confident and assertive in college and possessed the motivation and ability to adjust effectively (Helson et al., 1984).

Masculine Occupational Clock Women

As seniors, women who were on the MOC at both ages 28 and 42 scored significantly higher as college seniors on the traits of self-acceptance, capacity for status, dominance, empathy, independence, and social presence. Continued upward mobility on the MOC requires greater confidence, initiative, and intellectual independence than it does getting started on it (Helson et al., 1984).

Neither Social Clock Women

Women who adopted neither social clock in adulthood had vaguer and more distant plans for marriage than their classmates. These women scored lower than the

FSC college women on the traits of well-being, intellectual efficiency, self-acceptance, independence, and achievement via conformance scales. They appear to dwell on a negative self-image, feel they are at odds with themselves and others, and want the support and approval of others to compensate for their feelings of incompetence (Helson et al., 1984).

Taken as a whole, then, the data amassed by Helson and her colleagues have consistently found absolute personality trait changes in adulthood,[3] as did those studies reported above that looked at trait change from either a normative or life experience framework. What about the elderly? Do they also reveal the possibility of personality change in old age?

Change in the elderly: Elderly Swedish adults, ranging in age from 80 to 98 years, showed a significant absolute change in extraversion over a 6-year period. Participants, on average, were less extraverted compared to their earlier testing (Berg & Johansson, 2014).

An experiment among the elderly was conducted to find out if "an old dog can learn new tricks." Adults, ranging in age from 60 to 94 years (average age = 73), were randomly assigned to either a home-based intervention program or to a wait-list control group. The home intervention consisted of an inductive reasoning training program along with puzzles (that required inductive reasoning skills to solve) that were both fun and intellectually challenging (but not overwhelming). The training program lasted for 16 weeks. At the end of that time, the participants were given personality tests and tests of inductive reasoning ability. Can you guess what was found?

Participants who had experienced the home-based intervention training program were significantly more open to experience than those in the control group. These results suggest a decrease in the trait of openness is not inevitable if elderly adults are given a program that strengthens cognitive engagement and makes thinking fun (Jackson et al., 2012). Moreover, just spending a few minutes recalling a nostalgic event—one recalled with sentimental affection—can lead to greater openness to experience (van Tilburg, Sedikides, & Wildschut, 2015).

(d) *Trait change due to desire to change*

Are you completely satisfied with your personality the way it is now? Or, if you could, would you like to change one or more of your personality traits? Research indicates that most people would like to change one or more aspects of their personalities (Hudson & Roberts, 2014). Is this possible? What does research say? The results of the only published well-controlled investigation (as of this writing) on the question of volitional personality change revealed that we can change, to a limited extent, some aspects of our personalities (Hudson & Fraley, 2015).

Young adults (average age = 20 years) who wanted to change one or more of their personality traits participated in one of two 16-week-long programs. The first program did not help them change, but the second one did. The main difference between the two programs was that the second program required the participants to come up with *specific implementation intentions* every week (e.g., "Call Jack and ask him to go to lunch on Monday") as opposed to the general goals (e.g., "Be more sociable") of the first program. Prior research has shown that specific implementation plans are far more likely to lead to goal attainment than are vague goal intentions (Gollwitzer & Brandstatter, 1997).

This research found small but statistically significant absolute changes in extraversion, conscientiousness, and neuroticism over the second 16-week program. Specific implementation goals led to changes in daily behavior which led to changes in personality traits. By changing how they acted on a daily basis, participants may have altered their self-concept. Their new identity (of being more outgoing, more responsible, and/or more emotionally stable) then led them to continue to act in ways consistent with their new identity. After 16-weeks, they reported a change in those personality traits they wanted to change. If you want to change a personality trait, this research found, start by changing your daily behavior (Hudson & Fraley, 2015).

In summary, research shows that our personality traits are somewhat modifiable across the major points of our life course—adolescence, adulthood, and old age—whether the change is attributable to specific life experiences, is normative, or is desired. But not everyone agrees that traits can change. Some personality psychologists view those reported absolute changes to be quite small. After all, no one has yet reported that quiet, reserved introverts have morphed into life-of-the-party extraverts. The more accurate interpretation of these longitudinal investigations, they feel, is that our personality traits are far more stable across our life span than they change. What evidence do they have for this position?

Trait Continuity

The traits of the Five-Factor Model show stability over long time spans (for a complete review, see McCrae & Costa, 1993). For example, Conley (1984) found evidence for the stability of both neuroticism and extraversion. These traits were assessed on three occasions, when the participants were 24, 42, and 68 years old. Table 10.2 presents some of the stability coefficients obtained for men and women.

As shown in Table 10.2, stability coefficients ranging from .60 to .70 were found for both men and women for the traits of extraversion and neuroticism over the approximate 18-year time interval from ages 24 to 42. Even more impressive are the statistically significant[4] stability correlations found in the 44- to 45-year interval from ages 24 to 68. Although these correlations ranged from .25 to .34, they nevertheless indicate considerably more trait stability than might be assumed at first glance.

❖ **Table 10.2**   Stability Coefficients for Neuroticism and Extraversion Initially Measured at Age 24

	Age at Second Occasion (42 years old)		Age at Third Occasion (68 years old)	
	Men ($n = 212$)	Women ($n = 229$)	Men ($n = 181$)	Women ($n = 202$)
Neuroticism	.65	.60	.34	.31
Extraversion	.61	.70	.25	.27

Source: Data from Conley's (1984, p. 1331) Table 3.

Because the personality scales used to measure these traits are not perfectly reliable, stability coefficients will always give lower values than the true amount of stability actually present. Over a comparable 50-year interval, and correcting for unreliability, the true stability of these traits over the full adult life span is estimated to be .60 (Costa & McCrae, 1992b, 1994). A meta-analysis of longitudinal studies of personality traits suggests that Costa and McCrae underestimated the size of the stability coefficient. The corrected stability coefficient across all traits and all studies, over an average time interval of 80 months, is an impressive r = +0.79 (Ferguson, 2010).

McCrae and Costa (2008) note that absolute changes occur in all five personality traits after age 30. These changes, however, are quite gradual. If you are highly extraverted at age 20, you are likely to be extraverted at age 70, although perhaps not quite as strongly. Thus their position is that over the lifespan trait stability is more likely than any dramatic change. The gradual decline in neuroticism along with gradual increases in conscientiousness and agreeableness reflects a *maturity principle* as we travel the often bumpy road from adolescence to middle age. Slight changes in the direction of greater maturity may be normative (Caspi, Roberts, & Shiner, 2005).

So where do we stand? Do we change our traits or not? On the one hand, absolute changes in average trait scores have been reported by investigators from three different continents. On the other hand, the average trait change is unimpressively small. What can we conclude from these facts?

These nomothetic investigations may well be masking important individual differences. If the *average* change is only 2 points on an 18-point scale, some participants changed much more than that, while others changed less, not at all, or in the opposite direction. A productive next step in these large-scale longitudinal studies would be to identify those participants who changed a great deal and compare them, in a variety of ways, to those whose trait scores were unchanged. Is there a distinctive personality profile for those who really change?

Personal Concerns

Dan McAdams (1994) thinks personal concerns are more central to *who a person really is* than are her trait scores. *Personal concerns* is the level of personality that deals with our motives, hopes, and wishes for the future. This is the level where we are *agents* in the world. We act to get what we love and to avoid what we hate (McAdams & Olson, 2010).

Are your personal concerns related to your personality traits? Yes. Two longitudinal studies that measured both traits and goals found meaningful associations between them. In one study, the strongest correlations indicated that extraverts were more likely to endorse hedonistic goals (e.g., having fun, having an exciting lifestyle) and relationship goals (e.g., having a satisfying marriage/relationship, having harmonious relationships with parents) than were introverts. These introvert-extravert differences occurred both at time of first testing and four years later. Those who are high in agreeableness were likely to endorse social goals (e.g., helping others in need, volunteering for public service). Finally, those individuals who were open to experience strongly endorsed aesthetic goals (e.g., writing good fiction, becoming accomplished in one of the performing arts). The main difference between traits and goals was that, unlike personality traits, the average importance of specific goals declined over 4 years. Our specific goals change over time and circumstances; our personality traits are more stable (Roberts, O'Donnell, & Robins, 2004).

College students wrote personal narratives that revealed two of their major life goals. Those students whose narratives showed some form of personal growth reported greater satisfaction with life and overall happiness 3 years later. Students who expressed either an intellectual growth goal (e.g., to explore new concepts) or a socio-emotional growth goal (e.g., to contribute to the welfare of society), showed an increase in life satisfaction 3 years later. This was especially true for those students who were more conscientious at the start of the study. The growth goals of all students helped to create their future selves (Bauer & McAdams, 2010).

Similar results over a 5-year span were obtained in a sample of over 1,000 pairs of German twins. Participants were asked to indicate the importance of two types of goals: *Agency* goals (e.g., to hold a prestigious position; to develop skills) and *Communion* goals (e.g., to help other people; to have many friends). Agency goals correlated positively with the traits of extraversion, openness, and conscientiousness (but negatively with agreeableness). Communion goals correlated positively with extraversion, openness, and agreeableness.

Results also showed a tendency for goals assessed at time 1 to be related to changes in personality traits measured 5 years later. For example, individuals who expressed strong agency goals at time 1 were more conscientious 5 years later. Those who expressed strong communion goals at time 1 were more extraverted and open to experience 5 years later.

This finding, if replicated, would mean that our goals can lead us to modify our personality traits *in advance* of meeting future social demands (Bleidorn et al., 2010). This would constitute strong evidence for George Kelly's fundamental postulate (covered in the previous chapter): *A person's processes are psychologically channelized by the ways he anticipates events.* The Bleidorn et al. (2010) data suggest that the processes set in motion by anticipation include modifying one's personality traits. Your present goals may change your future personality.

Personality change at the level of personal concerns, however, may prove to be challenging. Nancy Cantor and John Kihlstrom (1987) view our learned cognitive procedures as organized in such a way as to resist changes in how we typically cope with our life task problems even if our coping efforts have not been successful.

An example of how difficult changing unhelpful cognitive strategies can be is found in academic settings. The strong positive correlations typically found among quiz scores in the same course indicate that most students who do not do well on their first quiz continue to get poor or failing grades throughout the semester. It seems they are unwilling to put in the necessary effort to change their procedural *rules for how to study* (even though they have not worked well so far). They are unwilling to accommodate their study habits to meet the new demands of the course. Since many of our "rules of thumb" for solving life's problems outside the classroom are equally well learned, Cantor and Kihlstrom (1987) anticipate that we are likely to apply them automatically to new situations, even if they don't work particularly well. Thus they pessimistically expect change at this level to be difficult.

McAdams (1994), however, is optimistic that personality change at the level of personal concerns is possible. Consistent with the views of Erik Erikson, personal concerns about *generativity* (concern for the welfare of the next generation) have been found to be greater in middle-aged and older adults than in younger ones (McAdams et al., 1993). By looking for personality changes in the context of major life tasks, as we saw in Helson's social clock project, future research may find long-term effects of a wide variety of personal concerns and the subsequent growth of personality at this level.

Life Narratives and the Making of the Self

The final level of personality proposed by McAdams is that of *life narratives*. McAdams notes that the creation of a meaningful narrative identity is the most important psychosocial challenge of adults in today's world (McAdams, 2008). Your life narrative is the story of your life.

McAdams (1994) expects personality change in adulthood to be quite likely at this level because changing circumstances create new opportunities and positions within which the person can live a meaningful life. This level of personality is thus explicitly concerned with the meaning we assign to our lives. Because we can always revise our interpretation of the meaning of past events in light of our present circumstances and anticipated future, we are able to revise our life narratives throughout adulthood.

For example, a woman who has been battered by her husband for many years may eventually take on a new identity as a counselor to other women in a similar situation. By so doing, she transforms her horrific prior life into a productively meaningful present one. As Mary Catherine Bateson (1990) observes in *Composing a Life*, "There is no way to know which fragments of the past will prove to be relevant in the future. Composing a life involves a continual reimagining of the future and reinterpretation of the past to give meaning to the present" (pp. 29–30).

Research strongly supports Bateson's idea: Survivors of traumatic events who can write about their experiences (a painful process at first) are better off in the long run for doing it. Their immune system improves, they need to visit their physician less often, they get better grades in college, and they miss less time at work (Frattaroli, 2006; Pennebaker, 2004).

Research on narrative identity shows that adults who arise strengthened from negative life experiences tend to engage in a two-step process. First, the individual explores the difficult experience in depth, remembering what it felt like, how it came about, what it led to and might still lead to, and how this negative experience fits into his or her total life story. Second, the individual creates and commits to a positive resolution of the incident. Research indicates the first step leads to personal growth and the second to happiness (McAdams & McLean, 2013).

Two theoretical orientations have contributed to our understanding of personality at the level of life narratives. Both orientations—the humanistic/existential and the psychodynamic—assume that personality change at this level is possible. As McAdams (1994) correctly points out, however, data on this point are virtually nonexistent. In other words, these theoretical views are interesting and important, but they are difficult to test empirically. We conclude the book, then, with answers to the question of continuity and change of personality in adulthood from theorists whose backgrounds as psychotherapists lead them to believe that motivated adults are able to change and create more satisfying stories of their lives.

Humanistic and Existential Approaches to Continuity and Change

The Fully Functioning Person

Perhaps the major reason I am willing to take chances is that I have found that in doing so, whether I succeed or fail, I learn. Learning, especially learning from experience, has been a prime element in making my life worthwhile. Such learning helps me to expand. So I continue to risk. . . . It seems to me that I am still—inside—the shy boy who found communication very difficult in interpersonal situations. . . . That boy is still very much part of me.

—Carl Rogers at age 75 (1980, pp. 78, 80)

These quotes from Carl Rogers illustrate some of his personal experiences with continuity and change in his personality. On the one hand, Rogers values taking risks because of the learning and growth of personality that ensue; on the other hand, Rogers still experiences significant continuity from his youth—the shy boy who finds interpersonal communication difficult.

Rogers' experience of both continuity and change is quite in keeping with the life narrative level of personality. Your life narrative will involve both continuity—after all, it is always *your* story—and change—your reevaluation of the meaning of past events in light of your new experiences.

Rogers, operating squarely in the humanistic tradition, begins with two major assumptions: (1) Every person is motivated to grow and become the person she is meant to be and (2) she can freely choose to change the direction of her life and create a new, more satisfying story of it. From his therapeutic experiences, Rogers (1961, pp. 167–175) identifies the following changes as typically involved in becoming a fully functioning person:

Away from facades. The individual moves away from pretending to be who she is not and comes closer to being herself.

Away from "oughts." The person moves away from a controlling image of who he should be and comes closer to finding who he is.

Away from meeting expectations. The person moves away from what her culture or social group expects her to be and become. She begins to resist pressures to conform.

Away from pleasing others. The person realizes that much of her life has been spent trying to please other people so they will like her rather than being true to what she really wants for herself.

Toward self-direction. The person becomes responsible for himself. He decides which activities have real meaning for him and which do not. He chooses and learns from the consequences of those choices.

Toward "being process." Individuals become more open to personal change from day to day. They begin to experience themselves as in processes of change rather than as static, fixed entities.

Toward "being complexity." The desire to be open to *all* of oneself in each moment, in all of one's complexity and contradictions, characterizes fully functioning individuals.

Toward openness to experience. The fully functioning person lives in a friendly and close relationship to his own experience. He becomes less afraid of his own spontaneous feelings and reactions.

Toward acceptance of others. As individuals accept themselves more fully, they tend to accept other individuals and their unique experiences for who and what they are, without needing to judge or evaluate them as good or bad, superior or inferior.

Toward trust of self. As individuals learn to accept themselves for who they are, they learn to know and trust their feelings, discover their own values, and express themselves in ways that are unique to them.

The issues of personal choice, free will, and taking responsibility for oneself that Rogers sees as integrally involved in becoming a fully functioning person are also central to the concerns of the existential psychologist Victor Frankl.

The Will to Meaning

Man does not simply exist but always decides what his existence will be, what he will become in the next moment . . . every human being has the freedom to change at any instant.

—Victor Frankl (1984, p. 133)

Victor Frankl himself is the foremost example of our freedom to change at any instant. Although he was daily surrounded by death in Nazi concentration camps for over 3 years, Frankl transformed his horrendous experiences into the life-affirming therapeutic approach he named *logotherapy*. How did Frankl accomplish this remarkable feat? By changing his attitude toward his suffering and changing his constant preoccupation with survival:

I forced my thoughts to turn to another subject. Suddenly I saw myself standing on the platform of a well-lit, warm and pleasant lecture room. In front of me sat an attentive audience on comfortable upholstered seats. I was giving a lecture on the psychology of the concentration camp! All that oppressed me at that moment became objective, seen and described from the remote viewpoint of science. By this method I succeeded somehow in rising above the situation, above the sufferings of the moment, and I observed them as if they were already in the past. Both I and my troubles became the object of an interesting psychoscientific study undertaken by myself. (1984, p. 82)

The creative process Frankl used to detach himself mentally from his gruesome situation (imagining he is giving a lecture in the future), can reliably elicit a sense of enhanced meaning in our own lives. Over a series of six studies, those individuals who imagined they were either doing something in the future or doing something in a different location (Frankl imaginatively changed both time and place) consistently reported greater meaning in their lives than individuals who focused on their present situation (Waytz, Hershfield, & Tamir, 2015). It appears that a key component of experiencing meaning in our lives involves mentally integrating our past and present experiences with our imagined future ones (Baumeister et al., 2013).

Logotherapy focuses on the meaning of human existence as well as on the individual's search for meaning in his or her life. The primary human motive, in Frankl's view, is to find meaning in one's life. Frankl sees the *will to meaning* as more fundamental to human existence than either Freud's *pleasure principle* (which Frankl calls "the will to pleasure") or Adler's *will to power*. Moreover, in sharp contrast to those drive-reduction models of personality, such as Freud's, that believe tension reduction to be the basis of all our motives, Frankl asserts that mental health is based on a certain amount of tension, the tension between what one has already accomplished and what one still ought to accomplish, or the gap between who one *is* and who one should *become*. Such a tension is inherent in the human being and therefore is indispensable to mental health. We should not, Frankl insists, be hesitant about challenging a person with a potential meaning for him or her to fulfill.

The results of an 18-year-long longitudinal study involving over 1,400 participants support Frankl's view that having a sense of purpose is therapeutic. Those older adults (average age = 77 years) with a stronger sense of purpose had fewer disabilities, did better on tests of cognitive functioning, reported better health and fewer depressive symptoms than those who did not. Although having a sense of purpose in life does not prevent those losses in health that are likely to occur among the oldest-old, purposeful living positively contributes to the health and well-being of older adults (Windsor, Curtis, & Luszcz, 2015).

Indeed, at the neurological level, older adults who stay engaged with life by continuing to learn and acquire new information show increased survival of new neurons. Cognitive neuroscience has shown that the aging human brain reorganizes itself to recruit new regions to support cognitive functions in ways that the brains of young adults do not. These neurological results have dramatically shifted the prevailing view of cognitive aging from inevitable decline to *plasticity*—the human brain qualitatively changes throughout the life span, showing less specialization in its recruitment of neural regions. For example, when our left frontal cortex loses some of its functionality, our right frontal cortex picks up the slack (Gutchess, 2014). Apparently then, having a sense of purpose not only helps to keep existing neurons alive, but it also seems to aid in the growth of new ones, a process called *neurogenesis* (Doidge, 2007).

Logotherapy is directed toward the future rather than the past. Each patient is asked, What tasks do you need to fulfill to give meaning to your life? Frankl notes that no universal answer to this question exists because each person needs to discover his or her own individual meaning at any particular point in his or her life. Research suggests that we are most likely to spend time thinking and analyzing the meaning of life precisely when such meaning is unclear to us. People who are living meaningful and purposeful lives intuitively know this without consciously dwelling on it (Heintzelman & King, 2015).

Frankl believes everyone has his or her specific mission in life, a set of concrete tasks that can be accomplished by no one else. The mission of logotherapy is to assist the person in finding meaning in his or her life.

"What's the purpose of my life? Could you Google it?"

There are general guidelines in logotherapy for discovering the meaning of one's life. Meaning can be found by

- *Creating* some product or doing something of value for others.
- *Loving* another person. In so doing, the loving person sees the traits and potentialities of the beloved person, and by her love she enables the loved person to actualize those potentials.
- *Suffering.* Within our *attitude* toward our *unavoidable*[5] suffering lies the key to finding meaning in our lives. "When we are no longer able to change a situation—just think of an incurable disease such as inoperable cancer—we are challenged to change ourselves" (Frankl, 1984, p. 116). By choosing to suffer bravely and search for the meaning that our unavoidable suffering holds for us, life has a meaning that endures until the end. In this way, we enable ourselves to continue to find satisfaction in our life narrative.

Psychodynamic Approaches to Continuity and Change

Donald Spence (1982) credits Freud with discovering the importance of synthesizing or bringing together apparently unconnected events in a person's life. Freud's method was to weave together a story for his patient, based on the facts of the case: the patient's dreams, his associations to the dream symbols, and "random" memories. From these data, Freud would construct a coherent narrative account of the patient's psychological life. Freud's story would show the patient how he consistently emotionally reacts to different people and events in his life (e.g., chronically feeling angry, disappointed, or anxious) because his major unconscious conflicts, originating in childhood, have not been resolved. As a result he unconsciously *transfers* his feelings (originally directed to his parents) to individuals in his present life.

Spence feels that a well-constructed story contains a certain level of truth, which he calls narrative truth. Narrative truth is real and immediate for the patient. By means of narrative truth the patient is able, for the first time, to see the patterns in his life that have inevitably led to interpersonal problems and dissatisfactions. By becoming clearly aware of the story of his past life, the patient is enabled to make his present life more satisfying. Similarly, Roy Schafer (1992) notes that the process of psychoanalysis is a dialogue between patient and analyst such that "each analysis amounts in the end to retelling a life in the past and present—and as it may be in the future. A life is re-authored as it is co-authored" (p. xv).

Carl Jung and Erik Erikson are two theorists from the psychodynamic tradition who have contributed to our understanding of personality growth throughout the second half of life. Both Jung and Erikson stress the necessity of finding personal meaning in our lives if we are to construct a life story that has a satisfying ending.

Jung and the Process of Individuation

From my eleventh year I have been launched upon a single enterprise which is my "main business." My life has been permeated and held together by one idea, and one goal . . . to penetrate into the secret of the personality.

—Carl Jung at age 83 (1965, p. 206)

This statement given by Jung in 1958, 3 years before his death, displays three features relevant to the narrative level of personality.

First, he wants to find the "secret" of personality. This suggests that there is something mysterious about it, a view that he had earlier expressed directly: "Yes, this thing we call personality is a great and mysterious problem" (Jung, 1954, p. 181). To Jung, personality refers to the very essence of an individual's unique nature. To become a personality is to achieve wholeness—to become complete. This is a lifelong process that requires a connection to one's social world but without total conformity to it. Total conformity destroys any possibility of discovering one's uniqueness. The secret of personality growth is to live a life that integrates freely chosen social obligations while remaining true to oneself.

Second, the mysterious quality of personality is hinted at in Jung's curious use of the passive voice in describing his main business of life—"I have been launched"—rather than asserting that he actively chose the "main business" of his life. If he did not launch himself, who did? To Jung, there is an "inner voice" in each person that is her own vocation—her own unique law of development. "In so far as every individual has the law of his life inborn in him, it is theoretically possible for any man to follow this law and so become a personality, that is, to achieve wholeness" (Jung, 1954, p. 179). This inner voice is part of our personality, because it is *our* inner voice and no one else's. Yet we also experience it as something objective or outside of us. This is part of the mystery of personality.

We can see the third revealing feature of Jung's quote when he proclaims that his own life "has been held together" by trying to solve the mystery of personality. He thereby summarizes his own personality and the necessity of achieving it. Jung (1954) maintains that we cannot realize our life's meaning without achieving personality—becoming a complete and unique individual. In this sense, then, Jung sees one's personality as intimately connected to one's life story and the meaning of one's life. Jung's term for the process of achieving personality is individuation:

Individuation means becoming a single, homogeneous being, and, in so far as "individuality" embraces our innermost, last, and incomparable uniqueness, it also implies becoming one's own self. Individuation means "coming to selfhood" or "self-realization" (Jung, 1956, p. 182).

Individuation and the Stages of Life

Jung (1931/1969b) divides the course of life into four stages: *childhood* (infancy to puberty), *youth* (puberty to middle life), *middle life* (starting around the ages 35–40), and *old age* (undefined starting point).[6] Jung finds the most interesting transition to be from the first to the second half of life, that is, from youth to middle life.

In the first half of life, men and women typically identify with and use their masculine and feminine qualities, respectively. Boys typically become men interested in engaging in "tough-minded" masculine pursuits. Girls typically become women interested in engaging in "tender-minded" feminine activities. But in the second half of life, if wholeness of personality is to be realized, we need to activate our unused talents, talents stereotypically identified as "belonging" to the opposite gender. So if a man thinks he needs to be tough and rugged, he will, in the first half of life, suppress his tender feelings. To achieve wholeness of personality, these "feminine" qualities need to be developed and allowed expression in the second half of his life. Similarly, if a woman thinks she should always be nurturant and care for others, the second half of her life is the time for her to bring out those undeveloped "masculine" traits (e.g., to become more assertive about satisfying her own needs) that she had suppressed during the first half of her life.

Our challenge in the second half of life, Jung notes, is to activate these suppressed features *without* losing our initial masculinity or femininity. Neither a weak, effeminate man nor a loud, manish woman demonstrates wholeness of personality. Achieving personality requires integrating all of our separate components into a unified, unique self. The goal is to live our lives as fully as possible.

Cultural norms can inhibit individuation in the second half of life, particularly during old age. For example, if a culture places great value on appearing to be youthful, then its elderly citizens will deny or even feel ashamed they are "old." They will obsess over their physical appearance. Many will elect painful surgeries to appear younger. This is, of course, regrettable. Old age is a time to continue looking forward to the next step of the journey. It is not a time to look backward, fruitlessly fighting the aging process in order retain one's youthful physical appearance. In 1931, Jung wrote,

Where is the wisdom of our old people, where are their precious secrets and their visions? For the most part our old people try to compete with the young. In the United States it is almost

an ideal for a father to be the brother of his sons, and for the mother to be if possible the younger sister of her daughter. (1931/1969b p. 400)

To Jung, wisdom involves a conscious return to those religious symbols, such as the idea of life after death, embedded deep within the unconscious mind. "It is only possible to live the fullest life when we are in harmony with these symbols" (1931/1969b, pp. 402–403). Unlike Freud, who held very negative views about religion, Jung strongly felt it is valuable to see death not as an end but rather as a transitional state to a new beginning. Jung maintains that only if we willingly accept the inevitable can we create a happy ending to our life narrative, a view with which Erik Erikson agrees.

Aging and Wisdom

Healthy children will not fear life if their elders have integrity enough not to fear death.

—Erik Erikson (1963, p. 169)

Erikson viewed old age as the last stage of personality development. In his view, the major psychosocial crisis of old age is *integrity versus despair*, as highlighted in Table 10.3.

Aging as a Psychosocial Process

How the children of a given culture feel about living is connected to how their elders feel about dying. Death is inevitable and thus is "that one aspect of the future that is both wholly certain and wholly unknowable" (Erikson, Erikson, & Kivnick, 1986, p. 72). How the elderly members of society typically think and feel about their

❖ **Table 10.3** Summary of Erikson's Stages of Development

Life Stage	Psychosocial Crisis	Adaptive Ego Quality	Ego Core Pathology
1. Infancy (0–2 years)	Trust vs. Mistrust	Hope	Withdrawal
2. Toddler (2–3 years)	Autonomy vs. Shame and Doubt	Will	Compulsion
3. Early School Age (4–5 years)	Initiative vs. Guilt	Purpose	Inhibition
4. Middle School Age (6–12 years)	Industry vs. Inferiority	Competence	Inertia
5. Adolescence	Identity vs. Identity Confusion	Fidelity	Repudiation
6. Young Adulthood	Intimacy vs. Isolation	Love	Exclusivity
7. Adulthood	Generativity vs. Stagnation	Care	Rejectivity
8. Old Age	Integrity vs. Despair	Wisdom	Disdain

Sources: Erikson (1963, 1978, 1982). Reprinted from *The Life Cycle Completed* by Erik H. Erikson, with the permission of W. W. Norton & Company Inc. Copyright© 1982 by Rikan Enterprises.

own personal death has an unavoidable impact on the expectations of its youngest members. Elders who accept the reality of death as an integral part of life implicitly send the message that all of life is good. But when the elderly fear death they send the message that the end of the life cycle brings nothing but anxiety and despair. The attitudes of the older generation necessarily affect those of the younger generation.

Erikson's (1978) psychosocial orientation to personality development is illustrated by three interdependent cycles of life:

1. The elderly individual's responses to her advanced age depend on her prior handling of the first seven psychosocial crises. A successful and fulfilling experience in old age necessarily depends on the ego strengths that have been developed earlier.

2. Successful fulfillment of one's life depends on being vitally concerned with the ongoing problems of the younger generation. This concern can manifest itself in such activities as assisting in the raising of the grandchildren, volunteering to help others, or actively working to protect the environment. The full development of the aging individual is thus intimately connected with the advancement of future generations.

3. This generational interdependence, "in turn, is vital to the maintenance of evolving *social structures* that must facilitate the emergence of the life stages or else suffer social and political pathology" (Erikson, 1978, p. 29, italics in original). Erikson believes that every society needs to provide opportunities for the elderly to become actively and productively involved in the lives of its younger members. At the same time, every society needs to evolve institutional structures for the physical and psychological care of its aging members. Erikson (1968) holds that a civilization can be measured by the meaning which it gives to the full cycle of life, for such meaning, or lack of it, cannot fail to reach into the beginnings of the next generation, and thus into the chances of others to meet ultimate questions with some clarity and strength. (pp. 140–141)

As a test of Erikson's eight-stage model of personality, adults (ages 62 to 92), were asked to write memories of their experiences that occurred within each decade (e.g., 0–9, 10–19, 20–29, etc.) of life. Those memories were then coded to see if they reflected the kinds of crises Erikson expects to arise at that age (e.g., the *Identity crisis* should first appear between 10–19 years of age).

Results supported Erikson's theory: The majority of memories reported by these adults (when they could be coded as reflecting one of the crises), fell within the expected age range. There was also considerable overlap across decades that support Erikson's epigenetic principle. Trust issues, for example, can appear at any time in the life cycle, particularly when the trust versus mistrust crisis was not satisfactorily resolved in early childhood. Finally, unique trajectories of memories revealed idiographic patterns of individual differences that Erikson expects: We are not clones of one other (Conway & Holmes, 2004).

In another, similar investigation, adults were given the Inventory of Psychosocial Development to assess their resolutions of the first six psychosocial crises (Constantinople, 1969) and an expanded version to cover the final two stages (Whitbourne & Waterman, 1979). The data revealed unique longitudinal trajectories consistent with Erikson's theory. While the identity crisis is felt initially and most intensely during the teenage years, it can continue to be an issue that is not fully resolved for many people until they are in their late 20s (or later). Erikson would not be surprised to learn that one size does not fit all (Carlsson, Wangqvist, & Frisen, 2015; Sneed, Whitbourne, & Culang, 2006).

Integrity Versus Despair

An elderly individual has integrity when she accepts her life as meaningful. The person who successfully resolves this final psychosocial crisis gains a sense of coherence and wholeness about herself and her life that will help her withstand the physical deterioration of very old age. Seeing one's entire life as meaningful is necessary, of course, to construct a satisfying conclusion.

Despair occurs when one is filled with regret at lost opportunities and realizes there is not enough time to create a new life. Despair in the elderly may also be a symptom of a mourning for failures to solve the earlier psychosocial crises: "for autonomy weakened, initiative lost, intimacy missed, generativity neglected—not to speak of identity potentials bypassed, or, indeed, an all too limiting identity lived" (Erikson, 1982, p. 63). The feelings of disgust and despair in old age indicate that one does not accept one's life as lived and does not accept death as the final end of this life. Fear of death is an inevitable outcome of the failure to resolve this last crisis.

Erikson asserts that the ego strength or virtue that accrues to those who do accept their lives as meaningful, thereby holding despair at bay, is wisdom. *Wisdom* is "a kind of informed and detached concern with life itself in the face of death itself" (1982, p. 61). Accepting one's death as inevitable, the elderly person nevertheless remains vitally concerned with life in a *detached* rather than egotistical manner. The elderly wise person shifts his thinking from a narrow concern with his personal life to a more general concern with life itself in all its various manifestations.

Could an attitude of detachment be a key to wisdom? Frankl's dramatic account of how he survived the Nazi concentration camps revealed that he was able (1) to

Ted Streshinsky/The LIFE Images Collection/Getty Images

Photo 10.1 Erik Erikson (1902–1994)

In addition to being the father of the identity crisis, Erikson recognized psychosocial issues that affect older adults. His concepts of *generative concerns* and *integrity* sparked major research programs that began about the time of his death.

Key publications:

Identity: Youth and Crisis (1968)
The Life Cycle Completed (1982)
Vital Involvement in Old Age (1986; with Joan Erikson and Helen Kivnick)

imagine being in a different time and place and (2) to detach himself, mentally and emotionally, from his present surroundings. He did not deny where he was. Instead, "All that oppressed me at that moment became objective, seen and described from the remote viewpoint of science" (1984, p. 82).

Evidence for the wisdom of detachment was obtained in two laboratory studies. Participants were randomly assigned to discuss complex social issues from one of two perspectives, an *ego immersed perspective* (e.g., imagine the events occurring as if you were there) or a *distanced perspective* (e.g., imagine the events occurring as if you were a distant observer). What effects did these perspectives have on their discussions?

Participants who were assigned to the distance perspective were more likely, compared to the ego immersed perspective, to (a) recognize and accept that the future was likely to change, (b) recognize that their own knowledge was limited, and (c) join a bipartisan political discussion group. The distance perspective allowed participants to be relatively free of their egos while discussing these issues. They could hash out the issues more objectively. In their discussions, they revealed aspects of wise reasoning, aspects that are far more difficult to achieve whenever we take things personally (Kross & Grossman, 2012).

Since wisdom is the virtue associated with solving the crisis of the eighth stage of life, does this mean Erikson thinks that we have to wait until we are very old before we can become wise? No, he does not. Erikson views that each virtue or ego strength is implicit at each stage of development. Wisdom, then, can be found within each successful resolution of every psychosocial crisis: The infant who trusts her trustworthy caregivers is wise; the toddler who begins to assert his will is wise; the older child who takes initiative is wise; the school-age child who industriously applies herself is wise; the adolescent who struggles with and attains a sense of identity is wise; the young adult who becomes intimate with another is wise; and the older adult who cares about nourishing others is wise. We continually create a satisfying ending to the story of our lives with each wise decision we make throughout the complete course of personality.

❖

QUESTIONS TO PONDER

1. Name three habitual behaviors you feel comfortable with and one habitual behavior you would like to change. How optimistic are you that you could change this behavior if you really wanted to? What keeps you from really wanting to?

2. From your observation of people you have known for a number of years, would you say any of them have changed in significant ways? Which levels of personality were involved in the changes you observed? What role might a more or less constant environment play in maintaining personality continuity?

3. What are some examples of wise choices you've made in your life? What do they have in common? How would you define wisdom?

4. Do you think elderly people, in general, are wiser than younger ones? Do you expect or want elderly people to share their wisdom with you? What does your answer tell you about the value your society places on wisdom?

5. In what ways does the law of cause-and-effect apply to your thoughts, expectations, feelings, and behavior? How often are your feelings directly caused by your own thoughts and expectations? If you change your expectations, what happens to your feelings?

❖

NOTES

1. I felt privileged to witness one aspect of this change. In riding together in a hospital elevator, a new mother (in a wheelchair hospitals use to exit their patients) was holding her newborn baby in her arms. I heard her say, with a slight surprise to her voice, "This is your first elevator ride." For the foreseeable future she will be viewing many events through the eyes of her child, which is one element in the growth of her own personality.

2. Surprisingly, there is little evidence for a personality constellation that might be called "The Addictive Personality." There seems to be a consensus among addiction researchers that no single pattern of personality traits is common to all addicts (DiClemente, 1994; Sutker & Allain, 1988). However, the APA Dictionary of Psychology identifies the traits of impulsivity and neuroticism as possibilities for this hypothetical personality pattern (American Psychological Association, 2007, pp. 18–19).

3. Reports of absolute trait change include: Helson & Moane, 1987; Helson & Picano, 1990; Helson & Roberts, 1994; Helson & Wink, 1992; Lilgendahl, Helson, & John, 2013; Roberts, Helson, & Klohen, 2002; Wink & Helson, 1993.

4. By applying various statistical tests to the obtained correlations, it can be shown that, given the large sample sizes of 181 men and 202 women, it is highly unlikely that the obtained coefficients would have reached those magnitudes if the true stability coefficients were actually zero.

5. Frankl is clear to distinguish unavoidable suffering from suffering that we can alleviate by taking appropriate corrective action. He is certainly not promoting a masochistic attitude toward pain. He is claiming that even within unavoidable suffering, we can find that our lives are meaningful.

6. "Elderly people" are always 20 years older than I am.

❖

SUGGESTIONS FOR FURTHER READING

Frankl, V. (1992). *Man's search for meaning: An introduction to logotherapy* (4th ed.). Boston, MA: Beacon Press.

Pennebaker, J. W. (2004). *Writing to heal: A guided journal for recovering from trauma and emotional upheaval.* Oakland, CA: New Harbinger Publications.

Seligman, M. E. P. (1994). *What you can change and what you can't.* New York, NY: Knopf.

Waymont, H. A., & Bauer, J. J. (Eds.). (2008). *Transcending self-interest: Psychological explorations of the quiet ego.* Washington, DC: American Psychological Association.

Wilson, T. D. (2011). *Redirect: The surprising new science of psychological change.* New York, NY: Little, Brown and Company.

INTERNET RESOURCES

1. To see how self-actualized you are at this stage of your life, go to http://www.blogthings.com/thefourfactorselfactualizationtest/.

2. To see how spiritual you are at this stage of your life, go to http://web.pdx.edu/~tothm/religion/Spiritual%20Quiz.pdf.

3. To find out how generative you are at this stage of life, go to http://www.sesp.northwestern.edu/foley/instruments/lgs/.

References

Aanes, M. M., Mittelmark, M. B., & Hetlan, J. (2010). Interpersonal stress and poor health: The mediating role of loneliness. *European Psychologist, 15,* 3–11.

Abramson, L. Y., Seligman, M. E. P., & Teasdale, J. D. (1978). Learned helplessness in humans: Critique and reformulation. *Journal of Abnormal Psychology, 87,* 49–74.

Adams, G. R., Abraham, K. G., & Markstrom, C. A. (1987). The relations among identity development, self-consciousness, and self-focusing during middle- and late-adolescence. *Developmental Psychology, 23,* 292–297.

Adams, G. R., & Fitch, S. A. (1982). Ego stage and identity status development: A cross-sequential analysis. *Journal of Personality and Social Psychology, 43,* 574–583.

Adler, A. (1929). *The science of living.* New York, NY: Greenberg.

Adler, A. (1930). Individual psychology. In C. Murchison (Ed.), *Psychologies of 1930* (pp. 395–405). Worchester, MA: Clark University Press.

Adler, A. (1939). *Social interest* (J. Linton & R. Vaughn, Trans.). New York, NY: G. P. Putnam.

Adler, A. (1957). *Understanding human nature* (W. B. Wolfe, ed., Trans.). New York, NY: Fawcett. (Original work published 1927)

Adolphs, R. (2003). Cognitive neuroscience of human social behavior. *National Review of Neuroscience, 4,* 165–178.

Aguilar, B., Sroufe, L. A., Egeland, B., & Carlson, E. (2000). Distinguishing the early-onset/persistent and adolescent-onset antisocial behavior types: From birth to 16 years. *Development and Psychopathology, 12,* 109–132.

Ainsworth, M. D. S. (1989). Attachments beyond infancy. *American Psychologist, 44,* 709–716.

Ainsworth, M. D. S., Blehar, M. C., Waters, E., & Wall, S. (1978). *Patterns of attachment: A psychological study of the Strange Situation.* Hillsdale, NJ: Lawrence Erlbaum.

Ainsworth, M. D. S., & Bowlby, J. (1991). An ethological approach to personality development. *American Psychologist, 46,* 333–341.

Alexander, R. D. (1989). Evolution of the human psyche. In P. Mellars & C. Stringer (Eds.), *The human revolution* (pp. 455–513). Princeton, NJ: Princeton University Press.

Allport, G. W. (1937). *Personality: A psychological interpretation.* New York, NY: Henry Holt and Company.

Allport, G. W. (1961). *Pattern and growth in personality.* New York, NY: Holt, Rinehart & Winston.

Allport, G. W., & Odbert, H. S. (1936). Trait-names: A psycho-lexical approach. *Psychological Monographs, 47* (Whole No. 211).

Amabile, T. M., Hennessey, B. A., & Grossman, B. S. (1986). Social influences on creativity: The effects of contracted-for-reward. *Journal of Personality and Social Psychology, 50,* 14–23.

Ambwani, S., & Morey, L. C. (2015). Food consumption as affect modulation in borderline personality. *Journal of Personality Disorders, 29,* 261–274.

American Psychiatric Association. (2013). *Diagnostic and statistical manual of mental disorders* (5th ed.). Washington, DC: Author.

American Psychological Association. (2007). *APA dictionary of psychology.* Washington, DC: Author.

Amiot, C., & Bastian, B. (2015). Toward a psychology of human-animal relations. *Psychological Bulletin, 141,* 6–47.

Anastasi, A. (1988). *Psychological testing* (6th ed.). New York, NY: Macmillan.

Anderson, C., Hildreth, J. D. J., & Howland, L. (2015). Is the desire for status a fundamental human motive? A review of the empirical literature. *Psychological Bulletin, 141,* 574–601.

Anderson, C., & Kilduff, G. J. (2009). The pursuit of status in social groups. *Current Directions in Psychological Science, 18,* 295–298.

Anderson, J. L., Sellbom, M., Sansone, R. A., & Songer, D. A. (2015). Comparing external correlates of DSM-5 Section III and Section II dimensional trait operationalizations of borderline personality disorder. *Journal of Personality Disorders.* In press.

Anderson, M. (1994). *Sexual selection.* Princeton, NJ: Princeton University Press.

Angus, L. E., & McCloud, J. (Eds.). (2004). *The handbook of narrative and psychotherapy: Practice, theory, and research.* London, UK: Sage.

Ansbacher, H. L., & Ansbacher, R. R. (Eds.) (1956). *The individual psychology of Alfred Adler.* New York, NY: Basic Books.

Arend, R., Gove, F. L., & Sroufe, L. A. (1979). Continuity of individual adaptation from infancy to kindergarten: A predictive study of ego-resiliency and curiosity in preschoolers. *Child Development, 50,* 950–959.

Asendorpf, J. B. (2015). Person-centered approaches to personality. In M. Mikulincer & P. R. Shaver (Eds.), *APA handbook of personality and social psychology. Vol. 4: Personality processes and individual differences* (pp. 403–424). Washington, DC: American Psychological Association.

Asendorpf, J. B., Penke, L., & Back, M. D. (2011). From dating to mating and relating: Predictors of initial and long-term outcomes of speed dating in a community sample. *European Journal of Personality, 25,* 16–30.

Ashton, M. C., & Lee, K. (2001). Empirical, theoretical, and practical advantages of the HEXACO model of personality structure. *European Journal of Personality, 15,* 327–353.

Ashton, M. C., & Lee, K. (2005). Honesty-humility and the Big Five, and the Five-Factor Model. *Journal of Personality, 73,* 1321–1351.

Ashton, M. C., Lee, K., & deVries, R. E. (2014). The HEXACO honesty-humility, agreeableness, and emotionality factors: A review of research and theory. *Personality and Social Psychology Review, 18,* 139–152.

Atkinson, J. W., & Birch, D. (1978). *Introduction to motivation* (2nd ed.). New York, NY: Van Nostrand Reinhold.

Avey, J. B., Luthans, F., Hannah, S. T., Sweetman, D., & Peterson, C. (2012). Impact of employees character strengths of wisdom on stress and creative performance. *Human Resource Management Journal, 22,* 165–181.

Avinum, R., & Knafo, A. (2014). Parenting as a reaction evoked by children's genotype: A meta-analysis of children-as-twins studies. *Personality and Social Psychology Review, 20,* 87–102.

Ayearst, L. E., Flett, G. L., & Hewitt, P. L. (2012). Where is multidimensional perfectionism in DSM-5? A question posed to the DSM-5 personality and personality disorders work group. *Personality Disorder: Theory, Research, and Treatment, 3,* 458–469.

Baddeley, A. D. (1986). *Working memory.* New York, NY: Oxford University Press.

Bakan, D. (1966). *The duality of human existence.* Boston, MA: Beacon.

Baker, R. R., & Bellis, M. A. (1995). *Human sperm competition.* London, UK: Chapman and Hall.

Ball, S. A. (1995). The validity of the alternative five-factor measure of personality in cocaine abusers. *Psychological Assessment, 7,* 148–154.

Baltes, P. B., & Staudinger, U. M. (2000). Wisdom: A metaheuristic to orchestrate the mind and virtue toward excellence. *American Psychologist, 55,* 122–136.

Bandura, A. (1971). Psychotherapy based on modeling principles. In A. E. Bergin & S. L. Garfield (Eds.), *Handbook of psychotherapy and behavior change.* New York, NY: John Wiley.

Bandura, A. (1977). Self-efficacy: Toward a unifying theory of behavioral change. *Psychological Review, 84,* 191–215.

Bandura, A. (1986). *Social foundations of thought and action.* Englewood Cliffs, NJ: Prentice-Hall.

Bandura, A. (1989). Human agency in social cognitive theory. *American Psychologist, 44,* 1175–1184.

Bandura, A. (1997). *Self-efficacy: The exercise of control.* New York, NY: Freeman.

Bandura, A., & Huston, A. (1961). Identification as a process of incidental learning. *Journal of Abnormal and Social Psychology, 63,* 311–318.

Bandura, A., Ross, D., & Ross, S. A. (1961). Transmission of aggression through imitation of aggressive models. *Journal of Abnormal and Social Psychology, 63,* 575–582.

Bandura, A., Ross, D., & Ross, S. A. (1963). Imitation of film-mediated aggressive models. *Journal of Abnormal and Social Psychology, 66,* 3–11.

Bandura, A., & Walters, R. H. (1963). *Social learning and personality.* New York, NY: Holt, Rinehart & Winston.

Barber, B. K. (Ed.). (2002). *Intrusive parenting: How psychological control affects children and adolescents.* Washington, DC: American Psychological Association.

Bargh, J. A. (1982). Automatic information processing and social perception: The influence of trait information presented outside of conscious awareness on impression formation. *Journal of Personality and Social Psychology, 43,* 437–439.

Barrett, H. C., & Kurzban, R. (2006). Modularity in cognition: Framing the debate. *Psychological Review, 113,* 628–647.

Barry, C. T., Doucette, H., Loflin, D. C., Rivera-Hudson, N., & Herrington, L. L. (2015). "Let me take a selfie": Associations between self-photography, narcissism, and self-esteem. *Psychology of Popular Media Culture.* In press.

Barry, H., & Blane, H. T. (1977). Birth order of alcoholics. *Journal of Individual Psychology, 62,* 62–79.

Bartholomew, K., & Horowitz, L. M. (1991). Attachment styles among young adults: A test of a four-category model. *Journal of Personality and Social Psychology, 61,* 226–244.

Bates, J. E., Schermerhorn, A. C., & Petersen, I. T. (2012). Temperament and parenting in developmental perspective. In M. Zentner & R. L. Shiner (Eds.), *Handbook of temperament* (pp. 425–441). New York, NY: Guilford.

Bateson, M. C. (1990). *Composing a life.* New York, NY: Plume.

Bauer, J. J., & McAdams, D. P. (2010). Eudaimonic Growth: Narrative growth goals predict increases in ego development and subjective well-being 3 years later. *Developmental Psychology, 46,* 761–772.

Bauer, J. J., McAdams, D. P., & Sakaeda, A. R. (2005). Crystallization of desire and crystallization of discontent in narratives of life-changing decisions. *Journal of Personality, 73,* 1181–1213.

Baughman, H. M., Jonason, P. K., Lyons, M., & Vernon, P. A. (2014). Liar liar pants on fire: Cheater strategies linked to the Dark Triad. *Personality and Individual Differences, 71,* 35–38.

Baumeister, R. F. (1987). How the self became a problem: A psychological review of historical research. *Journal of Personality and Social Psychology, 52,* 163–176.

Baumeister, R. F., Bratslavsky, E., Muraven, M., & Tice, D. M. (1998). Ego depletion: Is the active self a limited resource? *Journal of Personality and Social Psychology, 74,* 1252–1265.

Baumeister, R. F., Campbell. J. D., Krueger, J. I., & Vohs, K. D. (2003). Does high self-esteem cause better performance, interpersonal success, happiness, or healthier lifestyles? *Psychological Science in the Public Interest, 4,* 1–44.

Baumeister, R. F., DeWall, C. N., Ciarocco, N. J., & Twenge, J. M. (2005). Social exclusion impairs self-regulation. *Journal of Personality and Social Psychology, 88,* 589–604.

Baumeister, R. F., Gailliot, DeWall, C. N., & Oaten, M. (2006). Self-regulation and personality: How interventions increase regulatory success, and how depletion moderates the effects of traits on behavior. *Journal of Personality, 74,* 1773–1801.

Baumeister, R. F., & Heatherton, T. F. (1996). Self-regulation failure: An overview. *Psychological Inquiry, 7,* 1–15.

Baumeister, R. F., Heatherton, T. F., & Tice, D. M. (1994). *Losing control: How and why people fail at self-regulation.* San Diego, CA: Academic Press.

Baumeister, R. F., & Leary, M. R. (1995). The need to belong: Desire for interpersonal attachments as a fundamental human motivation. *Psychological Bulletin, 117,* 497–529.

Baumeister, R. F., Smart, L., & Boden, J. M. (1996). Relation of threatened egotism to violence and aggression: The dark side of high self-esteem. *Psychological Review, 103,* 5–33.

Baumeister, R. F., Vohs, K., Aaker, J., & Garbinsky, E. (2013). Some key differences between a happy life and a meaningful life. *The Journal of Positive Psychology, 8,* 505–516.

Baumgardner, A. H. (1990). To know oneself is to like oneself: Self-certainty and self- affect. *Journal of Personality and Social Psychology, 58,* 1062–1072.

Baumrind, D. A. (1971). Current patterns of parental authority. *Developmental Psychology Monographs, 4* (1, Pt. 2).

Baumrind, D. (1972). Socialization and instrumental competence in young children. In W. W. Hartup (Ed.), The young child: Reviews of research (Vol. 2, pp. 202–224). Washington, DC: National Association for the Education of Young Children.

Baumrind, D. (1973). The development of instrumental competence through socialization. In A. D. Pick (Ed.), *Minnesota symposium on child psychology* (Vol. 7, pp. 3–46). Minneapolis: University of Minnesota Press.

Beck, A. T. (1976). *Cognitive therapy and the emotional disorders.* New York, NY: New American Library.

Beck, A. T. (1983). Cognitive therapy of depression: New approaches. In P. Clayton & J. Barrett (Eds.), *Treatment of depression: Old and new approaches* (pp. 265–290). New York, NY: Raven Press.

Beck, A. T. (1984). Cognitive approaches to stress. In R. Wooford & P. Lehrer (Eds.), *Principles and practice of stress management.* New York, NY: Guilford.

Beck, L. A., Pietromonaco, P. R., DeBuse, C. J., Powers, S. I., & Sayer, A. G. (2013). Spouses' attachment pairings predict neuroendocrine, behavioral, and psychological responses to marital conflict. *Journal of Personality and Social Psychology, 105,* 388–424.

Beeney, J. E., Levy, K. N., Gatzke-Kopp, L. M., & Hallquist, M. N. (2014). EEG asymmetry in borderline personality disorder and depression following rejection. *Personality Disorders: Theory, Research, and Treatment, 5,* 178–185.

Bell, J. E. (1948). *Projective techniques.* New York, NY: Longmans, Green.

Bell, R. Q. (1968). A reinterpretation of the direction of effects in studies of socialization. *Psychological Review, 75,* 81–95.

Belsky, J. (1999). Modern evolutionary theory and patterns of attachment. In J. Cassidy & P. R. Shaver (Eds.), *Handbook of attachment: Theory, research, and clinical applications* (pp. 141–161). New York, NY: Guilford.

Belsky, J., Fish, M., & Isabella, R. A. (1991). Continuity and discontinuity in infant negative and positive emotionality: Family antecedents and attachment consequences. *Developmental Psychology, 27,* 421–431.

Belsky, J., Steinberg, L., & Draper, P. (1991). Childhood experience, interpersonal development, and reproductive strategy: An evolutionary theory of socialization. *Child Development, 62,* 647–670.

Bem, S. L. (1981). Gender schema theory: A cognitive account of sex-typing. *Psychological Review, 88,* 354–364.

Bem, S. L. (1985). Androgyny and gender schema theory: A conceptual and empirical investigation. In T. B. Sonderegger (Ed.), *Nebraska symposium on motivation, 1984: Psychology and gender.* Lincoln: University of Nebraska Press.

Bennett, R. J., & Robinson, S. L. (2000). Development of a measure of workplace deviance. *Journal of Applied Psychology, 85,* 349–360.

Ben-Porath, Y. S. (2012). *Interpreting the MMPI-2-RF.* Minneapolis: University of Minnesota Press.

Berg, A. I., & Johansson, B. (2014). Personality change in the oldest old: Is it a matter of compromised health and functioning? *Journal of Personality, 82,* 25–31.

Berg, J., Dickhaut, J., & McCabe, K. (1995). Trust, reciprocity, and social history. *Games and Economic Behavior, 10,* 122–142.

Berg, V., Lummaa, V., Lahdenpera, M., Rotkirch, A., & Jokela, M. (2014). Personality and long-term reproductive success measured by the number of grandchildren. *Evolution and Human Behavior, 35,* 533–539.

Bergman, S. M., Fearington, E., Davenport, S. W., & Bergman, J. Z. (2011). Millennials, narcissism, and social networking: What narcissists do on social networking sites and why. *Personality and Individual Differences, 50,* 706–711.

Berlin, L. J., & Cassidy, J. (2003). Mothers' self-reported control of their preschool children's emotional expressiveness: A longitudinal study of associations with infant-mother attachment and children's emotional regulation. *Social Development, 12,* 477–495.

Berlin, L. J., Cassidy, J., & Appleyard, K. (2008). The influence of early attachment on other relationships. In J. Cassidy & P. R. Shaver (Eds.), *Handbook of attachment: Theory, research, and clinical applications* (2nd ed., pp. 333–347). New York, NY: Guilford.

Bernier, A., Beauchamp, M. H., Carlson, S. M., & Lalonde, G. (2015). A secure base from which to regulate: Attachment security in toddlerhood as a predictor of executive functioning at school entry. *Developmental Psychology, 51,* 1177–1189.

Berreby, D. (2005). *Us and them: Understanding your tribal mind.* New York, NY: Little, Brown.

Berscheid, E. (2010). Love in the fourth dimension. *Annual Review of Psychology, 61,* 1–25.

Berscheid, E., & Hatfield, E. (1974). A little bit about love. In T. L. Huston (Ed.), *Foundations of interpersonal attraction* (pp. 157–215). New York, NY: Academic Press.

Berzonsky, M. D. (1992). Identity style and coping strategies. *Journal of Personality, 60,* 771–788.

Betzig, L. (1993). Sex, succession, and stratification in the first six civilizations. In L. Ellis (Ed.), *Social stratification and socioeconomic inequality* (pp. 37–74). Westport, CT: Praeger.

Bishop, S. R. (2002). What do we really know about mindfulness-based stress reduction? *Psychosomatic Medicine, 64,* 71–84.

Bjorklund, D. F., & Kipp, K. (1996). Parental investment theory and gender differences in the evolution of inhibition mechanisms. *Psychological Bulletin, 120,* 163–188.

Blackwell, L. S., Trzesniewski, K. H., & Dweck, C. S. (2007). Implicit theories of intelligence predict achievement across an adolescent transition: A longitudinal study and an intervention. *Child Development, 78,* 246–263.

Blanchard, D. C., Sakai, R. R., McEwen, B., Weiss, S. M., & Blanchard, R. J. (1993). Subordination stress: Behavioral, brain, and neuroendocrine correlates. *Behavioural Brain Research, 58,* 113–121.

Blanck, G., & Blanck, R. (1974). *Ego psychology: Theory and practice.* New York, NY: Columbia University Press.

Blease, C. R. (2015). Too many "friends," too few "likes,"? Evolutionary psychology and "Facebook" depression. *Review of General Psychology, 19,* 1–13.

Bleidorn, W., Kandler, C., Hulsheger, U. R., Riemann, R., Angleitner, A., & Spinath, F. M. (2010). Nature and nurture and the interplay between personality traits and major life goals. *Journal of Personality and Social Psychology, 99,* 366–379.

Block, J. (1971). *Lives through time.* Berkeley, CA: Bancroft Books.

Block, J. (1993). Studying personality the long way. In D. C. Funder, R. D. Parke, C. Tomlinson-Keasy, & K. Widaman (Eds.), *Studying lives through time: Personality and development* (pp. 9–41). Washington, DC: American Psychological Association.

Block, J. (1995). A contrarian view of the five-factor approach to personality description. *Psychological Bulletin, 117,* 187–215.

Block, J. H., & Block, J. (1980). The role of ego-control and ego-resiliency in the organization of behavior. In W. A. Collins (Ed.), *Minnesota symposia on child psychology* (Vol. 13, pp. 39–101). Hillsdale, NJ: Lawrence Erlbaum.

Blum, G. S. (1953). Psychoanalytic theories of personality. New York, NY: McGraw-Hill.

Bogg, T., & Roberts, B. W. (2004). Conscientiousness and health-related behaviors: A meta-analysis of the leading behavioral contributors to mortality. *Psychological Bulletin, 130,* 887–919.

Bokek-Cohen, Y., Peres, Y., & Kanazawa, S. (2007). Rational choice and evolutionary psychology as explanations for mate selectivity. *Journal of Social, Evolutionary, and Cultural Psychology, 2,* 42–55.

Bokenberger, K., Pedersen, Gatz, M., & Dahl, A. K. (2014). The type A behavior pattern and cardiovascular disease as predictors of dementia. *Health Psychology, 33,* 1593–1601.

Bolger, N. (1990). Coping as a personality process: A prospective study. *Journal of Personality and Social Psychology, 59,* 525–537.

Bolger, N., DeLongis, A., Kessler, R. C., & Wethington, E. (1989). The contagion of stress across multiple roles. *Journal of Marriage and the Family, 51,* 175–183.

Bolger, N., & Schilling, E. A. (1991). Personality and the problems of everyday life: The role of neuroticism in exposure and reactivity to daily stressors. *Journal of Personality, 59,* 355–386.

Bolle, F. (1998). Rewarding trust: An experimental study. *Theory and Decision, 45,* 83–98.

Bonnefon, J.-F., Hopfensitz, A., & DeNeys, W. (2013). The modular nature of trustworthiness detection. *Journal of Experimental Psychology: General, 142,* 143–150.

Booth-LaForce, C., & Kernis, K. A. (2009). Child-parent attachment relationships, peer relationships, and peer-group functioning. In K. H. Rubin, W. Bukowski, & B. Laursen (Eds.), *Handbook of peer interactions, relationships, and groups* (pp. 490–507). New York, NY: Guilford.

Bornovalova, M. A., Hicks, B. M., Iacono, W. G., & McGue, M. (2013). Longitudinal twin study of borderline personality disorder traits and substance use in adolescence: Developmental change, reciprocal effects, and genetic and environmental influences. *Personality Disorders: Theory, Research, and Treatment, 4,* 23–32.

Bornstein, M. H. (2014). Human infancy . . . and the rest of the lifespan. *Annual Review of Psychology, 65,* 121–158.

Bornstein, R. F., & Cecero, J. J. (2000). Deconstructing dependency in a five-factor world: A meta-analytic review. *Journal of Personality Assessment, 74,* 324–343.

Bouchard, T. J. Jr. (1997). Experience producing drive theory: How genes drive experience and shape personality. *Acta Paediatrica Supplement, 422,* 60–64.

Bouchard, T. J. Jr., & Loehlin, J. C. (2001). Genes, evolution, and personality. *Behavior Genetics, 31,* 243–273.

Bouchard, T. J., Jr., Lykken, D. T., McGue, M., Segal, N. L., & Tellegen, A. (1990). Sources of human psychological differences: The Minnesota Study of Twins Reared Apart. *Science, 250,* 223–228.

Bowers, K. S. (1973). Situationism in psychology: An analysis and critique. *Psychological Review, 80,* 307–336.

Bowlby, J. (1969/1982). *Attachment.* New York, NY: Basic Books.

Bowlby, J. (1973). *Separation: Anxiety and anger.* New York, NY: Basic Books.

Bowlby, J. (1979). *The making and breaking of affectional bonds.* London, UK: Tavistock/Routledge.

Bowlby, J. (1980). *Loss: Sadness and depression.* New York, NY: Basic Books.

Bowlby, J. (1982). *Attachment* (2nd ed.). New York, NY: Basic Books.

Bowlby, J. (1988). *A secure base: Parent-child attachment and healthy human development.* New York, NY: Basic Books.

Boyce, C. J., Wood, A. M., Daly, M., & Sedikides, C. (2015). Personality change following unemployment. *Journal of Applied Psychology.* In press.

Bradley, S. J., Oliver, G. D., Chernick, A. B., & Zucker, K. J. (1998). Experiment of nurture: Ablatio penis at 2 months, sex reassignment at 7 months, and a psychosexual follow-up in young adulthood. *Pediatrics, 102,* 1–5.

Brebner, J. (2003). Gender and emotions. *Personality and Individual Differences, 34,* 387–394.

Brennan, K. A, Clark, C. L., & Shaver, P. R. (1998). Self-report measurement of adult attachment. In J. A. Simpson & W. Steven Rholes (Eds.), *Attachment theory and close relationships* (pp. 46–76). New York, NY: Guilford.

Bretherton, I. (1990). Open communication and internal working models: Their role in the development of attachment relationships. In R. Thompson (Ed.), *Nebraska Symposium on Motivation: Vol. 36. Socioemotional development* (pp. 57–113). Lincoln: University of Nebraska Press.

Bretherton, I. (1991). Pouring new wine into old bottles: The social self as internal working model. In M. R. Gunnar & L. A. Sroufe (Eds.), *Self processes and development* (pp. 1–41). Hillsdale, NJ: Erlbaum.

Bretherton, I. (1992). The origins of attachment theory: John Bowlby and Mary Ainsworth. *Developmental Psychology, 28,* 759–775.

Bretherton, I., & Munholland, K. A. (2008). Internal working models in attachment relationships. In J. Cassidy & P. R. Shaver (Eds.), *Handbook of attachment* (2nd ed., pp. 102–127). New York, NY: Guilford.

Breuer, J., & Freud, S. (1895). *Studies on hysteria.* (Collected Works, Vol. II). London, UK: Hogarth.

Brewer, M. B., & Caporael, L. R. (2006). An evolutionary perspective on social identity: Revisiting groups. In M. Schaller, J. H. Simpson, & D. T. Kenrick (Eds.), *Evolution and social psychology* (pp. 143–162). New York, NY: Psychology Press.

Breznitz, S. (Ed.) (1983). *The denial of stress.* New York, NY: International Universities Press.

Bronfenbrenner, U. (1979). *The ecology of human development.* Cambridge, MA: Harvard University Press.

Brose, A., Schmiedek, F., Lovden, M., & Lindenberger, U. (2012). Daily variability in working memory is coupled with negative affect: The role of attention and motivation. *Emotion, 12,* 605–617.

Brown, D. E. (1991). *Human universals.* Philadelphia, PA: Temple University Press.

Brown, G. L., Mangelsdorf, S. C., & Neff, C. (2012). Father involvement, paternal sensitivity, and father–child attachment security in the first 3 years. *Journal of Family Psychology, 26,* 421–430.

Browne, J. (1995). *Charles Darwin: Voyaging.* Princeton, NJ: Princeton University Press.

Bruch, H. (1973). *Eating disorders.* New York, NY: Basic Books.

Bruehlman-Senecal, E., & Ayduk, O. (2015). This too shall pass: Temporal distance and the regulation of emotional distress. *Journal of Personality and Social Psychology, 108,* 356–375.

Buber, M. (1970). *I and thou.* New York, NY: Scribner.

Bue, S. L., Taverniers, J., Euwema, M., & Mylle, J. (2013). Hardiness promotes work engagement, prevents burnout, and moderates their relationship. *Military Psychology, 25,* 105–115.

Buelow, M. T., Okdie, B. M., Brunell, A. B., & Trost, Z. (2015). Stuck in a moment and you can't get out of it: The lingering effects of ostracism on cognition and satisfaction with basic needs. *Personality and Individual Differences, 76,* 39–43.

Buhrmester, M. D., Fraser, W. T., Lanman, J. A., Whitehouse, H., & Swann, W. B. (2015). When terror hits home: Identity fused Americans who saw Boston bombing victims as "family" provided aid. *Self & Identity, 14,* 253–270.

Burnstein, E. (2005). Altruism and genetic relatedness. In D. M. Buss (Ed.), *The handbook of evolutionary psychology* (pp. 528–551). Hoboken, NJ: Wiley.

Busch, H., & Hofer, J. (2012). Self-regulation and milestones of adult development. *Developmental Psychology, 48,* 282–299.

Bushman, B. J., & Baumeister, R. F. (1998). Threatened egotism, narcissism, self-esteem, and direct and displaced aggression: Does self-love or self-hate lead to violence? *Journal of Personality and Social Psychology, 75,* 219–229.

Buss, A. (1979). The trait-situation controversy and the concept of interaction. *Personality and Social Psychology Bulletin, 5,* 191–195.

Buss, D. M. (1995). Psychological sex differences: Origins through sexual selection. *American Psychologist, 50,* 164–168.

Buss, D. M. (2008). Human nature and individual differences: Evolution of human personality. In O. P. John, R. W. Robins, & L. A. Pervin (Eds.), *Handbook of personality: Theory and research* (3rd ed., pp. 29–60). New York, NY: Guilford.

Buss, D. M. (2012). *Evolutionary psychology: The new science of mind* (4th ed.). Boston, MA: Allyn & Bacon.

Buss, D. M., Abbott, M., Angleitner, A., Asherian, A., Biaggio, A., and 45 other coauthors. (1990). International preferences in selecting mates: A study of 37 cultures. *Journal of Cross-Cultural Psychology, 21,* 5–47.

Buss, D. M., & Greiling, H. (1999). Adaptive individual differences. *Journal of Personality, 67,* 209–243.

Buss, D. M., & Penke, L. (2015). Evolutionary personality psychology. In M. Mikulincer & P. R. Shaver (Eds.). *APA handbook of personality and social psychology* (Vol. 4, pp. 3–29). Washington, DC: American Psychological Association.

Buss, D. M., & Schmitt, D. (1993). Sexual strategies theory: An evolutionary perspective on human mating. *Psychological Review, 100,* 204–232.

Buss, D. M., Shackelford, T. K., Kirkpatrick, L. A., & Larsen, R. J. (2001). A half century of American mate preferences. *Journal of Marriage and the Family, 63,* 491–503.

Bussey, K., & Bandura, A. (1984). Influence of gender constancy and social power on sex- linked modeling. *Journal of Personality and Social Psychology, 47,* 1292–1304.

Bussey, K., & Bandura, A. (1999). Social cognitive theory of gender development and differentiation. *Psychological Review, 106,* 676–713.

Bussey, K., & Perry, D. G. (1982). Same-sex imitation: The avoidance of cross-sex models or the acceptance of same-sex models. *Sex Roles, 8,* 773–784.

Butler, J. M., & Haigh, G. V. (1954). Changes in the relation between self-concepts and ideal concepts, consequent upon client-centered counseling. In C. R. Rogers & R. F. Diamond (Eds.), *Psychotherapy and personality change* (pp. 55–75). Chicago, IL: University of Chicago Press.

Button, T. M. M., Corley, R. P., Rhee, S. H., Hewitt, J. K., Young, S. E., & Stallings, M. C. (2007). Delinquent peer affiliation and conduct problems: A twin study. *Journal of Abnormal Psychology, 116,* 554–564.

Byrne, D. (1971). *The attraction paradigm.* New York, NY: Academic Press.

Byrnes, J. P., Miller, D., & Schafer, W. D. (1999). Gender differences in risk-taking: A review. *Psychological Bulletin, 125,* 367–385.

Cacioppo, J. T., Hawkley, & Thisted, R. A. (2010). Perceived social isolation makes me sad: 5-year cross-lagged analyses of loneliness and depressive symptomatology in the Chicago Health, Aging, and Social Relations Study. *Psychology and Aging, 25,* 453–463.

Cacioppo, S., Capitanio, J. P., & Cacioppo, J. T. (2014). Toward a neurology of loneliness. *Psychological Bulletin, 140,* 1464–1504.

Camera, W. J., Nathan, J. S., & Puente, A. E. (2000). Psychological test usage: Implications in professional psychology. *Professional Psychology: Research and Practice, 31,* 141–154.

Campbell, D. T., & Fiske, D. W. (1959). Convergent and discriminant validation by the multitrait-multimethod matrix. *Psychological Bulletin, 56,* 81–105.

Campbell, J. D. (1990). Self-esteem and clarity of the self-concept. *Journal of Personality and Social Psychology, 59,* 538–549.

Campbell, W. K., & Miller, J. D. (2013). Narcissistic personality disorder and the Five-Factor Model: Delineating narcissistic personality disorder, grandiose narcissism, and vulnerable narcissism. In T. A. Widiger & P. T. Costa Jr. (Eds.), *Personality disorders and the Five-Factor Model of personality* (3rd ed., pp. 133–145). Washington, DC: American Psychological Association.

Canli, T. (2008). Toward a "molecular psychology" of personality. In O. P. John, R. W. Robins, & L. A. Pervin (Eds.), *Handbook of personality: Theory and method* (3rd ed., pp. 311–327). New York, NY: Guilford.

Cantor, N., Acker, M., & Cook-Flanagan, C. (1992). Conflict and preoccupation in the intimacy life task. *Journal of Personality and Social Psychology, 63,* 644–655.

Cantor, N., & Kihlstrom, J. F. (1987). *Personality and social intelligence.* Englewood Cliffs, NJ: Prentice-Hall.

Capitanio, J. P., Mendoza, S. P., & Baroncelli, S. (1999). The relationship of personality dimensions in adult male rhesus macaques to progression of simian immunodeficiency virus disease. *Brain, Behavior, and Immunity, 13,* 138–154.

Carlson, E. A. (1998). A prospective longitudinal study of disorganized/disoriented attachment. *Child Development, 69,* 1107–1128.

Carlson, E. N., Vazire, S., & Oltmanns, T. F. (2011). You probably think this paper's about you: Social perceptions of a narcissist. *Journal of Personality and Social Psychology, 101,* 185–201.

Carlson, R. (1988). Exemplary lives: The uses of psychobiography for theory development. *Journal of Personality, 56,* 105–138.

Carlson, V., Cicchetti, D., Barnett, D., & Brunwald, K. (1989). Disorganized/disoriented attachment relationships in maltreated infants. *Developmental Psychology, 25,* 525–531.

Carlsson, J. C., Wangqvist, M., & Frisen, A. (2015). Identity development in the late twenties: A never ending story. *Developmental Psychology, 51,* 334–345.

Carnelley, K. B., Pietromonaco, P. R., & Jaffe, K. (1994). Depression, working models of others, and relationship functioning. *Journal of Personality and Social Psychology, 66,* 127–140.

Carney, D. R., Hall, J. A., & Smith LeBeau, L. (2005). Beliefs about the nonverbal expression of social power. *Journal of Nonverbal Behavior, 29,* 105–123.

Carver, C. S., & Connor-Smith, J. (2010). Personality and coping. *Annual Review of Psychology, 61,* 679–704.

Carver, C. S., Johnson, S. L., & Joorman, J. (2008). Serotonergic function, two-mode models of self-regulation, and vulnerability to depression: What depression has in common with impulsive aggression. *Psychological Bulletin, 134,* 912–943.

Carver, C. S., & Scheier, M. F. (1981). *Attention and self-regulation: A control-theory approach to human behavior.* New York, NY: Springer-Verlag.

Carver, C. S., & Scheier, M. F. (1990a). Origins and functions of positive and negative affect: A control-process view. *Psychological Review, 97,* 19–35.

Carver, C. S., & Scheier, M. F. (1990b). Principles of self-regulation: Action and emotion. In E. T. Higgins & R. M. Sorrentino (Eds.), *Handbook of motivation and cognition* (Vol. 2, pp. 3–52). New York, NY: Guilford.

Carver, C. S., & Scheier, M. F. (1994). Situational coping and coping dispositions in a stressful transaction. *Journal of Personality and Social Psychology, 66,* 184–195.

Carver, C. S., & Scheier, M. F. (1998). *On the self-regulation of behavior.* New York, NY: Cambridge University Press.

Carver, C. S., & Scheier, M. F. (2009). Optimism. In M. R. Leary & R. H. Hoyle (Eds.), *Handbook of individual differences in social behavior* (pp. 330–342). New York, NY: Guilford.

Casey, B. J. (2015). Beyond simple models of self-control to circuit-based accounts of adolescent behavior. *Annual Review of Psychology, 66,* 295–319.

Caspi, A. (1998). Personality development across the life course. In N. Eisenberg (Ed.), *Handbook of child psychology* (5th ed., Vol. 3, pp. 311–388). New York, NY: Wiley.

Caspi, A., & Bem, D. J. (1990). Personality continuity and change over the life course. In L. A. Pervin (Ed.), *Handbook of personality* (pp. 549–575). New York, NY: Guilford.

Caspi, A., Bem, D. J., & Elder, G. H. Jr. (1989). Continuities and consequences of interactional styles across the life course. *Journal of Personality, 57,* 375–406.

Caspi, A., Elder, G. H. Jr., & Bem, D. J. (1987). Moving against the world: Life-course patterns of explosive children. *Developmental Psychology, 23,* 308–313.

Caspi, A., Elder, G. H. Jr., & Bem, D. J. (1988). Moving away from the world: Life-course patterns of shy children. *Developmental Psychology, 24,* 824–831.

Caspi, A., Roberts, B. W., & Shiner, R. (2005). Personality development: Stability and change. *Annual Review of Psychology, 56,* 453–484.

Caspi, A., & Shiner, R. L. (2006). Personality development. In N. Eisenberg (Ed.). *Handbook of child psychology* (6th ed., Vol. 3, pp. 300–365). Hoboken, NJ: Wiley.

Cassidy, J., Ziv, Y., Mehta, T. G., & Feeney, B. C. (2003). Feedback seeking in children and adolescents: Associations with self-perceptions, attachment representations, and depression. *Child Development, 74,* 612–628.

Cattell, R. B. (1965). *The scientific analysis of personality.* Chicago, IL: Aldine.

Cattell, R. J. (1957). *Personality and motivation structure and measurement.* New York, NY: World Book.

Centorrino, S., Djemai, E., Hopfensitz, A., Millinski, M., & Seabright, P. (2015). Honest signaling in trust interactions: smiles rated as genuine induce trust and signal higher earning opportunities. *Evolution and Human Behavior, 36,* 8–16.

Cerasoli, C. P., Nicklin, J. M., & Ford, M. T. (2014). Intrinsic and extrinsic incentives jointly predict performance: A 40-year meta-analysis. *Psychological Bulletin, 140,* 980–1008.

Champoux, M., Bennett, A., Shannon, C., Higley, J. D., Lesch, K. P., & Suomi, S. J. (2002). Serotonin transporter gene polymorphism, differential early rearing, and behavior in rhesus monkey neonates. *Molecular Psychiatry, 7,* 1058–1063.

Chaplin, T. M., & Aldao, A. (2013). Gender differences in emotion expression in children: A meta-analytic review. *Psychological Bulletin, 139,* 735–765.

Chaplin, W. F. (2007). Moderator and mediator models in personality research. In R. W. Robins, R. C. Fraley, & R. F. Krueger (Eds.), *Handbook of research methods in personality psychology* (pp. 602–632). New York, NY: Guilford.

Charnov, E. (1982). *The theory of sex allocation.* Princeton, NJ: Princeton University Press.

Charnov, E. (1993). *Life history invariants.* New York, NY: Oxford University Press.

Chemerinski, E., Triebwasser, J., Roussos, P., & Siever, L. J. (2013). Schizotypal personality disorder. *Journal of Personality Disorders, 27,* 652–679.

Chen, C., Hewitt, P. L., & Flett, G. L. (2015). Preoccupied attachment, need to belong, shame, and interpersonal perfectionism: An investigation of the Perfectionism Social Disconnection Model. *Personality and Individual Differences, 76,* 177–182.

Chen, C., Hewitt, P. L., Flett, G. L., Birch, S., Cassels, T. G., & Blasberg, J. S. (2012). Insecure attachment, perfectionistic self-presentation, and social disconnection in adolescents. *Personality and Individual Differences, 52,* 936–941.

Chen, S., Chen, K. Y., & Shaw, L. (2004). Self-verification motives at the collective level of self-definition. *Journal of Personality and Social Psychology, 86,* 77–94.

Cheng, J. T., Tracy, J. L., & Henrich, J. (2010). Pride, personality, and the evolutionary foundations of human society. *Evolution and Human Behavior, 31,* 334–337.

Cheung, F., & Miu-Chi Lin, V. (2015). Emotional labor and occupational well-being: A latent profile analytic approach. *Journal of Individual Differences, 36,* 30–37.

Chida, Y., & Hamer, M. (2008). Chronic psychosocial factors and acute physiological responses to laboratory-induced stress in healthy populations: A quantitative review of 30 years of investigations. *Psychological Bulletin, 134,* 829–855.

Chiu, M. M. (2007). Families, economies, cultures, and scientific achievement in 41 countries: Country-, school-, and student-level analysis. *Journal of Family Psychology, 21,* 510–519.

Chmielewski, M., Bagby, M., Markon, K., Ring, A. J., & Ryder, A. G. (2014). Openness to experience, intellect, schizotypal personality disorder, and psychoticism: Resolving the controversy. *Journal of Personality Disorders, 28,* 483–499.

Christiansen, P., Cole, J. C., & Field, M. (2012). Ego depletion increases ad-lib alcohol consumption: Investigating cognitive mediators and moderators. *Experimental and Clinical Psychopharmacology, 20,* 118–128.

Christie, R., & Geis, F. L. (1970). *Studies in Machiavellianism.* New York, NY: Academic Press.

Clark, D. A., & Beck, A. T. (1989). Cognitive theory and therapy of anxiety and depression. In P. C. Kendall & D. Watson (Eds.), *Anxiety and depression: Distinctive and overlapping features* (pp. 379–411). San Diego, CA: Academic Press.

Clark, L. A. (1990). Toward a consensual set of symptom clusters for assessment of personality disorders. In J. N. Butcher & C. D. Spielberger (Eds.), *Advances in personality assessment* (Vol. 8, pp. 243–266). Hillsdale, NJ: Erlbaum.

Clark, L. A. (2007). Assessment and diagnosis of personality disorder: Perennial issues and an emerging reconceptualization. *Annual Review of Psychology, 58,* 227–257.

Clark, L. A., & Watson, D. (2008). Temperament: An organizing paradigm for trait psychology. In O. P. John, R. W. Robins, & L. A. Pervin (Eds.), *Handbook of personality: Theory and research* (3rd ed., pp. 265–286). New York, NY: Guilford.

Clark, R. W. (1980). *Freud: The man and the cause.* New York, NY: Random House.

Claypool, H. M., & Bernstein, M. J. (2014). Social exclusion and stereotyping: Why and when exclusion fosters individuation of others. *Journal of Personality and Social Psychology, 106,* 571–589.

Cloninger, C. R. (2006). Differentiating personality deviance, normality, and well-being by the seven-factor psychobiological model. In S. Strack (Ed.), *Differentiating normal and abnormal personality* (pp. 65–81). New York, NY: Springer.

Coan, J. A. (2008). Toward a neuroscience of attachment. In J. Cassidy & P. R. Shaver (Eds.), *Handbook of attachment* (2nd ed., pp. 241–265). New York, NY: Guilford.

Cofta-Woerpel, L., McClure, J. B., Li, Y., Urbauer, D., Cinciripini, P. M., & Wetter, D. W. (2011). Early cessation success or failure among women attempting to quit smoking: Trajectories and volatility of urge and negative mood during the first postcessation week. *Journal of Abnormal Psychology, 120,* 596–606.

Cohen, C. R., Chartrand, J. M., & Jowdy, D. P. (1995). Relationships between career indecision subtypes and ego identity development. *Journal of Counseling Psychology, 42,* 440–447.

Cohen, T. R., Panter, A. T., Turan, N., Morse, L., & Kim, Y. (2014). Moral character in the workplace. *Journal of Personality and Social Psychology, 107,* 943–963.

Cole, E., & Stewart, A. J. (1996). Meanings of political participation among Black and White women: Political identity and social responsibility. *Journal of Personality and Social Psychology, 71,* 130–140.

Collins, N. L., & Feeney, B. C. (2004). Working models of attachment shape perception of social support: Evidence from experimental and observational studies. *Journal of Personality and Social Psychology, 87,* 363–383.

Collins, N. L., & Read, S. J. (1990). Adult attachment, working models, and relationship quality in dating couples. *Journal of Personality and Social Psychology, 58,* 644–663.

Collins, W. A., & Steinberg, L. (2006). Adolescent development in interpersonal context. In N. Eisenberg (Ed.), *Handbook of child psychology: Vol. 3. Social, emotional, and personality development* (6th ed., pp. 1003–1067). Hoboken, NJ: Wiley.

Conley, J. J. (1984). Longitudinal consistency of adult personality: Self-reported psychological characteristics across 45 years. *Journal of Personality and Social Psychology, 47,* 1325–1333.

Connor, T. S., Barrett, L. F., Tugade, M. M., & Tennen, H. (2007). Idiographic personality: The theory and practice of experience sampling. In R. W. Robins, R. C. Fraley, & R. F. Krueger (Eds.), *Handbook of research methods in personality psychology* (pp. 79–96). New York, NY: Guilford.

Connor-Smith, J. K., & Flachsbart, C. (2007). Relations between personality and coping: A meta-analysis. *Journal of Personality and Social Psychology, 93,* 1080–1107.

Constantinople, A. (1969). An Eriksonian measure of personality development in college students. *Developmental Psychology, 1,* 357–372.

Conway, M. A., & Holmes, A. (2004). Psychosocial stages and the accessibility of autobiographical memories across the life cycle. *Journal of Personality, 72,* 461–480.

Cook, R., Bird, G., Catmur, C., Press, C., & Heyes, C. (2014). Mirror neurons: From origin to function. *Behavioral and Brain Sciences, 37,* 177–192.

Coolidge, F. L., Thede, L. L., & Young, S. E. (2002). The heritability of gender identity disorder in a child and adolescent twin sample. *Behavior Genetics, 32,* 251–257.

Cooper, L. D., Balsis, S., & Oltmanns, T. F. (2014). A longitudinal analysis of personality disorder dimensions and personality traits in a community sample of older adults: Perspectives from selves and informants. *Journal of Personality Disorders, 28,* 151–165.

Cooper, M. L. (2010). Toward a person x situation model of sexual risk-taking behaviors: Illuminating the conditional effects of traits across sexual situations and relationship contexts. *Journal of Personality and Social Psychology, 98,* 319–341.

Copping, L. T., & Campbell, A. (2015). The environment and life history strategies: Neighborhood and individual-level models. *Evolution and Human Behavior, 36,* 182–190.

Cosmides, L. (1989). The logic of social exchange: Has natural selection shaped how humans reason? Studies with the Wason selection task. *Cognition, 31,* 187–276.

Cosmides, L., & Tooby, J. (2005). Neurocognitive adaptations designed for social exchange. In D. M. Buss (Ed.), *The handbook of evolutionary psychology* (pp. 584–627). Hoboken, NJ: Wiley.

Cosmides, L., & Tooby, J. (2013). Evolutionary psychology: New perspectives on cognition and motivation. *Annual Review of Psychology, 64,* 201–229.

Costa, P. T. Jr., & McCrae, R. R. (1992a). *Revised NEO Personality Inventory (NEO PI-R) and NEO Five-Factor Inventory (NEO-FFI) professional manual.* Odessa, FL: Psychological Assessment Resources.

Costa, P. T. Jr., & McCrae, R. R. (1992b). Trait psychology comes of age. In T. B. Sonderegger (Ed.). *Nebraska symposium on motivation: Psychology and aging* (pp. 169–204). Lincoln: University of Nebraska Press.

Costa, P. T. Jr., & McCrae, R. R. (1994). Set like plaster? Evidence for the stability of adult personality. In T. F. Heatherton & J. L. Weinberger (Eds.), *Can personality change?* (pp. 21–40). Washington, DC: American Psychological Association.

Cottrell, C. A., & Neuberg, S. L. (2005). Different emotional reactions to different groups: A sociofunctional threat-based approach to "prejudice." *Journal of Personality and Social Psychology, 88,* 770–789.

Covington, M. V. (1989). Self-esteem and failure in school: Analysis and policy implications. In A. M. Mecca, N. J. Smelser, & J. Vasconcellos (Eds.), *The social importance of self-esteem* (pp. 72–124). Berkeley: University of California Press.

Cox, K., & McAdams, D. P. (2014). Meaning making during high and low point life story episodes predicts emotion regulation two years later: How the past informs the future. *Journal of Research in Personality, 50,* 66–70.

Coyne, J. A. (2009). *Why evolution is true.* New York, NY: Penguin Books.

Cramer, P. (1998). Coping and defense mechanisms: What's the difference? *Journal of Personality, 66,* 919–946.

Cramer, P. (2006). *Protecting the self: Defense mechanisms in action.* New York, NY: Guilford.

Creasy, G. (2002). Associations between working models of attachment and conflict management behavior in romantic couples. *Journal of Counseling Psychology, 49,* 365–375.

Crego, C., Gore, W. L., Rojas, S. L., & Widiger, T. A. (2015). The discriminant (and convergent) validity of the personality inventory for DSM-5. *Personality Disorders: Theory, Research, and Treatment.* In press.

Crews, F. (1995). *The memory wars: Freud's legacy in dispute.* New York: The New York Review of Books.

Crittenden, P. M., & Ainsworth, M. D. S. (1989). Child maltreatment and attachment theory. In D. Cicchetti & V. Carlson (Eds.) Child maltreatment (pp. 432–463). New York, NY: Cambridge University Press.

Crockenberg, S., & Litman, C. (1990). Autonomy as competence in 2-year-olds: Maternal correlates of child defiance, compliance, and self-assertion. *Developmental Psychology, 26,* 961–971.

Cronbach. L. J. (1951). Coefficient alpha and the internal structure of traits. *Psychometrika, 16,* 297–334.

Cronbach, L. J., & Furby, L. (1970). How should we measure "change?"—Or should we? *Psychological Bulletin, 74,* 68–80

Cronbach, L. J., & Meehl, P. E. (1955). Construct validity in psychological tests. *Psychological Bulletin, 52,* 281–302.

Crooks, T. J. (1988). The impact of classroom evaluation practices on students. *Review of Educational Research, 58,* 438–481.

Crouter, A. C., & Head, M. R. (2002). Parental monitoring and knowledge of children. In M. H. Bornstein (Ed.), *Handbook of parenting: Vol. 3. Being and becoming a parent* (pp. 461–483). Mahwah, NJ: Erlbaum.

Crowell, J. A., Treboux, D., & Waters, E. (2002). Stability of attachment representations: The transition to marriage. *Developmental Psychology, 38,* 467–479.

Cullen, D. (2009). *Columbine.* New York, NY: Twelve.

Cummins, D. D. (1999). Cheater detection is modified by social rank: The impact of dominance on the evolution of cognitive functions. *Evolution and Human Behavior, 20,* 229–248.

Cummins, D. D. (2005). Dominance, status, and social hierarchies. In D. M. Buss (Ed.), *The handbook of evolutionary psychology* (pp. 676–697). Hoboken, NJ: Wiley.

D'Angelo, M. S., Pelletier, L. G., Reid, R. D., & Huta, V. (2014). The roles of self-efficacy and motivation in the prediction of short- and long-term adherence to exercise among patients with coronary heart disease. *Health Psychology, 33,* 1344–1353.

Damian, R. I., & Roberts, B. W. (2015). The association of birth order with personality and intelligence in a representative sample of U. S. high school students. *Journal of Research in Personality, 58,* 96–105.

Damm, V. J. (1969). Overall measures of self actualization derived from the Personal Orientation Inventory. *Educational and Psychological Measurement, 29,* 977–981.

Damon, W. (1983). *Social and personality development.* New York, NY: Norton.

Darwin, C. (1981). *The descent of man, and selection in relation to sex.* Princeton, NJ: Princeton University Press. (Original work published 1871)

De Haan, M., & Nelson, C. A. (1999). Brain activity differentiates face and object processing in 6-month-old infants. *Developmental Psychology, 35,* 1113–1121.

De Pauw, S. S., W., Mervielde, I., & Van Leeuwen, K. G. (2009). How are traits related to problem behavior in preschool children? Similarities and contrasts between temperament and personality. *Journal of Abnormal Child Psychology, 37,* 309–325.

De Raad, B., Barelds, D. P. H., Levert, E., Ostendorf, F., . . . Katigbak, M. S. (2010). Only three factors of personality description are fully replicable across languages: A comparison of 14 trait taxonomies. *Journal of Personality and Social Psychology, 98,* 160–173.

De Wolff, M., & van IJzendoorn, M. (1997). Sensitivity and attachment: A meta-analysis on parental antecedents of infant attachment. *Child Development, 68,* 571–591.

Deci, E. L., Koestner, R., & Ryan, R. M. (1999). A meta-analytic review of experiments examining the effects of extrinsic rewards on intrinsic motivation. *Psychological Bulletin, 125,* 627–668.

Deci, E. L., & Ryan, R. M. (1985). *Intrinsic motivation and self-determination in human behavior.* New York, NY: Plenum.

Deci, E. L., & Ryan, R. M. (1991). A motivational approach to self: Integration in personality. In R. Dienstbier (Ed.), *Nebraska symposium on motivation* (Vol. 38, pp. 237–288). Lincoln: University of Nebraska Press.

DeHart, T., Pelham, B., & Murray, S. (2004). Implicit dependency regulation: Self-esteem, relationship closeness, and implicit evaluation of close others. *Social Cognition, 22,* 126–146.

Dekovic, M., & Janssens, J. M. A. M. (1992). Parents' child-rearing style and child's sociometric status. *Developmental Psychology, 28,* 925–932.

Del Giudice, M. (2009). Sex, attachment, and the development of reproductive strategies. *Behavioral and Brain Sciences, 32,* 1–67.

Del Guidice, M., & Belsky, J. (2011). The development of life-history strategies: Toward a multi-stage theory. In D. M. Buss & P. H. Hawley (Eds.), *The evolution of personality and individual differences* (pp. 154–176). New York, NY: Oxford University Press.

Demarque, C., Apostolidis, T., & Joule, R-V. (2013). Consideration of future consequences and pro-environment decision making in the context of persuasion and binding commitment. *Journal of Environmental Psychology, 36*, 214–220.

Denollet, J. (2005). DS14: Standard assessment of negative affectivity, social inhibition, and Type D personality. *Psychosomatic Medicine, 67*, 89–97.

DeOliveira, C. A., Bailey, H. N., Moran, G., & Pederson, D. (2004). Emotion socialization as a framework for understanding the development of disorganized attachment. *Social Development, 13*, 437–467.

Derryberry, D., & Rothbart, M. K. (1988). Arousal, affect, and attention as components of temperament. *Journal of Personality and Social Psychology, 55*, 958–966.

Desmond, A., & Moore, J. (1991). *Darwin: The life of a tormented evolutionist.* New York, NY: Norton.

DeWall, C. N., Buffardi, L. E., Bonser, I., & Campbell, W. K. (2011). Narcissism and implicit analyses of social networking and online presentation. *Personality and Individual Differences, 52*, 482–486.

DeWall, C. N., Manor, J. K., & Rouby, D. A. (2009). Social exclusion and early-stage interpersonal perception: Selective attention to signs of acceptance. *Journal of Personality and Social Psychology, 96*, 729–741.

DeWall, C. N., Twenge, J. M., Gitter, S. A., & Baumeister, R. F. (2009). It's the thought that counts: The role of hostile cognition in shaping aggressive responses to social exclusion. *Journal of Personality and Social Psychology, 96*, 45–59.

DeYoung, C. G. (2011). Impulsivity as a personality trait. In K. D. Vohs & R. F. Baumeister (Eds.), *Handbook of self-regulation: Research, theory, and applications* (2nd ed., pp. 485–502). New York, NY: Guilford.

DeYoung, C. G., & Gray, J. R. (2009). Personality neuroscience: Explaining individual differences in affect, behavior, and cognition. In P. J. Corr & G. Mathews (Eds.), *The Cambridge handbook of personality psychology* (pp. 323–346). New York, NY: Cambridge University Press.

DeYoung, C. G., Grazioplene, R. G., & Peterson, J. B. (2012). From madness to genius: The openness/intellect trait as a paradoxical simplex. *Journal of Research in Personality, 46*, 63–78.

Diamond, S. (1974). *The roots of psychology: A sourcebook in the history of ideas.* New York, NY: Basic Books.

DiClemente, C. C. (1994). If behavior changes, can personality be far behind? In T. F. Heatherton & J. L. Weinberger (Eds.), *Can personality change?* (pp. 175–198). Washington, DC: American Psychological Association.

Diehl, M., Chui, H., Hay, E. L., Lumley, M. A., Gruhn, D., & Labouvie-Vief, G. (2014). Change in coping and defense mechanisms across adulthood: Longitudinal findings in a European American sample. *Developmental Psychology, 50*, 634–648.

Diener, E., & Fujita, F. (1995). Resources, personal strivings, and subjective well-being: A nomothetic and idiographic approach. *Journal of Personality and Social Psychology, 68*, 926–935.

Diener, M., Mangelsdorf, S., McHale, J., & Frosch, C. (2002). Infants' behavioral strategies for emotion regulation with fathers and mothers: Associations with emotional expressions and attachment quality. *Infancy, 3*, 153–174.

DiLalla, L. F., Bersted, K., & John, S. G. (2015). Evidence of a reactive gene-environment correlation in preschoolers' prosocial play with unfamiliar peers. *Developmental Psychology.* In press.

Docter, R. F. (1988). *Transvestites and transsexuals: Toward a theory of cross-gender behavior.* New York, NY: Plenum.

Doctor, R. M., Kahn, A. P., & Adamec, C. (Eds.) (2008). *The encyclopedia of phobias, fears, and anxieties* (3rd ed.). New York, NY: Facts on File.

Doidge, N. (2007). *The brain that changes itself: Stories of personal triumph from the frontiers of brain science.* New York, NY: Penguin.

Drake, K., Belsky, J., & Pasco Fearon, R. M. (2014). From early attachment to engagement with learning in school: The role of self-regulation and persistence. *Developmental Psychology, 50*, 1350–1361.

Dukes, W. F. N. (1965). *Psychological Bulletin, 64*, 74–79.

Dunbar, R. (1993). Coevolution of neocortex size, group size, and language in humans. *Behavioral and Brain Sciences, 16*, 681–735.

Dunbar, R. (1998). The social brain hypothesis. *Evolutionary Anthropology, 6*, 178–190.

Dunbar, R. (2010). *How many friends does one person need? Dunbar's number and other evolutionary quirks.* Cambridge, MA: Harvard University Press.

Dunkel, C. S., Mathes, E. W., Kessselring, S. N., Decker, M. L., & Kelts, D. J. (2015). Parenting influence on the development of life history strategy. *Evolution and Human Behavior, 36*, 374–378.

Dunning, D., Anderson, J. E., Schlosser, T., Ehlebracht, D., & Fetchenhauer, D. (2014). Trust at zero acquaintance: More a matter of respect than expectation of reward. *Journal of Personality and Social Psychology, 107,* 122–141.

Dutton, D. G., White, K. R., & Fogarty, D. (2013). Paranoid thinking in mass shooters. *Aggression and Violent Behavior, 18,* 548–553.

Dweck, C. S. (1999). *Self-theories: Their role in motivation, personality, and development.* New York, NY: Psychology Press.

Dyk, P. H., & Adams, G. R. (1990). Identity and intimacy: An initial investigation of three theoretical models using cross-lag panel correlations. *Journal of Youth and Adolescence, 19,* 91–110.

Dykas, M. J., & Cassidy, J. (2011). Attachment and the processing of social information across the life span: Theory and evidence. *Psychological Bulletin, 137,* 19–46.

Edmundson, M., & Kwapil, T. R. (2013). A Five-Factor Model perspective of schizotypal personality disorder. In T. A. Widiger, & P. T. Costa Jr. (Eds.), *Personality disorders and the Five-Factor Model of personality* (3rd ed., pp. 147–161). Washington, DC: American Psychological Association.

Effron, D. A., & Knowles, E. D. (2015). Entitativity and intergroup bias: How belonging to a cohesive group allows people to express their prejudices. *Journal of Personality and Social Psychology, 108,* 234–253.

Egan, P. M., Clarkson, J. J., & Hirt, E. R. (2015). Revisiting the restorative effects of positive mood: An expectancy-based approach to self-control restoration. *Journal of Experimental Social Psychology, 57,* 87–99.

Egan, S. J., Wade, T. D., & Sharfran, R. R. (2011). Perfectionism as a transdiagnostic process: A clinical review. *Clinical Psychology Review, 31,* 203–212.

Egan, S. K., & Perry, D. G. (2001). Gender identity: A multidimensional analysis with implications for psychosocial adjustment. *Developmental Psychology, 37,* 451–463.

Egan, V., & Angus, S. (2004). Is social dominance a sex-specific strategy for infidelity? *Personality and Individual Differences, 36,* 575–586.

Egeland, B., & Farber, E. A. (1984). Infant-mother attachment: Factors related to its development and changes over time. *Child Development, 55,* 753–771.

Ein-Dor, T., Perry-Paldi, A., Hirshberger, G., Birnbaum, G. E., & Deutsch, D. (2015). Coping with mate poaching: Gender differences in detection of infidelity-related threats. *Evolution and Human Behavior, 36,* 17–24.

Einolf, C. J. (2014). Stability and change in generative concern: Evidence from a longitudinal survey. *Journal of Research in Personality, 51,* 54–61.

Eisenberg, N., Fabes, R. A., Shepard, S. A., Gutherie, I. K., Murphy, B. C., & Reiser, M. (1999). Parental reactions to children's negative emotions: Longitudinal relations to quality of children's social functioning. *Child Development, 70,* 513–534.

Eisenberger, N. I. (2015). Social pain and the brain: Controversies, questions, and where to go from here. *Annual Review of Psychology, 66,* 601–629.

Eisenberger, N. I., Liberman, M. D., & Williams, K. D. (2003). Does rejection hurt? An fMRI study of social exclusion. *Science, 302,* 290–292.

Ellett, L., & Wildsschut, T. (2014). Are we all paranoid? *The Psychologist, 27,* 328–330.

Elliott, R., Newman, J. L., Longe, O. A., & Deakin, J. F. (2003). Differential response patterns in the striatum and orbitofrontal cortex to financial reward in humans: A parametric functional magnetic resonance imaging study. *Journal of Neuroscience, 23,* 303–307.

Ellis, A. (1962). *Reason and emotion in psychotherapy.* New York, NY: Lyle Stuart.

Ellis, L. (1994). *Social stratification and socioeconomic inequality, Vol. 2: Reproductive and interpersonal aspects of dominance and status.* Westport, CT: Praeger.

Elms, A. C. (1994). *Uncovering lives: The uneasy alliance of biography and psychology.* New York, NY: Oxford University Press.

Elms, A. C. (2007). Psychobiography and case studies methods. In R. W. Robins, R. C. Fraley, & R. F. Krueger (Eds.), *Handbook of research methods in personality psychology* (pp. 97–113). New York, NY: Guilford.

Else-Quest, N. M., Higgins, A., Allison, C., & Morton, L. C. (2012). Gender differences in self-conscious emotions: A meta-analysis. *Psychological Bulletin, 138,* 947–981.

Else-Quest, N. M., Hyde, J., Goldsmith, H. H., & Van Hulle, C. A. (2006). Gender differences in temperament: A meta-analysis. *Psychological Bulletin, 132,* 33–72.

Emmons, R. A. (1986). Personal strivings: An approach to personality and subjective well-being. *Journal of Personality and Social Psychology, 51,* 1058–1068.

Emmons, R. A. (1989). The personal striving approach to personality. In L. A. Pervin (Ed.), *Goal concepts in personality and social psychology* (pp. 87–126). Hillsdale, NJ: Lawrence Erlbaum.

Emmons, R. A. (1992). Abstract versus concrete goals: Personal striving level, physical illness, and psychological well-being. *Journal of Personality and Social Psychology, 62,* 292–300.

Emmons, R. A., & King, L. A. (1988). Conflict among personal strivings: Immediate and long-term implications for psychological and physical well-being. *Journal of Personality and Social Psychology, 54,* 1040–1048.

Ent, M. R., Baumeister, R. F., & Tice, D. M. (2015). Trait self-control and the avoidance of temptation. *Personality and Individual Differences, 74,* 12–15.

Erikson, E. H. (1958). *Young man Luther: A study in psychoanalysis and history.* New York, NY: Norton.

Erikson, E. H. (1959). *Identity and the life cycle: Selected papers.* New York, NY: International Universities Press.

Erikson, E. H. (1963). *Childhood and society* (2nd ed.). New York, NY: Norton.

Erikson, E. H. (1964). *Insight and responsibility.* New York, NY: Norton.

Erikson, E. H. (1968). *Identity: Youth and crisis.* New York, NY: Norton.

Erikson, E. H. (1969). *Gandhi's truth: On the origins of militant non-violence.* New York, NY: Norton.

Erikson, E. H. (1970). *Gandhi's truth: On the origins of militant non-violence.* New York, NY: Norton.

Erikson, E. H. (1978). Dr. Borg's life cycle. In E. H. Erikson (Ed.), *Adulthood* (pp. 1–31). New York, NY: Norton.

Erikson, E. H. (1982). *The life cycle completed.* New York, NY: Norton.

Erikson, E. H., Erikson, J. M., & Kivnick, H. Q. (1986). *Vital involvement in old age.* New York, NY. Norton.

Eschleman, K. J., Bowling, N. A., & Alarcon, G. M. (2010). A meta-analytic examination of hardiness. *International Journal of Stress Management, 17,* 277–307.

Esterson, A. (1993). *Seductive mirage: An exploration of the work of Sigmund Freud.* Chicago and LaSalle, IL: Open Court.

Eysenck, H. J. (1947). *Dimensions of personality.* London, UK: Routledge and Keegan Paul.

Eysenck, H. J. (1967). *The biological basis of personality.* Springfield, IL: Thomas.

Eysenck, H. J. (1976). *Sex and personality.* Austin, TX: University of Texas Press.

Eysenck, H. J. (1990). Biological dimensions of personality. In L. A. Pervin (Ed.), *Handbook of personality: Theory and research* (pp. 244–276). New York, NY: Guilford.

Eysenck, H. J., & Eysenck, S. B. G. (1964/1975). *Manuel of the Eysenck Personality Inventory.* San Diego, CA: Educational and Industrial Testing Service.

Eysenck, H. J., & Eysenck, S. B. G. (1976). *Psychoticism as a dimension of personality.* London, UK: Hodder & Stroughton.

Eysenck, S., & Zuckerman, M. (1978). The relationship between sensation-seeking and Eysenck's dimensions of personality. *British Journal of Psychology, 69,* 483–487.

Fagundes, C. P., & Way, B. (2014). Early-life stress and adult inflammation. *Psychological Science, 23,* 277–283.

Falbo, T., & Polit, D. F. (1986). Quantitative review of the only child literature: Research evidence and theory development. *Psychological Bulletin, 100,* 176–189.

Feather, N. T. (1975). Factor structure of the conservatism scale. *Australian Psychologist, 10,* 179–184.

Feeney, B. C., & Collins, N. L. (2015). A new look at social support: A theoretical perspective on thriving through relationships. *Personality and Social Psychology Review, 19,* 113–147.

Feeney, B. C., & Monin, J. K. (2008). An attachment-theoretical perspective on divorce. In J. Cassidy & P. R. Shaver (Eds.), *Handbook of attachment: Theory, research, and clinical applications* (2nd ed., pp. 934–957). New York, NY: Guilford.

Feeney, J. A. (2008). Adult romantic attachment: Developments in the study of couple relationships. In J. Cassidy & P. R. Shaver (Eds.), *Handbook of attachment: Theory, research, and clinical applications* (2nd ed., pp. 456–481). New York, NY: Guilford.

Fehr, B. (2015). Love: Conceptualization and experience. In M. Mikulincer & P. R. Shaver (Eds.), *APA handbook of personality and social psychology. Vol. 3: Interpersonal relations* (pp. 495–522). Washington, DC: American Psychological Association.

Fein, S., & Spencer, S. J. (2000). Prejudice as self-image maintenance: Affirming the self through derogating others. In C. Stanger (Ed.), *Stereotypes and prejudice* (pp. 172–190). Philadelphia, PA: Taylor and Francis.

Feldman, G., Harley, R., Kerrigan, M., Jacobo, M., & Fava, M. (2009). Change in emotional processing during a dialectical behavior therapy-based skills group for major depressive disorder. *Behaviour Research and Therapy, 47,* 897–912.

Feldman, S. S., & Aschenbrenner, B. G. (1983). Impact of parenthood on various aspects of masculinity and femininity: A short-term longitudinal study. *Developmental Psychology, 19,* 278–289.

Fenichel, O. (1945). *The psychoanalytic theory of the neuroses*. New York, NY: Norton.

Ferguson, C. J. (2010). A meta-analysis of normal and disordered personality across the life span. *Journal of Personality and Social Psychology, 98*, 659–667.

Field, T. (1989). Maternal depression effects on infant interaction and attachment behavior. In D. Cicchetti (Ed.) *The emergence of a discipline: Vol. 1. Rochester symposium on developmental psychopathology* (pp. 139–164). Hillsdale, NJ: Erlbaum.

Figner, B., Mackinlay, R. J., Wilkening, F., & Weber, E. U. (2009). Affective and deliberative processes in risky choice: Age differences in risk taking in the Columbia Card Task. *Journal of Experimental Psychology, 35*, 709–730.

Fillo, J., Simpson, J. A., Rholes, W. S., & Kohn, J. L. (2015). Dads doing diapers: Individual and relational outcomes associated with the division of childcare across the transition to parenthood. *Journal of Personality and Social Psychology, 108*, 298–316.

Fischer, A. H., Rodriguez Mosquerra, P. M., van Vianen, A. E., & Manstead, A. S. (2004). Gender and culture differences in emotion. *Emotion, 4*, 87–94.

Fisher, S., & Greenberg, R. P. (1996). *Freud scientifically reappraised: Testing the theories and therapy*. New York, NY: Wiley.

Fitch, S., & Adams, G. (1983). Ego identity and intimacy statuses: Replication and extension. *Developmental Psychology, 19*, 839–845.

Fleeson, W. (2001). Toward a structure- and process-integrated view of personality: Traits as density distributions of states. *Journal of Personality and Social Psychology, 80*, 1011–1027.

Fletcher, D., & Sarkar, M. (2013). Psychological resilience: A review and critique of definitions, concepts, and theory. *European Psychologist, 18*, 12–23.

Flett, G. L., & Hewitt, P. L. (Eds.) (2002). *Perfectionism: Theory, research, and treatment*. Washington, DC: American Psychological Association.

Flett, G. L., & Hewitt, P. L. (Eds.) (2013). *Perfectionism: Theory, research, and treatment* (2nd ed.). Washington, DC: American Psychological Association.

Flinn, M. V., Geary, D. C., & Ward, C. V. (2005). Ecological dominance, social competition, and coalitionary arms race: Why humans evolved extraordinary intelligence. *Evolution and Human Behavior, 26*, 10–46.

Fodor, J. (1983). *The modularity of mind*. Cambridge, MA: MIT Press.

Folkman, S., & Lazarus, R. S. (1985). If it changes it must be a process: Study of emotion and coping during three stages of a college examination. *Journal of Personality and Social Psychology, 48*, 150–170.

Fonagy, P., Target, M., Steele, M., & Steele, H. (1997). The development of violence and crime as it relates to security of attachment. In J. D. Osofsky (Ed.), *Children in a violent society* (pp. 150–177). New York, NY: Guilford.

Ford, M. B., & Collins, N. L. (2010). Self-esteem moderates neuroendocrine and psychological responses to interpersonal rejection. *Journal of Personality and Social Psychology, 98*, 405–419.

Fournier, M. A., Di Domenico, S. I., Westrate, N. M., Quitasol. M. N., & Dong, M. (2015). Toward a unified science of personality coherence. *Canadian Psychology/ psychologie canadienne, 56*, 253–262.

Fox, J., & Rooney, M. C. (2015). The Dark Triad and trait self-objectification as predictors of men's use and self-presentation behaviors on social networking sites. *Personality and Individual Differences, 76*, 161–165.

Fraley, R. C. (2007). Using the Internet for personality research: What can be done, how to do it, and other concerns. In R. W. Robins, R. C. Fraley, & R. F. Krueger (Eds.), *Handbook of research methods in personality psychology* (pp. 130–148). New York, NY: Guilford.

Frankl, V. E. (1984). *Man's search for meaning: An introduction to logotherapy* (3rd ed.). New York, NY: Simon & Schuster.

Frattaroli, J. (2006). Experimental disclosure and its moderators: A meta-analysis. *Psychological Bulletin, 132*, 823–865.

Freud, A. (1936). *The ego and the mechanisms of defense*. New York, NY: International Universities Press.

Freud, S. (1910/1964). *Leonardo da Vinci and a memory of his childhood*. Oxford, UK: Norton.

Freud, S. (1916/1957). On narcissism: An introduction. *Standard edition*, XIV. London, UK: Hogarth.

Freud, S. (1952). *A general introduction to psychoanalysis* (J. Riviere, ed., Trans.). New York, NY: Washington Square Press. (Original work published 1924)

Freud, S. (1959a). Inhibitions, symptoms, and anxiety. In J. Strachey (Ed. and Trans.) *Standard edition of the complete works of Sigmund Freud* (Vol. 20). London, UK: Hogarth Press. (Original work published 1926)

Freud, S. (1959b). On narcissism. In J. Strachey (Ed. and Trans.), *Standard edition of the complete works of Sigmund Freud* (Vol. 14). London, UK: Hogarth Press. (Original work published 1914)

Freud, S. (1959c). The ego and the id. In J. Strachey (Ed. and Trans.) *Standard edition of the complete works of Sigmund Freud* (Vol. 19). London, UK: Hogarth Press. (Original work published 1923)

Freud, S. (1960). *Jokes and their relation to the unconscious* (J. Strachey, Ed. and Trans.). New York, NY: Norton (Original work published 1905).

Freud, S. (1961). The ego and the id. In J. Strachey (Ed. and Trans.), *The standard edition of the complete psychological works of Sigmund Freud* (Vol. 19, pp. 12–66). London, UK: Hogarth Press. (Original work published 1923)

Freud, S. (1965). *The interpretation of dreams.* (J. Strachey, Ed. and Trans.). New York, NY: Avon Books. (Original work published 1900)

Freud, S. (1989a). In J. Strachey (Ed. and Trans.), *New introductory lectures on psycho-analysis.* New York, NY: Norton (Original work published 1933)

Freud, S. (1989b). In J. Strachey (Ed. and Trans.), *An outline of psycho-analysis.* New York, NY: Norton (Original work published 1940)

Frey-Rohn, L. (1974). *From Freud to Jung.* New York, NY: Dell.

Frias, M. T., & Shaver, P. R. (2014). The moderating role of attachment insecurities in the association between social and physical pain. *Journal of Research in Personality, 53,* 193–200.

Friedman, L. J. (1999). *Identity's architect: A biography of Erik H. Erikson.* New York, NY: Scribner.

Frison, E., & Eggermont, S. (2015). The impact of daily stress on adolescents' depressed mood: The role of social support seeking through Facebook. *Computers in Human Behavior, 44,* 315–325.

Funder, D. C., Block, J. H., & Block, J. (1983). Delay of gratification: Some longitudinal personality correlates. *Journal of Personality and Social Psychology, 44,* 1198–1213.

Funder, D. C., Furr, R. M., & Colvin, C. R. (2000). The Riverside Behavioral Q-sort: A tool for the description of social behavior. *Journal of Personality, 68,* 451–489.

Furnham, A., Richards, S. C., & Paulhus, D. L. (2013). The Dark Triad of personality: A 10 year review. *Social and Personality Psychology Compass, 7,* 199–216.

Furr, R. M., & Funder, D. C. (2007). Behavioral observation. In R. W. Robins, R. C. Fraley, & R. F. Krueger (Eds.), *Handbook of research methods in personality psychology* (pp. 273–291). New York, NY: Guilford.

Fuster, J. M. (2008). *The prefrontal cortex* (4th ed.). Boston, MA: Academic Press.

Galatzer-Levy, I. R., & Bonanno, G. A. (2013). Heterogeneous patterns of stress over the four years of college: Associations with anxious attachment and ego-resiliency. *Journal of Personality, 81,* 476–486.

Galione, J. N., & Oltmanns, T. F. (2013). Identifying personality associated with major depressive episodes: Incremental validity of informant reports. *Journal of Personality Assessment, 95,* 625–632.

Galla, B. M., & Duckworth, A. L. (2015). More than resisting temptation: Beneficial habits mediate the relationship between self-control and positive life outcomes. *Journal of Personality and Social Psychology.* In press.

Galla, B. M., & Wood, J. J. (2015). Trait self-control predicts adolescents' exposure and reactivity to daily stressful events. *Journal of Personality, 83,* 69–83.

Gangstad, S. W., & Buss, D. M. (1993). Pathogen prevalence and human mate preferences. *Ethology and Sociobiology, 14,* 89–96.

Gay, P. (1988). *Freud: A life for our time.* New York, NY: Norton.

Geary, D. C., & Huffman, K. J. (2002). Brain and cognitive evolution: Forms of modularity and functions of mind. *Psychological Bulletin, 128,* 667–698.

Gibbons, M. B. C., Crits-Cristoph, & Hearon, B. (2008). The empirical status of psychodynamic therapies. *Annual Review of Clinical Psychology, 4,* 93–108.

Gick, M. (2014). An exploration of the interactions of Conscientiousness and Consideration of Future Consequences on healthy eating. *Personality and Individual Differences, 66,* 181–187.

Gilligan, C. (1982). *In a different voice.* Cambridge, MA: Harvard University Press.

Gilliom, M., Shaw, D. S., Beck, J. E., Schonberg, M. A., & Lukon, J. L. (2002). Anger regulation in disadvantaged preschool boys: Strategies, antecedents, and the development of self-control. *Developmental Psychology, 38,* 222–235.

Gil-White, F. (2001). Are ethnic groups biological "species" to the human brain? *Current Anthropology, 42,* 515–554.

Glass, D. C., Neulinger, J., & Brim, O. G. (1974). Birth order, verbal intelligence, and educational aspiration. *Child Development, 45,* 807–811.

Goldberg, L. R., Johnson, J. A., Eber, H. W., Hogan, R., Ashton, M. C., Cloninger, C. R., & Gough, H. G. (2006). The international personality item pool and the future of public-domain personality measures. *Journal of Research in Personality, 40,* 84–96.

Goldberg, L. R., & Somer, O. (2000). The hierarchical structure of common Turkish person-description adjectives. *European Journal of Personality, 14,* 497–531.

Goldberg, L. R., & Velicer, W. F. (2006). Principles of exploratory factor analysis. In S. Strack (Ed.), *Differentiating normal and abnormal personality* (2nd ed., pp. 209–237). New York, NY: Springer.

Gollwitzer, P. M. (1999). Implementation intentions: Strong effects of simple plans. *American Psychologist, 54,* 493–503.

Gollwitzer, P. M. (2014). Weakness of will? Is a quick fix possible? *Motivation and Emotion, 38,* 305–322.

Gollwitzer, P. M., & Brandstatter, V. (1997). Implementation intentions and effective goal pursuit. *Journal of Personality and Social Psychology, 73,* 186–199.

Goma-i-Freixanet, M. (1995). Prosocial and antisocial aspects of personality. *Personality and Individual Differences, 19,* 829–832.

Goma-i-Freixanet, M. (2004). Sensation seeking and participation in physical risk sports. In R. M. Stelmack (Ed.), *On the psychobiology of personality: Essays in honor of Marvin Zuckerman* (pp. 185–201). Oxford, UK: Elsevier.

Gomez, A., Morales, J. F., Hart, S., Vazquez, A., & Swann, W. B. Jr. (2011). Rejected and excluded forevermore, but even more devoted: Irrevocable ostracism intensifies loyalty to the group among identity-fused persons. *Personality and Social Psychology Bulletin, 37,* 1574–1586.

Gomez, A., Seyle, D. C., Huici, C., & Swann, W. B. Jr. (2009). Can self-verification strivings fully transcend the self-other barrier? Seeking verification of ingroup identities. *Journal of Personality and Social Psychology, 97,* 1021–1044.

Goodman, G. S., Quas, J., A., & Ogle, C. M. (2010). Child maltreatment and memory. *Annual Review of Psychology, 61,* 325–351.

Goodwin, R. D., & Friedman, H. S. (2006). Health status and the five-factor personality traits in a nationally representative sample. *Journal of Health Psychology, 11,* 643–654.

Gordon, D. S., & Platek, S. M. (2009). Trustworthy? The brain knows: Implicit neural responses to faces that vary in Dark Triad personality characteristics and trustworthiness. *Journal of Social, Evolutionary, and Cultural Psychology, 3,* 182–200.

Gore, W. L., & Pincus, A. L. (2013). Dependency and the Five-Factor Model. In T. A. Widiger, & P. T. Costa Jr. (Eds.), *Personality disorders and the Five-Factor Model of personality* (3rd ed., pp. 163–177). Washington, DC: American Psychological Association.

Gosling, S. D. (2001). From mice to men: What can we learn about personality from animal research? *Psychological Bulletin, 127,* 45–86.

Gosling, S. D., & John, O. P. (1999). Personality dimensions in nonhuman animals: A cross-species review. *Current Directions in Psychological Science, 8,* 69–75.

Gosling, S. D., Kwan, V. S. Y., & John, O. P. (2003). A dog's got personality: A cross-species comparative approach to personality judgments in dogs and humans. *Journal of Personality and Social Psychology, 85,* 1161–1169.

Gosling, S. D., & Mason, W. (2015). Internet research in psychology. *Annual Review of Psychology, 66,* 877–902.

Gough, H. G. (1957). *California Psychological Inventory: Manual.* Palo Alto, CA: Consulting Psychologists Press.

Gough, H. G. (1987). *California Psychological Inventory: Administrator's guide.* Palo Alto, CA: Consulting Psychologists Press.

Gould, S. J. (2002). *The structure of evolutionary theory.* Cambridge, MA: The Belknap Press of Harvard University Press.

Greenaway, K. H., Haslam, S. A., Cruwys, T., Branscombe, N. R., Ysseldyk, R., & Heldreth, C. (2015). From "we" to "me": Group identification enhances perceived personal control with consequences for health and well-being. *Journal of Personality and Social Psychology.* In press.

Greenwald, A. G. (1980). The totalitarian ego: Fabrication and revision of personal history. *American Psychologist, 35,* 603–618.

Griffith, H. W. (2012). *Complete guide to symptoms, illnesses, and surgery* (6th ed.). New York, NY: Perigee.

Grijalva, E., Newman, D. A., Tay, L., Donnellan, M. B., Harms, P. D., & Robins, R. W. (2015). Gender differences in narcissism: A meta-analytic review. *Psychological Bulletin, 141,* 261–310.

Grillon, C., Quispe-Escudero, D., Mathur, A., & Ernst, M. (2015). Mental fatigue impairs emotion regulation. *Emotion.* In press.

Griskevicius, V., Cialdini, R. B., & Kenrick, D. T. (2006). Peacocks, Picasso, and parental investment: The effects of romantic motives on creativity. *Journal of Personality and Social Psychology, 91,* 63–76.

Gross, E. F. (2009). Logging on, bouncing back: An experimental investigation of online communication following social exclusion. *Developmental Psychology, 45,* 1787–1793.

Grossmann, T. (2015). The development of social brain functions in infancy. *Psychological Bulletin.* In press.

Grusec, J. E. (2011). Socialization processes in the family: Social and emotional development. *Annual Review of Psychology, 62,* 243–269.

Gueguen, N. (2012). Hair color and wages: Waitresses with blond hair have more fun. *The Journal of Socio-Economics, 41,* 370–372.

Gueguen, N., & Lamy, L. (2012). Men's social status and attractiveness: Women's receptivity to men's date requests. *Swiss Journal of Psychology, 71,* 157–160.

Gustavsson, L., & Johnsson, J. L. (2008). Mixed support for sexual selection theories of mate preferences in the Swedish population. *Evolutionary Psychology, 6,* 575–585.

Gutchess, A. (2014). Plasticity of the aging brain: New directions in cognitive neuroscience. *Science, 346,* 579–582.

Haggard, P., & Tsakiris, M. (2009). The experience of agency. *Current Directions in Psychological Science, 18,* 242–246.

Hagger, M. S., Wood, C., Stiff, C., & Chatzisarantis, N. L. D. (2010). Ego depletion and the strength model of self-control: A meta-analysis. *Psychological Bulletin, 136,* 495–525.

Hald, G. M., & Hogh-Oleson, H. (2010). Receptivity to sexual invitations from strangers of the opposite gender. *Evolution and Human Behavior, 31,* 453–458.

Hall, C. S., & Lindzey, G. (1957). *Theories of personality.* New York, NY: John Wiley & Sons.

Hall, C. S., & Lindzey, G. (1978). *Theories of personality* (3rd ed.). New York, NY: John Wiley.

Hallquist, M. N., & Lenzenweger, M. F. (2013). Identifying latent trajectories of personality symptom change: Growth mixture modeling in the longitudinal study of personality disorders. *Journal of Abnormal Psychology, 122,* 138–155.

Harackiewicz, J. M., Barron, K. E., Tauer, J. M., & Elliot, A. J. (2002). Predicting success in college: A longitudinal study of achievement goals and ability measures as predictors of interest and performance from freshman year through graduation. *Journal of Educational Psychology, 94,* 562–575.

Harden, K. P. (2014). Genetic influences on adolescent sexual behavior: Why genes matter for environmentally oriented researchers. *Psychological Bulletin, 140,* 434–465.

Hardin, E. E., Weigold, I. K., Nixon, A. E., & Robitschek, C. (2007). Self-discrepancy and distress: The role of personal growth initiative. *Journal of Counseling Psychology, 54,* 86–92.

Harlow, H. F., & Harlow, M. (1962). Social deprivation in monkeys. *Scientific American, 207,* 136–146.

Harrington, N. (2005). It's too difficult! Frustration intolerance beliefs and procrastination. *Personality and Individual Differences, 39,* 873–883.

Harris, J. R. (1995). Where is the child's environment? A group socialization theory of development. *Psychological Review, 102,* 458–489.

Harris, J. R. (1998). *The nurture assumption: Why children turn out the way they do.* New York, NY: Touchstone.

Harris, J. R. (2006). *No two alike: Human nature and human individuality.* New York, NY: Norton.

Harris, L. T., & Fiske, S. T. (2006). Dehumanizing the lowest of the low. *Psychological Science, 17,* 847–853.

Hart, J., Nailling, E., Bizer, G. Y., & Collins, C. K. (2015). Attachment theory as a framework for explaining engagement with Facebook. *Personality and Individual Differences, 77,* 33–40.

Harter, S. (1990a). Causes, correlates, and the functional role of global self-worth: A life-span perspective. In R. J. Sternberg & J. Kolligan Jr. (Eds.), *Competence considered* (pp. 67–97). New Haven, CT: Yale University Press.

Harter, S. (1990b). Self and identity achievement. In S. Feldman & G. Elliot (Eds.), *At the threshold: The developing adolescent* (pp. 352–387). Cambridge, MA: Harvard University Press.

Hartmann, H. (1958). *Ego psychology and the problem of adaptation.* New York, NY: International Universities Press. (Original work published 1939)

Hartmann, H., Kris, E., & Lowenstein, R. (1946). Comments on the formation of psychic structure. *Psychoanalytic Study of the Child, 2,* 11–38.

Haselton, M. G., & Buss, D. M. (2000). Error management theory: A new perspective on biases in cross-sex mind reading. *Journal of Personality and Social Psychology, 78,* 81–91.

Haselton, M. G., & Nettle, D. (2006). The paranoid optimist: An integrative evolutionary model of cognitive biases. *Personality and Social Psychology Review, 10,* 47–66.

Haselton, M. G., Nettle, D., & Andrews, P. W. (2005). The evolution of cognitive biases. In D. M. Buss (Ed.), *The handbook of evolutionary psychology* (pp. 724–746). Hoboken, NJ: Wiley.

Haslam, N. (2015). Dehumanization and intergroup relations. In M. Mikulincer & P. R. Shaver (Eds.), *APA handbook of personality and social psychology. Vol. 2: Group processes* (pp. 295–314). Washington, DC: American Psychological Association.

Haslam, N., & Loughnan, S. (2014). Dehumanization and infrahumanization. *Annual Review of Psychology, 65,* 399–423.

Hatfield, E. (1988). Passionate and companionate love. In R. J. Sternberg & M. L. Barnes (Eds.), *The psychology of love* (pp. 191–217). New Haven, CT: Yale University Press.

Hathaway, S. R., & McKinley, J. C. (1943a). *Manual for the Minnesota multiphasic personality inventory.* New York, NY: Psychological Corporation.

Hathaway, S. R., & McKinley, J. C. (1943b). *The Minnesota Multiphasic Personality Inventory* (rev. ed.). Minneapolis: University of Minnesota Press.

Hazan, C., & Shaver, P. (1987). Romantic love conceptualized as an attachment process. *Journal of Personality and Social Psychology, 52,* 511–524.

Heintzelman, S. J., & King, L. A. (2015). Meaning in life and intuition. *Journal of Personality and Social Psychology.* In press.

Helgeson, V. S. (2015). Gender and personality. In M. Mikulincer & P. R. Shaver (Eds.), *APA handbook of personality and social psychology. Vol. 4: Personality processes and individual differences* (pp. 515–534). Washington, DC: American Psychological Association.

Helgeson, V. S., & Fritz, H. L. (1998). A theory of unmitigated communion. *Personality and Social Psychology Review, 2,* 173–183.

Helson, R. (1993). Comparing longitudinal studies of adult development: Toward a paradigm of tension between stability and change. In D. C. Funder, R. D. Parke, C. Tomlinson-Keasey, & K. Widaman (Eds.), *Studying lives through time* (pp. 93–119). Washington, DC: American Psychological Association.

Helson, R., Jones, C., & Kwan, V. S. Y. (2002). Personality change over 40 years of adulthood: Hierarchical linear modeling analyses of two longitudinal samples. *Journal of Personality and Social Psychology, 83,* 752–766.

Helson, R., Kwan, V., S. Y., John, O. P., & Jones, C. (2002). The growing evidence for personality change in adulthood: Findings from research with personality inventories. *Journal of Research in Personality, 36,* 287–306.

Helson, R., Mitchell, V., & Moane, G. (1984). Personality and patterns of adherence and nonadherence to the social clock. *Journal of Personality and Social Psychology, 46,* 1079–1096.

Helson, R., & Moane, G. (1987). Personality change in women from college to midlife. *Journal of Personality and Social Psychology, 53,* 176–186.

Helson, R., & Picano, J. (1990). Is the traditional role bad for women? *Journal of Personality and Social Psychology, 59,* 311–320.

Helson, R., & Roberts, B. W. (1994). Ego development and personality change in adulthood. *Journal of Personality and Social Psychology, 66,* 911–920.

Helson, R., & Wink, P. (1992). Personality change in women from the early 40s to the early 50s. *Psychology and Aging, 7,* 46–55.

Hendrick, S. S., & Hendrick, C. (1992). *Liking, loving, and relating* (2nd ed.). Pacific Grove, CA: Brooks/Cole.

Henrich. J., & Gil-White, F. (2001). The evolution of prestige: Freely conferred deference as a mechanism for enhancing the benefits of cultural transmission. *Evolution and Human Behavior, 22,* 165–196.

Hetherington, E. M., & Frankie, G. (1967). Effect of parental dominance, warmth, and conflict on imitation in children. *Journal of Personality and Social Psychology, 6,* 119–125.

Hewett, P. L., & Flett, G. L. (2007). Diagnosing the perfectionistic personality. *Current Psychiatry, 6,* 53–64.

Hicks, B. M., & Patrick, C. J. (2006). Psychopathy and negative emotionality: Analyses of suppressor effects reveal distinct relations with emotional distress, fearfulness, and anger-hostility. *Journal of Abnormal Psychology, 115,* 276–287.

Higgins, E. T. (1987). Self-discrepancy: A theory relating self and affect. *Psychological Review, 94,* 319–340.

Higgins, E. T. (1997). Beyond pleasure and pain. *American Psychologist, 52,* 1280–1300.

Higgins, E. T. (2000). Making a good decision: Value from fit. *American Psychologist, 55,* 1217–1230.

Higgins, E. T., Kruglanski, A. W., & Pierro, A. (2003). Regulatory mode: Locomotion and assessment as distinct orientations. In M. P. Zanna (Ed.), *Advances in experimental social psychology* (Vol. 35, pp. 293–344). New York, NY: Academic Press.

Higgins, E. T., Tykocinski, O., & Vookles, J. (1990). Patterns of self-beliefs: The psychological significance of relations among the actual, ideal, ought, can, and future selves. In J. M. Olsen & M. P. Zanna (Eds.) *Self-inference processes* (pp. 153– 190). Hillsdale, NJ: Erlbaum.

Higgins, R. L., Snyder, C. R., & Berglas, S. (Eds.). (1990). *Self-handicapping: The paradox that isn't.* New York, NY: Plenum.

Higgins, T. J., Middleton, K. R., Winner, L., & Janelle, C. M. (2014). Physical activity interventions differentially affect exercise task and barrier self-efficacy: A meta-analysis. *Health Psychology, 33,* 891–903.

Hilbig, B. E., & Zettler, I. (2015). When the cat's away, some mice will play: A basic trait account of dishonest behavior. *Journal of Research in Personality, 57,* 72–88.

Hill, K., & Hurtado, A. M. (1996). *Ache life history.* New York, NY: Aldine de Gruyer.

Hinde, R. (1988). Continuities and discontinuities: Conceptual issues and methodological considerations. In M. Rutter (Ed.), *Studies of psychosocial risk: The power of longitudinal data* (pp. 367–383). New York, NY: Cambridge University Press.

Hobbes, T. (1997). *The leviathan.* New York, NY: Touchstone. (Original work published 1660)

Hobfoll, S. E., Rom, T., & Segal, B. (1989). Sensation seeking, anxiety, and risk-taking in the Israeli context. In S. Ebstein (Ed.), *Drugs and alcohol use: Issues and facts* (pp. 53–59). New York, NY: Plenum.

Hofer, J., Busch, H., Au, A., Solcova, I. P., Tavel, P., & Wong, T. T. (2014). For the benefits of others: Generativity and meaning in life in the elderly in four cultures. *Psychology and Aging, 29,* 764–775.

Hoffman-Plotkin, D., & Twentyman, C. (1984). A multimodal assessment of behavioral and cognitive deficits in abused and neglected pre-schoolers. *Child Development, 55,* 794–802.

Hogan, R. (1983). A socioanalytic theory of personality. In M. M. Page (Ed.), *Nebraska Symposium on Motivation* (pp. 336–355). Lincoln: University of Nebraska Press.

Hogan, R., & Nicholson, R. A. (1988). The meaning of personality test scores. *American Psychologist, 43,* 621–626.

Holahan, C. K., Holahan, C. J., & Belk, S. S. (1984). Adjustment in aging: The roles of life stress, hassles, and self-efficacy. *Health Psychology, 3,* 315–328.

Hollander, J. A. (2004). "I can take care of myself": The impact of self-defense training on women's lives. *Violence Against Women, 10,* 205–235.

Holloway, S. D. (1988). Concepts of ability and effort in Japan and the United States. *Review of Educational Research, 58,* 327–345.

Horner, T. (1985). The psychic life of the young infant: Review and critique of the psychoanalytic concepts of symbiosis and infantile omnipotence. *American Journal of Orthopsychiatry, 55,* 324–343.

Horney, K. (1945). *Our inner conflicts: A constructive theory of neurosis.* New York, NY: Norton.

Horney, K. (1950). *Neurosis and human growth: The struggle toward self-realization.* New York, NY: Norton.

Horney, K. (1967). *Feminine psychology.* New York, NY: Norton.

Horvath, P., & Zuckerman, M. (1993). Sensation seeking, risk appraisal, and risky behavior. *Personality and Individual Differences, 14,* 41–51.

Horwood, S., Anglim, J., & Tooley, G. (2015). Type D personality and the Five-Factor Model: A facet-level analysis. *Personality and Individual Differences, 83,* 50–54.

Hoyle, R. H., & Gallagher, P. (2015). The interplay of personality and self-regulation. In M. Mikulincer & P. R. Shaver (Eds.), *APA handbook of personality and social psychology* (Vol. 4, pp. 189–207). Washington, DC: American Psychological Association.

Hoyle, R., Fejfar, M. C., & Miller, J. D. (2000). Personality and sexual risk taking: A quantitative review. *Journal of Personality, 68,* 1203–1231.

Hudson, N. W., & Fraley, R. C. (2015). Volitional personality trait change: Can people choose to change their personality traits? *Journal of Personality and Social Psychology.* In press.

Hudson, N. W., & Roberts, B. W. (2014). Goals to change personality traits: Concurrent links between personality traits, daily behavior, and goals to change oneself. *Journal of Research in Personality, 53,* 68–83.

Huey, S. J., & Weisz, J. R. (1997). Ego control, ego resiliency, and the Five-Factor Model as predictors of behavioral and emotional problems in clinic-referred children and adolescents. *Journal of Abnormal Psychology, 106,* 404–415.

Hutteman, R., Nestler, S., Wagner, J., Egloff, B., & Back, M. D. (2015). Wherever I may roam: Processes of self-esteem development from adolescence to emerging adulthood in the context of international student exchange. *Journal of Personality and Social Psychology, 108,* 767–783.

Hyde, L. W., Byrd, A. L., Voltruba-Drzal, Hariri, A. R., & Manuck, S. B. (2014). Amygdala reactivity and negative emotionality: Divergent correlations of antisocial personality and psychopathy traits in a community sample. *Journal of Abnormal Psychology, 123,* 214–224.

Hyler, S. E., & Rieder, R. O. (1987). *Personality Diagnostic Questionnaire-Revised.* New York, NY: State Psychiatric Institute.

Hystad, S. W., Eid, J., & Brevik, J. J. (2011). Effects of psychological hardiness, job demands, and job control on sickness absence: A prospective study. *Journal of Occupational Health Psychology, 16,* 265–278.

Irons, W. (2005). How has evolution shaped human behavior? Richard Alexander's contribution to an important question. *Evolution and Human Behavior, 26,* 1–9.

Jackson, J. J., Hill, P. L., Payne, B. R., Roberts, B. W., & Stine-Morrow, E. A. L. (2012). Can an old dog learn (and want to experience) new tricks? Cognitive training increases openness to experience in older adults. *Psychology of Aging, 27,* 286–292.

Jaffe, L. T., & Archer, R. P. (1987). The prediction of drug use among college students from MMPI, MCMI, and sensation seeking scales. *Journal of Personality, 51,* 243–253.

James, W. (1890). *Principles of psychology* (Vols. 1–2). New York, NY: Dover.

James, W. (1961). *The varieties of religious experience.* New York, NY: Collier. (Original work published 1902)

Jang, K. L., Livesley, W. J., Angleitner, A., Riemann, R., & Vernon, P. A. (2002). Genetic and environmental influences on the covariance of facets defining the domains of the Five-Factor Model of personality. *Personality and Individual Differences, 33,* 83–101.

Jang, K. L., Livesley, W. J., & Vernon, P. A. (1996). Heritability of the big five personality dimensions and their facets. *Journal of Personality, 64,* 577–592.

Jeronimus, B. F., Riese, H., Sanderman, R., & Ormel, J. (2014). Mutual reinforcement between neuroticism and life experiences: A five-wave, 16-year study to test reciprocal causation. *Journal of Personality and Social Psychology, 107,* 751–764.

Jetten, J., Haslam, C., & Haslam, S. A. (Eds.). (2011). *The social cure: Identity, health, and well-being.* Hove, England: Psychogy Press.

Job, V., Walton, G. M., Bernecker, K., & Dweck, C. S. (2015). Implicit theories about willpower predict self-regulation and grades in everyday life. *Journal of Personality and Social Psychology, 108,* 637–647.

Jobin, J., Wrosch, C., & Scheier, M. F. (2014). Associations between dispositional optimism and diurnal cortisol in a community sample: When stress is perceived as higher than normal. *Health Psychology, 33,* 382–391.

John, O. P., Angleitner, A., & Ostendorf, F. (1988). The lexical approach to personality: A historical review of trait taxonomic research. *European Journal of Personality, 2,* 171–203.

John, O. P., Naumann, L. P., & Soto, C. J. (2008). Paradigm shift to the integrative Big Five trait taxonomy: History, measurement, and conceptual issues. In O. P. John, R. R. Robins, & L. A. Pervin (Eds.), *Handbook of personality: Theory and research* (3rd ed., pp. 114–158). New York, NY: Guilford.

John, O. P., & Robins, R. R. (1993). Determinants of interjudge agreement on personality traits: The Big 5 domains, observability, evaluativeness, and the unique perspective of the self. *Journal of Personality, 61,* 521–551.

Johnson, J. G., Cohen, P., Kasen, S., Skodol, A. E., Hamagami, F., & Brook, J. (2000). Age-related change in personality disorder trait levels between early adolescence and adulthood: A community-based longitudinal investigation. *Acta Psychiactrica Scandinavica, 102,* 265–275.

Johnson, S. M. (2008). Couple and family therapy: An attachment perspective. In J. Cassidy & P. R. Shaver (Eds.), *Handbook of attachment: Theory, research, and clinical applications* (2nd ed., pp. 811–829). New York, NY: Guilford.

Jokela, M., Puikki-Raback, L, Elovainio, M., & Kivimaki, M. (2014). Personality traits as risk factors for stroke and coronary heart disease mortality: Pooled analysis of three cohort studies. *Journal of Behavioral Medicine, 37,* 881–889.

Jonah, B. A. (1997). Sensation seeking and risky driving: A review and synthesis of the literature. *Accident Analysis and Prevention, 29,* 651–665.

Jonason, P. K., Hatfield, E., & Boler, V. M. (2015). Who engages in serious and casual sex relationships? An individual differences perspective. *Personality and Individual Differences, 75,* 205–209.

Jonason, P. K., Li, N. P., & Buss, D. M. (2010). The costs and benefits of the Dark Triad: Implications for mate poaching and mate retention tactics. *Personality and Individual Differences, 48,* 373–378.

Jonason, P. K., Lyons, M., & Blanchard, A. (2015). Birds of a "bad" feather flock together: The Dark Triad and mate choice. *Personality and Individual Differences, 78,* 34–38.

Jones, A., & Crandall, R. (1986). Validation of a short index of self-actualization. *Personality and Social Psychology Bulletin, 12,* 63–73.

Jones, J. D., Cassidy, J., & Shaver, P. R. (2015). Parents' self-reported attachment styles: A review of links of parenting behaviors, emotions, and cognitions. *Personality and Social Psychology Review, 19,* 44–76.

Jopp, A. M., & South, S. C. (2015). Investigating the personality inventory for DSM-5 using self and spouse reports. *Journal of Personality Disorders, 29,* 193–214.

Josephs, R. A., Markus, H. R., & Tafarodi, R. W. (1992). Gender and self-esteem. *Journal of Personality and Social Psychology, 63,* 391–402.

Juang, L. P., & Cookston, J. T. (2009). A longitudinal study of family obligations and depressive symptoms among Chinese American adolescents. *Journal of Family Psychology, 23,* 396–404.

Jung, C. G. (1906). The psychopathological significance of the association experiment. In *The Collected Works of C. G. Jung. Volume 2: Experimental Researches* (pp. 408–425). Princeton, NJ: Princeton University Press.

Jung, C. G. (1954). The development of personality. In *The collected works of C. G. Jung, Vol. 17: The development of personality* (pp. 167-186). Princeton, NJ: Princeton University Press. (Original work published 1934).

Jung, C. G. (1965). *Memories, dreams, and reflections.* (R. Winston & C. Winston, Trans.). New York, NY: Vintage.

Jung, C. G. (1969a). A review of the complex theory. In *The collected works of C. G. Jung. Vol. 8: The structure and dynamics of the psyche* (pp. 92–104). Princeton, NJ: Princeton University Press. (Original work published 1934)

Jung, C. G. (1969b). The stages of life. In *The collected works of C. G. Jung: Vol. 8: The structures and dynamics of the psyche* (pp. 387–403). Princeton, NJ: Princeton University Press. (Original work published 1931)

Jung, C. G. (1971). General description of the types. In *The collected works of C.G. Jung: Vol. 6: Psychological types* (pp. 330–407). Princeton, NJ: Princeton University Press. (Original work published 1921)

Kachadourian, L. K., Fincham, F., & Davila, J. (2004). The tendency to forgive in dating and married couples: The role of attachment and relationship satisfaction. *Personal Relationships, 11,* 373–393.

Kagan, J. (1989). Temperamental contributions to social behavior. *American Psychologist, 44,* 668–674.

Kagan, J. (2010). *The temperamental thread.* New York, NY: Dana Press.

Kagan, J., & Fox, N. A. (2006). Biology, culture, and temperament. In N. Eisenberg (Ed.). *Handbook of child psychology* (6th ed., Vol. 3, pp. 167–225). Hoboken, NJ: Wiley.

Kandler, C., Bleidorn, W., & Riemann, R. (2012). Left or right? Sources of political orientation: The role of genetic factors, cultural transmission, assortative mating, and personality. *Journal of Personality and Social Psychology, 102,* 633–645.

Kandler, C., Riemann, R., & Angleitner, A. (2013). Patterns and sources of continuity and change of energetic and temporal aspects of temperament in adulthood: A longitudinal twin study of self- and peer reports. *Developmental Psychology, 49,* 1739–1753.

Kaplan, H. S., & Gangestad, S. W. (2005). Life history theory and evolutionary psychology. In D. M. Buss (Ed.), *The handbook of evolutionary psychology* (pp. 68– 95). Hoboken, NJ: Wiley.

Kardum, I., Hudek-Knezevic, J., Schmitt, D. P., & Grundler, P. (2015). Personality and mate poaching experiences. *Personality and Individual Differences, 75,* 7–12.

Kashdan, T. B. (2007). Social anxiety spectrum and diminished positive experience: Theoretical synthesis and meta-analysis. *Clinical Psychology Review, 27,* 348–365.

Kashdan, T. B., & Silvia, P. J. (2009). Curiosity and interest: The benefits of thriving on novelty and challenge. In S. J. Lopez & C. R. Snyder (Eds.), *The Oxford handbook of positive psychology* (2nd ed., pp. 367–374). New York, NY: Oxford University Press.

Kasser, T. (2016). Materialistic values and goals. *Annual Review of Psychology, 67.* In press.

Kasser, T., & Ryan, R. M. (1993). A dark side of the American dream: Correlates of financial success as a central life aspiration. *Journal of Personality and Social Psychology, 65,* 410–422.

Keller, M. C., Coventry, W. L., Heath, A. C., & Martin, N. G. (2005). Widespread evidence for non-additive genetic variation in Cloninger's and Eysenck's personality dimensions using a twin plus sibling design. *Behavior Genetics, 35,* 707–721.

Keller, T. E., Spieker, S. J., & Gilchrist, L. (2005). Patterns of risks and trajectories of preschool problem behaviors: A person-oriented analysis of attachment in context. *Development and Psychopathology, 17,* 349–384.

Kelly, G. (1955). *The psychology of personal constructs.* New York, NY: Norton.

Kelly, J. F., & Greene, M. C. (2014). Where there's a will there's a way: A longitudinal investigation of the interplay between recovery motivation and self-efficacy in predicting treatment outcome. *Psychology of Addictive Behaviors, 28,* 928–934.

Kendler, K. S., Gardner, C. O., & Prescott, C. A. (2002). Toward a comprehensive developmental model for major depression in women. *American Journal of Psychiatry, 159,* 1133–1145.

Kenrick, D. T., & Funder, D. C. (1988). Profiting from controversy: Lessons from the person-situation debate. *American Psychologist, 43,* 23–34.

Kenrick, D. T., Griskevicius, V., Neuberg, S., & Schaller, M. (2010). Renovating the pyramid of needs: Contemporary extensions built upon ancient foundations. *Perspectives on Psychological Science, 5,* 292–314.

Kern, M. L., & Friedman, H. S. (2008). Do conscientious individuals live longer? A quantitative review. *Health Psychology, 27,* 505–512.

Kernberg, O. F. (1975). *Borderline conditions and pathological narcissism.* Northvale, NJ: Jason Aronson.

Kernberg, O. F., & Caligor, E. (2005). A psychoanalytic theory of personality disorders. In M. F. Lenzenweger & J. F. Clarkin (Eds.), *Major theories of personality disorder* (2nd ed., pp. 114–156). New York, NY: Guilford.

Kihlstrom, J. F. (2008). The psychological unconscious. In O. P. John, R. W. Robins, & L. A. Pervin (Eds.), *Handbook of personality: Theory and research* (3rd ed., pp. 583–602). New York, NY: Guilford.

Kilner, J. M., Neal, A., Weiskopf, N., Friston, K. J., & Frith, C. D. (2009). Evidence of mirror neurons in human inferior frontal gyrus. *The Journal of Neuroscience, 29,* 10153–10159.

Kim-Cohen, J., Moffitt, T. E., Caspi, A., & Taylor, A. (2004). Genetic and environmental processes in young children's resilience and vulnerability to socioeconomic deprivation. *Child Development, 75,* 651–668.

King, L. A. (2001). The hard road to the good life: The happy, mature person. *Journal of Humanistic Psychology, 41,* 51–72.

Kirkpatrick, L. E., & Davis, K. E. (1994). Attachment style, gender, and relationship stability: A longitudinal analysis. *Journal of Personality and Social Psychology, 66,* 502–512.

Kirkpatrick, L. E., & Hazan, C. (1994). Attachment styles and close relationships: A four-year prospective study. *Personal Relationships, 1,* 123–142.

Klein, K., & Boals, A. (2001). Expressive writing can increase working memory capacity. *Journal of Experimental Psychology: General, 130,* 520–533.

Klohnen, E. C., Vandewater, E. A., & Young, A. (1996). Negotiating the middle years: Ego-resiliency and successful midlife adjustment in women. *Psychology and Aging, 11,* 431–442.

Knapp, R. J. (1965). Relationship of a measure of self-actualization to neuroticism and extraversion. *Journal of Consulting Psychology, 29,* 168–172.

Kobak, R. R., & Hazan, C. (1991). Attachment in marriage: Effects of security and accuracy of working models. *Journal of Personality and Social Psychology, 60,* 861–869.

Kobasa, S. C. (1979). Stressful life events, personality, and health: An inquiry into hardiness. *Journal of Personality and Social Psychology, 37,* 1–11.

Kobasa, S. C., Maddi, S. R., & Kahn, S. (1982). Hardiness and health: A prospective study. *Journal of Personality and Social Psychology, 42,* 168–177.

Koch, E. J. (2002). Relational schemas, self-esteem, and the processing of social stimuli. *Self and Identity, 1,* 271–279.

Kochanska, G. (1998). Mother–child relationship, child fearfulness, and emerging attachment: A short-term longitudinal study. *Developmental Psychology, 34,* 480–490.

Kochanska, G. (2001). Emotional development in children with different attachment histories: The first three years. *Child Development, 72,* 474–490.

Koestner, R., & McClelland, D. C. (1990). Perspectives on competence motivation. In L. A. Pervin (Ed.), *Handbook of personality* (pp. 527–548). New York, NY: Guilford.

Kohut, H. (1971). *The analysis of the self.* New York, NY: International Universities Press.

Kort, C. (1981). Primal bond versus marriage bond. In R. Friedland, & C. Kort (Eds.), *The mother's book: Shared experiences* (pp. 123–127). Boston, MA: Houghton Mifflin.

Kosinski, M., Matz, S. C., Gosling, S. D., Popov, V., & Stillwell, D. (2015). Facebook as a research tool for the social sciences: Opportunities, challenges, ethical considerations, and practical guidelines. *American Psychologist, 70,* 543–556.

Kosson, D. S., Lorenz, A., & Newman, J. P. (2006). Effects of co-morbid psychopathy on criminal offending and emotional processing male offenders with antisocial personality disorder. *Journal of Abnormal Psychology, 115,* 798–806.

Kowaz, A. M., & Marcia, J. E. (1991). Development and validation of a measure of Eriksonian industry. *Journal of Personality and Social Psychology, 60,* 390–397

Kroger, J., Martinussen, M., & Marcia, J. E. (2010). Identity status change during adolescence and young adulthood: A meta-analysis. *Journal of Adolescence, 33,* 683–698.

Kross, E., & Grossman, I. (2012). Boosting wisdom: Distance from the self enhances wise reasoning, attitudes, and behavior. *Journal of Experimental Psychology: General, 141,* 43–48.

Kruger, J., & Dunning, D. (1999). Unskilled and unaware of it: How difficulties in recognizing one's own incompetence level lead to inflated self-assessments. *Journal of Personality and Social Psychology, 77,* 1121–1134

Kteily, N., Bruneau, E., Waytz, A., & Cotterill, S. (2015). The ascent of man: Theoretical and empirical evidence for blatant dehumanization. *Journal of Personality and Social Psychology.* In press.

Kuhl, J., & Fuhrmann, A. (1998). Decomposing self-regulation and self-control. In J. Heckhausen & C. Dweck (Eds.), *Motivation and self-regulation across the life span* (pp. 15–49). New York, NY: Cambridge University Press.

Kurzban, R. (2010). *Why everyone (else) is a hypocrite: Evolution and the modular mind.* Princeton, NJ: Princeton University Press.

Kurzban, R., & Aktipis, C. A. (2006). Modular minds, multiple motives. In M. Schaller, J. H. Simpson, & D. T. Kenrick (Eds.), *Evolution and social psychology* (pp. 39–53). New York, NY: Psychology Press.

Kurzban, R., & Leary, M. R. (2001). Evolutionary origins of stigmatization: The functions of social exclusion. *Psychological Bulletin, 127,* 187–208.

Kübler-Ross, E. (1969). *On death and dying.* New York, NY: Macmillan.

LaFreniere, P. J., Strayer, F. F., & Gauthier, R. (1984). The emergence of same-sex affiliative preferences among preschool peers: A developmental/ethological perspective. *Child Development, 55,* 1958–1965.

Langlois, J. H., Kalakanis, L., Rubenstein, A. J., Larson, A., Hallam, M., & Smoot, M. (2000). Maxims or myths of beauty: A meta-analysis and theoretical review. *Psychological Bulletin, 126,* 390–423.

Langston, C. A., & Cantor, N. (1989). Social anxiety and social constraint: When making friends is hard. *Journal of Personality and Social Psychology, 56,* 649–661.

Larsen, R. J., & Ketelar, T. (1991). Personality and susceptibility to positive and negative emotional states. *Journal of Personality and Social Psychology, 61,* 132–140.

Lasch, C. (1979). *The culture of narcissism.* New York, NY: Norton.

Lawton, E. M., Shields, A. J., & Oltmanns, T. F. (2011). Five-Factor Model personality disorder prototypes in a community sample: Self- and informant-reports predicting interview-based DSM diagnoses. *Personality Disorders: Theory, Research, and Treatment, 2,* 279–292.

Lazarus, R. S. (1993). From psychological stress to the emotions: A history of changing outlooks. *Annual Review of Psychology, 44,* 1–21.

Lazarus, R. S., & Folkman, S. (1984). *Stress, appraisal, and coping.* New York, NY: Springer-Verlag.

Leary, M. R., & Baumeister, R. (2000). The nature and function of self-esteem: Sociometer theory. In M. P. Zanna (Ed.), *Advances in experimental social psychology* (Vol. 32, pp. 1–62). San Diego, CA: Academic Press.

Leary, M. R., & Guadagno (2011). The sociometer, self-esteem, and the regulation of interpersonal behavior. In K. D. Vohs & R. F. Baumeister (Eds.), *Handbook of self-regulation: Research, theory, and applications* (2nd ed., pp. 339–354). New York, NY: Guilford.

Leary, M. R., & Toner, K. (2015). Self-processes in the construction and maintenance of personality. In M. Mikulincer & P. R. Shaver (Eds.), *APA handbook of personality and social psychology. Vol. 4: Personality processes and individual differences* (pp. 447–467). Washington, DC: American Psychological Association.

Lecky, P. (1945). *Self-consistency.* New York, NY: Island Press.

LeDoux, J. (1996). *The emotional brain: The mysterious underpinnings of our emotional life.* New York, NY: Touchstone.

Lee, J. A. (1973). *The colors of love.* Don Mills, Ontario, Canada: New Press.

Lee, J. A. (1988). Love styles: In R. J. Sternberg & M. L. Barnes (Eds.), *The psychology of love* (pp. 38–67). New Haven, CT: Yale University Press.

Lee, K., & Ashton, M. C. (2005). Psychopathy, Machiavellianism, and narcissism in the Five-Factor Model and the HEXACO model of personality inventory. *Personality and Individual Differences, 38,* 1571–1582.

Lee, K., & Ashton, M. C. (2007). Factor analysis in personality research. In R. W. Robins, R. C. Fraley, & R. F. Krueger (Eds.), *Handbook of research methods in personality psychology* (pp. 424–443). New York, NY: Guilford.

Lee, N. F., Rush, A. J., & Mitchell, J. E. (1985). Bulimia and depression. *Journal of Affective Disorders, 9,* 231–238.

Leerkes, E. M., Parade, S. H., & Gudmundson, J. A. (2011). Mothers' emotional reactions to crying pose risk for subsequent attachment insecurity. *Journal of Family Psychology, 25,* 635–643.

Leising, D., Erbs, J., & Fritz, U. (2010). The letter of recommendation effect in informant ratings of personality. *Journal of Personality and Social Psychology, 98,* 668–682.

Lenzenweger, M. F., Johnson, M. D., & Willett, J. B. (2004). Individual growth curve analysis illuminates stability and change in personality disorder features: The longitudinal study of personality disorders. *Archives of General Psychiatry, 61,* 1015–1024.

Lewis, M. (1992). *Shame: The exposed self.* New York, NY: Free Press.

Lewis, M., & Rosenblum, L. A. (Eds.). (1974). *The effect of the infant on its caregiver.* New York, NY: John Wiley & Sons.

Leyens, J.-P., Demoulin, S., Vaes, J., Gaunt, R., & Paladino, M. (2007). Infra-humanization: The wall of group differences. *Journal of Social Issues and Policy Review, 1,* 139–172.

Li, N. P., Yong, J. C., Tov, W., Sng, O., Fletcher, G. J. O., Valentine, K. A., Jiang, Y. F., & Balliet, D. (2013). Mate preferences do predict attraction and choices in the early stage of mate selection. *Journal of Personality and Social Psychology, 105,* 757–776.

Lichtenberg, J. D. (1981). Implications for psychoanalytic theory of research on the neonate. *International Review of Psycho-Analysis, 8,* 35–52.

Lieben, L. S., & Bigler, R. S. (2002). The developmental course of gender differentiation. *Monographs of the Society for Research in Child Development, 67*(2), 1–147.

Lieberman, M. D. (2013). *Social: Why our brains are wired to connect.* New York, NY: Crown Publishing.

Lilgendahl, J. P., Helson, R., & John, O. P. (2013). Does ego development increase during midlife? The effects of openness and accommodative processing of difficult events. *Journal of Personality, 81,* 403–416.

Linehan, M. (1993). *Cognitive-behavioral treatment of borderline personality disorder.* New York, NY: Guilford.

Liotti, G. (2004). Trauma, dissociation, and disorganized attachment: Three strands of a single braid. *Psychotherapy: Theory, Research, Practice, Training, 41,* 472–486.

Lissek, S., Baas, J. M., Pine, D. S., Orme, K., Dvir, S., Rosenberger, E., & Grillon, C. (2005). Sensation seeking and the aversive motivational system. *Emotion, 5,* 396–407.

Little, B. R. (1989). Personal projects analysis: Trivial pursuits, magnificent obsessions, and the search for coherence. In D. M. Buss & N. Cantor (Eds.), *Personality psychology: Recent trends and emerging directions* (pp. 15–31). New York, NY: Springer-Verlag.

Livesley, W. J., Jackson, D., & Schroeder, M. L. (1989). A study of the factorial structure of personality psychology. *Journal of Personality Disorders, 3,* 292-306.

Loehlin, J. C. (1997). A test of J. R. Harris's theory of peer influences on personality. *Journal of Personality and Social Psychology, 72,* 1197–1201.

Loehlin, J. C. (2010). Environment and behavior genetics: Let me count the ways. *Personality and Individual Differences, 49,* 302–305.

Loehlin, J. C., Willerman, L., & Horn, J. M. (1987). Personality resemblance in adoptive families: A 10-year follow-up. *Journal of Personality and Social Psychology, 53,* 961–969.

Loehlin, J. C., Willerman, L., & Horn, J. M. (1988). Human behavior genetics. *Annual Review of Psychology, 39,* 101–133.

Loevinger, J. (1976). *Ego development: Conceptions and theories.* San Francisco, CA: Jossey-Bass.

Londerville, S., & Main, M. (1981). Security of attachment, compliance, and maternal training methods in the second year of life. *Developmental Psychology, 17,* 289–299.

Lowe, J. R., Edmundson, M., & Widiger, T. A. (2009). Assessment of dependency, agreeableness, and their relationship. *Psychological Assessment, 21,* 543–553.

Lu, S. (2015). Great expectations. *Monitor on Psychology, 46,* 50–53.

Luborsky, L., & Barrett, M. S. (2006). The history and empirical status of key psychoanalytic concepts. *Annual Review of Clinical Psychology, 2,* 1–19.

Lucassen, N., Tharner, A., van IJzendoorn, M., Bakersmans-Kranenburg, M., Volling, B. L., Verhulst, F. C., Lambregtse-Van den Berg, M., & Tiemeier, H. (2011). The association between paternal sensitivity and infant-father attachment security: A meta-analysis of three decades of research. *Journal of Family Psychology, 25,* 986–992.

Luengo Kanacri, B. P., Pastorelli, C., Eisenberg, N., Zuffiano, A., Castellani, V., & Capara, G. V. (2014). Trajectories of prosocial behavior from adolescence to early adulthood: Associations with personality change. *Journal of Adolescence, 37,* 701– 713.

Lynam, D. R. (2013). Using the Five-Factor Model to assess disordered personality. In T. A. Widiger & P. T. Costa Jr. (Eds.), *Personality disorders and the Five-Factor Model of personality* (3rd ed., pp. 269–282). Washington, DC: American Psychological Association.

Lynman, D. R., & Widiger, T. A. (2001). Using the Five-Factor Model to represent the *DSM-IV* personality disorder: An expert consensus approach. *Journal of Abnormal Psychology, 110,* 401–412.

Lytton, H., & Romney, D. M. (1991). Parents' differential socialization of boys and girls: A meta-analysis. *Psychological Bulletin, 109,* 267–296.

Maccoby, E. E. (1992). The role of parents in the socialization of children: An historical overview. *Developmental Psychology, 28,* 1006–1017.

Maccoby, E. E. (2007). Historical overview of socialization research and theory. In J. E. Grusec & P. D. Hastings (Eds.), *Handbook of socialization: Theory and research* (4th ed., pp.13–41). New York, NY: Guilford.

Maccoby, E. E., & Martin, J. A. (1983). Socialization in the context of the family: Parent–child interaction. In E. M. Herrington (Ed.), *Handbook of child psychology* (Vol. 4, pp. 1–102). New York, NY: Wiley.

MacDonald, G., & Leary, M. R. (2005). Why does social exclusion hurt? The relationship between social and physical pain. *Psychological Bulletin, 131,* 202–223.

Macdonald, G., & Leary, M. R. (2012). Individual differences in self-esteem. In M. R. Leary & J. P. Tangney (Eds.), *Handbook of self and identity* (2nd ed., pp. 354–377). New York, NY: Guilford.

Macfarlane, J. W., & Tuddenham, R. D. (1951). Problems in the validation of projective techniques. In H. H. Anderson & G. L. Anderson (Eds.), *An introduction to projective techniques* (pp. 26–54). Englewood Cliffs, NJ: Prentice-Hall.

Machiavelli, N. (2003). *The prince* (R. Goodwin, Trans.). Wellesley, MA: Dante University Press. (Original work published 1515)

Macmillan, M. (1997). *Freud evaluated.* Cambridge, MA: The MIT Press.

Madigan, S., Bakermans-Kranenburg, M. J., van IJzendoorn, M. H., Moran, G., Pederson, D. R., & Benoit, D. (2006). Unresolved states of mind, anomalous parental behavior, and disorganized attachment: A preview and meta-analysis of a transmission gap. *Attachment and Human Development, 8,* 89–111.

Maher, B. (2008). Personal genomes: The case of the missing heritability. *Nature, 456,* 18–21.

Main, M. (1999). Epilogue. Attachment theory: Eighteen points with suggestions for future studies. In J. Cassidy & P. R. Shaver (Eds.), *Handbook of attachment: Theory, research, and clinical applications* (pp. 845–887). New York, NY: Guilford.

Main, M., & Hesse, E. (1990). Parents' unresolved traumatic experiences are related to infant disorganized attachment status: Is frightened and/or frightening parental behavior the linking mechanism? In M. T. Greenberg, D. Cicchetti, & E. M. Cummings (Eds.), *Attachment in the preschool years* (pp. 161–182). Chicago, IL: University of Chicago Press.

Main, M., & Solomon, J. (1990). Procedures for identifying infants as disorganized/ disoriented during Ainsworth's Strange Situation. In M. T. Greenberg, D. Cicchetti, & E. M. Cummings (Eds.), *Attachment in the preschool years* (pp. 121–160). Chicago, IL: University of Chicago Press.

Main, M., & Weston, D. R. (1982). Avoidance of the attachment figure in infancy: Descriptions and interpretations. In C. M. Parkes & J. Stevenson-Hinde (Eds.), *The place of attachment in human behavior* (pp. 31–59). New York, NY: Basic Books.

Makhanova, A., Miller, S. L., & Maner, J. K. (2015). Germs and the out-group: Chronic and situational disease concerns affect intergroup categorization. *Evolutionary Behavioral Sciences, 9,* 8–19.

Manuck, S. B., & McCaffrey, J. M. (2014). Gene–environment interaction. *Annual Review of Psychology, 65,* 41–70.

Marcia, J. E. (1980). Identity in adolescence. In J. Adelson (Ed.), *Handbook of adolescent psychology* (pp. 159–187). New York, NY: John Wiley.

Markon, K. E., Krueger, R. F., & Watson, D. (2005). Delineating the structure of normal and abnormal personality: An integrative hierarchical approach. *Journal of Personality and Social Psychology, 88,* 139–157.

Markus, H., & Nurius, P. (1986). Possible selves. *American Psychologist, 41,* 954–969.

Markus, H., & Ruvulo, A. (1989). Possible selves: Personalized representations of goals. In L. A. Pervin (Ed.), *Goal concepts in personality and social psychology* (pp. 211–241). Hillsdale, NJ: Lawrence Erlbaum.

Markus, H., & Wurf, E. (1987). The dynamic self-concept: A social psychological perspective. *Annual Review of Psychology, 38,* 299–337.

Marmot, M. (2004). *The status syndrome: How social standing affects our health and longevity.* New York, NY: Henry Holt.

Maslow, A. (1968). *Toward a psychology of being* (2nd ed.). New York, NY: Van Nostrand Reinhold.

Maslow, A. (1970). *Motivation and personality* (2nd ed.). New York, NY: Harper & Row.

Maslow, A. (1971). *The farther reaches of human nature.* New York, NY: Viking.

Massen, J. J. M, & Koski, S. E. (2014). Chimps of a feather sit together: Chimpanzee friendships are based on homophily in personality. *Evolution and Human Behavior, 35,* 1–8.

Masson, J. M. (1992). *The assault on truth: Freud's suppression of the seduction theory.* New York, NY: Harper/Perennial.

Masterson, J. F. (1988). *The search for the real self: Unmasking the personality disorders of our age.* New York, NY: The Free Press.

Matheny, A. P., & Phillips, K. (2001). Temperament and context: Correlates of home environment with temperament continuity and change, newborns to 30 months. In T. D. Wachs & G. A. Kohnstamm (Eds.), *Temperament in context* (pp. 81–101). Mahwah, NJ: Erlbaum.

Matheny, A. P., Wilson, R. S., & Thoben, A. S. (1987). Home and mother: Relations with infant temperament. *Developmental Psychology, 23,* 323–331.

McAdams, D. P. (1985). *Power, intimacy, and the life story: Personological inquiries into identity.* New York, NY: Guilford.

McAdams, D. P. (1989). *Intimacy: The need to be close.* Garden City, NY: Doubleday.

McAdams, D. P. (1993). The *Stories we live by: Personal myths and the making of the self.* New York, NY: William Morrow.

McAdams, D. P. (1994). Can personality change? Levels of stability and growth in personality across the life span. In T. F. Heatherton & J. L. Weinberger (Eds.), *Can personality change?* (pp. 299–313). Washington, DC: American Psychological Association.

McAdams, D. P. (2006). *The redemptive self: Stories Americans live by.* New York, NY: Oxford University Press.

McAdams, D. P. (2007). Personal narratives and the life story. In O. P. John, R. W. Robins, & L. A. Pervin (Eds.), *Handbook of personality: Theory and research* (3rd ed., pp. 242–262). New York, NY: Guilford.

McAdams, D. P. (2008). Personal narratives and the life story. In O. P. John, R. R. Robins, & L. A. Pervin (Eds.), *Handbook of personality: Theory and research* (3rd ed., pp. 242–262). New York, NY: Guilford.

McAdams, D. P. (2013). *The redemptive self: Stories Americans live by.* New York, NY: Oxford University Press.

McAdams, D. P., & Constantian, C. (1983). Intimacy and affiliation motives in daily living: An experience sampling analysis. *Journal of Personality and Social Psychology, 62,* 1003–1015.

McAdams, D. P., & de St. Aubin, E. (1992). A theory of generativity and its assessment through self-report, behavioral acts, and narrative themes in autobiography. *Journal of Personality and Social Psychology, 62,* 1003–1015.

McAdams, D. P., de St. Aubin, E., & Logan, R. L. (1993). Generativity among young, midlife, and older adults. Psychology and Aging, *8,* 221-230.

McAdams, D. P., Hart, H., & Maruna, S. (1998). The anatomy of generativity. In D. P. McAdams & E. de St. Aubin (Eds.), *Generativity and adult development: How and why we care for the next generation* (pp. 7–43). Washington, DC: American Psychological Association.

McAdams, D. P., & Manczak, E. (2015). Personality and the life story. In M. Mikulincer & P. R. Shaver (Eds.), *APA handbook of personality and social psychology. Vol. 4: Personality processes and individual differences* (pp. 425–446). Washington, DC: American Psychological Association.

McAdams, D. P., & McLean, K. C. (2013). Narrative identity. *Current Directions in Psychological Science, 22,* 233–238.

McAdams, D. P., & Olson, B. D. (2010). Personality development: Continuity and change over the life course. *Annual Review of Psychology, 61,* 517–542.

McClelland, D. C. (1961). *The achieving society.* New York, NY: Van Nostrand Reinhold.

McClelland, D. C. (1985). *Human motivation.* Glenview, IL: Scott, Foresman.

McClelland, D. C., & Franz, C. (1992). Motivational and other sources of work accomplishments in mid-life: A longitudinal study. *Journal of Personality, 60,* 679– 707.

McClelland, D. C., Atkinson, J. W., Clark, R. A., & Lowell, E. L. (1953). *The achievement motive.* New York, NY: Appleton-Century-Crofts.

McCrae, R. R. (2006). Psychopathology from the standpoint of the Five-Factor Model. In S. Strack (Ed.), *Differentiating normal and abnormal personality* (2nd ed., pp. 51–64). New York, NY: Springer.

McCrae, R. R., & Costa, P. T. Jr. (1986). Personality, coping, and coping effectiveness in an adult sample. *Journal of Personality, 54,* 385–405.

McCrae, R. R., & Costa, P. T., Jr. (1987). Validation of the Five-Factor Model of personality across instruments and observers. *Journal of Personality and Social Psychology, 52,* 81–90.

McCrae, R. R., & Costa, P. T. Jr. (1990). *Personality in adulthood.* New York, NY: Guilford.

McCrae, R. R., & Costa, P. T. Jr. (2003). *Personality in adulthood: A five-factor theory perspective* (2nd ed.). New York, NY: Guilford.

McCrae, R. R., & Costa, P. T., Jr. (2008). The five-factor theory of personality: In O. P. John, R. W. Robins, & L. A. Pervin (Eds.), *Handbook of personality: Theory and research* (3rd ed., pp. 159–181). New York, NY: Guilford.

McCrae, R. R., & Sutin, A. R. (2009). Openness to experience. In M. R. Leary & R. H. Hoyle (Eds.), *Handbook of individual differences in social behavior* (pp. 257–273). New York, NY: Guilford.

McCrae, S. M., & Hirt, E. R. (2001). The role of ability judgments in self-handicapping. *Personality and Social Psychology Bulletin, 27,* 1378–1389.

McCrae, S. M., Hirt, E. R., & Milner, B. J. (2008). She works hard for the money: Valuing effort underlies gender differences in behavioral self-handicapping. *Journal of Experimental Social Psychology, 44,* 292–311.

McElwain, N. L., Booth-LaForce, C., & Wu, X. (2011). Infant-mother attachment and children's friendship quality: Maternal mental-state talk as an intervening mechanism. *Developmental Psychology, 47,* 1295–1311.

McElwain, N. L., Cox, M. J., Burchinal, M. R., & Macfie, J. (2003). Differentiating among insecure mother-infant attachment classifications: A focus on child-friend interaction and exploration during solitary play at 36 months. *Attachment and Human Development, 5,* 136–164.

McGrath, R. E., & Carroll, E. J. (2012). The current status of "projective tests." In H. Cooper, P. M. Camic, D. L. Long, A.T. Panter, D. Rindskopf, K. J. Sher (Eds.), *APA handbook of research methods in psychology. Vol. 1: Foundation, planning, measures, and psychometrics* (pp. 329–348). Washington, DC: American Psychological Association.

McGrath, R. E., Mitchell, M., Kim, B. H., & Hough, L. (2010). Evidence for response bias as a source of error variance in applied assessment. *Psychological Bulletin, 136,* 450–470.

McGregor, I., & Little, B. R. (1998). Personal projects, happiness, and meaning: On doing well and being yourself. *Journal of Personality and Social Psychology, 74,* 494–512.

McGue, M., Bacon, S., & Lykken, D. T. (1993). Personality stability and change in early adulthood: A behavioral genetic analysis. *Developmental Psychology, 29,* 96– 109.

McGue, M., & Lykken, D. T. (1992). Genetic influence on risk of divorce. *Psychological Science, 3,* 368–373.

McGuire, W., & Hull, R. F. C. (Eds.). (1977). *C. G. Jung speaking.* Princeton, NJ: Princeton University Press.

McIntire, C. K., McGaugh, J. L., & Williams, C. L. (2012). Interacting brain systems modulate memory consolidation. *Neuroscience and Biobehavioral Reviews, 36,* 1750–1762.

Mealy, L. (1995). The sociobiology of sociopathy: An integrated evolutionary model. *Behavioral and Brain Sciences, 18,* 523–599.

Mealy, L., Daood, C., & Krage, M. (1996). Enhanced memory for faces of cheaters. *Ethnology & Sociobiology, 17,* 119–128.

Mecca, A. M., Smelser, N. J., & Vasconcellos, J. (Eds.). (1989). *The social importance of self-esteem.* Berkeley: University of California Press.

Meehl, P. E. (1962). Schizotaxia, schizotypy, schizophrenia. *American Psychologist, 17,* 827–838.

Meehl, P. E. (1990). Toward an integrated theory of schizotaxia, schizotypy, and schizophrenia. *Journal of Personality Disorders, 4,* 1–99.

Meehl, P. E. (1992). Factors and taxa, traits and types, differences of degree and differences in kind. *Journal of Personality, 60,* 117–174.

Meehl, P. E. (2004). What's in a taxon? *Journal of Abnormal Psychology, 113,* 39–43.

Meeus, W., Van de Schoot, R., Klimstra, T., & Branje, S. (2011). Personality types in adolescence: Change and stability and links with adjustment and relationships: A five-wave longitudinal study. *Developmental Psychology, 47,* 1181–1195.

Mellilo, D. (1983). Birth order, perceived birth order, and family position of academic women. *Individual Psychology, 39,* 57–62.

Mendolia, M., & Kleck, R. E. (1993). Effects of talking about a stressful event on arousal: Does what we talk about make a difference? *Journal of Personality and Social Psychology, 64,* 283–292.

Merrick, K. E., & Shafi, K. (2011). Achievement, affiliation, and power: Motive profiles for artificial agents. *Adaptive Behavior, 19,* 40–62.

Metcalfe, J., & Mischel, W. (1999). A hot/cool system analysis of delay of gratification: Dynamics of willpower. *Psychological Review, 106,* 3–19.

Meyer-Bahlburg, H. F. L. (2005). Gender identity outcome in female-raised 46, XY persons with penile agenesis, cloacal exstrophy of the bladder, or penile ablation. *Archives of Sexual Behavior, 34,* 423–438.

Meyers, S. A., & Landsberger, S. A. (2002). Direct and indirect pathways between adult attachment style and marital satisfaction. *Personal Relationships, 9,* 159–172.

Mikulincer, M., & Shaver, P. R. (2007). *Attachment in adulthood: Structure, dynamics, and change.* New York, NY: Guilford.

Miller, A. (1981). *The drama of the gifted child.* New York, NY: Basic Books.

Miller, G. (2000). *The mating mind.* New York, NY: Anchor Books.

Miller, G. (2009). *Spent: Sex, evolution, and consumer behavior.* New York, NY: Viking.

Miller, G. E., Chen, E., & Parker, K. J. (2011). Psychological stress in childhood and susceptibility to the chronic diseases of aging: Moving toward a model of behavioral and biological mechanisms. *Psychological Bulletin, 137,* 959–997.

Miller, J. D., & Campbell, W. K. (2008). Comparing clinical and social-personality conceptualizations of narcissism. *Journal of Personality, 76,* 449–476.

Miller, J. D., Hoffman, B. J., Gaughan, E. T., Gentile, B., Maples, J., & Campbell, W. K. (2011). Grandiose and vulnerable narcissism: A nomological network analysis. *Journal of Personality, 79,* 1013–1042.

Miller, J. D., & Lynman, D. R. (2008). Dependent personality disorder: Comparing an expert generated and empirically derived Five-Factor Model of personality disorder count. *Assessment, 15,* 4–15.

Miller, N., & Maruyama, G. (1976). Ordinal position and peer popularity. *Journal of Personality and Social Psychology, 33*, 123–131.

Miller, N., Maruyama, G., Beaber, R. J., & Valone, K. (1976). Speed of speech and persuasion. *Journal of Personality and Social Psychology, 34*, 615–624.

Millon, T. (1987). *Manual for the MCMI-II* (2nd ed.). Minneapolis, MN: National Computer Systems.

Millon, T. (1996). *Disorders of personality: DSM-IV and beyond* (2nd ed.). New York, NY: John Wiley & Sons.

Millon, T. (2011). *Disorders of personality: Introducing a DSM/CD spectrum from normal to abnormal* (3rd ed.). Hoboken, NJ: John Wiley & Sons.

Milne, E., & Graffman, J. (2001). Ventromedial prefrontal cortex lesions in humans eliminate implicit gender stereotyping. *Journal of Neuroscience, 8*, 294–300.

Minagawa-Kawai, Y., Matsuoka, S., Dan, I., Naoi, N., Nakamura, K., & Kojima, S. (2009). Prefrontal activation associated with social attachment: Facial-emotion recognition in mothers and infants. *Cerebral Cortex, 19*, 284–292.

Mischel, W. (1966). A social learning view of sex differences in behavior. In E. E. Maccoby (Ed.), *The development of sex differences* (pp. 56–81). Stanford, CA: Stanford University Press.

Mischel, W. (1968). *Personality and assessment.* New York, NY: Wiley.

Mischel, W. (1970). Sex typing and socialization. In P. H. Mussen (Ed.), *Carmichael's manual of child psychology* (Vol. 2, pp. 3–72). New York, NY: John Wiley.

Mischel, W. (1973). Toward a cognitive social learning reconceptualization of personality. *Psychological Review, 80*, 252–283.

Mischel, W. (1984). Convergences and challenges in the search for consistency. *American Psychologist, 39*, 351–364.

Mischel, W. (1990). Personality dispositions revisited and revised: A view after three decades. In L. A. Pervin (Ed.), *Handbook of personality* (pp. 111–134). New York, NY: Guilford.

Mischel, W. (1996). From good intentions to willpower. In P. Gollwitzer & J. Bargh (Eds.), *The psychology of action* (pp. 197–218). New York, NY: Guilford.

Mischel, W. (2004). Toward an integrative science of the person. *Annual Review of Psychology, 55*, 1–22.

Mischel, W., & Ayduk, O. (2011). Willpower in a cognitive affective processing system: The dynamics of delay of gratification. In K. D. Vohs & R. F. Baumeister (Eds.), *Handbook of self-regulation: Research, theory, and applications* (2nd ed., pp. 83–105). New York, NY: Guilford.

Mischel, W., & Ebbesen, E. B. (1970). Attention in delay of gratification. *Journal of Personality and Social Psychology, 16*, 329–337.

Mischel, W., & Moore, B. (1973). Effects of attention to symbolically presented rewards on self-control. *Journal of Personality and Social Psychology, 28*, 172–179.

Mischel, W., & Peake, P. K. (1982). Beyond déjà vu in the search for cross-situational consistency. *Psychological Review, 89*, 730–755.

Mischel, W., & Shoda, Y. (2008). Toward a unified theory of personality. In O. P. John, R. R. Robins, & L. A. Pervin (Eds.), *Handbook of personality: Theory and research* (3rd ed., pp. 208–241). New York, NY: Guilford.

Mischel, W., Shoda, Y., & Peake, P. K. (1988). The nature of adolescent competencies predicted by preschool delay of gratification. *Journal of Personality and Social Psychology, 54*, 687–696.

Mittal, C., & Griskevicius, V. (2014). Sense of control under uncertainty depends on people's childhood environment: A life history theory approach. *Journal of Personality and Social Psychology, 107*, 621–637.

Mittal, C., Griskevicius, V., Simpson, J. A., Sung, S., & Young, E. S. (2015). Cognitive adpatations to stressful environments: When childhood adversity enhances adult executive function. *Journal of Personality and Social Psychology, 109*, 604–621.

Monfort, S. S., Stroup, H., & Waugh, C. E. (2015). The impact of anticipating positive events on responses to stress. *Journal of Experimental Social Psychology, 58*, 11–22.

Morgan, C. D., & Murray, H. A. (1935). A method for investigating fantasies: The Thematic Apperception Test. *Archives of Neurology and Psychiatry, 34*, 289–306.

Morrison, A. P. (Ed.). (1986). *Essential papers on narcissism.* New York: New York University Press.

Mottus, R., Johnson, W., & Deary, I. J. (2012). Personality traits in old age: Measurement and rank-order stability and some mean-level change. *Psychology and Aging, 27*, 243–249.

Mullins-Sweatt, S., & Widiger, T. A. (2007). The Shedler-Westen Assessment Procedure from the perspective of general personality structure. *Journal of Abnormal Psychology, 116*, 618–623.

Munley, P. H. (1975). Erik Erikson's theory of psychosocial development of vocational behavior. *Journal of Counseling Psychology, 22*, 314–319.

Munro, G., & Adams, G. R. (1977). Ego-identity formation in college students and working youth. *Developmental Psychology, 13*, 523–524

Muraven, M., & Baumeister, R. F. (2000). Self-regulation and depletion of limited resources: Does self-control resemble a muscle? *Psychological Bulletin, 126*, 247–259.

Muraven, M., Baumeister, R. F., & Tice, D. M. (1999). Longitudinal improvement of self-regulation through practice: Building self-control strength through repeated exercise. *The Journal of Social Psychology, 139*, 446–457.

Muraven, M., Tice, D. M., & Baumeister, R. F. (1998). Self-control as a limited resource: Regulatory depletion patterns. *Journal of Personality and Social Psychology, 74*, 774–789.

Murray, H. A. (1938). *Explorations in personality.* New York, NY: Oxford University Press.

Murray, H. A. (1943). *The Thematic Apperception Test manual.* Cambridge, MA: Harvard University Press.

Neel, R., Kenrick, D. T., White, A. E., & Neuberg, S. L. (2015). Individual differences in fundamental human motives. *Journal of Personality and Social Psychology.* In press.

Nelissen, R. M. A., & Meijers, M. H. C. (2010). Social benefits of luxury brands as costly signals of wealth and status. *Evolution and Human Behavior, 32*, 343–355.

Nesse, R. M. (2005). Natural selection and the regulation of defenses: A signal detection analysis of the smoke detector principle. *Evolution and Human Behavior, 26*, 88–105.

Neuberg, S. L., & Cottrell, C. A. (2006). Evolutionary bases of prejudice. In M. Schaller, J. H. Simpson, & D. T. Kenrick (Eds.), *Evolution and social psychology* (pp. 163–187). New York, NY: Psychology Press.

Neuberg, S. L., Kenrick, D. T., & Schaller, M. (2010). Evolutionary social psychology. In S. T. Fiske, D. T. Gilbert, & G. Lindzey (Eds.), *Handbook of social psychology* (5th ed., pp. 761–796). Hoboken, NJ: John Wiley.

Newcomb, M. D., & McGee, L. (1991). Influence of sensation seeking on general deviance and specific problem behaviors from adolescence to young adulthood. *Journal of Personality and Social Psychology, 61*, 614–628.

O'Boyle, E. H., Jr., Forsyth, D. R., Banks, G. C., & McDaniel, M. A. (2012). A meta-analysis of the Dark Triad and work behavior: A social exchange perspective. *Journal of Applied Psychology, 97*, 557–579.

O'Connor, B. P. (2002). The search for dimensional structure differences between normality and abnormality: A statistical review of published data on personality and psychopathology. *Journal of Personality and Social Psychology, 83*, 962–982.

O'Donoghue, T., & Rabin, M. (1999). Incentives for procrastinators. *Quarterly Journal of Economics, 114*, 769–816.

Oaten, M., & Cheng, K. (2005). Academic examination stress impairs self-control. *Journal of Social and Clinical Psychology, 24*, 254–279.

Oaten, M., & Cheng, K. (2006). Longitudinal gains in self-control from regular physical exercise. *British Journal of Health Psychology, 11*, 717–733.

Ochse, R., & Plug, C. (1986). Cross-cultural investigation of the validity of Erikson's theory of personality development. *Journal of Personality and Social Psychology, 50*, 1240–1252.

Öhman, A., & Mineka, S. (2001). Fears, phobias, and preparedness: Toward an evolved module of fear and fear learning. *Psychological Review, 108*, 483–522.

Ohman, A., & Mineka, S. (2003). The malicious serpent: Snakes as a prototypical stimulus for an evolved module of fear. *Current Directions in Psychological Science, 12*, 5–9.

Oltmanns, T. F., & Carlson, E. (2013). Informant reports and the assessment of personality disorders using the Five-Factor Model. In T. A. Widiger & P. T. Costa Jr. (Eds.), *Personality disorders and the Five-Factor Model of personality* (3rd ed., pp. 233–248). Washington, DC: American Psychological Association.

Oltmanns, T. F., & Turkheimer, E. (2006). Perceptions of self and others regarding pathological personality traits. In R. F. Krueger & J. L. Tackett (Eds.), *Personality and psychopathology* (pp. 71–111). New York, NY: Guilford.

Orlofsky, J. L., Marcia, J. E., & Lesser, I. M. (1973). Ego identity status and the intimate versus isolation crisis of young adulthood. *Journal of Personality and Social Psychology, 27*, 211–219.

Osgood, C. E., Suci, G. J., & Tannenbaum, P. H. (1957). *The measurement of meaning.* Urbana: University of Illinois Press.

Ostrom, T. M., Carpenter, S. L., Sedikides, C., & Li, F. (1993). Differential processing of in-group and out-group information. *Journal of Personality and Social Psychology, 64*, 21–34.

Oxford, J., Ponzi, D., & Geary, D. C. (2010). Hormonal responses differ when playing violent video games against an ingroup and outgroup. *Evolution and Human Behavior, 31*, 201–209.

Oyserman, D., & Markus, H. R. (1990). Possible selves and delinquency. *Journal of Personality and Social Psychology, 59*, 112–125.

Oyserman, D., & Saltz, E. (1993). Competence, delinquency, and attempts to attain possible selves. *Journal of Personality and Social Psychology, 65*, 360–374.

Ozer, D. J. (2007). Evaluating effect size in personality research. In R. W. Robins, R. C. Fraley, & R. F. Krueger (Eds.), *Handbook of research methods in personality psychology* (pp. 495–501). New York, NY: Guilford.

Ozer, D. J., & Benet-Martinez, V. (2006). Personality and the prediction of consequential outcomes. *Annual Review of Psychology, 57,* 401–421.

Ozer, E. M., & Bandura, A. (1990). Mechanisms governing empowerment effects: A self-efficacy analysis. *Journal of Personality and Social Psychology, 58,* 472–486.

Pabian, S., De Backer, C. J. S., & Vandebosch, H. (2015). Dark Triad personality traits and adolescent cyber-aggression. *Personality and Individual Differences, 75,* 41–46.

Pailing, A., Boon, J., & Egan, V. (2014). Personality, the Dark Triad, and violence. *Personality and Individual Differences, 67,* 81–86.

Pallini, S., Baiocco, R., Schneider, B. H., Madigan, S., & Atkinson, L. (2014). Early child–parent attachment and peer relations: A meta-analysis of recent research. *Journal of Family Psychology, 28,* 118–123.

Palys, T. S., & Little, B. R. (1983). Perceived life satisfaction and the organization of personal projects systems. *Journal of Personality and Social Psychology, 44,* 1221– 1230.

Parke, R. D., & Buriel, R. (2006). Socialization in the family: Ethnic and ecological perspectives. In N. Eisenberg (Ed.), *Handbook of Child Psychology* (6th ed., pp. 429–504). Hoboken, NJ: Wiley.

Parker, S. L., Jimmieson, N. L., & Amiot, C. E. (2013). Self-determination, control, and reactions to changes in workload: A work simulation. *Journal of Occupational Health Psychology, 18,* 173–190.

Patrick, C. (2007). Getting to the heart of psychopathy. In H. Herve & J. Yuille (Eds.), *The psychopath: Theory, research, and practice* (pp. 287–299). Mahwah, NJ: Erlbaum.

Paulhus, D. L. (2014). Toward a taxonomy of dark personalities. *Current Directions in Psychological Science, 23,* 421–426.

Paulhus, D. L., & Vazire, S. (2007). The self-report method. In R. W. Robins, R. C. Fraley, & R. F. Krueger (Eds.), *Handbook of research methods in personality psychology* (pp. 224–239). New York, NY: Guilford.

Paulhus, D. L., & Williams, K. M. (2002). The Dark Triad of personality: Narcissism, Machiavellianism, and psychopathy. *Journal of Research in Personality, 36,* 556–563.

Paunonen, S. V., & Jackson, D. N. (2000). What is beyond the Big Five? *Journal of Personality, 68,* 821–835.

Paus, T., Keshavan, M., & Giedd, J. N. (2008). Why do many psychiatric disorders emerge during adolescence? *National Review of Neuroscience, 9,* 947–957.

Pavlov, I. P. (1906). The scientific investigation of the psychical faculties or processes in higher animals. *Science, 24,* 613–619.

Pawlow, L. A., & Jones, G. E. (2002). The impact of abbreviated progressive muscle relaxation on salivary cortisol. *Biological Psychology, 60,* 1–16.

Pelham, B. W. (1993). The idiographic nature of human personality. *Journal of Personality and Social Psychology, 64,* 665–677.

Pelham, B. W., & Swann, W. B. Jr. (1989). From self-conceptions to self-worth: On the sources and structure of global self-esteem. *Journal of Personality and Social Psychology, 57,* 672–680.

Penke, L. (2011). Bridging the gap between modern evolutionary psychology and the study of individual differences. In D. M. Buss & P. H. Hawley (Eds.), *The evolution of personality and individual differences* (pp. 243–279). New York, NY: Oxford University Press.

Pennebaker, J. W. (2004). *Writing to heal: A guided journal for recovering from trauma and emotional upheaval.* Oakland, CA: New Harbinger Publications.

Pennebaker, J. W., & Chung, C. K. (2007). Expressive writing, emotional upheavals, and health. In H. Friedman & R. Silver (Eds.), *Handbook of health psychology* (pp. 263–284). New York, NY: Oxford University Press.

Perusse, D. (1993). Cultural and reproductive success in industrial societies: Testing the relationship at proximate and ultimate levels. *Behavioral and Brain Sciences, 16,* 267–322.

Pervin, L. A. (1989). Goal concepts: Themes, issues, and questions. In L. A. Pervin (Ed.), *Goal concepts in personality and social psychology* (pp. 473–479). Hillsdale, NJ: Lawrence Erlbaum.

Peters, J. R., Geiger, P. J., Smart, L. M., & Baer, R. A. (2014). Shame and borderline personality features: The potential mediating role of anger and anger rumination. *Personality Disorders: Theory, Research, and Treatment, 5,* 1–9.

Peterson, B. E. (2002). Longitudinal analysis of midlife generativity, intergenerational roles, and caregiving. *Psychology and Aging, 17,* 161–168.

Peterson, B. E., & Duncan, L. E. (2007). Midlife women's generativity and authoritarianism: Marriage, motherhood, and 10 years of aging. *Psychology and Aging, 22,* 411–419.

Peterson, B. E., Smirles, K. A., & Wentworth, P. A. (1997). Generativity and authoritarianism: Implications for personality, political involvement, and parenting. *Journal of Personality and Social Psychology, 72,* 1202–1216.

Peterson, B. E., & Stewart, A. J. (1993). Generativity and social motives in young adults. *Journal of Personality and Social Psychology, 65,* 186–198.

Peterson, C., & Seligman, M. E. P. (Eds.). (2004). *Character strengths and virtues: A handbook and classification.* New York, NY: Oxford University Press.

Philippot, P., Chapelle, C., & Blairy, S. (2007). Respiratory feedback in the generation of emotion. *Cognition and Emotion, 16,* 605–627.

Piedmont, R. L., Bain, E., McCrae, R. R., & Costa, P. T., Jr. (2002). The applicability of the Five-Factor Model in a sub-Saharan culture. In R. R. McCrae & J. Allik (Eds.), *The Five-Factor Model of personality across cultures* (pp. 155–173). New York, NY: Kluwer Academic/Plenum.

Pierro, A., Giacomantonio, M., Kruglanski, A. W., Pica, G., & Higgins, E. T. (2011). On the psychology of time in action: Regulatory mode orientations and procrastination. *Journal of Personality and Social Psychology, 101,* 1317–1331.

Pietromonaco, P. R., & Beck, L. A. (2015). Attachment processes in adult romantic relationships. In M. Mikulincer & P. R. Shaver (Eds.), *APA handbook of personality and social psychology. Vol. 3: Interpersonal relations* (pp. 33–64). Washington, DC: American Psychological Association.

Pinker, S. (1994). *The language instinct.* New York, NY: HarperCollins.

Pinker, S. (1997). *How the mind works.* New York, NY: Norton.

Pipp, S., Easterbrooks, M. A., & Harmon, R. J. (1992). The relation between attachment and knowledge of self and mother in one- to three-year-old infants. *Child Development, 63,* 738–750.

Pisula, W., Turlejski, K., & Charles, E. P. (2013). Comparative psychology as unified psychology: The case of curiosity and other novelty-related behavior. *Review of General Psychology, 17,* 224–229.

Platt, J. R. (1964). Strong inference. *Science, 146,* 347–353.

Ploeger, A., & van der Hoort, B. (2015). Evolutionary psychology as a metatheory for the social sciences: How to gather interdisciplinary evidence for a psychological adaptation. *Review of General Psychology, 19,* 381–392.

Plomin, R. (2013). Child development and molecular genetics: 14 years later. *Child Development, 84,* 104–120.

Plomin, R., Pedersen, N. L., McClern, G. E., Nesselroade, J. R., & Bergeman, C. S. (1988). EAS temperaments during the last half of life: Twins reared apart and twins reared together. *Psychology and Aging, 3,* 43–50.

Popper, K. (1959). *The logic of scientific discovery.* New York, NY: Basic Books.

Posten, A.-C., & Mussweiler, T. (2013). When distrust frees your mind: The stereotype-reducing effects of distrust. *Journal of Personality and Social Psychology, 105,* 567–584.

Presnall, J. R. (2013). Disorders of personality: Clinical treatment from a Five-Factor Model perspective. In T. A. Widiger & P. T. Costa Jr. (Eds.), *Personality disorders and the Five-Factor Model of personality* (3rd ed., pp. 409–432). Washington, DC: American Psychological Association.

Puig, J., Englund, M. M., Simpson, J. A., & Collins, W. A. (2013). Predicting adult physical illness from infant attachment: A prospective longitudinal study. *Health Psychology, 32,* 409–417.

Pull, C. B. (2014). Personality disorders in Diagnostic and Statistical Manual of Mental Disorders-5: Back to the past or back to the future? *Current Opinion in Psychiatry, 27,* 84–86.

Putallaz, M. (1987). Maternal behavior and children's socioeconomic behavior. *Child Development, 58,* 324–340.

Putz, A., Palotai, R., Cserto, I., & Bereczkei, T. (2016). Beauty stereotypes in social norm enforcement: The effect of attractiveness on third-party punishment and reward. *Personality and Individual Differences, 88,* 230–235.

Quinn, S. (1987). *A mind of her own: The life of Karen Horney.* New York, NY: Summit Books.

Quoidbach, J., Gilbert, D. T., & Wilson, T. D. (2013). The end of history illusion. *Science, 339,* 96–98.

Raikes, H. A., & Thompson, R. A. (2006). Family emotional climate, attachment security, and young children's emotional understanding in a high-risk sample. *British Journal of Developmental Psychology, 24,* 89–104.

Rand, K. L., & Cheavens, J. S. (2009). Hope theory. In S. J. Lopez & C. R. Snyder (Eds.), *The Oxford handbook of positive psychology* (2nd ed., pp. 323–333). New York, NY: Oxford University Press.

Raskin, R. N., & Hall, C. S. (1981). The narcissistic personality inventory: Alternate form reliability and further evidence of construct validity. *Journal of Personality Assessment, 45,* 159–162.

Raskin, R., & Terry, H. (1988). A principal-components analysis of the Narcissistic Personality Inventory and further evidence of its construct validity. *Journal of Personality and Social Psychology, 54,* 890–902.

Rauthmann, J. F., Gallardo-Pujol, D., Guillaume, E. M., Todd, E., Nave, C. S., Sherman, R. A., . . . Funder, D. C. (2014). The situational eight DIAMONDS: A taxonomy of major dimensions of situation characteristics. *Journal of Personality and Social Psychology, 107,* 677–718.

Reichenbach, H. (1938). *Experience and prediction.* Chicago, IL: University of Chicago Press.

Reim, M. M. E., Bakersman-Kranenberg, M. J., van IJzendoorn, M. H., Out, D., & Rombouts, S. A. R. B. (2012). Attachment in the brain: Adult attachment representations predict amygdala and behavioral responses to infant crying. *Attachment and Human Development, 14,* 533–551.

Reiner, W. G., & Gearhart, J. P. (2004). Discordant sexual identity in some genetic males with cloacal exstrophy assigned to female sex at birth. *New England Journal of Medicine, 350,* 333–341.

Reio, T. G., & Wiswell, A. (2000). Field investigation of the relationship among adult curiosity, workplace learning, and job performance. *Human Resource Development Quarterly, 11,* 5–30.

Rennie, J. (1993). DNA's new twists. *Scientific American, 266,* 122–132.

Revelle, W., Amaral, P., & Turriff, S. (1976). Introversion/extraversion, time stress, and caffeine: Effect on verbal performance. *Science, 192,* 149–150.

Rhodewalt, F., Morf, C., Hazlett, S., & Fairfield, M. (1991). Self-handicapping: The role of discounting and augmentation in the preservation of self-esteem. *Journal of Personality and Social Psychology, 61,* 122–131.

Rickert, N. P., Meras, I. L., & Witkow, M. R. (2014). Theories of intelligence and students' daily self-handicapping behaviors. *Learning and Individual Differences, 36,* 1–8.

Rider, R. E., & Kosson, D. S. (2013), Criminal behavior and cognitive processing in male offenders with antisocial personality disorder with and without comorbid psychopathy. *Personality Disorders: Theory, Research, and Treatment, 4,* 332–340.

Riese, M. L. (1990). Neonatal temperament in monozygotic and dizygotic twin pairs. *Child Development, 61,* 1230–1237.

Riese, M. L. (1999). Effects of chorion type on neonatal temperament differences in monozygotic twin pairs. *Behavior Genetics, 29,* 87–94.

Rizzolatti, G., & Craighero, L. (2005). Mirror neuron: A neurological approach to empathy. In J.-P. Changeux, A. R. Damascio, W. Singer, & Y. Christen (Eds.), *Neurobiology of human values* (pp. 107–123). Berlin, Germany: Springer-Verlag.

Roberts, B. W., & Bogg, T. (2004). A longitudinal study of the relationships between conscientiousness and the social-environmental factors and substance abuse behaviors that influence health. *Journal of Personality, 72,* 325–354.

Roberts, B. W., Helson, R., & Klohen, E. C. (2002). Personality development and growth in women across 30 years: Three perspectives. *Journal of Personality, 70,* 79–102.

Roberts, B. W., O'Donnell, M., & Robins, R. W. (2004). Goal and personality trait development in emerging adulthood. *Journal of Personality and Social Psychology, 87,* 541–550.

Roberts, B. W., Walton, K. C., & Viechtbauer, W. (2006). Patterns of mean-level changes in personality across the life course: A meta-analysis of longitudinal studies. *Psychological Bulletin, 132,* 1–25.

Roberts, B. W., Wood, D., & Caspi, A. (2008). The development of personality traits in adulthood. In O. P. John, R. W. Robins, & L. A. Pervin (Eds.), *Handbook of personality: Theory and research* (3rd ed., pp. 375–398). New York, NY: Guilford.

Robertson, T. E., Delton, A. W., Klein, S. B., Cosmides, L., & Tooby, J. (2014). Keeping the benefits of group cooperation: Domain-specific responses to distinct causes of social exclusion. *Evolution and Human Behavior, 35,* 472–480.

Robins, R. W., Tracy, J. L., & Sherman, J. W. (2007). What kinds of methods do personality psychologists use? In R. W. Robins, R. C. Fraley, & R. F. Krueger (Eds.), *Handbook of research methods in personality psychology* (pp. 673–678). New York, NY: Guilford.

Rogers, C. R. (1951). *Client-centered therapy.* Boston, MA: Houghton Mifflin.

Rogers, C. R. (1954). The case of Mrs. Oak: A research analysis. In C. R. Rogers & R. F. Diamond (Eds.), *Psychotherapy and personality change.* Chicago, IL: University of Chicago Press.

Rogers, C. R. (1959). A theory of therapy, personality and interpersonal relationships as developed in the client-centered framework. In S. Koch (Ed.), *Psychology: A study of science: Formulations of the person and the social context* (pp. 184–256). New York, NY: McGraw-Hill.

Rogers, C. R. (1961). *On becoming a person.* Boston, MA: Houghton Mifflin.

Rogers, C. R. (1980). *A way of being.* Boston, MA: Houghton Mifflin.

Rohling, M. L., Larrabee, G. J., Greiffenstein, M. F., Ben-Porath, Y. S., Lees-Haley, P., Green, P., & Grieve, K. W. (2011). A misleading review of response bias: Comment on McGrath, Mitchell, Kim, and Hough (2010). *Psychological Bulletin, 137,* 708–712.

Rorschach, H. (1921). *Psychodiagnostik.* Bern, Germany: Bircher.

Rosen, K. S., & Rothbaum, F. (1993). Quality of parental caregiving and security of attachment. *Developmental Psychology, 29,* 358–367

Rosenberg, M. (1965). *Society and the adolescent self-image.* Princeton, NJ: Princeton University Press.

Rothbart, M. K. (2011). *Becoming who we are: Temperament and personality in development.* New York, NY: Guilford.

Rothbart, M. K., & Bates, J. E. (2006). Temperament. In N. Eisenberg (Ed.). *Handbook of child psychology* (6th ed., Vol. 3, pp. 99–166). Hoboken, NJ: Wiley.

Rottman, B. M., Woo-kyoung, A., Sanislow, C. A., & Kim, N. (2009). Can clinicians recognize DSM-IV personality disorders from Five-Factor Model descriptions of patient cases? *American Journal of Psychiatry, 166,* 427–433.

Rubin, Z. (1970). Measurement of romantic love. *Journal of Personality and Social Psychology, 16,* 265–273.

Ruble, D. N., Martin, C. L., & Berenbaum, S. A. (2006). Gender development. In N. Eisenberg (Ed.), *Handbook of child psychology* (6th ed., Vol. 3, pp. 858–932). Hoboken, NJ: Wiley.

Ruble, D. N., Martin, C. L., & Berenbaum, S. A. (2006). Gender development. In N. Eisenberg (Ed.), *Handbook of child psychology: Vol. 3. Social, emotional, and personality development* (6th ed., pp. 858–932). Hoboken, NJ: Wiley.

Runyon, W. M. (1982). *Life histories and psychobiography.* New York, NY: Oxford University Press.

Runyon, W. M. (1997). Studying lives: Psychobiography and the conceptual structure of personality psychology. In R. Hogan, J. Johnson, & S. Briggs (Eds.), *Handbook of personality psychology* (pp. 41–69). New York, NY: Academic Press.

Rutter, M. (1995). Clinical implications of attachment concepts: Retrospect and prospect. *Journal of Child Psychology and Psychiatry, 36,* 549–571.

Rutter, M., & Quinton, D. (1984). Long-term follow-up of women institutionalized in childhood: Factors promoting good functioning in adult life. *British Journal of Developmental Psychology, 2,* 191–204.

Ryan, R. M. (1993). Agency and organization: Intrinsic motivation, autonomy and the self in psychological development. In J. Jacobs (Ed.), *Nebraska symposium on motivation* (Vol. 40, pp. 1–56). Lincoln: University of Nebraska Press.

Ryan, R. M., & Deci, E. L. (2000). Self-determination theory and the facilitation of intrinsic motivation, social development, and well-being. *American Psychologist, 55,* 68–78.

Ryan, R. M., & Deci, E. L. (2008). Self-determination theory and the role of basic psychological needs in personality and the organization of behavior. In O. P. John, R. W. Robins, & L. A. Pervin (Eds.), *Handbook of personality: Theory and research* (3rd ed., pp. 654–678). New York, NY: Guilford.

Ryan, R. M., Mims, V., & Koestner, R. (1983). Relation of reward contingency and interpersonal context to intrinsic motivation: A review and test using cognitive evaluation theory. *Journal of Personality and Social Psychology, 45,* 736–750.

Saad, G. (2007). *The evolutionary basis of consumption.* Mahwah, NJ: Erlbaum.

Sadalla, E. K., Kenrick, D. T., & Vershure, B. (1987). Dominance and heterosexual attraction. *Journal of Personality and Social Psychology, 52,* 730–738.

Sagioglou, C., & Greitmeyer, T. (2014). Facebook's emotional consequences: Why Facebook causes a decrease in mood and why people still use it. *Computers in Human Behavior, 35,* 359–363.

Samuel, D. B., & Widiger, T. A. (2008). A meta-analytic review of the relationship between the Five-Factor Model and DSM-IV-TR personality disorders: A facet-level analysis. *Clinical Psychology Review, 28,* 1326–1342.

Sanson, A., Prior, M., Garino, E., Oberkaid, F., & Sewell, J. (1987). The structure of infant temperament. *Infant Behavior and Development, 10,* 97–104.

Sapolsky, R. M. (1990). Adrenocortical function, social rank, and personality among wild baboons. *Biological Psychiatry, 28,* 862–878.

Sapolsky, R. M. (2004). *Why zebras don't get ulcers: An updated guide to stress, stress-related diseases, and coping* (3rd ed.). New York, NY: Freeman.

Sapolsky, R. M. (2007). Stress, stress-related disease, and emotional regulation. In J. J. Gross (Ed.), *Handbook of emotional regulation* (pp. 606–615). New York, NY: Guilford Press.

Sarason, B. R., Pierce, G. R., Shearin, E. N., Sarason, I. G., Waltz, J. A., & Poppe, L. (1991). Perceived social support and working models of self and others. *Journal of Personality and Social Psychology, 60,* 273–287.

Saucier, G. (2003). Factor structure of English-language personality-type nouns. *Journal of Personality and Social Psychology, 85,* 605–708.

Saucier, G., & Srivastava, S. (2015). What makes a good model of personality? Evaluating the big five and alternatives. In M. Mikulincer & P. R. Shaver (Eds.), *APA handbook of personality and social psychology* (Vol. 4, pp. 283–305). Washington, DC: American Psychological Association.

Saulsman, L. M., & Page, A. C. (2004). The Five-Factor Model and personality disorder empirical literature: A meta-analytic review. *Clinical Psychology Review, 23,* 1055–1083.

Scarr, S., & McCartney, K. (1983). How people make their own environments: A theory of genotype → environmental effects. *Child Development, 54,* 424–435.

Schachter, S. (1959). *The psychology of affiliation.* Palo Alto, CA: Stanford University Press.

Schafer, R. (1992). *Retelling a life: Narration and dialogue in psycho*analysis. New York, NY: Basic Books.

Scheff, T. J., Retzinger, S. M., & Ryan, M. T. (1989). Crime, violence, and self-esteem: Review and proposals. In A. M. Mecca, N. J. Smelser, & J. Vasconcellos (Eds.), *The social importance of self-esteem* (pp. 165–199). Berkeley, CA: University of California Press.

Schmidt, L., Braun, E. K., Wager, T. D., & Shohamy, D. (2014). Mind matters: Placebo enhances reward learning in Parkinson's disease. *Nature Neuroscience, 17,* 1793–1797.

Schmitt, D. P., & Buss, D. M. (2001). Human mate poaching: Tactics and temptations for infiltrating existing relationships. *Journal of Personality and Social Psychology, 80,* 894–917.

Schmitt, D. P., Realo, A., Voracek, M., & Allik, J. (2008). Why can't a woman be more like a man? Sex differences in Big Five personality traits across 55 cultures. *Journal of Personality and Social Psychology, 94,* 168–182.

Schneider, B. H., Atkinson, L., & Tardiff, C. (2001). Child-parent attachment and children's peer relations: A quantitative view. *Developmental Psychology, 37,* 86–100.

Schneider, M. L. (1992a). The effect of mild stress during pregnancy on birth weight and neuromotor maturation in rhesus monkey infants (*Macaca mulatta*). *Infant Behavior and Development, 15,* 389–403.

Schneider, M. L. (1992b). Parental stress exposure alters postnatal behavioral expression under conditions of novelty challenge in rhesus monkey infants. *Developmental Psychobiology, 25,* 529–540.

Schneiderman, I., Zilberstein-Kra, Y., Leckman, J. F., & Feldman, R. (2011). Love alters autonomic reactivity to emotions. *Emotion, 11,* 1314–1321.

Schore, A. N. (1997). Early organization of the nonlinear right brain and development of a predisposition to psychiatric disorders. *Development and Psychopathology, 9,* 595–631.

Schore, A. N. (2002). The neurobiology of attachment and early personality organization. *Journal of Prenatal and Perinatal Psychology and Health, 16,* 249–263.

Schore, A. N. (2009). Relational trauma and the developing right brain. *Annals of the New York Academy of Sciences, 1159,* 189–203.

Schou, I., Ekeberg, O., & Ruland, C. M. (2005). The moderating role of appraisal and coping in the relationship between optimism-pessimism and quality of life. *Psycho-Oncology, 14,* 718–727.

Schwartz, A. (1992). *The man who could not kill enough: The secret murders of Milwaukee's Jeffrey Dahlmer.* New York, NY: Carol.

Schwinger, M., Withwein, L., Lemmer, G., & Steinmayr, R. (2014). Academic self-handicapping and achievement: A meta-analysis. *Journal of Educational Psychology, 106,* 744–761.

Sebastian-Enesco, C., & Warneken, F. (2015). The shadow of the future: 5-year-olds, but not 3-year-olds, adjust their sharing in anticipation of reciprocation. *Journal of Experimental Child Psychology, 129,* 40–54.

Sedikides, C. (1993). Assessment, enhancement, and verification determinants of the self-evaluation process. *Journal of Personality and Social Psychology, 65,* 317–338.

Seligman, M. E. P. (1994). *What you can change and what you can't.* New York, NY: Knopf.

Seligman, M. E. P., & Csikszentmihalyi, M. (2000). Positive psychology: An introduction. *American Psychologist, 55,* 5–14.

Selye, H. (1956). *The stress of life.* New York, NY: McGraw-Hill.

Selye. H. (1973). The evolution of the stress concept. *American Scientist, 61,* 672–699.

Serbin, L. A., & Sprafkin, C. (1986). The salience of gender and the process of sex typing in three- to seven-year-old children. *Child Development, 57,* 1188–1199.

Seyfarth, R. M., & Cheney, D. L. (2012). The evolutionary origins of friendship. *Annual Review of Psychology, 63,* 153–177.

Shapiro, D. (1965). *Neurotic styles.* New York, NY: Basic Books.

Sharma, L., Kohl, K., Morgan, T. A., & Clark, L. A. (2013). "Impulsivity": Relations between self-report and behavior. *Journal of Personality and Social Psychology, 104,* 559–575.

Shedler, J., & Block, J. (1990). Adolescent drug use and psychological health: A longitudinal inquiry. *American Psychologist, 45,* 612–630.

Shedler, J., & Westen, D. (2004). Refining personality disorder diagnosis: Integrating science and practice. *The American Journal of Psychiatry, 161,* 1350–1365.

Sheldon, K. M., & Kasser, T. (1998). Pursuing personal goals: Skills enable progress, but not all progress is beneficial. *Personality and Social Psychology Bulletin, 24,* 1319–1331.

Sheldon, K. M., & Kasser, T. (2001). Getting older, getting better? Personal strivings and psychological maturity across the life span. *Developmental Psychology, 37,* 491–501.

Sherman, G. D., Lerner, J. S., Josephs, R. A., Renshon, J., & Gross, J. J. (2015). The interaction of testosterone and cortisol is associated with attained status in male executives. *Journal of Personality and Social Psychology.* In press.

Shiner, R. L. (2015). The development of temperament and personality traits in childhood and adolescence. In M. Mikulincer & P. R. Shaver (Eds.), *APA handbook of personality and social psychology* (Vol. 4, pp. 85–105). Washington, DC: American Psychological Association.

Shostrom, E. L. (1963). Personal orientation inventory. San Diego, CA: EDITS/ Educational and Industrial Testing Service.

Shostrom, E. L. (1974). Manual for the personal orientation inventory. San Diego, CA: EDITS/Educational and Industrial Testing Service.

Sidanius, J., & Pratto, F. (1999). *Social dominance.* New York, NY: Cambridge University Press.

Siegel, D. J. (2012). *The developing mind: How relationships and the brain interact to shape who we are* (2nd ed.). New York, NY: Guilford.

Simpson, J. A. (1990). Influence of attachment styles on romantic relationships. *Journal of Personality and Social Psychology, 59,* 971–980

Singer, J. A. (2005). *Personality and psychotherapy: Treating the whole person.* New York, NY: Guilford.

Sipps, G. J., & DiCaudio, J. (1988). Convergent and discriminant validity of the Myers-Briggs type indicator as a measure of sociability and impulsivity. *Educational and Psychological Measurement, 48,* 445–451.

Sirois, F. M., & Kitner, R. (2015). Less adaptive or more maladaptive? A meta-analytic investigation of procrastination and coping. *European Journal of Personality, 29,* 433–444.

Skodol, A. E., Gunderson, J. G., Shea, M. T., . . . Stout, R. L. (2005). The Collaborative Longitudinal Personality Disorders Study (CLPS): Overview and implications. *Journal of Personality Disorders, 19,* 487–504.

Slavich, G. M., & Irwin, M. R. (2014). From stress to inflammation and major depressive disorder: A social signal transduction theory of depression. *Psychological Bulletin, 140,* 774–815.

Smith, A. J., Benight, C. C., & Cieslak, R. (2013). Social support and post deployment coping self-efficacy as predictors of distress among combat veterans. *Military Psychology, 25,* 452–461.

Smith, A. R., Chein, J., & Steinberg, L. (2014). Peers increase adolescent risk taking even when the probabilities of negative outcomes are known. *Developmental Psychology, 50,* 1564–1568.

Smith, G. T., & Guller, L. (2015). Psychological underpinnings to impulsive behavior. In M. Mikulincer & P. R. Shaver (Eds.), *APA handbook of personality and social psychology* (Vol. 4., pp. 329–350). Washington, DC: American Psychological Association.

Smith, T. W., Williams, P. G., & Segerstrom, S. C. (2015). Personality and physical health. In M. Mikulincer & P. R. Shaver (Eds.), *APA handbook of personality and social psychology. Vol. 4: Personality processes and individual differences* (pp. 639– 661). Washington, DC: American Psychological Association.

Sneed, J. R., Whitbourne, S. K., & Culang, M. E. (2006). Trust, identity, and ego integrity: Modeling Erikson's core stages over 34 years. *Journal of Adult Development, 13,* 148–157.

Sneed, J. R., Whitbourne, S. K., Schwartz, S. J., & Huang, S. (2012). The relationship between identity, intimacy, and midlife well-being: Findings from the Rochester Adult Longitudinal study. *Psychology and Aging, 27,* 318–323.

Snyder, C. R. (2003). *The psychology of hope.* New York, NY: The Free Press.

Sokol, D. K., Moore, C. A., Rose, R. J., Williams, C. J., Reed, T., & Christian, J. C. (1995). Intrapair differences in personality and cognitive ability among young monozygotic twins distinguished by chorion type. *Behavior Genetics, 25,* 457–466.

Solberg Nes, L., & Segerstrom, S. C. (2006). Dispositional optimism and coping: A meta-analytic review. *Personality and Social Psychology Review, 10,* 235–251.

Solomon, L. J., & Rothblum, E. D. (1984). Academic procrastination: Frequency, and cognitive-behavioral correlates. *Journal of Counseling Psychology, 31,* 503–509.

Song, A. V., & Simonton, D. K. (2007). Personality assessment at a distance. In R. W. Robins, R. C. Fraley, & R. F. Krueger (Eds.), *Handbook of research methods in personality psychology* (pp. 308–321). New York, NY: Guilford.

Sorokowski, P., Sorokowska, A., Oleszkiewicz, A., Frackowiak, T., Huk, A., & Pisanski, K. (2015). Selfie posting behaviors are associated with narcissism among men. *Personality and Individual Differences, 85,* 123–127.

South, S. C., Reichborn-Kjennerud, T., Eaton, N. R., & Krueger, R. F. (2015). Genetics of personality. In M. Mikulincer & P. R. Shaver (Eds.), *APA handbook of personality and social psychology* (Vol. 4, pp. 31–60). Washington, DC: American Psychological Association.

Spear, L. (2010). *The behavioral neuroscience of adolescence.* New York, NY: Norton.

Speiker, S. J., & Booth, C. L. (1988). Maternal antecedents of attachment quality. In J. Belsky & T. Nezworski (Eds.) *Clinical implications of attach*ment (pp. 95–135). Hillsdale, NJ: Erlbaum.

Spence, D. P. (1982). *Narrative truth and historical truth: Meaning and interpretation in psychoanalysis.* New York, NY: Norton.

Spoor, J. R., & Williams, K. D. (2006). The evolution of an ostracism detection system. In J. P. Forgas, M. G. Haselton, & W. Hippel (Eds.), *Evolution and the social mind* (pp. 279–292). New York, NY: Psychology Press.

Sporns, O., & Betzel, R. F. (2016). Modular brain networks. *Annual Review of Psychology.* In press.

Sroufe, L. A. (1988). The role of infant-caregiver attachment in development. In J. Belsky & T. Nezworski (Eds.) *Clinical implications of attachment* (pp. 18–38). Hillsdale, NJ: Lawrence Erlbaum.

Sroufe, L. A. (1990). An organizational perspective on the self. In D. Cicchetti & M. Beeghly (Eds.), *The self in transition* (pp. 281–307). Chicago, IL: University of Chicago Press.

Sroufe, L. A., Egeland, B., Carlson, E. A., & Collins, W. A. (2005). *The development of the person: The Minnesota study of risk and adaptation from birth to adulthood.* New York, NY: Guilford.

Sroufe, L. A., & Waters, E. (1977). Heart rate as a convergent measure in clinical and developmental research. *Merrill-Palmer Quarterly, 23,* 3–27.

Stagner, R. (1937). *Psychology of personality.* New York, NY: McGraw-Hill.

Stahl, C., Voss, A., Schmitz, F., Nuszbaum, M., Tuscher, O., Lieb, K., & Klauer, K. C. (2014). Behavioral components of impulsivity. *Journal of Experimental Psychology: General, 143,* 850–886.

Staudinger, U. M., & Gluck, J. (2011). Psychological wisdom: Commonalities and differences in a growing field. *Annual Review of Psychology, 62,* 215–241.

Steel, P. (2007). The nature of procrastination: A meta-analytic and theoretical review of quintessential self-regulatory failure. *Psychological Bulletin, 133,* 65–94.

Steele, H., Steele, M., & Croft, C. (2008). Early attachment predicts emotion recognition at 6 and 11 years. *Attachment and Human Development, 4,* 379–393.

Stephan, W. G. (2014). Intergroup anxiety: Theory, research, and practice. *Personality and Social Psychology Review, 18,* 239–255.

Stephens, N. M., Markus, H. R., & Phillips, L. T. (2014). Social class culture cycles: How three gateway contexts shape selves and fuel inequality. *Annual Review of Psychology, 65,* 611–634.

Stepp, D. D., Whalen, D. J., & Smith, T. D. (2013). Dialectical behavior therapy from the perspective of the Five-Factor Model of personality. In T. A. Widiger & P. T. Costa Jr. (Eds.), *Personality disorders and the Five-Factor Model of personality* (3rd ed., pp. 395–407). Washington, DC: American Psychological Association.

Stern, B. L., & Gershuny, B. S. (1998). A structured interview for the assessment of the Five-Factor Model of personality. *Psychological Assessment, 10,* 229–240.

Stern, D. N. (1985). *The interpersonal world of the infant.* New York, NY: Basic Books.

Sternberg, R. J. (1986). A triangular theory of love. *Psychological Review, 93,* 119–135.

Stillman, T. F., Maner, J. K., & Baumeister, R. F. (2009). A thin slice of violence: Distinguishing violent from non-violent sex offenders at a glance. *Evolution and Human Behavior, 31,* 298–303.

Stoller, R. J. (1985). *Presentations of gender.* New Haven, CT: Yale University Press.

Stone, M. H. (1998). Sadistic personality in murders. In T. Millon, E. Simonsen, M. Birket-Smith, & R. D. Davis (Eds.), *Psychopathy: Antisocial, criminal and violent behavior* (pp. 346–355). New York, NY: Guilford.

Stone, M. H. (2013). Treatment of personality disorders from the perspective of the Five-Factor Model. In T. A. Widiger & P. T. Costa Jr. (Eds.), *Personality disorders and the Five-Factor Model of personality* (3rd ed., pp. 133–145). Washington, DC: American Psychological Association.

Strathman, A., Gleicher, F., Boninger, D. S., & Edwards, C. S. (1994). The consideration of future consequences: Weighing immediate and distant outcomes of behavior. *Journal of Personality and Social Psychology, 66,* 742–752.

Strauman, T. (1996). Stability within the self: A longitudinal study of the structural implications of self-discrepancy theory. *Journal of Personality and Social Psychology, 71,* 1142–1153.

Strauman, T. J., Vookles, J., Berenstein, V., Chaiken, S., & Higgins, E. T. (1991). Self-discrepancies and vulnerability to body dissatisfaction and disordered eating. *Journal of Personality and Social Psychology, 61,* 946–956.

Strauss, R., & Goldberg, W. A. (1999). Self and possible selves during the transition to fatherhood. *Journal of Family Psychology, 13,* 244–259.

Sugiyama, L. S. (2005). Physical attractiveness in adaptationist perspective. In D. M. Buss (Ed.), *The handbook of evolutionary psychology* (pp. 292–343). Hoboken, NJ: Wiley.

Sulloway, F. J. (1992). *Freud, biologist of the mind.* Cambridge, MA: Harvard University Press.

Sulloway, F. J. (1996). *Born to rebel: Birth order, family dynamics, and creative lives.* New York, NY: Pantheon.

Suls, J., & Martin, R. (2005). The daily life of the garden-variety neurotic: Reactivity, stressor exposure, mood spillover, and maladaptive coping. *Journal of Personality, 73,* 1485–1509.

Sutin, A. R., Costa, P. T., Jr., Wethington, E., & Eaton, W. (2010). Turning points and lessons learned: Stressful life events and personality trait development across middle adulthood. *Psychology and Aging, 25,* 524–533.

Sutker, P. B., & Allain, A. N. J. (1988). Issues in personality conceptualizations of addictive behaviors. *Journal of Consulting and Clinical Psychology, 56,* 172–182.

Suzuki, A. S., Homma, Y., & Suga, S. (2013). Indelible distrust: Memory bias toward cheaters revealed as high persistence against extinction. *Journal of Experimental Psychology: Learning, Memory, and Cognition, 39,* 1901–1913.

Swann, W. B. Jr. (1987). Identity negotiation: Where two roads meet. *Journal of Personality and Social Psychology, 53,* 1038–1051.

Swann, W. B. Jr., & Buhrmester, M. D. (2015). Identity fusion. *Current Directions in Psychological Science, 24,* 52–57.

Swann, W. B. Jr., De La Ronde, C., & Hixon, J. G. (1994). Authenticity and positivity strivings in marriage and courtship. *Journal of Personality and Social Psychology, 66,* 857–869.

Swann, W. B. Jr., Gomez, A., Buhmeister, M. D., Lopez-Rodriguez, L., Jiminez, J., & Vazquez, A. (2014). Contemplating the ultimate sacrifice: Identity fusion channels pro-group affect, cognition, and moral decision making. *Journal of Personality and Social Psychology, 106,* 713–727.

Swann, W. B. Jr., Gomez, A., Dovidio, J. F., Hart, S., & Jetten, J. (2010). Dying and killing for one's group: Identity fusion moderates responses to intergroup versions of the trolley problem. *Psychological Science, 21,* 1176–1183.

Swann, W. B. Jr., Gomez, A., Huici, C., Morales, J. F., & Hixon, J. G. (2010). Identity fusion and self-sacrifice: Arousal as a catalyst of pro-group fighting, dying, and helping behavior. *Journal of Personality and Social Psychology, 99,* 824–841.

Swann, W. B. Jr., Gomez, A., Seyle, D. C., Morales, J. F., & Huici, C. (2009). Identity fusion: The interplay of personal and social identities in extreme group behavior. *Journal of Personality and Social Psychology, 96,* 995–1011.

Swann, W. B. Jr., Hixon, J. G., & De La Ronde, C. (1992). Embracing the bitter "truth": Negative self-concepts and marital commitment. *Psychological Science, 3,* 118–121.

Swann, W. B. Jr., Jetten, J., Gomez, A., Whitehouse, H., & Bastian, B. (2012). When group membership gets personal: A theory of identity fusion. *Psychological Review, 119,* 441–456.

Swann, W. B. Jr., Milton, L. P., & Polzer, J. T. (2000). Should we create a niche or fall in line? Identity negotiation and small group effectiveness. *Journal of Personality and Social Psychology, 79,* 238–250.

Swann, W. B. Jr., Stein-Seroussi, A., & McNulty, S. E. (1992). Outcasts in a white-lie society: The enigmatic words of people with negative self-conceptions. *Journal of Personality and Social Psychology, 62,* 618–624.

Sweeny, K., & Andrews, S. E. (2014). Mapping individual differences in the experience of a waiting period. *Journal of Personality and Social Psychology, 106,* 1015–1030.

Tackman, A. M., & Srivastava, S. (2015). Social responses to expressive suppression: The role of personality judgments. *Journal of Personality and Social Psychology.* In press.

Tajfel, H. (1970). Experiments in intergroup discrimination. *Scientific American, 223,* 96–102.

Tajfel, H., & Billig, M. (1974). Familiarity and categorization in intergroup behavior. *Journal of Experimental Social Psychology, 10,* 159–170.

Tandoc, E. C. Jr., Ferrucci, P., & Duffy, M. (2015). Facebook use, envy, and depression among college students: Is Facebooking depressing? *Computers in Human Behavior, 43,* 139–146

Tarabulsy, G. M., Larose, S., Bernier, A., Trottier-Sylvain, K., Girard, D., Vargas, M., & Noel, C. (2012). Attachment states of mind in late adolescence and the quality and course of romantic relationships in adulthood. *Attachment and Human Development, 14,* 621–643.

Tavris, C., & Aronson, E. (2007). *Mistakes were made (but not by me).* Orlando, FL: Harvest Book.

Taylor, S. E. (1989). *Positive illusions: Creative self-deceptions and the healthy mind.* New York, NY: Basic Books.

Taylor, S. E., & Brown, J. D. (1988). Illusions and well-being: A social psychological perspective on mental health. *Psychological Bulletin, 103,* 193–210.

Taylor, Z. E., Eisenberg, N., Van Schyndel, S. K., Eggum-Wilkens, N. D., & Spinrad, T. L. (2014). Children's negative emotions and ego-resiliency: Longitudinal relations with social competence. *Emotion, 14,* 397–406.

Taylor, Z. E., Larsen-Rife, D., Conger, R. D., Widaman, K. F., & Cutrona, C. E. (2010). Life stress, maternal optimism, and adolescent competence in single mother, African American families. *Journal of Family Psychology, 24,* 468–477.

Taylor, Z. E., Widaman, K. F., Robins, R. W., Jochem, R., Early, D. R., & Conger, R. D. (2012). Dispositional optimism: A psychological resource for Mexican-origin mothers experiencing economic stress. *Journal of Family Psychology, 26,* 133–139.

Tellegen, A., & Ben-Porath, Y. S. (2008/2011). *Minnesota Multiphasic Personality Inventory-2-Restructured Form: Technical manual.* Minneapolis: University of Minnesota Press.

Tellegen, A., Lykken, D. T., Bouchard, T. J. Jr., Wilcox, K. J., Segal, N. L., & Rich, S. (1988). Personality similarity in twins reared apart and together. *Journal of Personality and Social Psychology, 54,* 1031–1039.

Tenney, E. R., Logg, J. M., & Moore, D. A. (2015). (Too) optimistic about optimism: The belief that optimism improves performance. *Journal of Personality and Social Psychology, 108,* 377–399.

Tesch, S. A., & Whitbourne, S. K. (1982). Intimacy and identity status in young adults. *Journal of Personality and Social Psychology, 43,* 1041–1051.

Tesser, A. (1993). The importance of heritability in psychological research: The case of attitudes. *Psychological Review, 100,* 129–142.

The Dhammapada (1973). (J. Mascaro, Trans.). Suffolk, UK: Penguin.

Thomas, A., Chess, S., & Birch, H. G. (1968). *Temperament and behavior disorders in children.* New York, NY: New York University Press.

Thompson, R. A. (2006). The development of the person: Social understanding, relationships, conscience, self. In N. Eisenberg (Ed.), *Handbook of child psychology: Vol. 3. Social, emotional, and personality development* (6th ed., pp. 24–98). Hoboken, NJ: Wiley.

Thompson, R. A. (2008). Early attachment and later development. In J. Cassidy & P. R. Shaver (Eds.), *Handbook of attachment* (2nd ed., pp. 348–365). New York, NY: Guilford.

Thorne, A. (1987). The press of personality: A study of conversations between introverts and extraverts. *Journal of Personality and Social Psychology, 53,* 718–726.

Tice, D. M. (1991). Esteem protection or enhancement? Self-handicapping motives and attributions differ by trait self-esteem. *Journal of Personality and Social Psychology, 60,* 711–725.

Tice, D. M., & Baumeister, R. F. (1997). Longitudinal study of procrastination, performance, stress, and health: The costs and benefits of dawdling. *Psychological Science, 8,* 454–458.

Tomaka, J., Blascovich, J., Kibler, J., & Ernst, J. M. (1997). Cognitive and physiological antecedents of threat and challenge appraisal. *Journal of Personality and Social Psychology, 73,* 63–72.

Tomkins, S. S. (1979). Script theory: Differential magnification of affects. *Nebraska Symposium on Motivation, 26,* 201–236.

Tooby, J., & Cosmides, L. (1990). On the universality of human nature and the uniqueness of the individual: The role of genetics and adaptation. *Journal of Personality, 58,* 17–67.

Tooby, J., & Cosmides, L. (1992). The psychological foundations of culture. In J. H. Barkow, L. Cosmides, & J. Tooby (Eds.), *The adapted mind: Evolutionary psychology and the evolution of culture* (pp. 19–136). New York, NY: Oxford University Press.

Tooby, J., & Cosmides, L. (2005). Conceptual foundations of evolutionary psychology. In D. M. Buss (Ed.), *The handbook of evolutionary psychology* (pp. 5–67). Hoboken, NJ: Wiley.

Triebwasser, J., Chemerinski, E., Roussos, P., & Siever, L. J. (2012). Paranoid personality disorder. *Journal of Personality Disorders, 27,* 795–805.

Trull, T. J., Widiger, T. A., Useda, J. D., Holcomb, J., Doan, B-T., Axelrod, S. R., Trzseniewski, K. H., Donnellan, M. B., & Robins, R. W. (2008). Is "Generation Me" really more narcissistic than previous generations? *Journal of Personality, 76,* 903–916.

Trzseniewski, K. H., Donnellan, & Robins, R. W. (2008). Is "Generation Me" really more narcissistic than previous generations? *Journal of Personality, 76,* 903-916.

Tse, W. S., & Bond, A. L. (2002). Serotonergic intervention affects both social dominance and affiliative behavior. *Psychopharmacology, 161,* 324–330.

Tugade, M. M., & Frederickson, B. L. (2004). Resilient individuals use positive emotions to bounce back from negative emotional experiences. *Journal of Personality and Social Psychology, 86,* 320–333.

Tuk, M. A., Zhang, K., & Sweldens, S. (2015). The propagation of self-control: Self-control in one domain simultaneously improves self-control in other domains. *Journal of Experimental Psychology: General.* In press.

Turkheimer, E., Pettersson, E., & Horn, E. E. (2014). A phenotypic null hypothesis for the genetics of personality. *Annual Review of Psychology, 65,* 515–540.

Turner, J. C., & Onorato, R. S. (1999). Social identity, personality, and the self-concept: A self-categorization perspective. In T. R. Tyler, R. M. Kramer, & O. P. John (Eds.), *The psychology of the social self* (pp. 11–46). Mahwah, NJ: Erlbaum.

Tuschman, A. (2013). *Our political nature: The evolutionary origins of what divides us.* Amherst, NY: Prometheus Books.

Twenge, J. M., Baumeister, R. F., Tice, D. M., & Stucke, T. S. (2001). If you can't beat them, beat them: Effects of social exclusion on aggressive behavior. *Journal of Personality and Social Psychology, 81,* 1058–1069.

Twenge, J., Catanese, K. R., & Baumeister, R. F. (2002). Social exclusion causes self-defeating behavior. *Journal of Personality and Social Psychology, 83,* 606–615.

Tyson, P., & Tyson, R. L. (1990). *Psychoanalytic theories of development: An integration.* New Haven, CT: Yale University Press.

Urdan, T. (2004). Predictors of academic self-handicapping and achievement: Examining achievement goals, classroom goal structures, and culture. *Journal of Educational Psychology, 96,* 251–264.

Uskul, A. K, & Over, H. (2014). Responses to social exclusion in cultural context: Evidence from farming and herding communities. *Journal of Personality and Social Psychology, 106,* 752–771.

Vaillant, G. E. (1977). *Adaptation to life.* Boston, MA: Little, Brown.

Vaillant, G. E. (1993). *The wisdom of the ego.* Cambridge, MA: Harvard University Press.

Vaillant, G. E. (2000). Adaptive mental mechanisms: Their role in a positive psychology. *American Psychologist, 55,* 89–98.

Vallerand, R. J., & Bissonnette, R. (1992). Intrinsic, extrinsic, and amotivational styles as predictors of behavior: A prospective study. *Journal of Personality, 60,* 599–620.

Van den Tooren, M, & Rutte, C. (2015). Explaining emotional exhaustion and work engagement: The role of job demands-resources and Type D personality. *International Journal of Stress Management.* In press.

van der Schalk, J., Fischer, A., Doosje, B., Wigboldus, D., Hawk, S., Rotteveel, M., & Hess, U. (2011). Convergent and divergent responses to emotional displays of ingroup and outgroup. *Emotion, 11,* 286–298.

van Tilburg, W. A. P., Sedikides, C., & Wildschut, T. (2015). The mnemonic muse: Nostalgia fosters creativity through openness to experience. *Journal of Experimental Social Psychology, 59,* 1–7.

Vaughn, B. E., Bost, K. K., & IJzendoorn, M. H. (2008). Attachment and temperament. In J. Cassidy & P. R. Shaver (Eds.), *Handbook of attachment* (2nd ed., pp. 192–216). New York, NY: Guilford.

Vaughn, B. E., Stevenson-Hinde, J., Waters, E., Kotsaftis, A., Lefever, G. B., Shouldice, A., Trudel, M., & Belsky, J. (1992). Attachment security and temperament in infancy and early childhood: Some conceptual clarifications. *Developmental Psychology, 28,* 463–473.

Vazire, S. (2006). Informant reports: A cheap, fast, and easy method for personality assessment. *Journal of Research in Personality, 40,* 472–481.

Vazire, S., Gosling, S. D., Dickey, A. S., & Schapiro, S. J. (2007). Measuring personality in nonhuman animals. In R. W. Robins, R. C. Fraley, & R. F. Kruger (Eds.), *Handbook of research methods in personality psychology* (pp. 190–206). New York, NY: Guilford.

Veblen, T. (1994). *The theory of the leisure class: An economic study of institutions.* New York, NY: Dover. (Original work published 1899)

Verheul, R., & Widiger, T. A. (2004). A meta-analysis of the prevalence and usage of the personality disorder not otherwise specified (PDNOS) diagnosis. *Journal of Personality Disorders, 18,* 309–319.

Viken, R. J., Rose, R. J., Kaprio, J., & Koskenvuo, M. (1994). A developmental genetic analysis of adult personality: Extraversion and neuroticism. *Journal of Personality and Social Psychology, 28,* 463–473.

Vohs, K. D., Baumeister, R. F., Schmeichel, B. J., Twenge, J. M., Nelson, N. M., & Tice, D. M. (2008). Making choices impairs self-control: Limited-resources account of decision-making, self-regulation, and active initiative. *Journal of Personality and Social Psychology, 94,* 883–898.

Vroman, L. N., Lo, S. L., & Durbin, C. E. (2014). Structure and convergent validity of children's temperament traits as assessed by experimenter ratings of child behavior. *Journal of Research in Personality, 52*, 6–12.

Vukasovic, T., & Bratko, D. (2015). Heritability of personality: A meta-analysis of behavior genetic studies. *Psychological Bulletin, 141*, 769–785

Wagner, D. D., & Heatherton, T. F. (2015). Self-regulation and its failure: The seven deadly threats to self-regulation. In M. Mikulincer & P. R. Shaver (Eds.), *APA handbook of personality and social psychology. Vol. 1: Attitudes and social cognition* (pp. 805–842). Washington, DC: American Psychological Association.

Wagner, M. E., & Schubert, H. J. P. (1977). Sibship variables and United States presidents. *Journal of Individual Psychology, 62*, 78–85.

Wakslak, C. J., Smith, P. K., & Han, A. (2014). Using abstract language signals power. *Journal of Personality and Social Psychology, 107*, 41–55.

Wang, Q. (2001). Culture effects on adults' earliest recollection and self-descriptions: Implications for the relation between memory and the self. *Journal of Personality and Social Psychology, 81*, 220–233.

Wang, Q., & Conway, M. A. (2004). The stories we keep: Autobiographical memory in American and Chinese middle-aged adults. *Journal of Personality, 72*, 911–938.

Warren, S. L., Huston, L., Egeland, B., & Sroufe, L. A. (1997). Child and adolescent anxiety disorders and early attachment. *Journal of the American Academy of Child & Adolescent Psychiatry, 36*, 637–644.

Waterman, A. S. (1982). Identity development from adolescence to adulthood: An extension of theory and a review of research. *Developmental Psychology, 18*, 341– 358.

Waterman, A. S. (1985). Identity in the context of adolescent psychology. *New Directions for Child Development, 30*, 5–24.

Waterman, A. S. (1999). Identity, the identity status, and identity status development: A contemporary statement. *Developmental Review, 19*, 591–621.

Watson, D., & Clark, L. A. (1992). Affects separable and inseparable: On the hierarchical arrangement of the negative affects. *Journal of Personality and Social Psychology, 62*, 489–505.

Watson, D., & Clark, L. A. (1993). Behavioral disinhibition versus constraint: A dispositional perspective. In D. M. Wegner & J. W. Pennebaker (Eds.), *Handbook of mental control* (pp. 506–527). New York, NY: Prentice-Hall.

Watson, D., & Clark, L. A. (1997). Extraversion and its positive emotional core. In R. Hogan, J. Johnson, & S. Briggs (Eds.), *Handbook of personality psychology* (pp. 767–793). San Diego, CA: Academic Press.

Watson, D., & Humrichouse, J. (2006). Personality development in emerging adulthood: Integrating evidence from self-ratings and spouse ratings. *Journal of Personality and Social Psychology, 91*, 959–974.

Watson, J. (1924). *Behaviorism.* Chicago, IL: University of Chicago Press.

Watson, N., Bryan, B. C., & Thrash, T. M. (2014). Change in self-discrepancy, anxiety, and depression in individual therapy. *Psychotherapy, 51*, 525–534.

Waytz, A., Hershfield, H. E., & Tamir, D. I. (2015). Mental stimulation and meaning in life. *Journal of Personality and Social Psychology, 108*, 336–355.

Webster, R. (1995). *Why Freud was wrong: Sin, science, and psychoanalysis.* New York, NY: Basic Books.

Weiner, B. (1985). An attributional theory of achievement motivation and emotion. *Psychological Review, 92*, 548–573.

Weinfield, N. S., Sroufe, L. Alan, Egeland, B., & Carlson, E. (2008). Individual differences in infant-caregiver attachment. In J. Cassidy & P. R. Shaver (Eds.), *Handbook of attachment* (2nd ed., pp. 78–101). New York, NY: Guilford.

Weinstein, T. A. R., Capitanio, J. P., & Gosling, S. D. (2008). Personality in animals. In O. P. John, R. W. Robins, & L. A. Pervin (Eds.), *Handbook of personality: Theory and method* (3rd ed., pp. 328–348). New York, NY: Guilford.

Weisbuch, M., Sinclair, S. A., Skorinko, J. L., & Eccleston, C. P. (2009). Self-esteem depends on the beholder: Effects of a subtle social value cue. *Journal of Experimental Social Psychology, 45*, 143–148.

Weiss, A., & King, J. E. (2015). Great ape origins of personality maturation and sex differences: A study of orangutans and chimpanzees. *Journal of Personality and Social Psychology, 108*, 648–664.

Weiss, R. S. (1974). The provisions of social relationships. In Z. Rubin (Ed.), *Doing unto others* (pp. 17–26). Englewood Cliffs, NJ: Prentice Hall.

Westen, D. (1990). Psychoanalytic approaches to personality. In L. A. Pervin (Ed.) *Handbook of personality* (pp. 21–65). New York, NY: Guilford

Westen, D. (1991). Cultural, emotional, and unconscious aspects of the self. In R. C. Curtis (Ed.), *The relational self* (pp. 181–210). New York, NY: Guilford.

Westen, D. (1998). The scientific legacy of Sigmund Freud: Toward a psychodynamically informed psychological science. *Psychological Bulletin, 124*, 333–371.

Westen, D., Feit, A., & Zittel, C. (1999). Methodological issues in research using projective techniques. In P. C. Kendall, J. N. Butcher, & G. Holmbeck (Eds.). *Handbook of research methods in clinical psychology* (2nd ed., pp. 224–240). New York, NY: Wiley.

Westen, D., Gabbard, G. O., & Ortigo, K. M. (2008). Psychoanalytic approaches to personality. In O. P. John, R. W. Robins, & L. A. Pervin (Eds.), *Handbook of personality: Theory and research* (3rd ed., pp. 61–113). New York, NY: Guilford.

Westenberg, P. M., & Block, J. (1993). Ego development and individual differences in personality. *Journal of Personality and Social Psychology, 65*, 792–800.

Whitbeck, L. B., Hoyt, D. R., Simons, R. L., Conger, R. D., Elder, G. H., Lorenz, F. O., & Huck, S. (1992). Intergenerational continuity of parental rejection and depressed affect. *Journal of Personality and Social Psychology, 63*, 1036–1045.

Whitbourne, S. K., & Waterman, A. S. (1979). Psychosocial development during the adult years: Age and cohort comparisons. *Developmental Psychology, 15*, 373–378.

Whitbourne, S. K., Sneed, J. R., & Sayer, A. (2009). Psychosocial development from college through midlife: A 34-year sequential study. *Developmental Psychology, 45*, 1328–1340.

Whitbourne, S. K., Zuschlag, M. K., Elliot, L. B., & Waterman, A. S. (1992). Psychosocial development in adulthood: A 22-year sequential study. *Journal of Personality and Social Psychology, 63*, 260–271.

White, R. (1952). *Lives in progress: A study of the natural growth of personality.* New York, NY: Henry Holt.

White, R. W. (1959). Motivation reconsidered: The concept of competence. *Psychological Review, 66*, 297–333.

Whiteside, S. P., & Lynam, D. R. (2001). The five factor model and impulsivity: Using a structural model of personality to understand impulsivity. *Personality and Individual Differences, 30*, 669–689.

Whiteside, S. P., Lynam, D. R., Miller, J. D., & Reynolds, S. K. (2005). Validation of the UPPS Impulsive-Behavioral Scale: A four-factor model of impulsivity. *European Journal of Personality, 19*, 559–574.

Widiger, T. A. (2015). Assessment of DSM-5 personality disorder. *Journal of Personality Assessment, 97*, 456-466.

Widiger, T. A., & Costa, P. T., Jr. (2013a). Appendix: Description of the Revised NEO Personality Inventory (NEO-PI-R) facet scales. In T. A. Widiger & P. T. Costa, Jr. (Eds.), *Personality disorders and the Five-Factor Model of personality* (3rd ed., pp. 445–448). Washington, DC: American Psychological Association.

Widiger, T. A., & Costa, P. T, Jr. (2013b). Personality disorders and the Five-Factor Model of personality: Rationale for the third edition. In T. A. Widiger & P. T. Costa Jr. (Eds.), *Personality disorders and the Five-Factor Model of personality* (3rd ed., pp. 3–11). Washington, DC: American Psychological Association.

Widiger, T. A., & Costa, P. T. Jr. (Eds.). (2013c). *Personality disorders and the Five-Factor Model of personality* (3rd ed.). Washington, DC: American Psychological Association.

Widiger, T. A., Costa, P. T., Jr., Gore, W. L., & Crego, C. (2013). Five-Factor Model personality disorder research. In T. A. Widiger & P. T. Costa Jr. (Eds.), *Personality disorders and the Five-Factor Model of personality* (3rd ed., pp. 75–100). Washington, DC: American Psychological Association.

Widiger, T. A., & Mullins-Sweatt, S. N. (2009). Five-Factor Model of personality disorder: A proposal for DSM-5. *Annual Review of Clinical Psychology, 5*, 197–220.

Widiger, T. A., & Trull, T. J. (2007). Plate tectonics in the classification of personality disorder: Shifting to a dimensional model. *American Psychologist, 62*, 71–83.

Williams, J. E., & Best, D. L. (1990). *Measuring sex stereotypes: A multination study.* Newbury Park, CA: Sage.

Williams, K. D. (2007). Ostracism. *Annual Review of Psychology, 58*, 425–452.

Williams, K. M., Nathanson, C., & Paulhus, D. L. (2010). Identifying and profiling scholastic cheaters: Their personality, cognitive ability, and motivation. *Journal of Experimental Psychology: Applied, 16*, 293–307.

Williams, T. F., Thomas, K. M., Donnellan, M. B., & Hopwood, C. J. (2014). The aversive interpersonal behaviors associated with pathological personality traits. *Journal of Personality Disorders, 28*, 824–840.

Wilson, D. S., Near, D., & Miller, R. R. (1996). Machiavellianism: A synthesis of the evolutionary and psychological literature. *Psychological Bulletin, 119*, 285–299.

Wilson, M., & Daly, M. (1985). Competitiveness, risk-taking, and violence: The young male syndrome. *Ethology and Sociobiology, 6*, 59–73.

Windsor, T. D., Curtis, R. G., & Luszcz, M. A. (2015). Sense of purpose as a psychological resource for aging well. *Developmental Psychology, 51*, 975–986.

Winegard, B. M., Winegard, B., & Geary, D. C. (2014). Eastwood's brawn and Einstein's brain: An evolutionary account of dominance, prestige, and precarious manhood. *Review of General Psychology, 18*, 34–48.

Wink, P. (1992). Three types of narcissism in women from college to midlife. *Journal of Personality, 60,* 7–30.

Wink, P., & Helson, R. (1993). Personality change in women and their partners. *Journal of Personality and Social Psychology, 65,* 597–605.

Winter, D. (1973). *The power motive.* New York, NY: The Free Press.

Wondra, J. D., & Ellsworth, P. C. (2015). An appraisal theory of empathy and other vicarious emotional experiences. *Psychological Review, 122,* 411–428.

Wood, D. (2015). Testing the lexical hypothesis: Are socially important traits more densely reflected in the English Lexicon? *Journal of Personality and Social Psychology, 108,* 317–335.

Wood, W., & Runger, D. (2016). Psychology of habit. *Annual Review of Psychology, 67.* In press.

Woodruff, D. G., & Birren, J. E. (1972). Age changes and cohort differences in personality. *Developmental Psychology, 6,* 252–259.

Wortman, J., Lucas, R. E., & Donnellan, M. B. (2012). Stability and change in the Big 5 personality domains: Evidence from a longitudinal study of Australians. *Psychology and Aging, 27,* 867–874.

Wylie, R. C. (1974). *The self concept* (Vol. 1). Lincoln: University of Nebraska Press.

Wylie, R. C. (1979). *The self concept* (Vol. 2). Lincoln: University of Nebraska Press.

Yeager, D. S., Johnson, R., Spitzer, B. J., Trzesniewski, K. H., Powers, J., & Dweck, C. (2014). The far-reaching effects of believing people can change: Implicit theories of personality shape stress, health, and achievement during adolescence. *Journal of Personality and Social Psychology, 106,* 867–884.

Zahavi, A., & Zahavi, A. (1997). *The handicapping principle: A missing piece of Darwin's puzzle.* New York, NY: Oxford University Press.

Zahn-Waxler, C., Kochanska, G., Krupnick, J., & McKnew, D. (1990). Patterns of guilt in children of depressed and well mothers. *Developmental Psychology, 26,* 51–59.

Zanarini, M. C., Frankenberg, F. R., Hennen, J., Reich, D. B., & Silk, K. R. (2006). Prediction of the 10-year course of borderline personality disorder. *The American Journal of Psychiatry, 163,* 827–832.

Zapolski, T. C. B., Guller, L., & Smith, G. T. (2013). On the valid description of personality dysfunction. In T. A. Widiger & P. T. Costa Jr. (Eds.), *Personality disorders and the Five-Factor Model of personality* (3rd ed., pp. 29–42). Washington, DC: American Psychological Association.

Zelikovsky, N., & Lynn, S. J. (1994). The aftereffects and assessment of physical and psychological abuse. In S. J. Lynn & J. W. Rhue (Eds.), *Dissociation: Clinical and theoretical perspectives* (pp. 190–214). New York, NY: Guilford.

Zimmerman, M., Rothschild, L., & Chelminski, I. (2005). The prevalence of DSM-IV personality disorders in psychiatric outpatients. *The American Journal of Psychiatry, 162,* 1911–1918.

Zuckerman, M. (1971). Dimensions of sensation seeking. *Journal of Consulting and Clinical Psychology, 36,* 45–52.

Zuckerman, M. (1979). *Sensation-seeking: Beyond the optimal level of arousal.* Hillsdale, NJ: Erlbaum.

Zuckerman, M. (2005). *Psychobiology of personality* (2nd ed., Revised and updated). New York, NY: Cambridge University Press.

Zuckerman, M. (2007). *Sensation seeking and risky behavior.* Washington, DC: American Psychological Association.

Zuckerman, M. (2009). Sensation seeking. In M. R. Leary & R. H. Hoyle (Eds.), *Handbook of individual differences in social behavior* (pp. 455–465). New York, NY: Guilford.

Zuckerman, M., Kieffer, S. C., & Knee, C. R. (1998). Consequences of self-handicapping: Effects on coping, academic performance, and adjustment. *Journal of Personality and Social Psychology, 74,* 1619–1628.

Index

Shyness, 220
Siever, L. J., 238
Similarity–attraction relationship, 80
Similarity pole, 266–267
Sioux, 28–29
Situational arousal, 45–47, 46 (figure)
Situational Eight DIAMONDS, 8
Situational variability, 268
Situational variable x personality variable, 45–47,
    46 (figure)
Situationism, 6
Six trait solution, 32
Slavich, George, 200
Snyder, Charles "Rick," 141
Sociability, 54
Social clock project, 303–304
Social Darwinism, 197(n8)
Social desirability, 63
Social exclusion, 178–180, 246–247, 281–282
Social identity, 142, 158
Social interest, 105–106, 169
Social learning theory, 10, 33–34, 39 (table)
Socially prescribed perfectionism, 250
Social signal transduction theory of depression, 200
Social status, 180–183
Social support, 205, 206–207, 270
Sociometer theory, 159–161
Sociotropic depressives, 207
Sokol, D. K., 91
Somer, O., 32
Soto, C. J., 73(n14)
Specific implementation intentions, 304–305
Speiker, S. J., 117
Spence, Donald, 312–313
Spencer, Herbert, 197(n8)
Spinath, F. M., 307
Spouses, interacting with, 273–276
Stability, 97, 295–296
Stability coefficients, 300, 305–306, 305 (table)
Stagnation. *See* Generativity versus stagnation
Standard deviation, 93
Star Trek (television show), 25–26
States, 6
Statistical factor analytic programs, 54–55
Statistical significance, 72(n5)
Status, social, 180–183
Stereotyping, 109, 176
Stern, Daniel, 123
Stockholm syndrome, 125
Stone, Michael, 237, 257(n3)
Storge, 146
Strangers, interacting with, 268–269
Strange Situation, 115
Strathman, A., 281
Strengths, 221–225

Stress and coping:
    about, 199–201
    dispositional approaches, 200, 208–212
    emotional effects of stress, 200
    interpretational approaches, 200, 201–207
    personal projects and, 196
    physical effects of stress, 199–200
    physiological responses to stress, 181
    positive psychology and coping, 221–225
    psychodynamic approaches, 201, 213–221,
        215 (table), 219 (table)
    stress, defined, 204
Stress of Life, The (Selye), 200
Stressors, 200
Strivings, personal, 194–195
Strong Vocational Interest Blank, 60
Structural model of the mind, 20–22
Structural stability, 296
Structured interviews, 255
Style of life, 105
Subject variables, 47
Sublimation, 215, 215 (table)
Success, 162
Suci, G. J., 31
Suffering, 312, 319(n5)
Sulloway, Frank, 40(n2), 106–107
Superego, 21, 126
Superior function, 25, 26
Superiority, striving for, 166–167
Suppression, 215
Surgency, 96, 97
Survival of the fittest, 197(n8)
Swann, William, 136–137, 157–159
Synthesizing function of theories, 15

Tajfel, Henri, 175
Tannenbaum, P. H., 31
TAT. *See* Thematic Apperception Test
Taxa, 238
Temperament:
    about, 94–95, 94 (figure)
    gender differences, 97–98
    infancy and early childhood, 95–96
    older children, adolescents, and adults, 97
    stability and change, 97
Temper tantrums, 219
Tension reduction, 205
Testability of theories, 16
Test reliability, 61
Test validity, 61–62
Thematic Apperception Test (TAT), 66, 188
Thematic Perception Test, 65–66
Theories:
    defined, 14
    falsification of, 16